D0846147

The Essential Edmund Leach

The Essential Edmund Leach

Volume I: Anthropology and Society

edited by
Stephen Hugh-Jones and James Laidlaw

Yale University Press
New Haven and London

Set in Adobe Garamond by Best-set Typesetter Ltd, Hong Kong
Printed in Great Britain by Biddles Ltd, Guildford and Kings Lynn

ISBN 0-300-08124-3
Library of Congress Catalogue Card Number 00-043664

A catalogue record for this book is available from the British Library.

10 9 8 7 6 5 4 3 2 1

Contents

Figures and Tables

Acknowledgements

We are grateful to Louisa Brown, Edmund Leach's daughter and literary executor, for permission to publish this collection of his writings, and also for the information and practical help she has given us. Preparation of these volumes would have been a very great deal more onerous had not the Royal Anthropological Institute chosen to mark Leach's death by publishing a nearly complete bibliography. All those involved in that publication deserve our thanks. Our work has also been greatly aided by the staff in the Modern Archive Centre of the Library of King's College Cambridge, who run that valuable scholarly resource with great efficiency and friendliness.

References to works which are included in this collection are given, mostly in parentheses in the text, in the following form: (I.2.3: 45) – Volume I, Section 2, item number 3, page 45. Frequently, where relevant, we also give in parentheses the publication date of works cited or referred to. All other references are given by short titles in footnotes. Works which have not been previously published are marked with an asterisk on the contents pages. A full list of all works cited is included at the end of each volume. References to unpublished papers in the Leach Archive at King's College Cambridge are given as ERL followed by the archive catalogue number.

JAL/SH-J
Cambridge
July 1999

For permission to reprint articles, the Estate of Edmund Leach and Yale University Press would like to thank the following: 'Men and Ideas: Frazer and Malinowski. On the "Founding Fathers"', in *Current Anthropology*, Vol. 7 No. 5 (1966), reproduced by permission of The University of Chicago Press; 'The Epistemological Background to Malinowski's Empiricism', in *Man and Culture, An Evaluation of the Work of Bronislaw Malinowski* (1957), edited by Raymond Firth, reproduced by permission of Routledge; 'An Anthropologist's Trivia' (1967), copyright © *The Guardian*, reproduced by permission; 'Ritual', from the *International Encyclopaedia of the Social Sciences*, edited by David L. Sills, Vol. 13 (1968), Macmillan and the Free Press, and 'Raymond Firth', from the *International Encyclopaedia of the Social Sciences*, Vol. 18 (1979), copyright ©The Free Press, reproduced by permission of the Gale Group; 'The Ecology of Mental Process: A Life of Gregory Bateson', review of *Gregory Bateson: The Legacy of a Scientist*, by David Lipset, reproduced with permission from *Nature* (reference section), copyright © Macmillan Magazines Limited 1980; Review of Meyer Fortes, *The Web of Kinship*, in *Man* (1950), Vol. 50, and reviews of A. R. Radcliffe-Brown, *A Natural Science of Society* and S. F. Nadel, *The Theory of Social Structure*, in *Man* (1958), Vol. 58, reproduced by permission of the Royal Anthropological Institute; 'Social Anthropology: A Natural Science of Society?', copyright ©The British Academy 1977. Reproduced by permission from *Proceedings of the British Academy*, Vol. LXII (1976); 'Anthropology Upside Down', a review of *Reinventing Anthropology*, edited by Dell Hymes in *The New York Review of Books*, Vol. 21, No. 1 (1974), reprinted with permission from *The New York Review of Books*, copyright ©NYREV, Inc.; 'The Shangri-La That Never Was' (1953), 'The Cult of Informality', 'Models' (1964) and 'Barbar's Civilisation Analysed' (1962), reproduced by permission of the *New Statesman*, 2000; 'A Poetics of Power', a review of *Negara: The Theater State of Nineteenth-Century Bali*, by Clifford Geertz, in *The New Republic*, Vol. 184 (1981), reproduced with permission; Extracts from *Political Systems of Highland Burma* (1954/1977), 'Cronus and Chronus' (1953/1961/1966), 'Time and False Noses' (1955/1961/1966), and 'Rethinking Anthropology' (1959/1961/1966), reproduced by permission of Athlone Press; 'Ritualisation in Man in Relation to Conceptual and Social Development', in *Philosophical Transactions of the Royal Society of London*, Vol. 251, No. 772 (1966), reproduced by permission of the Royal Society; 'The Frontiers of "Burma"' (1961), reproduced by permission of *Comparative Studies in Society and History* and Cambridge University Press; 'Concerning Trobriand Clans and the Kinship Category *Tabu*', in *The Development Cycle in Domestic Groups*, edited by Jack Goody, *Cambridge Papers in Social Anthropology*, No. 1 (1958), and an extract from *Pul Eliya, A Village in Ceylon: A Study of Land Tenure and Kinship* (1961), reproduced by permission of Cambridge University Press; 'Anthropological Aspects of Language: Animal Categories and Verbal Abuse', in *New Directions in the Study of Language*, edited by Eric H. Lenneberg (1964), reproduced by permission of Massachusetts Institute of Technology Press.

With thanks to Lisa McQuail, Assistant Editor of the *American Ethnologist* and Ashgate Publishing Ltd for their help and useful advice.

Introduction

The aim of this collection is to make available in a convenient form a rounded and representative selection of the anthropological writings of Edmund Leach. Although Leach is well known among anthropologists, and is also a well-known anthropologist among both scholars in neighbouring disciplines and the educated public at large, the absence until now of a collection of this kind means that it is not well known, among anthropologists or others, just what kind of anthropologist he was. Cumulatively, the essays in this and its companion volume, *Culture and Human Nature*, reveal a thinker who not only made major contributions within academic anthropology, as theorist and as ethnographic interpreter, but who also developed, in direct and unpretentious language, an anthropological perspective on major philosophical questions about the human condition, and on some of the familiar political and moral questions which we encounter in our everyday lives.

Some of Leach's most important essays have been out of print for some years now, or were only ever published in relatively obscure journals or edited collections. His 1965 essay on 'The Nature of War' (I.4.3), for instance, was published in a short-lived journal dedicated to issues of disarmament and arms control. 'Pulleyar and the Lord Buddha' (II.2.1) appeared in a difficult-to-find psychoanalytic journal, and many anthropologists in Britain know it, if at all, from many-times-photocopied and barely legible offprints. His most influential book, *Political Systems of Highland Burma* (1954), is still in print and widely referred to, and still a staple of undergraduate teaching in social anthropology; as is his Fontana 'Modern Masters' on *Lévi-Strauss* (1970). But on their own these books give a misleading impression of Leach's practice as an anthropologist: of the sources of his theoretical inspiration; of the range of anthropological topics he explored and debates he provoked or did battle in; and in particular of his talents as an essayist and polemicist.[1]

Leach was a singular anthropologist, and this collection is an attempt to reflect his singular combination of characteristics and roles. He was an influential theorist during what has come to be seen as the classical era of British social anthropology; and here he combined an old-style ethnographer's fascinated insistence on the importance of ethnographic detail with a restless acquisitiveness and advocacy of new ideas, and an equally tireless combativeness in argument and debate. At the same time Leach was a public figure. As Provost of King's College

Cambridge he was head of an academic institution which, at least in England, is instantly recognisable outside the academic world. Leach exploited this position of paradigmatic 'Oxbridge don' to address a very wide educated public. He contributed frequently as essayist and reviewer to a range of publications from semi-specialist magazines (such as *New Society, New Scientist,* and *Nature*), through the political and literary weeklies both in the UK and the USA (*New Statesman, The Spectator, The Listener, New York Review of Books, New Republic,* etc.), to daily and weekly newspapers. He broadcast on radio and lectured to an astonishing range of educational, professional, and public institutions and gatherings.

In both his professional anthropological and his more public roles, Leach is in danger, with the passage of time, of being misunderstood. On the professional side, it is too easy to see Leach either as all of a piece with the other British 'structural-functionalists',[2] describing, as in an historical vacuum, 'indigenous' political institutions in the late colonial era; or as simply the man who 'introduced' Lévi-Straussian structuralist analysis of myth and symbolism into Anglophone anthropology. Both of these characterisations are widespread and, as the essays collected here make clear, both are misleading.

As an anthropologist, Leach had an exceedingly wide range of interests. Some of his earliest anthropological writings are on the interrelations between local political institutions and colonial governments. His first academic positions were in teaching about art and material culture, and in the curatorship of an ethnographical art collection. His writings about political institutions and about kinship were generally part of theoretical debates about how to model social systems and describe human action, and he was a searching critic of some of the most important bedrock assumptions of mid-century functionalist social theory. These writings also reflected his interests in human biology and its effect upon behaviour; in human cognition and how it is affected by culture; and in the effects of both long-term cultural history and environmental and ecological conditions on the life of local communities.

His 'structuralist' writings show an equally idiosyncratic set of preoccupations, and draw connections equally widely. A structuralist's approach to the analysis of myth and symbolism is combined with an interest in Freudian psychology, and the result is enquiries both into the place of the human body in religious thought, and into the role of the human senses in the appreciation of art. An interest in cognition and classification becomes for Leach a way of developing an anthropological understanding of ethnocentrism, racism, and war.

These two general aspects of Leach's anthropology – the functionalist and the structuralist – are reflected in the division of this collection into two volumes. Broadly speaking, this volume, in addition to some pieces on anthropology and anthropologists, contains a selection of Leach's writings on 'society'; while *Culture and Human Nature,* in addition to some of his attempts to address non-academic audiences, contains a selection of his writings about 'culture'. In many respects the distinction between 'society' and 'culture' is highly problematical, and Leach used both terms in his own in some respects idiosyncratic ways. It is nevertheless generally true that his studies of social structure, social relations, and social practices are heavily informed by the functionalism of Malinowski and Firth, while his studies of human cultural products and how they relate to human nature show the influence of Lévi-Strauss more markedly. And in general, as time went by, and as he came to work more and more on myth, art and architecture, and the body, so his writings became more markedly and recognisably structuralist. But although the balance is different in his different writings, in general these tendencies in his thinking – the empiricist and idealist as he sometimes put it – exist together in what is either a creative tension or a confusion, depending on one's point of view.

No matter what the subject matter or the theory under discussion, Leach always insisted that anthropology was not an arcane academic discipline that told us only about 'other' peoples living in distant lands. For him, anthropology stood at a crossroads between biology, psychology, cultural history, and political economy: it was, or at least aspired to be, an integrated study of human nature. Even, and indeed especially when it proceeds through detailed enquiry into the life of a very particular local community in a particular time and place, anthropology is always also the study of human nature. This meant for Leach not only that anthropological analysis should be turned on the very citadels of 'Western culture' – such as the Bible and the Sistine Chapel – but also that the lessons of anthropological enquiry were relevant to the everyday moral and political questions which were being debated all around him in the national press, and in the academic institutions in which he lived and worked.

So Leach set out to communicate with a wide educated public; to show them how 'his kind of anthropology' was relevant to understanding the changing world in which they lived. He achieved a level of fame – indeed notoriety – through his 1967 BBC Reith Lectures, entitled 'A Runaway World?'. In some ways these were a great success, in that they stimulated debate, as he certainly hoped that they would. But on the other hand public and press reaction was disproportionately focused on just a few remarks – some negative comments on the family, and what would now be called 'ageist' remarks about the need for elderly decision-makers to be replaced by younger people. Because these opinions seemed to place Leach so squarely in the 'trendy' and 'progressive' camp of the time, commentators tended to take positions for and against his lectures according to their general political position, and the more genuinely original aspects of his lectures attracted less attention than they otherwise might.

As is evident from the pieces reproduced in this collection, especially those in Volume II, Section 4, the lessons Leach drew from 'his kind of anthropology' did not fit easily into any one political camp. Certain things, notably racism, he was firmly, passionately, and consistently against; and he missed no opportunity to draw attention to its absurdities and its dangers, and to decry any attempt he saw to give it academic respectability. But for the most part Leach's comments on moral and political issues tend to cut across established lines of debate, to ask new questions, or to put familiar questions in a new context. He seems to have proceeded not from any consistent political position, but from a settled distrust of accepted pieties and a conviction that anthropology could help us to think new thoughts. More often than not his strategy was to unsettle his readership or audience, especially when they expected to agree with him. The image of the 'trendy-lefty don' is as misleading as that of the dry, academic, colonialist anthropologist.

One of the aims, then, of the editors of this collection, in presenting a representative cross-section of Leach's anthropology, is to enable readers to see for themselves the range of Leach's interests and the lines of argument he pursued. Neither of us comes even close to agreeing with everything that Leach wrote. Plainly, we find his writing interesting and thought-provoking, and we think that readers will do so too, whether they are professional anthropologists, students, or general readers interested in broadly anthropological questions. But we are not in the smallest degree interested in seeing a 'structuralist revival', or in re-discovering Leach as an anthropological hero, guru, or prophet. Our intention is not to promote or advocate any or all of Leach's views; but to present in accessible form a thinker who is somewhat more interesting than the simple stereotypes which have begun to appear in the literature, and who will be difficult to assimiliate into reductive and tendentious versions of anthropology's past.

We have arranged Leach's work thematically, rather than in chronological order (although there is often a chronological ordering within each section), and we have done this for a number of reasons. The first and most important is to bring out persistent but also changing and developing foci of interest in Leach's writings; themes and questions he returned to throughout his career. This incidentally brings out the extent to which he recycled certain arguments (and especially diagrams), applying old ideas to new material, or trying out a line of argument in a new and unfamiliar context.

Leach wrote fluently and was very prolific. As with many such authors, this was partly because he could easily trot out a version of a well-tried argument in new words for a new audience. He enjoyed addressing non-anthropological audiences, and worked persistently at making his arguments clear and comprehensible; at explaining abstruse ideas on familiar material, and in simple language. As a result, there is considerable repetition in his *oeuvre*. We have tried to select pieces which convey the fluency and versatility of his presentation, while avoiding too much actual repetition. At the same time, we have deliberately juxtaposed academic articles and more informal, popular presentations of the same ideas, or on the same material or theme.

Some of our thematic sections are devoted to areas of enquiry with which Leach's name is already familiarly associated. Ritual is one such, and another is classification and taboo; but in these cases we have included unpublished or obscure and unknown pieces which make a significant difference, in retrospect, to how we now read his thinking in this area, or which make the force and importance of what he had to say clearer. In other cases our themes would scarcely have been recognised as such by Leach's contemporaries. The pieces in Volume II, Section 3, for example, now seem clearly to be contributions to the anthropology of the body and the senses, though they were written before these fields of enquiry had been developed as such. Conversely, although several of the pieces included here reflect Leach's interest in ethnic conflict, racism, and the concept of race,[3] we have not grouped them together into a separate section.[4] The themes in Leach's work cross-cut in complex ways and it is only possible to cut the cake one way at a time.

Although much in this collection will be unknown, even to professional social anthropologists who reckon themselves familiar with Leach's work, only a few pieces are actually published here for the first time. He wrote quickly and often to order; and, partly because he did not much mind changing his opinions (once a controversy had died down, at least), he published readily whatever he wrote. As a result, there is rather little we have found that is unpublished, but we have chosen a few pieces which seem to us to be of interest.

There is one lengthy academic piece, 'Biblical Hair' (II.3.3), which is highly polemical in tone, constituting as it does a reply to some criticisms of an earlier piece by Leach ('Magical Hair', also reprinted here as II.3.2). It certainly shows Leach at his combative worst and best, but it also presents a significant development and clarification of his ideas. 'Once a Knight is Quite Enough' (I.2.7) is the only sustained piece of ethnographic interpretation among the unpublished pieces. This paper, which was given many times as a lecture to a variety of academic and non-academic audiences, is an analysis by Leach of the ceremony in which he was made a Knight Bachelor, and in it he reworked parts of an earlier still unpublished essay,[5] in order to compare that ceremony to a pig-sacrifice in Borneo. The piece shows many of Leach's greatest virtues: vivid and amusing description; analytical ingenuity and imaginative insight; playful presentation and humorous juxtaposition, but all used to make a serious point. 'Death of a Hero' (II.4.3) is another essay on a British state ritual, a radio talk Leach gave on the BBC at the time of Sir Winston Churchill's funeral.

Then there is a paper on Kurdistan delivered by Leach to Malinowski's now legendary anthropology seminar in the pre-war London School of Economics (II.4.1). This is interesting equally for showing us how some of the issues and dilemmas debated by anthropologists today (often enough, as if they were being raised for the first time) were talked about then, as it is for reminding us how little in some respects the situation in that area has changed in the intervening years. The 'Letter from Bhamo' (I.3.1) is Leach's first communication after he arrived in the Kachin Hills at the beginning of the Second World War. It records his first impressions of the area, and also the excitement of a young man embarking on an adventure which turned out to be more than merely anthropological. 'The Kachins of Burma' (II.4.2) shows how he explained the people he had lived with, studied, and fought among, to a radio audience shortly after the end of the war.

In our introductions to the individual sections of the collection, we have tried to draw out some themes and lines of argument that run through the pieces we have reprinted – that is, to illustrate why they can in our view be seen as thematic sets – and also to point out connections where appropriate to other of

Leach's writings. But our exegetical ambitions are strictly limited. We have not tried to argue that Leach always held to the same views, that he developed a consistent 'line' on given issues, or, and this is especially important, that the views he expressed across the huge range of his interests and concerns cohere into a single, consistent system. It seems clear that Leach had a definite vision of anthropology. He had strong intellectual propensities, and equally strong likes and dislikes in the thinking of other authors. And one can certainly see continuities between many disparate parts of his writing. But he was not in any degree a *systematic* thinker. His forte was for opportunistic use of a new idea; for seeing how an old question might be asked in a new way; for suddenly seeing that he could ditch a taken-for-granted assumption that everyone else was making: in short, for the quick and the clever, even at times the clever-clever. The last piece in our collection, 'Anthropos' (II.5), is probably the nearest Leach came to a synoptic statement of a philosophical anthropology, but even here he works through a series of mini-essays which progressively weave together separate strands of argument into an only loosely textured whole.

If this collection is not an exercise in systematic exposition, it is equally not an evaluation of Leach's anthropology. To date, the best short descriptive evaluation of his work is Fuller and Parry's 'Petulant Inconsistency?'.[6] Stanley Tambiah has written and will shortly be publishing an exposition and assessment of Leach's major writings, and that work and this will be complementary. For the most part, we have avoided agreeing or quarrelling with Leach's arguments, and assessing either individual essays or his contribution to any fields of enquiry as a whole. We have, very occasionally, pointed out where an argument has gone since Leach's day, but we have done so only sparingly, as our point is not artificially to magnify his influence, but simply to present in a collected form what he actually wrote and said. And we have forborne from censoring him where either his arguments or his language fail to conform to contemporary polite conventions: partly because there would be no end to such an exercise, once begun; and partly because our concern for historical fidelity anyway revolts against any such measure.

One final thing which these books are not is intellectual biography. The materials for such an exercise do now exist, in the Modern Archive Centre in the library of King's College Cambridge, where Leach's professional papers have been deposited. (His personal papers, it is hoped, will follow in due course.) The archive contains field notes, lecture notes, professional correspondence, and the texts of lectures and papers. There is a large amount of material and working through it would be a considerable exercise; as too would be tracing the influences on Leach's thinking from both within and outside academic anthropology, to say nothing of family and personal factors. Although we have made some use of this material, we cannot even begin to embark on an exercise of this kind here, but we shall end this introduction with a brief outline sketch of what appear to be the basic facts of Leach's life.[7]

Edmund Ronald Leach was born in Sidmouth in 1910. His immediate family was small – he was the youngest of three siblings – but it was part of a much larger clan of prosperous, inter-married, business families, descended from Rochdale mill owners but more recently with substantial sugar interests in Argentina. The youngest of twenty-eight cousins and two siblings in his generation, Leach was unusual among them in growing up in England, and therefore being unable to speak Spanish. His father, fifty-nine on the day Leach was born, was a remote figure and by all accounts his childhood was dominated by his much younger mother, a woman of artistic and intellectual leanings, and also a devout Anglican. His schooling followed family tradition – he became the twenty-first in a line of Leaches to attend Marlborough College. By his own account Leach had an unhappy time there, not being good at cricket. It was, he later recalled, 'a foretaste of hell on earth' (II.4.7: 301). In 1929 Leach went up as an exhibitioner to Clare College Cambridge, where he read first mathematics and then engineering. He found Cambridge much more to his liking – a 'glorious experience' was his judgement later in life[8] – and he left in 1932 with a first.

After Cambridge, Leach joined John Swire and Sons, one of the great British oriental trading houses. Following a year in London, he was posted to Hong Kong and then to various places in China: Shanghai, Chungking, Tsingtao, and Peking. At one point he was little more than 200 miles north of the Kachin Hills area of northern Burma, the area where he would spend the Second World War and which would be the subject of his first major book. Late in 1936 Leach resigned from Swires, but a plan to return to England by train through Russia had to be abandoned: Stalin's purges were in progress and the embassy was issuing no visas. Instead, after a chance meeting at an embassy party in Peking, he accepted an invitation from an American former Mormon missionary, Kilton Stewart, to accompany him and two others on an ethnographic expedition to the Yami, the aboriginal inhabitants of the island of Botel Tobago,[9] off the south-eastern coast of Taiwan, at that time part of the Japanese Empire.

This expedition was formative for Leach not only because the Yami were his first experience of what he jestingly referred to as 'real primitives', but also because it was his first significant experience of psychoanalysis. It was there that Kilton Stewart analysed his dreams. Leach later said of this expedition, 'I had no idea what I was up to. I made ethnographic notes as well as I could and drew accurate scale drawings of the boats and houses.'[10] In 1937 and 1938 he published a handful of articles on the Yami: on technology and economic life, on the construction of their spectacular and beautifully painted boats, and on the Japanese colonial government's 'development' policy towards them.[11]

When Leach returned from the Far East in 1937, he showed his notes to his childhood friend Rosemary Upcott, who had recently married the anthropologist Raymond Firth. Firth introduced him to Bronislaw Malinowski, and he joined Malinowski's seminar at the London School of Economics, where his contemporaries included William Stanner and Phyllis Kaberry. A short period of fieldwork followed in 1938 in Iraqi Kurdistan 'inspired by a love affair with an archaeologist'.[12] This was cut short and the projected doctoral dissertation never materialised, but he did publish a monograph, *Social and Economic Organisation of the Rowanduz Kurds*, in 1940.

By this time Leach was already on fieldwork again, in north-east Burma and, Malinowski having gone off to Yale, this time under the general guidance of Raymond Firth. Meyer Fortes, recently returned from West Africa, was also teaching at the LSE. During 1938/9 Leach had worked as a research assistant to Firth, and his new projected doctoral dissertation was to have been a Firthian socio-economic study of domestic organisation, local community, and trading networks. The Firths were undertaking a similar project in Malaya. As Leach later recalled, 'Segmentary lineages and cross-cousin marriage didn't come into the story at all. I think that if it had not been for the disasters of war we really would have produced volumes which were built around a common body of theoretical interests.'[13]

The choice of Burma seems to have arisen from Leach's acquaintance with H. N. C. Stevenson, a member of the Burma Frontier Service whom Leach had met at Malinowski's seminar.[14] Stevenson was in the hills of the north-east Burma frontier area, and had set up what would now be called a 'development project', dubbed the 'Kachin Regeneration Scheme'. Leach agreed to study and report on its effects. But the 'disasters of war' did indeed intervene. By the time Leach arrived in Burma in August 1939, war in Europe was clearly in sight and only a month away, and Stevenson had returned to England. Leach joined the Burma army and continued his research. He also married. Back in England, Kilton Stewart had introduced him to Celia Buckmaster. They had planned to marry in England in the summer of 1940 but when all leave was cancelled he telegraphed to her to join him in Burma instead, and they were married in Rangoon in February 1940. Celia remained in Burma until the spring of 1942 when she and their baby daughter were evacuated.

Leach did report, very negatively, on the 'Kachin Regeneration Scheme'. By the autumn of 1940 he was working as a recruiting officer among the Kachins and other hill peoples of the region. Then at the end of 1941, when the Japanese arrived, he was recruited into a behind-the-lines operation in the area under Stevenson. After an overland escape to Kunming, Leach was back in Burma late in 1942 continuing the work of raising the 'Kachin Levies'. Towards the end of the war he was in Civil Affairs, in the administration of areas of Burma won back from the Japanese. Leach's war experience involved extensive travel – throughout the Kachin Hills, in western Burma, Assam, and into Yunnan – and his researches into complex tribute systems – manipulated in the recruitment of allies – gave him a unique perspective on the Kachins and their neighbours, one quite different from that gained from the shorter-term, sedentary character of more conventional anthropological fieldwork. Added to this, Leach lost many of his field notes, one reason why he resorted to an in-depth reading of historical sources by missionaries, travellers, and government administrators. These unusual circumstances all played a key role in the formulation of his arguments concerning history, political change, and cultural variation, the hallmarks of *Political Systems of Highland Burma.*

Leach returned to England at the end of the war in the summer of 1945. His PhD dissertation, 'Cultural Changes with Special Reference to the Hill Tribes of

Burma and Assam', was completed in the spring of 1947. Radcliffe-Brown was the external examiner. In the meantime, in 1945, he published his first work in a discernibly structuralist style, 'Jinghpaw Kinship Terminology'.

In 1947, after the completion of his PhD, Leach was sent off almost immediately to Borneo. Raymond Firth appears to have persuaded the Colonial Office of the need for social and economic research in the new Crown Colony of Sarawak. On Firth's instructions, Leach carried out a pilot survey and recommended further research schemes.[15] The experience seems to have confirmed his antipathy to policy-oriented, colonial anthropology. Apart from some book reviews, he wrote only a small handful of essays, mostly on material culture, as a result of this trip.[16]

On his return from Borneo, Leach took up a teaching appointment in the Anthropology Department of the London School of Economics, where Firth was now Professor and head of department. Firth, Leach, and their colleague Audrey Richards were all disciples of Malinowski. But the publication in 1949 of Lévi-Strauss's *Structures élémentaires de la parenté* was a significant intellectual turning-point. The analysis of Kachin social structure put forward in that book caused Leach to rethink what he had written in his dissertation. He always maintained that Lévi-Strauss had got some of ethnographic detail crucially wrong, but he nevertheless felt that he had somehow grasped something quite profound about how the system worked. Leach responded in 1951 with his first Curl Prize Essay, 'The Structural Implications of Matrilateral Cross-Cousin Marriage'. He then resigned from his post at the LSE and spent a year at his house in Hertfordshire, re-reading historical sources on the Kachin area and writing *Political Systems of Highland Burma.*

He then returned briefly to the LSE, as a Reader in Anthropology, but in 1953 he took a demotion and a cut in salary to return as a Lecturer to Cambridge,[17] to the Department of Social Anthropology which Meyer Fortes had recently taken over as William Wyse Professor. *Political Systems* was published the following year. From this time also come his 'two essays on the symbolic representation of time'. The first, 'Cronus and Chronos' (I.2.4), appeared in 1953; 'Time and False Noses' (I.2.5) followed in 1955.

In 1954 Leach spent around six months in a village in north-central Ceylon. With a short return visit in 1956 this was his last major period of fieldwork. The first publications to result from this were a short report on land tenure and the milestone article, 'Polyandry, Inheritance, and the Definition of Marriage in Sinhalese Customary Law', both published in *Man* in 1955.

The year 1958 was representative of this period in terms of Leach's publications. He did not publish a major book – *Pul Eliya* would not appear until 1961 – but this year did see the publication of two major articles, both of which are included in this collection: 'Magical Hair' (II.3.2), which had been submitted the previous year and had won him a second Curl Prize Essay from the Royal Anthropological Institute; and 'Concerning Trobriand Clans and the Kinship Category *Tabu*' (I.3.4), a re-analysis of some of Malinowski's Trobriand ethnography. The latter was published in *The Developmental Cycle in Domestic Groups*, edited by

Jack Goody, which was the first of the 'Cambridge Papers in Social Anthropology', a new series of edited volumes launched in 1958 with Fortes, Leach, and Goody as general editors.[18]

Also in 1958 a third, slightly shorter essay, 'An Anthropologist's Reflections on a Social Survey', appeared in the inaugural volume of the *Ceylon Journal of Historical and Social Studies.* This article, both in its content and in its place of publication, shows the extent to which, in addition to the pursuit of his own concerns, Leach became caught up and interested while in Ceylon in the pressing issues of political and social development, as seen by local intellectuals at that time. During this period Leach struck up a number of long-lasting friendships with colleagues from Ceylon, including Gananath Obeyesekere and Stanley Tambiah. His interest in the general social and political situation in Ceylon is reflected also in two BBC radio talks, also delivered in 1958 and published in *The Listener*, on 'Ceylon Ten Years after Independence' and 'What the Rioting in Ceylon Means'. Leach's output of book reviews that year was also typically wide and varied. There is one of a book about Burma; two on works on the rural sociology of Ceylon; another on a book about Condorcet; plus a review of Louis Dumont's *Hierarchy and Marriage Alliance in South Indian Kinship*, and the review of works by Radcliffe-Brown and Nadel reprinted as I.1.7 in this volume. In addition to all this, Leach had time to reply in the pages of *Man* to criticisms of his 1954 paper 'A Trobriand Medusa?' (II.3.1); and to join the correspondence in *The Times Literary Supplement* on G. Morris Carstairs's book on a village in northern India.

The debates on kinship and social structure, between Leach and his Cambridge colleagues, Fortes and Goody, took on something of a legendary quality in social anthropology, even as they were going on; and Leach's use, in December 1959, of the first Malinowski Memorial Lecture to heighten the rhetoric and pursue his line of argument did nothing to calm matters down (see I.3.7 below). His Ceylon ethnography, *Pul Eliya* (see I.3.5), when it appeared in 1961, was written explicitly and directly as an attack on Fortes' view of kinship; and the essays collected in *Rethinking Anthropology*, published the same year, showed the increasing distinctiveness of Leach's position, and also the increasingly structuralist style of his thinking. One thing which many of his otherwise disparate major essays have in common – this is true especially of 'A Trobriand Medusa?' (II.3.1), 'Virgin Birth' (II.2.2), and 'Magical Hair' (II.3.2) – is that they provoked colleagues into critical replies, which Leach then took up as a challenge, whereupon furious debate would ensue. Leach was an enthusiastic and combative controversialist, and although he was willing to admit to having changed his mind on many issues, he also liked winning an argument, and would happily pursue one through reams of correspondence, riposte, and rejoinder.

The year 1960/1 was spent at the Center for Advanced Study in the Behavioral Sciences at Stanford, and Leach was generally an enthusiastic conference-goer and seminar participant, but he remained based in Cambridge for the whole of the rest of his career: from 1953 at the University's Department of Social Anthropology; and then also at King's College, where he was elected to a Fellowship in

1960. At this institutional level his career from now on was entirely uneventful, except for the steady accumulation of promotions and distinctions – his gradual transformation, as he himself put it, into an 'Establishment figure'. The University made him a Reader in 1957 and then a Professor in 1972. From 1964 to 1966 he was Vice-President of the Royal Anthropological Institute; and then President from 1971 to 1974. He was elected Provost of King's College in 1966, and thereupon became a Senior Fellow of Eton College. In 1968 he was elected a Fellow of the British Academy, and an Honorary Foreign Member of the New York Academy of Arts and Sciences. Other 'great-and-good' positions included Trustee of the British Museum, and President of the British Humanist Association. He was knighted in 1975.

By the early 1960s Leach was simultaneously giving enthusiastic airing to the work of Lévi-Strauss on myth,[19] and conducting acrimonious debate with him on his analysis of Kachin social structure.[20] Through the mid-to-late 1960s Leach was one of several authors writing in English – including Rodney Needham and S. J. Tambiah, and also though more problematically Mary Douglas and Victor Turner – who applied broadly structuralist ideas to the fields of social classification, taboo, and myth. In addition, Leach began to be more generally known as an interpreter of Lévi-Strauss through his reviews and popular essays in structuralist vein.[21]

Leach's reputation as expositor of what was then the height of intellectual fashion, added to his by now fairly extensive experience of broadcasting, and his recent election as Provost of King's, no doubt all combined in bringing an invitation from the BBC to deliver the 1967 Reith Lectures. This is an annual series of broadcast lectures in memory of the founding Director General of the BBC, given each year by a different distinguished artist or academic and at that time – rather less today – they were an important event in the cerebral calendar for the educated middle classes in Britain: alongside, roughly speaking, the beginning of a new Royal Shakespeare Company season, the Proms, and the Royal Academy Summer Exhibition. As mentioned above, Leach's lectures (one of which is reprinted as II.4.4, below) caused a considerable stir in the press, and gave him a slightly misleading reputation as a 'swinging sixties' progressive.

In 1968, the year after the Reith Lectures, Leach's serious academic output is rather less than ten years before. Four short essays appeared in the new *International Encyclopaedia of Social Sciences* (including 'Ritual', reprinted as I.2.3 below); as did a conference paper on 'the concept of sin' among the Kachin, and the important edited collection, *Dialectic in Practical Religion*, to which, however, Leach himself contributed only a short introduction. But he continued to review: books on anthropological theory, language, the anthropology of Buddhism, and human aggression and conflict. And the aftermath of the Reith Lectures was keeping him employed with newspaper articles and correspondence.

The following year saw the publication of the collection of essays *Genesis as Myth*, all of which were applications of Leach's own brand of structuralist analysis to Christian mythology. This was a persistent and growing interest through the 1970s and 1980s, and – along with some research on his own family history, little of which was published[22] – it was the main area of his work in the last years of his life (see *Structuralist Interpretations of Biblical Myth*, 1983). But he also found time for two popular and idiosyncratic introductory books designed for newcomers to anthropology: *Culture and Communication* (1976), an introduction to structuralist analysis; and *Social Anthropology* (1982), a primer, as he put it, in 'my kind of anthropology'. This was also the time when Leach discovered the work of Giambattista Vico, and he also continued his interest in ethology and evolution.

Leach retired from the University in 1978, and from the Provostship of King's College a year later. But even after retirement, he continued to review widely, keeping up with new developments across a wide range of anthropological topics; and he travelled and lectured extensively. In the late 1970s, in a series of lengthy articles for the Italian *Enciclopedia Einaudi*, he published a major synoptic overview of the broad philosophical questions underlying anthropological enquiry (see II.5). Leach also branched out from his study of biblical myth into Christian visual iconography, in his studies of the Sistine Chapel ceiling (II.2.4) and the windows of King's College Chapel.[23] This last was published in 1988, the last full year of his life.

Leach died on 6 January 1989 at the age of 78, leaving a widow and two adult children.

Notes

1. Four collections of Leach's essays were published in his lifetime, but none was representative of his anthropology as a whole. *Rethinking Anthropology* (1961), with the exception of two short essays on time, contains only relatively technical early essays on kinship and social structure; *Genesis as Myth* (1969) and *Structuralist Interpretations of Biblical Myth* (1983) were both, as their titles suggest, concerned exclusively with the interpretation of the Bible. In 1980 a collection of essays was published in French under the title *L'Unité de l'homme*. This collection does give a fair idea of the range of Leach's academic interests, but it contains only formal, academic pieces, and therefore does not reflect the range of ways in which he formulated and expressed his ideas.
2. For instance see Geertz, *Works and Lives*, in his chapter on Evans-Pritchard.
3. 'The Nature of War' (I.4.3); 'Only Connect . . .' (II.4.4); 'The Integration of Minorities' (II.4.6); 'Three Reviews' (II.4.8); and, most significantly, 'Anthropos' (II.5).
4. See also 'Some Prejudiced Thoughts on Race Prejudice' (1960); 'Integration, Race, and Ethnicity' (1974); 'Variation in Man: Culture and Breeding' (1974); 'Cultural Components in the Concept of Race' (1975); 'Etnocentrismi' (1978); not to mention dozens of book reviews.
5. The piece written in 1952, and entitled 'Temonggong Koh's Last Two Head Feasts' (King's College Cambridge, Leach Archive, 2/17; henceforth references to this archive will take the form ERL: 2/17).
6. Fuller and Parry, 'Petulant Inconsistency? The Intellectual Achievement of Edmund Leach'.
7. See also Hugh-Jones, *Edmund Leach*.
8. Leach in Kuper, 'Interview with Edmund Leach', p. 375.
9. What the drunken Stewart called 'Bottle the Bugger' is nowadays called Lanyu in Chinese and Orchid Island in English.
10. Leach in Kuper, 'Interview with Edmund Leach', p. 376.
11. See 'Boat Construction in Botel Tobago' (1937); 'The Yami of Koto-sho' (1937); 'Economic Life and Technology' (1938).
12. Leach in Kuper, 'Interview with Edmund Leach', p. 376.

13. Ibid., pp. 376–7
14. See Stevenson, *Economics of the Central Chin Tribes.*
15. See 'Pilot Survey of Sarawak' (1948), and the published version *Social Research in Sarawak* (1950).
16. See 'Some Features of Social Structure among Sarawak Pagans' (1948); 'A Melanau (Sarawak) Twine-Making Device' (1949); 'Some Aspects of Dry Rice Cultivation' (1949); 'A Kagaram Tomb Post' (1950).
17. See 'Glimpses of the Unmentionable' (1984), p. 11.
18. Leach was to edit two volumes in the series, *Aspects of Caste in South India, Ceylon, and North-West Pakistan* (1960), and *Dialectic in Practical Religion* (1968).
19. See 'Lévi-Strauss in the Garden of Eden' (1961); 'Genesis as Myth' (1962; see II.1.2, below).
20. See 'Asymmetric Marriage Rules' (1961).
21. Early examples include 'Beasts and Triangles' (1962); 'Babar's Civilisation Analysed' (1962; see I.4.1, below); 'Sins or Rules' (1963).
22. See the posthumously published 'Masquerade' (1990).
23. Leach and Drury, *The Great Windows of King's College Chapel* (1988).

Section 1
Intellectual Interactions

> The sequence is always dialectical. There was . . . a point in my anthropological development when Malinowski could do no wrong. In the next phase Malinowski could do no right. But with maturity I came to see that there was merit on both sides. I see this as an Hegelian process, a very fundamental element in the way that thinking in the humanities develops over time. But when this sequence leads you round in a circle, you are not just back where you started. You have moved on a bit, or you have moved somewhere else. But always the process involves the initial rejection of your immediate ancestors, the teachers to whom you are most directly indebted.[1]

> I reject the notion that I have swung back and forth between being a functionalist and being a structuralist; I have quite consistently been both at once. But both my functionalism and my structuralism derive from my grounding in mathematics and engineering.[2]

The writings included in this section contain many of Leach's most explicit and forceful general statements on anthropological theory. It is characteristic of his whole intellectual style that these statements should be made in the context of assessments of the writings of other anthropologists: his intellectual 'ancestors', his teachers, sparring partners, and *bêtes noires*; the heroes and the villains, as he saw it, in the continuing history of anthropology.

Leach typically thought in what he sometimes called 'dialectical' terms. It was natural to him to characterise an intellectual position in terms of what it was against, and in terms of the historical dynamics of intellectual debate. What was this or that author reacting against in the writings of the previous generation? What were the contradictions or inconsistencies that gave rise to a new line of thought? This gave him a strong sense of anthropology as a dynamical tradition and an abiding interest in the history and in the prehistory of anthropological thought. In the 1950s Leach's undergraduate lectures on 'The History of Anthropological Theory' began with Herodotus, Aristotle, and Lucretius; and continued through Hobbes, Montesquieu, Rousseau, Condorcet, Malthus, Pritchard, Comte, de Gobineau, Morgan, Darwin, Bastian, Bachofen, Maine, Tylor, Fustel de Coulanges, McLennan, Spencer, and Robertson Smith, before reaching Frazer and the Torres Straits Expedition.[3] Leach's interest in the dynamics of intellectual history is evident even in some of his earliest writings, but it became still more prominent in his later career (see II.5). And in later life he also wrote in a similar vein about his own life as an anthropologist, and about his professional relations with colleagues and contemporaries.[4]

Accordingly, Leach was often concerned with an author as much on account of what his influence had been, as with what he had actually written and said. Thus Frazer held his attention more because he had come to be widely regarded outside the discipline as representative of anthropology; and Radcliffe-Brown because Leach held him responsible for what he regarded as his colleagues' most damaging confusions. During one of his most vehement critical discussions of Radcliffe-Brown he remarked, 'I am not now concerned with what was right or wrong about Radcliffe-Brown's argument but rather with what has become of that argument in the context of the kind of debate which goes on among social anthropologists in 1976' (I.1.8: 83).

But Leach's most sustained and fruitful critical engagements were with those from whom he learned the most: his teachers Malinowski and Firth, and, though he never explicitly recognised his older contemporary as an 'ancestor', Lévi-Strauss. And to lesser extents and at different times in his life, Leach also went through the cycle he describes above of rapt fascination, critical rejection, and mature assimilated influence, with a number of other authors such as Freud, Vico, and Peirce.

Leach was quite conscious of the importance to his thought of Malinowski's influence, and of the quasi-Oedipal ambivalence with which he regarded his teachers. In his contribution to the *Festschrift* for Malinowski edited by Raymond Firth (I.1.2), Leach wrote, 'Malinowski, I have insisted, was "in bondage" to his predecessors; he resented their existence because he was so much indebted to them. Some of us perhaps feel the same about Bronislaw Malinowski.' And interestingly, Leach elsewhere attributed (or displaced?) the same feelings about Malinowski on to Firth himself (see I.1.4).

For decades after Malinowski's death, Leach kept up a one-sided debate with his former teacher. Many of his most successful and influential essays were based on reassessment and re-analysis of Malinowski's Trobriand ethnography (see I.3.4; I.3.7; II.2.2; and II.3.2).[5] And although Leach's own writings on Malinowski were often highly critical, he felt called upon to lead the defence when the latter was attacked by others. He was very hostile to the publication of Malinowski's fieldwork diaries (I.1.3), and readily attributed the decision by the executors to greed for financial gain. He saw immediately the uses to which the diary would be put, and the claims that would be made on the basis of it, and he did his best to rubbish them in advance (though his way of doing so hardly served to lower the temperature).[6]

Malinowski's Trobriand corpus and Firth's Tikopia were always among Leach's touchstone ethnographies of an 'ultra-primitive society'. But beyond that he remained entranced by the details of Trobriand ethnography – of which, at least outside those who conducted fieldwork there, he probably had an unrivalled mastery. As late as the early 1980s he was still thinking actively about the Kula, and encouraging others to do the same.[7]

If Leach put a lot of energy, in different ways, into maintaining Malinowski's importance as a 'founding father' of anthropology, he was almost equally tireless in doing what he could to lower the standing of Frazer.[8] There are a number of reasons for Leach's antipathy. Frazer certainly represented much that Leach disliked: what he saw as the pointless pedantry of his scholarship, the Establishment toadyism of his life and conduct; the tastelessness of his 'fine writing'; the threadbare racism underlying his intellectual system; and his failure to appreciate the importance of ethnographic context. But Leach could have more or less ignored Frazer. As he himself observed, by the time he got his teeth into him most of his professional colleagues were already doing just that. And equally, there were innumerable other earlier anthropologists who thought and wrote in roughly the same way. The reason he didn't do so is more or less explicit. Frazer was famous. He was the anthropologist most people had heard of, and when they thought of anthropology most people thought of Frazer. Therefore, it is as public figures as much as intellectual 'founding fathers' that Leach compares Malinowski and Frazer. Behind this lay a concern that anthropologists should be able to communicate with a wider reading public, and strong views about the proper way to do this. Again, Malinowski was an important reference point and Leach sought both to emulate and to surpass him.

Malinowski certainly resorted to some fairly low gimmicks in order to publicise his work: most notably in book titles such as *The Sexual Life of Savages*.[9] But in the books themselves his method was to show how information about how a 'primitive' society worked could change the way we should think about our own; and in this way to make informed discussion about other cultures a central part of general intellectual debate. This was different from that long tradition in which descriptions of more or less imaginary 'primitive societies' are presented as natural moral exemplars, and models for how to reform our own corrupt civilisation. That tradition, recast in new language by the Boasian doctrine of cultural determinism, gained special prominence for American cultural anthropology through the writings of Margaret Mead. Leach noted with evident satisfaction that Mead's cult status was restricted to the United States, and that her writings had always been regarded by professional anthropologists, especially in Britain, as slight and unreliable. In his view they scarcely merited, on academic grounds, Freeman's polemical demolition, but Leach nevertheless took the opportunity, in reviewing the latter, to drive the point home himself. What Mead had described, and impressed on the public mind in the United States, was a 'Shangri-la that never was' (I.1.12).[10] And he had equally little time for the neo-Marxist thesis, which began to be widely canvassed in the 1970s, that anthropologists should re-invent themselves as paid-up partisans of fashionable political causes (I.1.11; see also II.4.6 and II.5: 344)[11]

Malinowski, although sometimes seen as a prophet of sexual freedom, was more concerned to insist that a proper appreciation of, for example, how a matrilineal kinship system actually worked (in *Sex and Repression*), should affect, at a very basic level, how we think about the dynamics of human sexuality, and so present a challenge to the Freudian view of the Oedipus complex.[12] Similarly, the point of *Crime and Custom* is not to recommend anarchism, or any other specific political programme, and still less to tell us anything about prehistory or the origins of the state, but to present a challenge to legal theory: a difficult new case to think about and so a spur to new ideas. This was the model for popularising anthropology and addressing a wide non-professional audience that Leach himself tried to follow. The findings of anthropologists in distant places have direct relevance to life here at home, if we ask the right questions and think about them hard enough. 'If the peculiarities of crime and custom in savage society are interesting', he told the audience for his 1977 Munro Lectures in Edinburgh, 'it is because, if we look hard enough, we shall find these peculiarities close at hand in the streets of Edinburgh as well as in far away Melanesia.'[13] The lessons are general ones which are relevant to all humans everywhere. Almost the only good thing he has to say about Frazer is that he did at least ask 'the big questions', and that is why he held people's interest. Leach sought to do the same. The fields of enquiry that caught his attention – mathematical topology, psychoanalysis, structural linguistics, artificial intelligence, evolutionary biology, ethology, ecology, and so on – did so because they seemed to hold out the hope of providing new kinds of answers to 'the big questions', or at least of asking them in a new and interesting way.

This project for making anthropology 'relevant' involved a ready enthusiasm for controversy and often heated invective and argument. Leach pulled no punches where something he read had angered him (see I.1.11; II.4.2; II.3.3; and II.4.8); and especially from the mid-1960s onwards he appeared frequently on the lecturing platform taking his kind of anthropology to various public bodies, professional associations, and interest groups (II.4.5; II.4.6; and II.4.7); as well as writing for the public press and broadcasting (see I.2.6; I.2.7; I.3.6; I.4.1; I.4.4; II.4.2; II.4.3; II.4.4; II.4.8; and II.4.9). In all these contexts he delighted in challenging and sometimes shocking his audiences with far-fetched analogies, rhetorical questions, and sweeping generalisations. By these means, and especially in his role as expositor of Lévi-Strauss's structuralism in the educated press, he became for a while something of the same chic commentator among 'advanced' opinion-formers in England as Malinowski had been between the wars. And characteristically, he had no sooner achieved notoriety as an anti-Establishment radical than the tone of many of his writings and addresses started to change. Now it was as often as not 'progressive' assumptions and orthodoxies that he saw it as his duty to upset.[14] No wonder he described himself as 'both Radical and High Tory'.[15]

Leach's talent for controversy and invective was equally in evidence inside the professional world of social anthropology. For much of his career (until the advent of Marxism in the 1970s) he saw the social anthropology of his day as dominated by the 'school of Radcliffe-Brown'. He became famously embroiled in controversies with some of its leading members – notably his Cambridge colleagues Meyer Fortes and Jack Goody – which typically combined highly technical argument with intensely personal rhetoric. (People who knew both Leach and Fortes seem divided about just how personal the disagreements between them really were.) Leach used the opportunity of the 1976 Radcliffe-Brown Memorial Lecture to launch an unrestrained attack on the thinker he was supposed to be commemorating, and included fairly explicit suggestions that he was, personally, an intellectual fraud (I.1.8).[16] But the main target of attack, in this and in a host of other publications, was what Leach took to be the central theoretical presuppositions and procedures of the structural-functionalist approach: the organic analogy, the idea of a bounded social structure, the assumption of equilibrium, and the ambition to achieve 'scientific' knowledge by means of typological classification.

The organic analogy he regarded as a compound of several catastrophic errors: a sloppy analogy between an unsustainable, racist conception of the differences between human groups, and an out-of-date and superficial conception of biological species (I.1.8; see also II.5).[17] The use of the concept of 'function' by Radcliffe-Brown and his followers depended on this organic analogy. Their working assumption that societies existed in bounded and stable equilibrium could only be sustained by the 'dogmatic assertion' of social and cultural homogeneity within 'primitive' societies (I.1.6; see also Section 3 of this volume).

Leach was perhaps optimistically ahead of his time, but was nevertheless fundamentally correct, when he predicted in 1958 that the mid-century paradigm of a 'social science' had largely run its course (I.1.7). The ambition that social anthropology should be a typological science produced implausible portraits of societies peopled by clockwork marionettes, and would always be fundamentally at odds with the practice of fieldwork bequeathed to the discipline by Malinowski. 'The modern anthropologist is studying intercommunicating human beings, friends, fellow anthropologists, people who are in intimate personal relationships with himself as well as with one another, not specimens in glass bottles' (I.1.8: 93). Hence his objection to 'butterfly collecting' (I.3.7). There is a radical incompatibility between scientific detachment and participant observation. This has meant that for anthropologists the idea of a 'natural science of society', as Radcliffe-Brown conceived it, would never really carry conviction. As Leach remarks (I.1.11), that realisation goes back to Malinowski himself (I.1.2; I.1.8).

But while he was sceptical about the whole idea that anthropology could be a science, and hostile to the then fashionable conceptions of what that science might be like, these attitudes did not arise from hostility to science as such. It is clear that his enthusiasm for structuralism derived in part from the hope that it might provide anthropology with a more-or-less respectably scientific methodology for at least some of what it sets out to do.[18]

Leach had a sustained and informed interest in several branches of the natural sciences, he followed changing trends in scientific thinking fairly closely, and repeatedly and throughout his career he drew inspiration for his own work from new scientific developments. This was one of the sources of the affinity he felt with Gregory Bateson (I.1.5). He had an abiding interest in the history of technology and its impact on social change;[19] and he believed that psychology and biology bore directly on the social anthropologist's concerns. So he deplored what he saw as the widespread resort, especially in American cultural anthropology, to uninformed and dogmatic assertions that biology plays no determining role in human behaviour (I.1.12; I.1.13).

While his position was fairly consistently hostile to structural–functionalist theory, the focus of Leach's criticisms, and the rhetoric used to advance them, were anything but consistent; and the same is true of his equally well-known 'advocacy' of structuralism. In the 1950s, for the most part, Leach aligned himself with an 'empiricist' Malinowskian minority which stressed individual decision and economic interest, against the tidy abstractions of the theory of 'social structure'. Firth's notion of 'social organisation' he regarded, without much enthusiasm, as a compromise (I.1.4).[20] In the 1960s he championed Lévi-Straussian structuralism against what he portrayed as a near-sighted Anglo-Saxon obsession with empirical detail. In this guise he was happy to play the role of a herald of clever 'theory', whose opponents were just too stupid or slow to see the point (I.3.7). But he was equally happy to invoke Anglo-Saxon empiricist scepticism against Lévi-Straussian 'rationalism'. For this he was occasionally prepared to collapse the divisions within British social anthropology, which elsewhere he tended to play up, and even (see I.1.9) to cite with apparent approval Fortes' key paper, 'The Structure of Unilineal Descent Groups', from almost every major contention of which he dissented at one time or another.

Leach was frequently asked to review new works by Lévi-Strauss in both professional journals[21] and non-professional periodicals,[22] but objected to being referred to as a 'follower' of Lévi-Strauss. He never seems wholly comfortable in the role of exegete and expositor. 'Telstar and the Aborigines' (I.1.10), written in 1964, was a direct response to the publication two years earlier of Lévi-Strauss's *La Pensée sauvage*, but half of it is taken up with the extension of Lévi-Strauss's arguments to domains in which he himself had not applied them (see Introduction to Section 4). In 1967, in a review of *The Savage Mind* and *Mythologiques II* he wrote, 'I have put in that cautionary paragraph for the benefit of my anthropological colleagues, some of whom seem to think that I am such a devoted Lévi-Straussian that I can no longer exercise any scholarly detachment on the subject at all.'[23] As structuralism became more fashionable, his 'functionalist' doubts about Lévi-Strauss's use of ethnographic evidence, which he had voiced right from the start,[24] became progressively more prominent in his writings. His 1970 'Modern Masters' on Lévi-Strauss,[25] although part of a series of generally proselytising handbooks on currently fashionable intellectual luminaries, was highly critical in tone.

At the most basic level, Leach's biggest problem with Lévi-Strauss was the latter's anti-humanism: the reification of 'society' and attribution to this reified entity of agency comparable to that of the individual human being (I.1.9; II.1.3). Leach shared the deep hostility he finds in Malinowski (I.1.2) to any notion of a 'group mind', and in general to all fantasies of the 'supraorganic'. But for the most part such doubts take second place to his enthusiasm for the sheer grandeur and originality of Lévi-Strauss's thought. Comparing it to Freud's psychoanalysis, about which he was equally ambivalent, Leach declares Lévi-Straussian structuralism to be 'an innovation from which there can be no retreat' (I.1.10).[26]

It is perhaps worth mentioning in passing a figure who is notable for his absence from this section. Edward Evans-Pritchard was, at least until the early 1950s, as much a student of Radcliffe-Brown as was Fortes. But Leach never seems to have tried to pick a fight with him. In the 1960s, in reviews of late collections of Evans-Pritchard's essays, he unkindly rubs in the observation that the days of the latter's intellectual creativity seemed to have passed; but always acknowledged the achievements of his earlier works.[27] The nearest he seems to have come to explicit criticism in print was in *Pul Eliya* (1961), where he describes *The Nuer* as 'brilliantly simplified' (I.3.5). Late in life, Leach claimed to have admired Evans-Pritchard's later work, 'after he had shed his links with Radcliffe-Brown'[28] (meaning one supposes especially *Nuer Religion*), but he rarely seems to have referred to it. Even after Evans-Pritchard's death, Leach's comments on him are generally allusive to the point of mystery: like his unexplained assertion that in addition to his Roman Catholicism, Evans-Pritchard's homosexuality was 'crucial to his anthropology' (I.1.13).

Leach's most negative writing on Evans-Pritchard occurs in his review of Mary Douglas's 1980 'Modern Masters' volume on him.[29] It is relevant to an understanding of Leach's extremely critical review that Evans-Pritchard and Malinowski are known, latterly, to have loathed each other very cordially, and Leach begins his review by observing that there can be no sensible principle at work in selection of subjects for the series, since here we have a volume on Evans-Pritchard but there is none on Malinowski.

The review is set up, rhetorically, as a dispassionate empirical historian's complaint about an unscholarly devotional tract.[30] Douglas, whose Catholicism is an explicit element in her anthropological writings, is 'a very appropriate hagiographer' for her Catholic-convert teacher, who is presented in the book, Leach tells us, as a miraculous fount of infallible truths whose implications are still being explored by his disciples, notably Douglas herself. Thus Douglas claims that Evans-Pritchard invented the concept of negative feedback in *The Nuer*, thereby antedating Norbert Wiener by some eight years. 'For those of us who are less inclined to believe in miracles', says Leach, it seems obvious that what Evans-Pritchard does in that book is a straightforward application of Durkheim. The book is unhistorical, but then history is not the point: 'her task is to provide a new revelation'. But behind Leach's rhetoric, his real gripe about Douglas's book is that the influence and originality of his own teacher, Malinowski, is not sufficiently acknowledged. His complaint springs from his own sectarian loyalty: the apostolic succession of the true church of anthropology is being distorted and claimed by a rival sect! Leach is on hand to put things right: he puts forward an argument (actually rather plausible) for the strong influence of Malinowski on Evans-Pritchard's 'Cairo Essays', which Douglas had identified in her book as containing the kernel of all his later teachings.[31]

In the late 1960s and through the 1970s structuralism was largely displaced by Marxism as the leading intellectual fashion in anthropology. Leach clearly followed this development with interest, but it did not much influence his own anthropology.[32] The attempt by Jonathan Friedman to recast his Kachin ethnography in the language of structural Marxism he received with extreme hostility;[33] and he continued regularly to declare his opposition to any kind of 'historicism' or 'historical determinism'.[34] Leach was also impatient with the quasi-theological nature of much Marxist debate, in which conformity with holy writ was more important than either faithfulness to the facts or having new and interesting ideas. The essay 'Claude Lévi-Strauss: Anthropologist and Philosopher' (I.1.9) was written in 1965 for the *New Left Review*, and Leach was well aware that the question of whether or not Lévi-Strauss could be regarded as a Marxist of the approved fashion would have been of the first importance to his readers. He faithfully reports that Lévi-Strauss declared himself to be a Marxist, then notes that nevertheless Lévi-Strauss's position 'seems far removed from that of historical determinism in any simple sense' (1.9: 102). Leach was well aware that this last phrase would sound like a cracked bell amid the debates in that journal on what exactly is the correct interpretation of historical materialism; and he went on to give a fairly clear indication of what he thought of those debates: 'It is very difficult for anyone who is not highly expert in the appropriate form of discourse to say whether [Lévi-Strauss's] position can properly be said to be Marxist or even to understand where Marx comes into it at all' (1.9: 103).[35]

During the 1970s and 1980s Leach also watched trends within American cultural anthropology, and the increasing convergence between that tradition and the formerly rather separate world of British social anthropology. Opposition to what Leach took to be one of the foundational assumptions of cultural anthropology – that it makes sense to talk of 'cultures' in the plural – was a long-standing theme in his writing,[36] and this is evident in his ambivalent reaction even to the work of one of that tradition's greatest exponents (see I.1.13; I.1.14). Certain developments interested him very much. The distinctive treatment of structuralist ideas in the United States was one, differing from European versions as it did largely through the influence of Peirce.[37] Another was the theme of ethnography as fiction, though Leach tended to see this not as a radical new departure, but as an idea which had existed in anthropology, in creative tension with the aspiration to scientific knowledge, ever since the days of Malinowski (I.1.14).[38] But it is clear that as time went on, in describing and commenting on the contemporary scene in cultural anthropology, Leach was commenting on an intellectual world that was increasingly different from that in which he himself thought.

Notes

1. Leach in Kuper, 'Interview with Edmund Leach', p. 380.
2. Leach, 'Glimpses of the Unmentionable', p. 20.
3. ERL: 5/54.

4. See 'Glimpses of the Unmentionable'; 'Notes on the Mythology of Cambridge Anthropology' (1984).
5. See also *Custom, Law, and Terrorist Violence* (1977); 'The Kula: An Alternative View' (1983). In the former of these Leach says, 'I was a direct pupil of Malinowski and whatever I may say in criticism of his attitudes must be understood against the background fact that I consider him the greatest and most original of all social anthropologists' (pp. 5–6).
6. In addition to I.1.3 see 'Malinowskiana' (1980) and the subsequent correspondence; also 'Masquerade', p. 5.
7. See Leach and Leach (eds), *The Kula.*
8. In addition to 'Frazer and Malinowski' (I.1.1), see 'Golden Bough or Gilded Twig?' (1961); 'Frazer Reconsidered' (1970); 'All that Glitters is not Gold' (1977); 'Reconsiderations: *The Golden Bough*' (1978); 'Frazer' (1982); 'Reflections on a Visit to Nemi' (1985). See also the interesting discussion by Mary Beard, 'Frazer, Leach, and Virgil'.
9. Leach never did this in his books. His popular articles and reviews do often have rather witty titles – such as 'O Come All Ye Faithful' (1977) for his review of *Structural Anthropology II*; 'Long Pig: Tall Story' for his demolition of Arens's claim that no society has ever practised cannibalism (II.4.8) – not all of which may be due to clever sub-editors.
10. See also Leach, 'Middle America' (1985).
11. The themes in this piece are enlarged on by Leach in a magnificent, but quite extraordinarily vituperative (and never published) review, which he wrote for *Comparative Studies in Society and History*, of Stanley Diamond's *In Search of the Primitive* (ERL: 2/30). See also 'The Integration of Minorities' (II.4.6).
12. Leach of course was to continue this argument. See 'Virgin Birth' (II.4.2).
13. *Custom, Law, and Terrorist Violence*, p. 14.
14. Interesting examples include 'The Integration of Minorities' (II.4.6), 'Education and Social Conditioning' (II.4.7), and *Culture and Nature or La Femme sauvage* (1969).
15. Leach recalled how in the 1930s, along with many young intellectuals of the time, he was 'of a radical, near communist, political persuasion' (see 'Glimpses of the Unmentionable', p. 9). In the late 1980s, however, in an interview with M. Buchowski he remarked, 'All I can say is that I have always felt myself to be on the left in English politics but not very far to the left; and that is a pretty feeble position!' (English version ERL: 1/311).
16. See also *Custom, Law, and Terrorist Violence*, p. 6; and Needham, 'Surmise, Discovery, and Rhetoric'.
17. In an unpublished seminar paper from his time at the London School of Economics, Leach remarks that the 'dogma of equilibrium' in anthropology 'derives not from Darwin or Spencer or Lamarck but from Gobineau' (ERL: 5/1).
18. This is evident, for instance, in 'The Structure of Symbolism' (1972).
19. See Leach's early publications on the Yami: also 'Primitive Time Reckoning' (1954); and his Cantor Lectures, 'The Study of Man in Relation to Science and Technology' (1973).
20. See also the remarks in Leach's Preface to *L'Unité de l'homme* (pp. 19–20) in which he contrasts his own essay 'Magical Hair' (II.4.2) with Firth's paper on 'Hair' in his book *Symbols: Public and Private* (1973), and which Leach describes as being 'à la manière frazérienne'.
21. Review of Lévi-Strauss's edition of the works of Marcel Mauss (1951); Review of *Le Totémisme aujourd'hui* and *La Pensée sauvage* in *Man* (1963); Review of *Mythologiques I* in *American Anthropologist* (1965).
22. Review of *Totemism* and other books in *New Statesman* (1965); 'Brain-Twister': Review of *The Savage Mind* and *Mythologiques II* in *New York Review of Books* (1967); Review of Charbonnier, *Conversations with Claude Lévi-Strauss* in *The Listener* (1969); Review of *Tristes Tropiques* in *New Scientist* (1974); Review of *Structural Anthropology II* in *The Spectator* (1977); Reviews of *The View from Afar* in *Partisan Review* and *London Review of Books* (1986).
23. 'Brain-Twister' (1967). See also the Introduction to *The Structural Study of Myth and Totemism* (1967), where Leach both describes himself as 'personally more closely addicted to Lévi-Strauss's methods than are most of my colleagues as represented in this book' (p. x); and also insists, 'I do not consider that I am a slavish imitator of Lévi-Strauss' (p. xv).
24. See 'Structural Implications' (1951).
25. *Lévi-Strauss* (1970).

26. In his introduction to *The Structural Study of Myth and Totemism* Leach explicitly compares Lévi-Strauss to Malinowski in this respect. Responding to the charge that Lévi-Strauss was just 'a passing fashion', he wrote: 'But of course everything is a passing fashion. Malinowski's critics raised the same argument forty years ago and of course they were right. We no longer adhere to the doctrines which Malinowski espoused with such enthusiasm. Nevertheless, anthropology today would be a wholly different thing if Malinowski had never existed. Lévi-Strauss is important in this same sense' (pp. xv–xvi).
27. 'Nostalgia' (1962); 'Paths and Deserts' (1965).
28. Leach in Kuper, 'Interview with Edmund Leach', p. 380.
29. See Douglas, *Evans-Pritchard.* See the Introduction to Volume II for a discussion of the points of similarity and antipathy between Leach and Douglas.
30. Leach, 'Cairo Essays' (1980).
31. Another anthropologist of whom Leach said remarkably little in print is Victor Turner. The two shared many interests, not least the profound inspiration each found in the work of van Gennep, and their interest in psychoanalysis. But Leach hardly engaged at all with Turner's writings directly. It looks as if what Turner had to say just did not interest him very much. And the latter's marked hostility to structuralism (as expressed in *The Ritual Process*, for example) is unlikely to have endeared him to Leach.
32. In 'Cultura/Culture' (1978) Leach gives one of his more positive characterisations of Marxist anthropology, but it is positive just in so far as he identifies in it one of his own preoccupations, and it is unlikely to have made him very many friends among its practitioners; 'It is sometimes evolutionist–historicist in a nineteenth-century mode, sometimes neo-functionalist, sometimes even structuralist; it is polemical, ideological and full of outdated rhetoric denouncing the early twentieth-century anthropologists as lackeys of colonialist imperialism. Its strength lies in a willingness to recognise that the "tribes" of conventional ethnography are not static isolate systems with isolate histories, but dynamic sub-systems of larger social–political–economic complexes which are themselves in a continuous state of developmental flux.'
33. Friedman, 'Tribes, States, and Transformations'. Leach's unpublished response, in note form, is in the Leach Archive.
34. This is an important leitmotif throughout 'Anthropos' (II.5) for instance; and also in Leach's Reith Lectures (see II.4.4). See also the somewhat gratuitous declaration in *Structuralist Interpretations of Biblical Myth*, p. 10.
35. See also *Lévi-Strauss*, pp. 21–3.
36. It is worth noting, however, that he himself uses the idea of 'cultural boundaries', though admittedly only in passing, in 'Magical Hair' (II.3.2) and 'Levels of Communication and Problems of Taboo' (II.3.4).
37. See Leach, *Culture and Communication* (1976); also 'Sri Minaksi and her Tamil Cousins' (1984); Review of Singer, *Man's Glassy Essence* (1985); 'C. S. Peirce in Tamil Nadu' (1987).
38. See also *Social Anthropology* (1982); 'Tribal Ethnography' (1989).

1.1
Frazer and Malinowski (1965)

Between the basic absurdity Frazer attributed to primitive practices and beliefs and the specious validation of them in terms of the supposed common-sense invoked by Malinowski, there is scope for a whole science and a whole philosophy.

Claude Lévi-Strauss, *La Pensée sauvage*

The study of man must be central for everyone but anthropology is just another -ology. Opinion may be about evenly divided as to whether it is the study of apes or the name of an obscure religious sect. Even so, every now and then, a professional anthropologist becomes an international 'celebrity', and one wonders why. Of the living, only Margaret Mead has quite achieved this, but among the recent dead there are at least two others, Sir James Frazer, the author of *The Golden Bough*, and Bronislaw Malinowski, 'who wrote something or other about sex'.

Public renown need not imply professional esteem. Contemporary anthropologists for the most part consider Malinowski to be a major figure; they decry Frazer as a mere miser of facts. Anyone who doubts this need only take a look at the two latest general textbooks of the subject. Both authors[1] take for granted a whole set of Malinowski's concepts and build their thinking into this frame of reference; Frazer is treated as an historical figure of quite secondary significance, worth mentioning only because he was in grievous error.

But perhaps the experts are prejudiced. Dr Jarvie, a philosopher and pupil of Karl Popper, has recently presented Malinowski as the false prophet who led British anthropologists into the wilderness of profitless fact-collecting, whereas his Frazer appears as a hero of righteousness whose vigorous and original theories clearly marked out the path of scientific virtue.[2]

It is very natural that Dr Jarvie, as a good Popperite, should want to stimulate the thinking of his anthropological colleagues by challenging their dearest assumptions; and certainly he will be in no way abashed if I argue that his theses are false and untenable. It is just as well to get the record straight. There is a very wide discrepancy between Dr Jarvie's account of the recent history of British anthropology and what actually happened. The living prototypes of his 'Frazer' and 'Malinowski' died respectively in 1941 and 1942. The myth is worth investigating.

'Frazer' is admired by Dr Jarvie because he engaged in 'comparative sociology', the comparison of similar social phenomena occurring in different contexts of time and space. 'Frazer' was a man 'with lots of ideas' which is the Popperite way of saying that he was always ready to guess about causal connections linking together the facts at his disposal. The circumstance that very few of Frazer's 'conjectures' seem in the least plausible and that, on the rare occasions when they can be tested, they almost invariably prove to be wrong does not worry Dr Jarvie in the least. From his point of view, it is the method and not the truth that matters.

It seems that 'comparative sociology' can help us to understand regularities in historical sequences. When investigating an exotic institution from a primitive culture we should first consider the logic of the situation as it appears to us. This will give us a theory about how the members of such a culture might be expected to behave. If we then go on to interpret our actual observations, on a comparative basis and in the light of this same ethnocentric situational logic, we shall be led to discover regularities which will enable us to predict the circumstances under which institutions of this particular kind are likely to arise and develop. Now Frazer, too, was interested in historical process and his judgements about 'savages' were always based on a highly ethnocentric assessment of the logic of the savage's situation. So Frazer's 'evolutionism' must be considered sound as methodology even if it led to all the wrong conclusions.

Dr Jarvie also greatly admires the whole ethos of the library-bound scholar of which Sir James Frazer was such a superlative example. He believes, as Frazer believed, that first-hand experience of primitive peoples is a discomfort which the more intelligent anthropologist can well afford to do without. He thinks that the best anthropologists will do their best work while cogitating about the writings of others. This mental activity will (or may) lead to useful speculations about the nature of Human Society in general. Dr Jarvie does not claim that Frazer's own speculations were particularly illuminating, but he approves of what Frazer tried to do and of the way he tried to do it. He appreciates that this Frazerian manner may be linked with a deep-seated contempt for nine-tenths of the human race; that he is prepared to accept. He also accepts Frazer's literary style as 'exhilarating'; he supposes (quite erroneously) that Frazer was an unqualified atheist; and he credits Frazer with an academic status which he never possessed.

The complementary disapproval of 'Malinowski' is not so straightforward. In the Jarvie schema, 'Malinowski' is the hostile antithesis of 'Frazer'. In the early 1920s this aspiring and ambitious man was preoccupied with the destruction of 'Frazer's' reputation: the jealous 'son' had started a revolution against the all-powerful 'father'. This is bizarre – because the living Malinowski was the most persistent and devoted disciple of the real Frazer. In 1926 he wrote of *The Golden Bough* that

> No sooner had I begun to read this great work than I became immersed in and enslaved by it . . . and became bound to the service of Frazerian anthropology.

Even sixteen years later, although he could now take an objective view of Frazer's limitations, he was still in thrall:

> His [Frazer's] enormous creative influence surprises sometimes even his devoted admirer when confronted by one of the naïve theoretical arguments from *The Golden Bough* or some other of his volumes. His inability to convince seems to contradict his power to convert and to inspire.

Dr Jarvie also disapproves of Malinowski because of the way he emphasised the value of original fieldwork. Dr Jarvie appears to be an anthropologist *manqué*; philosophy was his second love. He now justifies his infidelity by saying that the first lady would have been most uncomfortable.

'Frazer the Evolutionist' and 'Malinowski the Functionalist' represent the contrast between a concern with how things have come to be as they are and a concern with how things, as they are, are interrelated with one another. For Dr Jarvie, functionalist investigations are pointless because they cannot give causal explanations of historical sequences; in contrast 'the evolutionists were answering different questions from those Malinowski was interested in, but theirs were satisfactory answers to the questions they had posed themselves'. This is a surprising opinion for a follower of Professor Popper.[3] What are the facts of the case?

The continuing celebrity of Sir James Frazer (Dr Jarvie apart) is an astonishing phenomenon. There are now two quite separate one-volume abridgments of the huge thirteen-volume *The Golden Bough*, and both apparently have a steady sale. Who are the buyers? What do they get from their reading?

From one point of view (the evolution of his world fame), the most important single fact in the career of the historical Frazer is that in 1896, at the age of forty-two, he married Lily Grove, a French widow, who thereafter made the enlargement of her husband's public image her sole preoccupation. It was an outstandingly successful public relations operation, and it has contributed to the distortions of the legend. Worldly success in the form of a knighthood, an Order of Merit, and strings of honorary degrees only started coming in around 1914, and it is this perhaps which has led Dr Jarvie to imagine that in the early 1920s, when Malinowski was in the ascendant, Frazer was the securely established leader of his profession. That was not the case; Frazer's personal influence was by that time insignificant. His strictly academic reputation had begun to fade before 1900. In later years he had great renown; he maintained a voluminous correspondence; and his books were always widely reviewed. But it does not appear that his views were highly regarded. Sometimes the style of his critics suggests that they might have been his close disciples, but this too is deceptive. The leading anthropologists of his time (including Frazer himself) were all close imitators of two much more brilliant men: E. B. Tylor and W. Robertson Smith. Frazer was an outstanding representative of the anthropology of his day, but that day had ended by 1910. For the next fifteen years British historical anthropology was completely dominated by the diffusionist views of Elliot Smith and W. J. Perry; as for the sociologists, they were taking all their cues from the school of Emile Durkheim in Paris. Frazer had ceased to matter.[4]

Frazer's original competence was in the classics and here his skill was very great indeed. Classical erudition is common enough but even so Frazer's carefully edited translations of Pausanias' *Description of Greece* and of Ovid's *Fasti* are outstanding of their kind. The source of Frazer's fame lay elsewhere; his colleagues were entranced by the novel use to which he applied the 'comparative method' which he had taken over from Tylor.[5] The first (two-volume) edition of *The Golden Bough* appeared in 1890. This was acclaimed on the quite specious ground that it revealed 'comparative anthropology [as] a serious study actually capable of elucidating a Greek or Latin text'. Classical scholars have always been frustrated by lacunae in the records, and perhaps the 'comparative method' could be used to make good this deficiency.

The avowed purpose of *The Golden Bough*, as expressed in the first chapter, was to investigate certain classical accounts concerning the rites associated with the worship of Diana at Nemi in southern Italy. The accounts are very incomplete, and Frazer agreed that there is not enough direct evidence to justify any particular interpretation. He proposed, however, to fill in the gaps by resorting to analogy. First he postulated that the Priest of Nemi was deemed to be the spouse of Diana; then, having cited examples of ritual theogamy from Babylon, Egypt, Athens, Eleusis, Russia, Sweden, Gaul, Peru, North America, Bengal, West and East Africa, and the Maldive Islands, he concluded:

> The evidence may, therefore, lend some countenance to the conjecture that in the sacred grove of Nemi where the powers of vegetation and of water manifested themselves in the fair forms of shady woods, tumbling cascades and glassy lake, a marriage like that of our King and Queen of May was annually celebrated between the mortal King of the Wood and the immortal Queen of the Wood, Diana. . . .

This, I may say, is a typical example of the style which admirers find so exhilarating. In fact, of course, the 'evidence' is totally irrelevant to the 'conjecture', and it was not very long before this irrelevance came to be fairly generally appreciated. Thereafter the interest of the professional classicists waned rather rapidly.

In the much narrower field of professional anthropology Frazer's standing was eminent and his phenomenal industry inspired awe; but his contributions to theory evoked no respect at all. Since he was a thoroughly bad public speaker, engaged in no teaching, and had no immediate pupils, his reputation rested exclusively on published work. This is bulky rather than profound, and even the bulk is deceptive.

Frazer's career as an author extended from 1884 to 1938. His output, excluding multiple editions of the same work, fills at least two yards of shelf space; yet in all this vast mass of print the total amount of material which represents a genuinely original contribution by Frazer himself probably adds up to only a few hundred pages. The rest consists of excerpts from the writings of others, sometimes quoted verbatim, but more often rephrased to suit the sentimental lilt which Frazer considered to be the essential quality of fine writing. Quite explicitly he thought of himself as making a contribution to literature rather than to science, and it does not seem to have occurred to him that in 'improving' his sources he might also be distorting them. He was perfectly frank about his procedures. Commenting on the difference between the original quotations recorded in his notebooks and the passages which appear in his own published works, Frazer wrote:

> [The notebook extracts] are written for the most part in a plain, straightforward way, the authors contenting themselves with describing in simple language the things which they have seen or had heard reported by competent native informants. Few, if any, possess that magic charm of style which, by firing the imagination or touching the heart, can alone confer what we fondly call immortality upon a work of literature.[6]

Frazer knew better, and how right he was! Clearly there have always been many who, like Dr Jarvie, 'find Frazer glorious and thrilling reading'.

All the same the diligence is quite extraordinary. A doubtful 'conjecture' does not become less doubtful by stating it twenty times over: but even the most sceptical critic finds himself yielding in fascinated incredulity as Frazer piles up his mountains of recondite 'evidence'.

Besterman's bibliography of Frazer's writings[7] (which is incomplete) runs to 266 items, but they are easily classified. With only minor exceptions all fall unambiguously into one or other of the following six categories:

(1) Translations and editions of the classics. These include Frazer's very first published work, a school edition of Sallust, and more substantially the Pausanias and Ovid already mentioned.

(2) Writings about the primitive concept of the soul. These start with two articles published in 1885 which were later expanded to a three-volume, *The Belief in Immortality and the Worship of the Dead.* The argument is reduced again to more manageable scale in *The Fear of the Dead in Primitive Religion* (1933). The whole of this series is derived from the second volume of Tylor's *Primitive Culture* (1871). Tylor's thesis is elaborately illustrated but not developed.

(3) Writings about totemism ('the worship of animal and plant species'). These start with an article commissioned by Robertson Smith as Editor of the *Encyclopaedia Britannica* and published in 1889. By 1910 this had become a four-volume work, *Totemism and Exogamy.* A fifth volume, *Totemica,* was added in 1937. Frazer propounded in all three quite different theories about the 'origin' of totemism. These he prints side by side in the 1910 volumes, but no fellow anthropologist has ever expressed any marked enthusiasm for any of them.

(4) Writings about folklore in the Old Testament (i.e. parallels between primitive customs as recorded by ethnographers and passages in the Bible). This work starts as a short essay in 1907 but had grown to three volumes by 1918. The whole is really a gloss upon what Robertson Smith had written in *Kinship and Marriage in Early Arabia* (1885) and *Lectures on the Religion of the Semites* (1889).

(5) A work entitled *Passages of the Bible: Chosen for their Literary Beauty and Interest by J. G. Frazer, M.A., Fellow of Trinity College, Cambridge.* Separate editions were issued in 1895, 1899, 1909, and 1927. A somewhat surprising publication for an allegedly atheistical rationalist. (The reissues were no doubt part of Lady Frazer's campaign to keep in well with the Establishment!)

(6) *The Golden Bough* itself. Two volumes in 1890, twelve by 1915, thirteen by 1937. The usual one-volume abridgement was first issued in 1922 and was reputedly the result of skilful scissor-work by Lady Frazer. A quite different abridgement appeared in the United States in 1959. *Psyche's Task* (1909) – reissued in 1928 as *The Devil's Advocate* – and *The Worship of Nature* (1926) merely rehash themes from the *magnum opus.* Malinowski claimed to be able to discern in the earlier of these two works the germ of his own functionalist theory.[8]

So far as the anthropological portion of this corpus is concerned the formative period was 1883–90. The dates are significant. The year 1883 was the one in which, after a notorious *cause célèbre*, W. Robertson Smith (who had been dismissed for heresy from his Chair of Old Testament Exegesis at the Free Church College in Aberdeen) moved to Cambridge as Professor of Arabic; 1890 was the year in which Robertson Smith was first struck down by the fatal illness which caused his death in 1894. The close association between Frazer and Smith was mutually acknowledged on numerous occasions. Smith's *Religion of the Semites* appeared in November 1889, with credits to Frazer; Frazer's *The Golden Bough* appeared in June 1890, with a dedication to Smith. The collaboration was widely recognised at the time and was remarked upon by reviewers both in *The Athenaeum* and in *Folklore.* The latter considered both books old-fashioned on account of their evolutionist bias! Even at this early date diffusionism was becoming an academic orthodoxy.

It is quite evident that in the Smith–Frazer teamwork all the inspiration and originality came from Smith. As soon as Smith's support was withdrawn Frazer's capacities were reduced to those of a voraciously diligent library mole. For the next fifty years he simply went on repeating himself over and over again on an ever-larger scale, adding nothing of significance in the process. Serious social anthropologists can still read *Religion of the Semites* with great advantage. Frazer's works may be examined for their bibliographies; otherwise they accumulate dust.

Frazer held a life fellowship in Trinity College, but he played no part in university affairs either in Cambridge or elsewhere. His title of Professor derived from a Chair at Liverpool University which he occupied only for one year (1908). Anthropology began to receive formal recognition in Cambridge around 1898 and achieved the status of a tripos subject in 1919. But Frazer had no part in this development which stemmed from the enthusiasms of A. C. Haddon and W. H. R. Rivers. One of Rivers's first pupils was 'a Mr Brown' who in 1908 became a Fellow of Trinity College where Frazer had already been installed for nearly thirty years. This was A. R. Radcliffe-Brown who was later to be Professor of Social Anthropology at Oxford; it is impossible to discern in his work the slightest trace of Frazerian influence.

Nor was this simply a case of a prophet without honour in his own country. The platforms for anthropological debate at this period were the meetings and publications of the Anthropological Institute, the Folklore Society, and Section H of the British Association; Frazer's name seldom appears in any of these places. In 1911, the year after the appearance of Frazer's four-volume *Totemism and Exogamy*, the British Association held a major international symposium on 'Totemism' under the chairmanship of A. C. Haddon; Frazer did not attend; his views were not represented; in the published report his name is never mentioned.

Frazer's strictly academic reputation seems, as I have said, to have passed its peak before 1900. That year saw the publication of the second (three-volume) edition of *The Golden Bough* which was widely reviewed. The anthropologists were notably cool. Andrew Lang was positively insulting; Hartland and Haddon praised Frazer's zeal but were caustic about his theories. Ten years later Frazer had become a bore; at the tail of a long review of *Totemism and Exogamy* Hartland (in *Man*) drops into mock Frazerian phraseology and hints that the great man has become prematurely old.[9]

Frazer could well afford this patronising disrespect by his professional colleagues, for he had other publics which were more rewarding and more influential. One of these came from the ranks of liberal-minded 'modern churchmen' who felt a special commitment to discover the true historical origins of Christianity. For them the passages in *The Golden Bough* which draw attention to parallels between Christianity and other Middle Eastern cults were both disturbing and fascinating. This material had originally occupied less than 100 pages, but in response to special demand it was blown up into a separate volume (*Adonis, Attis, Osiris*). By 1914 this book alone took up two volumes.

Frazer's upbringing had been rigorously Presbyterian; although in later life his attitude towards established religion became increasingly cynical, his direct references to Christianity are always carefully ambiguous. As a result, *The Golden Bough* was treated as an ammunition depot by members of the Rationalist Association – and as a source book of scholarly information by professional Christians.[10]

When the knighthood came in 1914, Frazer's fame must still have been narrowly confined, for *The Golden Bough*, now a work of twelve volumes, was surely a daunting prospect for librarian and reader alike. It was the publication of the 1922 abridgement, timed to synchronise with a flood of public honours, which finally made this classic work the kind of fashionable book which every educated man must at least pretend to have read. Thereafter Frazer became *the* anthropologist – and the merits of the case ceased to matter. Something of this cachet still remains.

Just what the book is all about it is difficult to say; there is something for everybody. The motif of the sacrifice of the Divine King (with its uncomfortable association with Christianity) and the entanglement of this theme with vegetation gods and the magical preservation of fertility persists throughout; but the author's more general concern is with the world-wide irrationality of custom. Huge chunks of highly elaborate and highly valued human behaviour serve no practical purpose (judged by the standard of late nineteenth-century European intellectuals). Frazer could not believe that people should consciously choose to waste their time in this way. Surely the actors who devote so much effort to 'ritual' must think they are doing something useful? They are mistaken, and Frazer will show us the nature of their error.

In his teens at Glasgow University, Frazer had studied under Sir William Thomson (Lord Kelvin) and through him had acquired a set of very simple mechanistic ideas about the nature of scientific truth. For Frazer, science is the true association of cause and effect. Magic is the corresponding false association. Primitive Man, being childish and ignorant, has much magic but little science. The modern European, being more adult and wiser, has less magic and more science. Religion, which is Frazer's third major category of action, is less precisely conceived. The notion of deity arises through an intellectual confusion. Primitive Man is groping after the definition of such abstract ideas as 'power', 'life', 'fertility', 'soul'; but he gets these ideas mixed up, and he fails to distinguish clearly between attributes of Man (e.g. authority, human sexuality) and attributes of Nature (e.g. vegetable fertility). Religious practices then develop out of magical techniques. When magical attempts to control the course of nature fail, the primitive mind conjures up deities, super-magicians from an unseen world, whose powers can be invoked to make good the deficiencies of mere human magic. By implication, the progress of science, which replaces magic, should make religion unnecessary. But even in the abridged edition it takes Frazer four closely printed pages to say this, and even then the argument is ambiguous. He does commit himself to the proposition that: 'In short, religion, regarded as an explanation of nature, is displaced by science.' Did he really suppose that religion is nothing more than 'an explanation of nature'? The reader of *The Golden Bough* is left to guess.

But this much is clear enough: for Frazer, all ritual is based in fallacy, either an erroneous belief in the magical powers of men or an equally erroneous belief in the magical powers of imaginary deities. The overall effect is to represent 'savages' as stupid. They have the simple-minded ignorance of children which is sharply contrasted with the sophisticated highly trained mind of the rational

European. Europeans, too, have their childish moments but, in general, the dichotomy is clear: the White man is wise; Black, Brown, and Yellow men are foolish. Frazer was writing precisely at the point when European colonial expansion had reached its peak; it must have been consoling for many liberal-minded imperialists to find that the 'White Man's Burden' could be justified by such detached scholarly procedures! And this may well be an important factor in the enduring popularity of the book.[11]

Perhaps, too, there are some who can still find pleasure in the sado-masochistic sexuality which is a prominent feature of much of Frazer's subject matter. Frazer was so anxious not to give offence that any reference to genitalia or an act of copulation is likely to be wrapped up in a complex periphrasis which lasts for half a page. But prudery of this sort is two-sided. The devotees of Attis sometimes expressed their faith by an act of self-castration: in recording the gory details of this ritual Frazer spreads himself over thirteen pages, including long, tantalising, small-printed footnotes in the original Latin and Greek. Such drawn-out agony offers all the delights of polite pornography.

Judged by modern standards Frazer's scholarly procedures are glaringly defective. While he was scrupulous in citing his authorities, he never assessed their quality. If we trouble to check up on his footnotes we find that the most trivial observation of the most ignorant traveller is given exactly the same weight and credibility as the most careful assessment of an experienced ethnographer. Worse still, he was constantly 'improving' his sources.

It is difficult to illustrate the consequences of such manipulations. Frazer started out with a number of basic assumptions: 'savages are afraid of the dead', 'savages have childlike imaginations', and so on. The 'evidence' was put in to illustrate these principles. Since the relevance of the 'evidence' to the principle is seldom obvious, Frazer helped the reader along with a liberal ration of 'conjectures'. Alternatively, he simply modified his source material so as to make it fit more closely with his hypothesis. The truth of the hypothesis is thus invariably demonstrated by the evidence!

Consider the following example. In the Trobriands, in Melanesia, every village holds a month-long harvest festival (*milamala*) during which the spirits of deceased ancestors (*baloma*) are supposed to return to their erstwhile homes. Malinowski's 7000-word ethnographic account of this ritual was published in 1916, and it is one of the most penetrating and convincing records in the whole of ethnographic literature. Malinowski asserts categorically that the Trobrianders feel no fear of their spiritual guests, who are there as friends. His own summary is:

> During the *milamala* the *baloma* are present in the village. They return in a body from Tuma to their own village, where preparations are made to receive them, where special platforms are erected to accommodate them, and where customary gifts are offered to them, and whence, after the full moon is over, they are ceremonially but unceremoniously driven away.[12]

The driving out of the spirits is a children's lark which Malinowski likens to Guy Fawkes Day.

Frazer's account antedates Malinowski's. His source is a missionary, the Rev. Dr George Brown, whose brief account is quite consistent with Malinowski's longer study:

> The dances and feasts lasted many days. When these were finished all the people gathered together, shouted, beat the posts of the houses, overturned everything where a spirit might be hiding, drove away the spirits and the feasts were over. The explanation given is that the spirits were thus made wealthy for another year. They had shared in the feasts, had seen the dances, and heard the songs. The spirits of the yams were theirs, the spirits of the property displayed were also theirs, and they were now made wealthy and fully provided for and so they were driven out.[13]

Frazer's citation of this material comes in a section entitled 'The periodic expulsion of evils'. Note carefully the modifications of Dr Brown's text (italics added):

> When the festivities were over, all the people gathered together and expelled the spirits from the village by shouting, beating the posts of the houses, and overturning everything under which *a wily spirit* might be supposed to lurk. The explanation which the people gave to the missionary was that they had entertained and feasted the spirits and provided them with riches, and it was now time for them to take their departure. Had they not seen the dances and heard the songs and *gorged themselves* on *the souls* of the yams, and appropriated the souls of the money and all the other fine things set out on the platform? What more could the spirits want? So out they must go. Among the Hos of Togoland in West Africa the expulsion of evils is performed annually before people eat the new yams.

By intruding emotive words like 'wily' and 'gorged', substituting 'soul' for 'spirit', and juxtaposing the 'expulsion of evils' by the Hos, the kindly Trobriand ancestors are adroitly converted into evil demons![14]

Such tampering with source materials seems to me indefensible. I find it quite impossible to accept Dr Jarvie's view that Frazer's explanations, though defective, were as good as could be expected in the circumstances of the time.

During the first twenty-five years of this [the twentieth] century, the monumental industry invested in *The Golden Bough* served to surround its author with an aura of veneration, so that he was often credited with insights which he never possessed.

Although the Divine King – also a Dying God, who is slain as his physical powers begin to wane in order that the fertility of the realm may be sustained – had been the hero of *The Golden Bough* from the very beginning, it is only in Vol. 4 of the third edition that we meet with a clear-cut example of this strange institution. All that went before had been only 'conjecture'. This was because it was only in 1910 that C. G. Seligman could claim to have verified that the Shilluk of the Sudan really did treat their kings just as Frazer said. This material was immediately incorporated into Frazer's new edition of *The Dying God* (this book rates as Vol. 4 of the twelve-volume edition of *The Golden Bough*). Likewise, Malinowski at first maintained that his studies of Trobriand garden magic fully confirmed the brilliant intuitive insights of the Master.[15] Such retrospective confirmations of hypothesis were felt to be clear demonstrations of Frazer's genius.

But the disciples were mistaken and bemused by faith. We now feel certain that the Shilluk did *not* murder their Divine Kings,[16] and we see quite plainly that Malinowski's view of magic is directly antithetical to that of his predecessor, for where Malinowski interpreted magic as an evocation of the mysterious, a procedure closely allied to religion, Frazer saw no more than a childishly mistaken attempt to achieve the technically impossible.

The trouble with Frazer is that he leaves no room for the imagination. A myth must always be a direct transcription of a rite and vice versa. If myth tells of the killing of a god–king, then the only possible origin of such a story is that an actual god–king was actually killed. The modern anthropologist, with his more immediate experience of how myth and ritual are interconnected, is much more cautious. For example, animal sacrifice is a very widespread human institution which, being irrational, must always be justified by myth. Observed *in situ*, two features of such sacrifice are easily recognised: firstly, the effect of the sacrifice is to improve the 'ritual condition' (the state of purity) of the donor; secondly, there is a direct symbolic association between the donor and the animal that is killed. In a mystical sense, the donor improves the state of his own divinity by destroying a mundane part of himself. This, of course, is a thoroughly non-rational procedure, but it is fully in accord with mythological stories which tell how 'in the beginning' there was a god–king who was killed (as a human being) in order that he should become an immortal god. *Some* of Frazer's 'dying god stories' are accountable in this way but others may have quite a different source. If, in any particular instance, we have detailed information about a set of sacrificial rituals and the mythology that goes with them, we are certainly likely to find a structural consistency between the ritual and the mythology; but we cannot take short cuts and infer rite from myth or myth from rite in the way that Frazer tried to do. In this respect he was quite fundamentally in error.

I suppose that Dr Jarvie might argue that it is precisely because Frazerian hypotheses have been refuted that they were worth making in the first place. No one can deny that when *The Golden Bough* first appeared in 1890 it caused a stir. It didn't actually say anything which had not been said before: but people took notice of it and started arguing: so it can be said to have advanced the subject of anthropology even if it added little to the sum of human knowledge. But Dr Jarvie's further defence of 'Frazer the Evolutionist' against 'Malinowski the

Functionalist' on the basis of the former's pre-Popperite enlightenment is pressing paradox too far.

In the first place, there is no more poverty-stricken form of historicism than late nineteenth-century anthropological 'evolutionism'. Lewis Morgan's *Ancient Society* (1877) was given the Marxist imprimatur by no less a figure than Friedrich Engels himself (in his *Der Ursprung der Familie* of 1884). On the other hand, the living Frazer was only a half-hearted sort of evolutionist. He tagged along with the assumptions of his predecessor, E. B. Tylor, and paid token respect to the notion that anthropology can reveal 'the origins' of institutions. But this for Frazer was never a central issue, and his accumulations of ethnographic quotation might have been fitted equally well to any other frame. *Folklore in the Old Testament* (1918) is not tied to an evolutionist framework at all, and even in the earlier works the matter of time-scale is irrelevant.

Frazer was concerned with what he called 'mental anthropology', or the universals of individual psychology. He thought he could explain savage customs by supposing that the mental processes of the savage are those of a modern child. The much more sociological emphasis of the orthodox evolutionist with its concern for whole 'stages of social development' lay quite outside Frazer's range of interests.

On the other hand, the living Malinowski was never seriously opposed to evolutionism though he was always willing to have a dig at the more preposterous form of conjectural history postulated by Lewis Morgan and Robert Briffault. Dr Jarvie seems to imagine that Malinowski's formal adoption of a 'functionalist' creed meant that thereafter he evaded all attempt to grapple with the sociological analysis of historical change. The facts are entirely otherwise. Not only is his posthumous book *Freedom and Civilisation* (1947) thoroughly evolutionist in tone but nearly all the writings of the last five years of his life are concerned with problems of developmental process ('culture change').[17]

Finally, we may note that whereas Frazer's 'ideas' ('conjectures'), which Dr Jarvie so admires, were only produced so as to force the ethnographic records into Frazer's determinist mould, Malinowski's theory of fieldwork, which Dr Jarvie so despises, corresponds very closely to that of Professor Popper's ideal scientist. When Dr Jarvie says 'you cannot collect facts without a theory', he is quoting Malinowski verbatim. Frazer thought exactly the opposite.

This does not mean that what Malinowski said corresponds exactly to what Malinowski did; nor does it mean that either Malinowski or Professor Popper is correct about the way that scientists actually achieve their results. It is simply that by his own criteria Dr Jarvie ought to judge Frazer's methodology deplorable. But then I am writing about Frazer and not 'Frazer', and there's the rub.

Bronislaw Kaspar Malinowski was of Polish aristocratic origin. His father was a professor of philology at the University of Cracow, where Malinowski himself obtained a PhD in mathematics and physics in 1908. The reasons which then led him to abandon an assured scientific career for the uncertain favours of 'sociology' are obscure, but after spending nearly two years at Leipzig working with Karl Bücher and Wilhelm Wundt, Malinowski moved to the London School of Economics where he came under the influence of Westermarck, L. T. Hobhouse, and C. G. Seligman. It was the last named who enabled him to find the financial support which, in 1914, took him to Australasia. He remained there for the next six years. Of this period two full years were spent on the Trobriand Islands in eastern New Guinea, a further six months being devoted to shorter spells of fieldwork among other primitive groups. Malinowski returned to London in 1920, and over the next two decades built up an outstanding reputation as a polemical writer and speaker.

His literary output was substantial but not vast; by far the greater part of it is devoted to the description and analysis of various aspects of life in the Trobriand Islands. Malinowski's style is vivid and full of colour but he was often careless, so that his writings provide many easy targets for a hostile and pedantic critic. It is this written work which provides the grist for Dr Jarvie's attack, but it needs to be stressed that during his lifetime Malinowski's main academic influence was through his teaching. Frazer's contribution to learning is to be discovered from his books; he passed on nothing by his social contacts; he had no pupils. With Malinowski, it was the other way around. He was a dynamically powerful personality, a 'charismatic leader' who aroused intense emotional feelings of love and hostility among all those with whom he became closely associated. What he taught in his seminars is only partly recoverable from what he wrote in his books, and it is no doubt on this account that Dr Jarvie's 'Malinowski' is so completely unrecognisable.

Like Frazer, Malinowski had several different publics. The reputation which made him a celebrity was quite different from that which gave him fame and notoriety among his professional colleagues.

The professional reputation was directly tied in with the unique quality of his field research which had been of a quite unprecedented intensity. No professional anthropologist had ever before spent two full years studying a single tribal group, actually living in a native village and sharing the native way of life. Malinowski's Trobrianders are not just dummy stereotypes with a formal set of customs; they are living human beings: they are villagers engaged in all the intricacies of village and domestic life. In his ethnographic monographs Malinowski was concerned to demonstrate two things: (1) that the Trobrianders' social life, at the ordinary domestic level, is based on entirely different assumptions from our own (e.g. Trobrianders deny that a child is genetically related to its mother's husband), and (2) that the patterns of customary behaviour which correspond to this different set of assumptions form a viable set. The quaint customs of these people, which Frazer would have judged to be palpable evidence of their childish ignorance, are shown to make logical, adult sense. They 'make sense' because they are mutually consistent with each other, and also with the framework of cognitive ideas through which the Trobrianders view their environment and their social world. These ideas, Malinowski thought, are in themselves no better or worse than those which we employ ourselves. Some of them, of course, are scientifically false. It is untrue that a child is genetically unrelated to its father; but our own social assumption that men are in all respects the physical and intellectual superiors of women is no better. The culture of each society makes sense in its own setting. It is neither true nor false, neither good nor bad, neither wise nor ignorant. Humanity is everywhere the same:

> When you enter a new cultural setting, the behaviour, individual or collective, of the new type of human beings seems strange, unmotivated, irrational, in short incomprehensible. You learn the language, you gradually adopt the strange habits and the new points of view – and imperceptibly what was alien becomes familiar and you feel at home in what recently had been an exotic milieu. The universally human running through all the cultures is the common measure of comprehension and adaptation. . . . Even in such cases as eating of human flesh, underdone beef, or plum pudding, playing golf, running amok, and the practice of the *couvade*, the anthropologist may attempt to survey the psychological raw material of the pursuit, can assume a certain diversity of taste in human beings, and define the pursuit in terms of the universally human.

Malinowski's unqualified acceptance of the doctrine of 'cultural relativism' has a vinegary taste for those who retain a lingering belief that one can make humane value-judgements and that the course of man's history suggests to us what they are; but his passionate insistence that technological sophistication implies neither moral superiority nor higher intelligence is still embarrassingly relevant.

In 1965, when most of us are prepared to recognise 'primitive people' as fully qualified human beings, Malinowski's programme, thus stated, does not seem very daring, but in 1920 it was unorthodox in the extreme.

Frazer, as I have suggested, had supposed that the savages, whom he had never seen, were simply grown-up children, and Malinowski himself started with Frazerian assumptions which he never fully abandoned. In 1922, he asserted that 'natives communally as well as individually never act except on traditional and conventional lines', and twenty years later he sentimentalised over 'the lowest primitives, the living representatives of archaic man' among whom 'war does not occur' and 'a somewhat higher level . . . the world of real savagery' where 'cannibalism, head-hunting, human sacrifice or scalping' is only a ritual game. But this kind of argument which stresses the 'otherness' of the primitive is completely at variance with his own major premise which insisted that the society of any primitive tribe of the present day is a normal society of fully adult rational human beings, who simply happen to run their affairs in a different way from ourselves:

> The most important thing to realise is that primitive man makes full use of his knowledge wherever he can. You must discard the notion that the savage is a child or a fool, a mystic or a nincompoop. I have seen the savage hunter at work: he knows his animals and their habits; he is familiar with the properties of his weapons, the strength of his spear and the flight of his boomerang. I have trusted myself to savage sailors in their frail craft over the dangerous seas and under trying conditions. They understand wind and weather, stability and tides, in a truly reliable, that is, in a scientific, way. It is only because he is able to observe correctly and to think clearly that, with his simple tools and limited co-operation, primitive man can master nature as well and as effectively as he actually does. . . .

Malinowski had difficulty in coming to terms with his own evolutionist assumptions, but his more immediate problem was to deal with the current orthodoxy of academic anthropology. The current vogue was *not* evolutionism in Frazerian or any other form, but 'diffusionism' in the exaggerated variant propounded by Sir Grafton Elliot Smith. In the pre-Malinowski era, all anthropologists had thought of themselves as engaged in the reconstruction of prehistory. If you assume that savages are stupid automata, bound in the chains of immemorial tradition, you can also assume that 'customs' are imperishable artifacts, as hard and enduring as flint tools and sherds of pottery. You can then set about reconstructing history from the data of anthropology by exactly the same procedures as are adopted by an archaeologist in reconstructing history from the data of an excavation.

Such an assumption may seem naïve, but to a certain kind of academic mind it is essentially 'sound', factual, scientific. It was precisely on this basis that anthropology was eventually accepted as an academic discipline of university status. Indeed it is because scholars of the 1900–20 period thought it sensible to treat customs as though they were potsherds and old bones that modern social anthropologists must still often share an uncomfortable *ménage à trois* with the prehistoric archaeologists and physical anthropologists! In the older universities, the psychologists are in much the same situation. It is always quite respectable to study the behaviour of rats under 'laboratory conditions' – that's science. To study human beings leading ordinary lives is mere frivolity.

In the early years of this century, a number of leading British anthropologists had a deep interest in psychology of the human sort. Rivers, who was, with Haddon, the founder of Cambridge academic anthropology, and Seligman, who had much the same role at the LSE, were both professionally qualified medical psychologists; this seems to have had little effect on academic sentiment. Rivers and Seligman themselves kept their 'psychological' and 'ethnological' interests sharply distinguished. The former were part of experimental science, the latter a part of prehistory. Consequently, Malinowski's first problem was how to get his subject recognised at all. He wanted to discuss the sociology of a primitive society. Who would listen? How could he persuade the academic world that it might be scholarly to treat 'savages' as adult human beings rather than fossilised survivals from a bygone age?

The convention of the 1920s was to think of 'customs' as free-floating entities which move about from place to place independently of the human groups to which they belong. On this basis anthropology had become a study of 'the distribution of customs' and the human beings were left out of account. Malinowski made a direct frontal assault on this mode of thought. In order to reaffirm that anthropology is the study of man and not the study of custom (in isolation from man), he threw the whole weight of his analysis upon the relation between culture and biology. Where his predecessors had been satisfied to write learned monographs on the distribution of string figures or the design of pipe stems, Malinowski disgusted everybody by discussing the pleasure of lice-hunting and varying styles in copulation.

It was this last form of shock tactic which finally established his reputation as a 'celebrity', though there was a preliminary more reputable and more academic phase.

Malinowski's first major ethnographic monograph was *Argonauts of the Western Pacific*, published in 1922 (Frazerian title; preface by Frazer; dedication to Seligman). Its central theme is the Trobriand system of ceremonial exchange. It was a truly revolutionary work which is still standard reading for undergraduate anthropologists. In France it was treated as a work of sociology and became the basis on which Marcel Mauss constructed his celebrated 'Essai sur le don', a study of the way in which reciprocal and obligatory gift-giving comes to reflect the structures of social relations.

Malinowski's 'functionalism', which was built up around the thesis that we can only understand social institutions if we take account of the fact that they must satisfy the needs of living human beings, was really a development out of Mauss's theme, though the biological twist which Malinowski gave to his 'principle of reciprocity' was quite alien to Mauss's more structural (even mathematical) train of thought.[18]

Argonauts was favourably and intelligently reviewed in the *American Anthropologist* (by Gifford), but in England the going was not so good. *Folklore* ignored it; A. C. Haddon in *Nature* was complimentary but treated it as simply another ethnography; *Man* passed the book to an American (F. R. Barton) who headed his notice 'Sociology' but largely missed the point: 'The book not only gives in picturesque detail the visible aspect of the various scenes and ceremonies pertaining to the Kula, but sheds also much light on the psychological mechanism on which the institution is based.' Malinowski must have felt a desperate need for a wider and less conventional audience.

In the following year his essay 'The Problem of Meaning in Primitive Languages' appeared as an appendix to *The Meaning of Meaning* by C. K. Ogden and I. A. Richards, a book which has had a lasting influence in many fields of thought, including philosophy, linguistics, psychology, and literary criticism. This work gave Malinowski the sort of general intellectual public he was looking for.

In the same year (1923) he contributed two pieces to *Nature*. The first was a long review of the one-volume edition of *The Golden Bough* (Dr Jarvie should study this item; Malinowski's praise of Frazer is exuberant and unqualified). The second was a 'Letter to the Editor' entitled 'Psychoanalysis and Anthropology', which was the opening broadside in a long series of publications on the psychology of sex in 'savage' society. The Trobriand Islanders happen to have a matrilineal organisation, and Malinowski claimed that in these special conditions the mother's brother and the mother's husband share between them the social role played by the father among Europeans. In such a situation the psychoanalytic concept of the Oedipus complex needs modification. Malinowski's presentation of this thesis was intentionally provocative, and Ernest Jones's hostile reaction was both predictable and welcome.[19] Psychoanalysis was at that time very much in vogue, a fashionable novelty among 'advanced' radicals. Malinowski's controversial challenge to the orthodox Freudian position put him right at the centre of London intellectual life.

In these very unanthropological circles it was immediately assumed that the Trobrianders' freedom from sexual restraint could provide moral lessons for ourselves. Before long, Malinowski's views became slogans of progressive education and the Trobrianders' sex life was being accepted as a model of virtue by such disparate propagandists as Havelock Ellis and Bertrand Russell.[20]

Malinowski delighted in the ensuing furore and went out of his way to create a sense of outrage. *The Sexual Life of Savages* is simply an account of Trobriand domestic organisation and is much less libidinous than the average modern novel. But its title assured it a place in Old Compton Street shop-windows where it is still to be found alongside sealed-up versions of *Fanny Hill* and the Marquis de Sade. The contemporary notices of this work are fascinating. *Man*, the official journal of the anthropological profession, ignored it altogether. In the highbrow weeklies the reviewers consistently missed all the anthropological points; they noticed only with astonished disbelief that Trobriand girls could fornicate without getting pregnant and that Trobrianders are ignorant of the biology of procreation. The reviewers' scepticism was justified; but the book itself remains a work of major scientific importance; it was the first (and is still the best) detailed study of family life in a matrilineal society.

The renown which flowed from this kind of publicity led to countless requests for public speeches, broadcasts, and journalistic articles. Malinowski willingly acted as his own populariser. At each repetition, the story became more simplified and more distorted. In the end the Trobriander merged with Rousseau's Noble Savage. Sexual laxity became a virtue in itself. This was all nicely in tune with the ethic of D. H. Lawrence, but it could hardly be claimed as a contribution to social science.

And there, perhaps, we can stop. For though Malinowski's rating as a professional anthropologist does not rest on his contribution to sexology, this was and is the context of his public celebrity.

Crudely summarised in this way neither Frazer nor Malinowski appears particularly laudable. Both men seem to have been more concerned with the plaudits of the gallery than with the pursuit of truth. Both made a cult of the outrageous, Frazer by cynical comments on religion, Malinowski by challenging English sexual morality. But in all other respects they at first seem notably different. Judged by what they did, what they wrote, and the way they set about propagating their views, they appear as polar types, and in the mythology of modern undergraduate anthropology (as well as in the pages of Dr Jarvie's book) they are just that: Frazer who deals in items of custom drawn out of context from here, there, and everywhere, and takes no account at all of individuals; Malinowski who constantly emphasises the importance of the total social context, and never for a moment forgets the essential unities of time and place and dramatis personae. Yet in an odd way the interests of the two men were very much the same, and at their grandest, they spoke in much the same language.

For both, the field of greatest professional renown was that of magic and religion and primitive psychology. There were important technical points of disagreement. Malinowski understood the expressive nature of ritual behaviour in a way that Frazer did not, and he is inclined to merge magic with religion rather than magic with science. He did not consider it a sign of intrinsic inferiority that a man should believe in miracles. Malinowski and Frazer both accepted Robertson Smith's thesis that ritual is to be understood as a manifestation of belief (dogma, myth); but they use this insight very differently. Frazer writes as if myth and ritual were interchangeable – if he finds the record of a myth, he 'conjectures' as to the nature of the corresponding ritual, and vice versa. Malinowski sticks firmly to the observable evidence; the myth is a 'charter for social action', but only if demonstrably so: no guessing. Yet so far as the Common Reader is concerned the similarities are more striking than the differences.

Frazer was eager to outline the psychology of Primitive Man, thought of as a unity. In all Frazer's writings the immense diversity of human culture is treated as a manifestation of just a single element – the simple-minded childishness of the savage, his ignorance, his lack of understanding of cause and effect. And why not? If there is indeed 'a psychic unity of mankind', Frazer was surely justified in developing a synthetic picture out of multiple parts. The parts come indifferently from all corners of the globe and have no chronological unity, but if Primitive Man is a unity then the diversity of source material cannot matter. We should be able to understand the Priest of Nemi by looking at what goes on in the Maldive Islands.

Malinowski went about things the other way round. He concentrated exclusively on one small group of 'savages' and looked at them under a sociological microscope. But he too, like Frazer, postulated a psychological unity of mankind and gradually step by step found himself talking, not about the Trobrianders in their uniqueness, but about Primitive Man in his generality. And why not? Why should a Trobriand Islander be deemed any more, or less, typical of the human race than the Priest of Nemi?

And here, perhaps, we begin to see the roots of their popularity. 'Typical Man' may not be a very satisfactory kind of concept from the scientific point of view, but it is surely of interest to all of us.

For the professional anthropologist, Malinowski has other virtues (and other vices) than those which I have considered here: and I need not pursue further my disagreements (and occasional agreements) with Dr Jarvie. Malinowski made contributions to many fields which Frazer never touched – language, kinship, primitive law, and economic relations in particular. Anyone with close knowledge of the subject must concede that Malinowski has left his personal mark on contemporary anthropology in a way that Frazer has not. He was a much less trivial scholar than my cursory and biased comments might suggest. But that is not the point.

My problem at the outset was to consider why, every now and then, an eminent anthropologist should rate as a 'celebrity'. What is there about a Frazer and a Malinowski (or a Margaret Mead) which gives public fame as well as professional distinction? My account suggests an answer.

Frazer and Malinowski in their different ways were both prepared to make sweeping generalisations about human nature itself. Frazer could never have seriously expected that his general reader would be terribly interested in what did or did not go on at Nemi in 200 BC, and the reader of Malinowski can get along very well without worrying as to whether the Trobriand Islands lie north or south of the Equator or east or west of longitude 180°. Both authors are really talking about Mankind, i.e. about you and me. It is because each of us can recognise in their pages the savage within us that we feel the excitement of insight, the unverifiable validity of a statement of genius.

There are many lesser, more pedantic men who in some ways can be considered much better anthropologists. But the public which has given these two a special accolade is not at fault.

Notes

This essay was written for the magazine *Encounter* and published in 1965, in a series entitled 'Men and Ideas'. Leach gave his essay the subtitle, 'On the "Founding Fathers"'.

1. Bohannan, *Social Anthropology*; Beattie, *Other Cultures*.
2. Jarvie, *Revolution in Anthropology*.
3. For Professor Karl Popper's views of 'evolutionism' and other forms of historical determinism see his *The Poverty of Historicism*.
4. In assessing Frazer's influence on his contemporaries we should note that although Freud obtained some of the ethnographic information employed in *Totem and Taboo* from Frazer's *The Golden Bough*, the key idea of the parricidal primal horde was borrowed from another British anthropologist, Atkinson, who is now rated entirely insignificant. See Lang and Atkinson, *Social Origins and Primal Law*. Freud's debt to this work was acknowledged.
5. Frazer's first anthropological publication was 'On Certain Burial Customs as Illustrative of the Primitive Theory of the Soul' (1885). Both in subject matter and manner this is quite explicitly modelled on Tylor's *Primitive Culture* (1871).
6. Frazer, *Anthologia Anthropologica*.
7. Besterman, *Bibliography of Frazer*.

8. Frazer's extreme repetitiveness was embarrassing to his publishers (Macmillan) and in the middle 1930s they formally declined to publish any further rehashed works – much to Lady Frazer's indignation. See Filby, 'Life with the Frazers'.
9. 'The preface amid the exquisite cadence of its sentences betrays perhaps a little weariness but no slackening of his indomitable energy . . . I at least decline to admit that his sun is yet prematurely westering.'
10. The widely held view that *The Golden Bough* 'explicitly set out to discredit present-day religion' (Jarvie) derives from hostile reviews of the second edition. Vol. 3, pp. 138–200 of that edition is a new section which discusses the Gospel story of the Crucifixion under the heading 'the Saturnalia and kindred festivals' which was plain heresy to orthodox Christians. Frazer suggests that the Gospel story of the Crucifixion is a folk record of a hypothetical Jewish festival at which a living malefactor was annually hanged to represent a ritual effigy of Haman.

    On the other hand, Frazer's more general thesis that the Gospel should not be interpreted as a record of historical fact but as a mythical background to a ritual drama has been found acceptable by a variety of Christian scholars. The latter have usually explained the cult similarities to which Frazer drew attention as being products of diffusion. See Brandon, 'The Myth and Ritual Position'.
11. Many who would never openly say so still sincerely believe that White superiority is a fact of Nature which depends upon a basic and intrinsic maturity of outlook. How often in the past two decades have we heard it argued that the African is not ready for self-government, that he is too inexperienced, too irresponsible, too ignorant . . . ? For those who really believe this (and Dr Jarvie gives hints that he may be one of them), Frazer must make congenial reading.
12. Malinowski, 'Baloma', pp. 370–1.
13. Brown, *Melanesians and Polynesians*, p. 414.
14. For another example of Frazer's improvement of his source see Leach, 'Golden Bough'; and Leach, 'Virgin Birth' (II.6.2, below).
15. Malinowski, 'Science and Superstition'. In a later, posthumous publication (*Scientific Theory of Culture*, p. 196) Malinowski said flatly that Frazer's 'theory of magic . . . is untenable'.
16. Evans-Pritchard, *Divine Kingship of the Shilluk.*
17. Malinowski, *The Dynamics of Culture Change.*
18. See Mauss, 'Essai sur le don'; Lévi-Strauss, 'Introduction à Marcel Mauss'. Malinowski's view that the 'functional method' was something specific and peculiar to his own brand of anthropology developed about 1928. He recognised the German ethnologist, Richard Thurnwald, and A. R. Radcliffe-Brown, as fellow 'functionalists'; but his considerable debt to the French sociologists was never stressed.
19. Jones, 'Mother-Right and Sexual Ignorance'. Malinowski's rejoinder appears in *Sex and Repression in Savage Society.*
20. Havelock Ellis, Preface to Malinowski's *Sexual Life of Savages*; Russell, *Marriage and Morals.*

1.2

Malinowski's Empiricism (1957)

Malinowski's contributions to the theory of social anthropology were of two sharply divergent kinds. In the first place he created a theory of ethnographic fieldwork. Although Malinowski's account of Trobriand culture is far from complete, his descriptions are so alive that we feel we know these people better than any other in the entire anthropological catalogue. The difference between the dry record of 'old-style ethnography' and the vivid life of 'Malinowskian ethnography' is not merely an artistic device, it is a matter of theoretical insight. This theory has become a fundamental element in the general body of doctrine propounded by British social anthropologists. We do not now seek to imitate the rather Frazerian style of fine writing which Malinowski adopted but, most definitely, we do all emphasise that we are studying contemporary societies of living human beings rather than fossilised relics from the prehistoric past. Malinowski transformed ethnography from the museum study of items of custom into the sociological study of systems of action.

But besides altering the whole mode and purpose of ethnographic enquiry Malinowski made numerous theoretical pronouncements of a general, abstract, sociological kind, which were supposed to be valid for all cultural situations regardless of time or space. Here, I consider, he was a failure. For me, Malinowski talking about the Trobrianders is a stimulating genius; but Malinowski discoursing on culture in general is often a platitudinous bore. The framework of concepts that is to be found in the posthumous *A Scientific Theory of Culture* (1944) or in the earlier article on 'Culture' (1931) provides us with few tools which the anthropological fieldworker can actually use in a practical situation. The 'principle of reciprocity', with its implied emphasis upon the priority of economic motives, may be descriptively preferable to Radcliffe-Brown's 'network of person-to-person relationships' but it doesn't get us very far. For most of us, 'functionalism' in its Malinowskian form has become repugnant. Nor can I believe that this is merely a passing phase; the abstract theoretical writings of Malinowski are not merely dated, they are dead.

Paradoxically, I consider that Malinowski's anthropological greatness is to be found precisely in this circumstance. That Malinowski was an imaginative genius of a high order there can be no doubt; but he had a bias against abstract theory which kept his imagination firmly earth-bound. The result was a unique and paradoxical phenomenon – a fanatical theoretical empiricist. After all, what was Malinowski's really fundamental contribution? Surely the intensive technique of field study? But of what does this consist? There was plenty of good ethnography long before Malinowski went to the Trobriands; Boas's work among the Kwakiutl, to take but one example, could hardly be described as anything but *intensive*. I should say that the special distinguishing characteristic of Malinowski's field technique lies in two things: firstly in the severely curtailed use of the professional informant, and secondly in the *theoretical* assumption that the total field of data under the observation of the fieldworker must somehow fit together and make sense.

Malinowski, of course, used informants, but only to supplement what he knew already; his first line of evidence was always first-hand observation by the fieldworker himself. Empiricism could hardly be carried further. Culture consists in what the fieldworker himself observes; it is intelligible in terms of the fieldworker's personal private intuitions. No data outside the immediate subjective–objective present need to be considered.

As a basis for abstract generalisation such an attitude to sociological materials is surely disastrous, but as a device for convincing the fieldworker that the minutiae of his present occupation are of supreme importance, it is magnificent. Malinowski trained his fieldworkers to observe the apparently unimportant in minute detail; the justification for so doing lay in a deeply rooted suspicion of every type of second-hand information. It is in the quality of the observation rather than in the interpretation that the merit of 'Malinowskianism' lies. The interpretations are mostly merely private intuitions, based in the minimal generalisation that human beings, as members of a biological species, must satisfy their biological needs.

Holding then that an 'obsessional empiricism' was both the strongest and the weakest element in Malinowski's intellectual equipment, I am concerned in this essay to examine the source and nature of this empiricism. It was dogma in the Malinowskian teaching that facts are only intelligible in their social context; let us then consider some of the elements in Malinowski's own social context.

Malinowski entered the British academic field in 1910. At this period, the late nineteenth-century cultus of mechanistic materialism, linked with naïve doctrines of the inevitability of progressive evolution, still held the field, but was under serious attack. In the realm of pure science, Einstein's formulation of the theory of relativity had shaken the simple world of Newtonian mechanics to its foundations, while Whitehead and Russell had just broken through the boundaries of Aristotelian logic which had held fast for over 2000 years. In psychology, Freud was busily engaged in cutting away the foundations of the ordinary man's common-sense idea of the rational individual. In social studies, the evolutionist comparative method had achieved a kind of massive futility in the vast tomes of Frazer and Westermarck and the only real stimulus was coming from the writings of Durkheim and his school, where the empirical content was often extremely low. Diffusionism with its superficial emphasis on material facts seemed likely to become the dominant vogue in the near future.

Malinowski, with his training in the pure sciences, was certainly keenly sensitive to all these trends, but above all it is his studies under Wundt that seem relevant here. For on the one hand Wundt was an objective empiricist, the founder of the science of experimental psychology, while on the other he was an evolutionist of the old school, who, in his anthropological studies, threw especial emphasis on the study of language and upon the unitary personality of the tribe as a whole.[1] Malinowski, I suggest, approved of Wundt's empiricism but was repelled by the 'group-mind' implications of his historicist approach. He searched therefore for a body of theory which could somehow combine the 'materialist' basis of nineteenth-century evolutionism with the attribution of free will to the individual soul.

It is my thesis that Malinowski found this body of theory in the pragmatism of William James. It was precisely in the period around 1910, when Malinowski first came to England to study sociology under Westermarck and Hobhouse, that James's philosophy had its maximum vogue, and it is at this period that Malinowski is most likely to have been receptive to the ideas of the English-speaking world.

Certainly the word 'pragmatic' was one which cropped up very frequently in Malinowski's discourse in later years, and certainly also there seems to be much in James's writing that finds a marked echo in the later Malinowski. The philosophic notion of pragmatism has an interesting history. The term was invented by the American philosopher C. S. Peirce to cover his own rather dry and detached method of logical inference. Though Peirce achieved only a meagre reputation in his own day, his work is now recognised as one of the major influences leading to the development of mid-twentieth-century logical positivism. William James was a friend and colleague of Peirce but a man of very different temperament. Where Peirce was austere, retiring, philosophic, James was a public figure, a missionary propagandist with a wide popular appeal. James's pragmatism is a creed rather than a philosophy; it is a practical guide to correct behaviour. In propounding it, James may well have supposed that he was merely elaborating his friend Peirce's ideas, but in fact he misrepresents and distorts Peirce out of all recognition. Significantly Peirce repudiated all connection with James's doctrine; after 1906 Peirce called himself a 'pragmaticist', a coinage which he dryly referred to as 'ugly enough to be safe from kidnappers'.

Malinowski's pragmatism is that of James rather than Peirce. Indeed James and Malinowski had a good deal in common. A recent extremely penetrating commentator has summarised James's position thus:

> First, from the plausible thesis that certain biological interests underlie, or provide some of the necessary conditions of, all our thinking, he (James) passed to the more exciting (and more ambiguous) thesis that the sole function of thought is to satisfy certain interests of the organism, and that truth consists in such thinking as satisfies these interests.[2]

Substitute *behaviour* and *behaving* for *thought* and *thinking* in this quotation and we have in a nutshell the whole essence of Malinowski's functionalism.

The same author contrasts Peirce's more metaphysical approach in the following terms:

> For Peirce . . . ideas, ideals, movements of thought and feeling, traditional wisdoms, life-tendencies, and above all the life that is inherent in symbols – these were to him every bit as real as the individuals who apply them or, rather, as the individual occasions, the actions and reactions, in which they are applied.[3]

The contrast here drawn between the pragmatism of James and the pragmatism of Peirce surely parallels closely the analogous contrast between the functionalism of Malinowski and the functionalism of Durkheim, Mauss and Radcliffe-Brown? The heart of the matter is that James was deeply suspicious of any abstraction that could not immediately be referred to directly observable facts; so was Malinowski. This suspicion led Malinowski to his valuable emphasis on first-hand observation as a field technique but it also led him to cast most of his theoretical ideas in a shape which makes sociological comparison nearly impossible.

It will be useful here if we distinguish three main types of epistemological thinking. Down to the end of the nineteenth century most philosophies were based in Aristotelian logic, which assumes that all Truth is of one kind and that the validity of statements about God can be tested by the same criteria that might apply to statements about the sun. Today, largely as a result of the development of logical positivism, the technique of making scientific statements is becoming increasingly specialised. It has come to be recognised that the language of science deals with propositions quite different in kind from those of ordinary speech. Conversely, we see now that statements that concern metaphysics cannot be expressed in scientific language at all.

In terms of this contrast, James's pragmatism occupies a kind of middle ground. On the one hand it recognises that strict logic cannot lead directly to metaphysical judgements; yet metaphysical judgements are still supposed to have a psychological basis in reason. James maintained that we are entitled to believe whatever can be shown to be biologically satisfying even though the belief in question may be metaphysical and incapable of verification either by experiment or rational argument. He explicitly maintained that where proof is impossible it is 'reasonable' to hold beliefs that are arrived at by other than rational means.[4]

There is here a serious failure to distinguish clearly between several distinct meanings of the term *reasonable. Reasonable* may be held to mean *rational* – the outcome of logical analysis in the strictest sense, or *plausible* – a guess that is justifiable on the grounds of probability, or *sensible* – convenient in the given circumstances. *Reasonable propositions* of the first two kinds are meaningful in the language of science, because they are potentially verifiable; but *reasonable propositions* of the third kind might well include all sorts of metaphysical hypotheses which fall outside the field of scientific analysis altogether.

James is ambiguous, and a very similar ambiguity confuses much of Malinowski's theoretical argument.

We are all kidnappers of ideas. Any attempt to diagnose the epistemological context of Malinowski's functionalism runs into the difficulty that Malinowski borrowed the concept of social function from Durkheim,[5] but transmuted it in the process. Durkheim's use of the term is unambiguous, it equates with utility: 'the function of a social fact ought always to be sought in its relation to some social end (*fin*)'.[6] But Malinowski changed 'social end' to 'biological end' and thereby loaded the argument with value-judgements. Durkheim was simply concerned to investigate the relationship between social facts and their social consequences – he did not presuppose that the consequences were good, they were simply moral or a-moral according as to whether they fitted with the prevailing conditions of society. But for Malinowski social phenomena exist in order to satisfy needs of the biological organism. Functions are thus both purposive and positive and to detect them requires intuitive judgement. Functionalism, in Malinowski's hands, became something very like a religious creed;[7] it is presented to us as reasonable (practically useful) rather than reasonable (logical or plausible). The 'truth' of functionalism is itself simply a matter of functional utility.

The fervour that functionalism aroused among a limited intellectual circle was not based in reasoned analysis. Malinowski had many of the qualities of a prophet, he was a 'charismatic' leader and such men always express their creed in slogans, which have a certain characteristic quality. These slogans assert in a clear-cut but crassly oversimplified form, a state of affairs which their followers would all like to be true. Malinowski's thesis that cultures are functionally integrated is no more true, empirically speaking, than Hitler's thesis that Germans are the master race, but both assertions *could* be true and both appeal to their respective adherents for somewhat similar reasons – they express a Utopian state of affairs.

Prophets are conscious of their powers. Malinowski had no doubts about his own greatness; he regarded himself as a missionary, a revolutionary innovator in the field of anthropological method and ideas. Like all such revolutionaries he tended to belittle the significance of his more conservative contemporaries and their immediate predecessors. His published comments on fellow anthropologists are seldom flattering[8] and in verbal discourse he was even more explicit; he claimed to be the creator of an entirely new academic discipline. A whole generation of his followers was brought up to believe that social anthropology began in the Trobriand Islands in 1914.

Yet it is a matter of objective fact that the revolutions which innovators achieve seldom extend over a very wide field. The decisive steps, though all-important, are usually quite small. In retrospect the original genius tends to look strikingly like his less imaginative conventional contemporaries. We can observe this over the whole range of science, art and philosophy. Newton, Masaccio, and Occam are cases in point. So too with Malinowski. We may grant that he was the originator of 'a new age' in social anthropology, yet we need to recognise that he was a scholar who reached maturity in the first decade of the twentieth century, and that consequently he took for granted most of the fads and prejudices of the men of that particular generation.

A significant example is his use of the term *savage*. Malinowski habitually refers to the Trobrianders as *savages*, implying thereby a whole catalogue of value-judgements about the intrinsic superiority of European culture, which few of us today would unhesitatingly accept, but which were an unquestioned anthropological dogma at least as late as about 1925. True enough, Malinowski ridiculed the missionary view that the Trobriander was 'lawless, inhuman and savage',[9] but when he himself spoke of the Trobrianders as savages he did not do so only in mockery. Tacitly, for all his anti-historicism, Malinowski used the word *savagery* as Morgan has done, to denote a 'stage' in cultural evolution: 'When we move in our survey from the lowest primitives to a somewhat higher level, we are met by a complexity of forces and facts. We enter the world of real savagery . . . .'[10] There was, admittedly, an important middle phase in his career when Malinowski formally recanted from evolutionary presuppositions. Writing in 1932[11] he draws the reader's attention to the fact that the evolutionary premises present in his work down to 1927 were dropped when he came to write *The Sexual Life of Savages* in 1929. Even so, a paper dated 1930 makes a simple equation between 'savage societies' and 'early societies' and half seriously compares 'my present-day Stone Age savages of the South Seas' with our European ancestors of 'forty thousand years back or thereabouts', a viewpoint borrowed straight from Tylor and Lubbock.[12]

Now whether or not evolutionary doctrine is true, it is certainly quite irrelevant for the understanding of present-day human societies, and Malinowski was perfectly well aware of this, but somehow the categories of his thinking were still partially trapped in the cage of nineteenth-century orthodoxy. Along with his insistence that the fieldworker must recognise the tribe under observation as consisting of living human beings, he still used the verbal conventions of the evolutionists which set a great gulf between the savage primitives of ethnography and the civilised European intellectual who was observing them.

The notion that the culture of primitive peoples represents in some sense a *survival* from the past was of course a basic premise of the Tylorian anthropology which Malinowski considered it his duty to overthrow. The fact that the same premise was incorporated as a dogma into the very roots of 'functionalism' had important and logically fatal consequences.

Thus: 'This (functional) method has been worked out with the purpose of describing and analysing one culture, and a culture at that, which *through age-long historical development* has reached a state of well-balanced equilibrium'.[13] It was Malinowski's proud boast that he had taught anthropologists the futility of the pursuit of conjectural history, yet all the time, the primary assumption of the functionalist creed – the dogma that there is an intrinsic integration between the institutional mechanisms of any one cultural whole – called for a major historical conjecture, namely that equilibrium had been achieved through 'age-long historical development'.

Oddly enough this is an hypothesis that is particularly inappropriate to the Trobriand situation. Chieftainship is quite abnormal in Melanesia and this circumstance suggests strongly that the political structure observed by Malinowski in 1914 may have been of recent origin and perhaps a quite transient phenomenon.

This is one of the cases where Malinowski's ethnography is strikingly superior to his theory. In *Coral Gardens* he actually describes in some detail the process by which the Tabalu chiefly clan was, at the time of his visit, actively expanding its political influence, a condition of affairs hardly consistent with 'a state of well-balanced equilibrium'.[14]

The very notion of the 'cultural whole', which is, at all stages, central to Malinowski's thesis, is a concept taken over uncritically from earlier writers (e.g. Wundt) whose 'tribes' were clear-cut, easily distinguishable entities, with completely stereotyped characteristics. Malinowski professed to ridicule the resultant picture of bodies of men conforming to meticulously detailed customs in a rigid and mechanical manner. He sought to replace the notion of custom as an accidental product of history by the notion of custom as a rationally designed tool.

Yet when he indulged in cultural comparisons outside the immediate context of Trobriand functionalism, he made statements just like those of his predecessors. What, for example, could be more untrue than the following?

> Were we to take the map of any continent, Australia, Africa, Asia or America we would be able to divide it neatly into ethnographic tribal boundaries. Within each such ethnographic area we would find people of 'the same' tribe. On the other side of the boundary another tribe would be found, distinguishable from the first by a different language, different technologies and material objects, different customs and forms of grouping.[15]

There is almost no part of the world in which recent first-hand accounts have not tended to contradict this assertion in every particular.[16]

The simple fact is that intercultural comparison was not a field which Malinowski ever bothered to think about or investigate at all carefully. When he expressed an opinion on such a topic he merely repeated the stock dogmas of an earlier generation.

This paradox is a geniune one which might be documented by numerous quotations. On the one hand it was Malinowski's outstanding contribution that he 'brought ethnography to life'. In the pages of *Argonauts* and its successors, the 'savage' ceases to be a marionette 'bound in the chains of immemorial tradition'.[17] He is a live human being operating a bizarre system of social organisation through the exercise of rational choices about alternative means to alternative ends. Yet somewhere at the back of Malinowski's mind there still seems to have persisted the earlier convention that savages are mechanical dolls surviving from the Stone Age. It was in *Argonauts*, of all places, that he wrote: 'It must not be forgotten that there is hardly ever much room for doubt or deliberation, as natives communally, as well as individually, never act except on traditional and conventional lines.'[18]

Let me then sum up this part of my argument. Briefly it is that Malinowski, like William James, was a rebel against the mechanistic implications of later nineteenth-century thought and that his 'functionalism', like James's 'pragmatism', was an aspect of this revolt.[19] Yet at the same time Malinowski was intellectually a 'child of his time', rationalist and materialist in his outlook, and he was himself much influenced by, and even a victim of, those very epistemological windmills against which he charged so valiantly.

The particular aspect of this thesis which I now propose to discuss concerns Malinowski's views of rationality and the effect of those views upon his theories of magic, technology, and kinship.

It may fairly be said of Malinowski, as it has been said of James, that 'he was an individualist, interested in the experiences, perplexities, and satisfactions of individual souls, and anything claiming to be more-than-individual he distrusted from the depth of his soul'.[20] Malinowski's biggest guns are always directed against notions that might be held to imply that, in the last analysis, the individual is not a personality on his own possessing the capacity for free choice based in reason. Morgan is repeatedly lacerated for postulating group marriage;[21] Durkheim's sin is that he emphasises religious euphoria, with its implication of a group mind;[22] Freud gets it in the neck for postulating a collective unconscious;[23] Hartland is attacked for suggesting that primitive man is a legal automaton,[24] and so on.

It was dogma for Malinowski that all human beings are reasonable (sensibly practical) individuals. To understand the significance of this belief we need to remember that at the beginning of Malinowski's anthropological career the 'savage' was commonly regarded as a sub-rational human being. Marett's criticism of Tylor was then in vogue and the *mana* concept was bearing fruit in Durkheim's *représentations collectives* and Lévy-Bruhl's 'pre-logical mentality', abstractions utterly repugnant to Malinowski's way of thinking.

It is against this background that we need to consider Malinowski's attempt to impose 'rationality' upon his savages – for that is what it amounts to. He maintains persistently that primitive man makes a fundamental category distinction between fact and fiction, using criteria that might have been acceptable to John Stuart Mill.

In all Malinowski's writings concerning the relation between magic and science this argument is latent. He himself found the conceptual distinction between the rational and the metaphysical self-evident; he insisted that it must be self-evident to the Trobriander also:

> Thus there is a clear-cut division: there is first the well-known set of conditions, the natural course of growth, as well as the ordinary pests and dangers to be warded off by fencing and weeding. On the other hand there is the domain of the unaccountable and adverse influences, as well as the great unearned increment of fortunate coincidence.[25]

Malinowski accused Tylor of treating primitive man as 'a ratiocinating philosopher'[26] yet this simple dichotomy between the objective–rational and the subjective–metaphysical is strictly in the Tylor–Frazer tradition.

Actually Malinowski went one better than Tylor, for he postulated that the Trobriander was more rational than himself. Although he maintained that, for the Trobriander, there is a clear-cut division between the domain of knowledge and work and the domain of magic, he later confessed that 'I was not able to judge for myself where rational procedure ended and which were the supererogatory activities, whether magical or aesthetic.'[27]

In Malinowski's analysis magical procedures are distinguished from non-magical procedures according to the kind of reasonableness involved. All behaviour is regarded as a means to an end (functionally orientated) but whereas non-magic is reasonable because it is based in scientific fact, magic is reasonable because it is based in psychological need:

> Experience and logic teach man that within definite limits knowledge is supreme; but beyond them nothing can be done by rationally founded

> practical exertions. Yet he rebels against inaction because *although he realizes his impotence* he is yet driven to action by intense desire and strong emotions.[28]

Notice the insistence that the actor himself distinguishes between the strictly rational and the psychologically sensible.

It is in accord with Malinowski's dogma that reasonableness is natural to mankind that witchcraft beliefs – being neither sensible nor rational – were never effectively incorporated into the functionalist schema. Such beliefs had been reported in the Massim area by Seligman.[29] Malinowski at first expressed complete scepticism,[30] then he moved to a position of partial agreement,[31] and finally accepted Seligman's views in their entirety.[32] Yet he seems never to have adjusted his other ideas to this empirical discovery. Trobriand witches (*mulukuausi*) do not fit into the rationalist schema. In *Coral Gardens*, where magical beliefs and practices are dealt with at length and treated as functionally positive practical working tools, the existence of witchcraft beliefs is completely ignored, the word *witchcraft* being used merely as a synonym for sorcery, in the sense of negative magic.

Malinowski maintained, no doubt rightly, that Trobrianders are at least as rational as twentieth-century Europeans. He stressed that 'civilised' as well as 'savage' life is packed with magical practices.[33] Where he seems to err is in maintaining that the ordinary man distinguishes consistently between the magical and non-magical.

Here we need to remember that in Malinowski's youth non-rationality had been deemed to be one of the characteristic marks of the savage; it was likewise deemed to be characteristic of civilised man that he could distinguish clearly between the logical and the non-logical. Frazer's description of magic as 'bastard science' epitomises this view. In seeking to break down the dichotomy between savagery and civilisation Malinowski argued that primitives were just as capable as Europeans of making such distinctions. 'Since the superstitious or pre-logical character of primitive man has been so much emphasised, it is necessary to draw clearly the dividing line between primitive science and magic.'[34] He would have had a much better case if he had insisted that Europeans are ordinarily just as incapable as Trobrianders of distinguishing the two categories. In seeking to prove that Trobriand savages are not really savages after all, he endeavours to impose upon them a precision of mental classification such as is ordinarily demanded only of professional logicians.

A striking example of this is the doctrine of homonyms which became very prominent in Malinowski's writing during the *Coral Gardens* period.[35] According to this thesis, it is incorrect to suppose that 'native terminologies represent native mental categories'. This very surprising proposition is developed by saying that when the Trobrianders use the word *taytu* to mean (1) a plant, (2) the food derived from it, (3) the crops, (4) the year in which the crops ripen, they do not 'lump these meanings together in one confused category'. On the contrary 'there is no confusion in the use of these terms; the series is really a series of homonyms, each of them invariably well indexed in actual usage by the context of speech'.[36]

Malinowski alleges that 'armchair anthropologists' have inferred that primitive peoples have a 'pre-logical mentality' because they make verbal categorisations unfamiliar to modern Europeans.[37] His way of repudiating this allegation is to assert that these verbal categories do not really exist at all; they are merely accidental homonyms which the armchair anthropologists mistakenly assume to constitute a single word.

The same doctrine can be applied to kinship terminologies: 'to correlate kinship terms with kinship facts is based on the mistaken assumption that when there is one term for two people these two people must somehow be lumped together or telescoped or united in the mind of the native, or even that they must be one and the same person'.[38] This is the equivalent of saying that because the English subsume under a single word 'tree' a number of different botanical species, it is a 'mistaken assumption' to suppose that Englishmen find anything common as between one tree and another, and that those who hold a contrary opinion are seeking to maintain that all members of the class 'tree' are one and the same.

It is certainly a curious argument. Perhaps because they lend themselves so easily to a kind of abstract algebra, kinship terminologies, as such, were repugnant to Malinowski. It is significant that the volume on formal kinship structure, promised in *The Sexual Life of Savages*, was never written. Classificatory systems somehow 'stood for' Morgan and Rivers and everything out of date and antiquated in anthropological theory. They were a type example of non-rational behaviour – judged by European standards – and Malinowski seems to have felt impelled to do away with them root and branch, even though the Trobrianders inconveniently possessed such a system of terminology themselves. The facts were inconvenient but he could deny the implications. Without a vestige of proof, he asserts categorically the unlikely proposition that for the Trobrianders 'the word *tabu* in the sense of "grandmother", in the sense of "maternal [*sic*] aunt", and in the sense of "taboo" are accidental homonyms',[39] meaning thereby that the three meanings here listed are in no way associated.

Now this assertion that the several meanings of *tabu* represent separate words rather than variant meanings of the same word is something which Malinowski projected on to the data in the light of his homonym theory. It is indeed a rational but not a reasonable (sensible) argument! The separate words were not obvious to Malinowski the fieldworker, nor even to Malinowski the author of *The Sexual Life of Savages.* Thus: 'The primary meaning of this word (*tabu*) is "father's sister". It also embraces "father's sister's daughter" or "paternal cross cousin" or, by extension, "all the women of the father's clan"; and in its widest sense, "all the women not of the same clan".'[40]

The whole doctrine of homonyms, with the added arguments about 'metaphorical extensions' to the 'primary meanings' of terms, seems to me very much on a par with the artificial rational–metaphysical dichotomy upon which

I have commented above. Here again Malinowski seems to be trying to force Trobriand categories of thought into the watertight logical containers fashionable among rationalist European thinkers around the beginning of the century. He would surely have disapproved most strongly of certain important trends in contemporary anthropological thinking.

Consider for example the following remarks by Godfrey Lienhardt:

> If I report without further comment that some primitive men speak of pelicans as their half-brothers, I do little more than offer the reader a form of words which, as it stands in English, suggests the atmosphere of fairy tale and nonsense. . . . In order to make this understood in English it would be necessary to give a full account of views about the relations of the human and non-human quite different from those we entertain, but not therefore, necessarily, less reasonable.[41]

This reaches to the very heart of the matter. Lienhardt finds it quite possible to suppose that his primitive peoples are reasonable (sensible) men although they order their world by principles of logic different from those current in contemporary Europe. Malinowski on the other hand insisted that, belief or dogma apart,[42] all intelligent behaviour must be based in nineteenth-century logic. The doctrine of homonyms is brought in as a *deus ex machina* to explain away the fact that Trobrianders do not, on the face of it, use nineteenth-century logic. In a similar way Malinowski would doubtless have got rid of Lienhardt's example by saying that, among the tribes in question, the word for pelican and the word for half-brother are accidental homonyms!

Malinowski's contributions to the sociology of language are very relevant here. A linguist of outstanding brilliance, he emphasised that the effect of the spoken word is entirely dependent upon the context in which it is uttered. 'The meaning of words consists in what they achieve by concerted action, the indirect handling of the environment through the direct action on other organisms.'[43] 'Language in its primitive function and original form has an essentially pragmatic character.'[44] 'It is a type of behaviour strictly comparable to the handling of a tool';[45] it operates as an instrument of communication, as a tool does, 'by direct action'. The symbolic significance of language, its use as a vehicle of thought, is consistently minimised – 'to regard it as a means for the embodiment or expression of thought is to take a one-sided view of one of its most derivate and specialized functions'.[46]

On the other hand, despite the important insistence that 'language is an integral part of culture. . . . body of vocal customs'[47] Malinowski isolated spoken language as a thing in itself and gave it special importance – 'the spell is the most important element in magic'.[48] For Malinowski, the 'meaning' of every type of custom was to be seen in its 'pragmatic effect', but there was a tendency to maintain that every type of custom had a special type of effect (function) peculiar to itself. Mere communication – symbolic statement – was not one of the effects which Malinowski considered to be of any importance.

We arrive here at a very important source of confusion. Malinowski's notion of pragmatic function differs radically not only from the 'organic function' concept of Durkheim and Radcliffe-Brown,[49] but also from the 'symbolic function' concept employed by mathematicians and logicians.[50] In logic, if we have a symbolic equivalence such that *X* stands for *Y*, then the form of the symbolisation – that is to say the description of *Y* in terms of *X* – is referred to as a function. For example, if we write $y = \log x$ then y is a function of x, and if x has the particular value 3 then the expression $\log x$ stands for, or is a description of, the number 0.4771. The expression 'log' ('the logarithm of') is here 'the function'. Since, in principle, anything can symbolise anything else the number of forms in which any particular proposition or statement can be expressed is limitless. In any particular case the problem of determining 'the function' is that of ascertaining the symbolic rules and conventions that link the thing described with the form of its description. When Malinowski propounded his extremely valuable thesis that the function of myth is to provide a charter for proper social relationships[51] he seems to have been using function in this *logical* sense, but in most other contexts he uses the term as very nearly the equivalent of *purpose*. In Malinowskian theory, the function of a custom is the direct effect it produces. In practice, because of the impossibility of establishing causal relationships, Malinowski's 'functions' were determined intuitively, with a very general tendency to allocate one specific function to one specific aspect of culture.

This part of the Malinowskian scheme seems seriously defective.

If culture be regarded as a set of tools (institutions), designed for specific purposes, or causing specific effects, one must face up to the epistemological problems involved in distinguishing the 'designer' and in separating out 'purpose' from 'cause' and from 'consequence', and this Malinowski most signally fails to do.

Moreover even if we take a pragmatist position and say that Malinowski's system is justifiable on grounds of utility, though defective in strict logic, we must still recognise the narrowness of his exposition. Let us concede that speech can have direct empirically observable effects, does that lessen the importance of communication of a less 'pragmatic' kind?

Malinowski's savage has no time for philosophy. For him, culturally defined behaviour is concerned only with *doing* things, not with saying or thinking. But surely all culture (both verbal and non-verbal) is also concerned with 'making statements' about the social order? In many ritual contexts non-verbal symbolic communication seems to be an end in itself quite independent of the practical–technical outcome (the 'pragmatic function'). Persistently right through his work Malinowski manages to minimise the significance of this aspect of social behaviour.

His treatment of the Kula provides an example. Malinowski's description represents the Kula as primarily an economic institution, though the economic principles involved differ from those axiomatically assumed by professional European economists. The picture presented is that of a vigorously competitive market in which the 'currency' consists of 'social debts' of all descriptions. Yet, as Mauss points out, Malinowski's account 'tells us very little about the sanction behind these transactions'.[52] In Malinowski's own terms, the Kula, as described, is pragmatically useless; why then is it maintained? Malinowski's reaction to this criticism was to complain that it is no part of an ethnographer's task to inject private theoretical interpretations into his material, though he proposed to reveal his views in a further work – which never materialised.[53] In retrospect, one feels that Malinowski was here handicapped by his conviction that all behaviour must have a practical end – using the term practical in a narrow mechanistic sense. Mauss's interpretation though not 'pragmatic' provides a most important supplement to Malinowski. Mauss, in essence, sees 'potlatch' behaviour of the Kula type as 'symbolising' the ambivalent friendship–hostility aspects of the relationship ties which constitute the component elements in the social structure. It is an abstract interpretation which implies that Trobrianders, in carrying out their Kula rituals, are also, in a symbolic way, 'saying things' to one another which they certainly could not put into words.

Of course there is a large measure of agreement between Malinowski and Mauss; both are talking about the same material, and the material is that provided by Malinowski. But the underlying difference of basic viewpoint is very fundamental – Mauss sees gift-giving as symbolic behaviour, a way of making statements; Malinowski sees it exclusively in operational terms, a way of achieving desired results. Today we can learn from both masters, but that should not blind us to their differences.

So far as I know Malinowski's only published comment on *Essai sur le don* is a footnote.[54] He here accepts Mauss's criticism of the concept of 'pure gift' but claims that he revised his views independently.

This brings me back to a point I made much earlier, Malinowski's deep suspicion of 'abstract theory' as such. I would emphasise again that this prejudice proved both an advantage and a handicap.

The advantages are clear. Consider for example the opening paragraphs of Chapter XI of *Coral Gardens* which carries the title 'The Method of Field-Work and the Invisible Facts of Native Law and Economics'. Here Malinowski lays down rather precisely the relationship, as he saw it, between theory and observation, and the limits to which abstract theorising might legitimately proceed:

> The main achievement of fieldwork consists, not in a passive registering of facts, but in the constructive drafting of what might be called the charters of native institutions. . . . While making his observations the fieldworker must constantly construct: he must place isolated data in relation to one another and study the manner in which they integrate . . . 'Facts' do not exist in sociological any more than in physical reality; that is they do not dwell in the spatial and temporal continuum open to the untutored eye. The principles of social organisation, of legal constitution, of economics and religion have to be constructed by the observer out of a multitude of manifestations of varying significance and relevance. It is these invisible realities, only to be discovered

> by inductive computation, by selection and construction, which are scientifically important in the study of culture.[55]

Malinowski, then, approved of the use of sociological theory in the interpretation of first-hand fieldwork observations; what he objected to was 'armchair theorising' about behaviour recorded in hearsay statements. On the face of it this is a sensible and scientific attitude, and yet it has implications which are entirely paradoxical. Logically speaking, Malinowski would need to maintain that, for the Trobrianders themselves, 'Trobriand culture as a whole' does not exist. It is not something that can be reported on by Trobrianders, it is something that has to be discovered and constructed by the ethnographer. It is entirely consistent with this position that the most intelligible account of the total social structure of Trobriand society which Malinowski gives us occupies the *last* fifty pages of the *last* book he published on the subject.[56]

In an earlier work he specifically mocked at the account of Trobriand social structure that one might expect to obtain from a professional Trobriand informant,[57] though when he himself attempted to write a concise description of 'The Constitution of Trobriand Society'[58] the result resembles most strikingly that given by his imaginary despised 'informant'.

Now it is certainly true that in recognising quite specifically that there is a marked divergence between 'ideal' and 'actual' behaviour, Malinowski made explicit a fact of the greatest sociological importance:

> The hasty fieldworker who relies completely upon the question-and-answer method, obtains at best that lifeless body of laws, regulations, morals and conventionalities which *ought* to be obeyed, but in reality are often only evaded. For in actual life rules are never entirely conformed to, and it remains, as the most difficult but indispensable part of the ethnographer's work, to ascertain the extent and mechanism of the deviations.[59]

Moreover he was perfectly justified in asserting that most of his predecessors had relied heavily on hearsay statements so that existing ethnographic accounts of tribal custom consisted everywhere of abbreviated descriptions of idealised behaviour. But he went much too far in the other direction. He appears to have regarded the ideal construct of the native informant as simply an amusing fiction, which could at best serve to provide a few clues about the significance of observed behaviour. Truth was 'pragmatic', objectively observable; it lay in what men did, not in what they said they did. Yet surely in Malinowski's own analysis of myth a counter-argument is already apparent? If myths are to be regarded as charters for social institutions, surely the intelligent informant's descriptions of his own society are also 'a kind of myth', a charter for human action, none the less important because the rules are not precisely obeyed?

In the case I have cited, Malinowski uses the fact that Trobrianders frequently have love affairs with their clan sisters (*kakaveyola*) but only very seldom with their lineage sisters (*veyola*), as evidence for the uselessness of general statements about clan exogamy. But in recent years facts strikingly similar to those recorded by Malinowski have been reported from other societies, and have been shown to be meaningful precisely because they provide differentiating criteria in terms of which the different segments of the formal social structure become apparent.[60] The same is certainly true in the Trobriand case also. In this instance, as in a number of others, Malinowski's pupils have progressed further than Malinowski himself largely because of their willingness to recognise that symbolic functions are at least as relevant as pragmatic ones.

In writing this essay, the impression I have been trying to convey is that Malinowski was a highly original thinker who was nevertheless held in bondage by the intellectual conventions of his youth. But did he point the way to escape from the dilemmas with which he was faced?

It would be absurd to suggest that Malinowski's thinking was 'permanently stuck at 1910'. Although his last books, written in illness, give the impression of regression to a position formally repudiated in 1932,[61] there is otherwise a very noticeable 'development' throughout Malinowski's work. If we take *Mailu* (1915), *Argonauts* (1922) and *Coral Gardens* (1935) as three points on a time-scale, the increase in sophistication is very marked indeed, and is an indication of the extent to which Malinowski's famous seminars were a vehicle for learning as well as for teaching.

But we need to see this development as part of an intellectual problem: Malinowski's persistent struggle to break out of the strait-jacket of nineteenth-century historicist theory without getting hopelessly bogged in empirical detail. Despite his advocacy of empiricism Malinowski was really searching all the time for concepts of the middle range of generality, not so abstract as to amount to mere verbal speculation, not so concrete as to defy generalised comparison. Culture is too abstract; the individual too concrete.

Now if we compare the stated content of 'functionalism' at different stages of Malinowski's career we find an interesting and significant shift of emphasis. The original stress on 'culture' as a unitary integrated whole seems gradually to lessen, as also the emphasis on the simple family as the basic unit of social structure, while in their place we find a new 'concrete isolate of organised behaviour' – the 'institution'.[62] Here, I would suggest, Malinowski was pointing the road for his successors.

Sociologists have used the concept of 'institution' in a variety of senses.[63] Malinowski's version tends to confuse the individual with his institutionalised role. As a result his institutions emerge as collections of individuals (personnel) who possess a common vested interest,[64] a conception closely analogous to Weber's 'corporate group' (*Verband*).[65] A recent American study makes this parallel very clear.[66]

Since Malinowski's death British social anthropologists have increasingly tended to think of their special field as the study of the behaviour of small groups operating within a defined structural–cultural matrix.

It is in line with this that the concept of the 'corporation' with its associated hereditable estate – its 'bundle of rights' over things and people – is tending to become central to our analysis. We have reached this position by borrowing ideas from the lawyers and the theoretical sociologists – Maine, Durkheim, Weber, Talcott Parsons in particular, but the resulting development seems to parallel that of Malinowski in same respects. Malinowski's 'institution', as he left it, is not a precise isolate, but it does provide a kind of bridge between the crude intuitive functionalism of the 1930s and the increasingly sophisticated structural analysis of today. It is in concepts of this type that we find a meeting point between the arguments of those who stress the importance of the ideal order conceived as a system of jural relationships and those who see social behaviour as the outcome of competitive individual self-interest. To that extent we may now be coming back to where Malinowski left off.

One thing at any rate we should remember. All the authors of this book were 'grounded in Malinowski', just as I have suggested that Malinowski himself was grounded in William James. If I am correct in thinking that Malinowski was partly frustrated by the persistence of youthful intellectual prejudices, the same certainly applies to ourselves. Malinowski, I have insisted, was 'in bondage' to his predecessors; he resented their existence because he was so much indebted to them. Some of us perhaps feel the same about Bronislaw Malinowski.

Notes

This essay was written for a *Festschrift* for Malinowski entitled *Man and Culture: An Evaluation of the Work of Bronislaw Malinowski.* The volume, published in 1957, was edited by Raymond Firth, a student of Malinowski's and one of Leach's own teachers. Leach's essay was entitled, 'The Epistemological Background to Malinowski's Empiricism'.

1. See Vierkandt, 'Wundt', p. 506.
2. Gallie, *Peirce and Pragmatism*, p. 25.
3. Ibid., p. 29.
4. Ibid., pp. 25–6.
5. Malinowski, *Family among Australian Aborigines*, p. 303. This first reference to social function follows directly on a discussion of Durkheim's work and is cast in strictly Durkheimian form.
6. Durkheim, *Rules*, p. 110. Earlier in *Division of Labour* (p. 49), Durkheim introduced the notion of social function by drawing the analogy with organic function which 'expresses the relation existing between (a system of vital movements) and corresponding needs (*besoins*) of the organism'. Durkheim consistently makes social facts relate to social ends/needs on the analogy that biological facts relate to biological ends/needs. In contrast, Malinowski uses 'function' to relate social facts to biological ends/needs.
7. In the Foreword to the third edition of *Sexual Life of Savages*, Malinowski wrote, 'The magnificent title of the Functional School of Anthropology has been bestowed by myself, in a way on myself, and to a large extent out of my own sense of irresponsibility' (p. xxix). Self-mockery though this be, it nevertheless reflects Malinowski's belief in himself as the prophet of a new creed.
8. Consider for example, from this point of view, the first twenty pages of *Crime and Custom.* The posthumous *Scientific Theory of Culture*, ch. 3, is, on the other hand, quite unexpectedly tolerant.
9. Malinowski, *Argonauts*, p. 10n.
10. *Freedom and Civilisation*, p. 280; cf. also *Scientific Theory of Culture*, pp. 16–17.
11. Foreword to 3rd edn, *Sexual Life of Savages*, pp. xxii–xxiii.

12. 'Parenthood', pp. 113, 123. The use of 'evolutionist' phraseology in this essay is particularly revealing, since the essay itself is largely concerned with the demolition of evolutionist presuppositions.
13. Malinowski, 'Anthropology of Changing African Cultures', p. xxxvi – my italics.
14. *Coral Gardens*, i, pp. 365–6.
15. *Freedom and Civilisation*, pp. 252–3.
16. For example, see recent accounts of Arnhem Land by R. M. and C. H. Berndt (*Sexual Behaviour in Western Arnhem Land*), of New Guinea by Hogbin (*Law and Order in Polynesia*), of North Burma by Leach (*Political Systems of Highland Burma*), of West Africa by Nadel (*The Nuba*), and of Bechuanaland by Schapera (*Native Land Tenure in the Bechuanaland Protectorate*; *Migrant Labour and Tribal Life*).
17. Malinowski, *Crime and Custom*, p. 10.
18. *Argonauts*, p. 62.
19. Gallie, *Peirce and Pragmatism*, pp. 23–4.
20. Ibid., p. 29.
21. Malinowski, Foreword to 3rd edn, *Sexual Life of Savages*, p. xxxii.
22. 'Magic, Science, and Religion', p. 55.
23. *Sex and Repression*, pp. 156ff.
24. *Crime and Custom*, pp. 10, 55ff.
25. 'Magic, Science, and Religion', p. 31.
26. *Scientific Theory of Culture*, p. 27.
27. *Coral Gardens*, i, p. 460; cf. ii, p. 113.
28. 'Culture', p. 635 – my italics.
29. Seligman, *Melanesians*, ch. 47.
30. Malinowski, 'Natives of Mailu', p. 648n.
31. 'Baloma', p. 356, n. 2.
32. *Argonauts*, pp. 237ff.
33. 'Culture', p. 636.
34. Ibid.
35. See index reference to *homonyms* in *Coral Gardens*, ii, but esp. pp. 65–73. Cf. 'Parenthood', p. 159. The germ of the homonym argument is present in *Sexual Life of Savages* (1929), but is not obvious in the 'Problem of Meaning' article in 1923.
36. *Coral Gardens*, ii, pp. 69, 73, 124.
37. Ibid., p. 69n.
38. Ibid., p. 65, n. 2.
39. Ibid., p. 28. The word 'maternal' is here a mistake for 'paternal'. [Eds.: This disagreement with Malinowski is pursued further by Leach in 'Concerning Trobriand Clans', I.3.4. below.]
40. *Sexual Life of Savages*, p. 423.
41. Lienhardt, 'Modes of Thought', p. 97.
42. Malinowski, 'Baloma', p. 418n.
43. 'Culture', p. 622.
44. 'Problem of Meaning', p. 480.
45. 'Culture', p. 622.
46. 'Problem of Meaning', p. 481.
47. 'Culture', p. 622.
48. 'Magic, Science, and Religion', p. 68.
49. Radcliffe-Brown, 'Concept of Function', p. 3.
50. Stebbing, *Introduction of Logic*, pp. 128ff.
51. Malinowski, *Myth in Primitive Psychology*.
52. Mauss, *The Gift*, p. 24.
53. See Malinowski, *Coral Gardens*, i, pp. 455–6. Malinowski seems to have oscillated between thinking that the ultimate practical reason for the Kula was economic and the potentially much more structural idea that it 'is to a large extent a surrogate and substitute for head-hunting and war'.
54. *Crime and Custom*, p. 41n.
55. *Coral Gardens*, i, p. 317.
56. Ibid., pp. 328–81.

57. *Sexual Life of Savages*, pp. 416–24, gives the formal description of the structure; pp. 425–9 are devoted to ridiculing the validity of this native description.
58. *Coral Gardens*, i, pp. 33–40.
59. *Sexual Life of Savages*, pp. 428–9.
60. Evans-Pritchard, *Kinship and Marriage among the Nuer*, ch. 2; cf. also Fortes, *Web of Kinship*, pp. 101, 115.
61. Both *Freedom and Civilisation* and *A Scientific Theory of Culture* are strangely 'evolutionist' in tone when compared with his explicit repudiation of 'speculations about origins' in the 1932 edition of *The Sexual Life of Savages*, pp. xxii–xxiii.
62. *Scientific Theory of Culture*, p. 52; 'Culture', p. 626.
63. Cf. Nadel, *Foundations of Social Anthropology*, p. 108.
64. Malinowski, *Scientific Theory of Culture*, pp. 52ff. and 62–3.
65. Weber, *Social and Economic Organisation*, pp. 124ff.
66. Gerth and Mills, *Character and Social Structure*, p. 13 *et passim*; Vidich, Review of Gerth and Mills.

1.3

An Anthropologist's Trivia (1967)

An anthropologist on a South Sea Island! How romantic! But the reality entails a kind of squalid loneliness which might otherwise be encountered only by a victim of political torture in solitary confinement. The anthropologist's position is highly anomalous. He wants to understand the values of the society which he observes around him, yet his ultimate purpose is to translate those values into his own. He must *not* be totally absorbed – he must *not* be brainwashed. So the more deeply he comes to know his tribal families the more desperately he clutches at any tenuous straw which may help him to remember that he is still, in his own right, a member of modern civilisation. Letters from home become treasures beyond price; the company of missionary bigots, crooked traders and drunken remittance men is made to function as a surrogate for academic discussion; and, finally, when all this fails, some sanity can still be preserved by talking to oneself. The private diaries of fieldwork anthropologists record torments of loneliness, fantasies of love, dreams of past life and fears of coming death, and above all the torments of sexual frustration; but they are devices for retaining a grip on reality, a kind of catharsis, they should never be interpreted as a balanced record of the writer's inner personality.

Bronislaw Malinowski, the originator of modern anthropological field method, kept such diaries in New Guinea and Melanesia in 1914–15 and 1917–18, and it is to the discredit of all concerned that they have been committed to print. The originals were written in Polish telegraphese with a mixture of other languages. The translator has pedantically sorted it all out as if it were a sacred text worth putting most (but not all) of the 'wrong' words in italics and dolling up the results with footnotes and glossary and learned bibliography. The net effect can best be seen by comparing p. 260 of the English text with the facsimile Polish reproduced on the frontispiece. It will be seen that the non-dictionary word *nigrami* appears twice. Throughout the diary Malinowski uses this word to mean 'the blacks' (i.e. Trobrianders) as distinct from 'the whites' (i.e. the missionaries, traders, etc.). The translator turns this into *niggers* written in italics! Like any other anthropologist exhausted by lack of privacy and the inconsequential unpunctuality of native assistants Malinowski certainly felt that he could quite happily have murdered all his informants, but to suggest, by this use of the word *nigger*, that under the skin he was a white supremacist from Alabama is quite outrageous.

The context of the diary adds nothing at all to our understanding of Malinowski's work as an anthropologist. Most of Part I was written while he was still learning his craft in and around Mailu. There is only one short entry which relates to his major Trobriand expedition which lasted from May 1915 to May 1916. Part II was written during his final Trobriand expedition. It is entirely dominated by the author's passionate yearnings for his fiancée (who later became his first wife) and by guilty remorse at the fact that memories and fantasies of other women keep intruding on his thoughts.

A psychiatrist could doubtless find entertainment here, noting, for example, the frequent references to Malinowski's mother and the somewhat unexpected areas where reticence intervenes. But the plain fact is that most of the rest is trivial in the extreme.

> 29 April, 1918. In the morning wrote letter to E.R.M. and worked with Raffael. Mrs Mahoney came by, wasted the whole day with her. Went to see Auerbach. Conversation: Headon killed Dr Harse's dog; the doctor sued him. Samarai sympathises with Headon. Dr H. is a shark . . .

Why such stuff should be preserved for posterity is hard to understand. Certainly there are passages of another kind such as:

> Since Thursday I have been in a state of utter distraction. I must absolutely stop this. It is caused by too violent and too passionate contact with people, by an unnecessary communion of souls.
>
> I don't think much about E.R.M., but all my erotic impulses centre on her. Also moments of strong emotional longing for N.S.

Malinowski's widow, who holds the copyright, justifies the publication by claiming that these documents give 'direct insight into the author's inner personality'. They do nothing of the sort, but both Malinowski and his loved ones survive their sacrifice to Mammon remarkably well.

Notes

This short piece was published in *The Guardian* newspaper on 11 August 1967 as a review of *A Diary in the Strict Sense of the Term*, which was a posthumously published edited version of the diaries kept by Malinowski during some of his periods of fieldwork in New Guinea and Melanesia during the 1910s.

1.4

Raymond Firth (1979)

Raymond William Firth was born in 1901 near Auckland, New Zealand; he was educated at Auckland Grammar School and Auckland University College. Since 1932 he has resided in England, but he preserves his links with New Zealand relatives. The unpretentious style of living and the no-nonsense rationalism which have been characteristic of Firth throughout his academic life have their roots in the modest simplicity of his colonial background.

At Auckland University College Firth specialised in economics, and his first publication was a short monograph on the economics of the kauri-gum industry.[1] In 1924, he came to England to work for a higher degree in economics at the London School of Economics (LSE); his planned field of research was the frozen meat industry of New Zealand. At that time, Bronislaw Malinowski had just been appointed to a readership at the University of London, tenable at the LSE. Malinowski's various writings on the Kula exchange system prevailing in the archipelagos of eastern New Guinea had been published between 1920 and 1922, and had aroused great interest among economic historians, notably R. H. Tawney, who was at that time an influential member of the LSE academic staff. It was probably a combination of Tawney's breadth of vision concerning the scope of economics, Malinowski's personal magnetism, and Firth's long-standing interest in the ethnography and archaeology of the New Zealand Maori which led Firth to change the topic of his PhD dissertation to 'The Primitive Economics of the New Zealand Maori'. It was completed in 1927 and published as a book in 1929.

This thesis, written under Malinowski's supervision, is based on bookwork rather than fieldwork – that is to say, the facts of Maori ethnography derive from published records concerning the 'traditional' society rather than from first-hand enquiry among present-day Maori. Malinowski's influence on Firth's general reading in anthropology can be seen from the bibliography, where more than three-quarters of the entries in the general non-Maori section are in German and refer to authors of whom Malinowski approved. The extension to this bibliography which appears in the substantially revised edition published in 1959 reflects not only the expansion of the field of economic anthropology, largely as a response to Firth's own activities, but also the extent to which Firth's anthropological vision had broadened out once he was free of the restricting influence of Malinowski.

During the decade 1925 to 1935, Malinowski's celebrated graduate seminar became a magnet for young scholars of the most diverse backgrounds. Embryo anthropologists who were either regular or occasional participants included E. E. Evans-Pritchard, Raymond W. Firth, Isaac Schapera, Audrey I. Richards, Meyer Fortes, Reo F. Fortune, Ian Hogbin, and Gregory Bateson. From the start, Firth stood closest to Malinowski, and his subsequent achievements reflect most clearly the goals that Malinowski presented to his students. The memorial volume to Malinowski which Firth edited is an enduring expression of Firth's indebtedness to his mentor.[2]

After obtaining his PhD Firth returned to New Zealand, where he prepared his thesis for publication and planned what proved to be one of the most important anthropological field trips ever undertaken. This was his 1928 visit to the tiny island of Tikopia, which is geographically located within the Solomon Islands, though its population, then numbering approximately thirteen hundred, are of Polynesian race and culture. Firth made further, briefer visits in 1952 and 1966.

Firth's first three publications concerning Tikopia were a general field report and a paper on 'Totemism in Polynesia' which appeared in the first volume of *Oceania* (1930–1) and a paper entitled 'Marriage and the Classificatory System of Relationship' which first appeared in the *Journal of the Royal Anthropological Institute* (1930). The first major monograph, *We, the Tikopia* (1936), was concerned with kinship organisation. Since then Tikopia has been the subject of five further monographs, an essay collection, and a score of uncollected articles.[3]

Although these writings add up to a truly formidable achievement, Firth's Tikopia studies have had less impact on the development of anthropological thinking than their bulk might suggest. Firth's written style is sometimes florid, but seldom elegant. His closely packed paragraphs make no concessions to the novice reader. He hardly ever resorts to diagrammatic simplification of the argument; indeed he is opposed in principle to model-building or reductionism in any form. Firth's general view of the nature of culture remains close to that of Malinowski, but whereas the latter, while stressing the involuted complexity of the 'system as a whole', implied that the functional implications of cultural conventions are mutually consistent, Firth's emphasis is on the inconsistencies. He presents his individual Tikopian as faced with a dense mesh of alternative avenues of cultural expression. Faced with such choices the individual makes decisions and it is this process of decision making within a cultural matrix that Firth claims to be able to analyse in his numerous writings on the theme of social organisation. But Firth's reader has to work hard to understand what is being said.

On returning from the field, Firth joined the staff of the Department of Anthropology at the University of Sydney, which was then headed by A. R. Radcliffe-Brown. Firth was active as editorial promoter of the newly established journal *Oceania*, which was based in the Sydney department. He was acting head of the department in 1931/2.

Firth then returned to London to take up a post under Malinowski at the LSE. He had the status of Lecturer from 1932 to 1935, and Reader from 1935 to 1944. Malinowski died in the United States in 1942 and Firth was appointed to a full professorship in his stead in 1944.

In the immediate pre-war period, Firth was a particularly active member of the Royal Anthropological Institute of which he was Honorary Secretary from

1936 to 1939. He was President from 1953 to 1955 and has played a prominent role in the Institute's affairs ever since.

In 1938, Firth completed the text of *Primitive Polynesian Economy* (1939), which is wholly devoted to Tikopia. Firth describes it as 'in a sense a supplement to my *Primitive Economics of the New Zealand Maori* (1929)', and his next enterprise was designed as a further supplement. The idea was to study the economics of a community still relatively 'primitive' in terms of technological organisation, but which was caught up in the world-wide monetary system and international trade in a way that the 'traditional' Maori and the Tikopia were not.

In late 1939, Firth and his wife Rosemary Upcott, daughter of Sir Gilbert Upcott, embarked on field research in a fishing community in Trengganu on the north-east coast of the Malay Peninsula. The research was partially frustrated by the outbreak of the Second World War, but it resulted in a major monograph by Firth, *Malay Fishermen: Their Peasant Economy* (1946), and an additional volume, *Housekeeping among Malay Peasants* (1943), written by his wife. Firth made brief return visits to Malaya in 1947 and 1963, and the 1966 revision of his book is substantially enlarged.

During the war, the LSE was evacuated to Cambridge, where Firth was also posted in a subcentre of the Naval Intelligence Division of the British Admiralty, which was run by the geographer H. C. Darby and which was responsible for the production of a series of geographical handbooks designed as tools for the contingency planning of naval operations throughout the world. Firth was the principal compiler and editor of the four volumes of this series which relate to the Pacific islands. Originally issued as internal Admiralty documents in 1943, 1944, and 1945, they became more generally available ten years later. Much of the information which they contain would still be hard to obtain from any other source.[4]

As the war progressed, the British authorities began to consider the effects that the war would have on the far-flung British colonial empire. While few people foresaw the rapidity of post-war colonial dissolution, there was a widespread appreciation that radical changes were impending. Yet it was apparent that in many of the colonial dependencies sensible planning for the future was hopelessly prejudiced by a basic lack of information concerning fundamental social and economic facts. Through his work on the Admiralty handbooks, Firth understood the seriousness of these gaps in information and he actively promoted a consciousness of this situation in government circles. The outcome was the formation in 1944 of the Colonial Social Science Research Council, of which Firth was the first Secretary. In the immediate post-war period an immense amount of really first-class anthropological research was carried out under the auspices of the British Colonial Office on the recommendations of this body. Its successor, the centrally financed Social Science Research Council, of which Firth was again a founding member, continues to be the principal agency for funding the field research of British social anthropologists.[5]

By the end of 1945, the LSE had been re-established in London, and Firth took on the full responsibility for running Malinowski's former department, which he chaired until his retirement in 1968. During much of this period he was the guide and sponsor of an ambitious long-term project to study, by the methods of social anthropology, the operations of kinship in urban settings in London. The publications which have resulted from this enterprise were disappointing.[6]

Firth has subsequently been a visiting professor at universities in the United States, Canada, and New Zealand. Earlier in his career, he was a visitor at the Australian National University at Canberra, where he played a leading part in the discussions that led to the establishment of the important chair of anthropology and sociology in the Research School of Pacific Studies. Since 1965, Firth has accumulated a notable string of honorary degrees, has been a fellow of the British Academy since 1949, and was awarded a knighthood in 1973.

In post-war Britain, the number of graduate students working for research degrees in social anthropology grew rapidly, and before long a vigorous rivalry developed between the two leading centres, Firth's department at the LSE, which became the stronghold of a slightly modified Malinowskian orthodoxy, and the Institute of Social Anthropology at Oxford, which was first directed by Radcliffe-Brown, Malinowski's long-standing rival, and later by Evans-Pritchard. At a later date, the pre-eminence of the LSE was challenged by the creation of a vigorous new department at the University of Manchester, under the leadership of Max Gluckman, and by the success of Meyer Fortes in reviving the fortunes of the long-established, but languishing, department at Cambridge University. There was also a veritable mushroom growth of lesser institutions. By the early 1960s, social anthropology, which had been virtually an LSE monopoly as late as 1939, was being taught in at least eighteen different universities in the British Isles.

In intellectual terms, Firth responded negatively to the new styles of anthropological presentation represented in the work of Evans-Pritchard, Fortes, Gluckman, and their students, but he recognised, more clearly than some of his senior colleagues, that despite their different approaches to the Durkheimian notion of the functional interdependence of institutions, the various emergent cliques of social anthropologists all had a great deal in common. Moreover he saw very clearly that, in the new post-war circumstances, the miniscule private trust funds through which most British anthropological research had been funded prior to 1939 would prove wholly inadequate. He also recognised that if social anthropologists were to gain access to the much more substantial resources at the disposal of the government research councils, they would have to demonstrate some degree of corporate identity. The point was not lost on his Oxford opponents and in 1946 all of the professional social anthropologists in the country – still numbering fewer than a score – met together at the LSE to form the Association of Social Anthropologists of the Commonwealth, with Radcliffe-Brown as its first Chairman. In 1962, Firth, then Chairman of the Association, took the initiative that led to the important international conference of social anthropologists held in Cambridge in 1963. As a result of this conference, a distinctive series of symposia publications known as the ASA Monographs (subsequently ASA Series, ASA Essays) first appeared. This collection, in its variety and homogeneity, provides a specification of what British social anthropology is all about. Appropriately Firth is the Life President of the Association.

All of this might give the impression that Firth's principal historical significance for the history of the social sciences is that he showed the entrepreneurial and organisational flair that converted British social anthropology from being the brand name of a rather quirkish style of anthropological practice peculiar to a handful of individuals – which was the state of affairs in the 1930s – into an internationally accepted, widely practised, and highly respected branch of study, which ranks high in the generally accepted hierarchy of the various social sciences.

Certainly this side of Firth's work deserves emphasis and is of sociological interest in itself. In the dialectical development of British social anthropology, the ancestral doctrine of Malinowski generated the rival creeds of Radcliffe-Brown, Evans-Pritchard, Fortes, and Gluckman. In this mêlée, Firth was from the start a peacemaker among the factionalists, a leader who was more concerned with the future of social anthropology as an academic discipline than with his own academic reputation. But precisely because Firth chose to be a leader without disciples, it is difficult to spell out with any clarity just where he stands in the spectrum of anthropological opinion. He has not been the founder of a 'school'; he has no immediate imitators.

The extraordinary detail of his description of Tikopia culture and society has been mentioned already and is a lasting monument. But though the Tikopia can be cited as examples (or perhaps counter-examples) of all kinds of generalising anthropological theories, Firth's Tikopia studies did not in themselves serve to break new theoretical ground.

The succession of monographs, essays, and editorial initiatives relating to economic anthropology, and their revisions, are another matter.[7] In the ongoing debate between the 'formal theorists' and the 'substantivists', Firth has consistently adopted a 'formal theorist' stance – that is to say he has maintained that economics is a unified science containing basic principles that have world-wide application. Any persisting mode of human organisation, whether primitive or sophisticated, monetary or non-monetary, market-oriented or subsistence-oriented, capitalist or socialist, has an economic aspect, and general principles relating to such factors as production, distribution, and exchange, the ownership of goods, and command over the means of production are comparable right across the board. In particular, Firth holds that economics is the study of the allocation of scarce resources among alternative ends and that the concept of scarcity is essential to any meaningful study of economics. Firth has viewed with persistent scepticism the various contrary opinions, many of which have their roots in Marxist ideology, which argue that scarcity is simply a product of the particular social formation with which we are most familiar – that of the world-wide, capitalist, market economy – and that there are different types of economy which differ as do species.

The formidable corpus of Firth's writings includes contributions to almost every aspect of social anthropology. Apart from economics, the most prominent themes are social change and religion. A crucial element in his treatment of these topics is the special meaning that he attributes to the concept of social organisation.

Firth began to use this expression as early as 1930, but in the period from 1949 to 1960, he employed it as a polemical weapon of attack against 'the rigidity and limitations of a simple structuralism' alleged to be propounded by the Oxford followers of Radcliffe-Brown.[8] If viewed in its historical context, this phase of Firth's writings was an attempt to rescue from oblivion certain undervalued individualist aspects of Malinowski's functionalism, and in this regard it must be rated a failure. Admittedly structuralism in social anthropology has now become the brand name of the anthropology of Claude Lévi-Strauss rather than that of Radcliffe-Brown, but this transformation was not brought about by the empiricist criticisms that Firth levelled against the latter. But the importance of the concept of social organisation for an understanding of the distinctive characteristics of Firth's personal brand of anthropological argument may be inferred from the fact that the expression appears not only in the title of his textbook, but also in that of the *Festschrift* offered to him by his former pupils shortly before his retirement.[9]

Two quotations may serve to introduce our discussion of this key concept.

> (1) A theoretical framework for the analysis of social change must be concerned largely with what happens to social structures. But to be truly dynamic it must allow for individual action. . . .[10]
>
> (2) . . . so far from the religion of the Tikopia merely reflecting or maintaining the social structure, in some of its aspects it offers avenues of *escape from* society, into personal fantasy, which is then allowed social recognition and credited with social functions.[11]

These are both typical examples of what Firth means by social organisation. It is a concept which has a binary relationship with Radcliffe-Brown's social structure. 'Structure' is here conceived of as a stable, inflexible system of jural rules; 'organisation' is the set of cultural conventions which allows individuals to interpret the rules with sufficient flexibility to make the system of structural rules viable at the level of empirical behaviour. Changes in these conventions over time provide Firth with his principal tool for the analysis of social change both in the secular and religious spheres of practical activity.

Firth, like Malinowski, has consistently assumed that the core of every serious piece of anthropological research must consist of the detailed field study of a particular culture considered as a total system. The task of the anthropologist is to show not only how the system fits together but how it works. Most of Firth's younger colleagues now interpret the 'how it works' component of this doctrine very loosely. The mechanistic notion that particular social institutions have particular identifiable functions which can be shown to serve the egocentric needs of the individual (Malinowski) or the socio-centric needs of society (Radcliffe-Brown) have been abandoned. Indeed, the word function seldom appears in any of their writings. Firth's position, on the other hand, is a compromise between the two earlier standpoints, with 'social organisation' serving as the mediating term.

Closely linked with this special brand of functionalism, which puts so much emphasis on the individual as decision-maker, is Firth's consistent empiricist bias, which is reflected in an equally consistent antipathy towards psychoanalytic and structuralist (i.e. Lévi-Straussian) explanations of symbolic action, which emphasise unconscious rather than conscious motivations on the part of the individual. The weakness of such arguments from Firth's point of view is that they evade the guiding principle that speculation must always be tested against the fieldworker's direct and detailed observations.

This empiricist commitment has proved inhibiting. Thus, Firth's restudies of Tikopia and Trengganu culture, after an interval of years, are contributions to the particular histories of these two societies, but they have not led to conclusions about the general processes of cultural change which are other than commonplace. It should be noted, however, that Firth has entered into direct and well-informed debate with the Marxists over their treatment of anthropological data.[12]

Much the same applies to Firth's writings on primitive religion, which are based on Tikopia data. As an atheist, Firth assumes that any honest anthropological fieldworker must start out from the premise that in 'real' terms, all religious belief is illusion. The task of the functional anthropologist is therefore to discover utility (or disutility) in the social consequences of religious performance.

Firth is very far from being insensitive to the aesthetic nuances of religion, but he has repeatedly attempted to separate aesthetic activity from religious activity, apparently because, while he approves of the former he views all forms of the latter as a kind of self-deception.[13]

Here is a paradox. Although Firth is clearly fascinated by the relationship between art and religion, he remains deeply sceptical about all discussions of intangible reality. The overall point of his most recent major monograph, *Symbols* (1973), is that because there has been a plethora of general anthropological theories about symbolism (both religious and other), and because it is easy to find ethnographic counter-examples to any scheme which postulates a general systemic ordering of human symbols, the anthropologist's proper role should be to demonstrate the non-logical inconsistency rather than the logical consistency of this major aspect of human self-expression, which 'not only blurs relationships in the orders of reality; [but] it also has historically been a potent trigger of social conflict.'[14] Sometimes one has the impression that Firth looks upon current structuralist fashions of the Lévi-Straussian sort as manifestations of religious superstition, and evil at that!

Finally, there remains for consideration Firth's role as a teacher. Here his influence has been very great indeed. Firth is not at his best in the setting of a formal lecture. He has too many facts at his disposal and his empiricist honesty drives him to put too many of them on show at the same time. But, as the chairman of a seminar discussion, his performance is superb. During his years at the LSE, it was above all through the medium of the academic seminar that Firth made his influence felt. In this setting, he treats the contributors to a debate as if they were informants in an unstructured session of Tikopia fieldwork. He manages to extract sense from the ramblings of even the most uninteresting informants. Over and over again, as scores of participants can bear witness, Firth's summing-up of a long discursive argument has had the magical effect of converting what had seemed to be a tediously pointless discussion into an innovating discovery procedure of real significance. If he had done nothing else, and he has of course done a very great deal, Firth would by this competence alone have demonstrated that he was a thoroughly worthy successor to the formidable Malinowski.

Notes

This short biographical sketch and assessment was written by Leach as an entry for the *International Encyclopaedia of the Social Sciences* (1979). It describes the life and work to that time of Sir Raymond Firth, one of Leach's own teachers and one of the great British anthropologists. Readers should note that in the more than twenty years since Leach's piece was written, Sir Raymond has added many other distinguished publications to his oeuvre.

1. Firth, *Kauri-Gum Industry.*
2. Firth (ed.), *Man and Culture.*
3. See *Primitive Polynesian Economy*; *The Work of the Gods in Tikopia*; *Social Change in Tikopia*; *History and Traditions of Tikopia*; *Tikopia Ritual and Belief*; *Rank and Religion in Tikopia.*
4. See, Great Britain Naval Intelligence Division, *Pacific Islands.*
5. [Eds: In the early 1980s the Social Science Research Council was replaced by the Economic and Social Research Council.]
6. Firth (ed.), *Two Studies of Kinship in London*; Firth, Hubert, and Forge, *Families and their Relatives.*
7. See, Firth, *Economics of the New Zealand Maori*; *Primitive Polynesian Economy*; *Malay Fishermen*; Firth (ed.), *Themes in Economic Anthropology*; Firth and Yamey (eds), *Capital, Savings, and Credit.*
8. Firth, *Essays on Social Organization and Values*, chs 4, 5, 6.
9. *Elements of Social Organization*; Freedman (ed.), *Social Organisation.*
10. Firth, *Elements of Social Organization*, p. 83.
11. *Essays on Social Organization*, p. 254.
12. 'The Sceptical Anthropologist?'.
13. *Essays on Social Organization*, pp. 138–9.
14. *Symbols*, pp. 427–8.

1.5

The Ecology of Mental Process (1980)

Review of David Lipset, *Gregory Bateson: The Legacy of a Scientist*

Margaret Mead died in November 1978, Reo Fortune in November 1979, Gregory Bateson in July 1980. The conjunction of these three most unusual anthropologists in New Guinea at the end of 1932 drastically restructured their private lives.

Mead, who was then married to Fortune, was later married to Bateson for fourteen years. The consequences for scholarship are still difficult to assess. Fortune ceased altogether to be an effective anthropologist; Mead became an international celebrity, mainly by virtue of highly impressionistic, easy-to-read, accounts of field research which had already been completed when she first met Bateson. Bateson's principal contribution to anthropology, the awkwardly complex but highly original *Naven* (1936), was also based on fieldwork that had been completed by late 1932, and which was written up in Cambridge before his marriage to Mead. But although it is a very different sort of book from anything that either Mead or Fortune might have written, it would probably never have been written at all without their stimulus.

In 1936 the dominant style in British anthropology was the extreme empirical functionalism adopted by Malinowski and his pupils, Raymond Firth and Audrey Richards. Bateson, while declaring his respect for the work of this school, also argued that the best ethnography has the artistic merits of a great novel. In his opening pages he invoked the names of Jane Austen and Charles Doughty's *Arabia Deserta.*

Naven was an attempt to capture what Bateson called the ethos of Iatmul culture rather than simply to describe, in Malinowskian manner, how everything fitted together. The general attitude to ethnographic evidence which Bateson adopted, which was made to seem quite unnecessarily obscure through his mode of presentation, had much more in common with the later work of Evans-Pritchard and of Levi-Strauss than it had with then current fashions. But although *Naven* was ridiculed at the time by Malinowski, along with Mead's *Sex and Temperament in Three New Guinea Societies* and Benedict's *Patterns of Culture,* it was a book that was read with great interest by Malinowski's younger pupils, as I can vouch from my experience.

Bateson usually described himself as an anthropologist, but he also had polymathic interests in such fields as animal behaviour, cybernetics, and the psychology of schizophrenia. His enduring reputation, which may well prove to be very considerable, is likely to derive as much from these other interstitial activities as from his direct contributions to anthropology.

Lipset's biography, which was published a few weeks before Bateson's death, is a brilliant performance. He had the full collaboration of Bateson himself and of all members of his entourage, including access to family papers and letters, but many of the most interesting passages in the book derive from the personal recollections of those who had known Bateson and whose opinions, as expressed in unstructured interviews, were recorded by Lipset on tape. A great variety of people collaborated in this way, including both Mead and Fortune, and the author has shown astonishing skill and tact in deducing, from what must often have seemed very contradictory and prejudiced evidence, a balanced account of the life and intellectual development of a man whose persistent curiosity about matters which most of us take for granted sometimes came close to genius.

Bateson's family background was academic Cambridge in high degree. His grandfather, W. H. Bateson, was Master of St John's College from 1857 to

1882; his father, William Bateson, was the celebrated zoologist whose renown stemmed from his pugnacious vindication of the genetics of Mendel against the statistical biometrics of Weldon and Pearson. William Bateson invented much of the technical language of modern genetics including the word 'genetics' itself. Gregory was clearly greatly influenced by his father; indeed his first publication was a joint-authorship contribution to the *Journal of Genetics* 'On certain aberrations of the red-legged partridges . . .' (1926), published when Gregory was twenty-two.

But Gregory's intellectual heritage was not restricted to biology. It was William Bateson who first introduced Geoffrey Keynes to the art of William Blake, a field in which Sir Geoffrey, at the age of ninety-three, is now an acknowledged world authority. This was an enthusiasm which Gregory shared and which is somehow reflected in much of his later work. But probably the most important influences on Bateson's thinking came from his close friend C. H. Waddington, the Edinburgh geneticist. Gregory never adopted the Marxist view of science favoured by Waddington, but he did share many of the latter's humanist concerns. What these concerns were is summed up in the titles of Gregory's last two substantial publications, an essay collection, *Steps to an Ecology of Mind* (1972), and *Mind and Nature: A Necessary Unity* (1979), the latter written at a time when Gregory was fully aware that he was suffering from terminal cancer.

Gregory was not a vitalist; he saw very clearly that the scientific explanation of human behaviour must be of essentially the same kind as the scientific explanation of the behaviour of dolphins. But he was too good a cultural anthropologist to be taken in by the kind of reductionism that is favoured by some of the more simple-minded sociobiologists. The human mind cannot be explained away either as a genetically pre-programmed machine or as an illusory side-effect of conditioned reflexes.

Gregory's interests always remained biological; but the focus of his attention was not confined to the human being as a biological organism. It was man in his social interactions and man as a species adapted to extremely sophisticated forms of interpersonal communication that provoked his most challenging suggestions. But they were suggestions rather than proven facts. His theories about the nature of schizophrenia and about 'the double bind' influenced a wide variety of practising psychotherapists, but they were often misunderstood and they were not of a sort which lend themselves to verification.

Academically he was always a loner; he seldom occupied any position which called for formal teaching. He exercised his influence in private informal seminars and conference discussions and it is difficult to pin down just what that influence was. Gregory was a guru. I know that I myself found him one of the most exciting and inspiring 'teachers' I have ever met.

Gregory himself would probably have claimed that his main claim to fame was his application of ideas borrowed from cybernetics to an understanding of the feedback which occurs in person-to-person interactions. But what he had to say on such matters often contained a good deal of blarney; he had a scientific attitude, but he was not an exact scientist and he was not a mathematician.

Lipset recognises these limitations. Inspired in his youth by the art of Blake and the laws of Mendel, Gregory aspired to make comparable innovations. He did not succeed, but his contributions to our understanding of the position of mind in the physical world and to the complex relationships which link form and process are far from negligible.

There is much more to Lipset's book than I have been able to summarise here. The account of the intellectual atmosphere in which Gregory grew up is particularly impressive. The book as a whole makes a most timely and fitting memorial.

Notes

This is Leach's review, written in 1980 for the science journal *Nature*, of a biography of Gregory Bateson by David Lipset.

1.6

Review of Meyer Fortes, *The Web of Kinship* (1950)

The first part of this important work, *The Dynamics of Clanship among the Tallensi*, was published as long ago as 1945. Neither book can usefully stand alone and some briefer title such as *Tallensi Social Structure*, Vols 1 and 2, might have been more appropriate. This initial comment is not merely captious. The existing titles of the two books are somewhat characteristic of the writing of the books themselves; in both volumes a wealth of penetrating analysis and at times brilliant generalisation is embedded in too many words and often tortuous analogies. This second volume certainly is decidedly easier to digest than the first – the terminological overprecision which produced 'incipient patri-segments' and 'effective minimal lineages' obtrudes only occasionally – but even so, the merits and limitations of the book are only likely to be fully appreciated by those thoroughly familiar with the current controversies of social anthropology. Likewise it is difficult to discuss the book except in terms of these controversies.

Broadly speaking, social anthropologists may be divided into those who consider that individual behaviour results from the incentive of self-interest, as culturally determined, and those who emphasise the external discipline imposed by moral and jural pressures. The first group tend to frame their argument around the cultural determinants of economic systems or, alternatively, around the cultural determinants of psychological personality; the second group are prone to ignore culture in its generally accepted anthropological sense and to concern themselves with the internal logic of social systems: they discuss not culture, but social structure.

In writing of the Tallensi Dr Fortes has aligned himself whole-heartedly with the latter group of writers, and to my mind the primary importance of his book is that it is a most carefully worked out attempt to give concrete examples of structurally paired relationships which have previously been discussed only in abstract or at any rate largely formal terms. For example, when Dr Fortes comes to discuss the relation of mother's brother to sister's son (e.g. pp. 283ff.), he gives us not only the formal socially approved behaviour, but also concrete examples of such behaviour, and he even attempts to consolidate his argument by resort to statistics. The reader is thus able to judge for himself just what the concepts of social structure mean in real-life situations. I should add, however, that the attempt, though worthy, is not altogether successful. The figures given on pp. 288ff. have very little meaning; in the absence of data as to the total numerical size of the different clans mentioned it is impossible to determine how far the distribution cited deviates from the purely haphazard.

Whereas in Vol. 1 the Tallensi social system was considered in its large-scale ramifications as manifested in lineage segmentation and the balanced opposition of ritual and secular leadership, here in Vol. 2 we are concerned with the same system in its impact upon the developing family and household. Throughout both volumes one particular key theme of structural analysis is stressed repeatedly, namely the proposition that Tallensi society is an 'equilibrium' resulting from the 'polar opposition' of sundry collectivities. These range in kind from such universals as the contrast between male and female, or the psychological hostility between father and son, to the specifically Tallensi distinction between Namoo chiefs and Tali priest leaders (*tendaana*). I do not admit myself that this concept of a social equilibrium is acceptable, but Dr Fortes has eliminated many of the theoretical objections by his dogmatic assertion that the Tallensi are culturally and economically homogeneous. This enables him virtually to dismiss economics from the field of discussion, and to interpret Tallensi social organisation wholly in terms of cleavages and combinations in the fields of kinship and ritual.

Personally I feel sceptical about this alleged economic homogeneity; I do not understand for example how the Chief of Tongo, who appears to possess thirty wives, forty-odd sons and ten times as many cattle as the average Tallensi (pp. 72, 82, 270), can be regarded as a member of an economically undifferentiated community; proportionately speaking, the rich men of a capitalist society are always only 'a handful' of the total. All the same, I readily concede that many of the concepts which Dr Fortes develops in the course of his study of structural oppositions may prove to be valuable analytical tools, with an applicability to cultural situations far removed from West Africa. Especially thought-provoking is the sharp distinction which he draws between agnatic (lineage-based) and cognatic (biologically based) kinship ties (pp. 13ff.) and also the demonstration that, in this patrilineally ordered society, differentiation, both at the lineage and at the personal level, is expressed through contrasted female descent (pp. 229, 328; cf. Vol. 1).

Even so, despite or even because of his protestations to the contrary (p. 223), I have a suspicion that Dr Fortes is not entirely satisfied with the somewhat mechanical appearance of the Tallensi puppets that emerge from his sometimes overformalised analysis. Paradoxically, we find him repeatedly claiming to interpret not only the structural relations of his subjects but also their personal emotions. I need cite only one example. In Chapter 4 the difficulties of Tallensi married life are presented as 'arising out of the cleavages inherent in the structure of the family' (p. 79); the formal relations which link husband and wife to one another and to the individual members of their respective families are examined in detail with great analytical precision, yet every now and then we come upon a paragraph which does not seem to form part of this logical analysis at all. The following, for example, appears to be a straight projection of European sentiments into the Tallensi situation: 'The real foundation of a lasting marriage is not custom or jural or ritual sanctions, but a satisfactory relationship between the married pair. . . . The sexual bond is of vital importance in this relationship' (p. 87). So in the end, it seems, despite the beautiful symmetries of their social system, the Tallensi are faced with the same psychological difficulties as middle-class Englishmen! Is not this tantamount to an admission that structural analysis only touches the outermost superficialities of behaviour?

The book, then, has negative as well as positive virtues. On the one hand it is a brilliant exposition of the methods of social analysis that have been developed from the teachings of Professor Radcliffe-Brown; on the other it demonstrates, even if unintentionally, the inadequacy of this method as a tool of total social analysis. Some of the remarks in the final chapter of the book suggest that Dr Fortes may himself have reached a very similar conclusion (p. 339).[1]

No doubt the basic argument of these two volumes could have been presented in simpler and much more readily understandable form if the author had been prepared to admit from the start that he was describing a logical system to which real-life behaviour is only a rather remote approximation, but the result might then have been much less instructive. What Dr Fortes actually does is first to describe a formal system; then recognise the vagaries of actual behaviour; and then seek to justify these aberrations in terms of the system. It is this last mental gymnastic which makes the argument often difficult to follow, yet it is crucially important, for it is precisely here that we can recognise both the value and the limitations of structural concepts. What Dr Fortes has really described is the moral code of the Tallensi with all its logical ramifications (p. 346); he has also shown, if only in passing, that the Tallensi do not obey their own moral rules. Without this corrective, structural analysis is liable to reduce human beings to mechanical automata and to reassert the classic anthropological fiction that 'the native is a slave to custom'. Dr Fortes has avoided, if only just, this pitfall of his own method.

Notes

This review of *The Web of Kinship among the Tallensi* was published in the leading British academic anthropology journal, *Man*, in 1950.

1. [Eds. The passage Leach refers to reads as follows: 'All kinship institutions have two major facets or, if we like, functions. They serve as a mechanism for organising social activities and coordinating social relations, either in a limited sector of social life or in relation to all social

interests; and they at the same time constitute the primary mould of the individual's psychosocial development . . . . We are concerned with two distinct levels of organisation and expression in the structure of human social behaviour. . . . A complete understanding of the significance of its institutions for a particular society calls for an investigation on both levels. That is not what we have attempted in this book'.]

1.7

Review of Radcliffe-Brown, *A Natural Science of Society*, and Nadel, *The Theory of Social Structure* (1958)

The simultaneous publication of these two posthumous volumes is both a symptom and a portent. Taken together they perhaps mark the beginning and the end of a special phase in the development of social anthropology. The two books are strictly comparable. Both originated in a course of university lectures, both are concerned with the general theory of social structure at the highest possible level of abstraction. But, in origin, they are separated by nearly twenty years.

The Radcliffe-Brown volume is a verbatim transcript of lectures delivered at the University of Chicago in 1937. A restricted duplicated edition of the same text has circulated since 1948 under the title *The Nature of a Theoretical Natural Science of Society*. The theme was the author's favourite topic of discourse and this fact is reflected on every page. Each sentence has a gem-like polish, every statement takes the form of an all-embracing generalisation. But the sense is aphoristic rather than exact; through repeated repetition, all facts of ethnography or history have become moulded to what Radcliffe-Brown believed must necessarily be the case. Such beautiful lucidity is entrancing; all the more reason to ask: does the acknowledged merit of 1937 still endure twenty years later?

Radcliffe-Brown's general viewpoint is today sufficiently well known. Human societies throughout the world differ in their systemic organisation. Systems can be classified according to their structure. The taxonomic classification of social structures is a scientific end in itself and constitutes the first essential step towards the formation of a 'science of human society', the exact nature or purpose of which is left conveniently obscure.

The book presents an elegant façade of widely ranging scholarship. The author plays by turn the roles of historian, physicist, and mathematical logician but always with one central aim in view. His book is a plea for the scientific utility of a comparative taxonomy of *total* social structures. Although, in practice, these totalities are much more difficult to identify than Radcliffe-Brown was prepared to admit, this is a gospel which has had extremely important consequences for social anthropology. At least four well-known symposia[1] are directly in line with the doctrine here laid down.

Yet one may wonder. Why, after all, should similarity of 'structure' – if we are certain what we mean by that – be scientifically so important? Might it not be as well to take warning from the botanists? In that field, over the past two centuries, the concept of 'species' has been laboriously constructed on purely structural principles but it now transpires that, in the most significant of all botanical enquiries, that of cross-breeding and reproduction, structurally defined species are not specific at all! Botanists still resort to classification but the principles on which this classification is based are no longer exclusively structural.[2]

The following quotation from a botanist,[3] if taken to apply to social anthropology, is in direct contradiction to Radcliffe-Brown's thesis:

> Comparative morphology cannot in fact exist as an independent scientific discipline: it must make the fullest possible use of the data and conclusions of causal morphology, which in fact involves physiology, genetics and ecology.

Doubts of this general kind seem to have been present in Nadel's mind when he wrote *The Theory of Social Structure* for he is plainly sceptical concerning the scientific value of 'a structural frame of reference' unless it can somehow incorporate 'concepts connoting purpose and utility' (p. 158).

Nadel's book is an enlarged version of a course of lectures delivered at the London School of Economics in the spring of 1955. At the time of his death the text was already in proof but the absence of an index and one or two blatant errors (e.g. p. 121) in the 'mathematics' with which some chapters are liberally bespattered suggest that final revision was still lacking.

Although Professor Fortes, at the end of his interesting memoir, expresses the opinion that this will become 'one of the great theoretical treatises of twentieth-century social anthropology' my own view is much less optimistic. Those who are not devotees of the subject are likely to find the book unreadable. Nadel seems to have aimed at doing three quite separate things. Firstly, he examines in great detail the implications of 'role theory' which has found its way into social anthropology chiefly through the writings of Radcliffe-Brown, Linton, and Max Weber. Secondly he attempts, towards the end of his book, to arbitrate between the diverse views of social structure advanced by a number of different social anthropologists, notably Radcliffe-Brown, Firth, Fortes, Lévi-Strauss, and myself. But thirdly he has used his book as a platform from which to propound his highly personal view that the future of abstract anthropological theory lies in the development of an appropriate calculus of symbolic logic. It is this last feature which is disastrous.

Every now and then the argument is interrupted to present a series of generalised propositions expressed in a symbolic logic of the author's own devising. None of these symbolic statements has any meaning until Nadel has himself explained them in his accompanying text and none of them leads to conclusions which are not much more readily propounded in simple English. The only positive effect of this excursion into 'mathematics' is to deter the reader from trying to understand the argument.

Those who are tough-minded enough to ignore the calculus will find the discussion of role theory very stimulating. There is much here with which I personally do not agree – e.g. the notion that societies can be usefully distinguished according to the number of different roles which they contain (pp. 61f.) – and unfortunately the most personal and original section (pp. 115–21) is the worst entangled with symbolism. Who on earth is going to work his way through the following?

$$\begin{aligned} &\text{if E: A}[\gtrless (crb)] \text{ is such that} \\ &\quad \text{ErA} \supset \text{E } (ca) \text{ A} \\ &\therefore \text{ ErA} \rightarrow \text{A } [\gtrless (crb)] \end{aligned}$$

Even with the clues that *ca* stands for 'command over the actions of others' and *crb* for 'command over services and benefits' the reader is not likely to be much the wiser. But the cross-cutting taxonomy of role types (summarised in the charts at pp. 53, 73) and the integration of this taxonomy with the distinction between 'leadership roles' and 'expressive roles' which appears in the work of Parsons and Bales[4] marks a genuine step forward.

Yet in the outcome, my total reaction is one of scepticism. For Radcliffe-Brown, it was a methodological dogma to assume that 'a social system is not purposive' (p. 155). Dismayed at the implications of such detachment, Nadel would have us abandon the carefully formulated distinction between role and status (p. 109). Despite his fondness for mathematics Nadel still wants to stick closely to the empirical facts; an office, it seems, has no existence apart from the individuals who fill it. In fact Nadel does not really admit that there is anything abstract about social structure at all. 'Empirical constancies do exist and are observable' (p. 145). Perhaps. But do anthropologists in fact observe them? I cannot help remembering that Nadel's excellent volume *The Nuba*, which records a very large number of structural constancies for no fewer than ten different tribes, is based on empirical observations covering about twelve months.

I think that both these books deserve to be read and read together, for they pose a question. Has the too narrow pursuit of Radcliffe-Brown's principles led to a dead end? Was Nadel pointing the road ahead? I myself would answer the first question with a 'yes' and the second with a 'no', but that is just a matter of opinion.

Notes

This review was published in *Man* in 1958.

1. Eggan (ed.), *North American Tribes*; Fortes and Evans-Pritchard (eds), *African Political Systems*; Eggan, *Social Organization of Western Pueblos*; Radcliffe-Brown and Forde (eds), *African Systems of Kinship and Marriage*.
2. Lam, 'Classification and the New Morphology'.
3. Wardlaw, *Phylogeny and Morphology*.
4. Parsons and Bales, *Family Socialization and Interaction*.

1.8

Social Anthropology: A Natural Science of Society? (1976)

As a start let me emphasise the query at the end of my title. In my view the scientific status of social anthropology is very much an open question.

In part my argument will be historical. I am concerned with changes in the theoretical attitudes of social anthropologists so dates are relevant.

A. R. Radcliffe-Brown died in 1955. His career as a professional anthropologist had begun in 1906.[1] His publications were not extensive. Apart from two important items which I shall mention presently, virtually all his significant published work had been written before 1949.[2]

My contrasted hero Claude Lévi-Strauss began his anthropological career in 1932.[3] He has written a great deal. His distinction as a theorist first became apparent as the result of work published in the United States between 1943 and 1945. His status as an international celebrity dates from 1955, the year that saw the publication in French of *Tristes tropiques*, a collection of autobiographical reflections on the nature of anthropology.

The practical overlap between these two figures is thus very minor. Lévi-Strauss has recognised a limited debt to Radcliffe-Brown; there was no feedback influence the other way.

The work of Radcliffe-Brown was an important influence in British social anthropology from about 1910 onwards and over the decade 1945–55 it was dominant. It was a weakening influence thereafter.

Lévi-Strauss's work began to affect British social anthropology some time around 1950 and, despite persistent denunciation, became a dominant influence about ten years later. This influence has not yet been replaced.

Perhaps I can best explain my theme by analogy with another pseudo-science. In the summer of last year a congress of 1,500 Freudian psychoanalysts assembled in London and, if press reports are to be believed, devoted most of its energies to internal feuding. The argument was not really about what psychoanalysts do but about the models they should use in the interpretation of their observations.

On the one side there were the conservative traditionalists who held that the old Freudian model, which assumes an identity between psychic phenomena and the forces and quantities of the empirical sciences, is still, with minor modifications, quite good enough. On the other there were the radical reformers, led by a contingent from Paris, who rejected the assumption that causal–deterministic principles derived from the physical sciences can be usefully applied to the study of human beings who exercise conscious choice. These latter, the radical reformers, deployed the language of contemporary semiology. Psychoanalysis was to be regarded as a 'biological theory of meaning'. Psychoanalytic theory needs to be reformulated in terms of communication theory . . . and so on.[4] All of which will sound very familiar to the professional social anthropologists in my audience.

To those outside the profession the definitional limits of what social anthropology is often seem very obscure. This does not worry the professionals themselves. Social anthropology *is* what social anthropologists *do*; academic debate is all focused around styles in interpretation and explanation.

The concept of 'explanation' is itself very slippery. Academics of all kinds clearly feel that they are engaged in a kind of jigsaw-puzzle activity. 'Explanation' consists of fitting together a number of isolated pieces of information so that they begin to look as if they formed part of a larger pattern. There are many different kinds of explanation and all of them are provisional, that is to say, they express what is probable rather than what is certain, though many things are so highly probable that we can ignore the uncertainty.

As indicated by the congress of psychoanalysts, debate about the nature of explanation leads to polarisation.

One such polarity is that which divides *conservatives* and *radicals. Conservatives* will cling desperately to their accustomed models and persuade themselves, in defiance of all probability, that all newly discovered facts will fit in with what they think they know already. *Radicals* have a prior commitment to destroy whatever model of reality had seemed acceptable to their predecessors; they therefore concentrate all their attention on the lack of fit between the new information and the old. As Thomas Kuhn and Michel Foucault have both argued in their different ways, the two sides never really carry on a dialogue; they talk past one another.[5] In the end the conservatives die off and the counter-culture viewpoint of the radicals becomes a new orthodoxy. With hindsight, historians then recognise an intellectual revolution.

Another major polarity is that which distinguishes *rationalists* from *empiricists.* In terms of my jigsaw-puzzle analogy, *rationalists* start out with a clear-cut idea of the picture they are going to construct and then search around for pieces to fit into it. *Empiricists* work the other way round. They start with a pile of pieces which they assume will fit together and develop their picture *ad hoc* as they go along.

The radical rationalists are obsessed with the need to develop new theories without regard for the utility of old ones, while the radical empiricists constantly demand the collection of new facts, the implication being that if only you have enough facts you will be able to see that reality is chaos and that all search for systematic order is futile self-deception.

By contrast a conservative empiricist tends to get hooked on to a model which he formulated early on out of the first pieces of practical evidence that he happened to pick up. Thereafter he will either ignore all exceptions or resort to statistics to show that they are so unusual that they can be ignored. But for a conservative rationalist facts of any kind are just a nuisance. He may even adopt the stance that since explanation is only concerned with models in the human mind the empirical evidence does not matter at all.

My professional colleagues in this audience will, I think, agree that the practice of social anthropology, as it has developed over the past forty years, has exhibited each of these several polarities in very clear-cut form. In particular Lévi-Strauss often behaves as a prototypical conservative rationalist while Radcliffe-Brown was the perfect example of a conservative empiricist.

The old-guard conservative empiricists are not yet all dead and it may well be that by the time they are gone the whole discipline of social anthropology will have disappeared and transformed itself into something else – a general theory of linguistics for example – but meanwhile it may be of interest to take a look at the transformation in process.

Most forms of explanation in contemporary social anthropology can be typecast under one or other of four labels: functionalist, structuralist, Marxist, and structural-functionalist. In part a particular author's characteristic style will be determined by the nature of his interests and his position on the rationalist–empiricist continuum.

Orthodox *functionalist* explanation of the 'everything fits together like the gearwheels of a watch' variety is especially compatible with a relatively detached interest in the political and economic organisation of small-scale local communities and appeals to those who are themselves, by temperament, far out on the empiricist wing.

Structuralism, which tends to reinterpret interpersonal economic and political transactions as acts of communication, appeals most strongly to those who feel that the elementary forms of the religious life are of greater fundamental interest than primitive economics. Its practitioners claim that the ultimate objective of social anthropology is to gain an understanding of the workings of the human mind. Its appeal is to those who are rationalist by temperament.

Marxist explanation of the sort which Raymond Firth has labelled 'gut Marxism' is likely to take over whenever an anthropologist who has started out with functionalist assumptions tries to give his economic and political interests a wider spatial and temporal context. This is especially the case if he allows his human sympathies to get the better of his supposedly scientific judgements, so that participant activity replaces participant observation. But 'cerebral Marxism', which has all the hallmarks of an intellectual religious exercise, is often hard to distinguish from structuralism.[6]

Finally, *structural-functionalism* is a style congenial to those who still hope that there might some day emerge a *social science* with clear-cut causal deterministic laws as precisely spelled out as those of Newtonian physics. As is the case with Marxism, rationalists and empiricists both feel that they can accommodate themselves to this style of argument but then engage in bitter dialectical debate with one another.

Structural-functionalism was in large measure the personal invention of A. R. Radcliffe-Brown who is commemorated in the lecture series to which I am now contributing. Twenty years ago, as I have indicated already, it was the dominant viewpoint in British social anthropology.

I would hesitate to pronounce a funeral oration and declare that structural-functionalism is now completely dead, but it is certainly on the way out. My concern for the remainder of this lecture will be to consider what has become of the explanatory fashion which Radcliffe-Brown first established.

So that brings me to my title.

Radcliffe-Brown's book *A Natural Science of Society*, with no question mark, was published in 1957 and is a posthumous work. Its history is as follows.

In 1931, in the course of a highly peripatetic academic career, Radcliffe-Brown reached the University of Chicago in the status of Visiting Professor of Anthropology. He stayed on in the capacity of Distinguished Scholar. In the spring of 1937 he was still at Chicago but had just been appointed to the newly established Chair of Social Anthropology at the University of Oxford which he was due to take up the following October. From this prestigious position he took the floor at a senior faculty seminar to deliver his views on the scientific status of social science in general. Radcliffe-Brown spoke without manuscript and almost without notes but the proceedings were transcribed in shorthand. With Radcliffe-Brown's approval the resulting digest of this stenographic record was later put on sale in mimeograph form in the faculty bookshop. The text ran to eighty pages of single-spaced type and carried the full title: 'The Nature of a Theoretical Natural Science of Society: Notes on a Discussion in a Seminar at the University of Chicago, 1937'.

From time to time over the next fifteen years or so Radcliffe-Brown expressed his intention to revise the text for formal publication but since he never got round to doing so it must be assumed that, despite the *ad hoc* circumstances of its production, he considered the existing text to be a fair representation of his opinions. The posthumous, 1957, book version is substantially the same as the mimeograph.

The fact that Radcliffe-Brown talked rather than wrote *A Natural Science of Society* gives it a special kind of historical importance. Radcliffe-Brown's academic influence depended much more on what he said than on what he wrote. He had a large imposing physical presence, he was very fluent, and he was superficially knowledgeable about a great variety of subjects. In his talk he put himself forward as a polymath know-all, and got away with it far more often than he deserved. But it was, I think, precisely because a great many of the things he *said* in this way were never written down and made available for close inspection that his 'influence' over his immediate disciples persisted in the way it did. If they had more generally *read* rather than listened to the kind of argument that is presented in *A Natural Science of Society* they would surely have been less impressed?

But let me emphasise again. I am not now concerned with what was right or wrong about Radcliffe-Brown's argument but rather with what has become of that argument in the context of the kind of debate which goes on among social anthropologists in 1976.

I do not propose to give you a full digest of Radcliffe-Brown's book though I shall presently discuss certain features of it. But first let me say something about Radcliffe-Brown's overall viewpoint.

He was emphatically a conservative. He claimed explicitly that the 'theory' that he expounded in Chicago in 1937 was directly derived from the pages of the early volumes of Durkheim's *L'Année sociologique* published in Paris before the First World War. On other occasions, when anxious to claim priority over Malinowski, he maintained that the whole essence of his system had already been incorporated in a course of lectures delivered in Sydney in 1910!

In practice the cast of his argument was probably not quite so inflexible as he pretended but there can be no doubt that when Radcliffe-Brown talked about 'natural science' he was recapitulating ideas which he had picked up in his undergraduate days at Cambridge right at the beginning of the century. That was the heyday of museums. Science teaching was focused around showcases exhibiting specimens classified by types – fossils, rocks, insects, stuffed birds, caged animals in zoos – fixed entities, changeless, everlasting.

But although Radcliffe-Brown laid great stress on the supposed empirical basis for what he called 'the abstract structural principles of the social system', his theorising fitted pretty badly with the available evidence even in 1910. It did not fit at all with what was known by 1937.

Radcliffe-Brown did not try to escape from this difficulty, as some of his successors have done, by claiming that his structural principles apply only to statistical norms rather than particular cases. Instead he slipped, perhaps almost unconsciously, into a semi-rationalist position. He had started out by talking about facts; he ended up talking about concepts. But it was the showcases of Cambridge museums at the beginning of the century which provided the model for those concepts. 'The fundamental problems' of a theoretical social science, he declared, 'must depend on the systematic comparison of a number of societies of sufficiently diverse types.'[7]

This simplistic, nineteenth-century view of the relationship between the natural order of things and the taxonomies which scientists employ to describe them bears directly on my thesis that there has recently been a basic shift in the epistemological assumptions that anthropologists make about their subject matter.

From 1960 onwards Lévi-Strauss has made a number of unexpectedly complimentary remarks about Radcliffe-Brown's contributions to anthropological theory. In particular, he has claimed that the latter's 1951 Huxley Lecture applies to the analysis of Australian totemism a transformational view of structure closely akin to Lévi-Strauss's own, and that this represented a major breakthrough in Radcliffe-Brown's thinking.[8]

To those who were present on that occasion it seemed that Radcliffe-Brown was in fact saying precisely what he had said a great many times before. Indeed only one year *after* this event, in a letter addressed to Lévi-Strauss in 1952, Radcliffe-Brown roundly declared: 'I use the term "social structure" in a sense so different from yours as to make discussion so difficult as to be unlikely to be profitable.'[9]

I suspect that it was this *ex cathedra* statement more than anything else which led Radcliffe-Brown's most immediate disciples to ignore Parisian heresy for the next twenty years.

However, if we look at the available evidence it would seem that Radcliffe-Brown's ideas about structure, although significantly different from those which Lévi-Strauss eventually developed, were nothing like *so* different as he himself seems to have supposed.

In the letter in question, Radcliffe-Brown explains what he means by structure as an empirical pattern of consistency by reference to the shapes of sea-shells. I will quote at some length. Radcliffe-Brown writes:

> While for you [Lévi-Strauss] social structure has nothing to do with reality but with models that are built up, I [Radcliffe-Brown] regard the social structure as a reality. When I pick up a particular sea-shell on the beach, I recognise it as having a particular structure. I may find other shells of the same species which have a similar structure, so that I can say there is a form of structure characteristic of the species. By examining a number of different species, I may be able to recognise a certain general structural form or principle, that of a helix, which could be expressed by means of a logarithmic equation. I take it that the equation is what you mean by 'model'. I examine a local group of Australian aborigines and find an arrangement of persons in a certain number of families. This I call the social structure of that particular group at that moment of time. Another local group has a structure that is in important ways similar to the first. By examining a representative sample of local groups in one region, I can describe a certain form of structure. . . . The structural form may be discovered by observation, including statistical observation, but cannot be experimented on. . . . In dealing with Australian kinship systems, I am really only concerned with arriving at *correct* descriptions of particular systems and arranging them in a *valid* typological classification. I regard any genetic hypothesis as being of very little importance, since it cannot be more than a hypothesis or conjecture.[10] [My italics.]

Notice the fundamental point that Radcliffe-Brown is here taking it for granted that his sea-shell *species* are naturally existing, real entities naturally distinct from one another, and not, as Buffon would have argued,[11] simply the arbitrary product of the application of rules of taxonomic classification.

Though written in 1952, the general style of the argument is indistinguishable from that of the 1937 Chicago discourse. However, in this 1952 case, the actual metaphors employed, with their references to forms, helical shells, logarithmic equations, and conjectural genetic hypotheses make it almost certain that the immediate source of Radcliffe-Brown's phraseology is D'Arcy Thompson's *On Growth and Form*, first issued in 1916 and revised in 1942. I do not know when

Radcliffe-Brown first read Thompson's classic or how often he consulted it afterwards, but the echoes in 1952 seem very clear.[12]

Let me comment briefly on this latter book.

Like Radcliffe-Brown, Thompson posed as an empiricist. He starts with the precise description of material objects and moves step by step towards analytical and mathematical generalisation. But he wrote this way because he was a biologist addressing other biologists. He in fact called himself 'a biologist with an inkling of mathematics' while insisting that the real task was for mathematicians who would eventually have to develop a general systems theory into which practical reality would be seen to fit.

In his final chapter entitled 'On the theory of transformations and the comparison of related forms', which I can recommend to you all, Thompson makes clear what sort of mathematics he had in mind.

Considering the immense changes in biological viewpoint that have come about as a result of the discovery of the genetic code and of recent developments in the mathematical theory of classification, Thompson's arguments have stood up amazingly well. But what is especially interesting and relevant for my present purposes is that the first reference to Thompson in the whole of Lévi-Strauss's massive four-volume *Mythologiques* comes fifteen pages from the end of the final volume.[13] He there quotes from Thompson's own concluding paragraphs:

> A 'principle of discontinuity' is inherent in all our classifications, whether mathematical, physical or biological; and the infinitude of possible forms, always limited, may be further reduced and discontinuity further revealed by imposing conditions, as, for example, that our parameters must be whole numbers or proceed by *quanta*, as the physicists say.[14]

It is on the basis of this quotation that Lévi-Strauss launches into his final coda, in the course of which he recapitulates in splendid oratory all the essentials of his structuralist thesis that binary coding is the basic universal principle of both nature and culture. No précis could do justice to the metaphysical exultation with which the reader is invited to recognise how the wonders of nature are grasped by the metaphors and metonymic associations of the human mind through the transformations of common structures.

I certainly do not propose to guide this audience through the labyrinth of rhetoric by which in the course of the final six pages we move rapidly from the big bang origin of the universe to the reproductive mechanism of orchids, pass by a renewed denunciation of Sartre, return again to D'Arcy Thompson, reflect on the binary structure of the visual mechanism of cats, and end up with a contemplation of Hamlet contemplating a universe of not-being. But what is here said, in convoluted form, about the principle of discontinuity inherent in all classifications is very relevant to my present theme.

Very roughly, Lévi-Strauss seems to argue as follows. He agrees with Thompson that, in the sensible world out there, the processes of evolution, physical and genetic, operated upon by mathematical constraints of probability and quantum jumps, has produced a discontinuous field. He would accept Thompson's comment that 'We cannot transform an invertebrate into a vertebrate by any simple or legitimate transformation . . . not by anything short of reduction to elementary principles'.[15] On the other hand, at the level of elementary principles, *everything* is possible. The universe of myth, which is the creation of the human mind, differs from the sensible world out there in the following respects: the discontinuities are arbitrary not given, they are unambiguous and binary with no fuzzy overlap at the edges, there are no transformational constraints, any pattern can (at least in theory) be transformed into any other.

In practice it does not really work out like that. The concepts which make up the tidily organised universe of myth are modelled on percepts which we receive through our senses. But what we perceive is not just a mirror of what really is. Perception is already worked upon by the intellect before it passes messages to the brain. To some extent at least we see what we expect to see. For example, seventeenth-century scientists working with early microscopes managed to see fully formed homunculi within the human spermatozoa which they examined. One consequence of such intellectual modification of perception is that when we project our conceptual image of the world back on to the world out there in order to work upon it, the constructed discontinuities of the one do not fit with the natural discontinuities of the other. The world of reality out there then appears to us to be fuzzy at the edges, disjointed in the wrong places. Ritual, according to Lévi-Strauss (though perhaps I misrepresent him), is a procedure we adopt to overcome the anxieties which are generated by this lack of fit between how things really are and how we would like to think about them.[16]

The argument between the Radcliffe-Brownian structural-functionalists and the Lévi-Straussian structuralists, around which my present lecture is focused, turns on just this point, the lack of fit between ideal categories and empirical discontinuities. Should recognised discontinuities of social structure be thought of as naturally existing – like the distinction between vertebrate and invertebrate – or should they be seen as arbitrary impositions of the human intellect, like the left and right sections of a straight line notionally bisected in the middle?

Before going back to Radcliffe-Brown's Chicago seminar let me draw your attention to one or two other features of his simile between *species* of sea-shells and varieties of Australian kinship systems.

It must be remembered that at this point in time Radcliffe-Brown must have read Lévi-Strauss's *Elementary Structures of Kinship* which had appeared in 1949. The first part of that book contains an account of Australian kinship systems which is quite close to the version which Radcliffe-Brown had himself published in 1930,[17] but then, by an adroit variation of parameters, Lévi-Strauss tries to persuade his readers that the Australian systems, regarded as a set, can be treated as a particular transformation of a much more general phenomenon, that of 'alliance', which is manifested in an entirely different form in another set of kinship systems located empirically in mainland eastern Asia. It is this kind of conjuring trick that Radcliffe-Brown is objecting to when he says: 'Structural form may be discovered by observation, including statistical observation, but cannot be experimented with.'[18]

Moreover, as I have remarked already, it is a fundamental point in Radcliffe-Brown's argument that species differences in nature are 'real' and not just something that has been imposed on the data to suit the convenience of taxonomists. It is against this background assumption that there is one, and only one, correct way of providing a true scientific description of the contents of the external world that he applies the analogy to human societies. 'I am really only concerned with arriving at *correct* descriptions of particular systems and arranging them in *valid* typological classification.'[19] It would not have been in any way surprising if Radcliffe-Brown had argued this way in 1910, but he wrote this in 1952!

Let us get back to Chicago in 1937.

I won't attempt to summarise the whole argument about a theoretical natural science of society, but will pick out some key points.

At the outset Radcliffe-Brown insists that the starting-point of all scientific enquiry is observation rather than speculation or inspired hunch. The scientist always moves from the particular to the general, not the other way round. The selection of modes of generalisation is to some extent arbitrary but this is where the skill of the great scientist lies; genius is a matter of finding the *right* rules and the *right* abstractions.

Explicitly we are told that 'the method of science is one involving observation, classification, and generalisation, not as separate processes but as parts of a single complex procedure'.[20]

The prototype exponent of this method of science is declared to be Galileo. What Radcliffe-Brown tells us about his hero's intellectual standpoint is contradicted by the historical evidence but Radcliffe-Brown's own position emerges quite clearly: 'Systems of *a* man, *a* cell, *a* society, exist. They are real concrete phenomena. [The concepts] "man", "cell", "society" exist in the abstract, but not as abstract *systems*. You never have abstract social systems.'[21] In other words, the Durkheimian metaphor 'a society is like an organism' is taken to be true in a literal empirical sense. It is not an abstract analogy. Relations are empirical facts out there in the world, not ideas in the mind.

The difficulties of this position were just as obvious to Radcliffe-Brown as they are to everyone else. His way of dealing with the matter was to pile on additional metaphors and hope that his listeners' scepticism would be worn down in the process. Since his audience has been assured that 'the first step in the development of any science is taxonomic' it follows that the would-be social scientist must classify. But what should he classify? On this occasion Radcliffe-Brown talked about animals instead of sea-shells. I quote again: 'What is a zoologist doing when he is defining a lion? He is giving you the characteristics of all systems which fall into the class lion. All he has to do is to look at certain animals, perhaps not even dissect them, and he is then able to classify them quite soundly.'[22] From this base Radcliffe-Brown then develops the inference that 'a society' is a self-perpetuating natural system strictly comparable to an animal species.

Notice that it is lion as species rather than any individual lion that provides the model for a society. This is because both a species and a society exhibit continuity through time. Radcliffe-Brown refers to the genetic relationships between 'a father lion, a mother lion, a son lion' and finally to 'the inner relationships of the lion through periods of time and through a series of reactions'[23] but there is no mention of the lion's adaptive relationship to its environment or to other species. The whole discussion focuses on the natural separateness of a class of real objects. Definition of the class is treated as discovery. The implication is that in specifying the characteristics of a human society we are recognising (discovering) the distinctiveness of something which is there already.

The argument is at best defective, at worst fraudulent. The listener naturally supposes that he is being asked to believe that one society differs from another society as the species lion differs from the species elephant. But the constituents of the species lion are individual lions while the constituents of the species elephant are individual elephants, and even if you work downwards to more and more general comparisons, lion and elephant remain immutably distinct, even to the level of chromosome and gene. But, on the same basis, the constituents of *a* society are individual human beings and as such are completely interchangeable between any one society and any other.

You may perhaps think that this weakness of analogy is so obvious as to be trivial but this is not so. Radcliffe-Brown's simplistic comparison between 'a society as a system' and 'an animal species as a system' carries with it the fundamental racialist assumption that was so deeply embedded in nineteenth-century anthropology, the belief that not only is every primitive tribe a naturally separate thing in itself but that the constituent members of such tribes are likewise naturally distinct as kinds, so that each tribe is quite properly described as a separate race.

There is no suggestion in any of Radcliffe-Brown's published work that he harboured racialist sentiments of this kind yet it would seem that he had never really thought through the implications of his early anthropological training and this failure to fit his model to his own experience seems to have inhibited his thinking to a very marked degree. It is surely very surprising that despite his emphasis on the notion of system and his fondness of biological analogies, he never seems to have shown any interest in the Darwinian notion of adaptation through continuous natural selection. It was the separateness and differences between human societies that interested him, not their interactions with each other or with the rest of their environment.

Incidentally, it is only during the last ten years or so that anthropologists have begun to break out of this straitjacket and to think seriously about human ecology, not just as a relationship between a society and a static environment but as a whole set of continuously adaptive sub-systems within an unbounded matrix. It has long been obvious that man is always modifying any environment he occupies, often at a precipitate rate, but anthropologists have been very slow to recognise that any modification of the environment is also, by feedback, a modification of the human social system within it.

I dare say Radcliffe-Brown would have accepted this proposition but he preferred to concern himself with what he considered to be more fundamental problems.

Some time in the future the study of history in process might become a proper subject for anthropological investigation, but that time had not yet arrived:

> it is absolutely necessary to study separately how societies persist in maintaining their type in spite of internal change and how societies change their type. . . . The first major task of analysis I conceive to be the synchronic study of the society. Such a study is more fundamental than the diachronic one.[24]

So let us get back to the basic analogy: *a* human society is like an animal species, both need to be viewed as closed, ongoing, self-perpetuating systems.

The most obvious difficulty about this metaphor lies in the problem of boundaries. A lion, considered as an individual, is a free-standing natural entity separated from its environment by a natural skin. Until we get down to rather sophisticated levels of physiology there is really no problem about deciding on the difference between the inside and the outside of a lion.

But this is not the case with species. Modern research in genetics and applied probability theory shows that clear-cut boundaries between one species and another do not emerge as a natural inference from empirical facts. It is only the *idea* of species that is unambiguous. By *definition* members of one species do not interbreed with members of any other species. But definition is not discovery. A species is a rational construct, not a 'real concrete phenomenon'. Leaving aside the new complexities which have been introduced through the techniques of genetic engineering, it has always been the case that the species of empirical reality lack objective homogeneity and are blurred at the edges. The way that the human observer slots empirical individuals into one species category rather than another is determined by his definitions, not the other way round.

But what happens to this concept of a defined natural boundary in the case of the so-called organic analogy of society?

We have been told that the social scientist must establish a taxonomy of naturally existing social systems. He must therefore be able to know where one system ends and another begins. But what is there in social affairs which might be considered to constitute a natural boundary in this sense? Admittedly modern sovereign states have national frontiers. There are objective criteria by which the traveller can know whether he is in France or Switzerland but this sort of thing is not the norm for human society as a whole.

In his Chicago discourse Radcliffe-Brown was in no hurry to tackle this seemingly fundamental issue but he did get round to it in the end. He then pretended that there was no problem. I will quote again at some length:

> I am suggesting that the most expedient abstraction we can make of *a* society is to take a territorially delimited group which seems to be not only clearly

> marked off from other groups but which is also sufficiently homogeneous in most respects of the behaviour of its individuals, if not in all of them, so that the similarities can be discovered and constitute a material which can be adequately described.
>
> The anthropologist does this fairly simply with savage tribes. He generally takes the abstractions made by the savages themselves. I go into a savage country and say 'Who are you?' As a matter of fact, what I say is, 'What language do you talk?'. They give me the name of their language, 'We are the Kariera people.' They have given themselves a name. Then I ask 'Do these people over the river speak Kariera also?' – 'Yes.' 'Are these people over the hump Kariera?' – 'No.' They will offer details, and they will mark off for you a definite territory and people who talk the same language and say those are Kariera. On the whole, language usually constitutes the line of demarcation. There is a single region which can be described as Kariera by the fact that Kariera is spoken there.[25]

Radcliffe-Brown then goes on to admit that 'in certain regions of Africa it becomes difficult to decide what unit to take'. Then, in the next paragraph, he qualifies his argument still further: 'I am insisting again that the procedure contains an arbitrary element', and finally, in complete anticlimax, we are told 'a society is a body of people, in certain relations, which we study as a unit – as a *conceptually* isolated system – to compare with other similar units. . . . I do not believe there is any more precise definition which can be given.'[26]

Notice that the method of verbal delivery has allowed Radcliffe-Brown to contradict himself quite directly. At p. 31 of the printed text we were told that 'a society is a system' and all systems are 'real concrete phenomena'. 'You never have abstract social systems.' But now at p. 60 'a territorially delimited group' is 'the most convenient abstraction we can make of a society'. Admittedly he has covered himself by pointing out at p. 31 that we use the notion of abstraction in more than one sense, but he has fudged the argument just the same!

Furthermore, having first led his listener to suppose that the coincidence of territorially delimited group and language group is normal for the Australian Aborigines as well as for 'most savages', we end up by discovering that what we have to compare are not 'concrete phenomena' at all but '*conceptually* isolated systems'.

The trick is a verbal trick. In print the self-contradiction is obvious, but by skilful oratory – and one must suppose that the passages I have compared were probably spoken on different days of the week – the listener is led to imagine that the facts on the ground (the concrete phenomena) are really quite close to the idealised set of conceptually isolated systems.

I have not drawn attention to these passages simply as a means of poking fun at the ghost of Radcliffe-Brown, but because they illustrate very well the semi-rationalist stance which Radcliffe-Brown finally came to adopt. Radcliffe-Brown remained consistently conservative; he never qualified his original view that his hypothetical social science would reveal an orderly universe governed by natural laws. But in the light of experience he came to modify his original expectation that if he arranged his empirical facts in their proper natural classes then the natural regularities would be revealed. The connection between the facts on the ground and the natural order of things was evidently more complicated than he had supposed. But having thus qualified his empiricism he ended up talking about an imaginary world of ideal social types.

This shift of view was not peculiar to Radcliffe-Brown; it was predictive of what was to happen in social anthropology as a whole.

I do not want to suggest that we have *all* become out-and-out rationalists in the Lévi-Straussian manner. On the contrary, and particularly in Cambridge under the guidance of Professor Fortes and Professor Goody, the tradition of British empiricism has been most staunchly upheld, but there is now a much greater willingness to recognise that the way we cut up the empirical cake for the purposes of analysis is a matter of convenience rather than something that is given by nature, and that however we choose to make discriminations between one social system and another there will always be a fuzziness at the edges, and that it is in this fuzzy boundary area, where our typological assumptions do *not* fit, that the problems of real theoretical interest are likely to be found.

A case in point is provided by Professor Goody himself who has devoted a whole series of publications to the relationship between local group nomenclature and rules of inheritance in an area of north-western Ghana where a zone of patrilineal inheritance and a zone of matrilineal inheritance abut. Professor Goody does not contradict himself, but his emphases have changed. At the start, despite a guarded dissociation from the views of his mentors, Radcliffe-Brown and Fortes, he was much concerned to distinguish types of social system in a Radcliffe-Brownian manner.[27] But at the beginning of his latest paper on this theme he lays stress on the inhibitions that have been imposed upon social anthropologists by their general commitment to the 'idea that they are examining "societies", "social structures" or "cultures" which operate in some sense as "systems", as boundary maintaining units'.[28] He then goes on to apply himself specifically to the problem of boundaries – with what happens, for example, when as a result of intermarriage across a jural frontier such as this, an individual has relatives in both camps.

Perhaps, even by my insults,[29] I have myself contributed something to this change of view. Like other British social anthropologists Professor Goody has moved beyond the phase of butterfly collecting – that is of docketting types of society – to a more rewarding investigation of the actual processes of historical development.

Let me go back to Radcliffe-Brown in Chicago. You will have noticed that in my earlier quotation from *A Natural Science of Society* Radcliffe-Brown refers to named groups of Australian Aborigines such as the Kariera as 'savage tribes'. Comparably Malinowski regularly referred to the Trobriand Islanders as 'savages'.[30] Nobody worried about such usages at the time, but when Lévi-Strauss's *La Pensée sauvage*, which should perhaps have been decoded as 'thought in the wild', was put out as *The Savage Mind* nearly all English-speaking anthropologists of my acquaintance were appalled.

This new squeamishness is another indicator of changing views. The use of the term 'savages' by Radcliffe-Brown and Malinowski was again a part of the nineteenth-century tradition by which it was taken for granted that anthropologists are primarily concerned with 'primitive' peoples, species apart, who are *ipso facto* inferior, and who can on that account be treated as experimental objects, like animals in zoos. Radcliffe-Brown's analogy 'a social system is like a species' was wholly consistent with this tradition.

By contrast, the highly elaborated techniques of fieldwork by participant observation, which have gradually been developed out of Malinowski's original innovating procedures, are wholly inconsistent with this sort of purported 'objectivity'. The modern anthropologist is studying intercommunicating human beings, friends, fellow anthropologists, people who are in intimate personal relationship with himself as well as with one another, not specimens in glass bottles. How can you study people who answer back and change their minds if you persist in thinking of them as specimens dissected on a laboratory bench or observed at a distance through a microscope?

Whatever links there may be between social anthropology and natural science it is certainly not *that* sort of natural science. So one palpable necessity is a change of metaphor, and it may be worth considering the metaphors which the natural scientists themselves now tend to employ.

Radcliffe-Brown's schoolboy conviction that the central concern of all science is the discovery of natural laws was, after all, abandoned by the natural scientists themselves a great many years ago, certainly long before 1937! The universe, physical, chemical, and biological, which scientists now seek to understand is *not* a changeless vista of the Great Chain of Being governed by immutable laws imposed by the nature of Nature at the beginning of time. It is an evolving system in which the relations between the ever-changing constituent elements are constantly assuming new patterns in new combinations. In a universe of this sort the most interesting events, the events that generate change, are those which are statistically improbable.

The improbable, change-generating events occur at random against a background of imperfect order. We now know that, in general, biological systems reproduce themselves with quite extraordinary precision and just how this comes about is certainly very interesting. But we also know that every now and again the precision breaks down, and that is much *more* interesting!

With the increasing attention paid to uncertainty, natural scientists have come to recognise that mechanical analogies are quite inappropriate. Ordinary machines cannot make mistakes. So the mathematical general systems theory which D'Arcy Thompson envisaged is now discussed in the language of communication engineers; serious experts speculate about the attributes of an ideal computer which might be endowed with 'artificial intelligence'.[31]

And this rationalist, mathematical view of a universe of intercommunicating entities possessing the essentially *human* characteristic of intelligence has begun to feed back into the scientist's perception of empirical things.

In molecular biology the error-making replicating link is described as 'message-bearing RNA'. Such language is surely highly significant? Everyone's prototype model for a message-generating entity is the human mind. So instead of social anthropology becoming a theoretical natural science of society, biology seems to have become a theoretical social science of nature!

Radcliffe-Brown would, I imagine, have reacted to this inversion of his basic premiss much as he reacted to Lévi-Strauss's rationalist use of the concept of structure; yet in some ways these developments make the notion of a Natural Science of Society more rather than less plausible.

I have stressed throughout this lecture that we are all of us *both* rationalist and empiricist. Individual bias apart, we are all concerned with the interplay between ideal constructs and the way they are interpreted in social behaviour. Once that is recognised it should be obvious that a typology of mechanically articulated modes of social integration such as Radcliffe-Brown envisaged becomes as irrelevant as the theory of phlogiston. But if our concern is with these *two* levels, with how things are thought about versus how things really are, with jural rules versus what men actually do, with myth versus ritual, with practices versus praxis, then it makes sense to say that, in some very general but not easily specifiable sense, the whole of human culture operates 'like a language'.

This at least gives the social anthropologist a reasonably specific set of problems – what are the limits of the analogy 'culture operates like a language'? Hopefully at the end of the day he will find that in fact there are no limits – that is to say that the language-like character of human culture is a quality shared by biological systems in general, and that the ultimate theoretical natural science of society turns out to be a kind of general linguistics which incorporates non-verbal communication at one extreme and Darwinian notions of natural selection at the other.

This is more than verbal rhapsody.

At the beginning of this lecture I suggested that most contemporary work in social anthropology can be typecast as relying on one of four major types of explanation, functionalist, structuralist, Marxist, and structural-functionalist. The weakness of functionalism in its earlier forms, as developed by Malinowski and his pupils, was similar to that of the structural-functionalism of Radcliffe-Brown. It conceived of human society as consisting of closed, discrete, integrated systems with fixed boundaries functioning within a stable environmental matrix. But a modified functionalism, which views the environmental matrix as itself part of a total network of pliable unbounded relationships – an *ecological* anthropology as its practitioners describe it – is, both in method and in aim, not at all unlike 'ethology', that is the scientific zoological study of the evolution of the behaviour of wild animals in their natural environment. So it might almost seem as if we were back once more at Radcliffe-Brown's biological analogy between animal species and types of society.

But anthropologists need to handle this new vogue in sociobiology with extreme caution. In its more sensational forms it has the effect of reducing social anthropology to a crude behaviourism.[32] Men are once again reduced to the status of impotent machines activated by laws of nature over which they exercise no control. Moreover sociobiological model-building embodies very obvious racialist presuppositions – every social group has its proper social station, just as every animal species has its proper environmental niche.

On the other hand, an ecological anthropology, which takes into account the fact that, as man modifies his environment, he also modifies himself and his society, could, in principle, take over from both Vico and Karl Marx the doctrine that

> It is a truth beyond all question that the world of civil society has certainly been made by men and that its principles are therefore to be found within the modifications of our own human mind.[33]

If a natural science of society must for ever be searching for cosmic laws of nature – supernatural forces in face of which man is impotent – then I for one am quite uninterested. But a scientific anthropology which could explain not only how man could live in his environment without destroying it, but also how the conscious control of civil society could establish a fit between what is actually the case and what we desire – that would be quite another matter.

But that again implies a humanisation of natural science, and here I am an optimist.

Any type of anthropological explanation which concentrates attention on the actual processes of economic transactions within small-scale, face-to-face communities necessarily takes us back to Malinowski's 'principle of reciprocity', and from there it is only half a step to Mauss's 'general theory of gift exchange' and to Lévi-Strauss's transformation which reinterpreted the reciprocity of economic exchange as the reciprocity of interpersonal communication.[34]

And indeed, in their different ways, contemporary functionalist, structuralist, and Marxist social anthropologists are all tending to converge on a type of explanation which views social behaviour as a network of communication. So far, so good; but if anthropologists are to make the most of this kind of metaphor they need to acquire a much better understanding not only of structural linguistics but also of the thought processes of computer programers and communication engineers.

The two key scientific principles that are common to all these fields are *transformation* and *feedback*. What happens when a message in one language is translated into another language? What is the nature of bilingualism? What happens when we switch codes either verbal or non-verbal? These are not just transformational processes; the responses are interactional and cybernetic.

Each of us regularly adapts his or her behaviour to a whole range of special situations. According to where we are, we speak differently, we act differently;

but at the same time we learn by experience. In this cultural sense all of us are polylingual to a most marked degree. We know very little indeed about how such code switching is accomplished or how it comes about that some transformations are acceptable as within the bounds of normality while others are rejected as incomprehensible and foreign, or how what was once abnormal later becomes normal. But these are scientific problems which should be capable of scientific investigation and analysis.

You see, I have come back once again to the problem of social boundaries. Radcliffe-Brown's formula that 'language usually constitutes the line of demarcation' needs to be heavily qualified, but the related statements by D'Arcy Thompson and Lévi-Strauss remain very much to the point.

The empirical transformations of structure which occur among things in the world out there are subject to limitation and discontinuity. In principle, the operations of human thought are subject to no such limitation. But such freedom of thought is only 'in principle'. The practical, scientific, dare I say Marxist, task of social anthropology is to understand better how, at any given time, our modes of thinking are in fact conditioned by the state of the environment in which we operate. Where Radcliffe-Brown talked about taxonomy, we should be thinking about feedback. That too is a part of a theoretical natural science of society.

Notes

The British Academy hosts a regular series of lectures in honour of the memory of A. R. Radcliffe-Brown, who was a Fellow of the Academy and Professor of Social Anthropology at Oxford. Leach gave his lecture on 20 May 1976 and this is the text as published in the *Proceedings* of the Academy.

1. For an outline of Radcliffe-Brown's career see Firth, 'Alfred Reginald Radcliffe-Brown'.
2. See bibliography in Fortes (ed.), *Social Structure.*
3. For a skeletal outline of Lévi-Strauss's career see Leach, *Lévi-Strauss.*
4. Fuller, 'A Chat of Analysts'.
5. See Kuhn (*Structure of Scientific Revolutions*) on changing paradigms; Foucault (*Les Mots et les choses*) on changing epistemes.
6. I have borrowed the distinction between 'gut' and 'cerebral' Marxism from Firth ('Sceptical Anthropologist?').
7. Radcliffe-Brown, *Natural Science of Society*, p. 141.
8. Lévi-Strauss, *Le Totémisme*, pp. 155–64; cf. Radcliffe-Brown, 'Comparative Method'.
9. Radcliffe-Brown, 'Letter to Lévi-Strauss'.
10. Ibid.
11. 'Il n'existe, dit il, réellement dans la nature que des individus; les genres, les ordres et les classes n'existent que dans notre imagination.' This frequently cited opinion is given in Flourens (*Histoire des travaux de Buffon*), as if it were a direct quotation from de Malesherbes (*Observations*, i, p. 38). The quotation does not in fact appear at that reference but it corresponds in a general way to Malesherbes's detailed account of Buffon's views about natural and artificial classifications.
12. Professor Fortes, who knew Radcliffe-Brown very well during the latter part of his life, tells me that he is not aware that Radcliffe-Brown ever referred to Thompson either in talking or in writing, but he also tells me that he himself was long ago struck by a parallelism between some of Radcliffe-Brown's formulations and those of Thompson. He suggests that 'some of his thinking went back to sources he had in common with Thompson in the first decade of this century'. In any case the similarity between the condensed argument in Radcliffe-Brown's 1952 letter and the extended exposition in ch. 11 of Thompson's book seems to me much too close to be entirely accidental.

13. Lévi-Strauss, *L'Homme nu*, p. 604.
14. Thompson, *Growth and Form*, p. 1094.
15. Lévi-Strauss, *L'Homme nu*, pp. 615–21.
16. Ibid., p. 603. The whole discussion of pp. 593–603 is relevant. Since my own view of the relation between myth and ritual, thought and action, is very different from that of Lévi-Strauss it is very likely that I have misrepresented his argument. [Eds.: On Leach's views about the relation between myth and ritual see Section 6 below.]
17. Radcliffe-Brown, 'Social Organisation of Australian Tribes'.
18. Radcliffe-Brown, 'Letter to Lévi-Strauss'.
19. Ibid.
20. Radcliffe-Brown, *Natural Science of Society*, p. 28. In the citations which follow I give the pagination in the 1957 book and not the 1948 mimeograph.
21. Ibid., p. 31.
22. Ibid., p. 32.
23. Ibid., p. 33.
24. Ibid., p. 88.
25. Ibid., pp. 60–1.
26. Ibid., p. 62.
27. Goody, *Social Organization of LoWiili*, pp. iii, 16–26, and 'Social Control among the Lo Dagaba', *passim.*
28. Goody, *Comparative Studies in Kinship*, and 'Inheritance, Social Change, and the Boundary Problem'.
29. See Leach, 'Rethinking Anthropology' (I.3.7, below). The repudiation of the idea that societies 'operate in some sense as "systems", as boundary maintaining units' is the central theme of Leach, *Political Systems of Highland Burma* (I.3.2).
30. For example, *The Sexual Life of Savages in North West Melanesia.*
31. Winograd, 'Processes of Language Understanding'.
32. Wilson (*Sociobiology*) only refers in passing to the implications of sociobiology for social anthropology, but his references to Robin Fox, Lionel Tiger, Desmond Morris, and Robert Ardrey as anthropologists who are working on the right lines, from his point of view, are not reassuring. [Eds.: See II.4.8 below, for Leach's views on the work of Tiger and Fox, and Ardrey).
33. Vico, *New Science*, para 331.
34. Malinowski, *Crime and Custom*, esp. chs 2–3; Mauss, 'Essai sur le don'; Lévi-Strauss, *Les Structures élémentaires*, ch. 5.

1.9

Claude Lévi-Strauss: Anthropologist and Philosopher (1965)

As with Darwin and Freud and many other famous men Claude Lévi-Strauss, Professor of Social Anthropology at the Collège de France, needs to be judged on two quite different levels. First we may ask: 'What has he contributed to the particular scientific discipline in which he is a professional expert?' and secondly: 'What is the basis of his public celebrity?' The treatment which is now being accorded to Lévi-Strauss's work in French intellectual journals suggests that he should be looked upon as an original thinker of the first rank. He is beginning to be spoken of as a philosopher, the founder of 'structuralism', on a par with Sartre, the founder of existentialism. How should we judge him in this role?

A fellow anthropologist like myself is not perhaps the best kind of person to answer this sort of question. I can make judgements about Lévi-Strauss's skill as an analyst of ethnographic materials, but when it comes to his still embryonic but potentially much more grandiose reputation as a philosopher I am not only out of my depth but somewhat unsympathetic to his position.

In this twentieth century, 'idealist' attitudes are not at all respectable and Lévi-Strauss himself emphatically rejects any suggestion that his arguments must imply an idealist foundation. But this is awkward. The elements in Lévi-Strauss's thought which I find most interesting all seem to me to be idealist in tone; yet these are precisely the points at which Lévi-Strauss feels that I misunderstand his intentions. Readers of this essay should bear this discrepancy in mind.

At the outset of his academic career Lévi-Strauss was associated with Marcel Mauss, the principal pupil and collaborator of Emile Durkheim. This means that there is substantial common ground between the social anthropology of Lévi-Strauss and the social anthropology of his British colleagues, for the latter likewise trace their intellectual descent in a direct line back to Durkheim. But the common ground is treated in very different ways. Whereas the British show an obsessional interest in particulars and an exaggerated suspicion of generalisation, Lévi-Strauss is at his best when talking in completely general terms and at his weakest when demonstrating the fit of his general theory with the tiresome details of particular cases. This difference is partly a matter of national temperament, the French love of logical order, the British love of practical experiment, but it is also the outcome of history. In all countries the twentieth-century Founding Fathers of anthropology favoured grandiose generalisation. They thought of anthropology as the study of Man, the whole species of *Homo sapiens*, and their objective was to discover facts which were universally true of all men everywhere, or at least of all men at 'a particular stage of development'. They showed great ingenuity in the construction of logically plausible schemes of universal human evolution and they then used ethnographic evidence simply as 'illustration', arguing (without justification) that the primitive peoples of the modern world were really very ancient peoples whose development had somehow been arrested. Lucretius had managed just as well in the first century BC without dragging in the ethnography at all.

But with the turn of the century, British social anthropologists executed a complete volte-face. Under the influence of W. H. R. Rivers, an experimental psychologist, they began to concentrate their efforts on the detailed ethnographic description of particular societies. The history and social organisation of a single tribe is not perhaps a subject of such general and enthralling interest as the History of Mankind but, for a scientist, a few verifiable facts about the former are worth any number of mere guesses about the latter. Generally speaking, things have stayed that way. For over half a century the distinguishing quality of British social anthropology has been the superlatively high standards of its ethnographic description and analysis. But along with this bias towards empiricism goes a limitation of objectives. Pushed to define his subject a British social anthropologist is likely to say that his concern is with 'the principles of organisation in small-scale societies'. For him *social structure* is something which 'exists' at much the same level of objectivity as the articulation of the human skeleton or the functional–physiological interdependence of the different organs of the human anatomy. In contrast, Lévi-Strauss still retains the grander more macrocosmic viewpoint of the nineteenth century; he is concerned with nothing less than the structure of the human mind, meaning by 'structure' not an articulation which can be directly observed but rather a logical ordering, a set of mathematical equations which can be demonstrated as functionally equivalent (as in a model) to the phenomenon under discussion.

The total transaction

Some of the critical formative influences on Lévi-Strauss's thinking are quite easy to detect. An early item is Mauss's 'Essai sur le don' (1923). In this celebrated essay Mauss used two detailed ethnographic descriptions of primitive systems of ritual exchange (Malinowski's account of the Trobriand Kula and Boas' account of the Kwakiutl potlatch) as the foundation for a broad generalisation about the nature of social action. Sociologists (and social anthropologists) are concerned with 'man in society', with systems of relationships rather than with individuals in isolation. Mauss's insight was to recognise that the concept of 'relationship' is itself an abstraction from something quite concrete. We say of two individuals that they are 'in relationship' when we can see that they are in communication, that is when they pass 'messages' to one another, and these messages are conveyed through material media, sound waves in the air, ink scribbles on a piece of paper, the symbolic value embodied in a gift of flowers. The 'gift', that is to say the material thing which passes from one individual to the other, is an 'expression' of the relationship, but the quality of the relationship is something both more abstract and more mysterious. The recipient of a gift, whether of words or of things, feels coerced by it, he is not only compelled to receive he is also compelled to reciprocate. Mauss's original treatment of this theme borders on the mystical and Lévi-Strauss's own much more subtle elaborations of the idea always hover on the edge of metaphysics. This perhaps is unavoidable.

Mauss's essay contains another very fundamental idea, that of the *prestation totale*. A person-to-person interaction is never an isolated event but only part of a total set of transactions widely dispersed through space and through time. A particular gift has significance because of its comparability and contrast with other transactions, not only those between the same actors, but also those which are taking place round about between other members of the same communication system.

As developed by Lévi-Strauss this theme links up directly with his view that in any cultural system the conventional modes of person-to-person interaction constitute a language which can be decoded like any other language. But a language is not just an inventory of words, it is a complex structure of syntax and grammar which is all of a piece. Indeed individual words have little or no meaning in themselves; the meaning arises from the context in which they appear and the grammatical conventions of the language as a whole. One does not need to be a professional linguist to see that this is true of *words*; Lévi-Strauss's originality is that he applies the same kind of argument to all kinds of conventional action and also to the thematic symbols which appear in myth and ritual. This doctrine, that actions, events, ideas can never be assessed in isolation but only as part of a total system, is not peculiar to Lévi-Strauss, it was present much earlier in the writings of the theoretical sociologists (e.g. Comte, Marx, Durkheim, Weber) and of the functionalist social anthropologists (e.g. Malinowski and Radcliffe-Brown) and even in Freud's view of the human personality, but it contrasts sharply with the philogenetic view of history in which each event is unique in itself, a derivative of its chronological antecedents, and also with various brands of historical anthropology in which each 'custom' is treated as an isolate with a particular discoverable 'origin'. Earlier varieties of functionalism have assumed that the 'purpose' or 'need' served by the interconnectedness of cultural phenomena is of an economic or political or physiological kind . . . the parts of the social system function together so as to

(1) preserve the system in its struggle against the natural environment (Marx);
(2) preserve the system as such 'in good health' (Durkheim, Radcliffe-Brown);
(3) satisfy the biological needs of the individual members of society (Malinowski).

Lévi-Strauss's functionalism is not only of larger scale, in that his 'totality' is, generally speaking, the whole of humanity rather than the whole of one particular society, but his emphasis on 'communication' gives the whole argument a novel twist and suggests a possible utility for other concepts taken over direct from general communication theory, e.g. binary oppositions, Markov chains, redundancy. But while Lévi-Strauss's anthropology has a new look, he has not really made any fundamental new discoveries; rather he has presented familiar materials in a different way, so that modern technological discoveries in other fields, such as those which are ordinarily associated with computer languages and systems theory, suddenly acquire a possible relevance for the understanding of human behaviour in general.

The prototype of 'primitive man'

Between 1935 and 1939 Lévi-Strauss held a post as Professor of Sociology at the University of São Paulo, Brazil. In successive long vacations he conducted anthropological fieldwork among a variety of primitive tribal peoples of the interior, notably a tiny group of Amazonian nomads, the Nambikwara.

In a strictly academic sense the resulting formal monograph[1] seems of rather indifferent quality when compared with the sort of thing that English writers (influenced by Malinowski) had already produced at a much earlier date,[2] but the direct experiences of primitive life left a deep and lasting impression. The curious autobiographical travel book *Tristes tropiques*, which first established Lévi-Strauss's reputation as an intellectual (as distinct from being an anthropologist) is principally an account of his personal reaction to the situation of the Amazonian Indians as he saw them. In retrospect these people have become for Lévi-Strauss the prototype of 'primitive man', and when, as in his latest volume, *Le Cru et le cuit*, he discusses the myths of the Bororo and the Munduruсu he writes as if he were displaying for our attention the characteristics of untutored savages everywhere. It is this kind of generality which gives Lévi-Strauss's work its wide appeal. Anthropologists become interesting when they talk about man – all men, including you and me. Yet it is precisely this same generality which makes Lévi-Strauss's professional (British) colleagues suspicious. They have carefully cultivated an expertise by which one culture is sharply distinguished from another; they are alarmed by those strands in the Lévi-Strauss brand of structuralism which seem to reduce all men to a single pattern.

'Seem to' is the operative expression here. Lévi-Strauss constantly wobbles precariously between the study of man and the study of particular peoples. When he is talking about man, it is the 'human mind' which becomes the creative agent responsible for the miracle of culture and this 'human mind' is an aspect of the human brain, something shared by all members of the species *Homo sapiens*. But when he is talking about particular peoples, a slightly different kind of entity has to be reified. One of the most interesting chapters in *Tristes tropiques* is entitled 'A Native Society and its Style'. I can warmly recommend it to anyone trying to get to grips with the 'variations-on-a-theme' aspects of the structuralist thesis. But this chapter starts off as follows:

> The ensemble of a people's customs has always its particular style; they form into systems. I am convinced that the number of these systems is not unlimited and that human societies, like individual human beings (at play, in their dreams, or in moments of delirium) never create *absolutely*: all they can do is to choose certain combinations from a repertory of ideas which it should be possible to reconstitute. For this one must make an inventory of all the customs which have been observed by oneself or others, the customs pictured in mythology, and the customs evoked by both children and grown-ups in their games. The dreams of individuals, whether healthy or sick, and psychopathological behaviour should also be taken into account.[3]

Note how, in this quotation, 'human societies' are credited with a limited creative capacity directly analogous to that of 'individual human beings'. This is very difficult. Lévi-Strauss claims that he does not share Durkheim's very idealist concept of a 'group mind' or 'collective conscience' yet it is hard to see how a passage such as the above can be given any sense without the introduction of some such metaphysical formulation.

A third landmark experience in Lévi-Strauss's development was his association in New York, during the latter part of the war, with the linguist Roman

Jakobson. The latter was responsible for introducing into America the concepts and procedures of the Prague school of structural linguistics, and the emphasis on 'binary opposition' and 'distinctive features' which permeates Jakobson's linguistics has been assimilated *en bloc* into Lévi-Strauss's system of structural anthropology. A paper written at that time and published in the second issue of *Word*, a journal originally launched by Jakobson and his friends, has become a key reference for anyone interested in Lévi-Strauss's ideas.[4] Sixteen years later the same two authors collaborated on a lemon-squeezer analysis of the structure of a poem by Baudelaire.[5] Those who find the peculiarities of marriage preferences and South American mythology too far off the beaten track may learn something of structuralism by studying this exercise in literary criticism, which most people find preposterous, exasperating, and fascinating all at once.

Marx and Freud

Freud has a place in the Lévi-Straussian scheme but it is not easy to assess. He is extensively referred to only in one book,[6] yet a number of Lévi-Strauss's more difficult arguments seem to parallel comparable obscurities in the Freudian system. Freud's final model of the human psyche postulated an opposition between an animal Id and a human Ego, mediated by the Super-Ego, an internalised parent, an 'unconscious conscience'. The Super-Ego is a precipitate of the cultural environment but it only needs a slight deviation from Freudian orthodoxy to turn Super-Ego into a metaphysical Jungian 'collective unconscious'. As indicated already, Lévi-Strauss's system entails a rather similar triad: Nature, Culture and a mediator which is mostly a structural aspect of the human brain, but sometimes a much more generalised *Geist*-like entity the *esprit humain* – the Human Mind – which seems hardly distinguishable from a personified human society.

Finally Marx. Lévi-Strauss persistently maintains that he is a Marxist and on occasion he will use specific Marxist terms such as *praxis*. Likewise he refers to the 'undeniable primacy of the infrastructures'[7] which I interpret as meaning that the style of a culture is limited by the state of its technology in relation to the physical environment and by the degree to which that environment has already been modified by human action. But Lévi-Strauss's position seems far removed from that of historical determinism in any simple sense. On the contrary he is constantly emphasising the enormous variability of culture and laying stress on the mutual interdependence of the variations rather than on their chronological development or on the superiority of one system as against another. Cultural differences, in Lévi-Strauss's analysis, are analogous to the differences between the individual pieces in Bach's thirty Goldberg variations: they are played in sequence one after another and there is a sense in which the last is an evolutionary development from the first, but the later variations are neither superior nor inferior to the earlier ones and the elimination of any one would reduce the merit of all.

It is very difficult for anyone who is not highly expert in the appropriate form of discourse to say whether such a position can properly be said to be Marxist or even to understand where Marx comes into it at all. Marx, it is said, 'stood Hegel on his head' and if Lévi-Strauss has turned Marx inside out we are perhaps more or less back at the beginning. A strain of Hegelian dialectic is very prominent in all of Lévi-Strauss's writing. Every thesis serves to generate its own antithesis and the opposition between thesis and antithesis will then be resolved by a mediating synthesis which in turn generates a new antithesis. For Hegel this was a process in the development of ideas, for Marx it is a process in the development of political–economic systems, for Lévi-Strauss it is simply 'dialectic', a basic characteristic of the human mind which expresses itself in verbal classifications, in the structure of myth, in varieties of marriage regulation.

Any reader of Lévi-Strauss must find it very difficult to decide just how he views the role of the historical situation as an active factor in the historical process. In some of his earlier writings there is a definite undertow of evolutionism – 'generalised' exchange is more highly evolved than 'restricted' exchange, class structures may evolve out of 'generalised' exchange. I don't think that he has ever actually repudiated this position; he has simply talked about something else. His chosen field is the analysis of 'elementary' structures; 'complex' structures are left to others. On the other hand he can hardly be said to be an enthusiast for the idea of Progress.

The conclusion of *Tristes tropiques* stresses the transitoriness of all human endeavour. 'The world began without the human race and will end without it. The institutions, manners and customs which I shall have spent my life in cataloguing and trying to understand are an ephemeral efflorescence of the creative process in relation to which they are meaningless, unless it be that they allow humanity to play its destined role' . . . . And a few lines later we learn that civilisation is a 'prodigiously complicated mechanism' whose 'true function' is simply to increase the entropy of the universe.[8] Whatever meaning one may attach to such rhetoric, this is not the voice of Marxist optimism. Yet this position does involve a kind of historical determinism: 'As he moves forward within his environment, Man takes with him all the positions that he has occupied in the past, and all those he will occupy in the future'.[9] As in a Greek drama, destiny will work itself out in the end no matter how the individual characters exercise their free choices meanwhile. The last move of the game is checkmate whatever you do. Despite the implicit pessimism, the passage which I have just cited really contains the nub of the structuralist argument. Social phenomena are to be thought of as particular expressions of persistent generalised mathematical functions. What happens in the future is not predetermined in its details but it is predestined in its overall shape since it is simply a transformation of what is already existent and of what has already happened in the past. The more we go forward, the more we stay in the same place; the last act of Hamlet is already foreshadowed in the opening scene even though the beholder is still quite unaware of that which is to come. Nineteenth-century brands of evolutionism assumed that, by ratiocination and planning, man could not only know where he was heading for but could ensure that he got there in the shortest possible time. Lévi-Strauss's brand of destiny is of a much more ambiguous kind but it is far from being an unprecedented novelty. Sophocles and the authors of the Old Testament and the legendary Lord Buddha would all have understood his thesis very well.

The model

Lévi-Strauss's first really major work was *Les Structures élémentaires de la parenté* (1949). It is a work of technical anthropology mainly devoted to making a wide ranging set of comparisons between the formal marriage rules of Australian Aborigines and those of various tribal peoples of southeast Asia. Marriage, for Lévi-Strauss, is not simply a matter of establishing a legal basis for the domestic family, it is an *alliance* resulting from a contractual exchange between two groups – the group of the husband and the group of the bride. The exchange can take different forms . . . it may involve direct reciprocity, an exchange of sisters between two men, or delayed reciprocity: 'We give you a woman now; you give back to us one of her daughters', or generalised reciprocity within a larger system: 'We give you a woman in exchange for cattle; we will use the cattle to obtain a woman from elsewhere.'

Although British social anthropologists admire the way that Lévi-Strauss displays these systems, which are distributed seemingly at random over vast areas of the map, as dialectical variations of a single theme, many would question whether formal marriage rules can have the importance which Lévi-Strauss supposes and some would challenge quite radically his whole approach to kinship behaviour and kinship terminology. They also question the evolutionist undercurrent. As mentioned already Lévi-Strauss has argued that different systems of marital organisation can have different absolute merit in that one may be more resistant than another to the ravages of history, or one may serve to hold together larger agglomerations of people than another. On this basis generalised marriage exchange is to be regarded as a later more sophisticated development than the direct reciprocal type. But generalised exchange also has its weaknesses which must lead towards the development of a class hierarchy in which inferiors render women as tribute to their superiors, and this is the beginning of caste hypergamy. Such condensation of what is really a rather subtle argument is outrageously unfair but it will indicate why the empirically minded British anthropologists have not responded very favourably to this extreme exercise in grand scale theory.

In the decade before Lévi-Strauss published his book his British colleagues, working mainly from African data, had developed a substantial body of theory about the importance of principles of descent and inheritance as factors in maintaining the continuity of society.[10] In the African systems where descent functions as a principle of group solidarity (e.g. 'the children of Israel', 'the house of David'), marriage is usually looked upon as a personal matter serving to distinguish the individual from his fellow group members. Lévi-Strauss certainly added something important when he showed that marriage alliance, like descent, *can* function so as to preserve the structural continuity of a social system and he also took a genuine step forward when he showed that the south-east Asian kinship systems which he talks about can be thought of as 'variations on a theme' in relation to the better-known systems of the Australian Aborigines, but in the British view, his generalisations were far too sweeping. Since the 'elementary structures' which he discusses are decidedly unusual they seem to provide a rather flimsy base for a general theory. The British, who pride themselves on their detailed studies of particular systems, have also been horrified by the scale and superficiality of Lévi-Strauss's comparisons. In order to cover so much ground in such small space Lévi-Strauss was ruthlessly selective in his selection of what he took to be significant evidence and there are places when he seems to have misread his sources altogether.

But though *Structures* is best regarded as a splendid failure it does contain one fundamental idea of great importance; this is the notion, distilled from Mauss and Freud and Jakobson, that social behaviour (the transactions which take place between individuals) is always conducted by reference to a conceptual scheme, a model in the actor's mind of how things are or how they ought to be. And the essential characteristic of this model is that it is logically ordered. Lévi-Strauss recognises that the actual behaviour of actual individuals may be full of irregularity and improvisation. But these practices are nevertheless an expression of the actors' orderly ideal scheme just as the ideal scheme is itself a programme for action produced by the *praxis* of the whole society. As his ideas have developed Lévi-Strauss has come to see himself more and more as being concerned with the logical structures which are to be found not *in* the empirical facts themselves but *at the back of* the empirical facts.

The analogy is with language. The grammar and syntax and sound discriminations of a language are what make it possible for a sentence to convey a meaning, but the linguist who seeks to investigate such structures has to go to the patterning of the sounds not to the meaning of the message. And so also in psychoanalytical dream interpretation. The basic assumption is that the actual dream, which here corresponds to a 'practice', is an ephemeral trivial matter, but it is at the same time a precipitate of something much more important and more enduring, a logical puzzle in the dreamer's conceptual system.

If we accept this approach, it is understandable that Lévi-Strauss should have moved directly from a study of overformalised ideal systems of marriage regulation, which he presumed to provide the logic at the back of actual kinship behaviour, to a study of the structure of myth. Lévi-Strauss's first essay in this field was published in English in 1955,[11] and in the intervening years he has published a great deal on the subject both in English and in French. So far as ordinary anthropology is concerned his procedures represent a radical departure from previous orthodoxies though there are links with George Dumezil's comparative studies of Indo-European religions and also with techniques employed for many years by students of European folk-tales.

The inner structure of myths

For the past fifty years the orthodox British anthropological view has been quite unambiguous. Myth can only be understood in its cultural context; within that context it provides the 'charter for social action', that is to say it stands behind social practice in much the same way as Lévi-Strauss's 'structurally ordered conceptual scheme' stands behind actual social behaviour. But where, for Lévi-Strauss and the Marxists, words like *structure*, *praxis*, and *ideology* are very broad notions corresponding to the thoughts and actions of whole classes of humanity at a particular stage of development, the British anthropologists' ordinary use of *myth* is narrowly specific; a myth is a particular tale about the past which serves to justify a particular type of action in the present within the context of a particular cultural milieu. Against this background the two fundamental peculiarities of Lévi-Strauss's myth analysis are, firstly his nineteenth-century willingness to talk about myths in themselves without close reference to social context, and secondly his view that significance can only emerge from a study of contrast. This second principle implies that while he is never prepared to expound a single myth considered in isolation he will readily tackle the seemingly much more difficult task of analysing and interpreting a whole set of marginally related tales. He presumes that such tales, considered as a total set, develop out of repeated transformations of the elements of a single persisting structural theme, and it is this persisting structure which must be the analyst's chief concern.

The significance of a set of myths does not lie in the meaning of the stories in any straightforward sense but in the relations between the stories. There is an analogy with music. What we first hear is a tune, a melody; but the experience of music is not just a collection of tunes. What the musically sensitive person responds to is the structure of the music as a totality, the complexities of counterpoint and of harmony, and the relations between a theme and its variations. Likewise in drama, what distinguishes a powerful, emotionally significant play from a triviality is not a quality of the story but a quality of the inner structure to which we can respond even when we cannot consciously recognise what it is. Lévi-Strauss's thesis is that the inner structures of myth systems are everywhere much the same and he is concerned to show us what these structures are. The analogy with linguistics is very close. There are linguists who are solely concerned with the analysis of the grammar, syntax, phonology, etc., of particular languages, and there are other linguists who set out to discover general principles which apply to all forms of human speech. The two kinds of study are mutually interdependent but, up to a point, they are separate fields of investigation. As Lévi-Strauss sees it, the type of localised functionalist analysis favoured by British anthropologists corresponds to the particular description of a particular language; his own contribution to social anthropology corresponds to general linguistic theory. But just as general linguistics is in no way concerned with the particular meaning of particular sentences but only with the mechanics of how sentences can convey information, so also the logic of Lévi-Strauss's position leads him to lose interest in the meaning of particular myths. Instead he concentrates all his attention on how myths come to mean anything at all.

Even so there are certain fundamental contradictions in the human situation with which all human beings must come to terms. In so far as myth provides a way of dealing with these universal puzzles, there is a limited sense in which even the meaning of all mythical systems is the same. For example it is universally true that man is both an animal (a creature of nature) and different from an animal (in that he is a creature of culture); it is universally true that although all sensible men are fully aware that every individual is destined to die, yet many sensible men manage to persuade themselves that, on a metaphysical plane, some form of immortality is possible; it is universally true that through a process of enculturation men come to believe, at a subliminal level, that 'mothers' and 'sisters' and 'wives' are women of quite different kinds towards whom quite distinct types of sexual behaviour are appropriate. One common function of myth is to provide a deeply felt justification for such culturally basic yet non-rational attitudes as these.

An orderly world

Anyone who wishes to see how this doctrine works out in practice must examine for himself some of Lévi-Strauss's own writings. The principle is expounded in 'The Structural Study of Myth'; the most satisfying practical exercises are 'La Geste d'Asdiwal' and *Le Cru et le cuit.*

Parallel with investigations into the structure of myth Lévi-Strauss has pursued investigations into the structure of human thought as such. *La Pensée sauvage* with its separate preface *Le Totémisme aujourd'hui* does not postulate, in nineteenth-century evolutionist manner, a mythopoeic phase of civilisation which we have left behind, it assumes rather that the style of thinking which is typical of very primitive societies is present also in much of our own thinking process; we too are totemites only at one remove.

The essentials of Lévi-Strauss's argument here seem to me to be the following:

(1) The world of Nature, the unmodified environment into which man is born, exists in its own right and is governed by order; the processes of biology are not just random accidents. In this respect the human brain is a part of Nature.

(2) Nevertheless this order in Nature is to a large extent inaccessible to us as conscious beings. The human brain is not in the least like a camera. Our capacity to achieve technological mastery over our surroundings does not derive from any capacity to see things as they actually are, but rather from the fact that the brain is capable of reproducing transformations of structures which occur 'out

there' in Nature and then responding to them. In other words Lévi-Strauss seems to postulate that the structure and workings of the human brain are analogous to those of a very complicated kind of computer; it is the nature of this computer that it sorts out any information which is fed into it through the sense organs in accordance with the 'programme' to which it is adjusted. The result of this sorting process is to present to the individual consciousness an impression of an orderly world, but this orderliness of the perceived world is not necessarily closely fitted to the orderliness of Nature, it is an orderliness that has been imposed on the sensory information by the structures built into the computer program. The 'program' (this is my term not Lévi-Strauss's) is partly an endowment of heredity . . . that is to say it arises from the intrinsic characteristics of the brain of *Homo sapiens* and partly it is a feedback from the cultural environment in which the individual has been raised. Particularly important here are the categories of the individual's ordinary spoken language which have the effect of presenting the speaker's sense perceptions to himself as an organised system. Lévi-Strauss likens this organising capacity of the human brain to the activities of a *bricoleur* or handiman who creates fantastic and only partly useful objects out of old junk, the residues of history and anything that comes to hand. All that one can affirm about the final product is that, to the beholder, the world will appear to be an organised place, but there is an almost unlimited range of possibilities about just how the organisation will be achieved. Hence the extraordinary variety of human culture despite the unity of human nature. The basic bricks out of which cultural order is constructed are verbal categories and *La Pensée sauvage* is really an enquiry into just how far the content of such categories is arbitrary and how far it is predetermined by the nature of the real objects which are being categorised.

Lévi-Strauss claims to be a Marxist materialist and he firmly rejects any suggestion that he believes in 'idealism' – the view that things only exist in so far as they are known. Yet his position seems in some respects akin to that of an idealist in that he appears to argue that what we know is only very marginally related to what actually exists. Moreover since our actions are governed by what we know (or rather by what we think) it would seem logical to conclude that it doesn't really matter very much what kind of reality lies at the back of the verbal categories. It is worth reflecting that the famous mediaeval controversy between the realists (idealists) and the nominalists (empiricists) arose over an argument about the meaning of a passage on Porphyry's *Introduction to the Categories of Aristotle* which raised the question of whether species (1) exist of themselves or only in the mind, (2) whether if subsistent they are corporeal or incorporeal, and (3) whether they are separated from sensible things or placed in them. This seems a very good description of the theme of Lévi-Strauss's *La Pensée sauvage*. The fact that his topic is a very old one does not mean that he has nothing new to say, but it does perhaps suggest that the novelty of his style of presentation should not lead us into excessive enthusiasm.

Totemism

From the anthropological (as distinct from the philosophical) point of view the most interesting aspect of this part of Lévi-Strauss's work is that he has brought back into fashion an out-of-date topic, the study of totemism. In its new guise 'totemism', as such, really disappears; it becomes just one specialised variety of a universal human activity, the classification of social phenomena by means of categories derived from the non-social human environment.

The process by which words can be made to convey information is vastly more complex than is ordinarily understood by those who lack linguistic sophistication. The meaning of a word is not just the gloss which is attached to it in a dictionary, it is also something that derives from the social situation in which the word is uttered, its position in relation to other words in the sentence, and the punning associations which the word denotes subliminally both for the speaker and listener. We ourselves use language in a variety of different ways but, in particular, we have a literary language as well as a spoken language. 'Written speech' is addressed to strangers who are out of sight; it must therefore be unambiguous; whatever information is to be conveyed must be there in the pattern of the words. But 'spoken speech' is addressed to acquaintances in direct face-to-face relations, and, in this case, the exchange of words is only a part of the total communicative transaction which is also conducted by other forms of action such as 'gesture', 'gift-giving', 'role-playing', etc. One distinguishing feature of *La Pensée sauvage* is that the individuals who are in communication are always in face-to-face relationships so that speech and action are not nearly so sharply distinguished as is commonly the case among 'educated' (i.e. literate) people. But, in literate civilisations, words are not *just* a means of *transmitting* information, they are *also* a means of *storing* information. By inversion, this raises a problem which Lévi-Strauss has thought about in a new and very interesting way. Every culture, primitive as well as sophisticated, is faced with problems of information storage and information retrieval. Primitive savages, such as Australian Aborigines or Kalahari Bushmen, are very far from being ignorant fools. On the contrary, they have such an intimate knowledge of the resources of the local environment that they are able to live with considerable comfort in terrain which more 'civilised' people consider uninhabitable. How is this done? In the absence of books, how is the essential 'scientific' information stored away and transmitted from generation to generation?

Lévi-Strauss's answer to this problem runs something like this: When sophisticated people store information in books or computer tapes or gramophone records they do so by means of structured codes. Specially designed objects in the external world (books, etc.) are subjected to an ordering process which serves as a store of information; other men using the same codes can then read back the information by analysing the patterns which have been imposed on the material objects.

But in primitive society, as in any other, *all* objects in the external world are ordered by the mere process of subjecting them to verbal categories, and the way things in the world are classified is *itself* a form of information storage. The words of an ordinary vernacular language do not reflect natural kinds but sets of things which are of value and relevance for the speaker of the language, and the way such words are associated and patterned in relation to one another serves to store information in the same way as the information on this printed page is stored in the patterning of the conventional printed signs.

In addition to its dual function of imposing order on, and storing up information about, the external world, verbal classification has the further important function of imposing order upon the speaker's own human society. In an objective sense, a human society is just an undifferentiated crowd of human individuals, but this is not how it seems to the actor who is a member of the system. For this human actor, society as a whole is divided into named groups, within which individuals have different named statuses, and it is these groups and statuses which determine how individuals shall react towards one another. The novelty of Lévi-Strauss's approach to totemism (which is a development from a position adopted a generation earlier by Radcliffe-Brown) lies in his recognition that a major characteristic of totemic systems is that the actors use the same verbal classifications to impose order upon the human society as they use to impose order on the natural environment.

In all normal colloquial languages all species of living things, recognised as existing in the natural environment, are treated as elements in a single total system. The members of a particular species are not then distinguished by a simple list of positive characteristics but rather by a list of binary discriminations.

Thus for us 'the dog is the companion of man' and the word 'dog' connotes a whole set of discriminations such as:

dog is like man in that it is organic not inorganic, warm-blooded not cold-blooded, inedible not edible, mammal not bird, tame not wild, lives in the house not outside, is a personality with a name not just a member of a species.

dog is unlike man in that it is four-footed not two-footed, furry not hairless, incapable of speech, has a personal name which is similar to but usually different from that of a man, and so on.

What I am saying here is that, in arriving at any particular discrimination, such as: 'What is the difference between a dog and a man?' we really use a kind of matrix classification which simultaneously distinguishes one set of criteria which are common to both dog and man and another set of criteria which differentiate dog and man. In the computer-like language of the mind the word 'dog' instantaneously embodies this whole matrix of binary discriminations as well as many more.

The peculiarity of totemic societies is that the discriminations which are applied to animal species are of a kind that are applicable also to human groups so that the difference between one human group and another is felt to be of the same kind as the difference between one animal species and another. This is not a *stupid* way of thinking, it is simply an *economical* way of thinking; it is analogous to running several different programs through the same computer at the same time, all using the same computer language. If the programs have been set up correctly there will be no confusion.

Lévi-Strauss's importance

Lévi-Strauss has not resolved all the anthropological problems posed by totemism. In particular it has been argued that by concentrating his attention on objective distinctions such as those in his formula *fresh: putrid:: raw: cooked:: natural process: cultural process* he has pushed on one side those subjective distinctions which are at the base of religious attitudes (e.g. clean/dirty, good/bad, sacred/profane) and that in consequence, in Lévi-Strauss's analysis, the mystical aspects of totemism (which have traditionally been considered its very essence) are not so much explained as simply ignored. All the same, by shifting attention away from the oddity of religious attitudes being addressed to animal species to the much more general problem of the relation between social classifications and natural kinds, he has made a very old hat suddenly look fresh and interesting.

This is where Lévi-Strauss's importance lies. He puts familiar facts together in unfamiliar ways and thereby provokes thought about fundamentals. *La Pensée sauvage* contains an astonishing chapter in which the author sets out to demonstrate that the structure of the Indian caste system is a logical transformation from the structure of the totemic order of the Australian Aborigines. Intellectual fireworks of this kind do not in themselves enlarge our understanding of either the caste order or of Australian totemism, but they do challenge us to think more deeply about what is specifically human about human society. In Lévi-Strauss's view it is much more important to understand the difference between culture and nature than to bother with scholastic arguments about how oriental despotism is related to feudalism in the sequence of historical determinism.

Finally I should like to offer a brief warning to those who, like myself, find it a lot easier to read English than to read French. Lévi-Strauss chooses and arranges his words with scrupulous care so that in the original the result often has a poetic quality in that a sentence may contain a variety of harmonic ambiguities over and above what appears to be said on the surface. This faces his translators with a difficult if not impossible task. Paradoxically some of the really difficult passages seem quite straightforward in English simply because the built-in opacity cannot be reproduced in translation. Philosophers who attempt in this way to talk about the unsayable are almost bound to be misunderstood. But even misunderstanding can be a mental stimulus. I think we can pin down fairly precisely just where the misunderstanding is most likely to arise.

To go back to the beginning. In supposing that the individual human brain operates somewhat after the fashion of a computer in selecting and sorting and comparing patterned structures Lévi-Strauss is very much in contemporary fashion,[12] but the philosophical difficulty is how to move from the level of the individual to the level of the group. Social anthropologists are primarily interested in behaviours which are characteristic *not* of individuals acting in isolation and *not* of the whole human species but of individuals in the context of their cultural situation; and human cultures vary to a quite astonishing degree. Lévi-Strauss seems to be trying to use the model of the computer-like human brain to provide a representation of the workings of whole societies within a system of such societies. At a conscious level he apparently rejects the abstract metaphysical notion of 'group mind', which an equivalance between individual and society might invite, yet he seems to come back to the same point from two directions, firstly by reifying society and treating it as an active creative entity *like* an individual, and secondly by asserting that the pure individual, the 'I', has no separate existence at all.

This seems to me a strictly anti-nominalist position in the classical sense and one which is surely very hard to square with materialism or empiricism or any other down-to-earth concern with observable facts. It is this aspect of the matter which makes British social anthropologists cagey if not actively hostile.

Notes

This piece was written for the *New Left Review* in 1965. *New Left Review*, which is still in publication, was the most prominent high-brow forum in Britain in the 1960s for the then fashion for the writings of the early Marx, especially as filtered through French Marxist thinkers.

1. Lévi-Strauss, *La Vie familiale des indiens Nambikwara.*
2. Firth, *We, the Tikopia*; Bateson, *Naven.*
3. Lévi-Strauss, *Tristes Tropiques*, p. 182.
4. Lévi-Strauss, 'L'Analyse structurale', in *Anthropologie structurale.*
5. Jakobson and Lévi-Strauss, 'Les Chats de Charles Baudelaire'.
6. Lévi-Strauss, *Les Structures élémentaires de la parenté.*
7. *La Pensée sauvage*, p. 173.
8. *Tristes Tropiques*, pp. 448–9.
9. Ibid., p. 446.
10. For a survey of this work see Fortes, 'Structure of Unilineal Descent Groups'.
11. Lévi-Strauss, 'Structural Study of Myth'.
12. The following is part of a report in *The Times*, 7 September 1965, p. 11, on the British Association meeting:

    > Dr M. B. Clowes, of the Medical Research Council Psycholinguistics Research Unit, Oxford, said that research on the analysis of structure in languages had led them to begin developing by analogy, a system of analysing pictures.
    >
    > Without a computer the system could not even be tested. The operations of the computer in deriving a structural description of pictures showed similarities to the visual systems of higher animals.
    >
    > Dr L. Uhr, of the Medical Health Research Institute of Michigan University, expanded on both these speakers. Some of the models that had been arrived at to account for the recognition of patterns, the account of theorems, and playing games already exhibited 'fairly complex and general behaviour'. Some of the methods used in pattern recognition were reminiscent of 'associations', 'ideas', 'images', and 'meaningful properties'.

    Lévi-Strauss was already saying this sort of thing around 1950.

1.10

Telstar[1] and the Aborigines, or *La Pensée sauvage* (1964)

Lévi-Strauss's book is like a Chinese puzzle box in which a number of bits of wood of seemingly random and eccentric shape can with ingenuity and patience be fitted together to form a perfect cube. Turn the whole thing upside down; the total shape is the same but the combination seems quite different. I have now read *La Pensée sauvage* from beginning to end at least three times and on each occasion I have obtained a very different impression of how it all fits together. It all depends on what you take to be the leading theme. In this essay I am writing with the prejudices of an English social anthropologist and it could be that, from the author's point of view, I have altogether missed the point. The considerable section of the final chapter which is taken up with a commentary upon Jean-Paul Sartre's *Critique de la raison dialectique* is certainly quite outside my comprehension.

I will start with two quotations. The first comes from an article published in 1917, in which A. L. Kroeber reaffirmed his scepticism as to whether the category systems implicit in kinship terminologies could be expected to 'make sense' in terms of the wider social system. To clinch his argument Kroeber used the following linguistic analogy:

> We have in English the curious habit of designating an oyster or a lobster as a 'shell fish'. The word 'fish' unquestionably calls up a concept of a smooth elongated free-swimming water animal with fins. The only conceivable reason why a flat and sessile mollusk without any of the appendages of a fish or a legged and crawling animal of utterly different appearance should be brought in terminology into the class of fishes is the fact that they both live in the water and are edible. Now these two qualities are only a small part of those which attach to the generic concept that the word 'fish' carries in English; and yet the wide discrepancy has not prevented the inclusion of the other two animals under the term. All speech is full of just such examples, and no one dreams of explaining the multitudinous phenomena of this kind by reference to social institutions, former philosophies, or other formulated manifestations of non-linguistic life, or of reconstructing the whole of a society from a vocabulary.[2]

One way of describing the subject matter of *La Pensée sauvage* would be to say that Lévi-Strauss is setting out to do precisely that which Kroeber held to be absurd.

My second quotation comes from Professor Gilbert Ryle's *Concept of Mind* (1949):

> This trick of talking to oneself in silence is acquired neither quickly nor without effort: and it is a necessary condition of our acquiring it that we should

> have previously learned to talk intelligently aloud and have heard and understood other people doing so. Keeping our thoughts to ourselves is a sophisticated accomplishment. It was not until the Middle Ages that people learned to read without reading aloud . . .[3]

More briefly, Ryle's view is that: 'thinking is talking'. Lévi-Strauss carries the argument one stage further back; words are just sound patterns conjured out of the air, they are sound patterns which relate to objects and categories in the external world. Even more basic to logical thought than the operation of words is the operation of the concrete entities to which the words correspond. Arithmetic begins with the manipulation of an abacus rather than with simply 'saying' 'two plus two equals four'. Ryle was concerned to demolish the Cartesian distinction between abstract mind and concrete body – 'the dogma of the Ghost in the Machine'; Lévi-Strauss is similarly concerned to break down the conventional distinction between verbal and non-verbal aspects of culture, his argument being that both are equally a means of communication, a language. In recent years theoretical studies in structural linguistics and the closely related applied studies of communication engineers have enormously advanced our understanding of the way in which verbal forms of language actually operate as a means of communication. Lévi-Strauss is suggesting that we apply strictly comparable forms of analysis to the 'language' aspect of non-verbal culture.

Two propositions are crucial. The first, as stated on the dust cover, is that the subject matter of the book is 'La pensée sauvage' and not 'la pensée des sauvages'. The fact that the author draws many of his examples from the ethnography of exotic peoples does not mean that he supposes that the thought processes of Australian Aborigines are in any fundamental way different from our own. If we exclude from consideration the specialised technical languages employed by modern intellectuals and scientists of various kinds then the generalisations which Lévi-Strauss derives from the speech patterns and beliefs of the Menomini Indians apply equally to a Chinese or to a Western European. He is concerned with the elementary principles common to all thinking, and not simply with the thoughts of 'primitive peoples'. Generalisations on such a grandiose scale are likely to provide many easy targets for the hostile critic and there are some weak patches in Lévi-Strauss's argument but I cannot see that this really matters. In a comparable way it is easy to show that Freud was very often wrong on points of detail; this does not detract from the massive validity of Freud's major generalisations. Even if time should show that some of the items of evidence have been misplaced, the fundamental method of Lévi-Strauss's analysis is an innovation from which there can be no retreat.

The second essential proposition is that which I have mentioned already. The non-verbal content of human culture is to be understood as a system of communication to which the principles of a general theory of communication may be applied. The elements of culture constitute a language full of redundancies by means of which 'senders' transmit 'information' to 'receivers' against a background of 'noise'. Lévi-Strauss is not the first to draw an analogy between 'culture' and 'language' but he takes the argument much further than his predecessors.

In presenting his case he hangs a great deal of the discussion around the class of institutions which anthropologists have been accustomed to group together under the label 'totemism' – a system of belief in which real components of the universe external to man (e.g. animal species) appear to be drawn into and merged with human society itself. The implied equation might be represented thus:

things in the external world	words in the verbal language	the operations of human 'thought'
categories of things in the external world (e.g. totems)	beliefs as expressed in mythology	the operations of culturally defined behaviour

This is an immensely difficult and intricate theme. For centuries past sophisticated societies have sustained their superiority by maintaining a store of information in the form of written documents, which are a special category of material things subject to human manipulation. It is a common assumption that this ability to communicate by means of the written word is a unique cultural phenomenon peculiar to 'civilised' societies. But Lévi-Strauss denies that this is so. 'Uncivilised' societies likewise have their categories of material things which serve as a store of knowledge and a means of communication. Indeed in primitive thought 'the universe consists of messages' ('l'univers des primitifs consiste principalement en messages'). The categories into which the primitive world is ordered have the same function as the words of a sentence. Only a short while ago it would have seemed purely fanciful to argue in this way but now, in the age of electronics, it is much easier to understand that written documents are only one specialised and very inefficient device for storing information.

The combinations of binary oppositions which make up the universe of a totemic society might seem to constitute a very crude and restricted vocabulary yet the latest miracles of the communication engineer operate within the precisely similar restrictions. In a delightful passage Lévi-Strauss recalls the poetic evocation of a time

> . . . où le ciel sur la terre
> Marchait et respirait dans un peuple de dieux.[4]

Is this the golden age of the primitive past or the vital age of the electronic present? 'This time is now restored to us, thanks to the discovery of a universe of information where the laws of savage thought reign once more: "heaven" too "walking on earth" among a population of transmitters and receivers whose messages, while in transmission, constitute objects of the physical world and can be grasped both from without and from within.'[5]

This particular passage illustrates in an extreme form a not infrequent feature of Lévi-Strauss's method. His most telling generalisations are often achieved by opposing the characteristics of sharply contrasted cultural situations. Earlier exponents of the 'comparative method' in anthropology (e.g. Sir James Frazer) illustrated their a priori propositions by pointing out obvious superficial similarities between spatially dispersed customs; in contrast Lévi-Strauss demonstrates *structural* similarity by comparing clusters of custom which are not only spatially separate but also, in a superficial sense, totally dissimilar. In my quotation the unstated opposition seems to be between Telstar and the Aborigines. Elsewhere in the book one of the most effective chapters is that in which the author discusses structural parallels between Australian totemism and the Indian caste system, two modes of social organisation which, by any conventional taxonomy, would appear as different as chalk from cheese.

The effect of such work is to break up the traditionally accepted categories of anthropological analysis including totemism itself. This is salutary, for we are thereby reminded of an essential fact which is very easily forgotten. *Any* taxonomy in any academic discipline is only a heuristic device; it is an aid to clear thinking, not a permanent fact of nature.

This aspect of Lévi-Strauss's argument is very much in line with current developments in many of the natural sciences. Botanists, zoologists, bacteriologists, soil scientists, and many others are all searching for structural identities which cross-cut the neat discrimination of conventional taxonomic systems.[6] Linnaeus's concept of 'species' is suddenly very much out of fashion. It is easy to see how this has come about. Increasing familiarity with the programing requirements of digital computers has made the ordinary scientific worker familiar with the notion that 'similarity' may be thought of in statistical terms as representing a clustering rather than an identity of characteristics. Such similarities, which show up in a matrix computation, are often very different from those which might be inferred from direct inspection. Traditional taxonomies have necessarily depended upon the presence or absence of a small number of 'obvious' characteristics. This has meant that a very large number of apparently minor yet possibly significant variables have been excluded from all consideration. Until the coming of computers any other routine would have proved impossibly cumbersome. But now, in the computer era, it is the previously neglected variables which are receiving priority attention. In the long run this reaction may prove to have been exaggerated but, for the time being, the taxonomic 'shake-up' is proving most invigorating.

What has all this to do with the thinking of Lévi-Strauss? The particular system of factorial analysis which has influenced Lévi-Strauss most directly is that of the structural linguists (especially R. Jakobson and M. Halle), and the particular feature of general communication theory which he finds best adapted to his purposes is that of binary discrimination. The most fundamental proposition here is that, in any kind of code, every 'message' may be analysed into a series of cross-cutting binary discriminations such that

Any *x* may be slotted as

(i) either '*p*' or 'not *p*'

(ii) if '*p*' then either '*q*' or 'not *q*'
if 'not *p*' then either '*q*' or 'not *q*'

(iii) if '*p* and *q*' then either '*r*' or 'not *r*'
if '*p* and not *q*' then either '*r*' or 'not *r*'
if 'not *p* and *q*' then either '*r*' or 'not *r*'
if 'not *p* and not *q*' then either '*r*' or 'not *r*'

(iv) if '*p* and *q* and *r*' then either '*s*' or 'not *s*'
if '*p* and *q* and not *r*' then either '*s*' or 'not *s*'

and so on.

For the communication engineer the importance of this highly cumbersome way of arriving at the facts is that any message can be encoded as a series of positive and negative impulses. For the linguist the same kind of argument implies that any sound pattern which adds up to a piece of meaningful speech can be analysed into a series of phonemic 'distinctive features' which are distinguished as binary opposites: e.g. vocalic/non-vocalic, consonantal/non-consonantal, compact/diffuse, tense/lax.[7] Lévi-Strauss looks for comparable 'distinctive features' in non-verbal patterns of culture which will likewise sort out the facts by means of binary discriminations.

In practice, Lévi-Strauss has used these ideas in a great many different ways with increasing sophistication. In *Les Structures élémentaires de la parenté* (1949) the principle of binary discrimination is present in the notions of harmonic versus disharmonic organisation and also in the opposition between *échange restreint* and *échange généralisé*. But at this stage Lévi-Strauss had made no radical break with conventional procedures; the argument was a fairly straightforward development from themes already present in the writings of Durkheim and his pupils, Mauss and Hertz in particular.

In the various essays on myth, the earliest of which appeared in 1953, the influence of linguistic analysis is much more obvious; in the present volume it is dominant. A striking example occurs at pp. 140–9 where a vast body of ethnography relating to the Osage, an American Indian tribe, is tentatively reduced to a three-dimensional matrix so as to form at least the outline of an explicit computer program.

This merging of linguistics and social anthropology is something far more important than merely 'bringing Mauss up to date', and we need to understand clearly just what is entailed.

It is widely accepted that the specifically human characteristic which differentiates man from all other living creatures is the inferiority of his instinctive apparatus and his consequent total dependence upon culture, that is, upon patterns of behaviour which are learned from others. The humanity of man does not rest in the *capacity* to communicate but in the *necessity* to do so. A mere dependence upon communication is in itself a limiting factor; the circumstance which makes man superior to all other creatures is not the faculty to communicate but the faculty to operate with the symbols through which he communicates.

The mathematical transformation by means of which a particular sound pattern, 'man kills dog', is made to mean precisely the opposite to another sound pattern, 'dog kills man', is a characteristic which appears in all kinds of human communication systems. No non-human creature, so far as we are aware, can 'play games' with the elements of its communication system in this way.

Now this seems highly paradoxical. I am saying that the uniquely human characteristic is a capacity to perform logical transformations, to perform such mental exercises as:

$$\text{if } a + b = c \quad \text{then} \quad c - a = b$$

But if this is really true, if it is its *mathematical* quality which differentiates culture from nature, how can it begin? How does mathematical (logical) thinking first grow in the minds of unsophisticated man? This, it seems to me, is the core of Lévi-Strauss's problem.

It is a basic part of the argument that mathematical relations, linguistic relations, kinship relations and transactional relations of all types are really 'all of the same kind'. Mauss's 'Essai sur le don' (1924) is here of cardinal significance. Mauss lived before the coming of computers and matrix algebra, but he perceived a very fundamental truth. Individuals communicate with one another by 'giving'. The 'gifts' may be words or things, services or women, but in every case the act of giving sets up a 'relationship', and patterns of giving establish whole structures of relationship, networks of debtors and creditors, of rights and obligations. When an anthropologist studies a social system he is concerned with individuals whose lives are governed by a system of relationships and who conduct their mutual affairs by means of strategies defined by rules, as if all concerned were engaged in a multidimensional cosmic game of chess. In such a context, the rules of the game, the system of relationships, the network of exchange, the total system of communication are all aspects of the same 'thing' – the culture of society.

But here we face a problem. When we describe the ordering of society as a 'system of relationships' we are using the special technical language of the professional anthropologist. What is the objective reality to which this description refers? The anthropologist's notion of relationship is highly abstract; how are such 'relationships' perceived to be by those who employ them in their most rudimentary form?

It is not just a question of perceiving the nature of the relationships between man and man, there is also the question of the relations between man and his environment. To become aware of himself, man must differentiate himself from nature. But, furthermore, if man is to have a position in the order of the universe, the universe must at the same time itself be given a sense of order. How is this done? Whence does the orderliness spring?

Scholars who are unfamiliar with ethnographic literature commonly suppose that the formulation of taxonomies is a peculiar mark of the true scientist: indeed there are eminent anthropologists who have themselves held this to be the case (e.g. Radcliffe-Brown[8]). But this is a fundamental error. Modern ethnographic research has shown that even the most 'primitive' peoples are prone to discriminate the elements of their environment by means of extremely elaborate, logically ordered taxonomies. Although the 'species' categories which result are different from those of modern science, the procedures by which a particular species is distinguished are the same as those which an orthodox scientist would employ:

> Many times I have seen a Negrito, who, when not being certain of the identification of a particular plant, will taste the fruit, smell the leaves, break and examine the stem, comment upon its habitat, and only after all of this, pronounce whether he did or did not know the plant.[9]

The comprehensiveness of this kind of classification may be formidable. Conklin has observed that the Hanonoo of Mindanao discriminate 1800 mutually exclusive botanical species among a range of plants in which orthodox botany finds only 1300 taxa.

I have already noted how Western scientists have been tending to lose their confidence in the absolute validity (or utility) of conventional taxonomies. It is more and more widely recognised that a taxonomy simply represents a convenient (though sometimes misleading) summary of information which could more satisfactorily be presented in matrix form in a shape which could be digested by a digital computer. It is part of Lévi-Strauss's argument that the 'non-scientific yet logical' taxonomies of primitive peoples are likewise summaries of information which could very well be presented in matrix form.

One of our difficulties here is that we have got so used to thinking of the concept of 'species' as corresponding to a true fact of nature that it is now difficult to recognise that the word means no more than 'kind' or 'sort'. The statement: 'a kangaroo is a different species of mammal from a wallaby' is really just the same type of statement as: 'a Parisian is a different kind of man from a Lyonnais'. Thus we might merge the two formulae and say 'a kangaroo–Parisian is a different species of man–mammal from a wallaby–Lyonnais'. This makes nonsense in conventional French or English but is just the kind of statement that has repeatedly been reported by the ethnographers of Australian Aborigines under the heading of 'totemism'.

Lévi-Strauss argues that the reason that anthropologists have discerned a mystery in the phenomena which they lump together under the label 'totemism' is that they have been inhibited by the special conventions of syntax customary in modern Western European languages. 'Totemism', according to Lévi-Strauss, is really just one aspect of a more complex and more important phenomenon, the general classificatory process which is essential for all thought. 'Totemism' seems mysterious to us because it merges into one taxonomy (1) a system of classification of natural things external to human society and (2) a system of classification of categories of human being internal to human society. We find this absurd because our own equally arbitrary linguistic conventions imply that (1) and (2) are, self-evidently, of 'different kinds'.

Though such conventions vary as between one language system and another, a classification of type (1) is a necessity for any ordered society. Lévi-Strauss's novel insight is to perceive that, at the level of 'la pensée sauvage', the linguistic apparatus in terms of which categories of human grouping are arranged *must* be integral with, and in certain respects derivative from, the linguistic apparatus which is employed for establishing a description of the world. This comes about because the 'stuff' of which messages are made as they pass from one human being to another is itself a material stuff, a part of the external world:

> Above all, during the period of their transmission, when they have an objective existence outside the consciousness of transmitters and receivers, messages display properties which they have in common with the physical world. (p. 268)

As Lévi-Strauss has himself recognised, his view that the essence of totemism is to be seen in the ordering of the world into logical categories has some resemblance to the view propounded many years ago by the British functionalist anthropologists. The latter tended to argue that the constituent objects distinguished by any cultural system are intrinsically valuable because of their utility. Totemism serves not only to classify but also to express the value of useful things, especially foodstuffs. Lévi-Strauss has shifted the emphasis. In his view things have value in themselves because of the requirements of logic; utility is a secondary matter. Totems he says are 'bonnes à penser' rather than 'bonnes à manger'.[10]

I believe that Lévi-Strauss may here have evaded some issues of importance, but certainly his insistence that all systems of classification are essentially similar in that they imply a logically ordered set of binary discriminations has far-reaching implications for the anthropologist. As an example let me cite one particular case where Lévi-Strauss applies his argument to a problem of ethnographic analysis. At some stage Lévi-Strauss seems to have asked himself: By what criteria do the Aborigines of central Australia feel themselves to be of different kinds (tribes) (e.g. Arabanna, Aranda, Kaitish, Warramunga)? According to his interpretation of the ethnography, these distinctions depend upon a variety of factors (distinctive features) involving patterns of belief, marriage, ritual, and temporal periodicity. These factors can be displayed on a matrix as follows (p. 87):

		'Tribe'		
Factor	Arabanna	Aranda	Kaitish	Warramunga
A	+	−	−	+
B		+		−
C	+	−		+
D		+	−	+
E			+	−
F		+		−
G		+		−

Presumably, if the ethnography were more complete and the patience of the analyst more enduring, the empty spaces in the matrix could be filled in and the list of distinctive features further extended. This is not just an example of anthropological cleverness; it is, in Lévi-Strauss's view, a true key to the way in which the native Aborigines think about themselves.

I find an unexpected convergence here between Lévi-Strauss's work and that of some of his English colleagues. The English 'structuralist' anthropologists, notably Evans-Pritchard in *The Nuer* (1940), have made extended use of an argument already implicit in Durkheim's *De la Division du travail social* (1893). In that book Durkheim's discussion of mechanical solidarity amounts to a thesis that the binary discrimination between *we* and *they* depends upon context; those who are members of 'our group' at one level of (lineage) segmentation will be felt to be members of the 'other group' at a different level of (lineage) segmentation. Since 1940, English social anthropologists have applied these ideas very extensively to the dimension of political relations, and, latterly, some have attempted to link up the political frame of reference with other dimensions. To this end Gluckman has coined the expression 'multiplex relationships',[11] a notion which implies that we/they discriminations can simultaneously manifest themselves within many different fields which are not necessarily co-extensive. Even at one specific level of group segmentation the we/they discrimination which is derived from ritual relations may be quite different from the we/they distinctions which emerge from political, or economic, or kinship obligations. In Gluckman's view the sum of such binary distinctions is always cohesive in effect because of the resultant inconsistency of mutual obligations.

This no doubt somewhat distorts Gluckman's thesis but I have twisted it into this form merely to show that there is some convergence between Lévi-Strauss's argument and the superficially quite different British view. The differences also deserve attention. The British remain crudely empirical – their problem is: 'How does society work' ('function')? Lévi-Strauss's interest is much more that of the philosopher: 'How does man perceive himself to be in relation to the world and to society?'

But now let me raise certain objections. I was myself first attracted to Lévi-Strauss's work by the circumstance that the ethnography of the Kachins of North Burma is of central importance for the argument of *Les Structures élémentaires de la parenté*, and I happened to have first-hand knowledge of the Kachin facts. What amazed me at the time was that Lévi-Strauss had somehow perceived much more clearly than I had myself certain essential features of the structure of Kachin society, but that he had done so on the basis of a very cursory and sometimes quite misleading review of the ethnographic evidence.

Something of the same problem troubles me now. The range of Lévi-Strauss's ethnographic reading is vast, and his use of ethnographic evidence is extremely ingenious but it is also very selective, and, in particular cases, the selectivity produces a bad fit between the analysis and the evidence.

One example of this occurs at pp. 191–8, where Lévi-Strauss claims to resolve the logical puzzle presented by the extremely complex material relating to Penan teknonyms and 'death-names' (necronyms). Lévi-Strauss's discussion here is a profoundly illuminating contribution to the general theory of naming procedures but it does not satisfy me as a solution to the particular problem provided by the Penan ethnography.[12] Or again there is the material at pp. 204–8 which presents a fascinating discussion of 'our' customs regarding the naming of birds and dogs and racehorses and cattle. Fascinating as an illustration of the way in which 'species of words' may correspond to categories of social origin, but somehow doubtful as an interpretation of the evidence? Presumably English naming customs are sufficiently different from the French to spoil the bite of the argument as soon as it crosses the Channel.

Details of this kind are liable to exasperate the specialist but they should not be overrated. Lévi-Strauss has been engaged in a reconnaissance of largely unexplored territory. When a cadastral survey comes to be made, some of the finer points are bound to need revision.

But there are more serious difficulties, and I propose to consider one of these in some detail.

There is a sense in which the central theme of the book is the grandiose problem of the nature of man. What distinguishes man from non-man? Lévi-Strauss claims that his answer to this problem is akin to that of Rousseau. The *Discours sur l'origine et les fondéments de l'inégalité parmi les hommes* distinguishes the characteristics of man by means of a three-dimensional binary opposition:[13]

(i) *animalité* / *humanité*
(ii) *nature* / *culture*
(iii) *affectivité* / *intellectualité*

The first of these distinctions is that which is involved in the concept of 'totemism'. Lévi-Strauss argues that the anthropologists have erred in trying to isolate totemism as a one-dimensional phenomenon; Rousseau's larger frame of reference needs to be taken into account. Despite the amount of space which he devotes to its consideration, Lévi-Strauss takes the view that totemism does not deserve to be classed as a special category of behaviour because it is only one facet of something much wider and more fundamental – the *total* process by which man uses categories of words and categories of objective things to place himself in an ordered world. For Lévi-Strauss totemic species are simply logical operators.

I grant that Lévi-Strauss demonstrates in a most brilliant and convincing way that totems are in fact used as the 'stuff of thinking' and this previously neglected aspect of totemism is of great importance. But that is not the whole of the matter. This treatment of the ethnographic facts seems to evade the central problem (as it has formerly been understood) which is: Why are totemic species held to be sacred?

I agree that the earlier functionalist theories of the British anthropologists which Lévi-Strauss criticises were inadequate, but to this particular question they provided some sort of answer. They suggested that totems are sacred because they are useful, that they are, to use Lévi-Strauss's phrase, 'bonnes à manger'. But here it seems to me Lévi-Strauss has been trapped by his fondness for binary discriminations. He distinguishes things which are 'bonnes à manger' from things which are 'bonnes à penser' as opposite categories, and opts for the latter rather than the former. But surely totems may very well be both at once?

Binary discrimination is a very powerful tool of analysis. Any kind of information whatsoever *can* be discriminated in this way. But binary analysis is a possible rather than a necessary procedure. It has important disadvantages. One of these is that it tends to minimise problems of value. Lévi-Strauss's use of the communication theory analogy is very illuminating, but he seems to have overlooked the fact that there are types of communication problem which are more conveniently handled by analog computers (which answer questions in terms of *more* or *less*) than by digital computers (which can only answer *yes* or *no*). Lévi-Strauss's treatment hardly allows for the fact that in a society which orders living creatures into sets of 'species' which serve as a paradigm for corresponding sets of human groups, the individual members of any set may be valued in very different ways. The distinction is not just a binary matter of tame/wild, sacred/profane, prohibited/allowed, but of a subtle and many-sided graduation between 'more sacred' and 'less sacred', and this may bring into consideration factors which have so far escaped Lévi-Strauss's attention.

As I have remarked above, Lévi-Strauss argues that totemic species are 'bonnes à penser' rather than 'bonnes à manger'. Food preferences and food taboos are simply logical counters, 'bits' of information (p. 103: 'Eating prohibitions and obligations thus seem to be theoretically equivalent means of "denoting significance" in a logical system some or all of whose elements are edible species'). So also in the discussion of caste, food taboos, exogamy, endogamy are treated simply as digital indicators like the plus and minus signs on a computer tape.

Here again the point of my criticism is not that Lévi-Strauss is wrong but that he does not pursue the implications of his insights far enough. Thus in the chapter entitled 'Totem et caste' he demonstrates with superlative elegance how a structure of categories composed of endogamous sub-castes which are interdependent by virtue of their specialised cultural activities may resemble a structure of categories composed of exogamous totemic groups which are made interdependent through the pattern of marriage and which are differentiated because of the natural differences between the totemic species with which they are identified (pp. 123–5), a dialectic which leads to the generalisation (p. 128) that: 'the "system of women" is, as it were, a middle term between the system of (natural) living creatures and the system of (manufactured) objects' – a statement from which I personally can derive immense illumination.

In this discussion Lévi-Strauss very naturally takes note of the 'food prohibitions' which are commonly associated with totemism and he even notes (p. 126) that in caste systems the rules regarding 'culinary operations and utensils' are in some degree the 'equivalent' of such food taboos. Nevertheless he consistently plays down the importance of food customs as cultural indicators. 'Systems of names deriving from the natural kingdoms are not always accompanied by food prohibitions: they can be "stressed" (*marqués*) in diverse fashions' (p. 129). This is true but it leads Lévi-Strauss to overlook the fact that the food customs of Indian castes fit superbly well with his general argument.

Beals gives the following chart to show the interrelations of the caste groups in a South Indian village.[14] It seems clear from column 1 that, in this instance at least, 'bonnes à manger' are also 'bonnes à penser'.

	Economic status		
Ceremonial rank	Landlord	Middle class	Landless
Vegetarian	Brahmin	Lingayat priest Carpenter Blacksmith	Lingayat farmer
Mutton no beer		Saltmaker	Saltmaker
Mutton and beer		Farmer Shepherd Barber	Farmer Shepherd
Beef no pork		Muslim priest Muslim butcher Muslim weaver	
Pork no beef		Stoneworker	Stoneworker Basketweaver
Beef and pork			Leatherworker

Let me repeat: I do not disagree with what Lévi-Strauss says on this theme but I feel he is leaving something out.

He observes, for example, that there is a world-wide tendency to make some kind of verbal equation between eating and sexual intercourse. As a consequence the ritual attitudes evoked by food taboos and by sex taboos are interrelated. The linkage he asserts is metaphorical rather than causal (p. 105). The human mind perceives a logical similarity between the acts of eating and copulation – 'the lowest common denominator of the union of the sexes and union of eater and eaten is that they both effect a conjunction by complementarity' (pp. 105–6). I understand what he means. I can accept the proposition. But it seems to me to miss the point.

For most anthropologists the most interesting aspect of taboo is its relation to sacredness. A taboo has a qualitative value; it is not just a trap door that is either open or shut.

Lévi-Strauss wants to use the rules of sex and the rules of eating as binary discriminators which say 'yes' or 'no':

> Item A is allowed. The answer is 'yes'. The sign is +
> Item B is prohibited. The answer is 'no'. The sign is –

But, what about item C which is also prohibited but against which the sanctions are of quite a different kind and strength from those that are raised against item B?

It is here that I would bring in the issue of edibility.

It is surely always true that edibility is a very important factor in determining the way any particular animal species is categorised. But such categories are intricate. Lévi-Strauss (p. 205) notes that there is a food taboo which inhibits us from eating pet dogs. True, but the matter is complicated. The rule which prevents us from eating dog is tacit, unstated; the rule which prevents a Jew from eating pork is explicit. The valuations are quite different and these valuations deserve attention.

The complexity of the problem is obvious. Clearly the environment of any society contains a vast number of plants and living things which are dietetically nourishing but which are none the less treated as inedible. Taboo establishes discriminations but not in any simple fashion. Europeans do not eat rats; Hindus do not eat beef. There are similarities between the two cases but also radical differences, and Lévi-Strauss has, as yet, scarcely suggested how we should investigate such matters.

Goody has pointed out that a satisfactory analysis of the rules of incest calls for a consideration of the whole system of permissible, prohibited, and undesirable sex relations,[15] and in a comparable way Lévi-Strauss is himself insisting that totemism needs to be considered within the setting of a wider set of categories. So far so good. But if we are considering the relationships of man to animals – and that after all is what totemism is all about – then the edibility of the animals from the viewpoint of man is a very important part of the story. We need to consider the whole range of dietetic possibilities; every society distinguishes not only between food and non-food but also between food that is good and food that is bad and between food that is pleasant and food that is unpleasant. For such an ordering of materials the binary discriminations of which Lévi-Strauss is so fond seem clumsy and inappropriate. Indeed, it seems to me that the limitations of binary analysis have infected Lévi-Strauss's own thinking in a rather serious way. He has been engaged in expounding to us the logic of religious categories, but in the process he has come to ignore precisely those aspects of the matter which are most specifically religious.

Sir James Frazer's first study of totemism might have been criticised on somewhat similar grounds.[16] Frazer in that book distinguishes between 'The Religious Side of Totemism' and 'The Social Side of Totemism' but does not succeed very well in tying the two together. In discussing 'The Social Side of Totemism' Frazer recognises that the totemic categories might be expected to reflect in some way the segmentary structure of the society with which they are associated, but he despairs of discovering the logical key to the system.

Lévi-Strauss's analysis shows us that logical ordering of categories may after all be embedded in even the most confusing ethnographic evidence, and it is a further great step forward to be able to recognise that this 'totemic style' of logic can be discerned not only in systems composed of exogamous unlineal descent groups but also in the converse type of segmentary structure represented by an endogamous caste system. But this leaves out of account those social structures which are not 'segmentary' in any straightforward sense and which, on that account, do not readily lend themselves to binary analysis. Where, for example, do we meet with a totemic style of logic in the collective representations of societies which have a bilateral (cognatic) pattern of kinship organisation?

I believe that Lévi-Strauss's theory can be developed so as to provide an answer to this question which will at the same time tie in the 'sacred' aspect of totemism with its 'category-forming' aspect. But in the present volume this synthesis has not been achieved.

Professor Lévi-Strauss might well reply that I should confine my attention to what he has written and not concern myself with hypothetical missing chapters. But that is just my point. I consider that *La Pensée sauvage* is one of the most illuminating and potentially germinal contributions to anthropology that has been published within the last forty years, but its importance lies in its innovations and beginnings, not in its conclusions. That surely is the best kind of merit that any book can ever have?

Notes

This piece was originally published in French, in the 1964 volume of the historical journal *Annales*, then a highly influential mouthpiece for a school of mostly Marxist historians specialising in the analysis of long-term economic and social history. The English version was published in 1970 in *Sociological Theory and Philosophical Analysis*, edited by Dorothy Emmet and Alasdair MacIntyre.

1. [Eds.: Telstar was the first communications satellite ever launched (in 1962)].
2. Kroeber, 'California Kin Terms', p. 391.
3. Ryle, *The Concept of Mind*, p. 27.
4. Lévi-Strauss, *La Pensée sauvage*, p. 354.
5. Lévi-Strauss, *The Savage Mind*, p. 267. Unless otherwise stated, page references in this essay to works by Lévi-Strauss are to *The Savage Mind*.
6. See Aslib, 'Symposium on Classification'.
7. Jakobson and Halle, *Fundamentals of Language*, pp. 29ff.
8. Radcliffe-Brown, *A Natural Science of Society*.
9. Fox, 'Pintubo Negritos'; quoted by Lévi-Strauss, p. 4.
10. Lévi-Strauss, *Le Totémisme aujourd'hui*, p. 128.
11. Gluckman, *Judicial Process among the Barotse*, p. 156, and 'Les Rites de passage', p. 40.
12. If this comment seems unduly curt the interested reader may compare Lévi-Strauss's remark, p. 259: 'The proper name is the reverse of the necronym' with the original evidence provided by Needham ('System of Teknonyms of the Penan', pp. 422–3), which shows that a 'proper name' and a 'necronym' are commonly held by the same individual at the same time either as alternatives or in combination.
13. See Lévi-Strauss, *Le Totémisme aujourd'hui*, p. 144.

14. Beals, *Gopalpur*, p. 38.
15. Goody, 'Comparative Approach to Incest'.
16. [Eds: Leach refers here to Frazer's *book* published in 1887. Frazer's first *essay* on 'Totemism' was published in 1888; his book *Totemism and Exogamy* was published in 1910.]

1.11
Anthropology Upside Down (1974)

Review of Dell Hymes (ed.), *Reinventing Anthropology*

The enigmatic title of this antitextbook may best be explained by an analogy. In the flush of radical enthusiasm which was briefly dominant in England between 1645 and 1660, left-wing religious sectarians – Diggers, Seekers, Quakers, Ranters, Muggletonians, Fifth Monarchy Men, and what have you – vied with one another to reinvent Christianity. They proclaimed a 'world turned upside down', a New Heaven and a New Earth. Mutual recrimination apart, the vitriolic pamphlets, sermons, and denunciations of these reformers have much in common; there is a universal flavour of witch-hunting paranoia, an insistence that the new Christianity must be relevant to the mundane affairs of seventeenth-century rural England, an extreme intolerance of past orthodoxies of all kinds, a marked provincialism and lack of sophistication in the theology.

The teachings of these hot gospellers had derived from radical Continental theologians of the previous century, men such as Zwingli and Thomas Münzer, but the English enthusiasts showed hardly any interest in the history of their dogma. They were committed to the belief that what they were saying was of immediate relevance and entirely new. For their purposes history was not a record of what had actually happened but simply an instrument for political propaganda. If necessary the facts of the case could be turned completely back to front. King Charles I was tried and executed by the Puritan-dominated Parliament in 1649; in less than a decade 'sober and eminent persons' were saying that the whole episode had been engineered by the Jesuits as part of a Papist plot!

The new anthropology is very similar. Dell Hymes's contributors are of diverse sectarian affiliation but all tend to quote from Marx's *Theses on Feuerbach* with the same glib out-of-context reverence which their seventeenth-century predecessors exhibited toward passages of Holy Writ. They do not describe the virtues of the New Jerusalem in any detail but imply them, by contrast, simply by reciting a dreary catalogue of the vices of Vanity Fair. The anthropology about which these authors write is provincial and exclusively American. All concerned display an amazing ignorance of the European foundations of the doctrines that they proclaim. In consequence Franz Boas is mentioned more than fifty times but

Marcel Mauss and Edward Evans-Pritchard do not appear at all; Emile Durkheim and Raymond Firth are mentioned in passing once. In compensation the editor invents for our consideration a wholly imaginary character, 'the early ethnologist Elliot Rivers', evidently an ellipsis of W. H. R. Rivers, the founding originator of British social anthropology, and his close friend, the anatomist Sir Grafton Elliot Smith.

Likewise, just as the seventeenth-century sectarians interpreted their Bible reading in the homely context of contemporary rural England, so also these modern authors transpose the writings of the classical ethnographers into the anachronistic setting of twentieth-century America. William S. Willis, Jr, for example, who is an American Negro anthropologist, moves Melanesia to Mississippi. Preoccupied with the racial prejudices of his white colleagues past and present, he repeats the allegation that Malinowski, in a private diary, 'confessed a "need to run away from the niggers".' In fact Malinowski's diaries were written in a polyglot of Polish–German–English–Kiriwinan. The word translated as 'niggers' in the published text is the Polish term for 'blacks', a word which is repeatedly used by Dr Willis himself in passages where he clearly believes that he is writing without racial prejudice. I would not want to deny that anthropological writing is full of white middle-class bias but it is naive to imagine that everything will be put right if we turn the world upside down and extol the virtues of black lower-class bias.

As for the misuse of history, I will mention only that Stanley Diamond blandly assures us that 'certainly nothing could be clearer than that imperialism was the source of the idea of the inferior savage' in a context which identifies 'imperialism' with the 'nineteenth-century bourgeois colonialist epoch' (p. 409). How should one refute such a fantasy? Will Shakespeare suffice, whose prototype savage, Caliban, 'gabbles like a thing most brutish'? Or Daniel Beeckman, writing of Hottentots in 1714 as 'these filthy creatures [who] hardly deserve the name of rational creatures'? But to what end? For mere ignorance is not the issue; it is simply that Messrs Diamond and Co., like religious zealots everywhere, feel that they are entitled to mould their history to suit contemporary objectives. All references to the past are means by which the new anthropologists may 'declare themselves partisans in the movements for national liberation . . . and social reconstruction' (p. 426).

But millenarian enthusiasm apart, what is the argument all about?

Most of the assembled authors are middle-aged professors of anthropology in American universities, and I can only assume that many of their sillier statements are no more than shibboleth utterances designed to appease student militants. There is an excessive larding of the text with Marxist rhetoric, e.g. 'Anthropologists . . . may now decide to turn to the arena in which the generality of men, notably peasants and primitives, the conventional "objects" of study, are now recreating themselves as subjects of the revolutionary dramas of our time.' But meshed in with the slogans there is in these essays matter of more serious moment. Let me try to decipher what these worries are.

The basic complaint is that, somewhere around the beginning of this century, American cultural anthropologists and their British counterparts set themselves the goal of establishing a *science* of social man. From the beginning of recorded history literate travellers have delighted in recording the quaint customs of exotic peoples. This is not a European peculiarity. Herodotus had his Chinese and Indian equivalents. Likewise, from the days of Plato and Confucius onward, moral philosophers have been prone to cite ethnographic evidence to illustrate, as in a mirror, both the frailties and the virtues of literate civilisation. The intellectual fashion of the present century has been different. From the start, Boas in America and Rivers in England, in their contrasted styles, set out to create a *scientific* anthropology which would take as its model the experimental laboratory research that is normal in the physical and biological sciences. The new watchword was 'objectivity'. It was taken for granted that, as a scientist, the anthropological observer could be, and should be, in a position of privileged detachment, external to the material of his observation.

The cosmology implicit in such attitudes is crudely materialistic. Nature, out there, is presumed to consist of hard facts, organised into patterned structures governed by natural laws. These laws are ultimately mathematical; they are open to discovery by human minds but they are not open to manipulation. The Cartesian dichotomy between the mind of the observer and the stuff which he observes is absolute. The purpose of research is to discover the true nature of the facts and their interrelations, uncontaminated by errors introduced by the observers' fallibility or defects in the overall experimental situation.

The immediate consequence of applying such an ideology to the study of ethnography was to sharpen the distinction between the 'civilised' observer and the 'primitive' observed, and, as these writers often point out, to reinforce existing forms of racial prejudice by implying that native peoples in subordinate political positions could properly be looked upon as laboratory animals rather than as human beings who can make rational choices and tell lies. The culture which these anthropologists sought to study was traditional culture; its essence was that it was static, remote, and irrelevant to the observer's normal existence.

However, as this scientific ethnography developed in sophistication, a contrary trend became apparent. As a legacy from Malinowski, all modern forms of social anthropology are based on field research involving 'participant observation'. In this case the anthropological observer tries to understand the ramifications of an exotic alien culture by involving himself at first hand in the activities of those who are providing him with information. And whether the anthropologist likes it or not, the alien culture is in this case immediate and emergent, an element in the totality of twentieth-century human society. As Malinowski himself discovered – and as Mr Hymes's contributors have been rediscovering – there is a radical incompatibility between the demands of scientific objectivity and the personal human involvement which participant observation necessarily entails.

Because of local circumstances American anthropologists were slow to recognise this paradox. For most of the first half of the century, American anthropological research was heavily concentrated on the study of North American Indians. Its explicit purpose was historical reconstruction; the anthropologist aimed at producing a description of how 'traditional' Indian society had worked, on its own, before it had been crushed by the frontier wars of the nineteenth century. The object of study was thus already remote; participant observation was seldom an option that was open to the white investigator, and there was no stimulus to look closely at the uncomfortable political realities of present-day life on Indian reservations.

Outside America the setting of anthropological research was very different. Throughout the first half of this [the twentieth] century British ethnographers in Africa, Asia, and Oceania operated as specially protected persons under the aegis of the paramount colonial power, but the autonomy of action of their tribal 'objects of study' was of quite a different order from that which existed in North American Indian reservations.

Like their American contemporaries the British anthropologists usually ended up by writing monographs about idealised 'traditional' societies, but they were much less oblivious of the social realities of the *de facto* situation. As early as 1936 they had begun to explore the sociology of colonialism.[1] In many well-known cases their pupils were to become the leaders of post-colonial independent governments. The latter included the present President of Kenya, whose 1938 PhD thesis was dedicated 'to all the dispossessed youth of Africa'.[2]

The trouble with all the essays in Hymes's collection is their denial of historical reality. The authors have been shocked by the fact that, in south-east Asia and South America, professional anthropologists have functioned as intelligence agents on behalf of the CIA and the American armed forces, from which they have inferred that a politically neutral anthropology is an impossibility. They take it for granted that the 'others' whom anthropologists study are, by definition, in a state of political subjection. Since they hold that attempts at objectivity in social studies are positivist illusions, it follows that the anthropologist must always be 'involved' in his research situation. He then has a simple moral choice; he can side either with the oppressors or with the oppressed. From this it is readily deduced that it is always morally deplorable to serve any established authority and always morally virtuous to side with liberation movements. That sympathies may be divided or solutions elusive does not seem to occur to these writers. All the anthropologist's actions must be immediately relevant to the manifest problems of those whom he observes.

If this kind of 'relevance' is accepted as dogma, all the existing textbooks can be thrown away. We must change the whole curriculum. E. N. Anderson puts it this way:

> Some establishment of priorities is needed. Is cross-cousin marriage really a more vital issue than the world food problem? If not, why do we not change editorial and instructional policies which imply this?

Well one of the reasons is that it is the function of mature scholars to warn their students that altruism and enthusiasm are not enough. Until we adequately understand the fundamentals of the situations in which people live – which we do not – we are not likely to get very far with solving anything. Direct assault is not a sensible strategy in intellectual war. Very few major advances in human understanding have come about as the result of a conscious effort to solve a particular practical problem. It may indeed turn out that an understanding of cross-cousin marriage bears on the problem of food production. The conditions of creativity, in learning as well as in art, are not predictable in advance. We would not now be better off if someone had persuaded the altruistic Einstein that he ought to devote his great abilities to the design of farm machinery.

But the malaise of which these essays are a symptom is very general. In English universities anyway, anthropology is today a very 'popular' subject, but it is not only the students who feel that there is something radically wrong with the syllabus of anthropology as it is now taught. I feel that way myself and I fully sympathise with the frustrated exasperation of Hymes's contributors. The fragmentation of the study of man into component 'subjects', as in the dissection theatre of an anatomy school, dehumanises the whole enterprise.

I go along with the reformers when they argue that the central problem is how to convey the idea that in learning about other societies we are, at one remove, learning about our own. Most certainly every budding anthropologist must understand that the observer is part of the scene that he observes. But God forbid that we should propose the search for mystical experience as a proper substitute for the pretensions of objectivity. I have no wish to muddle up my scholarly concerns with the ethics of a Franciscan friar. So I am quite unmoved by the self-flagellation with which Robert Jay declares that his earlier work has been a 'shallow, distorted, even arrogant effort at understanding the problems' of his informants and that 'in future fieldwork I shall place first a mutual responsibility to my whole self and to those I go to learn from'.

The purpose of such rhetoric is to generate fervour and commitment but, like the monotonous din in a Tibetan temple, the ultimate effect is soporific; the words flow on and on . . .

> . . . the process of comparative differentiation and discrimination does not itself suggest any compelling criteria for critical judgment. If these are to be found at all, I would advocate that we seek them in the normative and emancipatory interests of anthropological praxis, that is, in the degree to which anthropological activity violates or sustains pertinent 'life-preserving' values and in the extent to which it inhibits or realises human freedom.

And then on the next page:

> The emancipatory interest is not only integral to anthropological praxis, the latter also contributes to making that emancipation possible.

And on the next:

> The comparative understanding of others contributes to self-awareness; self-understanding, in turn, allows for self-reflection and (partial) self-emancipation; the emancipatory interest, finally, makes the understanding of others possible.

So writes Bob Scholte. But what does this repetitive circular argument actually imply for 'anthropological praxis'? Simply that we turn the clock back 120 years and take our inspiration from *The Communist Manifesto*. 'Its empirical and analytic function would be to provide causal explanations for cultural processes, to suggest hypothetical predictions of socio-historical events and to define the infrastructural determinants of human behaviour.' None of which would be subject to any sort of empirical verification. If this is anthropology reinvented, give me cross-cousin marriage every time.

The interconnections between the Puritan ethic, which expressed itself in the sound and fury of the seventeenth-century Ranters, and the Spirit of Capitalism are still a matter for debate. The rantings of the twentieth-century anthropological Puritans may likewise be symptomatic of things to come, but just what will emerge from such turmoil none of us can tell, except perhaps that it will not be what we expect.

Notes

This review of Dell Hymes's edited volume, *Reinventing Anthropology*, was published in the *New York Review of Books* on 4 April 1974.

1. See the papers reprinted in *Africa*, Memorandum XV (1938). [Eds: The volume, entitled *Methods of Study of Culture Contact in Africa*, was published by the International Institute of African Languages and Cultures, with an introduction by Malinowski. The essays are: Lucy Mair on 'The Place of History in the Study of Culture Contact'; essays by Monica Hunter and Isaac Schapera on culture contact in, respectively, Pondoland and Bechuanaland; a paper by A. T. and G. M. Culwick entitled 'Culture Contact on the Fringe of Civilisation'; Audrey Richards, 'The Village Census in the Study of Culture Contact'; Meyer Fortes, 'Culture Contact as a Dynamic Process'; and Günter Wagner, 'The Study of Culture Contact in its Practical Applications'.]
2. Kenyatta, *Facing Mount Kenya.*

1.12

The Shangri-La That Never Was (1983)

Review of Derek Freeman, *Margaret Mead and Samoa: The Making and Unmaking of an Anthropological Myth*

In the United States, because of a remarkable feat of advance publicity on the part of the publishers, this book is likely to prove a *succès de scandale.*

Although the publication date was originally announced as April 1983 the *New York Times* had, by the end of January, published a review, several letters, and even a leading article on the topic and other journals, including *New Society*, followed suit.

The result was, as I can personally testify, that by mid February, in localities as far apart as Dunedin, New Orleans, and San Francisco, wherever a congregation of anthropologists might be gathered together, 'Derek Freeman's vicious attack on Margaret Mead' was a prime and passionate topic of conversation, made all the more heated by the fact that at that time hardly anyone had read the book.

All this is only comprehensible when it is realised that immediately following her death in November 1978, at the age of nearly 77, Mead was treated as a national heroine. Posthumous honours of all kinds were showered upon her including the Presidential Medal of Freedom, 'the nation's highest civilian honour'.

On this side of the Atlantic, where the name of Margaret Mead carries none of these cult-figure associations, the reception of Freeman's book is likely to be more sedate. It is a genuine contribution to the history of twentieth-century anthropology couched in a very polemical style, but the focus of discussion is extremely narrow and the excitement that has been generated in the United States can in no way be justified on academic grounds.

Margaret Mead's field research in Samoa lasted only seven months. It was carried out in 1925–6 at a time when she was an inexperienced graduate student at Barnard College (Columbia University) working under Franz Boas, the founding father of modern American anthropology.

By modern standards it was clearly a very defective piece of fieldwork. Mead pointedly avoided living in a Samoan household, choosing instead to lodge with the family of the chief pharmacist's mate of the American naval medical dispensary. On her own declaration she did not have 'any political participation in village life'. Her knowledge of the Samoan language was very limited and she evidently relied heavily on English-speaking informants, in particular the American-educated Samoan who was at the time the district governor of Manu'a and girls attending the government school on the same island. The local American colonial regime evoked her unstinted admiration.

The results of her research were mainly published in two monographs, *Coming of Age in Samoa* (1928), which was reprinted many times and had an enduring influence on various aspects of American education, and *Social Organisation of Manu'a* (1930), which is unlikely to have had many readers who were not professional anthropologists.

Some of the deficiencies of these works have been widely known to anthropologists for many years, but the monumental scale of the errors of ethnographic fact which Freeman now displays has not been appreciated, except perhaps by the readers of certain hard-to-find, unpublished, doctoral dissertations. Freeman maintains that Mead's account contained radical errors in almost every dimension of discussion. So much so that he concludes that many of Mead's adolescent informants must have engaged in systematic deception by way of a joke and that their victim was successfully taken for a ride.

If it be asked why we should now prefer the word of Freeman, a retired senior professor of social anthropology, to that of Mead, an inexperienced graduate student at the age of twenty-four, we must consider the probabilities. Samoan society and its associated culture is not uniform and it has certainly changed greatly over time. Mead herself emphasised that the easygoing social system she described seemed to be very different from the rank-conscious society portrayed in the literature of the pre-Christian era. But in fact, while these reports from Ancient Samoa and many more recent descriptions all seem fully compatible with what Freeman now tells us about the Samoa that he himself has studied, hardly any of it fits the Mead story.

Moreover the time gap is not large. Freeman first engaged in field research in Samoa in the period 1940–3 and, in all, he has spent more than six years in the territories. He has a comprehensive knowledge of both the classical and the modern colloquial languages. He is a very experienced researcher. He has talked with Samoans who remembered Mead's visit.

But why should it matter? All inexperienced graduate students engaged on their first piece of field research are liable to make mistakes. The full bibliography of Mead's writings includes some 1400 items. Why should Freeman have chosen to concentrate his attack on just two or three items published at the beginning of her long career?

The answer to that is that, despite the gossip, Freeman's book is not designed as 'a vicious attack on Margaret Mead' at all. His purpose is simply to show that the research findings reported in *Coming of Age in Samoa* were certainly invalid and the long-term influences which that book exercised in certain fields of American academic thinking must be wholly disregarded.

It is just possible, though it's very unlikely, that the theoretical position which Boas supported around 1925 and which he believed to be convincingly validated by Margaret Mead's Samoan evidence is still supportable on other grounds, but it is now quite clear that the Samoan material does not support Boas's theory at all.

But what was that theory? Why did Boas adopt it? Why did he (or Margaret Mead) suppose that the study of adolescent girls in Samoa would clinch the case?

It is the answers to these questions, which Freeman offers in the first five chapters of his book, which provide its justification rather than the more titillating issue of whether the youthful Margaret Mead was or was not quite exceptionally naive.

Freeman's view of the matter runs something like this. He traces Boas's persistent aversion to evolutionist theories to his early association in Berlin with Rudolf Virchow and his indirect adoption of the ideas of Theodor Waitz, a celebrated professor at the University of Marburg. In the earlier part of his academic career Boas was principally concerned simply to clarify the distinction between biological nature and cultural nurture as influences on human behaviour. But as time went on he increasingly came to assert the absolute pliability of biology and the overriding importance of cultural factors. Even the vagaries of human personality were supposed to be culturally determined.

That, over the years, the dogma of cultural determinism came to assume greater and greater importance in Boasian anthropology is a clearly established fact of history. The novelty of Freeman's account is the suggestion that the increasing rigidity of this position developed in direct dialectical response to an opposite form of extremism, the racialist dogma of biological determinism as expounded by Darwin's cousin, Francis Galton, and his followers in the Eugenics Society.

The doctrines of the eugenicists eventually led to atrocious laws concerning the sterilisation of the (morally) unfit, not only in Hitler's Germany but also in various parts of the United States. As Freeman sees it, Boas's eagerness during the 1920s period to have his pupils 'demonstrate' that personality disturbances associated with the biological development of the individual are subject to cultural conditioning was a humanistic response to his dismay at the increasing respect that was being paid to eugenicist doctrines in medical, psychological, and political circles.

The test case was to be adolescence. In capitalist industrial America it had become almost a cliche that adolescence is likely to be a period of intergenerational conflict and extreme individual distress manifested in feelings of sexual guilt with frequent symptoms of neurosis. If one could find a 'negative instance' of a cultural environment in which adolescence was free and easy and the 'happiest time of one's life' the case for cultural determinism would surely be established. But why Samoa?

Freeman seems to believe that Mead's realisation that the sexual mores of 'traditional' Samoa, as indeed of other parts of western Polynesia, had been of almost Calvinist severity was retrospective. He suggests that she had originally gone to Samoa inspired by romantic notions of free love in the South Seas, having previously gained extensive knowledge of the ethnographic literature relating to eastern Polynesia (for example, Tahiti). Certainly Samoa would seem to have been an improbable place to expect to find Boas's 'negative instance'. However, when Mead reported back to her mentor in New York she claimed to have discovered the hoped-for Shangri-la and *Coming of Age in Samoa* took its place as one of the major classics of psychological anthropology.

I have no doubt that other reviewers will take a very different view of Freeman's book from that which I have adopted here, for much is at stake. *Coming of Age in Samoa* provided the founding myth of a whole school of cultural anthropology and the idea that human culture is packaged in separate boxes, each of which is liable to generate its own form of 'basic personality', is still around. Only a few weeks ago in New Zealand I heard a professor of international repute expatiating on the special characteristics of 'the Maori mind'.

My own queries would be of a different kind; p. 320 n. 37 calls for expansion. As far as I am aware Mead's book does not anywhere mention the names of either Sigmund Freud or Bronislaw Malinowski, but both of them surely lurk somewhere in the background? The latter's *The Father in Primitive Psychology* and *Sex and Repression in Savage Society* had both appeared in 1927. The young Margaret Mead was not just telling lies as some modern Samoans have averred, nor was she simply discovering what Boas had told her to find; she was also responding to influences which were already 'in the air' in other parts of the academic world besides the cosy coterie that had its focus in the Department of Anthropology at Columbia University.

I also find it a pity that Freeman is so solemnly committed to the revelation of scientific truth. If he had written his story as a satire on the frailty of academic researchers he could have made his points just as well and it would have been much more fun.

Notes

This is a review of Derek Freeman's de-bunking book on Margaret Mead, *Margaret Mead and Samoa*, and was published in *New Society* on 24 March 1983.

1.13

A Poetics of Power (1981)

Review of Clifford Geertz, *Negara: The Theater State in Nineteenth-Century Bali*

In the special bicentennial programme of the American Academy of Arts and Sciences to be held in May 1981, the lead speaker on behalf of the social sciences will be Professor Clifford Geertz of the Institute of Advanced Study at Princeton University. This provides some indication of the high regard in which the author of *Negara* is held by academic colleagues. His new book can only enhance that reputation.

Geertz explicitly addresses himself to several kinds of reader, and this produces an unusual format. The book is quite short, less than 300 pages in all, but fewer than half of these are devoted to the book proper. These are written in ordinary narrative discourse and can be read with understanding by anyone who possesses some degree of scholarly sophistication. The argument calls for only a modest knowledge of Indonesian history and only a bare-bones understanding of anthropological theory. The other half of the book is for the expert. It consists of notes, glossary, and bibliography, which add up to a specialised scholarly apparatus designed both to justify and to comment upon the arguments which are taken for granted in the main text.

From both points of view Geertz earns full marks. He once described the task of the anthropologist as the art of 'thick description', but his own writing combines elegance, brevity, and lucidity to an unusual degree.[1] The range of his scholarship is very extensive but seldom employed in a contentious manner. He is fortunate in holding a post at Princeton which allows him to devote his whole time to research, and he makes good use of his time. For the anthropological specialist in Indonesian affairs there is not a great deal in this book that is strictly new; some parts of it are rewritten versions of materials Geertz himself has presented elsewhere, but there is a functional coherence to the different strands of his argument which is welcome and in some ways unexpected.

It needs to be stressed that Geertz is a cultural anthropologist whose first commitment is to a specifically American academic tradition which must be distinguished from the social anthropology which is represented by the work of the present reviewer and which is generally practised by British exponents of the art of anthropology.

The distinction is not easy to explain in simple language. Very roughly, social anthropology is concerned with the analysis of networks of interpersonal relationships; cultural anthropology, with the description of styles of life and the interpretation of such 'styles of life' as meaningful systems of symbols. Social anthropologists ordinarily pay much more attention to the structural/functional interdependence of the different facets of the social system they are describing than do cultural anthropologists, whose viewpoint (in the eyes of their critics) is unduly intuitive and impressionistic. However, there are many bridge points between the two approaches and one of these is of particular importance in this book.

Because Geertz was at one time a pupil of Talcott Parsons, he always has been much influenced by the writings of Max Weber, a sociological theorist who is also greatly admired by the social anthropologists. A central theme in *Negara* is that the assumptions concerning the nature and objectives of political power, which most social anthropologists have taken over from Weber and which they share with most political theorists of European background, are inadequate to explain the observed facts in the case of the nineteenth-century Indonesian state.

Hitherto British anthropologists have shown only qualified respect for Geertz's work. They have recognised the excellence of *Islam Observed* (1968) which, in very brief compass, makes a highly insightful comparison between Islam as interpreted by Indonesians and Islam as interpreted by Moroccans. But this was a particular case to which the 'impressionism' of cultural anthropological analysis was particularly well suited. But in other writings, such as the early *Peddlars and Princes* (1963), a comparison of economic developments in two Indonesian towns, and *Kinship in Bali* (1975), written jointly with Hildred Geertz, it has seemed to the British that the means were ill-adapted to the end and that a social anthropological approach would have been much more appropriate. The are not likely to have reservations of this sort with regard to the present book.

Although Weber is criticised, his influence remains very strong. The book is about nineteenth-century Bali, but the *negara* that is described (the word denotes the miniature 'state' which constituted the unit of political identity in most parts of pre-colonial Indonesia) is an 'ideal type' in the Weberian style, many features of which were to be found not only in other parts of Indonesia but also in many other parts of south-east Asia. For example, in general form, there is little difference between the *negara*, as here described, and the corresponding units of Thai/Burmese society usually referred to as *mong* or *maing*.[2]

The model for the whole is provided by Tabanan, one of seven tiny 'kingdoms', each only a few miles across, which constituted the South Bali heartland that was annexed by the Dutch colonialists only in 1906. As each of the kingdoms was captured the respective royal families managed, in one way or another, to commit spectacular suicide. It was, as Geertz puts it, 'quite literally the death of the old order. It expired as it had lived: absorbed in a pageant.'

The content of the book is formally concerned with how these royal families were constituted, their relationship to the endogamous kin groups (*dadia*) of which they were components, the structure and mode of operation and control of the irrigated rice lands on which the economy of the system depended, and, above all, the nature of the political relationship that linked royalty to land and people. In places the detail is very impressive, but the account remains that of an ideal type rather than of an actual system. The close observer will notice that only one of the maps is marked with a scale.

But Geertz's objective goes far beyond that of providing us with a model of how an Indonesian *negara* might actually have worked. In the concluding chapter, which carries the title 'Bali and Political Theory', he argues that his model presents a challenge to the whole body of 'power-centred' political theory which runs from Machiavelli through Hobbes to Marx, Pareto, and de Jouvenel.

I am not prepared to go very far down this road, though I agree with some parts of the argument, but Geertz's position on this general issue deserves attention. In the book this piece of 'inverted Weber' political theory is put at the end, as if it were a logical inference from the details of Bali ethnography that have gone before. This is fair enough. But there are many potential readers who may initially be more interested in the general theory than they are in Bali. I would encourage such readers to read the conclusion first. They will then understand more easily just what the fine detail of ethnography, the 'thick description' that has been given in earlier chapters, is really all about.

There are two main targets for Geertz's criticism. The first is Karl Wittfogel's link between 'hydraulic society', 'the Asiatic mode of production', and 'Oriental despotism' operating through a hierarchy of officials responsible for the maintenance of the irrigation works. Here Geertz has an unanswerable, but not very original, case. Bali was, in its small way, a 'hydraulic society', but the Wittfogel formula about the inevitable despotic power which accrues to the controlling manager of an elaborate irrigation system did not work out. But then it is very doubtful whether it ever worked out anywhere else. In recent years versions of operational 'hydraulic systems' in China, Burma, Sri Lanka, and elsewhere have been carefully analysed. In some cases the maintenance of these systems has entailed the existence of a permanent administrative bureaucracy, but no example has come to light in which the political authority of the 'despot' at the centre was critically dependent on control of the irrigation system.[3]

Geertz's other major general theme needs to be viewed with greater caution. The hereditary kings of Indonesian *negara* were divine kings in the prototypical sense exhibited many years ago in A. M. Hocart's various writings about kingship. Everything connected with their royal office was surrounded by pageantry. Political theorists tend to take such pageantry for granted, treating it as mere play-acting. What politics is really all about is the struggle for power: the control of men by other men exercised through control over primary economic resources of land and water.

But Geertz points out that even European forms of centralised authority have not always fitted tidily into this pattern. In modern English the word 'state' and its adjectival adjuncts have a number of different meanings but the sense 'a sovereign state' is relatively recent; 'stateliness' in the sense of pomp and splendour is much older. The normal view of the political theorists, of the right as well as the left, is that the pomp and ceremony of monarchy is a fraud, 'a dark noise to impress the impressionable and induce in them a trembling awe'. The reality of state politics is concerned with 'the capacity of elites to extract surpluses from the less well-placed and transfer them to themselves'. In such a view state ceremony is seen as a business of 'mystification, in the sense of the spiritualising of material interests and the fogging over of material conflicts'. In all varieties of such theory what Geertz calls 'the semiotic aspects of the state' (i.e. the patterning of symbolisation associated with ideas concerning royal authority) 'remain so much mummery. They exaggerate might, conceal exploitation, inflate authority, or moralise procedure. The one thing they do not do is actuate anything.'

Geertz does not deny that in Bali, as everywhere else, ambitious and powerful men exploited and oppressed their weaker neighbours, but the fantastic imagery of Balinese kingship was not, he insists, just play-acting.

> To understand the *negara* is to . . . elaborate a poetics of power, not a mechanics. The idiom of rank not only formed the context within which the practical relationships of the major sorts of political actors . . . took their shape and had their meaning; it permeated as well the dramas they jointly mounted, the *décor théâtral* amid which they mounted them, and the larger purposes they mounted them for. The state drew its force, which was real enough, from its imaginative energies, its semiotic capacity to make inequality enchant. . . . The notion that politics is an unchanging play of natural passions, which particular institutions of domination are but so many devices for exploiting, is wrong everywhere; in Bali, its absurdity is patent. The passions are as cultural as the devices; and the turn of mind – hierarchic, sensory, symbolistic, and theatrical – that informs the one informs the other.

These quotations all come a few pages from the end of the book. I have quoted them here at length not simply because they summarise the essence of Geertz's theoretical position but because they indicate where, as anthropologists, Geertz and I part company. That final quotation is, in my view, complete rubbish. I can make no sense of a line of thought which claims that 'passions' are culturally defined. From my prejudiced position as a social anthropologist this passage reveals with startling clarity the ultimately radical weakness of the basic assumption of cultural anthropology, namely, that not only are cultural systems infinitely variable, but that human individuals are products of their culture rather than of their genetic predisposition.

What Geertz has to tell us about the role of competitive display in traditional Indonesian politics is not only interesting in itself but is very often of comparative interest for parts of the world many thousands of miles from Bali. But for Geertz 'culture' is ultimately a patterned system of symbols in individual human minds rather than a set of techniques for wresting a living from the environment. Again and again he implies that the superstructure of ideology is of greater significance than the infrastructure of basic economic need. One does not have to be a whole-hearted Marxist to feel that this argument is flawed at its roots.

So for me, as a fellow professional anthropologist, it is the earlier part of the book with its ethnographic detail rather than the later part with its overstretched cultural theory that provides the focus of interest.

Here criticism is difficult because the book is a historical study. Geertz has undertaken fieldwork in Bali, but it was under the post-war, Javanese-dominated, Indonesian government, which was much closer to that of the Dutch colonialists than it was to indigenous nineteenth-century Balinese rule. So his presentation of the Balinese *negara* in terms of ideal types and models was not just a matter of making complicated matters easy to understand, it was unavoidable. Geertz provides a very convincing account of how such a system *might* have worked; in this respect his account is unexpectedly 'functionalist', showing, in a now unfashionable way, how very different types of institutions fit together to form a meaningful and economically viable whole. Nevertheless it remains a model. There is hardly any evidence about actual individuals, actual land holdings, actual systems of irrigation and their control. It seems to me altogether improbable that the facts on the ground really bore a close relationship to the patterns in the model. I am not challenging the model; I would just like to know what sort of compromises were introduced to make fact and fiction fit together.

But that is a pedantic objection. As a matter of fact Geertz has managed to discover a certain amount of on-the-spot, directly observed material, the most remarkable being that provided by the journals of Ludvig Helms, who was in Bali as a merchant's assistant in the late 1840s and who published his recollections in English in 1882. These records include a detailed account of the funeral of the king of Gianjar in December 1847, in the course of which

> the body was burned with great pomp, three of his concubines sacrificing themselves in the flames. It was a great day for the Balinese. It was some years since they had had the chance of witnessing one of these awful spectacles, a spectacle that meant for them a holiday with an odour of sanctity about it; and all the remaining Rajahs of Bali made a point of being present, either personally or by proxy, and brought large followings.

The words are those of Helms and provide the opening of a four-page citation from Helms's book. It is Geertz's achievement that, without sentimentalising the issue, he is able to transform this scene, which provoked Helms's deep disgust, into a poetic imagery which arouses our respect for a wholly alien way of life in which even the 'barbarities' of obligatory suicide attain a kind of aesthetic perfection.

As the reader of this review will have noticed, this book offends against some of my deepest anthropological prejudices, but it is certainly a book that deserves to be read, and not only by anthropologists.

Notes

This review of Clifford Geertz's book on the state in nineteenth-century Bali, *Negara*, was published in the American journal, *The New Republic*, on 4 April 1981.

1. [Eds: In Geertz, *The Interpretation of Cultures*.]
2. [Eds: See Leach, 'The Frontiers of "Burma"' (I.3.3, below) and Tambiah, 'The Galactic Polity'.]
3. [Eds: See Leach, 'Hydraulic Society in Ceylon' (1959).]

1.14

Writing Anthropology (1989)

Review of Clifford Geertz, *Works and Lives: The Anthropologist as Author*

One of the most celebrated pieces of fictitious ethnography ever written is J. G. Frazer's account of the Priest–King of Nemi awaiting his execution by his as yet unknown successor. It comes in the first chapter of *The Golden Bough* but its immense verbosity, even in the abridged edition, makes it unquotable. I refer to it now only because the status of Clifford Geertz as Priest–King of American cultural anthropology seems to me to be rather similar.

The book under review originally formed a sequence of Harry Camp Lectures delivered at Stanford University in the spring of 1983; the subsequent editing seems to have been minor but various footnotes refer to work published later than 1983. The symposium of essays edited by James Clifford and George E. Marcus entitled *Writing Culture: The Poetics and Politics of Ethnography*, which reports on the proceedings of a seminar held at Santa Fe in April 1984, is especially relevant. The following is a quotation from an essay by Paul Rabinow in this latter volume:

> There is a curious time lag as concepts move across disciplinary boundaries. The moment when the historical profession is discovering cultural anthropology in the [unrepresentative] person of Clifford Geertz is just the moment when Geertz is being questioned in anthropology [one of the recurrent themes in the Santa Fe seminar that gave rise to this volume]. So, too, anthropologists

> . . . are now discovering and being moved to new creation by the infusion of ideas from deconstructionist literary criticism, now that it has lost its cultural energy in literature departments and Derrida is discovering politics.[1]

And then on p. 243: 'Despite Geertz's occasional acknowledgements to the ineluctability of fictionalising, he has never pushed that insight very far.'

These comments need to be borne in mind by the readers of my essay. Geertz's own name for his personal style is 'interpretive anthropology'. What he means by that has shifted over the years and may now be on the way out, at any rate among his younger colleagues.

There is a certain ambiguity about the identity of the subtitled 'Anthropologist as Author' whose work is under discussion. Clifford Geertz himself might fill that role though I am sure that was not what he intended. So I shall outline the shape of his book as a whole but my readers should not be surprised if I take an occasional sideswipe at Geertz himself.

The book is quite short. Only 150 pages of main text. Six chapters, the first and last being comments by Geertz on the contemporary anthropological (ethnographical) scene and the other four presenting compressed cameos of what purports to be representative work by Lévi-Strauss, Evans-Pritchard, Malinowski, and Ruth Benedict – in that order. Geertz's choice of authors suggests that, in his view, each of these celebrated figures had/has a distinctive and contrastable style of writing that is epitomised in Geertz's text.

I doubt if Geertz really believes this and though he claims to admire the work of all four of his targets, his admiration is clearly limited. He writes without obvious malice but somehow the 'new criticism' apparatus, which Geertz employs in the manner of Kenneth Burke, does not come off. The theory requires that the critic should pay especially close attention to the small details of what the author actually writes but, as we shall see, Geertz often fails to do precisely this and, on that account, comes to seem untrustworthy.

His investigation has several facets: How does the anthropological author perceive his/her own 'text'? What is it about that text that has led the informed reader to regard its author as a master (as compared with other authors who use similar stylistic devices but are not so reckoned)? Just what is the relationship between the objective ethnographic 'reality' out there and the artistic fiction that the text conjures up? These are important questions. What sort of answers does Geertz provide?

The first chapter, entitled 'Being There', successfully explains what we are to expect though it never comes to grips with what seems to me to be the crux of the whole matter: Does ethnography have an objective subject matter at all? Ever since the days of Herodotus, who is supposed to have started it all, ethnographers have written as if customs were normally static. When change occurs it has to be explained as if it were an anomaly. But historical records everywhere suggest that what would need to be explained is an ethnography that did not change. I shall come back to that. But Geertz does not discuss this issue. Why should history be made up of descriptions of one happening after another, the individual happenings being quite different, whereas the sequences reported by ethnographers are supposed to be endlessly repetitive?

Chapter 2 is about Lévi-Strauss, especially *Tristes tropiques.* I agree that this is a good representative work of Lévi-Strauss as author. The French text contains all the peculiar stylistic features that characterise the author's *oeuvre.* It was designed from the start as a work of literature to be read by Parisian intellectuals rather than simply by anthropologists. It proved to be a best-seller. Geertz quotes extensively but always in English. He uses Russell's translation, *A World on the Wane,* but notes that Lévi-Strauss prefers the Weightman version. He gives the page references of both English versions and of the French original as well. What more could one ask of a serious scholar? But actually it is very odd because the Russell translation lacks four chapters of the original, a fact that Geertz does not report. How can those of his potential readers who do not read French be expected to pay close attention to the text if large parts of it are missing?

All the same I think that Geertz is right to emphasise the 'extraordinary air of abstracted self-containment' that is characteristic not only of *Tristes tropiques* but also of Lévi-Strauss's more explicitly anthropological writings. The ethnography is nearly always second-hand. A report from before the First World War that makes everything seem neat and tidy will always be preferred to more recent accounts in which the data is palpably contaminated by European influence. The ethnographic 'not-here/ not-us' exists only in Lévi-Strauss's text, not in his experience, which, ethnographically, has been rather meagre.

Chapter 3 focuses on Evans-Pritchard. Whereas *Tristes tropiques* was a best-seller, at any rate in France, Evans-Pritchard's stylistic oddities are here represented by a very short (nine pages), little-known article in *The Army Quarterly* for July 1973 entitled 'Operations on the Akobo and Gila Rivers, 1940–1'. It seems to be Geertz's thesis that it is characteristic of Evans-Pritchard's ethnography that the scene is built up by recollection, as one might tell stories about the pictures in a photograph album. The objective reality as experienced is decorated but not actually invented. Geertz shrewdly suggests that the Akobo battle piece was composed by trying it out on various attentive audiences in an Oxford pub!

What Geertz says about this Akobo paper intrigues me greatly for quite a different reason. My own military adventures in the far north of Burma from the summer of 1942 to the winter of 1943 were strikingly similar. My guerrillas were untrustworthy Kachins; E-P's were untrustworthy Anuak. My largely invisible enemy were Japanese; E-P's were Italians. The guerrillas in both cases were armed with antique rifles. Both E-P and I got on very badly with our military superiors while colluding well with the civilians (both white and non-white) . . . and so on. But these similarities of military experience have not led to any similarity of anthropological style, and I cannot see why they should.

Consequently Geertz's claim that the British 'school' of social anthropology – whom he lists by name as Evans-Pritchard, Radcliffe-Brown, Meyer Fortes, Max Gluckman, Edmund Leach, Raymond Firth, Audrey Richards, S. F. Nadel, Godfrey Lienhardt, Mary Douglas, Emrys Peters, Lucy Mair, and Rodney Needham – 'is held together far more by this manner of going about things in prose than it is by any consensual theory or settled method . . .' seems to me very astonishing. Is there really a British school of social anthropology? What are its characteristics? The persons named do not (did not) even speak English in the same way, let alone write it in the same way. Raymond Firth and Meyer Fortes were both my teachers and former colleagues and I admire the work of both, but I do not admire the written style of either. If, from the other side of the Atlantic, my own texts appear to resemble those of either of these scholars, then all my literary efforts for the past thirty-five years have been completely in vain.

But Geertz's long list of names deserves another comment that relates to his own literary style. A psychiatrist friend of mine once told me that he had a patient who spent all his waking hours copying lists of names out of a telephone directory. Geertz writes like that. Every point of argument is reinforced as if it needed to be supported by a thesaurus. The resulting garrulity quickly becomes intolerable. Where should one stop? For example, even if the social anthropologists in Geertz's list do have some kind of social solidarity, why leave it like that? What about Bronislaw Malinowski, Isaac Schapera, Ian Hogbin, Monica Wilson, Elizabeth Colson, Phyllis Kaberry, William Stanner, Jack Goody . . . and Uncle Tom Cobley and all . . . ?

That Evans-Pritchard's renown rests on his work relating to the Azande and the Nuer and Sanusi is mentioned, but its connection with the Anuak campaign seems to exist only in Geertz's imagination. Geertz does refer to the deep hostility that developed between Malinowski and Evans-Pritchard, but he does not discuss the marked difference between the Azande witchcraft book where the stylistic influence of Malinowski is still strong, the early Nuer publications where the model is Radcliffe-Brown, and the later publications where there begins to be a strong whiff of Lévi-Straussian structuralism. There is no explicit reference to Evans-Pritchard's Catholicism or to his homosexuality, both of which had a marked influence on his style of writing.

Chapter 4 is entitled 'I-Witnessing: Malinowski's Children'. In these days I suspect that the only work of Malinowski's that gets a reading from the potential audience of a series of Harry Camp Memorial Lectures is *A Diary in the Strict Sense of the Term*, so perhaps it was predictable that Geertz would use this lamentable and easily misunderstood work to display what he claims to be the peculiarities of Malinowski's thought and style.

Geertz does not seem to be worried that Malinowski, as author, never had any intention that this document should be published nor does he comment on the fact that the first half of the *Diary* has nothing whatever to do with the Trobriand Islands and was written before Malinowski had had any significant fieldwork experience or had developed anything resembling a distinctive anthropo-literary style. He does not mention that the expression 'Exterminate the brutes', which has been cited against Malinowski (by Francis Hsu when giving a Presidential address to the AAA) is a quotation from Conrad which, in context, is a rebuke by Malinowski against himself! (*Diary*, 21 January 1915; Geertz, p. 74.)[2]

Even more misleading is the passage quoted here at p. 133 (in the final chapter) and said to come from the *Diary* at p. 150. In fact it comes from p. 140. The quote from Geertz reads as follows: 'Malinowski's happy "Eureka!" when first coming upon the Trobrianders – "Feeling of ownership: it is I who will describe them . . . [I who will] create them".' It is a remarkable example of *not* paying close attention to the text! The *Diary* entry is dated 1 December 1917. It does not contain the word 'Eureka!'. The people whom Malinowski plans to 'create' (by writing about them) are not the Trobrianders at all but the pot-makers of the Amphlett Islands. By that date Malinowski spoke fluent Kiriwinan and had lived among Trobrianders for more than eighteen months. That Geertz, whom many consider to be the most distinguished ethnographer in the United States, should write as carelessly as this seems to me absolutely extraordinary.

But let us get back to Geertz's Chapter 4. The title refers not to Malinowski but to 'Malinowski's Children'. Who are they? First, Kenneth Read, author of *The High Valley* (1965). Actually Read's links with Malinowski, whom he never met, are somewhat remote. He is by birth an Australian and he learned his basic anthropology from Ian Hogbin, one of Malinowski's first-generation pupils. He obtained his PhD at the London School of Economics in 1948 when Raymond Firth was the senior professor. His subsequent academic career was mostly on the faculty at the University of Washington, Seattle. The 'High Valley' is located in the Eastern Highlands of New Guinea. I share Geertz's views about the excellence of this book, which is one of the first anthropological monographs to be frankly subjective and autobiographical. Read went back to the High Valley for brief visits in 1981 and 1982 but was unable to recapture the romance of his original fieldwork. Read had personal problems that might account for this but Geertz seems to suggest that it is an inevitable consequence of pursuing Malinowski's style of 'immersionist ethnography' and attempting to be honest about it that the high romance should end by going completely flat.

At any rate Geertz includes among 'Malinowski's Children' three recent works of Moroccan ethnography by P. Rabinow (1977), V. Crapanzano (1980), and K. Dwyer (1982). None of these authors has any sort of connection with Malinowski. Geertz's claim that there is a common stylistic thread but that the whole thing has gone rotten because the author has put too much of himself into his text is a very personal invention. Geertz is of course himself a specialist on Morocco so perhaps he should know; but he is not an entirely unprejudiced witness. The alleged link with Malinowski shows once again how difficult it is for anthropologists who have been reared in the American tradition running from Boas to Kroeber to Talcott Parsons to Edward Shils to grasp what Malinowski thought he was up to.

Chapter 5 is about Ruth Benedict. She is not an author who is widely read on this side of the Atlantic. Even *Patterns of Culture* has now been dropped from undergraduate reading lists and *Chrysanthemum and the Sword* was never on them; but Geertz, by picking up an early minor text preserved by Margaret Mead, has managed to convince me that Benedict deserves comparison with Swift. The chapter title 'US/NOT-US: Benedict's Travels' is intended as a trope for 'Gulliver's Travels' and Geertz would apparently put Benedict in the same class as Montaigne, Montesquieu, Voltaire, W. S. Gilbert, Veblen, and Saul Bellow (pp. 107–8). Note again Geertz's thesaurus-type approach! All the same this is the best chapter in the book. Benedict's long-lasting love affair with Margaret Mead is not mentioned, though, as it has been vouched for by Mead's daughter, Catherine Bateson, it is now in the public domain.

The final chapter carries the title 'Being Here: Whose Life Is It Anyway?' It is very hard to read because of the repeated listing of names – 'a shelved beach in Polynesia, a charred plateau in Amazonia; Akobo, Meknes, Panther Burn . . .' – 'the *suffisance* of Lévi-Strauss, the assuredness of Evans-Pritchard, the brashness of Malinowski, the imperturbability of Benedict . . .' The sceptic in me reacts to this sort of thing by muttering, 'Why Polynesia?' – 'What is brash about Malinowski?' But the argument seems to be that in the post-colonial era the kind of ethnography that was pursued (or at least attempted) by Geertz's four protagonists no longer has any relevance to anything. In those far off days 'Here' and 'There' were in quite different parts of the map. Geographical difference was reflected in cultural difference. Cultures had hard edges. They could be thought of as entirely separate. But now no more.

Being a fully certified member of 'the British "school" of social anthropology' (whatever that means!), this does not worry me very much. I have always taken the line that, in ethnographic writing, cultural differences, though sometimes convenient, are temporary fictions. Recently I have become more explicit about this.[3] An ethnographic monograph has much more in common with an historical novel than with any kind of scientific treatise. As anthropologists we need to come to terms with the now well-recognised fact that in a novel the personalities of the characters are derived from aspects of the personality of the author. How could it be otherwise? The only ego that I know at first hand is my own. When Malinowski writes about Trobriand Islanders he is writing about himself; when Evans-Pritchard writes about the Nuer he is writing about himself. Any other sort of description turns the characters of ethnographic monographs into clockwork dummies. I cannot fathom whether Geertz would agree with this statement or not. Sometimes he seems to be saying something rather like this, but at other times it is quite the reverse.

Perhaps the underlying problem is the one I mentioned earlier. Why should anthropologists take it for granted that history never repeats itself but persuade themselves that, if left alone, ethnographic cultures never do anything else? The answer is that it is often convenient so to believe. Malinowski believed that the Trobriand Kula, as he observed it, had been working like that for hundreds if not thousands of years. He mentions this belief only in a footnote. The evidence is that it had in fact been in existence for less than fifty years and was changing rapidly all the time. But even the archaeologists would not accept that assertion 100 per cent. It was necessary for Malinowski's style of writing about the Kula that it should have existed for a long time. Without that improbable assumption we would never have had *Argonauts of the Western Pacific*. Ethnographers as authors are not primarily concerned with factual truth; they convince by the way they write. Montaigne writing about cannibals in the sixteenth century is still far more convincing than is W. Arens writing on the same topic from Stony Brook in 1979.[4] I suspect that Geertz would agree.

Notes

This is a review of Clifford Geertz's book, *Works and Lives*, which is the text of a series of lectures given by Geertz at Stanford in 1983, updated for publication in 1988. Leach's review was published in the leading American academic anthropology journal, *American Ethnologist*, in 1989.

1. Rabinow, 'Representations are Social Facts', pp. 241–2.
2. [Eds: See Leach, 'An Anthropologist's Trivia' (I.1.3, above).]
3. [Eds: See Leach, 'Tribal Ethnography'.]
4. [Eds: See Leach, 'Long Pig, Tall Story' (II.4.8).]

Section 2
The Aesthetic Frills: Ritual

The first three pieces in this section are general and theoretical; the rest gradually introduce the theme of rites of passage and become more concrete and ethnographical.

Ritual occupied a central place in Leach's thought: he was fascinated by it but also deeply suspicious of it – especially when it involved himself.[1] When Leach describes ritual as 'an aesthetic frill' (I.2.1: 154), in no sense does he mean to imply that it was trivial or optional or something that could be dispensed with. In 'Ritualisation in Man' (I.2.2), a piece written for an interdisciplinary conference, he notes that human ritual differs from that of animals precisely because it is subject to the kind of manipulations he explored in *Political Systems*. There Leach assumed maximisation as a general human propensity but what was maximised was not simply economic benefit but rather a matter of ritual: power, prestige, status, recognition, esteem, and display; what you are seen to do and seen to be able to do. People maximise power, ritual is power, and 'the potency of ritual action is by no means an illusion' (I.2.3: 173). Ritual lies at the heart of the Kachins' political manoeuvring – and what goes for the Kachins' sacrificial feasts goes equally for the formality of bureaucratic committees and expensive weddings in otherwise informal modern Britain (I.2.6).

In 'Ritual' (I.2.3) Leach develops arguments sketched out in the preceding two pieces. *Pace* Durkheim, ritual is not a special kind of (sacred) behaviour, nor is myth a special kind of (religious) narrative. Myth and ritual 'say' the same things. Myth is verbal ritual; the verbal and behavioural aspects of ritual are inseparable. 'Ritual', defined broadly, is an aspect of action, the communicative aspect of behaviour; the communication expresses the status of the actor in relation to his physical and social environment. While in this sense all human actions have a 'ritual aspect', in some this aspect becomes predominant, and it is these we most easily recognise as 'ritual'. This, according to Leach, results from the stylisation of action – potentially any action – a stylisation which must in some sense increase the meaningfulness of the action itself since that is what turns secular activity into ritual (I.2.3: 173).[2] Though Leach makes no explicit mention of this, his view is also compatible with speech act theory.[3] Just as speech acts can alter states of affairs in the world, so ritual can alter the actor's status – hence its real power (I.2.1: 157). Authors such as Ahern, Bloch, and Tambiah went on to develop this insight further.[4]

Leach's view of ritual is presupposed in his view on social structure. Ritual expresses a particular state of affairs at a particular moment of time – a reminder of the proper order of things ('social structure') and of people's places within it. Because rituals are staged by particular individuals, these 'reminders' are also political acts: people may use the same ritual form to make rival assertions concerning the proper social order, and contesting claims concerning their own positions. Thus seen, ritual is no longer merely the paean of a stable social order but rather a basic mechanism alike of social reproduction and social change. By the same token, a common structural pattern may be dressed up in the symbolic forms of different cultures – as when Kachins become Shans.

Leach's ambivalence towards ritual is consistent with his ambivalence towards culture more generally. Culture on its own is superficial 'dress' – often literally as clothing (see I.2.5; I.2.6; and I.2.7) – and the exploration of culture as belief detached from action is a dead end: 'to ask questions about the content of belief which are not contained in the content of ritual is nonsense' (I.2.1: 155); 'all attempts to make a rational analysis of the irrational must necessarily be fallacious' (I.2.3: 172). But what makes behaviour social is the cultural form that it takes. It is precisely this dressing up, this quality of 'masquerade' (see I.2.5) that makes ritual at once both illusory and superficial yet potent and profound.

In different ways, these essays all display Lévi-Strauss's influence on Leach and also Leach's efforts to rethink Lévi-Strauss's ideas. The central place given to ritual by Leach stands in marked contrast to its peripheral status in Lévi-Strauss's work. For Leach, ritual puts categories into action; initially, Lévi-Strauss sees ritual as working together with myth to produce structural pieces from events;[5] later and more pessimistically, he sees it as working in the opposite direction – a vain and irrational effort to recapture the continuity of lived experience already irredeemably fragmented by the logical operations of mythic thought.[6]

Leach never explicitly abandoned his position that myth and ritual were both one and the same and intimately linked to social concerns but, in practice, in his more structuralist guise, he did go on to analyse myth, metaphysics, and systems of ideas with only relatively little reference to 'the material world of observable human behaviour' (I.2.1: 155). When compared with the more complex and profound treatment in *Political Systems* and early essays, some of his later formulations of ritual (notably in his 1976 *Culture and Communication*) appear at once more woodenly Durkheimian – 'ritual as a symbolic representation of social relations' – and more mechanically semiotic – 'ritual as the exemplification of classificatory systems'.

Lévi-Strauss's influence must be set against that of Arnold van Gennep. Though Leach never wrote an extended piece about him, the last four essays, notably 'Cronus and Chronos' (I.2.4) and 'Time and False Noses' (I.2.5), all show the influence of *Les Rites de passage*, a work from which much of Leach's structuralism, especially his structuralist treatment of ritual, derives. The stylisation of behaviour in ritual takes two general forms, the ascetic and the ecstatic, the formal and the informal (see I.2.6; II.2.1; and II.3.3)[7] only one of which fits easily with Durkheim's 'sacred'. Together these provide a major component of ritual's communication code. Thus far we are still in the realm of Lévi-Strauss's 'binary oppositions' but Leach takes us further, to the temporal alternation between the two and to what lies in between and out of time – the zone of masquerade, false noses, and taboo. Van Gennep's tripartite schema, recast as Leach's favourite diagram (see I.2.7; I.4.2; II.2.4; II.3.4; and II.4.1), crops up time and again. These essays on time were the tip of an iceberg, a monograph on the subject of which Leach never completed.[8] Van Gennep wrote on thresholds and compared rites of passage to movement between the rooms of a house; Leach went on to write an essay about gateways and gatekeepers in religious architecture (II.2.3).

The last, most recent piece is arguably also the first: it borrows from an extended analysis of a Borneo head feast, written in 1952 and reworked again twenty years later. This early essay is probably now the only substantial piece of Leach's writing which remains unpublished. But the obsession with head-hunting, of which this essay is a symptom (see also II.4.1), goes back further. In 1937/8 Leach wrote a seminar entitled 'The Problem of the Head-Hunter in the Wild Wa Area, An Area to Which I Shall Return'. This obsession goes together with references to 'ultra-primitive human societies' (see I.2.2: 160), the ones that 'real anthropologists' study.[9] He would use this stereotype as a thought experiment only to declare in the same breath that it was a wholly indefensible fiction: 'the central problem for late twentieth century academic anthropology is . . . whether we can fully convince ourselves, as well as our non-anthropological colleagues, that all men and women, past, present, and future, are of equal standing and that the distinction between the savage and the civilised upon which the whole edifice of traditional anthropology was constructed deserves to be consigned to the trash can.[10]

The real point was to use the Other as a mirror to reveal the arbitrariness of our own conventions. The reflection could be unsettling. In 'Once a Knight' (I.2.7), Leach appears as a subject in the masquerade of ritual; his analysis reveals not only his own personal ambivalence but also a more general ambivalence about all such proceedings. In 'Masquerade', a paper published after his death, he asks wistfully 'if *all* the world's a stage; if we are *always* social persons rather than individual selves, where is the *true* self? Does it exist? Can we ever know it?'.[11]

Notes

1. As Provost of King's College Leach presided over the abolition of several aspects of College ceremonial. He also introduced compromise. As Provost he was obliged to admit new Fellows in a ceremony in the College chapel. The ceremony was retained, but Leach substituted English for Latin as the language of the central performative (a change which has since been reversed).
2. For a directly contrary view see Bloch, 'Symbols, Song, Dance', and *From Blessing to Violence.*
3. See Austin, *How to Do Things with Words*; Searle, *Speech Acts.*
4. Ahern, 'The Problem of Efficacy'; Bloch, 'Symbol, Song, Dance'; Tambiah, 'A Performative Approach to Ritual'. See also the critique by Gardner, 'Performativity in Ritual'.

5. Lévi-Strauss, *The Savage Mind*, pp. 32–3.
6. Lévi-Strauss, *The Naked Man*, p. 679.
7. See also Leach, 'Of Ecstasy and Rationality' (1979).
8. Time also appears as a significant interest in 'Anthropos' (II.5).
9. See Kuper, 'Interview with Edmund Leach'; and Leach, *Social Anthropology*, ch. 4.
10. 'Masquerade', p. 47.
11. Ibid., p. 50.

2.1

Ritual as an Expression of Social Status (1954)

Ritual, I assert, 'serves to express the individual's status as a social person in the structural system in which he finds himself for the time being'. Clearly the significance of such an aphorism must depend upon the meaning that is to be attached to the word *ritual.*

English social anthropologists have mostly followed Durkheim in distinguishing social actions into major classes – namely, religious rites which are *sacred* and technical acts which are *profane.* Of the many difficulties that result from this position one of the most important concerns the definition and classification of magic. Is there a special class of actions which can be described as magical acts and, if so, do they belong to the category 'sacred' or to the category 'profane', have they more of the nature and function of religious acts or of technical acts?

Various answers have been given to this question. Malinowski, for example, places magic in the terrain of the sacred;[1] Mauss seems to regard it as profane.[2] But no matter whether the major dichotomy is seen to lie between the magico-religious (sacred) and the technical (profane), or between the religious (sacred) and the magico-technical (profane), the assumption remains that somehow sacred and profane situations are distinct as wholes. Ritual is then a word used to describe the social actions which occur in sacred situations. My own use of the word is different from this.

From the observer's point of view, actions appear as means to ends, and it is quite feasible to follow Malinowski's advice and classify social actions in terms of their ends – i.e. the 'basic needs' which they appear to satisfy. But the facts which are thereby revealed are technical facts; the analysis provides no criterion for distinguishing the peculiarities of any one culture or any one society. In fact, of course, very few social actions have this elementary functionally defined form. For example, if it is desired to grow rice, it is certainly essential and functionally necessary to clear a piece of ground and sow seed in it. And it will no doubt improve the prospects of a good yield if the plot is fenced and the growing crop weeded from time to time. Kachins do all these things and, in so far as they do this, they are performing simple technical acts of a functional kind. These actions serve to satisfy 'basic needs'. But there is much more to it than that. In Kachin 'customary procedure', the routines of clearing the ground, planting the seed, fencing the plot, and weeding the growing crop are all patterned according to formal conventions and interspersed with all kinds of technically superfluous frills and decorations. It is these frills and decorations which make the performance a *Kachin* performance and not just a simple functional act. And so it is with every kind of technical action; there is always the element which is functionally essential, and another element which is simply the local custom, an aesthetic frill. Such aesthetic frills were referred to by Malinowski as 'neutral custom',[3] and in his scheme of functional analysis they are treated as minor irrelevancies. It seems to me, however, that it is precisely these customary frills which provide the social anthropologist with his primary data. Logically, aesthetics and ethics are identical.[4] If we are to understand the ethical rules of a society, it is aesthetics that we must study. In origin the details of custom may be an historical accident; but for the living individuals in a society such details can never be irrelevant, they are part of the total system of interpersonal communication within the group. They are symbolic actions, representations. It is the anthropologist's task to try to discover and to translate into his own technical jargon what it is that is symbolised or represented.

All this of course is very close to Durkheim. But Durkheim and his followers seem to have believed that collective representations were confined to the sphere of the sacred, and since they held that the dichotomy between the sacred and the profane was universal and absolute, it followed that it was only specifically sacred symbols that called for analysis by the anthropologist.

For my part I find Durkheim's emphasis on the absolute dichotomy between the sacred and the profane to be untenable.[5] Rather it is that actions fall into place on a continuous scale. At one extreme we have actions which are entirely profane, entirely functional, technique pure and simple; at the other we have actions which are entirely sacred, strictly aesthetic, technically non-functional. Between these two extremes we have the great majority of social actions which partake partly of the one sphere and partly of the other.

From this point of view technique and ritual, profane and sacred, do not denote *types* of action but *aspects* of almost any kind of action. Technique has economic material consequences which are measurable and predictable; ritual on the other hand is a symbolic statement which 'says' something about the individuals involved in the action. Thus from certain points of view a Kachin religious sacrifice may be regarded as a purely technical and economic act. It is a procedure for killing livestock and distributing the meat, and I think there can be little doubt that for most Kachins this seems the most important aspect of the matter. A *nat galaw* ('nat making', a sacrifice) is almost a synonym for a good feast. But from the observer's point of view there is a great deal that goes on at a sacrifice that is quite irrelevant as far as butchery, cooking, and meat distribution are concerned. It is these other aspects which have meaning as symbols of social status, and it is these other aspects which I describe as ritual whether or not they involve directly any conceptualisation of the supernatural or the metaphysical.[6]

Myth, in my terminology, is the counterpart of ritual; myth implies ritual, ritual implies myth, they are one and the same. This position is slightly different from the textbook theories of Jane Harrison, Durkheim, and Malinowski. The classical doctrine in English social anthropology is that myth and ritual are conceptually separate entities which perpetuate one another through functional interdependence – the rite is a dramatisation of the myth, the myth is the sanction or charter for the rite. This approach to the material makes it possible to discuss myths in isolation as constituting a system of belief, and indeed a very large part of the anthropological literature on religion concerns itself almost wholly with a discussion of the content of belief and of the rationality or otherwise of that content. Most such arguments seem to me to be scholastic nonsense. As I see it, myth regarded as a statement in words 'says' the same thing as ritual regarded as a statement in action. To ask questions about the content of belief which are not contained in the content of ritual is nonsense.

If I draw a rough diagram of a motor-car on the blackboard and underneath I write 'this is a car', both statements – the drawing and the writing – 'say' the same thing – neither says more than the other and it would clearly be nonsense to ask: 'Is the car a Ford or a Cadillac?' In the same way it seems to me that if I see a Kachin killing a pig and I ask him what he is doing and he says '*nat jaw nngai*' – 'I am giving to the nats', this statement is simply a description of what he is doing. It is nonsense to ask such questions as: 'Do nats have legs? Do they eat flesh? Do they live in the sky?'

In parts of this book I shall make frequent reference to Kachin mythology but I shall make no attempt to find any logical coherence in the myths to which I refer. Myths for me are simply one way of describing certain types of human behaviour; the anthropologist's jargon and his use of structural models are other devices for describing the same types of human behaviour. In sociological analysis we need to make frequent use of these alternative languages, but we must always remember that a descriptive device can never have an autonomy of its own. However abstract my representations, my concern is always with the material world of observable human behaviour, never with metaphysics or systems of ideas as such.

Interpretation

In sum, then, my view here is that ritual action and belief are alike to be understood as forms of symbolic statement about the social order. Although I do not claim that anthropologists are always in a position to interpret such symbolism, I hold nevertheless that the main task of social anthropology is to attempt such interpretation.[7]

I must admit here to a basic psychological assumption. I assume that all human beings, whatever their culture and whatever their degree of mental sophistication, tend to construct symbols and make mental associations in the same general sort of way. This is a very large assumption, though all anthropologists make it. The situation amounts to this: I assume that with patience I, an Englishman, can learn to speak any other verbal language – e.g. Kachin. Furthermore, I assume that I will then be able to give an *approximate* translation in English of any ordinary verbal statement made by a Kachin. When it comes to statements which, though verbal, are entirely symbolic – e.g. as in poetry – translation becomes very difficult, since a word-for-word translation probably carries no associations for the ordinary English reader; nevertheless I assume that I can, with patience, come to understand *approximately* even the poetry of a foreign culture and that I can then communicate that understanding to others. In the same way I assume that I can give an approximate interpretation of even *non-verbal* symbolic actions such as items of ritual. It is difficult entirely to justify this kind of assumption, but without it all the activities of anthropologists become meaningless.

From this point we can go back to the problem I raised near the beginning of this chapter,[8] namely the relation between a social structure considered as an abstract model of an ideal society, and the social structure of any actual empirical society.

I am maintaining that wherever I encounter 'ritual' (in the sense in which I have defined it) I can, as an anthropologist, interpret that ritual.

Ritual in its cultural context is a pattern of symbols; the words into which I interpret it are another pattern of symbols composed largely of technical terms devised by anthropologists – words like lineage, rank, status, and so on. The two symbol systems have something in common, namely a common *structure*. In the same way, a page of music and its musical performance have a common structure.[9] This is what I mean when I say that ritual makes explicit the social structure.

The structure which is symbolised in ritual is the system of socially approved 'proper' relations between individuals and groups. These relations are not formally recognised at all times. When men are engaged in practical activities in satisfaction of what Malinowski called 'the basic needs', the implications of structural relationships may be neglected altogether; a Kachin chief works in his field side by side with his meanest serf. Indeed I am prepared to argue that this neglect of formal structure is essential if ordinary informal social activities are to be pursued at all.

Nevertheless if anarchy is to be avoided, the individuals who make up a society must from time to time be reminded, at least in symbol, of the underlying order that is supposed to guide their social activities. Ritual performances have this function for the participating group as a whole;[10] they momentarily make explicit what is otherwise a fiction.

Social structure and culture

My view as to the kind of relationship that exists between social structure and culture[11] follows immediately from this. Culture provides the form, the 'dress' of the social situation. As far as I am concerned, the cultural situation is a given factor, it is a product and an accident of history. I do not know *why* Kachin women go hatless with bobbed hair before they are married, but assume a turban afterwards, any more than I know *why* English women put a ring on a particular finger to denote the same change in social status; all I am interested in is that in this Kachin context the assumption of a turban by a woman does have this symbolic significance. It is a statement about the status of the woman.

But the structure of the situation is largely independent of its cultural form. The same kind of structural relationship may exist in many different cultures and be symbolised in correspondingly different ways. In the example just given, marriage is a structural relationship which is common to both English and Kachin society; it is symbolised by a ring in the one and a turban in the other. This means that one and the same element of social structure may appear in one cultural dress in locality A and another cultural dress in locality B. But A and B may be adjacent places on the map. In other words there is no intrinsic reason why the significant frontiers of social systems should always coincide with cultural frontiers.

Differences of culture are, I admit, structurally significant, but the mere fact that two groups of people are of different culture does not necessarily imply – as has nearly always been assumed – that they belong to two quite different social systems. In this book I assume the contrary.

In any geographical area which lacks fundamental natural frontiers, the human beings in adjacent areas of the map are likely to have relations with one another – at least to some extent – no matter what their cultural attributes may be. In so far as these relations are ordered and not wholly haphazard there is implicit in them a social structure. But, it may be asked, if social structures are expressed in cultural symbols, how can the structural relations between groups of different culture be expressed at all? My answer to this is that the maintenance and insistence upon cultural difference can itself become a ritual action expressive of social relations.

In the geographical area considered in this book the cultural variations between one group and another are very numerous and very marked. But persons who speak a different language, wear a different dress, worship different deities, and so on are not regarded as foreigners entirely beyond the pale of social recognition. Kachins and Shans are mutually contemptuous of one another, but Kachins and Shans are deemed to have a common ancestor for all that. In this context cultural attributes such as language, dress, and ritual procedure are merely symbolic labels denoting the different sectors of a single extensive structural system.

For my purposes it is the underlying structural pattern and not the overt cultural pattern that has real significance. I am concerned not so much with the structural interpretation of a particular culture, but with how particular structures can assume a variety of cultural interpretations, and with how different structures can be represented by the same set of cultural symbols. In pursuing this theme I seek to demonstrate a basic mechanism in social change.

Notes

This is an extract from Leach's book *Political Systems of Highland Burma* (1954), pp.10–17.

1. Malinowski, *Magic, Science, and Religion*, p. 67.
2. Mauss, *Manuel d'ethnographie*, p. 209.
3. Malinowski, 'Introduction' to Hogbin, *Law and Order in Polynesia*, p. xxvi.

4. Wittgenstein, *Tractatus*, 6.421.
5. Durkheim, *Formes élémentaires* (2nd edn), p. 53.
6. Cf. the distinction made by Merton (*Social Theory*) between *manifest* and *latent* function.
7. The concept of *eidos* as developed by Bateson (*Naven*) has relevance for this part of my argument.
8. [Eds: See the extract from *Political Systems of Highland Burma* reproduced here as I.3.2.]
9. Russell, *Human Knowledge*, p. 479.
10. For the individual, participation in a ritual may also have other functions – e.g. a cathartic psychological one – but this, in my view, is outside the purview of the social anthropologist.
11. As this book may be read by American as well as by English anthropologists I need to emphasise that the term *culture*, as I use it, is not that all-embracing category which is the subject matter of American cultural anthropology. I am a social anthropologist and I am concerned with the social structure of Kachin *society*. For me the concepts of culture and society are quite distinct. 'If society is taken to be an aggregate of social relations, then culture is the content of those relations. Society emphasises the human component, the aggregate of people and the relations between them. Culture emphasises the component of accumulated resources, immaterial as well as material, which the people inherit, employ, transmute, add to, and transmit.' Firth, *Elements of Social Organisation*, p. 27. For the somewhat different use of the term culture current among American anthropologists see Kroeber, *Nature of Culture*, and Kroeber and Kluckhohn, *Culture*.

2.2

Ritualisation in Man (1966)

It has become plain that the various contributors to this symposium use the key term *ritual* in quite different ways. The ethologists are consistent with one another; Professor Hinde's definition will serve for all: 'ritualisation refers to the evolutionary changes which the signal movements of lower vertebrates have undergone in adaptation to their function in communication'. Such a definition has no relevance for the work of social anthropologists. Unfortunately, although *ritual* is a concept which is very prominent in anthropological discourse, there is no consensus as to its precise meaning. This is the case even for the anthropologist contributors to this symposium; for example, I myself use the term in a different way from Professor Fortes whose paper immediately follows my own.[1] Even so certain major differences between the positions of the ethologist and the social anthropologist need to be noted. For the ethologist, ritual is adaptive repetitive behaviour which is characteristic of a whole species; for the anthropologist, ritual is occasional behaviour by particular members of a single culture. This contrast is very radical. Professor Erikson has suggested, by implication, that we may bridge the gap by referring to 'culture groups' as 'pseudo-species'.[2] This kind of analogy may be convenient in certain very special kinds of circumstance, but it is an exceedingly dangerous kind of analogy. It is in fact precisely this analogy which provides the basis for racial prejudice wherever we encounter it. It cannot be too strongly emphasised that ritual, in the anthropologist's sense, is in no way whatsoever a genetic endowment of the species.

Anthropologists are in the main concerned with forms of behaviour which are not genetically determined. Three types of such behaviour may be distinguished:

(1) Behaviour which is directed towards specific ends and which, *judged by our standards of verification*, produces observable results in a strictly mechanical way . . . we can call this 'rational technical' behaviour.

(2) Behaviour which forms part of a signalling system and which serves to 'communicate information' not because of any mechanical link between means and ends but because of the existence of a culturally defined communication code . . . we can call this 'communicative' behaviour.

(3) Behaviour which is potent in itself in terms of the cultural conventions of the actors but *not* potent in a rational-technical sense, as specified in (1), or alternatively behaviour which is directed towards evoking the potency of occult powers even though it is not presumed to be potent in itself . . . we can call this 'magical' behaviour.

These distinctions commonly apply to aspects of individual acts rather than actions considered as wholes, but crude examples are: (1) cutting down a tree, (2) an Englishman shaking hands, (3) an Englishman swearing an oath.

The orthodox convention in anthropology, to which Professor Fortes still adheres, is to reserve the term *ritual* for behaviours of class (3) only and to call behaviours of class (2) by some other term, e.g. etiquette, ceremonial. For complex reasons which cannot be developed here I myself hold that the distinction between behaviours of class (2) and behaviours of class (3) is either illusory or trivial so that I make the term *ritual* embrace both categories.

Although swearing an oath can be a brief and simple action which all anthropologists would rate as ritual, a 'typical' ritual, as conceived by most anthropologists, would be a performance of a much more prolonged and complex kind . . . e.g. the whole sequence of operations surrounding the disposal of the dead. It is characteristic of such complex ritual sequences that they have a 'structure' which is in a crude sense analogous to a prose passage in that the sequence as a whole is self-segmented into elements of decreasing scale. Where, in a prose passage, we can distinguish successively paragraphs, sentences, phrases, words, syllables, phonemes, so in a complex ritual we can distinguish sub-sequences and ritual elements of different 'levels'. Professor Turner's paper provides some illustrations of this point.[3] Professor Turner's paper also demonstrates the enormous complexity of the problems which face the anthropologist who seeks to interpret or decode the 'messages' embodied in a ritual sequence. One feature, however, is very plain and virtually universal. A ritual sequence when performed 'in full' tends to be very repetitive; whatever the message may be that is supposed to be conveyed, the redundancy factor is very high.

Here it is worth reflecting on a general point of communication theory. If a sender seeks to transmit a message to a distant receiver against a background of noise, ambiguity is reduced if the same message is repeated over and over again by different channels and in different forms. For example, suppose that on a windy day I want to say something to a companion standing on a hill some distance away. If I want to make sure that my message has been understood I will not only repeat it several times over in different forms, but I will add visual signals to my verbal utterances. In so far as human rituals are 'information-bearing procedures' they are message systems of this redundant, interference-loaded, type.

From an ethologist's point of view an example of ritualised adaptation in *Homo sapiens* is the capacity for speech, but the evolutionary developments which resulted in this capacity took place a very long time ago and the findings of contempory anthropology have absolutely no bearing on the matter. Nevertheless, the relation between speech and ritual (in the anthropologist's sense) deserves close attention. When anthropologists talk about ritual they are usually thinking, primarily, of behaviours of a non-verbal kind, so it is worth reminding my anthropologist colleagues that (as I use the term) speech itself is a form of ritual; non-verbal ritual is simply a signal system of a different, less specialised, kind. To non-anthropologist readers I would simply say that the focus of interest in this paper is the relation between ritual as a communication system and ordinary speech as a communication system.

Professor Lorenz told us that the ethologists have two prime questions to ask about any ritual sequence.[4] The philo-genetic question 'How come?' and the functional question 'What for?'. The enormous complexity of the ritual sequences which anthropologists have to study makes any guesses of the 'How come?' type more or less absurd. Functional explanations of the 'What for?' kind may look more plausible. A very general, very plausible, functional proposition is that an isolated human society must be so organised and so adapted to its environment that it can survive. For the sake of simplicity let us then confine our attention to ultra-primitive human societies as they existed in their erstwhile self-sufficient economic condition.

One common characteristic of such primitive peoples is that they are illiterate. Another is that each particular primitive society seems to be very well adapted to the environmental conditions in which it exists. Thus the Eskimos, the Australian Aborigines, and the Kalahari Bushmen all manage to live quite comfortably in conditions in which an ordinary white man would find himself incapable of sustaining life at all. This is possible because these people are somehow capable of transmitting from generation to generation an extremely elaborate body of information about the local topography, and its contents and how it may best be utilised. How is this achieved in the absence of any written documents or of any kind of formal schooling? In brief, my answer is that the performance of ritual serves to perpetuate knowledge which is essential for the survival of the performers. But this is altogether too slick. I need to explain how.

The first point to understand is an important difference between the kind of verbal classifications which we employ and those found in primitive society.

We act as if we believed that all the things in the world belonged to 'natural kinds' – I am not concerned here with the truth or falsity of this proposition but only with the fact that in our ordinary life we tend to assume that we can ask of any object whatsoever: 'What is it?', and that there is a unique particular correct answer to that question. In primitive society, on the other hand, it is broadly true that only things which are in some sense useful or significant to the speaker have names. With this limitation it is still possible for the classification of the things in the world to be enormously complex, but in general the vocabulary of primitive peoples is not cluttered up with concepts which are wholly irrelevant to the user – as is invariably the case with written languages.

Put in a different way one may say that when man attaches a particular category word to a class of objects he *creates* that class of objects. If an object has no name it is not recognised as an object and in a social sense 'it does not exist'. Thus the world of primitive man's experience contains fewer kinds of things than the world of our experience; but the fewer things all have names and they are all of social significance.

It is characteristic of many ritual and mythical sequences in primitive society that the actors claim to be recapitulating the creation of the world and that this act of creation is mythologised as a list of names attached to persons, places, animals, and things. The world is created by the process of classification and the repetition of the classification of itself perpetuates the knowledge which it incorporates.

The next point I would emphasise is that although the languages of primitive non-literate peoples contain relatively few concepts which are purely abstract, this does not mean that primitive man is incapable of apprehending abstract notions. To take a case in point which is of cardinal importance to anthropologists the words nature and culture are both high-level abstractions. The social anthropologist sees his task as being specifically concerned with what is cultural rather than natural. I think it goes almost without saying that concepts such as nature and culture do not occur in primitive languages, yet primitive people must still be aware of the distinction nature/culture, for a concern with the distinction between man and non-man must always have a central place in any system of human knowledge. But how? I only have time to provide a single illustration. Professor Lévi-Strauss has recently drawn attention to a group of South American Indian myths which constantly harks back to a contrast between raw meat and cooked meat on the one hand (that is a human – i.e. *cultural* – mode of transformation) and a contrast between fresh vegetables and putrid vegetables on the other (that is a non-human – i.e. *natural* – mode of transformation).[5] Raw meat, cooked meat, fresh vegetables, putrid vegetables are all explicit concrete things, but placed in a pattern these few categories can serve to express the highly abstract idea of the contrast between cultural process and natural process. Furthermore, this patterning can be expressed *either* in *words* (*raw, cooked, fresh, putrid*) and displayed in a myth, *or* alternatively it can be expressed in *things* with the ritual manipulation of appropriate objects. *In such ways as this the patterning of ritual procedures can serve as a complex store of information.*

We ourselves ordinarily store our information by patterned arrangements of a small number of simple signs marked on paper or punched cards or computer tape. Primitive peoples use the objects which they employ in ritual in analogous ways – the message is not conveyed by the objects as such but by their patterned arrangement and segmental order.[6]

Non-literate peoples have every incentive to economise in their use of information-storing messages. Since all knowledge must be incorporated in the stories and rituals which are familiar to the living generation, it is of immense advantage if the same verbal categories (with their corresponding objects) can be used for multiple purposes.

Broadly speaking the information which must be stored and transmitted from generation to generation is of two kinds: (1) information about nature: that is about the topography, the climate, usable and dangerous plants, animals, inanimate things, and so on; (2) information about society: the relations of men to other men, the nature of social groups, the rules and constraints which make social life possible. These broad categories of 'information about nature' and 'information about society' belong to separate fields, and no great ambiguity is likely to be introduced if we express both kinds of information in the same kind of language. Australian totemism which has fascinated but baffled several generations of anthropologists seems to be a phenomenon of this kind. Australian Aborigines classify the categories of human society by means of the same words which they use to classify the categories of nature so that a group of human beings, a verbal concept, and a class of natural objects may all be thought of as representations of the same entity. It is only because we use words in a different way that we find this strange. For example, it makes sense in English to say: 'A kangaroo is a different species of mammal from a wallaby.' It also makes sense to say: 'A Londoner is a different kind of man from a Parisian.' But in English it does *not* make sense to economise with concepts and say: 'A kangaroo–Londoner is a different species-kind of mammal–man from a wallaby–Parisian.' But it is only because of our linguistic conventions that this last sentence does not make sense – it is in no way ambiguous. The peculiarity of Australian totemic myths and rituals is that they constantly make condensed statements of precisely this kind.[7] Since modern computers do the same thing I cannot really feel that our own normal mode of expression can properly be said to be the more highly developed; it merely takes up more verbal space.

A rather similar point is that in primitive society it is hardly possible to make any clear-cut distinction between information which is expressed in verbal form and information which is expressed in non-verbal action.

A generation ago Jane Harrison, Malinowski, and others made a clear distinction between myth on the one hand and ritual on the other, and argued that ritual was the dramatisation of myth, while myth was a recapitulation of the drama, but this seems to me too simple. 'Ritual' as one observes it in primitive communities is a complex of words and actions. There are doubtless some purposes for which it is useful to distinguish, within this complex, actions which are ritual, words which are spells, and words which are myth. But it is not the case that the words are one thing and the rite another. The uttering of the words is itself a ritual.

Educated peoples in our society have such a mastery of grammatically ordered speech that they can put *all* forms of information into words – and most of us tend to imagine that this is a normal capacity. But I think that Dr Bernstein will bear me out if I say that it is not.[8] For ordinary non-literate people there are many kinds of information which are never verbalised but *only* expressed in action. Verbal utterance then consists of chunks of conventionalised and often wholly non-grammatical 'noise behaviour'. *In its proper context* the totality of the behaviour – words plus action – conveys meaning, but the meaning is conveyed because of what we know already about the context; if you record the performance on a tape and play it back, you will often find that what was said, taken by itself, was virtually gibberish.

This is true even of 'ordinary conversation' among intimates but it is much more true of ritual sequences. In any ritual performance some of the actors are likely to be novices but the majority will have participated in the 'same kind' of ritual many times before; indeed the stability of the form of the ritual through time is dependent on the fact that it is familiar to most of the actors. But while the familiarity of the actors makes it possible to reproduce past performances with little variation this same familiarity allows the combination of words and actions to be drastically condensed without final loss of communication value . . . precisely as happens in the conversation of intimates.

One implication of this is that attempts to interpret the 'meaning' of ritual by anthropological intuition must be viewed with great scepticism. This kind of interpretation has been very common in the past and we have had some examples put forward even in this symposium. I would assert quite categorically that no interpretation of ritual sequences in man is possible unless the interpreter has a really detailed knowledge of the cultural matrix which provides the context for the rite under discussion. The gap between Sir James Frazer and Professor Turner is very wide and it seems to me that Sir Maurice Bowra has not fully appreciated this fact.[9]

The distinction between condensed, action-supported, ritual utterance and fully grammatical ordered utterance does not lie between primitive man and modern man but between the thought of non-literate, partially verbalised man, and that of fully literate, fully verbalised man. Both types occur in our own society. In the latter mode concepts are apprehended as *words* which exist as distinct abstract entities capable of manipulation by themselves irrespective of any particular referent; in the former mode concepts lie in the relations between things, and between persons, and between persons and things, so that words are a kind of amalgam linking up things and persons. In this mode of thought the name of a thing or of an action is not separable from that to which it refers, and things and persons which belong to the same verbal category are thereby fused together in a manner which to us seems 'mystical' or 'non-logical'. I do not rate this as *primitive* thinking but rather as *economical* thinking. In primitive society the whole of knowledge has to be encapsulated into a memorisable set of formalised actions and associated phrases: in such circumstances the use of a separate word for every imaginable category (which is the normal objective of literate people) would be a thoroughly wasteful procedure.

These really are the main points I want to make in this brief paper:

(1) In ritual, the verbal part and the behavioural part are not separable.

(2) As compared with written or writable speech the 'language' of ritual is enormously condensed; a great variety of alternative meanings being implicit in the same category sets. This is also an attribute of mathematics. Primitive thought is transformational in the sense that mathematics is transformational.

(3) We tend to think this odd because of our own speech habits, but in fact our writable speech contains a vast amount of redundancy. This redundancy is valuable when, as is normally the case with us, we wish to convey information at a distance by means of speech alone without reference to context. In contrast the more condensed message forms which are characteristic of ritual action are generally appropriate to all forms of communication in which speaker and listener are in face-to-face relations and share a common body of knowledge about the context of the situation. In these restricted circumstances, which are normal in primitive society, the condensed and multi-faceted concepts to which I have been referring do not lead to ambiguity. In any event in ritual sequences the ambiguity latent in the symbolic condensation tends to be eliminated again by the device of thematic repetition and variation. This corresponds to the communication engineer's technique of overcoming noisy interference by the use of multiple redundancy.

Notes

Under the auspices of the Royal Society, Sir Julian Huxley organised a discussion on 'Ritualisation of Behaviour in Animals and Man', in June 1965. There were contributions from ethologists (including Robert Hinde and Konrad Lorenz), psychologists (Erik Erikson and R. D. Laing), sociologists (including Edward Shils), cultural and art historians (Sir Maurice Bowra and E. H. Gombrich), as well as several contributions on film (including two by David Attenborough). The anthropologists present included G. Morris Carstairs, Meyer Fortes, and Victor Turner, as well as Leach. This is Leach's paper, as published in the *Philosophical Transactions of the Royal Society of London*, Series B, 251 (1966). The references made by Leach in this paper are mostly to other presentations made at that discussion.

1. Fortes, 'Religious Premises in Divinatory Ritual'.
2. Erikson, 'Ontogeny of Ritualisation'.
3. Turner, 'Syntax of Symbolism'.
4. Lorenz, 'Ritualisation in Psycho-Social Evolution'.

5. Lévi-Strauss, *Le Cru et le cuit.*
6. Here again Professor Turner's paper ('Syntax of Symbolism') provides some exemplification of what I mean.
7. Lévi-Strauss, *Le Totémisme aujourd'hui.*
8. [Eds.: This is presumably a reference to Basil Bernstein who must have been at the conference. No paper by him is published in the proceedings but see his *Class, Codes, and Control.*]
9. Bowra, 'Dance, Drama, and the Spoken Word'.

2.3

Ritual (1968)

Citations in the *Oxford English Dictionary* from the fourteenth century on reveal two distinct trends of common usage for the words *rite* (*ritual*), *ceremony* (*ceremonial*), and *custom* (*customary*). On the one hand, these terms have been used interchangeably to denote any non-instinctive predictable action or series of actions that cannot be justified by a 'rational' means-to-ends type of explanation. In this sense the English custom of shaking hands is a ritual, but the act of planting potatoes with a view to a harvest is not. But rationality is not easily defined. A psychiatrist may refer to the repeated hand-washing of a compulsive neurotic as a 'private ritual' even when, in the actor's judgement, the washing is a rational means to cleanliness. Likewise, a high-caste Hindu is required by his religion to engage in elaborate washing procedures to ensure his personal purity and cleanliness; the rationality or otherwise of such actions is a matter of cultural viewpoint. In this case, anthropologists who distinguish between ritual cleanliness and actual cleanliness are separating two aspects of a single state rather than two separate states. The distinction between cleanliness and dirt is itself a cultural derivation that presupposes an elaborate hierarchy of ritual values. If 'non-rationality' is made a criterion of *ritual*, it must be remembered that the judge of what is rational is the observer, not the actor.

The other trend of usage has been to distinguish the three categories: ritual, ceremony, and custom. Ritual is then usually set apart as a body of custom specifically associated with religious performance, while ceremony and custom become residual categories for the description of secular activity. Where religion is the specific concern of fully institutionalised churches, as in Europe, a religious delimitation of ritual is unambiguous and easy to apply; in the exotic societies studied by anthropologists this is not the case. Recognising this problem, some contemporary authors have argued that ambiguity in the data may be overcome by the multiplication of analytic concepts.[1] Gluckman, in particular, favours an elaborate vocabulary giving clearly distinguishable meanings to *ceremony*, *ceremonious*, *ritual*, *ritualism*, and *ritualisation*, but the circumstances in which precision might be useful are hard to imagine. Ritual is clearly not a fact of nature but a concept, and definitions of concepts should be operational; the merits of any particular formula will depend upon how the concept is being used.

In short, to understand the word *ritual* we must take note of the user's background and prejudices. A clergyman would probably assume that all ritual necessarily takes place inside a church in accordance with formally established rules and rubrics; a psychiatrist may be referring to the private compulsions of individual patients; an anthropologist will probably mean 'a category of standardised behaviour (custom) in which the relationship between the means and the end is not "intrinsic" ',[2] but he will interpret this definition loosely or very precisely according to individual temperament. The associated terms *ceremonial* and *customary* are also used in very varied ways, even by professionals from the same discipline.

Historical usage of the concept

The views of Robertson Smith[3] are of particular relevance in arriving at a definition of terms. As a former professor of divinity, he advocated the study of comparative religion. He assumed that the boundaries between what is religion and what is not religion are self-evident. Modern religion (Christianity) consists of beliefs (dogma) and practices (ritual); 'in the antique religions mythology takes the place of dogma'. Myth is merely 'an explanation of a religious usage'. Hence, 'the study of ancient religion must begin, not with myth, but with ritual and traditional usage'. The thesis that religion consists essentially of beliefs *and* rituals and that, of the two, ritual is in some sense prior has influenced many later writers in many different fields.

Durkheim[4] defined religion as 'a unified system of beliefs and practices (rites) relative to sacred things, that is to say, things set apart and forbidden – beliefs and practices which unite into a single moral community called a Church, all those who adhere to them'. Rites, for Durkheim, are 'the rules of conduct which prescribe how a man should comport himself in the presence of these sacred objects'.[5] Negative (ascetic) rites are the customs that we commonly label *taboo.* Positive rites include 'imitative rites', which are in fact the same practices that Frazer called 'homeopathic magic'; 'representative or commemorative rites', which are the cults of ancestor worship; sacrifice; and piacular rites, or memorials to misfortune, such as mourning. The overprecision of Durkheim's classification leads to some difficulties. He asserts dogmatically that 'the division of the world into two domains, the one containing all that is sacred, the other all that is profane, is the distinctive trait of religious thought'.[6] In his system, magic belongs to the sphere of the profane, even though 'magic, too, is made up of beliefs and rites'.[7]

The same set of rituals may readily be classified in other ways. Thus van Gennep proposed a category to cover all individual life-crisis ceremonials (e.g. those associated with birth, puberty, marriage, death) and also recurrent calendric ceremonials such as birthdays and New Year's Day.[8] He called these 'rites of passage'. In practice, van Gennep's schema has proved more useful than Durkheim's.[9]

If Durkheim seems to be excessively rigid, Frazer, who was Robertson Smith's pupil, errs in the opposite direction. In the pages of *The Golden Bough* (1890) the words *custom*, *ceremonial*, *rite*, and *ritual* seem to be interchangeable. Belief and rite are assumed to be so closely interdependent that if evidence concerning either is available the author may confidently 'conjecture' as to the other, which he does very freely. Employing similar assumptions, later writers have felt entitled to make the most sweeping reconstructions of ancient religious systems on the basis of slender archaeological residues of ritual practice.[10]

A more profitable development of Robertson Smith's theme was the enquiry by Jane Harrison into the relationship between ritual and art.[11] Harrison noted that the Greek word *drama* is derived from *dromenon* (religious ritual, literally: 'things done'). She attached special importance to Durkheim's category of 'imitative rites': 'Primitive man . . . tends to re-enact whatever makes him feel strongly; any one of his manifold occupations, hunting, fighting, later ploughing and sowing, provided it be of sufficient interest and importance, is material for a *dromenon* or rite.'[12] Thus ritual is seen as a magical dramatisation of ordinary activities, while in turn the drama is a secular recapitulation of ritual. Although ritual is distinguished from non-ritual by the presence or absence of a religious context, the details of this distinction remain imprecise.

Harrison was a classical scholar who profited from the writings of anthropologists; the succeeding generation of anthropologists in turn profited from hers. Malinowski and Radcliffe-Brown introduced the concept of functionalism into British social anthropology; they were both indebted to Harrison, though both were also, and quite independently, the propagators of Durkheim's ideas. The concept of 'ritual value', which Radcliffe-Brown developed in *The Andaman Islanders* and later writings, is essentially that espoused by Harrison. Objects to which ritual value attaches are objects that are socially important for secular reasons. Radcliffe-Brown, however, added the proposition that the performance of ritual generates in the actors certain 'sentiments' that are advantageous to the society as a whole. In their discussions of this theme both Radcliffe-Brown and Malinowski tend to assume that economic value depends upon utility rather than scarcity, and they attempt to distinguish ritual value as something other than economic value. Radcliffe-Brown shows that the Andamanese attached 'ritual value' to objects (including foods) that were scarce luxuries, but he makes an unnecessary mystery of this fact. Karl Marx had a much clearer understanding of what is, after all, our common experience. Marx (in *Capital*) observed that the value of commodities in the market is quite different from the value of the same goods considered as objects of utility. He distinguishes the extra value that goods acquire by becoming market commodities as 'fetishistic value'. This concept is closely akin to Radcliffe-Brown's 'ritual value', though in Marx's argument the magical element is only an aspect of the commodity value, rather than the value as a whole. Furthermore, where Radcliffe-Brown urged that ritual is to the advantage of society, Marx claimed that it is to the disadvantage of the individual producer. The Marxist thesis is that in the activities of the secular market – where all values are supposed to be measured by the strictest canons of rationality – judgements are in fact influenced by mystical non-rational criteria. A full generation later

Mauss (in *The Gift*), developing his general theory of gift exchange from an entirely different viewpoint, reached an identical conclusion. Exchanges that *appear* to be grounded in secular, rational, utilitarian needs turn out to be compulsory acts of a ritual kind in which the objects exchanged are the vehicles of mystical power.

Of the authors I have mentioned, Durkheim, Harrison, Radcliffe-Brown, and Mauss all started out with the assumption that every social action belongs unambiguously to one or the other of two readily distinguishable categories: the non-rational, mystical, non-utilitarian, and sacred or the rational, common-sense, utilitarian, and profane. Each author would clearly like to distinguish a specific category, *ritual*, which could refer unambiguously and exhaustively to behaviour relevant to things sacred. Each author ends up by demonstrating that no such discrimination is possible – that all 'sacred things' are also, under certain conditions, 'profane things', and vice versa. Malinowski sought to avoid this dilemma. For him, the essential issue was that of rationality rather than religion. Those who followed Frazer in thinking of magic as 'a false scientific technique' necessarily classed magic as a profane activity, but according to Malinowski, primitive man has a clear understanding of the difference between a technical act and a magical rite. Magic and religion both belong to a single sphere, the magico-religious; '. . . every ritual performance, from a piece of primitive Australian magic to a Corpus Christi procession, from an initiation ceremony to the Holy Mass, is a traditionally enacted miracle. . . . Man needs miracles not because he is benighted through primitive stupidity, [or] through the trickery of a priesthood . . . but because he realises at every stage of his development that the powers of his body and of his mind are limited'.[13]

But if ethnography offers little support to Durkheim, it offers still less to Malinowski. Most people in most societies have only the haziest ideas about the distinction either between sacred and profane or between rational and non-rational; it is a scholastic illusion to suppose that human actions are everywhere ordered to accord with such discriminations. Some authors still hold that a specific category is delimited by the phrase 'behaviour accounted for by mystical action': in my view they are mistaken.

Ritual and communication

In this whole discussion two elements are involved which have so far been scarcely mentioned. Human actions can serve to *do* things, that is, alter the physical state of the world (as in lighting a bonfire), or they can serve to *say* things. Thus, the Englishman's handshake makes a complicated statement such as, 'I am pleased to meet you and willing to converse.' All speech is a form of customary behaviour, but, likewise, all customary behaviour is a form of speech, a mode of communicating information. In our dress, in our manners, even in our most trivial gestures we are constantly 'making statements' that others can understand. For the most part these statements refer to human relationships and to status.

The actions that 'say things' in this way are not as a rule intrinsically different from those that 'do things'. If I am cold, I am likely to put on more clothes, and this is a rational action to alter the state of the world; but the kinds of clothes I put on and the way I wear them will serve to 'say things' about myself. Almost every human action that takes place in culturally defined surroundings is divisible in this way; it has a technical aspect which does something and an aesthetic, communicative aspect which says something.

In those types of behaviour that are labelled ritual by any of the definitions so far discussed, the aesthetic, communicative aspect is particularly prominent, but a technical aspect is never entirely absent. The devout Christian eats and drinks as part of a sacrament, but he also says grace as a preface to an ordinary meal. These are plainly 'ritual' matters. But it is equally a matter of 'ritual' that whereas an Englishman would ordinarily eat with a knife and fork, a Chinese would use chopsticks, and an Indian his right hand (but not his left, which for complex reasons is deemed polluted).

The meaning of ritual

Whether we use a narrow or a broad definition of ritual, one major problem is that of interpretation. What does ritual mean? If a ritual act be deemed to say something, how do we discover what it says? Clearly the actor's own view is inadequate. With minor variations the ritual of the Christian Mass is the same throughout Christendom, but each individual Christian will explain the performance by reference to his own sectarian doctrine. Such doctrines vary quite widely; the social scientist who seeks to understand why a particular ritual sequence possesses the content and form that he observes can expect little help from the rationalisations of the devout. But intuition is equally unreliable. Sacrifice, in the sense of the ritual killing of an animal victim, is an institution with a world-wide distribution. How can we explain this? Why should this particular kind of rite be considered an appropriate kind of action in the situations in which it is observed? There is no lack of theory. Some argue that the victim is identified with God and then sacramentally eaten; others that the victim is a gift or a bribe to the gods; others that the victim stands in substitution for the giver of the sacrifice; others that the victim is a symbolic representation of sin; and so on. All these explanations may be true or partly true for particular situations, but they cannot all be true at once, and none of them reaches into the heart of the problem, which is, Why should the killing of an animal be endowed with sacramental quality at all?

Some interpretative approaches are more clearly formulated than others and deserve special attention. Radcliffe-Brown postulated that human beings always manipulate their thought categories consistently.[14] We can discover what a ritual symbol means by observing the diverse uses of that symbol in both ritual and secular contexts. This is a powerful but by no means foolproof interpretative device. For example, the English speak of 'high' status versus 'low' status. We might then suppose that in ritual drama the person who is 'higher' will always be superior. Up to a point this applies. Persons of authority are raised on a dais; a suppliant kneels; an orator stands when his audience sits. But there are also situations where persons of extreme eminence sit (e.g. a king on his throne) when all others stand. The regularities are not simple.

This should not surprise us. In seeking to understand ritual we are, in effect, trying to discover the rules of grammar and syntax of an unknown language, and this is bound to be a very complicated business.

Lévi-Strauss is inclined to see ritual procedures as integral with processes of thought.[15] The drama of ritual breaks up the continuum of visual experience into sets of categories with distinguishable names and thereby provides us with a conceptual apparatus for intellectual operations at an abstract and metaphysical level. Such an approach implies that we should think of ritual as a language in a quite literal sense. Various theorems of communication engineering and of structural linguistics should thus be applicable. We can, for example, start to investigate the role played by 'redundancy' in ritual. Do binary contrasts in ritual correspond to phonemic contrasts in verbal speech forms? Can we discover, in any particular culture, rules concerning the development of a ritual sequence that would be comparable to the rules of generative grammar which Chomsky suggests must govern the modes by which each individual composes a verbal utterance?[16] This is a field in which exploration has hardly begun.

Ritual as social communication

Most modern anthropologists would agree that culturally defined sets of behaviours can function as a language, but not all will accept my view that the term *ritual* is best used to denote this communicative aspect of behaviour. Although we are still very much in the dark as to how ritual behaviours manage to convey messages, we understand roughly what the messages are about and at least part of what they say. Social anthropologists and sociologists alike claim that their special field is the study of systems of social relationship. This notion of social relationship is a verbal derivation based on inference. We do not observe relationships; we observe individuals behaving towards one another in customary, ritually standardised ways, and whatever we have to say about social relationships is, in the last analysis, an interpretation of these 'ritual' acts. All of us in our private daily lives manipulate the symbols of an intricate behavioural code, and we readily decode the behavioural messages of our associates; this we take for granted. Comparable activities on a collective scale in the context of a religious institution are rated mysterious and irrational. Yet their functional utility seems plain enough. Our day-to-day relationships depend upon a mutual knowledge and mutual acceptance of the fact that at any particular time any two individuals occupy different positions in a highly complex network of status relationships; ritual serves to reaffirm what these status differences are. It is characteristic of all kinds of ritual occasion that all participants adopt special forms of dress, which emphasise in an exaggerated way the formal social distinctions that separate one individual from another. Thus, ritual serves to remind the congregation just where each member stands in relation to every other and in relation to a larger system. It is necessary for our day-to-day affairs that we should have these occasional reminders, but it is also reassuring. It is this reassurance perhaps that explains why, in the absence of scientific medicine, ritual forms of therapy are often strikingly successful.

Here the argument seems to have come full circle. For if ritual be that aspect of customary behaviour that 'says things' rather than 'does things' (cf. Parsons's instrumental–expressive dichotomy), how is it that, in the view of the actors (and even of some analysts), ritual may 'do things' as well as 'say things'. The most obvious examples are healing rituals which form a vast class and have a world-wide distribution, but here we may also consider role-inversion rituals, which Gluckman has classed as 'rituals of rebellion' and which he perceives as fulfilling a positive cathartic function.[17]

Ritual as power

From the viewpoint of the actor, rites can alter the state of the world because they invoke power. If the power is treated as inherent in the rite itself, the analyst calls the action magic; if the power is believed to be external to the situation – a supernatural agency – the analyst says it is religious. Current argument on this theme is highly contentious, and I must declare my own position: I hold that the rite is prior to the explanatory belief. This will be recognised as essentially the view of Robertson Smith.

The concept of power itself is a derivation. We observe as an empirical fact that an individual A asserts dominance over another individual B, we observe that B submits to A, and we say that 'A has power over B.' And then in a ritual context we observe another individual A^1 going through a performance that he believes will coerce a fourth individual B^1; or alternatively, we observe B^1 making a ritual act of submission to an unseen presence C^1. The normal classification declares that the acts of A and B are rational but that the acts of A^1 and B^1 are irrational. To me it seems that they are all actions of the same kind. The 'authority' by which A is able to coerce and control the behaviour of B in a secular situation is just as abstract and metaphysical as the magical power by which A^1 seeks to coerce B^1 or the religious power that B^1 seeks to draw from C^1. Ideas about the relations between supernatural agencies and human beings or about the potency of particular ritual behaviours are modelled on first-hand experience of real-life relationships between real human beings. But conversely, every act by which one individual asserts his authority to curb or alter the behaviour of another individual is an invocation of metaphysical force. The submissive response is an ideological reaction, and it is no more surprising that individuals should be influenced by magical performances or religious imprecations than that they should be influenced by the commands of authority. The power of ritual is just as actual as the power of command.

Ritual as belief

Unlike Robertson Smith, Tylor assumed the priority of belief over ritual.[18] In England a neo-Tylorian view has a number of contemporary advocates. According to their argument, it is the belief accompanying the behaviour, rather than any quality of the behaviour itself, that distinguishes ritual. Since the participants in a religious ritual claim that their actions are designed to alter the state of the world by bringing coercive influence upon supernatural agencies, why should we not accept this statement at its face value? Why invoke the proposition that the actions in question are, as Durkheim would have it, 'symbolic representations of social relationships'? Goody counterposes the intellectualised interpretation of social behaviour made by the observer to the statement of the actor himself. 'What happens, then,' writes Goody, 'is that symbolic acts are defined in opposition to rational acts and constitute a residual category to which "meaning" is assigned by the observer in order to make sense of [the] otherwise irrational. . . .'[19] Ritual acts are to be interpreted in the context of belief: they mean what the actors say they mean. This commonsense approach clearly has its attractions. Yet it may be argued that if culturally defined behaviour can only be interpreted by the actors, all cross-cultural generalisation is impossible, and all attempts to make a rational analysis of the irrational must necessarily be fallacious.[20] In contrast, I, along with other Durkheimians, continue to insist that religious behaviour cannot be based upon an illusion.

Jane Harrison's thesis that 'ritual is a dramatisation of myth' was reformulated by Malinowski in the assertion that 'myth is a charter for social action'. According to this argument, myth and ritual are not merely interdependent; they jointly provide a model for 'correct' moral attitudes in secular life. But although it is easy to cite examples in which rituals enshrine in a quite straightforward way the most strongly felt values of society, there are many striking exceptions. The characters of myth frequently break all the moral conventions of mundane society in the most glaring way, and in many rituals the actors are required to behave in a manner precisely contrary to that which they would be expected to adopt in ordinary life. Two very different types of explanation have been offered for facts of this kind. One sees this role inversion as symbolic; the events of myth and ritual refer to the space–time of 'the other world'; they belong to Durkheim's category of the *sacred*, and to express this fact their content systematically inverts whatever is appropriate to 'this world', the *profane*. In contrast, Gluckman, in an argument that has wide application,[21] stresses the aggressive elements present in role-reversal ceremonies, which he aptly names 'rituals of rebellion'.[22] The performers, he suggests, act out in dramatic form hostilities that are deeply felt but may not be expressed in normal secular relationships. This acted aggression serves as a cathartic release mechanism, and by relieving tension these inverted behaviours actually serve to strengthen the moral code they appear to deny. It is an ingenious argument but hard to validate. Once again we are faced with the difficulty that sharply contrasted interpretations seem to afford partial explanations of the same ethnographic facts, so that choice of theory becomes a matter of personal predilection.

Nineteenth-century positivist thinkers made a triadic distinction between reason, magic, and religion. Various authors have attempted to fit ritual to this triad and also to the two dichotomies: sacred–profane, rational–non-rational. Some of the resulting difficulties have been considered. It is argued that no useful distinction may be made between ritual acts and customary acts but that in discussing ritual we are concerned with aspects of behaviour that are expressive (aesthetic) rather than instrumental (technical). Ritual action, thus conceived, serves to express the status of the actor *vis-à-vis* his environment, both physical and social; it may also serve to alter the status of the actor. When ritual functions in this latter sense, it is a manifestation of power; thus, the universal belief in the potency of ritual action is by no means an illusion. No attempt has been made to discuss the forms of ritual. Any form of secular activity, whether practical or recreational, can be stylised into dramatic performance and made the focus of a ritual sequence. Such stylisation tends to distort the secular norm in either of two directions: the emphasis may be ascetic, representing the intensification of formal restraint, or ecstatic, signifying the elimination of restraint. Ascetic and ecstatic elements are present in most ceremonial sequences, and the contrast may form part of the communication code.[23] Finally, it has been stressed that even among those who have specialised in this field there is the widest possible disagreement as to how the word ritual should be used and how the performance of ritual should be understood.

Notes

This essay was written as an entry for *The International Encyclopaedia of Social Sciences*, published in 1968.

1. For example Firth, 'Ceremonies for Children', p. 46; Wilson, 'Nyakyusa Ritual', p. 240; Gluckman, 'Les Rites de passage', pp. 20–4.
2. Goody, 'Religion and Ritual', p. 159.
3. Smith, *Religion of the Semites.*
4. Durkheim, *Elementary Forms*, p. 47.
5. Ibid., p. 41.
6. Ibid., p. 37.
7. Ibid., p. 42.
8. van Gennep, *Les Rites de passage.*
9. Gluckman, 'Les Rites de passage'.
10. Hooke (ed.), *Myth, Ritual, and Kingship.*
11. Harrison, *Themis*, and *Ancient Art and Ritual.*
12. Durkheim, *Elementary Forms*, p. 49.
13. Malinowski, *Sex, Culture, and Myth*, pp. 300–1.
14. Radcliffe-Brown, *The Andaman Islanders.*
15. Lévi-Strauss, *The Savage Mind.*
16. Chomsky, *Syntactic Structures.*
17. Gluckman, 'Les Rites de passage'.
18. Tylor, *Primitive Culture.*
19. Goody, 'Religion and Ritual', p. 157.
20. Ibid., p. 155.
21. See Norbeck, *Religion in Primitive Society*, pp. 205–11.
22. Gluckman, 'Les Rites de passage'.
23. Leach, 'Cronus and Chronos' (I.2.4, below), and 'Time and False Noses' (I.2.5, below).

2.4

Cronus and Chronos (1953/1961)

My starting point in this essay is simply *time* as a word in the English language. It is a word which we use in a wide variety of contexts and it has a considerable number of synonyms, yet is oddly difficult to translate. In an English–French dictionary *time* has one of the longest entries in the book; time is *temps*, and *fois*, and *heure*, and *age*, and *siècle*, and *saison*, and lots more besides, and none of these is a simple equivalent; *temps* perhaps is closest to English *time*, but *beau temps* is not a 'lovely time'!

Outside of Europe this sort of ambiguity is even more marked. For example, the language of the Kachin people of North Burma seems to contain no single word which corresponds at all closely to English *time*; instead there are numerous partial equivalents. For example, in the following expressions the Kachin equivalent of the word *time* would differ in every case:

The *time* by the clock is	*ahkying*
A long *time*	*na*
A short *time*	*tawng*
The present *time*	*ten*
Spring *time*	*ta*
The *time* has come	*hkra*
In the *time* of Queen Victoria	*lakhtak, aprat*
At any *time* of life	*asak*

and that certainly does not exhaust the list. I do not think a Kachin would regard these words as in any way synonyms for one another.

This sort of thing suggests an interesting problem which is quite distinct from the purely philosophical issue as to what is the *nature* of Time. This is: How do we come to have such a verbal category as *time* at all? How does it link up with our everyday experiences?

Of course in our own case, equipped as we are with clocks and radios and astronomical observatories, time is a given factor in our social situation; it is an essential part of our lives which we take for granted. But suppose we had no clocks and no scientific astronomy, how then should we think about time? What obvious attributes would time then seem to possess?

Perhaps it is impossible to answer such a very hypothetical question, and yet, clocks apart, it seems to me that our modern English notion of time embraces at least two different kinds of experience which are logically distinct and even contradictory.

Firstly, there is the notion of repetition. Whenever we think about measuring time we concern ourselves with some kind of metronome; it may be the ticking of a clock or a pulse beat or the recurrence of days or moons or annual seasons, but always there is something which repeats.

Secondly, there is the notion of non-repetition. We are aware that all living things are born, grow old, and die, and that this is an irreversible process.

I am inclined to think that all other aspects of time, duration for example or historical sequence, are fairly simple derivatives from these two basic experiences:

(1) that certain phenomena of nature repeat themselves;
(2) that life change is irreversible.

Now our modern sophisticated view tends to throw the emphasis on the second of these aspects of time. 'Time', says Whitehead, 'is sheer succession of epochal duration': it goes on and on.[1] All the same we need to recognise that this irreversibility of time is psychologically very unpleasant. Indeed, throughout the world, religious dogmas are largely concerned with denying the final 'truth' of this common-sense experience.

Religions of course vary greatly in the manner by which they purport to repudiate the 'reality' of death; one of the commonest devices is simply to assert that death and birth are the same thing – that birth follows death, just as death follows birth. This seems to amount to denying the second aspect of time by equating it with the first.

I would go further. It seems to me that if it were not for religion we should not attempt to embrace the two aspects of time under one category at all. Repetitive and non-repetitive events are not, after all, logically the same. We treat them both as aspects of 'one thing', *time*, not because it is rational to do so, but because of religious prejudice. The idea of Time, like the idea of God, is one of those categories which we find necessary because we are social animals rather than because of anything empirical in our objective experience of the world.[2]

Or put it this way. In our conventional way of thinking, every interval of time is marked by repetition; it has a beginning and an end which are 'the same thing' – the tick of a clock, sunrise, the new moon, New Year's Day . . . but every interval of time is only a section of some larger interval of time which likewise begins and ends in repetition . . . so, if we think in this way, we must end by supposing that 'Time itself' (whatever that is) must repeat itself. Empirically this seems to be the case. People *do* tend to think of time as something which ultimately repeats itself; this applies equally to Australian Aborigines, Ancient Greeks, and modern mathematical astronomers.[3] My view is that we think this way not because there is no other possible way of thinking, but because we have a psychological (and hence religious) repugnance to contemplating either the idea of death or the idea of the end of the universe.

I believe this argument may serve to throw some light upon the representation of time in primitive ritual and mythology. We ourselves, in thinking about time, are far too closely tied to the formulations of the astronomers; if we do not refer to time as if it were a coordinate straight line stretching from an infinite past to an infinite future, we describe it as a circle or cycle. These are purely geometrical metaphors, yet there is nothing intrinsically geometrical about time as we actually experience it. Only mathematicians are ordinarily inclined to think of repetition as an aspect of motion in a circle. In a primitive, unsophisticated community the metaphors of repetition are likely to be of a much more homely nature: vomiting, for example, or the oscillations of a weaver's shuttle, or the sequence of agricultural activities, or even the ritual exchanges of a series of interlinked marriages. When we describe such sequences as 'cyclic' we innocently introduce a geometrical notation which may well be entirely absent in the thinking of the people concerned.

Indeed in some primitive societies it would seem that the time process is not experienced as a 'succession of epochal durations' at all; there is no sense of going on and on in the same direction, or round and round the same wheel. On the contrary, time is experienced as something discontinuous, a repetition of repeated reversal, a sequence of oscillations between polar opposites: night and day, winter and summer, drought and flood, age and youth, life and death. In such a scheme the past has no 'depth' to it, all past is equally past; it is simply the opposite of now.

It is religion, not common sense, that persuades men to include such various oppositions under a single category such as *time*. Night and day, life and death are logically similar pairs only in the sense that they are both pairs of contraries. It is religion that identifies them, tricking us into thinking of death as the night-time of life and so persuading us that non-repetitive events are really repetitive.

The notion that the time process is an oscillation between opposites – between day and night or between life and death – implies the existence of a third entity – the 'thing' that oscillates, the 'I' that is at one moment in the daylight and at another in the dark, the 'soul' that is at one moment in the living body and at another in the tomb. In this version of animistic thinking the body and the grave are simply alternative temporary residences for the life-essence, the soul. Plato, in the *Phaedo*, actually uses this metaphor explicitly: he refers to the human body as the *tomb* of the soul (psyche). In death the soul goes from this world to the underworld; in birth it comes back from the underworld to this world.

This is of course a very common idea both in primitive and less primitive religious thinking. The point that I want to stress is that this type of animism involves a particular conception of the nature of time and, because of this, the mythology which justifies a belief in reincarnation is also, from another angle, a mythological representation of 'time' itself. In the rest of this essay I shall attempt to illustrate this argument by reference to familiar material from classical Greece.

At first sight it may appear that I am arguing in a circle. I started by asking what sort of concrete real experience lies at the back of our abstract notion of time. All I seem to have done so far is to switch from the oscillations of abstract time to the oscillation of a still more abstract concept, soul. Surely that is worse than ever. For us, perhaps, yes. We can 'see' time on a clock; we cannot see people's souls; for us, souls are more abstract than time. But for the Greeks, who had no clocks, time was a total abstraction, whereas the soul was thought of as a material substance consisting of the marrow of the spine and the head, and forming a sort of concentrated essence of male semen. At death, when the body was placed in the tomb this marrow coagulated into a live snake. In Greek ancestor cults the marked emphasis on snake worship was not a residue of totemism: it was simply that the hero–ancestor in his chthonic form was thought to be an actual snake. So for the Greeks, of the pre-Socratic period anyway, the oscillation of the soul between life and death was quite materially conceived – the soul was either material bone-marrow (in the living body) or it was a material snake (in the tomb).[4]

If then, as I have suggested, the Greeks conceived the oscillations of time by analogy with the oscillations of the soul, they were using a concrete metaphor. Basically it is the metaphor of sexual coitus, of the ebb and flow of the sexual essence between sky and earth (with the rain as semen), between this world and the underworld (with marrow-fat and vegetable seeds as semen), between man and woman. In short, it is the sexual act itself which provides the primary image of time. In the act of copulation the male imparts a bit of his life-soul to the female; in giving birth she yields it forth again. Coitus is here seen as a kind of dying for the male; giving birth as a kind of dying for the female. Odd though this symbolism may appear, it is entirely in accord with the findings of psychoanalysts who have approached the matter from quite a different point of view.[5]

All this, I suggest, throws light upon one of the most puzzling characters in classical Greek mythology, that of Cronus, father of Zeus. Aristotle (*de Mundo*, ch. 7) declared that Cronus (Kronos) was a symbolical representation of Chronos, Eternal Time – and it is apparently this association which has provided our venerable Father Time with his scythe.[6] Etymologically, however, there is no close connection between *kronos* and *chronos*, and it seems unlikely that Aristotle should have made a bad pun the basis for a major issue of theology, though this seems to be the explanation generally put forward. Whatever may have been the history of the Cronus cult – and of that we know nothing – the fact that at one period Cronus was regarded as a symbol for Time must surely imply that there was something about the mythological character of Cronus which seemed appropriate to that of a personified Time. Yet it is difficult for us to understand this. To us Cronus appears an entirely disreputable character with no obvious temporal affinities.

Let me summarise briefly the stories which relate to him:

(1) Cronus, King of the Titans, was the son of Uranus (sky) and Ge (earth). As the children of Uranus were born, Uranus pushed them back again into the body of Ge. Ge to escape this prolonged pregnancy armed Cronus with a sickle with which he castrated his father. The blood from the bleeding phallus fell into the sea and from the foam was born Aphrodite (universal fecundity).

(2) Cronus begat children by his sister Rhea. As they were born he swallowed them. When the youngest, Zeus, was born, Rhea deceived Cronus by giving him a (phallic) stone wrapped in a cloth instead of the new-born infant. Cronus swallowed the stone instead of the child. Zeus thus grew up. When Zeus was adult, Cronus vomited up his swallowed children, namely: Hades, Poseidon, Hestia, Hera, Demeter, and also the stone phallus, which last became a cult object at Delphi. Zeus now rebelled against King Cronus and overthrew him; according to one version he castrated him. Placed in restraint, Cronus became nevertheless the beneficent ruler of the Elysian Fields, home of the blessed dead.[7]

(3) There had been men when King Cronus ruled but no women; Pandora, the first woman, was created on Zeus' instructions. The age of Cronus was a golden age of bliss and plenty, when the fields yielded harvests without being tilled. Since there were no women, there was no strife! Our present age, the age of Zeus, will one day come to an end, and the reign of Cronus will then be resumed. In that moment men will cease to grow older: they will grow younger. Time will repeat itself in reverse: men will be born from their graves. Women will once more cease to be necessary, and strife will disappear from the world.[8]

(4) About the rituals of Cronus we know little. In Athens the most important was the festival known as Kronia. This occurred at harvest time in the first month of the year and seems to have been a sort of New Year celebration. It resembled in some ways the Roman Saturnalia (Greek Cronus and Roman Saturn were later considered identical). Its chief feature seems to have been a ritual reversal of roles – masters waiting on slaves and so on.[9]

What is there in all this that makes Cronus an appropriate symbol for Time? The third story certainly contains a theme about time, but how does it relate to the first two stories? Clearly the time that is involved is not time as we ordinarily tend to think of it – an endless continuum from past to future. Cronus' time is an oscillation, a time that flows back and forth, that is born and swallowed and vomited up, an oscillation from father to mother, mother to father, and back again.

Some aspects of the story fit well enough with the views of Frazer and Jane Harrison about Corn Spirits and Year Spirits (*eniautos daimon*).[10] Cronus, as the divine reaper, cuts the 'seed' from the 'stalk' so that Mother Earth yields up her harvest. Moreover, since harvest is logically the end of a sequence of time, it is understandable enough that, given the notion of time as oscillation, the change over from year's end to year's beginning should be symbolised by a reversal of social roles – at the end point of any kind of oscillation everything goes into reverse. Even so the interpretation in terms of vegetation magic and nature symbolism does not get us very far. Frazer and Jane Harrison count their Corn Spirits and Year Spirits by the dozen and even if Cronus does belong to the general family this does not explain why Cronus rather than any of the others should have been specifically identified as a symbol of Time personified.

My own explanation is of a more structural kind. Fränkel has shown that early Greek ideas about time underwent considerable development.[11] In Homer *chronos* refers to periods of empty time and is distinguished from periods of activity which are thought of as days (*ephemeros*). By the time of Pindar this verbal distinction had disappeared, but a tendency to think of time as an 'alternation between contraries', active and inactive, good and bad, persisted. It is explicit in Archilochus (seventh century BC). In the classical period this idea underwent further development so that in the language of philosophy, time was an oscillation of vitality between two contrasted poles. The argument in Plato's *Phaedo* makes this particularly clear. Given this premise, it follows logically that the 'beginning of time' occurred at that instant when, out of an initial unity, was created not only polar opposition but also the sexual vitality that oscillates between one and the other – not only God and the Virgin but the Holy Spirit as well.[12]

Most commentators on the Cronus myth have noted simply that Cronus separates sky from earth, but in the ideology I have been discussing the creation of time involves more than that. Not only must male be distinguished from female but one must postulate a third element, mobile and vital, which oscillates between the two. It seems clear that the Greeks thought of this third element in explicit concrete form as male semen. Rain is the semen of Zeus; fire the semen of Hephaestos; the offerings to the dead (*panspermia*) were baskets of seeds mixed up with phallic emblems;[13] Hermes the messenger of the gods, who takes the soul to Hades and brings back souls from the dead, is himself simply a phallus and a head and nothing more.

This last symbolic element is one which is found to recur in many mythological systems. The logic of it seems clear. In crude pictorial representation, it is the presence or absence of a phallus which distinguishes male from female, so, if time is represented as a sequence of role reversals, castration stories linked up with the notion of a phallus trickster who switches from side to side of the dichotomy 'make sense'. If Kerényi and Jung are to be believed there are psychological explanations for the fact that the 'messenger of the gods' should be part clown, part fraud, part isolated phallus[14] but here I am concerned only with a question of symbolic logic. If time be thought of as alternation, then myths about sex reversals are representations of time.

Given this set of metaphors Cronus' myth *does* make him 'the creator of time'. He separates sky from earth but he separates off at the same time the male vital principle which, falling to the sea, reverses itself and becomes the female principle of fecundity. The shocking part of the first story, which at first seems an unnecessary gloss, contains, as one might have expected, the really crucial theme. So also in the second story the swallowing and vomiting activities of Cronus serve to create three separate categories – Zeus, the polar opposites of Zeus, and a material phallus. It is no accident that Zeus' twice-born siblings are the five deities named, for each is the 'contrary' of Zeus in one of his recognised major aspects:

the three females are the three aspects of womanhood, Hestia the maiden, Hera the wife, Demeter the mother; they are the opposites of Zeus in his roles as divine youth (*kouros*), divine husband, divine father and divine son (Dionysus). Hades, lord of the underworld and the dead, is the opposite of Zeus, lord of the bright day and the living; Poseidon, earth shaker, god of the sea (salt water), is the opposite of Zeus, sky shaker (thunderer), god of rain and dew.

The theme of the child which is swallowed (in whole or part) by its father and thereby given second birth, crops up in other parts of Greek mythology – e.g. in the case of Athena and of Dionysus. What is peculiar to the Cronus story is that it serves to establish a mythological image of interrelated contraries, a theme which recurs repeatedly in mature Greek philosophy. The following comes from Cary's translation of the *Phaedo*:

> 'We have then,' said Socrates, 'sufficiently determined this – that all things are thus produced, contraries from contraries?'
>
> 'Certainly.'
>
> 'What next? Is there also something of this kind in them, for instance, between all two contraries a mutual twofold production, from one to the other, and from the other back again . . . ?'[15]

For men who thought in these terms, 'the beginning' would be the creation of contraries, that is to say the creation of male and female not as brother and sister but as husband and wife. My thesis then is that the philosophy of the *Phaedo* is already implicit in the gory details of the myth of Cronus. The myth is a creation myth, not a story of the beginning of the world, but a story of the beginning of time, of the beginning of becoming.

Although the climate may seem unfamiliar, this theme is not without relevance for certain topics of anthropological discussion. There is for instance Radcliffe-Brown's doctrine concerning the identification of alternating generations, whereby grandfather and grandson tend to exhibit 'solidarity' in opposition to the intervening father. Or there is the stress which Lévi-Strauss has placed upon marriage as a symbol of alliance between otherwise opposed groups.[16] Such arguments when reduced to their most abstract algebraic form may be represented by a diagram such as this:

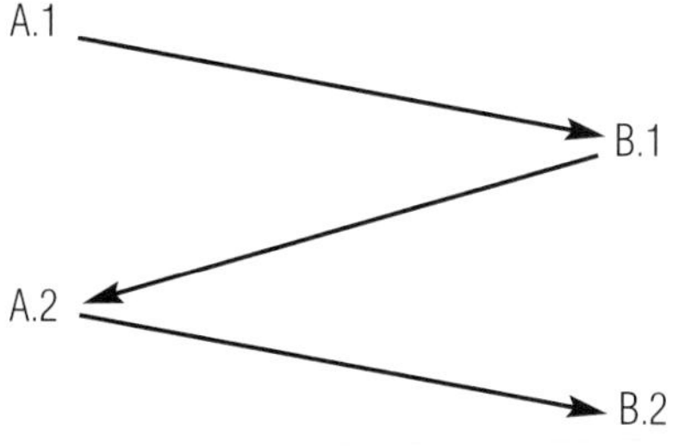

In Radcliffe-Brown's argument the As and the Bs, that are opposed yet linked, are the alternating generations of a lineage; in Lévi-Strauss's, the As and the Bs are the males of contending kin groups allied by the interchange of women.

My thesis has been that the Greeks tended to conceptualise the time process as a zigzag of this same type. They associated Cronus with the idea of time because, in a structural sense, his myth represents a separation of A from B and a creation of the initial arrow A→B, the beginning of life which is also the beginning of death. It is also nicely relevant that Heraclitus should have defined 'a generation' as a period of thirty years, this being calculated 'as the interval between the procreation of a son by his father and the procreation of a son's son by the son', the interval, that is A.1→B.1→A.2.[17]

I don't want to suggest that all primitive peoples necessarily think about time in this way, but certainly some do. The Kachins whom I mentioned earlier have a word *majan*, which, literally, ought to mean 'woman affair'. They use it in three main contexts to mean (1) warfare, (2) a love-song, and (3) the weft threads of a loom. This seems to us an odd concatenation yet I fancy the Greeks would have understood it very well. Penelope sits at her loom, the shuttle goes back and forth, back and forth, love and war, love and war; and what does she weave? You can guess without looking up your *Odyssey* – a *shroud* of course, the time of Everyman. 'Tis love that makes the world go round; but women are the root of all evil.[18]

Notes

This essay, and 'Time and False Noses' which follows it, first appeared, in 1953 and 1955 respectively, in *Explorations*, a journal published from Toronto University. The texts which appear here are based on those which were republished in *Rethinking Anthropology* in 1961, as 'Two Essays Concerning the Symbolic Representation of Time'. Leach took the opportunity to incorporate some comments and corrections from the Cambridge classicist, M. I. (later Sir Moses) Finley.

1. Whitehead, *Science and the Modern World*, p. 158.
2. Hubert, 'Le Rituel', p. 248; Hubert and Mauss, 'Étude de la représentation du temps'.
3. Hoyle, *Nature of the Universe*, p. 108.
4. Onians, *Origins of European Thought*; Harrison, *Prolegomena*.
5. Roheim, *Animism, Magic, and the Divine King*, pp. 20–6.
6. Rose, *Handbook of Greek Mythology*, p. 69, n. 1.
7. Frazer, *Gloden Bough*; Roscher, *Lexikon der Griechischen Mythologie*; Nilsson, *Geschichte der Griechischen Religion*, i, pp. 510–17.
8. Hastings, *Encyclopaedia of Religion and Ethics*, i, pp. 192–200.
9. In general see Nilsson, *Griechischen Religion*.
10. Frazer, *Golden Bough*; Harrison, *Themis*.
11. Fränkel, *Früh-Griechischen Denkens*.
12. Cf. Cornford, 'Mystery Religions'.
13. Harrison, *Themis*, and *Prolegomena*.
14. See Radin, *The Trickster*, pp. 173–211 and the commentaries by Jung and Kerényi.
15. Plato, *Phaedo* (Cary trans.), p. 141.
16. Lévi-Strauss, 'L'Analyse structurale'.
17. Fränkel, *Früh-Griechischen Denkens*, pp. 251–2.
18. See Onians, *Origins of European Thought*, refs. to *kairos*. The Greek Ares, god of war, was paramour of Aphrodite goddess of love.

2.5

Time and False Noses (1955/1961)

Briefly my puzzle is this. All over the world men mark out their calendars by means of festivals. We ourselves start each week with a Sunday and each year with a fancy-dress party. Comparable divisions in other calendars are marked by comparable behaviours. The varieties of behaviour involved are rather limited yet curiously contradictory. People dress up in uniform, or in funny clothes; they eat special food, or they fast; they behave in a solemn restrained manner, or they indulge in licence.

Rites de passage, which mark the individual's social development – rituals of birth, puberty, marriage, death – are often similar. Here too we find special dress (smart uniform or farcical make-believe), special food (feast or fast), special behaviour (sobriety or licence). Now why?

Why should we demarcate time in this way? Why should it seem appropriate to wear top hats at funerals, and false noses on birthdays and New Year's Eve?

Frazer explained such behaviours by treating them as survivals of primitive magic. Frazer may be right, but he is inadequate. It is not good enough to explain a world-wide phenomenon in terms of particular, localised, archaic beliefs.

The oddest thing about time is surely that we have such a concept at all. We experience time, but not with our senses. We don't see it, or touch it, or smell it, or taste it, or hear it. How then? In three ways:

Firstly we recognise repetition. Drops of water falling from the roof; they are not all the same drop, but different. Yet to recognise them as being different we must first distinguish, and hence define, time-intervals. Time-intervals, durations, always begin and end with 'the same thing', a pulse beat, a clock strike, New Year's Day.

Secondly we recognise ageing, entropy. All living things are born, grow old, and die. Ageing is the irreversible fate of us all. But ageing and interval are surely two quite different kinds of experience? I think we lump these two experiences together and describe them both by one name, time, because we would like to believe that in some mystical way birth and death are really the same thing.

Our third experience of time concerns the rate at which time passes. This is tricky. There is good evidence that the biological individual ages at a pace that is ever slowing down in relation to the sequence of stellar time. The feeling that most of us have that the first ten years of childhood 'lasted much longer' than the hectic decade from forty to fifty is no illusion. Biological processes, such as wound healing, operate much faster (in terms of stellar time) during childhood than in old age. But since our sensations are geared to our biological processes rather than to the stars, time's chariot appears to proceed at ever-increasing speed. This irregular flow of biological time is not merely a phenomenon of personal intuition; it is observable in the organic world all around us. Plant growth is much faster at the beginning than at the end of the life cycle; the ripening of the grain and the sprouting of the sown grain proceed at quite different rates of development.

Such facts show us that the regularity of time is not an intrinsic part of nature; it is a man-made notion which we have projected into our environment for our own particular purposes. Most primitive peoples can have no feeling that the stars in their courses provide a fixed chronometer by which to measure all the affairs of life. On the contrary it is the year's round itself, the annual sequence of economic activities, which provides the measure of time. In such a system, since biological time is erratic, the stars may appear distinctly temperamental. The logic of astrology is not one of extreme fatalism, but rather that you can never be quite sure what the stars are going to get up to next.

But if there is nothing in the principle of the thing, or in the nature of our experience, to suggest that time must necessarily flow past at constant speed, we are not required to think of time as a constant flow at all. Why shouldn't time slow down and stop occasionally, or even go into reverse?

I agree that in a strictly scientific sense it is silly to pretend that death and birth are the same thing, yet without question many religious dogmas purport to maintain precisely that. Moreover, the make-believe that birth follows death is not confined to beliefs about the hereafter, it comes out also in the pattern of religious ritual itself. It appears not only in *rites de passage* (where the symbolism is often quite obvious) but also in a high proportion of sacrificial rites of a sacramental character. The generalisations first propounded by Hubert and Mauss and van Gennep have an extraordinarily widespread validity; the rite as a whole falls into sections, a symbolic death, a period of ritual seclusion, a symbolic rebirth.

Now *rites de passage*, which are concerned with demarcating the stages in the human life cycle, must clearly be linked with some kind of representation or conceptualisation of time. But the only picture of time that could make this death–birth identification logically plausible is a pendulum-type concept. All sorts of pictorial metaphors have been produced for representing time. They range from Heraclitus' river to Pythagoras' harmonic spheres. You can think of time as going on and on, or you can think of it as going round and round. All I am saying is that in fact quite a lot of people think of it as going back and forth.

With a pendulum view of time, the sequence of things is discontinuous; time is a succession of alternations and full stops. Intervals are distinguished, not as the sequential markings on a tape measure, but as repeated opposites, tick-tock tick-tock. And surely our most elementary experiences of time flow are precisely of this kind: day–night day–night; hot–cold hot–cold; wet–dry wet–dry? Despite the word *pendulum*, this kind of metaphor is not sophisticated; the essence of the matter is not the pendulum but the alternation. I would maintain that the notion that time is a 'discontinuity of repeated contrasts' is probably the most elementary and primitive of all ways of regarding time.

All this is orthodox Durkheimian sociology. For people who do not possess calendars of the Nautical Almanac type, the year's progress is marked by a succession of festivals. Each festival represents, for the true Durkheimian, a temporary shift from the Normal–Profane order of existence into the Abnormal–Sacred order and back again. The total flow of time then has a pattern which might be represented by such a diagram as this (Fig. 1):

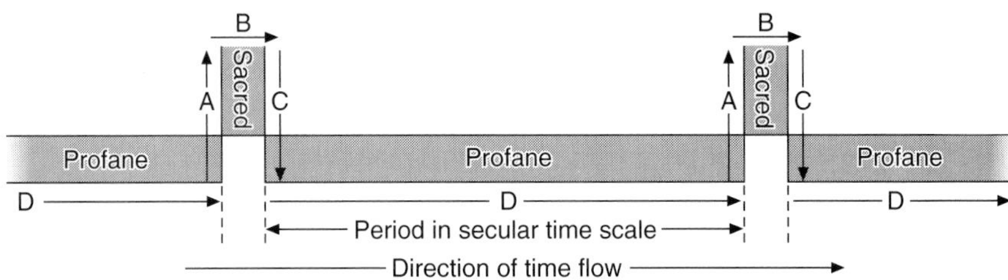

Fig. 1. Flow of Time.

Such a flow of time is man-made. It is ordered in this way by the societies (the 'moral persons' to use Durkheimian terminology) which participate in the festal rites. The rites themselves, especially sacrificial rites, are techniques for changing the status of the moral person from profane to sacred, or from sacred to profane. Viewed in this Durkheimian way, the total sequence embraces four distinct phases or 'states of the moral person'.

> Phase A. The rite of sacralisation, or separation. The moral person is transferred from the Secular–Profane world to the Sacred world; he 'dies'.
>
> Phase B. The marginal state. The moral person is in a sacred condition, a kind of suspended animation. Ordinary social time has stopped.
>
> Phase C. The rite of desacralisation, or aggregation. The moral person is brought back from the Sacred to the Profane world; he is 'reborn', secular time starts anew.
>
> Phase D. This is the phase of normal secular life, the interval between successive festivals.

So much for Durkheim, but where do the funny hats come in? Well, let me draw your attention to three features in the foregoing theoretical argument.

Firstly let me emphasise that, among the various functions which the holding of festivals may fulfil, one very important function is the ordering of time. The interval between two successive festivals of the same type is a 'period', usually a named period, e.g. 'week', 'year'. Without the festivals, such periods would not exist, and all order would go out of social life. We talk of measuring time, as if time were a concrete thing waiting to be measured; but in fact we *create time* by creating intervals in social life. Until we have done this there is no time to be measured.

Secondly, don't forget that, just as secular periods begin and end in festivals, so also the festivals themselves have their ends and their beginnings. If we are to appreciate how neatly festivity serves to order time, we must consider the system as a whole, not just individual festivals. Notice for example how the forty days between Carnival (Shrove Tuesday) and Easter is balanced off by the forty days between Easter and Ascension, or how New Year's Eve falls precisely midway between Christmas Eve and Twelfth Night. Historians may tell you that such balanced intervals as these are pure accidents, but is history really so ingenious?

And thirdly there is the matter of false noses, or to be more academic, role reversal. If we accept the Durkheimian analysis of the structure of ritual which I have outlined above, then it follows that the rituals of Phase A and the rituals of Phase C ought, in some sense, to be the reverse of one another. Similarly, according to the diagram, Phase B ought somehow to be the logical opposite to Phase D. But Phase D, remember, is merely ordinary secular life. In that case a logically appropriate ritual behaviour for Phase B would be to play normal life back to front.

Now if we look at the general types of behaviour that we actually encounter on ritual occasions we may readily distinguish three seemingly contradictory species. On the one hand there are behaviours in which formality is increased; men adopt formal uniform, differences of status are precisely demarcated by dress and etiquette, moral rules are rigorously and ostentatiously obeyed. An English Sunday, the church ceremony at an English wedding, the Coronation procession, university degree-taking ceremonials are examples of the sort of thing I mean.

In direct contrast we find celebrations of the fancy-dress party type, masquerades, revels. Here the individual, instead of emphasising his social personality and his official status, seeks to disguise it. The world goes in a mask, the formal rules of orthodox life are forgotten.

And finally, in a few relatively rare instances, we find an extreme form of revelry in which the participants play-act at being precisely the opposite to what they really are; men act as women, women as men, kings as beggars, servants as masters, acolytes as bishops. In such situations of true orgy, normal social life is played in reverse, with all manner of sins such as incest, adultery, transvestitism, sacrilege, and *lèse-majesté* treated as the natural order of the day.

Let us call these three types of ritual behaviour (1) formality, (2) masquerade, (3) role reversal. Although they are conceptually distinct as species of behaviour, they are in practice closely associated. A rite which starts with formality (e.g. a wedding) is likely to end in masquerade; a rite which starts with masquerade (e.g. New Year's Eve; Carnival) is likely to end in formality. In these puritanical days explicit role reversal is not common in our own society but it is common enough in the ethnographic literature and in accounts of mediaeval Europe. You will find such behaviours associated with funerals, or with *rites de passage* (symbolic funerals) or with the year's end (e.g. in Europe: Saturnalia and the Feast of Fools).

My thesis is then that *formality* and *masquerade*, taken together, form a pair of contrasted opposites and correspond, in terms of my diagram, to the contrast between Phase A and Phase C. *Role reversal* on the other hand corresponds to Phase B. It is symbolic of a complete transfer from the secular to the sacred; normal time has stopped, sacred time is played in reverse, death is converted into birth. This Good King Wenceslas symbolism is something which has a world-wide distribution because it makes logical sense independently of any particular folklorish traditions or any particular magical beliefs.

2.6

The Cult of Informality (1965)

Formality is something about which each of us is constantly making judgements. Every incident of regular social life has its proper position. I can no more attend a wedding in a dressing gown than I can take breakfast in a top hat, but, in the new society of 1965, dressing gowns are felt to be preferable. Stiff shirtedness in dress goes with diplomatic manoeuvres and incomprehensible legal contracts in small print; if I trust my neighbour I should not have to fake appearances by acting a part; honesty implies informality. Some people certainly feel that way, but is this cult of informality a general valuation or simply an aspect of the conflict of generations?

I find this difficult. The concepts formality–informality are ill defined, and used in different senses. Perhaps my response to these words is narrowly personal. I myself associate formality with two particular kinds of context; first, elaborate uniforms and etiquette such as are characteristic of court life in a centralised monarchy; and secondly, 'the formalities of the law' – customs sheds, lawyers offices, filling out forms in the Post Office – in other words, the whole apparatus of Weber's rational–legal bureaucracy.

Since we live no longer in a centralised monarchy but in a rational–legal bureaucracy, I am predisposed from the start to think that formality may be both decreasing and increasing at the same time according to its field of operation.

But my assumption that formality equates with aristocratic snootiness and bureaucratic red tape is not shared by all. Some hold that formality is typical of simple rather than complex social systems. Professor Max Gluckman, for example, has recently given a very elaborate definition of what he calls 'ritualisation', a concept close to 'formality'. For Gluckman 'ritualisation' is particularly characteristic of primitive societies in which the majority of individuals fill a wide variety of social roles in association with the same sets of associates. In such situations a high incidence of ritualisation is necessary in order to distinguish the particular role that any one individual is playing at any one time.[1] Well, it may be so, but let us stick to European history and a less academic vocabulary.

So far as formal etiquette is concerned the facts of the case seem plain enough. Ever since the middle of the eighteenth century the scope and rigour of formality has been on the decline, modes of dress and of address have become increasingly casual, precedence and protocol increasingly irrelevant, and this is generally true for most of western Europe. Significantly the same tendency is apparent in modern Japan, a newly 'westernised' country in which polite formality was at one time carried to extremes.

Some of the causal factors seem obvious. When all political power is vested in a narrowly delimited aristocracy it is functionally essential that the members of this elite shall be clearly distinguishable from all the rest, and that, within the elite itself, subtle differences of rank shall be precisely discriminated. Where so much may depend upon personal influence, deportment can assume a terrible significance. The extraordinary elaborations of costume and etiquette which prevailed among the ruling classes of the eighteenth century, or for that matter among the governing elite of British India during the twentieth century, are understandable in these terms. And so also in reverse, the lessening of the individual's dependence upon personal favour has gone along with a general decay in the interest paid to details of formal politeness; servility and polite formality go together.

But the correlation is not a simple one. There are some modern countries – Sweden is a case in point – which are egalitarian and permissive in some respects but exceptionally formal in others; and we ourselves are far from consistent. Most of us are no longer concerned as to whether the Lady Amelia is Lady Amelia X or Amelia, Lady X, yet the number of people who feel it appropriate that they should announce their births, marriages, deaths and betrothals in *The Times* or the *Daily Telegraph* seems constantly to increase and there are certainly many readers of *New Society* who are acutely sensitive to such magical letter combinations as FRS, DSc, and HonLittD. Since I hold a London and not an Oxbridge PhD/DPhil my Cambridge hostesses are constantly in a quandary. Is it Dr Leach or Mr Leach?[2] But how much worse the *faux pas* if an American acquaintance addresses me as Professor! These academic niceties are no less absurd than those of dukes and duchesses. Polite formality still has a place, though perhaps rather a different place.

Periwigs and anoraks

In this country, although the decline from periwigs and swords has been long term, the total collapse of the more traditional tricks of formality is quite recent. Among gentry and would-be gentry the complicated game of visiting cards was still in general vogue right up to the last world war – and even later in the surviving colonies and protectorates. For that matter gentlemen wore a white tie if they sat in the stalls at Covent Garden (they still do on first nights or if they are posing as an audience on TV); debutantes were presented at court, and so on and so forth. In contrast the established upper class now lean over so far in the opposite direction that their young will wear jeans and a dirty anorak in almost any situation; Savile Row suits are left to social climbers. Is this a matter of economics, of infuriating Dad, or merely a symptom of general loss of nerve among the former ruling class? As the Warden of All Souls recently remarked of Oxbridge donnery, such people are now besotted with 'Fear of Being Thought Behind the Times, Fear of Seeming to Claim Privilege, and Fear of Questioning the Equality of Everybody with Everybody Else'. And all these fears carry the implication that informality is the best policy.

It is intriguing to note just where bits and pieces of the once complex pattern of genteel etiquette have managed to survive. Manners in dress provide some striking examples. Messrs Moss Bros still hire out the appropriate grey toppers and morning suits (1) for weddings and (2) for the Royal Enclosure at Ascot, a curious but perhaps significant combination. The male dinner jacket is still a badge of formality but the occasions for its use have greatly changed; except among the very affluent it has become a public not a private garment. The once quite essential operation of 'dressing for dinner' *at home* is quite on its last legs. On the other hand the use of the much more uncomfortable (and therefore more formal?) white tie and tails has dwindled almost to the point of disappearance. In Cambridge, a former home of the most elaborate social snobberies, one can meet with gentlemen in lounge suits even at College Feasts and May Balls. On present showing tails will shortly be restricted to waiters, orchestra leaders, and Presidents of the Union.

There remains a variety of public functions for which a man will still put on evening dress (dinner jacket only) to provide his wife with an excuse for doing likewise, but the social obligation to conform precisely to a set style of dress is weakening all the time. There is a contrary aspect to this. Thirty years ago the dinner-jacket-wearing class was the only smart class and was narrowly defined by economic as well as social criteria; this is no longer true. Every man can now afford to be smart and a well-dressed Mod can spend just as much on his clothes as a well-dressed Etonian. But among the newly affluent it is only the very young who cultivate new fashions; the middle-aged imitate quite uncritically the dinner jacket conventions of their social superiors and society has conveniently created a whole new set of institutions of the Masonic-Rotary-Business-Firm-Convention type to provide opportunity for the wearing of formal dress. But these organisations are modelled on American rather than European prototypes and their membership is very definitely *not* drawn from the English upper and upper-middle strata which formerly set the standard of manners.

Up to a point the decline of formality in the context of domestic entertainment is a simple matter of economics. Cooking and evening dress do not go together. The cult of the formal dinner party at home could nowhere survive the end of domestic service. What then should we make of the elegant ladies and gents who still turn up in films and on the telly and in the glossy advertisements of weekend magazines? The advertisers presumably know their business. Perhaps the image of formality with its suggestion of a life of ease and luxury and dozens of servants in the background is competitive democracy's idea of Heaven, an unattainable Other World where peptic ulcers are no more. But if so, the climate of Heaven must change according to circumstance. An exuberant 'it was heavenly' can be applied equally to the informality of sunshine at St Tropez or the formality of tea at Buckingham Palace. So how do we distinguish one from the other? Given the proper context, bikinis on the beach are just as *correct* as the wigs and gowns in a court of law. Is a Beatle haircut any less of a uniform than that of a Louis XIV marquis?

Transition rites

Evidently we need to define our terms. Let us go back to the beginning where I noted that we use the contrast formality–informality in several different ways, not only to differentiate status, and to mark special occasions – especially transition rites such as funerals, weddings, and coronations – but also to create unambiguous precedents. It is not simply that a Major-General must be distinguished from a Lieutenant-Colonel or a bride from a widow; there is also the matter of getting the record straight.

How does this last category, legal formality, tie in with the polite formality of my earlier discussion? Legal formality is not something which we meet with only in government offices. It permeates our whole society and is constantly increasing. Its most typical and impressive manifestation is the English committee, with its elaborate apparatus of agenda, minutes, and attached documents, which has now penetrated right across the class system. The subtle use of 'on a point of order, Mr Chairman' is as powerful a political instrument on the parish council as it is in the House of Commons. The very people who acclaim informality in domestic relations are the first to object to informality in committee.

Although the majority of committees do not have the standing of organs of government they have intrinsically the same nature. Their proceedings must be conducted with due formality because they involve the exercise of power. Formerly, in England, all power derived from control over land and was the exclusive prerogative of a small landed aristocracy. Today the means of production have proliferated and the instruments of control have tended to become vested in corporate institutions. Committees, as the executive agents of such corporations, are the arbiters of property relations and they have taken upon themselves the mantle of formality which was formerly only appropriate to a Lord of the Manor adjudicating copyhold title in his Court Baron. In his own petty sphere every Secretary of Committee has the powers and functions of the Master of the Rolls.

A tricky point

The analysis so far shows that we are concerned with two cross-cutting pairs of variables, etiquette versus legalism and privacy versus publicity. The distinction formality–informality straddles all four categories. This raises a tricky point. How far is it consistent to set value on privacy and informality at the same time? If it is true that in England royalty is always the fountainhead of formal attitudes, how does the private–public antithesis apply to their case? The answer is distinctly skew.

Palaces are not private places; eighteenth-century monarchs took all their meals in public and hardly escaped the public gaze even in bed. Their modern successors are only slightly better off; telephoto cameras and an enthusiastic press ensure that all cats may look at kings. Yet the kind of formal behaviour which such people are required to exhibit has changed drastically. Half a century ago the most royal of royal functions required the monarch to dress up in imperial finery and sit on an elephant at a durbar in New Delhi; the modern equivalent is a fireside chat on Christmas afternoon. And here is the paradox; from the Queen's point of view the Christmas talk in front of arc lights and television cameras must be the most formal of formal occasions, but by our plebeian scheme of values the success of her performance is measured by the degree to which she manages to appear informal!

Perhaps the antithesis formality–informality is itself too simple. What do these words really mean?

One possible definition of a formal occasion might be: 'a situation in which individual behaviour is narrowly defined by social expectations and the compulsion to conform precisely to these social expectations is exceptionally high'. I leave on one side the Durkheimian question: what is the source of the expectation or the compulsion? Suffice that formal behaviour is predictable in form and restricted in scope. *Formality* is always role-defining; we recognise what the individual is by what he does. Sometimes the formality specifies the individual's role as a member of a class. 'That man in a funny conical hat is a policeman' and sometimes as the holder of a particular office. 'The man with the wig reaching down to his shoulders is the judge; the smaller wigs are only barristers.'

The contrasted state of *informality* is much less specific; it sometimes means unpredictable, sometimes anonymous.

In the intimate context of home life roles are fully defined by prior knowledge so that behaviour is roughly predictable without formality. This creates the illusion that an individual may act 'as he chooses'. In line with this it is now polite to offer the same freedom to even the most temporary member of the household. As in the case of royalty such a code of informality is self-destructive for it brings in its trail a denial of all privacy. The grand ladies of the eighteenth century held court for all and sundry in their bedrooms. This did not make their lives informal; very much the reverse.

But sometimes we stress 'informality' not because we want to be homely but because we want to be faceless. The prototype of this latter kind of behaviour is the masquerade – the actual wearing of masks in public places, and it is the explicit counterpart of formal rectitude. Where the public figure in his proper uniform must conform exactly to the moral conventions of his social position the same figure in a mask may indulge in all manner of licence – indeed he is expected to do so. But 'informal' behaviour in this sense is, in its way, just as

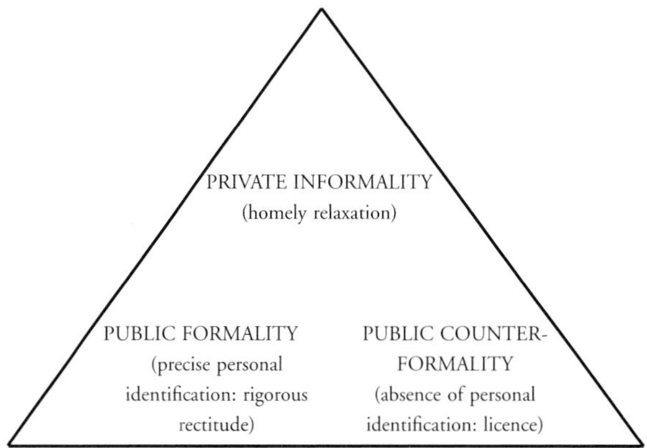

Fig. 1. Triad of Formalities.

narrowly defined and predictable and role-defining as 'formal' behaviour; Rockers and Mods have their uniforms as well as policemen and guardees.

So we have come back full circle to St Tropez and Buckingham Palace. Perhaps it may help if we re-sort our categories. Instead of a dichotomy formality–informality I suggest a triad (1) Private Informality; (2) Public Formality which emphasises individual status within a group of actors; and (3) Public Counter-formality which emphasises membership of an unstructured, unorganised group but does not distinguish the group into a hierarchy of castes and particular offices.

These three labels correspond to ideal types located at the corners of a triangle (see Fig. 1). Most actual situations will combine elements of all three.

We use these behaviour contrasts to express facts about the social system in which we live and if our valuations of such behaviours are changing it is because of underlying changes in the social system.

Eighteenth-century aristocratic formality with its subtle uniforms and etiquette and total lack of privacy served to distinguish minute differences in the social hierarchy. It concentrated all polite behaviour into the bottom left-hand corner of my diagram. The compulsive formalities of fashion now have a different function. Dominated as we are by bureaucratic assumptions concerning promotion according to merit, we like to deny the relevance of class while giving added emphasis to seniority. Hence, in all contexts, we tend to classify by age instead of by nobility. 'Teenagers', a newly defined group with a new name and a new place in society, must be distinguished by their formal attributes and so they wear special clothes and make special kinds of noise. But such labels distinguish the group not the individual; behaviours are predictable but faceless. In terms of my diagram they express *counter-formality* rather than *formality*.

The denial of class values has other aspects. We are not in fact entering a classless society but the significant class groupings are changing and our apparent informality in some traditionally formal contexts is a function of this fluidity.

Weird invention

In ossified class systems, classes tend to be endogamous and various social mechanisms ensure that this shall be so. Characteristically the pattern of inter-dining and the pattern of inter-marriage is then very similar. In the relatively rigid class structure which prevailed in this country at least as late as 1930 formal entertainment among the wealthy had a great deal to do with match-making; that weird upper class invention 'the London season' was concerned with nothing else. But today the erosion of educational privilege and the much greater opportunities of economic and social mobility have drastically modified the advantages of a class-endogamous marriage. The reshaping of formal dining patterns is a function of this particular social change. In America where this process has gone much further than in Europe, the new structures of power rest firmly on a base of common economic or occupational interest rather than on ties of kinship. The solidarity of such groups is much more easily expressed by saying 'people like us are the people who go to the same church and attend the same dining club (which meets once a month at the XYZ Hotel)' than by the earlier formula that 'people like us are those we ask to our homes, with whom our children inter-marry'. The locale of formal behaviour is adjusted accordingly.

But what about the grey toppers and the morning coats? So far the gist of my argument has been that in public matters, formality proper stays close to the locus of power. It has changed its place in society and become more diffuse but not necessarily less rigorous in its application. On the other hand, private domestic life among the relatively affluent seems genuinely to be more relaxed. How can we account for the exceptions to this principle? The dress-up dinner party is nearly dead; the grand wedding is very much alive.

The persisting and even expanding demand for formal marriage ceremonies is quite remarkable. There must be thousands of couples who never go near a church in the whole of their lives except to get christened, get married, or to watch a relative get buried. Why should it be felt worthwhile to spend a small fortune on a wedding get-up which will never be used again? The facts are difficult to quantify but I have the impression that over a wide spectrum of our society expensive weddings are replacing expensive funerals as a major status symbol; in any case both institutions remain very important. This is curious. One can make out some kind of rational case for a scheme of values in which owning a car and a telly is more important than having a house with decent plumbing and heating, but weddings are straight conspicuous consumption. Is there any more to it than that? How can one judge?

Change of status

There are, of course, very general grounds why weddings and funerals should always be formalised. The bride and the widow are persons whose social status is being changed. The new personality must be publicly displayed. Property relations are affected; everything must be done in a regular manner. Certainly too the details of the performance are very appropriate: these are the only two occasions on which an English woman wears a veil – on entering the married state and on leaving it. And at the crucial moment of transition, when she has no social personality, her face is veiled. But this still does not explain why a secular society, which tends in general to debunk all domestic formality, should make such a marked exception of these two cases. Anthropologists offer no help; they point out that what is at stake in a wedding is the legitimacy of the ultimate children rather than the status of the bride, and that funerals declare the interests of the heirs rather than their love for the deceased. True enough, but in contemporary English custom it is on the bride and the widow *as individuals* that fomality is concentrated. Why? The psychological and religious ramifications of that one lie outside the scope of this essay, but it may be significant that while we equate the bride with royalty, we should attempt to reduce royalty itself to a prototype of the domestic family.

So let me sum up. The editor who launched me on this journey posed what seemed a simple question: 'Why should informality be gaining in social prestige?' My answers are largely equivocation.

Firstly, I challenge the proposition itself, at least as a general rule. I admit that the values of a meritocracy have tended to replace the values of face and favour and that in the process, the personal relations of those who would formerly have been in a position to grant favours have become more relaxed, but at the same time the legal machinery through which the meritocracy itself selects its favoured sons has become more and more formalised. In providing opportunities for higher education or other forms of social advancement we act as if what mattered is not that justice be done but that justice should seem to be done. Every office-holder must have the correct diploma.

Secondly, I have emphasised that a break with previously established formal codes does not in itself indicate informality. The young of all social classes are as fashion conscious and convention bound as they have ever been. Both in hairstyle and in other ways their manners hark back to swashbuckling models from the sixteenth century, a period of most elaborate formalities.

But the uniforms of our contemporary young assert anonymous membership of an unstructured group (for example, Rockers) rather than status in a paramilitary organisation (for example, Boy Scouts) and I think we should distinguish accordingly between counter-formality and formality proper.

Thirdly, I admit that there has been a heightened evaluation of informal homeliness as an index of hospitality and friendliness. But here I feel doubtful. If such 'informal' behaviour becomes self-conscious it can quickly turn into a new kind of formality. The overall result could be a destruction of privacy rather than an enhancement of domesticity.

Yet finally, when one has said all this, a central puzzle remains. Some of the formal conventions of the old society survive in modified form as status symbols in the new. The most obvious are the formalities of birth, marriage, and death. Of these I have not been able to say anything except that the ancestors knew best.

Notes

This piece was first published in *New Society* on 8 July 1968, and was the first in a series under the title, 'Notions in Transition'.

1. [Eds: See Gluckman, 'Les Rites de passage'.]
2. [Eds: Leach here plays upon the point that Oxford, Cambridge, and Trinity College Dublin gave formal recognition only to each other's degrees.]

2.7

Once a Knight is Quite Enough (1981)

I have given this lecture on a number of previous occasions in a variety of different localities; my qualifications for doing so are personal and exceptional. Although there are parts of the City of London where British Knights of the Realm come two a penny, academic anthropologists of that ilk are uncommon. Among socio-cultural (as distinct from physical) anthropologists I can think of only four others besides myself: Sir Edward Tylor the nineteenth-century founder of British socio-cultural anthropology, Sir James Frazer the author of *The Golden Bough*, the late Sir Edward Evans-Pritchard, and his still-living contemporary, Sir Raymond Firth. And I seem to be quite alone in having attempted to use my expertise as a participant observer of exotic rituals to analyse the actual proceedings of initiation into knighthood. This may not strike you as an altogether serious lecture but it is, I can assure you, perfectly serious anthropology. What that indicates about the general nature of anthropology I leave you to decide!

To avoid any possible misunderstanding, let me emphasise that my lecture is in no way intended as a sideswipe at the British monarchy. Symbolic Heads of State play an important role in modern national and international relations and our British version of that frustrating office has much to be said in its favour as compared with the versions which we encounter elsewhere; the absolute distinction between symbol and reality which the British have achieved in their separation of hereditary Monarch and elected Prime Minister has a great deal to be said in its favour as compared with, say, your own system of elected Presidents. I am not one of the small band of British Republicans.

My first teacher in anthropology was Bronislaw Malinowski. The key point about Malinowski's anthropology was his thesis that the fieldworker must use his eyes and his personal experiences rather than just ask 'informants' about 'customs' which, for all he knew, might just be figments of the imagination. The data of anthropology come from real life not from travellers' tales. My present exercise is given in this same spirit. At a certain level of abstraction initiation rites the world over exhibit a marked similarity of structure. To demonstrate this fact I propose to make a comparison between a head-hunting ritual, which I observed in Borneo in 1947 just shortly after I had obtained my PhD degree, and the investiture into knighthood, which I underwent in London in 1975. The crucial episode in the former affair was the sacrifice of a large pig; in the latter it is the initiate knight who is the sacrificial pig.

In Britain an enthusiast can collect titles like other people collect postage stamps and even if you are not a philatelist of this sort you are still liable to accumulate these things one after another once you get on to the appropriate network. Some titles signify more than others. If a scientist is entitled to put the letters FRS after his name you can be sure that he really is a scientist of great distinction, though the duties of most Fellows of the Royal Society, as such, amount to very little except to decide which other scientists shall be entitled to a like honour. By contrast, the letters FBA which I myself can append to my name, though they purport to be indicators of a like sort, in fact provide a much less reliable guide to genuine distinction.

The Royal Society and the British Academy are private institutions, the Monarch's Honours List is a different matter. Every six months, at New Year and on the Queen's Birthday (which needless to say is not her real birthday!), and sometimes more frequently if there is a change of government, an Honours List is issued in the Queen's name. Most such lists contain several hundred names, ranging in distinction from peerages and Orders of Merit, at the top, to Police Medals for Bravery, at the bottom. The peers are later inducted into office in a special ceremony in the House of Lords, and Knights of the Garter and Knights of the Thistle have their own rigmarole at Windsor and in Edinburgh, and a fair number of people at the bottom end of the list receive their badges of honour locally by delegation. However the Queen herself deals with all the other more senior titles and a fair proportion of the minor ones. During 1975, when I myself received my knighthood, I reckon that she must personally have invested at least 500 of her faithful servants with their appropriate badges of honour. She clearly takes the job very seriously and does her homework. On the occasion that I am about to describe she initiated about 130 individuals and had something personal and relevant to say to each one of them.

Just precisely how the victims are selected is shrouded in mystery. A branch of the Prime Minister's Office known as the Office of the Patronage Secretary sifts the lists of nominees which are put forward by official bodies and also by members of the general public. Senior civil servants and officers in the armed forces collect badges of honour almost automatically as they move up in rank though there is a complex pecking order about the various sequences of letters; in the eyes of the recipient there is all the difference in the world between a KCB and a KCMG though for the rest of the public a knight is a knight and an oddity at that.

The acquisition of titles by unofficial individuals is more chancey. I have no idea just why I was nominated for a knighthood or by whom; however the network is such that any Provost of King's College Cambridge is likely to fetch up with a title of some sort in due course. If you are offered a title you can refuse, but I doubt if many people do; that would be taking matters too seriously. There are no perks except by accident. The only one that has come my way was that on one occasion a check-in clerk at Heathrow, noticing that I was a 'Sir',

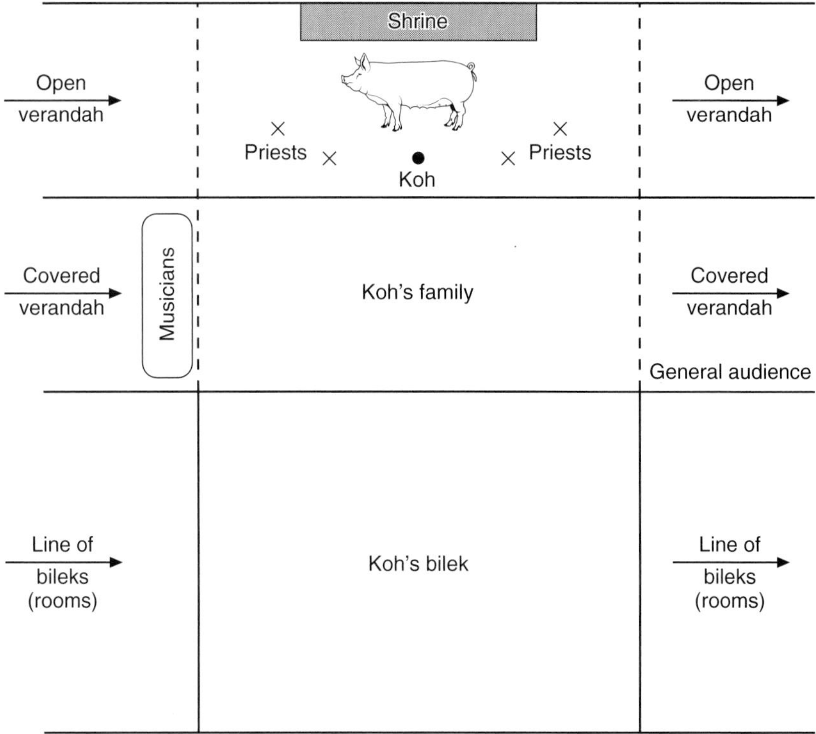

Fig. 1. Layout of penultimate episode of Pengulu Koh's head feast, Rijang River, Sarawak, September 1947.

immediately sent me off to the First Class lounge, where you get free drinks, even though I was travelling 'Tourist'. Alas it has never happened again![1]

But tonight I will leave on one side the finer subtleties of the present-day social significance of British knighthood. My concern is simply with the ethnography of the rite of initiation.

Let me start then (if only briefly) with the head feast which was performed in the house of Penghulu Koh on the Rejang River in Sarawak in September 1947.

On the basis that he had provided background support for an expedition which claimed to have taken two Japanese heads in 1944 Koh was giving what anthropological literature describes as a feast of merit. He was celebrating, in the most ostentatious style, his assumption of a new title of honour, the highest in rank that any Iban had claimed within living memory. The proceedings lasted for several days and culminated with the sacrifice of a large pig which was directly identified with Koh himself as donor of the sacrifice. This identity was indicated by the fact that Koh, who otherwise played a very passive role, placed his foot on the pig's back immediately before it was despatched. The pig had lain all night and for most of the previous day under an awning on the longhouse verandah in front of Koh's dwelling room (*bilek*) where it had received the tender attention of the women of Koh's domestic group. Behind the awning was a temporary construction of bamboo and decorative grass. This was described as 'the seat of Lang', Lang being the name of the ancestor–head-hunter–hero–deity to whom the pig was being sacrificed and whose blessings would, in return, bring beatitude to Koh's and his household. My first diagram shows this general layout. Notice that the donor and the sacrificial animal and the priests are in an area that lies midway between the secular congregation who were the witnesses of the deed and the throne of Lang which appeared to ordinary human eyes to be empty.

After the pig had been killed the donor withdrew and various things were done to the pig's blood and liver in order to take auspices. At the end of the day only a few token pieces of the pig's carcass were placed on Lang's shrine; the rest was removed and eventually distributed among the spectators. But these matters do not here concern us. Notice however the presence of an orchestra. The local equivalent of a Javanese gamelan played continuously throughout the sacrificial proceedings.

I have witnessed a variety of animal sacrifices in a variety of cultural contexts. The layout of the scene of action was always more or less the same and it included the following features: (1) a shrine, which, either in appearance or by name, was treated as a throne on which the deity had temporarily taken up his or her abode; (2) a place of sacrifice, which was reserved for the priestly participants including the donor and the victim; and (3) a lay congregation of onlookers or witnesses.

The place of sacrifice was in every case located mid-way between the shrine proper and the congregation. Other common features were that the whole area in which the sacrificial proceedings took place was marked off from the ordinary everyday world by boundary markers of some kind, and the presence of some kind of noise-making machinery which also functioned as a marker of discontinuity with normality. The noise sources varied – orchestras, drums, firecrackers, shotguns, human singers. The scale of such arrangements may vary enormously but the layout of a typical English parish church conforms to the general pattern and will give you an idea of what I am getting at.

The church precinct as a whole, including the churchyard, is fenced off from 'ordinary ground'. The churchyard commonly functions as a cemetery and is often thought to be haunted on that account. It is 'betwixt and between' the House of God and the World of Mammon.

But when we get inside the church we find that it is again marked off into segments of differentiated sacredness. The main altar is ordinarily at the extreme east end. During church services this part of the church (the sanctuary) may only be entered by the officiating priests. It is separated from the rest of the church by a railing and often by a raised step. The nave, which forms the west end of the church, is occupied by the congregation but most of the ritual action takes place in the intermediate area, the chancel, which lies between the nave and the sanctuary. This again is usually clearly demarcated by a raised step and was formerly separated from the nave by a screen.

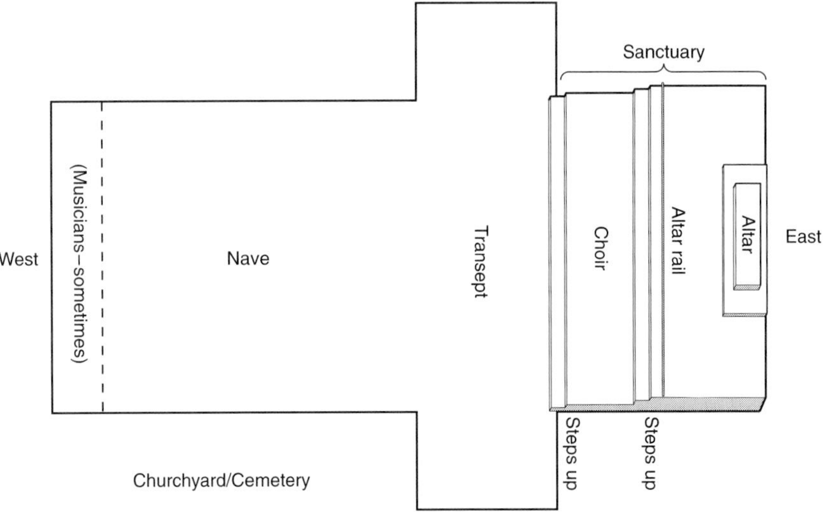

Fig. 2. Layout of typical English village church.

The noise-making apparatus of the church, consisting of a choir or an organ or both, is usually located in the chancel area thus marking a separation of the sacred from the profane. But sometimes the organ (or the choir or both) is located immediately above the entrance to the church at the west end.

In various publications I have maintained that the principle that is involved here is extremely general. Power is manifested at the interface of separable categories. The principle applies whether the potency that is made manifest is physical – as in the case of electricity or other prime movers – sexual, political, or metaphysical. I usually illustrate my argument with an Euler diagram. The real world is continuous. By the use of categories we separate physical and social space into areas of differentiated power-potential, creating the illusion of discontinuity. At the interface there is a region which belongs to neither category and yet to both. It is an area of danger, of taboo, of manifested power. You will see what I mean if you clutch an electric power cable with your hands while your feet are on the ground and you are not wearing rubber boots. But here we are discussing the potency of divinity and of royalty, rather than of things in the world.

In this frame of thinking any shrine which is treated as a throne of an invisible deity is a source of potential power. It is, for the time being, a part of the other world of immortal gods rather than of this world of mortal men. The penumbra of the shrine area, the betwixt and between region where most of the ritual action takes place, is both in this world and in the other world. The whole area is dangerous and loaded with taboo but, as you approach closer to the core,

The real world of experience is continuous but it is cut up into discontinuous segments by our use of verbal categories. The boundary layer is ambiguous and becomes the focus of taboo.

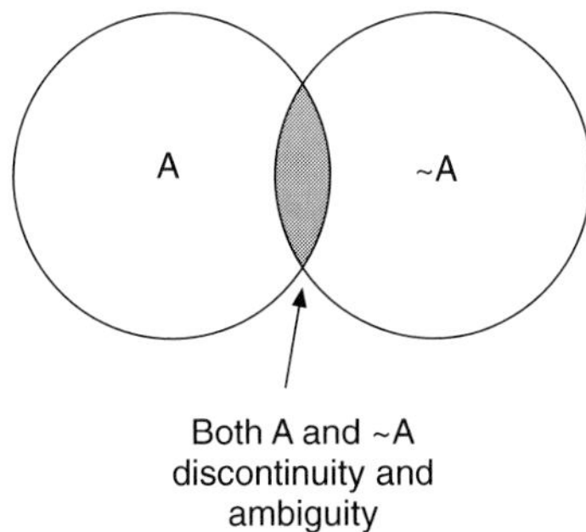

The cosmos of imagination is likewise continuous but 'this world' is separated from/connects with the 'other world' by a zone of ambiguity which is the focus of the ritual process.

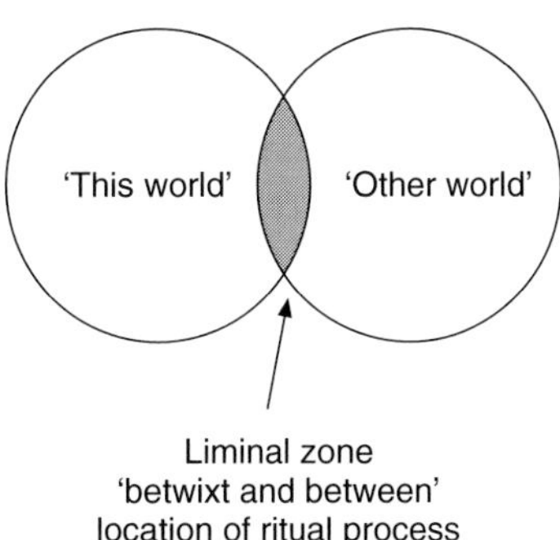

Fig. 3. The real world of experience and the cosmos of imagination.

the throne of the deity, the ultimate source of power, the intensity of the taboo increases.

This model fits very well with my diagrams both for the Borneo head feast and for the English parish church; but how about Buckingham Palace?

Architecturally speaking, I consider that Buckingham Palace is a shocker. The building started out as Buckingham House built by a Duke of Buckingham in the eighteenth century. It then faced the other way round, with the frontal to the west. The house was bought by George III for his wife. It was then known as The Queen's House. The present west front of the building, which opens onto extensive gardens, dates from 1825 when the architect was John Nash. But the present public aspect, which faces east, dates only from 1911 when it was redesigned as a backcloth for the outrageously hideous memorial to Queen Victoria which stands at the end of The Mall.

The Palace has been a regular residence of the reigning monarch since about 1850. One can only hope that the private apartments are more comfortable than the ornate splendours of the rooms which are open to the public.

The furnishing of these public rooms is quite comic in its ghastliness, a mixture of the gilded decadent baroque favoured by George IV and Victoriana of the 1860s. The Throne Room, which is an immense rectangle 64 feet in length, dates from 1856 and retains all its original furnishings including medallions of Prince

Albert and the young Victoria worked into the panelling. In the labyrinthine passageways through which the visitor must pass on his way to the heart of things, the inevitable statuary consists very largely of masterpieces of the 1850s, a truly astonishing period during which both British and American sculptors achieved the seemingly impossible feat of producing completely nude white marble ladies who are entirely devoid of any semblance of sexuality.

In terms of the theory which I am propounding this is very appropriate since these rooms and passages lie in an area of social ambiguity. At the time of the actual Investiture this ambiguous imagery was intensified by the fact that the stairs and other points on the visitors' journey were guarded by sentries. The sentries were members of Her Majesty's Household Cavalry, on foot but otherwise dressed in their full regalia, which includes an armoured breastplate appropriate to cavalry charges in the seventeenth century. Their function on the present occasion was to stand absolutely immobile for hours on end. As we went up the stairs I heard a small child whisper to its mother 'Mummy, is it alive?'.

As I remarked earlier, the Investiture involved about 130 recipients of honours. At the head of the list came one recipient of an Order of Merit (this really is a badge of distinction; there are never more than twenty-four at any one time and they come from all walks of life); then about a dozen knights of various grades; and then all kinds of lesser orders. What I have to say applies, in the main, only to the knights, and, in particular, to the order of Knights Bachelor to which I myself, like most other civilian knights, in fact belong.

The British institution of knighthood is very ancient; its history is mixed up with the emergence of European feudalism out of the remnants of Roman imperialism. In the battles of the eleventh-century Crusades armoured knights on armoured horses were the equivalent of the modern tank. But knighthood had ceased to have any military significance at least as early as the middle of the fifteenth century. Ninety-nine per cent of the present day ritual fal-de-lal which is governed by an august body called the College of Heralds was invented in the early part of the nineteenth century at a period when the ravages of the Industrial Revolution produced (by dialectical reaction) an enthusiasm for antiquarian revivalism of all kinds.

In detail, I have no idea how Queen Elizabeth I initiated her knights at the end of the sixteenth century but I feel pretty sure that, apart from changes in costume, Queen Elizabeth II, in 1975, was doing very much what her great-great-grandmother Victoria had done a century earlier. Just who invented the proceedings and what they had in mind when they did so is an interesting but largely unanswerable question; my concern is with the structure of the outcome, and to some extent with its mythology, but not immediately with its true history.

As I shall explain presently, there are bits and pieces of the ritual which appear to be very old.

Initiation into a knighthood is today a thoroughly secular affair but in its historical origins it was an explicitly religious rite closely allied to the ordination of priests and the enthronement of bishops. In the late Middle Ages one of the central issues in the struggle between the Pope and the Emperor was the question whether secular authorities had the right to hold investitures and thereby endow feudal knights with fiefdoms. The Pope maintained that investiture was an exclusive prerogative of the Church but secular leaders successfully usurped this right together with the patronage that went with it.

But enough of all this; let us get down to the ethnography. How does one become a knight?

The first thing that happens is that you receive a letter from the Patronage Secretary of the Prime Minister saying that the Prime Minister is minded to recommend to the Queen that you be appointed to a knighthood. Please sign on the dotted line to confirm that, if so appointed, you will accept the offer!

About a month later the actual list appears in *The Times*. At much the same time you receive a letter from some official in the College of Heralds asking for a subscription and instructing you to attend at the College to sign the roll. Once you have done this you are authorised to use your title. This however is a recent innovation; in the past you were not 'actually' a knight until you had been dubbed by the monarch.

In due course you will receive instructions from quite a different official about the date and procedure for the Investiture at the Palace. The instructions specify time and style of dress and call for the names of guest witnesses, who can be any two persons, but three, if two of them are your children. The dress instructions apply to the guests as well.

In the past when Investitures were much smaller and confined to knights only, they were also much grander and more elitist and males were all required to turn up in the fancy-dress costume known as Court Dress. Even a generation ago this was usually hired for the occasion. The requirements are now much more lenient. Members of the armed services and the police appear in uniform but civilians are simply advised: 'Morning dress or dark lounge suit'.

In these plebeian days 'morning dress' for most people still implies a visit to a firm of dress-hire specialists. The ladies among the guests are advised to wear hats but other details of dress are not specified. On this occasion they dressed to match their husbands; that is to say they put on costumes which they would have felt to be appropriate to a smart wedding. As to the males, a fair proportion of the guests, that is to say males in the audience, took advantage of the let-out and appeared in 'dark lounge suits'. However all the recipients of honours, right down the list (with one exception) appeared either in uniform or in morning dress. Appropriately, the one exception was the recipient of the highest honour of all, the Order of Merit. Since he had been through similar performances on a number of previous occasions he was now so endowed with the potency of honour in his own right that he could ignore the rules altogether. He was dressed in a light-coloured suiting appropriate to the hot summer weather outside.

And so, on the appointed day, at 10 a.m., a queue of overdressed local and national celebrities, with their spouses and offspring, or perhaps less legitimate associates, gathered outside Buckingham Palace on the east side. In due course

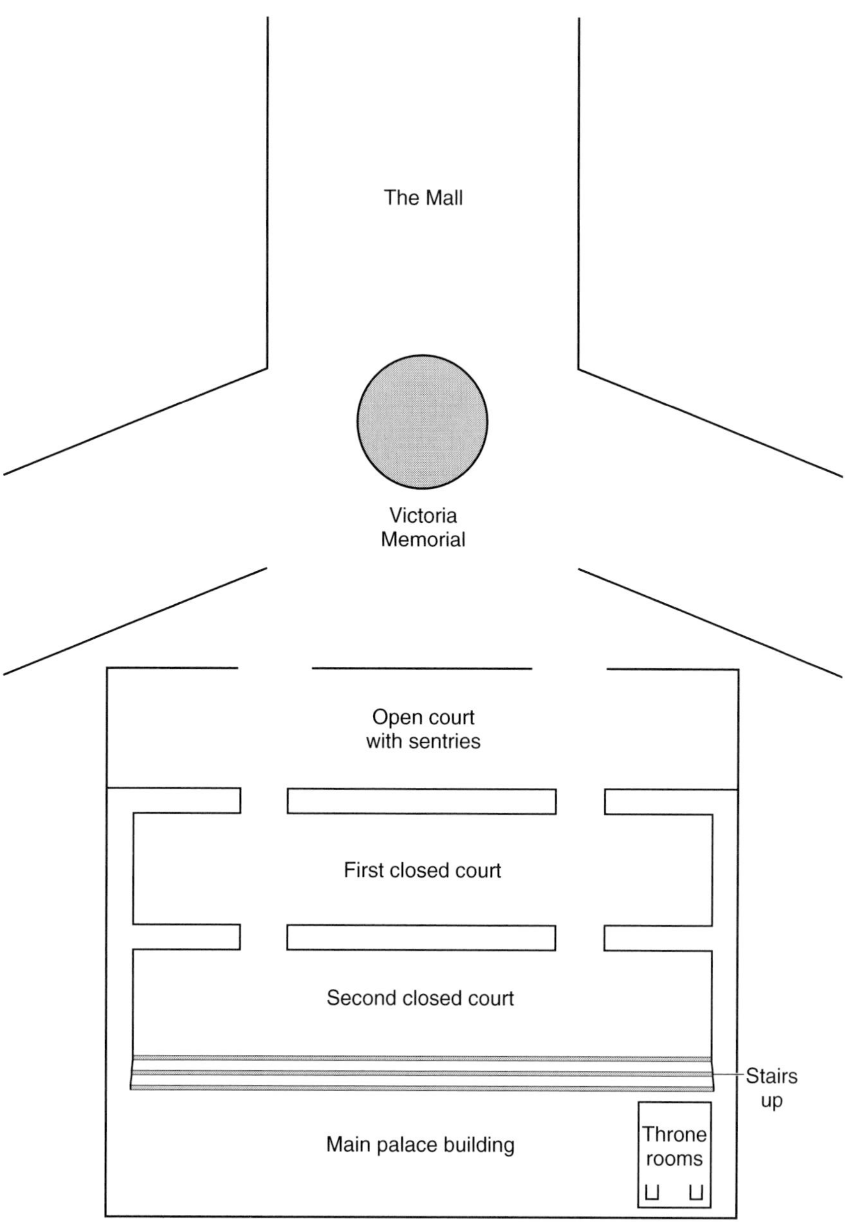

Fig. 4. Schematic layout of Buckingham Palace precincts.

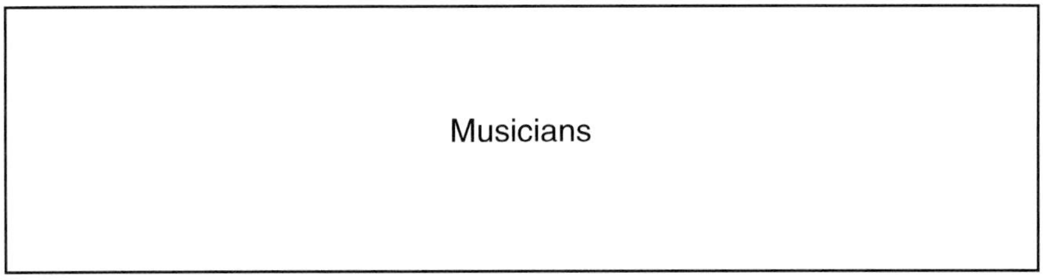

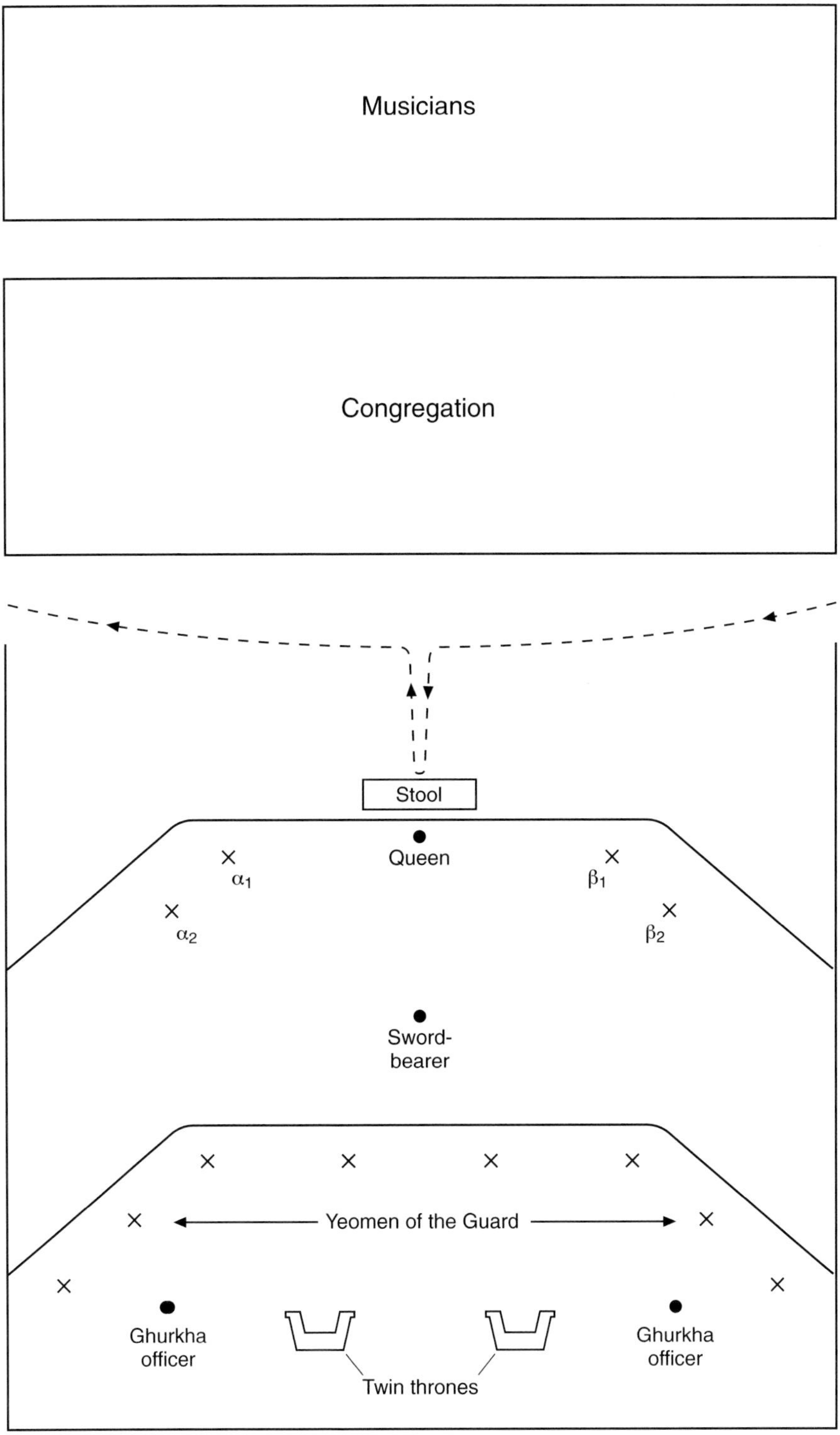

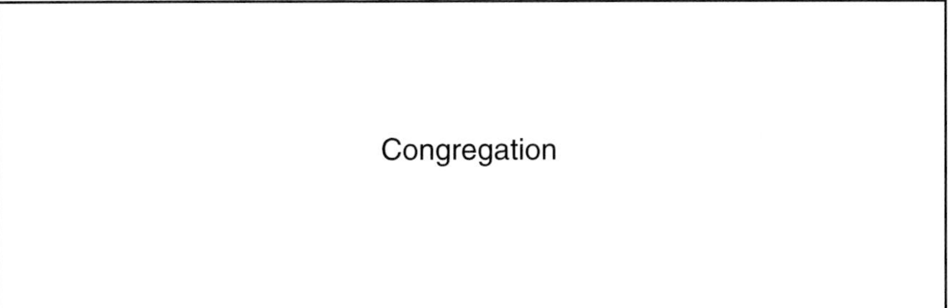

Musicians
Congregation
Stool
Queen
α1
β1
α2
β2
Sword-
bearer
Yeomen of the Guard
Ghurkha
officer
Ghurkha
officer
Twin thrones

Fig. 5. Layout of Throne Room for Knights' Investiture.

they entered the Palace through a succession of courtyards appropriately decorated with seventeenth-century cavalrymen on foot.

Once inside the Palace the initiates and the guests were separated. The guests proceeded direct to the Throne Room where they took up seats which would be appropriate for the lay congregation in the nave of a parish church. Secular light music dating from around 1900 was provided by the military band orchestra located, as can be seen, at the opposite end of the room from the empty thrones. The initiates meanwhile were conducted to another part of the building where they were individually rehearsed in what they had to do.

At this point we need to look more closely at the layout of the Throne Room bearing in mind the analogy with the general format of a sacrificial shrine and of a church to which I have already drawn your attention.

The band was placed in a kind of minstrels' gallery in what would have been the west end of a church. At the opposite end, located where the altar would be in a church setting, were the two ornate but empty thrones. There are, I suppose, occasions when the Queen actually sits on her throne though I don't know what they are. On such occasions I feel sure she would be dressed in her full regalia, robes, crown, and all. But on this occasion the Queen was dressed like an ordinary mortal; indeed, though elegantly attired, she had clearly gone to some trouble not to upstage the female members of her audience. In terms of my general theory she was officiating as the priestess of a metaphysical divinity called 'sovereignty' whose unseen presence was symbolised by the empty thrones, but she was emphatically not masquerading as 'sovereignty' itself in her own person.

When the Queen appeared she was accompanied by a covey of high-ranking service officers and palace functionaries together with a sword-bearer and a personal bodyguard. The sword-bearer, carrying the ceremonial Sword of State which the Queen is to use in dubbing her new knights, moved in the procession immediately in front of the Queen. By the time that everyone was positioned on the dais area, the sword-bearer stood midway between the Queen and the empty thrones. The Sword, like the Crown, is a specific symbol of the Queen's sovereignty.

The bodyguard consisted, in the first place, of five members of the elite corps of much bemedalled retired officers who form the Yeomen of the Guard, dressed in their splendidly picturesque but unauthentic sixteenth-century costumes, which resemble those worn by the Yeomen Warders of the Tower of London which are blazoned abroad by the posters of the British Tourist Agency. In addition there were two Gurkha officers. I don't know whether this is a regular feature or whether there was some special reason for their presence.

But the really interesting detail, from my point of view, was that when the members of the guard had taken up their stations on the daised area they were quite clearly guarding the empty thrones and not the physical person of the Queen herself who stood out in front (Fig. 5).

At the same time the two Gurkha officers, a uniformed admiral, and the Chief Gentleman Usher of the Court took up positions at the four corners of a rectangle, thereby demarcating the limits of the territorial space within which the ritual process was about to take place.

Notice carefully the arrangements within this rectangle. Viewed from the Queen's orientation, the Thrones are to the rear, the audience out in front. The initiates approach one at a time through a doorway to the right. They walk between the audience–congregation and the front of the defined ritual space.

Having reached the centre of the room the initiate then turns to face the Queen and the Thrones and walks forward into the ritual space. He there kneels on a stool in front of the Queen who is standing on the dais at a slightly higher level. The Queen dubs the kneeling knight on each shoulder with the flat of her Sword of State; he rises; she hangs the badge of his order round his neck (another recent innovation); they shake hands; the Queen says something appropriate to the particular initiate; the initiate bows, withdraws backwards out of the ritual space, and then moves off to the left. Once he is outside the Throne Room another functionary removes the badge of honour which the Queen has just bestowed, puts it in a case, and gives it back. The initiate then walks round to the back to join the audience.

On the dais on which the Queen is standing (which is a step lower than that on which the Thrones are placed) are her various functionary assistants. They comprise (1) the Lord Chamberlain, the holder of an office which dates back at least 700 years, whose function on this occasion was to read out the names of the initiates as they appeared, (2) a checker who seemed to be reading the same list to make sure that there was no slip-up, (3) another admiral in uniform who handed the Queen the appropriate badges of honour, one by one, on a velvet cushion, and (4) a backer-up for the Admiral to make sure that he didn't get it wrong. The actual badges had been laid out on a table in advance.

All this is much as might have been expected. The Queen in her priestess role is a sacred person who cannot actually be touched even by an admiral. Hence the velvet cushion. Her role in the dubbing ceremony is to convey an element of the power of sovereignty through the sword to the person of the initiate knight. But a detail which I had not appreciated until the performance was that the Queen would place the flat of her sword first on one shoulder and then on the other. In a symbolic sense the action is sacrificial. The priestess cuts off the victim's head.

I dare say that most of you will feel that this is just silly; but from an anthropological point of view it makes a lot of sense. For here we are in the middle of a *rite de passage* and in such contexts, as is well known, the use of death and rebirth symbolism is extremely common. The initiate 'dies' in his old status and is 'reborn' in his new status. Moreover sacrificial rites – the 'making sacred' of the initiate – regularly form part of such initiatory proceedings. Where the sacrifices are real, the initiate dies vicariously because he is identified with the sacrificial victim; in our present example no animal or human victim is actually killed, so it is appropriate that the symbolic killing should be directed against the initiate himself instead of against a vicarious substitute.

But, if the dubbing implies the symbolic death of the knight-to-be, where is the symbolic rebirth? I shall come back to that point presently but for the moment let me draw your attention to the several distinct sections of the Queen's performance: (1) she dubs the kneeling knight with the sword, (2) she hangs a badge round the neck of the standing knight, (3) she shakes the knight by the hand – that is she makes physical contact with him in her person, (4) she says something; she exhibits the magical power of words; in Malinowski's language, she utters a spell.

Another key point, which I shall elaborate presently, is that a knight's investiture is sometimes referred to as a *dubbing ceremony* and sometimes as *receiving the accolade*. Contrary to some popular misconceptions, these are not just two names for the same thing; they refer to two distinct parts of a single sequence. The first is a symbolic slaying; the second a symbolic restoration to life.

For the present that is all I propose to say about the Buckingham Palace ethnography but it seems to me that the structural parallels between my two cases, the Borneo slaughter of a pig and the London investiture of a knight, are very close. But if we want to understand why this should be so then the key symbol in both cases is an empty throne, the seat of Deity, the ancestor–hero Lang in the one case, the metaphysical concept of 'sovereignty' in the other. Both are viewed as sources of power. The purpose of the ritual performance is to convey some part of this power to the initiate who thereby becomes properly qualified to assume his new title, his new social status. The argument of course presupposes the appropriateness of Durkheim's formula which declares that, in the last analysis, 'God is Society itself'. In the London example the sovereignty, which is exhibited in the symbols of the empty thrones and the sword, and made manifest in the Queen's execution of her royal function, is a very clear example of this principle.

But why should we carry on in this way? Is the whole business just antiquarian, mediaeval, make-believe? I don't think so at all. For it is from the validity of this symbolism that the legitimacy of the whole machinery of the state derives. This is Max Weber's point which he elaborated in particular with reference to the office of the Emperor of China. It was the charisma of the throne, rather than of the Emperor as individual, that was the ultimate source of the bureaucratic legitimacy of the Chinese literati. And so it is with us except that, since the reigning monarch does not exercise any actual political power, it has become sociologically essential that the capacity of the monarch to legitimise status must be constantly reiterated by public demonstration.

A constitutional detail which is followed very punctiliously is that every new minister of the Government of the day must attend personally at the Palace to 'kiss hands'. I have no idea what really happens on such occasions. But two points stand out: firstly there is the clear implication that the legitimacy of the minister's authority as a servant of 'the Crown' requires initiation by physical contact with the monarch, and secondly these ceremonials are private. Investitures, which, relatively speaking, are performed in public, are the counterpart of such private goings-on. Public approval of the seeming nonsense of Birthday and New Year Honours demonstrates indirectly a respect for the constitution as a whole.

But enough of Durkheim and Weber, let us get back to some contemporary anthropology. My ethnography bears on Victor Turner's association of *rites de passage* not only with liminality (which I have already shown) but with what he calls *communitas*, the breakdown of the hierarchical distinctions which separate the holders of public office in ordinary life.[2]

Notice, for example, that the Queen was in ordinary dress not ceremonial dress. She was separated from those who were seated at the front of her audience only by a passageway a few yards wide; she stood above them only by the height of the dais, a matter of six inches or so. She was representative of 'the Throne', but in fact she herself was separated from the actual thrones by a line of guardsmen and a covey of functionaries. As a result she was among, or almost among, the ordinary people, or at any rate some of the more or less ordinary people. Nevertheless she remained a sacred person: the badges of honour through which she conveyed the *charisma* of the Throne to the initiates had to be handed to her on a velvet cushion by an admiral. But again, to emphasise the *communitas* angle, the various grades of initiate were all treated more or less alike. Only the knights were required to kneel and be tapped with a sword and only the knights subsequently had their badges hung around the neck. In all the other cases the Queen simply pinned the badge on the initiate's left breast. But the shaking of hands and the personal word of commendation were common to all. It is relevant here that it is only the knights who actually change their names and hence their social identity as a result of the ceremony. The others acquire an honour but not a new title.

Which brings us back to the matter of the dubbing and the accolade and my improbable thesis that the dubbing symbolises the cutting off of the knight's head.

As I said earlier there are no grounds for thinking that the ceremonial which is now performed is ancient, though it does seem to contain ancient elements. At least since the seventeenth century the expression *dubbing* has referred to the hitting on the shoulder of a kneeling knight with a sword held by the monarch. However, although the *accolade*, which evidently refers to the neck (French, *col*), was formerly described as an 'embrace' or 'kiss', this is not its present form.

In present-day England shaking hands is the equivalent of the continental embrace around the neck so I presume that both the shaking hands element in the present ritual and the 'kissing of hands' required of initiate Ministers of State are derivative versions of the earlier accolade.

The earliest documentary reference to the dubbing of a knight goes back to 1085; unfortunately, it is not clear what was involved. Initiate monks at that period were buffeted on each cheek by their ecclesiastical superior; the hitting of the initiate knight was the secular equivalent. The present practice of hanging a badge of office around the knight's neck is very recent. It has the effect of reducing to a minimum the difference between the investiture of a knight and the investiture of lesser orders.

It seems possible that whoever invented the new procedure supposed that, since the knight's investiture needed to include an accolade, and an accolade has to do with the neck, then hanging a badge around the neck could serve as the accolade! If this is what happened then they were misinterpreting the rules. The point about the accolade (if you accept my thesis) is that, in van Gennep's language, it is 'a rite of aggregation'; the initiate, having been 'killed' in his old role, must be 'restored to life' in his new one. To achieve this the power of sovereignty must flow through the Queen to the initiate. It is the physical contact with the Queen's body which achieves this end. It is the shaking of hands which is the modern accolade!

But having asserted my opinion in this categorical way I need to consider a question which must be worrying the non-anthropological members of my audience. What is the status of interpretations of this sort? None of the participants (other than the sole anthropologist present) had any conception that they were participating in a religious rite, and most of them would have been highly indignant if anyone had suggested that they were. And by their criteria they were surely right. The band was not playing hymn tunes but music-hall melodies of the era of 'A Bicycle Made for Two'! And anyway, they would one and all have laughed to scorn my suggestion that the dubbing of a knight is analogous to a heathen animal sacrifice. So what is my justification for reshuffling the cards in this way?

Well, quite clearly my assertions are not scientific statements; they cannot be validated in any way; they cannot be disproved. They are more like the free associations of a patient on a psychoanalyst's couch. Yet they seem to me to increase my insight into what was going on. I do not believe that people attempt to preserve 'ye olde customes' just because they are old or just because they are customary; they do so because such behaviour tends to give satisfaction to some kind of socio-psychological need. As Malinowski often asserted, all customary behaviour is functional in the present; it is not just an odd survival from the past. But the problem of course is to know what that function is.

Opinions will differ here even among anthropologists of similar general orientation, but my own view is that an analysis of this sort, even though it may appear trivial, gives me a better understanding of why such archaic institutions as knighthood and investiture show the vitality that they do and why even cynics like myself can feel genuinely pleased, genuinely honoured, by initiation into an office which carries with it no rewards or responsibilities of any kind.

And, by feedback, I feel that this kind of mental and structural association tells me, as a professional anthropologist, something about the essential nature of sacrifice that I did not know before.

But of course the general point is very much simpler. You do not have to go all the way to the Trobriand Islands or to Sarawak either to observe the exotic or to practise anthropology.

Notes

Leach read several versions of this unpublished lecture in different North American universities. The version printed here is based on the text delivered at the University of Illinois, Urbana–Champaign in April 1981.

1. [Eds: A short following paragraph in the original typescript has been omitted.]
2. [Eds: see Turner, 'Liminality and Communitas'.]

Section 3

The Hard Core: Kinship and Social Structure

This section begins with Leach's first recorded attempt to describe the culturally complex situation he found in highland Burma when he arrived there at the beginning of the Second World War. His attempt to understand this situation – described here with evident excitement as 'an absolute anthropological zoo' – was a crucial formative influence on his whole style of anthropology, not least because his introduction to the work of Claude Lévi-Strauss was through the latter's use of ethnographic data from that region. The piece itself is a letter home, of which carbon copies were sent to friends and family. Plainly, this is not in any sense a serious considered analysis (the self-presentation, on the other hand, is highly-wrought and deliberate). But there are several points about Leach's observations as recorded here which in retrospect appear significant.

First, it is notable that Leach is already speaking of the 'ravages' of the Kachin Regeneration Scheme, and foreseeing difficulties with his superiors when he came to present the eventual results of his researches on its effects. Even though, the scheme being new, it is 'difficult to be dogmatic', Leach has nevertheless already adopted the firmly negative attitude to 'development anthropology' which he was to hold throughout his life.[1]

Although he dutifully declares an intention to 'limit any particular line of enquiry to manageable dimensions', Leach seems to take it for granted that the situation he has to grasp ('Could anything be simpler?') is the total cultural and ethnic mix. And after a brief and robustly sceptical overview of the policies and procedures of British colonial rule, he is naturally drawn to the possibility of systematic comparison between groups living under different political regimes. His thinking seems clearly informed by the issue of 'culture contact' as discussed in Malinowski's LSE seminars, and reflects the line of argument Leach himself had adopted there (see II.4.1).

The end result, famously, is the rejection of the notion of bounded, homogeneous 'unit societies' that was one of the main themes of *Political Systems of Highland Burma*. This was not merely a point about the social and cultural situation in Burma. Leach had become convinced that the problem lay in the very way social anthropologists had come to think about social structure. As he later summarised the problem, 'I needed a new terminology. Everyone kept talking about "tribes" as if they were closed systems. As you moved across the road you moved from Tribal Area "A" to Tribal Area "B". This was plain nonsense as far as south-east Asia is concerned, and I suspected that it was nonsense too in many parts of Africa where "tribes" were credited with hard-edged boundaries.'[2] Leach felt his colleagues had consistently exaggerated the stability of the societies they had studied; and had explained away evident social change of quite fundamental kinds as merely the internal workings of a stable social structure. In what is clearly a reference to the studies of 'segmentary lineage systems' by his Africanist colleagues, he wrote, 'the essence of my argument is that the process by which the small units grow into larger ones and the large units break down into smaller ones is not simply part of the process of structural continuity; it is not merely a process of segmentation and accretion, it is a process involving structural change' (I.3.2: 221).

The question of how an anthropologist might give an account of structural social change occurring through historical time was one which occupied Leach throughout his career, and he approached it in different ways. In *Political Systems* he emphasises the internal dynamics of Kachin social structure. He later saw Sahlins's and Valeri's work on Hawaii[3] as attempts to solve the same problem.[4] In 'The Frontiers of "Burma"' (I.3.3) the emphasis is on the external constraints and influences of ecology, trade, and cultural influence from India and China.[5] In the 1970s, Leach welcomed the development of models of human ecology, 'not just as a relationship between a society and a static environment but as a whole set of continuously adaptive sub-systems within an unbounded matrix . . . any modification of the environment is also, by feedback, a modification of the human social system within it' (I.1.8: 89). Either way, a prerequisite was to abandon the notion of a bounded social system, which could be thought of having a singular 'relation' to its surrounding socio-political and natural environment.

This theme was closely bound up with two others, which emerged with increasing clarity in Leach's writings in the 1950s and 1960s. First, he argued that kinship is not a distinct field within social life, not 'a thing in itself'. This of course was in direct conflict with the position held and developed by Fortes and others who followed Radcliffe-Brown (and through him Durkheim and Morgan) in seeing kinship relations as the basic skeleton of social structure in a 'primitive society', and the basis, to the extent that they existed at all, of political offices and institutions. Just as Leach insisted that, from the outside so to speak, social structures were not neatly separable entities; so he insisted that, from the inside, there was no set of isolable 'kinship relations' of which social structures were composed.

Of course, none of this should be taken to suggest that Leach wanted to downplay or marginalise the study of kinship. In *Pul Eliya* he describes kinship as 'by far the most sophisticated tool of analysis which the social anthropologist possesses' (I.3.5). And he went so far in 1967 as to regret Lévi-Strauss's move from kinship studies, the 'hard core' of anthropological study, to exclusive interest in classification, cosmology, and mythology.[6] Leach's point was just that this 'hard core' was not a separate 'thing in itself' which could be analysed in isolation.

There were several aspects to Leach's position on the autonomy of 'kinship'. At one level it arose from the breadth of his interests, which embraced geography and ecology, as well as material culture, including technology. In *Political Systems*, in 'The Frontiers of "Burma"', and in *Pul Eliya* he pays close attention to the effects on behaviour of what he refers to in the last of these works as, 'such crude nursery facts as that water evaporates and flows downhill' (I.3.5: 270). Geography and ecology shape political culture and institutions in profound and long-term ways (I.3.3); a theme explored further in 'Hydraulic Society in Ceylon' (1959). No set of moral or jural rules – and thus no set of purely 'kinship relations' – could exist or be properly understood in isolation from these brute facts.

At another level Leach's position was an expression of his humanistic and individualist conception of persons (one he shared with Malinowski) which saw them as broadly rational, deliberating, and decision-making agents, and not as bound by rules and customs to behave in pre-programmed ways. People always have considerable latitude as to which rights and duties they choose to claim and to recognise. Economic interest and ambition for status and honour will take different forms in different social contexts, and they will be shaped by ecology and culture, but they will always affect how people perceive, interpret, and act upon conventional expectations or responsibilities. Kinship relations are not immune to these influences. This was a constant theme in his writings. It is there in *Political Systems* and, more explicitly, in one of his other major Kachin publications, 'The Structural Implications of Matrilateral Cross-Cousin Marriage' (1951). It was an important theme in his re-analysis of Trobriand kinship (I.3.4) where he placed more emphasis than Malinowski had done on residence and property (they are integral to his notion of 'social distance'). And it is the central thrust of *Pul Eliya.* In his 1977 public lectures, 'Custom, Law, and Terrorist Violence', Leach is perhaps at his most unguarded and explicit: 'It is the very essence of being a human being that the individual should resent the domination of others and seek to exercise choices of his own.'[7]

The final theme, which connects with Leach's views on unit societies and the autonomy of kinship relations, is his conception of social structure. When anthropologists or other social scientists describe a 'social structure' they are, according to Leach, describing an abstraction, a formal model of a smoothly functioning system and this is in effect an hypothesis about 'how the system works'. What is the relation between this model and what actually happens 'on the ground'? In *Political Systems* Leach says the following: 'I hold that social structure in practical situations (as contrasted with the sociologist's abstract model) consists of a set of ideas about the distribution of power between persons and groups of persons' (I.3.2: 220). So one important difference between the analyst's model of social structure and social structure 'in practical situations' is that because the latter set of ideas is held by the social actor, who is conceived by Leach to be a roughly rational and self-interested individual, they are about the distribution of power. The analyst might hypothesise that some other dimension of social life is the final explanatory factor, but from the actor's point of view it is likely to be differences in power and status that are the focus of interest.

But in the context of 1950s social theory the most striking thing about Leach's description of social structure 'in practical situations' is not this difference from, but a similarity which it bears to his view of the theorist's model of social structure. For like the latter the former is, in his words, 'a set of ideas'. For Leach, social structure, even social structure 'in practical situations', is a logical ordering of categories and concepts. Typically it is found in implicit rather than explicit form, and is expressed in ritual (including the telling of myth), rather than in theoretical discourse, but it is none the less basically a conceptual object. It is what he referred to in 1964 as a 'cognitive model' (I.3.6). This is why the analysis of social structure takes the form of analysis of verbal categories (I.3.2; I.3.4) and why theoretical comparison between social systems can only be conducted once the logical relations between key concepts have been identified (I.3.7).

And because social structures, conceived in this way, are ideas which are carried in cultural forms, most especially in ritual, it is possible and indeed according to Leach it is the normal state of affairs for individuals to have at their disposal more than one such 'structure'. 'In situations such as we find in the Kachin Hills Area, any particular individual can be thought of as having a status position in several different social systems at one and the same time' (I.3.2: 222–3). These systems may be radically inconsistent, as indeed the ideal models of a Shan autocracy and *gumlao* democracy are, and the real social and political situation in any given locality at any particular time may be an uneasy combination of the two. Such is the case in highland Burma, where villages or village clusters of the *gumsa* type (which are greatly the majority) are inherently unstable and contradictory combinations of *gumlao* and Shan social structures. What it means in practice for an individual to be part of two status systems at the same time is that he always has a choice of at least two different courses of action, each of which is suggested as the way to advancement within one system, but which are not compatible one with the other. We must not imagine that this is unusual. 'In our own society the ethically correct action for a Christian business man is often equally ambiguous' (I.3.2: 224).

This brings us back to the decision-making and self-interested individual. Leach is careful to qualify this conception. It is not a simple cross-cultural constant. 'The social anthropologist is never justified in interpreting action as unambiguously directed towards one particular end . . . but I consider it necessary and justifiable to assume that a conscious or unconscious wish to gain power is a very general motive in human affairs . . . Esteem is a cultural product. What is admired in one society may be deplored in another' (I.3.2: 224). In addition, as we saw in Section 2, Leach was highly conscious that the pervasiveness of games of self-presentation, deception, and masquerade means that 'the true self' is a highly elusive notion. But at the centre of Leach's system is the flesh-and-blood individual. For Leach, the 'unity of mankind' is both a moral and a methodological postulate (see II.4.6; II.4.8; and II.5).

A social structure, even one 'in practical situations', describes the relations between 'social persons', that is to say not particular flesh-and-blood individuals but abstract categories of persons who occupy specified roles (chief and commoner, or wife-giver and wife-taker, and so on). But while social structures are made up of these abstracted social persons, real societies are not. It is individuals who think with these models, choose between them, manipulate them, and take advantage, where they can, of the contradictions between them. The patterns of behaviour that emerge from all these decisions and actions are what, in *Pul Eliya*, Leach refers to as 'quantitative' or 'statistical' orders, and their relation to the ideal orders of structural value systems will always be highly complex.

In *Political Systems* the actual state of affairs in most political units (the 'statistical order', although Leach did not use this expression in that book) fell somewhere between two radically different ideal 'social structures', in each case it showed some influence from both, and also changed over time. In *Pul Eliya* the statistical order was shown by Leach to be remarkably stable over time, and to be quite contrary to the commonly asserted scheme of norms and values, which therefore, he declared, did not exert a determining effect upon behaviour. In both cases, political or economic self-interest motivated individual actions, and in the radically different ecological, economic, and historical contexts of the two cases the results were correspondingly different. In both cases Leach set out to describe the 'social structure' he found there: 'social structure', in the sense now of 'the sociologist's abstract model'. Whereas, in *Political Systems*, what this abstract model described was long-term oscillation between two extreme ideal types of political organisation, in *Pul Eliya* it was a statistical norm which is not explicit in any local ideal model. 'It is a by-product of the sum of many individual human actions, of which the participants are neither wholly conscious nor wholly unaware' (I.3.5: 275).

Thus Leach's preference for an explicitly abstract, mathematical notion of social structure ('structuralist rationalism', as he sometimes called it) was for him perfectly compatible with his focus on economic interest and the concrete individual ('empiricist functionalism').[8] Both were part of a critique of the structural-functionalist paradigm, whose practitioners mistook their abstract models of social structure for concrete reality (forgetting that 'The model in a matchbox won't fly' (I.3.6: 285)), and, by descriptively squeezing real individuals into the 'roles' provided for in the model, presented the societies they described in a falsely homogeneous way (I.1.6; I.1.8). The basic intellectual error was not to see that some level of abstraction is a necessary part of what the anthropologist has to do (I.3.6; I.3.7). The structural-functionalists fondly imagined that their models of social structures were simple descriptions of something that actually existed in the fabric of the societies they had studied. They assumed they were describing real things: as unproblematically real, they mistakenly imagined, as biological species; and their exercises in typological comparison resembled a similarly naïve and outdated kind of natural history (I.3.7).

As Tim Ingold has remarked, 'More than any other recent anthropologist, it was Edmund Leach who contrived to place the status of "society" at the top of the theoretical agenda, at a time when – for most of his colleagues – the existence of societies "on the ground" was a simple fact of life that required no further justification."[9] The arguments Leach employed, in order to try to make his colleagues see that there was a problem, changed over time, and he came at the matter from different angles in his major ethnographic studies. But he had no objection to repeating himself and deliberately provocative declarations of the central point sound as a refrain through his writings. For purposes of description there is nothing wrong with calling any territorially defined political unit 'a society', even if for some purposes it is part of a larger such unit,[10] but only so long as we remember that in reality: 'Every real society is a process in time' (I.3.2: 220); 'society is a concept rather than a concrete thing' (I.3.6: 279); 'Society is not a "thing"; it is a way of ordering experience' (I.3.5: 277).

Notes

1. See *Social Anthropology*, p. 50: 'It follows that I consider "development anthropology" a kind of neo-colonialism'. See also II.4.6.
2. Leach in Kuper, 'An Interview with Leach', p. 378.
3. Sahlins, *Islands of History*; Valeri, *Kingship and Sacrifice.*
4. Leach in Kuper, 'Interview with Leach', p. 378; also 'Masquerade', p. 3.
5. This essay directly influenced Tambiah's model of political relations in south-east Asia, as developed in 'The Galactic Polity'.
6. Leach, 'Brain-Twister'.
7. *Custom, Law, and Terrorist Violence*, p. 19.
8. Much later (*Social Anthropology*, p. 44), Leach described *Political Systems* as 'organised as a kind of dialogue between the empiricism of Malinowski and the rationalism of Lévi-Strauss'. However, Leach also wrote as follows of *Political Systems*: 'The structuralism of that book derived from Vaihinger (1924) and Pareto (1916). Lévi-Strauss's influence was present only as a dialectical irritant' (Preface to *L'Unité de l'homme*, p. 18).
9. Ingold, 'The Concept of Society is Theoretically Obsolete'.
10. See I.3.2; and *Social Anthropology*, p. 41.

3.1

Letter from Bhamo(1939)

Bhamo, 8.9.39

Apologies to anyone who objects to getting a carbon copy, but most of this has to be said several times over. The future is exciting and slightly fantastic.

Since I reached Rangoon my plans have been more or less in abeyance. Stevenson's sudden departure was damping enough in itself, since he was my only contact with the Kachins and so far as I know there was no one else who had any interest in my activities. Certainly the Government people in Rangoon were not encouraging (though it appears now that if I had been more enterprising and tackled the Governor himself, I should have got a better reception) – their questions inevitably took the form 'Yes, but what exactly are you going to do?' – to which any ten-word answer is inevitably quite inane. Anyway they were in the midst of crisis and had no time for me. Then while I was on the way up river the war started and I was confronted with a further set of moral and practical complications. There were two aspects of the thing; What ought I to do? What was it possible to do? I felt I ought to serve 'King and Country' somehow or other; I have no more enthusiam [*sic*] for the war than anyone else, and I admit that the dishonest motives on our side our [*sic*] just about as scurrilous as those on the other, but since I have for years been quite sincerely anti-Hitler, it's my battle as much as anyone else's and it doesn't seen very valiant just to retire into the jungle and be comfortably safe. On the other hand it became increasingly obvious after a day or two that inside Burma King and Country hadn't much use for me, while at the same time it had become virtually impossible to get out of the country. I decided that when I got to Bhamo I would ask the D.C. for advice as to my best course of action. However when I got here I found that the D.C. too was away – was up in Sinlum in fact looking after Stevenson's affairs – so I was no further. Still the easygoing attitude of the tiny European community here was very calming to the nerves, and the war began to seem a long way off after all, and with the mountains so invitingly near . . . I decided to go up to Sinlum and have a talk to the D.C. So I went; ten miles in a car and sixteen miles on a mule, and almost immediately Hitler became a myth.

I should explain here that the plains area around Bhamo is part of Burma proper and is controlled by the Burmese Government, the inhabitants solemnly elect MPs and so forth – (the Westminster-model Burmese Constitution is incidently a complete and ludicrous farce but that's by the way); all the surrounding mountains on the other hand come under the Burma Frontier Service who are responsible only to the Governor. The D.C. at Bhamo however operates in both spheres – for the sub-division of Bhamo he is responsible to the Burmese Government; for the sub-division of Sinlum he is responsible to the Governor. All a bit complicated, but you see the idea.

There is no start to these mountains – they go straight up sheer out of the plain of the river – a dense steamy jungle forrest [*sic*] of bamboo and teak full of fantastic birds and beasts and enormous butterflies . . .

In due course I reached Sinlum, and found Wilkie the D.C. dressed in grey flannels and a sports coat sitting in front of a roaring fire 6000 feet up in the air and on top of everything with glorious Alpine views in all directions. . . . It was wildly exciting, I had found my heart again; it was like being back on Omei, the same jungle, the same flowers and butterflies, the same views, indeed very nearly the same mountains – (Omei I think is only about 300 miles north from here).

Wilkie is an entirely marvellous person, entirely unperturbed by the war, and enormously enthusiastic about everything connected with his job, especially where it concerns the Kachins. I had soon forgotten that I had contemplated starting off for England again. Plans for my future are all cut and dried. A house is being built for me in a Kachin village about three miles from the China border, fifteen miles from Sinlum, and about forty miles from anywhere else; I have a chinese [*sic*] speaking cook – fortunately Yunnanese is first cousin to Szechwanese as far as dialect is concerned; I borrow Stevenson's pony and probably his dog. What more could I want?

And the place is an absolute anthropological zoo; – I knew [of]course that there were supposed to be 340-odd different tribes between here and Szechwan – but I had imagined them as being merely variants of the same theme. Now I am not so sure. There was a bazaar in Sinlum the day I was there and there were present Shans from the plains (culturally very close to the Chinese); Chinese from Yunnan, Jingpaws, Atsis, Hkauris (three varieties of Kachin); Yawyins (apparently the same as the Chinese *lisu*, but all I can tell you at the moment is that they have extraordinarily pretty faces and wear the most complicated costume I ever seen [*sic*] anywhere); Palawngs (?); and then just a few odd individual Burmese, Indians, and Karens. Could anything be simpler?

Until a few years ago the administartion [*sic*] didn't bother about the Kachins, but powerful bands of American Babtist [*sic*] and R.C. missionaries were hard at work until today in this area about half the population are Christians of some sort or other. Then suddenly for reasons which I haven't quite fathomed the authorities got bitten with the bug of 'indirect rule' and it was decided to 're-establish the power of the Chiefs' (ominous phrase), Stevenson was put in charge and the 'Kachin Regeneration Scheme' was born. Well as you know I haven't met Stevenson but he must be an individual of positively volcanic energy. He seems to have begged, borrowed, or stolen money from a dozen government departments and now has 999 schemes all going at once. The thing has only been going two years, so its [*sic*] difficult to be dogmatic. All the schemes – which range in scope from supplying the services of a pedigree bull to forcibly amalgamating half a dozen villages – are enterprising, some of them highly ingenious. Whether the consequences will be what is intended is another matter; but what is undoubtedly the case is that it has made the local Kachins extremely proud of themselves, they naturally feel that if the Government is prepared to take so much interest they must be pretty fine chaps – and that is probably worth all the other 998 stunts put together. But its [*sic*] the hell of a muddle. Obviously the root trouble is the existence of the rival missions, one is bad enough, but two!! Still what a chance for sociological comparison. You see just across the border there are Kachins who are not christian and not administered at all, while just to the south there is another lot who are in British territory all right but who are outside the Sinlum sub-division and therefore escape the ravages of the 'Regeneration Scheme'. Wilkie's idea seems to be that I should report upon the consequences of the steps already taken, and then go on to make suggestions as to what ought to be done next – I can see I shall have to tread delicately!!

The trouble will be of course to limit any particular line of enquiry to managable [*sic*] dimensions – if forty anthropologists with 4000 notebooks studied for half a year, do you believe the Walrus said that they's [*sic*] get anywhere. Persoanlly [*sic*] I doubt it. But the vistas of exciting possibilities are almost endless . . .

Anyway I am taking all my goods and chattels up to Sinlum next week, where I can get down to it and start learning Kachin. Once my house is built I shall say goodbye to radios and newspapers and everything else.

So much for my patriotic principles!!

Notes

This is a letter sent by Leach shortly after his arrival in Burma in 1939. The copy in King's College Library, from which this is reproduced, is a carbon copy (presumably one of several), which also has a short typed addendum addressed to Leach's mother.

3.2

Models in Equilibrium and Societies in Change (1954)

What is meant by continuity and change with regard to social systems? Under what circumstances can we say of two neighbouring societies A and B that 'these two societies have fundamentally different social structures' while as between two other societies C and D we may argue that 'in these two societies the social structure is essentially the same'?

The argument in brief is as follows. Social anthropologists who, following Radcliffe-Brown, use the concept of social structure as a category in terms of which to compare one society with another, in fact presuppose that the societies with which they deal exist throughout time in stable equilibrium. Is it then possible to describe at all, by means of ordinary sociological categories, societies which are *not* assumed to be in stable equilibrium?

My conclusion is that while conceptual models of society are necessarily models of equilibrium systems, real societies can never be in equilibrium. The discrepancy is related to the fact that when social structures are expressed in cultural form, the representation is imprecise compared with that given by the exact categories which the sociologist, *qua* scientist, would like to employ. I hold that these inconsistencies in the logic of ritual expression are always necessary for the proper functioning of any social system.[1]

Most of my book is a development of this theme. I hold that social structure in practical situations (as contrasted with the sociologist's abstract model) consists of a set of ideas about the distribution of power between persons and groups of persons. Individuals can and do hold contradictory and inconsistent ideas about this system. They are able to do this without embarrassment because of the form in which their ideas are expressed. The form is cultural form; the expression is ritual expression. The latter part of this introductory chapter is an elaboration of this portentous remark.

But first to get back to social structure and unit societies.

Social structure

At one level of abstraction we may discuss social structure simply in terms of the principles of organisation that unite the component parts of the system. At this level the form of the structure can be considered quite independently of the cultural content.[2] A knowledge of the form of society among the Gilyak hunters of Eastern Siberia[3] and among the Nuer pastoralists of the Sudan[4] helps me to understand the form of Kachin society despite the fact that the latter for the most part are shifting cultivators inhabiting dense monsoon rain forest.

At this level of abstraction it is not difficult to distinguish one formal pattern from another. The structures which the anthropologist describes are models which exist only as logical constructions in his own mind. What is much more difficult is to relate such abstraction to the data of empirical fieldwork. How can we really be sure that one particular formal model fits the facts better than any other possible model?

Real societies exist in time and space. The demographic, ecological, economic, and external political situation does not build up into a fixed environment, but into a constantly changing environment. Every real society is a process in time. The changes that result from this process may usefully be thought of under two heads.[5] Firstly, there are those which are consistent with a continuity of the existing formal order. For example, when a chief dies and is replaced by his son, or when a lineage segments and we have two lineages where formerly there was only one, the changes are part of the process of continuity. There is no change in the formal structure. Secondly, there are changes which do reflect alterations in the formal structure. If, for example, it can be shown that in a particular locality, over a period of time, a political system composed of equalitarian lineage segments is replaced by a ranked hierarchy of feudal type, we can speak of a change in the formal social structure.

When, in this book, I refer to changes of social structure, I always mean changes of this latter kind.

Unit societies

In the context of the Kachin Hills Area the concept of 'a society' presents many difficulties which will become increasingly apparent in the course of the next few chapters. For the time being I will follow Radcliffe-Brown's unsatisfactory advice and interpret 'a society' as meaning 'any convenient locality'.[6]

Alternatively, I accept Nadel's arguments. By 'a society' I really mean any self-contained political unit.[7]

Political units in the Kachin Hills Area vary greatly in size and appear to be intrinsically unstable. At one end of the scale one may encounter a village of four households firmly asserting its right to be considered as a fully independent unit. At the other extreme we have the Shan state of Hsenwi which, prior to 1885, contained forty-nine sub-states (*möng*), some of which in turn contained over a hundred separate villages. Between these two extremes one may distinguish numerous other varieties of 'society'. These various types of political system differ from one another not only in scale but also in the formal principles in terms of which they are organised. It is here that the crux of our problem lies.

For certain parts of the Kachin Hills Area genuine historical records go back as far as the beginning of the nineteenth century. These show clearly that during the last 130 years the political organisation of the area has been very unstable. Small autonomous political units have often tended to aggregate into larger systems; large-scale feudal hierarchies have fragmented into smaller units. There have been violent and very rapid shifts in the overall distribution of political power. It is therefore methodologically unsound to treat the different varieties of political system which we now find in the area as independent types; they should clearly be thought of as part of a larger total system in flux. But the essence of my argument is that the process by which the small units grow into larger ones and the large units break down into smaller ones is not simply part of the process of structural continuity; it is not merely a process of segmentation and accretion, it is a process involving structural change. It is with the mechanism of this change process that we are mainly concerned.

There is no doubt that both the study and description of social change in ordinary anthropological contexts present great difficulties. Field studies are of short duration, historical records seldom contain data of the right kind in adequate detail. Indeed, although anthropologists have frequently declared a special interest in the subject, their theoretical discussion of the problems of social change has so far merited little applause.[8]

Even so it seems to me that at least some of the difficulties arise only as a by-product of the anthropologist's own false assumptions about the nature of his data.

English social anthropologists have tended to borrow their primary concepts from Durkheim rather than from either Pareto or Max Weber. Consequently they are strongly prejudiced in favour of societies which show symptoms of 'functional integration', 'social solidarity', 'cultural uniformity', 'structural equilibrium'. Such societies, which might well be regarded as moribund by historians or political scientists, are commonly looked upon by social anthropologists as healthy and ideally fortunate. Societies which display symptoms of faction and internal conflict leading to rapid change are on the other hand suspected of 'anomie' and pathological decay.[9]

This prejudice in favour of 'equilibrium' interpretations arises from the nature of the anthropologist's materials and from the conditions under which he does his work. The social anthropologist normally studies the population of a particular place at a particular point in time and does not concern himself greatly with whether or not the same locality is likely to be studied again by other anthropologists at a later date. In the result we get studies of Trobriand society, Tikopia society, Nuer society, *not* 'Trobriand society in 1914', 'Tikopia society in 1929', 'Nuer society in 1935'. When anthropological societies are lifted out of time and space in this way the interpretation that is given to the material is necessarily an equilibrium analysis, for if it were not so, it would certainly appear to the reader that the analysis was incomplete. But more than that, since, in most cases, the research work has been carried out once and for all without any notion of repetition, the presentation is one of *stable* equilibrium; the authors write as if the Trobrianders, the Tikopia, the Nuer are as they are, now and for ever. Indeed the confusion between the concepts of equilibrium and of stability is so deep-rooted in anthropological literature that any use of either of these terms is liable to lead to ambiguity. They are not of course the same thing. My own position is as follows.

Model systems

When the anthropologist attempts to describe a social system he necessarily describes only a model of the social reality. This model represents in effect the anthropologist's hypothesis about 'how the social system works'. The different parts of the model system therefore necessarily form a coherent whole – it is a system in equilibrium. But this does not imply that the social reality forms a coherent whole; on the contrary the reality situation is in most cases full of inconsistencies; and it is precisely these inconsistencies which can provide us with an understanding of the processes of social change.

In situations such as we find in the Kachin Hills Area, any particular individual can be thought of as having a status position in several different social systems at one and the same time. To the individual himself such systems present themselves as alternatives or inconsistencies in the scheme of values by which he orders his life. The overall process of structural change comes about through the manipulation of these alternatives as a means of social advancement. Every individual of a society, each in his own interest, endeavours to exploit the situation as he perceives it and in so doing the collectivity of individuals alters the structure of the society itself.

This rather complicated idea will receive frequent illustration in the pages which follow but the argument may be illustrated by a simple example.

In matters political, Kachins have before them two quite contradictory ideal modes of life. One of these is the Shan system of government, which resembles a feudal hierarchy. The other is that which in this book is referred to as the *gumlao* type organisation; this is essentially anarchistic and equalitarian. It is not uncommon to meet an ambitious Kachin who assumes the names and titles of a Shan prince in order to justify his claim to aristocracy, but who simultaneously appeals to *gumlao* principles of equality in order to escape the liability of paying feudal dues to his own traditional chief.

And just as individual Kachins are frequently presented with a choice as to what is morally right, so also whole Kachin communities may be said to be offered a choice as to the type of political system which shall serve as their ideal. Briefly, my argument is that in terms of political organisation Kachin communities oscillate between two polar types – *gumlao* 'democracy' on the one hand, Shan 'autocracy' on the other. The majority of actual Kachin communities are neither *gumlao* nor Shan in type, they are organised according to a system described in this book as *gumsa*,[10] which is, in effect, a kind of compromise between *gumlao* and Shan ideals. In a later chapter I describe the *gumsa* system as if it were a third static model intermediate between the *gumlao* and Shan models, but the reader needs clearly to understand that actual *gumsa* communities are not static. Some, under the influence of favourable economic circumstances, tend more and more towards the Shan model, until in the end the Kachin aristocrats feel that they 'have become Shan' (*sam tai sai*), as in the case of the Möng Hko elder [whom we encountered on p. 2]; other *gumsa* communities shift in the opposite direction and become *gumlao*. Kachin social organisation, as it is described in the existing ethnographic accounts, is always the *gumsa* system; but my thesis is that this system considered by itself does not really make sense, it is too full of inherent inconsistencies. Simply as a model scheme it can be represented as an equilibrium system,[11] yet as Lévi-Strauss has perceived the structure thus represented contains elements which are 'en contradiction avec le système, et doit donc entraîner sa ruine'.[12] In the field of social reality *gumsa* political structures are essentially unstable, and I maintain that they only become fully intelligible in terms of the contrast provided by the polar types of *gumlao* and Shan organisation.

Another way of regarding phenomena of structural change is to say that we are concerned with shifts in the focus of political power within a given system.

The structural description of a social system provides us with an idealised model which states the 'correct' status relations existing between groups within the total system and between the social persons who make up particular groups.[13] The position of any social person in any such model system is necessarily fixed, though individuals can be thought of as filling different positions in the performance of different kinds of occupation and at different stages in their career.

When we refer to structural change we have to consider not merely changes in the position of individuals with regard to an ideal system of status relationships, but changes in the ideal system itself: changes, that is, in the power structure.

Power in any system is to be thought of as an attribute of 'office holders', that is of social persons who occupy positions to which power attaches. Individuals wield power only in their capacity as social persons. As a general rule I hold that the social anthropologist is never justified in interpreting action as unambiguously directed towards any one particular end. For this reason I am always dissatisfied with functionalist arguments concerning 'needs' and 'goals' such as those advanced by Malinowski and Talcott Parsons,[14] but I consider it necessary and justifiable to assume that a conscious or unconscious wish to gain power is a very general motive in human affairs. Accordingly I assume that individuals faced with a choice of action will commonly use such choice so as to gain power, that is to say they will seek recognition as social persons who have power; or, to use a different language, they will seek to gain access to office or the esteem of their fellows which may lead them to office.

Esteem is a cultural product. What is admired in one society may be deplored in another. The peculiarity of the Kachin Hills type of situation is that an individual may belong to more than one esteem system, and that these systems may not be consistent. Action which is meritorious according to Shan ideas may be rated as humiliating according to the *gumlao* code. The best way for an individual to gain esteem in any particular situation is therefore seldom clear. This sounds difficult, but the reader need not imagine that such uncertainty is by any means unusual; in our own society the ethically correct action for a Christian business man is often equally ambiguous.

Notes

This is an extract from Leach's book *Political Systems of Highland Burma* (1954), pp. 3–10.

1. [Eds: See I.2.1 above for elucidation of what Leach means by 'ritual expression'.]
2. Cf. Fortes, 'Time and Social Structure', pp. 54–60.
3. Lévi-Strauss, *Structures élémentaires* (1st edn), ch. 18.
4. Evans-Pritchard, *The Nuer*.
5. Fortes, 'Time and Social Structure', pp. 54–5.
6. Radcliffe-Brown, 'On Social Structure'.
7. Cf. Nadel, *Foundations of Social Anthropology*, p. 187.
8. Malinowski, *Dynamics of Culture Change*; G. and M. Wilson, *Analysis of Social Change*; Herskovits, *Man and his Works*.
9. Homans, *The Human Group*, pp. 336f.

10. Except where otherwise stated, all native words used in this chapter are words of the Jinghpaw language spelt according to the system of romanisation devised by Hanson; cf. Hanson, *Dictionary of the Kachin Language.*
11. Leach, 'Structural Implications', pp. 40–5.
12. Lévi-Strauss, *Structures élémentaires*, p. 325.
13. For this use of the expression 'social person' see especially Radcliffe-Brown, 'Social Structure', p. 5.
14. Malinowski, *Scientific Theory of Culture*; Parsons, *Essays in Sociological Theory*; Parsons and Shils, *General Theory of Action*, part 2.

3.3

The Frontiers of 'Burma' (1961)

The thesis underlying this essay may be summarised as follows: the modern European concepts *frontier*, *state*, and *nation* are interdependent but they are not necessarily applicable to all state-like political organisations everywhere. In default of adequate documentary materials most historians of south-east Asia have tended to assume that the states with which they have to deal were nation–states occupied by named 'Peoples' and separated from each other by precise political frontiers. The inferences that have been made on the basis of these initial assumptions sometimes conflict with sociological common sense. It is not the anthropologist's task to write history, but if history is to be elaborated with the aid of inspired guesses then the special knowledge of the anthropologist becomes relevant so as to point up the probabilities.

What then do we mean by a frontier? In modern political geography a frontier is a precisely defined line on the map (and on the ground) marking the exact division between two adjacent states. Most such frontiers, as they exist today, are the outcome of arbitrary political decision or military accident; very few correspond to any economically significant feature of the natural topography. Yet wars are fought to defend such frontiers and from such wars there has emerged a European myth which asserts, not only that every political state must, *ipso facto*, have a definite boundary, but also that the frontiers in question *ought* in some way to correspond with differences of culture and language.

This attitude to frontiers ties in with the dogma of sovereignty. In the ideology of modern international politics all states are sovereign and every piece of the earth's surface must, by logical necessity, be the rightful legal possession of one and only one such state. There are no longer any blank spaces on the map and, in theory at least, there can be no overlap between the territories of two adjacent states. Whatever practical difficulties this may entail – as for example in Antarctica – the principle is not in doubt; territorial sovereignty is absolute and indivisible.

The universality of this dogma is quite a recent development. In its present form it is a by-product of the clash of European imperialist interests. In Asia and

Africa nearly all the present political frontiers were first established during the nineteenth or early twentieth centuries either as a compromise between the rival aspirations of European Great Powers or else as an *ad hoc* invention designed to suit the administrative convenience of some colonial agency. Even today in the few cases in which genuinely non-European regimes still survive, the determination of frontiers is often impossible. The boundaries between Saudi Arabia and Trucial Oman are a case in point; the boundary between north-east Burma and China is another. This last instance is relevant to my theme.

By the 'Burma' of my title I wish to imply the whole of the wide imprecisely defined frontier region lying between India and China and having modern political Burma at its core.

In this region the indigenous political systems which existed prior to the phase of European political expansion were not separated from one another by frontiers in the modern sense and they were not sovereign nation–states. The whole of 'Burma' is a frontier region continuously subjected to influences from both India and China and so also the frontiers which separated the petty political units within 'Burma' were not clearly defined lines but zones of mutual interest. The political entities in question had interpenetrating political systems, they were not separate countries inhabited by distinct populations. This concept of a frontier as a border zone through which cultures interpenetrate in a dynamic manner is not a new one[1] but it needs to be distinguished clearly from the precise MacMahon lines of modern political geography.

Existing histories of the Burma region do not interpret the facts in this way. Instead it is constantly assumed that frontiers of language correspond to frontiers of culture and of political power. The population is said to consist of a large number of separate 'peoples': Mons, Arakanese, Karens, Burmese, Kachins, Shans, Lisu, and so on, each group being assumed to have a separate history. Such peoples are never treated as indigenous to Burma; each group arrived separately by migration from some remote original homeland. Such fables are like saying that the original home of Man was in the Garden of Eden. The theory that the Burmese came from Tibet is based on linguistic similarities between the modern Burmese and Tibetan languages. Similar arguments might be used to demonstrate that the original home of the English was in Italy or Persia or even Iceland.

This myth of philological origins, with its illusion of multiple discontinuities, has distracted the historian's attention from those elements of the modern Burmese social scene which have been persistently present throughout the last 2000 years. In particular, the historians have tended to neglect the continuing interaction between processes of political action and the permanent structure of ecological relationships.

In what follows I shall ignore the problems posed by language distributions and I do so intentionally for I insist that very few valid inferences can be constructed solely on the basis of knowledge thus provided. Anyone who doubts this need only consider the relations between history and the facts suggested by a linguistic map of contemporary Europe. Language groupings are of sociological rather than historical significance.

Those who speak one mother-tongue necessarily share a certain sense of social solidarity with one another, but this has no necessary implications for the historical antecedents of the individuals concerned. In present-day Ceylon most of the ruling elite speak English in their homes and have Portuguese surnames; it would be completely erroneous to suppose that any significant proportion of these people are of European descent.

The analysis and classification of the languages and language distributions of 'Burma' is an important scientific exercise, it cannot be a contribution to history.

As an alternative I argue that the historically significant contrasts in present-day 'Burma' are differences of ecology and differences of social organisation. The two sets of differences nearly coincide; roughly speaking the Hill People are patrilineal and hierarchical, the Valley People have a non-unilineal kinship organisation linked with charismatic despotism. This coincidence is not a *necessary* coincidence; if we are to explain why it exists then we must seek an historical explanation. The explanation which I offer is that the Valley People took their social organisation and their politics from India while the Hill People took their social organisation along with their trade and their kinship system from China. It is a possible explanation; I do not claim more than that.

In place of the usual linguistic categories I would substitute ecological categories and these I shall now specify.

'Hill People' and 'Valley People'

The terrain of Burma is very mountainous but not uniformly so. There are parts of the area where the valleys between the mountain ridges are narrow gorges where no human habitation is possible except for those who are prepared to scrape a livelihood from the steep mountain face. But elsewhere the valleys form flat well-watered alluvial basins perfectly adapted to the needs of the rice farmer. My terms 'Hill People' and 'Valley People' are intended to denote the diametrically opposed modes of subsistence associated with these two types of terrain. These two modes of subsistence have been present in the area throughout historical times[2] and any hypothesis concerning historical process must take this into account.

The term Hill People is unambiguous; the people so described do in fact live in steep hill country. In the main they enjoy a somewhat meagre standard of living sustained through the aid of shifting cultivation, though certain exceptions to this generalisation will be considered later. Among the Hill People there is a great range of variety both in language and tribal organisation. The indigenous religion of most groups comes within Tylor's category of animism; it usually involves some form of ancestor worship. Over the past century the Christian missions have made many converts, but true Hill People are never Buddhists.

The term Valley People is not quite so straightforward; it is not the equivalent of 'Lowlander'. The major populations of the lowland plains of Burma, Thailand, and Assam are Valley People, but so also are the dominant elements in the population of the Shan states, south-west Yunnan, and Laos – all of which are upland districts. The characteristic alluvial terrain which makes wet rice cultivation a profitable enterprise often occurs at high altitudes. Some settlements of Valley People are located nearly 6000 feet above sea level.

My term Valley People also covers other ambiguities. The greater part of 'Burma' is a region of high annual rainfall, in which every level stretch of ground can readily be developed into a rice field. But 'Burma' also includes certain dry zones in which the characteristic rice farming techniques of the Valley People are only possible in association with large-scale irrigation engineering. Consequently, in these dry-zone valleys, the population is divided between two distinct sociological categories. On the one hand there are the prosperous rice farmers who are concentrated around the areas of artificial irrigation; on the other there are the people of the parched outlands, whose living standards are at an altogether lower level. In this essay I shall ignore this distinction. My Valley People are all assumed to be wet rice cultivators living in conditions highly favourable to wet rice cultivation.

The languages of the Valley People are diverse but much less so than is the case with the Hill People. The majority of Valley People speak Khmer (Cambodian), Thai, and Burmese dialects;[3] these languages are not spoken by any Hill People as a mother-tongue, though bilingualism is common.

The most distinctive cultural characteristic of the Valley People – apart from the practice of wet rice farming – is their adherence to Hinayana Buddhism. The Valley People think of themselves as the civilised sector of the total 'Burma' population, and in that context Buddhism and civilisation are synonymous. In Burma proper, the Valley People are mostly either Burmese or Shan; they express their contempt for their hill neighbours by using the epithet *Kha* ('slave', 'savage'). Nevertheless, a *Kha* who becomes a Buddhist is thereby civilised, he has 'become a Shan', and within a generation or two the barbarian origin of his descendants may be forgotten. This type of assimilation has been going on for centuries. What is recorded of Cambodia in the thirteenth century is strictly in accord with what we know of North Burma in the nineteenth century.[4]

My generalisation that Hill People are never Buddhist needs further qualification. Apart from individual conversions there are certain exceptional circumstances in which whole groups of Hill People have become economically sophisticated and have adopted the religion and manners of their Valley neighbours. For example, the Palaung inhabitants of Tawngpeng in the Burma Shan States who are prosperous cultivators of tea have become Buddhists and have organised their Tawngpeng State in exact imitation of the political model provided by their Shan neighbours – who are typical rice-growing Valley People.[5] In general however it is only the true Valley People who can afford to be civilised and Buddhist.

The fully documented history of 'Burma' goes back only for a few centuries and is very largely concerned with the relations between European colonialists and native rulers. For periods more remote than the fifteenth century we have only a kind of proto-history, a mixture of legend and inspired guesswork comparable to those histories of Troy which ingeniously manage to fit the stories of the *Iliad* to the latest findings of Turkish archaeology. If such proto-history is to be convincing it must be sociologically probable; it must not neglect the fixity of ecological facts and it must not postulate sharp cultural and political boundaries in a region where none exists even to this day.

Besides the two internal continuities – the ecological categories Hill People and Valley People – there have been two external continuities, the persisting influence of India and China. What is their nature?

India and China

Throughout recorded history there have been two main foci of cultural development in eastern Asia; one in India and the other in China. Every society in south-east Asia of which we have knowledge which has possessed even a modest degree of cultural sophistication has been quite emphatically subject to Indian or Chinese influence; usually to both.

The manifestations of such influence are very diverse and I only propose to consider certain major aspects. Within these limits I shall propound the theses that the influence of China has been mainly in the fields of trade and communication and has affected the Hill People rather than the Valley People and that, in contrast, the influence of India has been felt particularly in the fields of politics and religion and has affected the Valley People rather than the Hill People.

There is no mystery about this – the Chinese have never been interested in 'Burma' as a potential dominion – they have believed it to be too unhealthy. But they have had a persistent interest in overland routes to India and also in the natural resources of 'Burma's' mountains and forests. The early Chinese records tell us nothing about the political organisation of the region but they record detailed itineraries[6] and also such facts as that the land of the *b'uok*[7] tribes living south-west of Yung Chang produced rhinoceros, elephant, tortoise-shell, jade, amber, cowries, gold, silver, salt, cinnamon and cotton, hilly-paddy and panicled millet, a catalogue which, apart from the cinnamon, is accurate and comprehensive to this day.

Even in the thirteenth century when China under the Mongols was adopting blatantly imperialistic policies her ambassador remarks of Cambodia that 'this country has long had commerical relations with us'. He does not claim any ancient political suzerainty.[8]

So also in recent centuries when northern Burma had been the main source of jade for all China, the jade mines were owned and worked by Hill People and Chinese interests remained basically commercial rather than political. The Valley People of the jade mines area benefited only indirectly.

I shall return again to this matter of the economic interrelations between the Chinese and the northern Hill Peoples, but first let us consider some features of the political structure.

Already in early Han times, in the first millennium BC, the Chinese had developed an idea of the nation–state comparable to the concept of *imperium* which the Romans developed in Europe a few centuries later. This ideology postulates a central government which is the ultimate political authority for the whole of a large territorial area delimited by frontiers. The administration of this empire is in the hands of office-holders, an Emperor with an administrative staff of bureaucrats.[9] The authority of the central government is maintained by military force, exercised by garrison troops permanently dispersed throughout the country and at appropriate positions on the frontier. Administration is financed by taxation which is levied in a systematic 'legitimate' manner and not according to the arbitrary whim of local war-lords.

No doubt the practical application of such theories often deviated very far from the ideal, yet the basic structure of both the Chinese and the Roman systems possessed an extraordinary degree of stability. In both cases the Empire was able to survive long phases of catastrophic incompetence and corruption at the centre; the structure of administrative authority was almost impervious to the effects of palace revolutions and dynastic change.

The Indian political model is very different. Here the ideal ruler is not an office-holder, the Emperor, but an individual, Asoka; the pattern is one of charismatic leadership rather than bureaucratic continuity. Now it is an established fact that all the early historical states of the Burma region which achieved any international renown were of an Indian style. Coedès calls them *les états hindouisés*, and Hall, elaborating this, says that their organisational pattern always had four common elements which he lists as:

(1) a conception of royalty characterised by Hindu or Buddhist cults;
(2) literary expression by means of the Sanskrit language;
(3) a mythology taken from the Epics, the Puranas, and other Sanskrit texts containing a nucleus of royal tradition and the traditional genealogies of royal families of the Ganges region;
(4) the observance of the Dharmashatras, the sacred laws of Hinduism and in particular that version known as the Laws of Manu.[10]

It is quite outside my field to discuss just how this Indian colonisation came about but what I must emphasise is the pervasiveness and wide extent of the political influence in question.

In the second century BC the western border of China lay along the Salween but after AD 342 the official frontier was withdrawn much further to the north-east. This was a consequence of the development of Nanchao as an independent political entity centred near modern Tali. Now Nanchao, despite its remote position, was unquestionably a state of Indian rather than Chinese type. It had no bureaucratic stability and its fortunes fluctuated violently according to the individual aggressiveness of successive rulers.

Nanchao provides an excellent example of the confusion which arises when such states are thought of as nation–states of modern type. Nanchao was inhabited by people of Thai speech; it ceased to exist as an independent political entity in 1253, following conquest by Kublai Khan. In the centuries which follow, monarchs with Thai-sounding names are recorded as the rulers of petty principalities all over 'Burma'. This has been interpreted as evidence that, following the destruction of Nanchao, there was a mass migration of Thai-speaking peoples to the south-west.[11] This in turn is linked with the more general thesis that since Thai is a language of Chinese type it must have 'originated' somewhere in central China.

Yet in fact there is no evidence at all of any migration of Thai-speaking peoples into 'Burma' from the north-east, and recent trends in linguistic research seem to indicate that Thai speech has no close affinities with Chinese. Its closest links appear to be with languages further south such as Mon and Indonesian.[12]

Moreover Nanchao should not be thought of as a state with borders but as a capital city with a wide and variable sphere of influence. The inhabitants of Nanchao had no specific identification with the state, there was no Nanchao nation which would be dispersed by the elimination of Nanchao as a separate political entity. Indeed Kublai Khan's occupation of the capital – which was notably peaceful – need have had no effect on the population whatsoever.

The common-sense assumption is that there must have been Valley People in 'Burma' in the fifth century just as there were Valley People in 'Burma' in the fifteenth century and that the Valley People of the two periods spoke much the same sort of language or set of languages. The migration hypothesis of the historians is both improbable and unnecessary.

Charismatic kingship

What then are the empirical characteristics of *les états hindouisés*? Most of them have been small, most of them have been short-lived; the continuity of the state depends upon the personality of the monarch; every monarch has a successor, but every succession is an issue of dispute; the state dies with the King, the successor must create a new state from his own personal endeavours.

There was continuity of a sort, for the states were in every case built up around a heartland of irrigated rice cultivation and, whatever the vicissitudes of politics, the rice-land stayed in one place. But the state had no fixed frontier, no permanent administrative staff.

Scott's comment on the Shans is applicable to all the Valley Peoples of 'Burma':

> Shan history more than that of any other race, seems to have depended on the character and personal energy of the Sawbwa (Prince). An ambitious ruler

> seems always to have attempted, and often to have effected, the subjugation of his neighbours. When there were two or more such there was perpetual war; when there was none there were a number of practically independent chieftains dwelling in their own valleys. Hence the astounding number of huge ruined cities which are found all over Indo-China.[13]

In this respect the historical kingdoms of Arakan, Pagan, Pegu, Thaton, Ava, Ayut'ia, Manipur, and Assam (as well as some hundreds of smaller principalities located within the same general area) all had much in common. Hinayana Buddhism was everywhere the state religion mixed, as in Ceylon, with many explicit elements of Saivite Brahmanism. Everywhere royal polygyny was an exaggerated feature of the royal prerogative. The King was regarded as a Chakravartin – a 'Universal Emperor' – or else as an incipient Buddha.[14] Ritual and myth both implied that he was playing the role of the secular Gaudama prior to his enlightenment. Every feature of the system implied that government was regarded as personal rule by a divinely inspired monarch considered as an individual.

Let me elaborate these sweeping generalisations so as to bring out the difference between the Indian model and the Chinese.

In China the succession was governed by law; each Emperor had a single legitimate heir specified by rules of descent. If the heir was a minor at the time of his succession he still became Emperor even though a close relative might act as regent. Usurpation was relatively rare and occurred only with a change of dynasty or in times of political chaos. Day-to-day government was in the hands of the literati, persons whose status as bureaucrats was, in theory, based on personal merit and not on royal favour or aristocratic blood. In practice the literati constituted a largely hereditary class but they were not close relatives of the Emperor. The Princes of the blood royal held highly privileged positions but this did not give them office as administrators.

In the 'Indian' states of 'Burma' any one of a King's very numerous offspring might 'legitimately' succeed him and palace murders were the norm. The first act of any successful claimant was to carry out a holocaust of his most immediate rivals – that is to say, his half-brothers and step-mothers. He then apportioned out his realm in fiefs to those of his close relatives who had survived and were considered trustworthy; that meant, in the main, the King's own wives and sons. The nature of this fiefdom is well indicated by the Burmese term for a fief holder – *myosa* – 'the eater of the township'. Since the *myosa*'s tenure of office was notoriously short-lived, he made the most of his opportunities.

It is true that in addition to these licensed royal plunderers the structure of government included a hierarchy of commoner officials with fanciful and elaborate titles – the Burmese *wun*, Shan *amat*, Siamese *brahya*. But these offices too were directly in the King's personal gift. There was no criterion of achieved qualification as in the case of the Chinese literati. In thirteenth-century Cambodia the two recognised ways of obtaining administrative office were (1) to make oneself the client of a royal prince or (2) to donate a daughter to the royal harem.[15]

First-hand observers of Thai and Burmese monarchs during the nineteenth century were all unanimous in emphasising the complete absolutism of the monarch's authority[16] and the arbitrariness of the resulting administration. The position is thus summed up by Scott:

> The coolie of today may be the minister of tomorrow; and a month hence he may be spread-eagled in the court of the palace with a vertical sun beating down upon him and huge stones piled on his chest and stomach . . . When King Tharrawaddy succeeded, he made Ba-gyee-daw's ministers work as slaves on the roads for a time, and when this exercise had quite worn them out, charitably put them to death . . . When an official displeased the king (Mindohn Min) in some way, he said emphatically 'I don't want to see that man any more' . . . A day or two afterwards his majesty would ask where so-and-so was. 'Alas Sire,' was the answer, 'he died of chagrin shortly after the lord of the earth and ocean cast eyes of displeasure on him.'[17]

Absolute tyranny was tempered only by the fact that the King, though also head of the Buddhist Church, had relatively limited power to manipulate clerical offices. A hierarchy of relatively permanent Church officials operated in parallel to the secular hierarchy of royal appointees and seems to have introduced at least a few elements of stability and mercy into a governmental system ordinarily controlled by arbitrary whim.

The typical 'Burma' state consisted of a small fully administered territorial nucleus having the capital at the centre. Round about, stretching indefinitely in all directions, was a region over which the King claimed suzerainty and from the inhabitants of which he extracted tribute by threat of military force. These marginal zones all had the status of conquered provinces, and their populations were normally hostile to the central government. Insurrections were endemic and the political alignments of local leaders possessed the maximum uncertainty. Practically every substantial township in 'Burma' claims a history of having been at one time or another the capital of a 'kingdom', the alleged frontiers of which are at once both grandiose and improbable.

It is consistent with this general pattern that those who are now remembered as great kings were practitioners of banditry on a grand scale whose fame rests solely on their short-term success in carrying fire and slaughter into the territory of their more prosperous neighbours. The 'Just Ruler', that archetypal figure upon whom the Confucian ethic lays much stress, had no place in the value system of 'Burma' kingship. The kings of Ava, Arakan, Pegu, and Ayut'ia were forever pillaging each other's capitals, but conquest by the sword was never followed up by any serious attempt to establish a permanent political hegemony. Military success was simply a manifestation of the monarch's personal power, it did not serve to establish authority and it did not alter political frontiers.

But in what sense did these explosive, ephemeral, yet recurrent states really possess 'frontiers' at all?

Political interdependence of hills and valleys

Let us go back and resume our consideration of the ecological as distinct from the politico-historical factors in the situation. The political states which we have been discussing have always included elements of both my main population categories, Hill People as well as Valley People. The heartland of the state, with the King's capital, was *always* a rice-growing valley inhabited by Valley People but the outlying parts of the state normally included Hill sectors as well as Valley sectors. The pattern of development was as follows. The King would first establish authority over his own home valley – ideally by succession, but more frequently by usurpation. He would then spread his authority to a neighbouring valley. This might be achieved by conquest or by marriage treaty or sometimes simply by colonisation. Finally the King would claim sovereignty over all the hill country separating the two valley sectors of his total domain. Thus most Hill People were, at least in theory, the subjects of a Valley Prince.

But the control which the Valley Princes were able to exercise over the Hill subjects was seldom more than marginal, and the Hill People were quite indiscriminate in their favours. If it suited his convenience a Hill chieftain would readily avow loyalty to several different Valley Princes simultaneously. There were two recognised methods by which the Valley Prince might assert his authority; he could organise a punitive expedition and levy tribute, or he could pay protection money to the Hill tribesmen as a reward for their loyalty.[18] Some form of the latter procedure seems to have been the most common.

What I must emphasise is that the nominal overlordship of a Valley prince over a tract of Hill country did not entail the merging of the Valley People with the Hill People in any cultural sense. Whatever the overall political structure the two categories remained distinct in language, religion, and ecological adaptation. It is true that the manners and customs of the Valley People provided, in certain respects, a model of politeness even for the Hill barbarians. In Burma proper the Hill chieftains whom the first European travellers encountered were often dressed in Chinese, Shan, or Burmese style and took pride in listing the honorific titles which had been bestowed upon them by their elegant Valley overlords, but at the same time they themselves claimed to be lords in their own right, subject to no outside authority.

But it would be equally misleading to represent the Valley People and the Hill People as permanently ranged in implacable hostility. The two categories of population are symbiotic on one another; they interpenetrate territorially and politically as well as culturally for, in the course of centuries, 'civilisation', as represented by the culture of the Valley People, has fanned out along the river valleys and infiltrated upwards into isolated pockets right in the heart of the hill country.

Some of these small pockets of upland Valley People may have originated as military garrisons guarding a strategic route, others may have been started by private colonists seeking to escape the burdens of war and tyranny, but the fact that they have survived and still managed to retain their characteristic Valley Culture shows that the professed hostility of the surrounding Hill People is seldom carried to extremes.

The high degree of political interconnectedness between adjacent groups of Valley People and Hill People may best be demonstrated from an example. The far north-west of Burma is dotted with tiny Shan settlements surrounded by vast areas of mountain country inhabited only by Kachins. Chinese documents show that some of these Shan settlements were already in existence in the eighth century AD. Though widely scattered, these various Shan statelets claim a cultural unity; they are Hkamti Shans and formerly fell within the domain of the Prince of Mogaung. The Kachins of the surrounding hill country admit no kinship with the Shans nor do they admit that they were ever the subjects of the Prince of Mogaung. They point out that the jade and amber mines which were the main source of Mogaung prosperity lie in Kachin and not in Shan territory. The Kachins, they say, were the allies but not the servants of Mogaung. It is a matter of history that the independent principality of Mogaung was extinguished by military force in 1765, but the ancient ideology persists. The present-day Kachin chieftain who owns the jade mines has appropriated to himself the title of Hkamti Prince (Kansi Duwa).

The Shan statelets of the former Mogaung realm were widely scattered as the table below shows.

Modern map names	*Distance (miles) and direction from Mogaung*
Mogaung	–
Kamaing	22 NW
Mohnyin	50 SW
Mainghkwan	73 NNW
Möng Kong (Maing Kaing)	93 WSW
Singkaling Hkamti	90 NW
Taro	90 NNW
Hkamti (Headwaters Irrawaddy)	140 NNE
Hkamti (in Assam)	160 NNW

Each of these localities is a small rice plain inhabited by a Thai-speaking Buddhist population ranging in numbers from a hundred to a few thousand. In addition the Mogaung Prince claimed suzerainty over all the hill country lying in between, that is an area of some 10,000 square miles. For that matter, he also claimed overlordship over all Assam. In turn the Prince himself offered ambivalent allegiance to both the Emperor of China and the King of Ava, a circumstance which proved disastrous when, in the latter part of the eighteenth century, the King of Ava went to war with China over the control of the jade trade.

My point is this. The seventeenth–eighteenth-century realm of Mogaung may be regarded as a typical 'Burma' state. It had from certain points of view a very real existence; there *was* a Mogaung Prince and his kingdom had a name (it appears in the records as Nora, Pong, etc.); yet in another sense the kingdom was a fiction. Its Shan inhabitants were widely scattered and by no means numerous. The Prince could only undertake effective military or political action with the aid and consent of the Hill 'subjects', who were not subjects at all. His claims regarding territorial suzerainty were optimistic in the extreme.

This Mogaung example is in no way an extreme or atypical instance nor have the conditions which prevailed in the eighteenth century altered substantially in recent times. The authority exercised by the central government of the Independent Sovereign State of Burma over its outlying regions in the year 1959 is of a very similar kind. I believe that nearly all the Indian style states of 'Burma' history have been of this general type.

My main purpose in citing this example was to indicate the kind of relationship which existed between the civilised, nominally dominant Valley People on the one hand and their barbarous Hill neighbours on the other. In the Mogaung case, Kachins fought in the Shan armies and they traded in the Shan markets and they admitted the lordship of the Shan Prince. But the Shan Prince exercised no administrative authority and levied no tribute. Shans and Kachins did not intermarry and the Kachins had no truck with the Buddhist priesthood. Yet assimilation could and did take place. The labourers on the Shan ricefields were mostly settled Kachins living in voluntary serfdom. We have actual historical evidence that such groups, by adopting the manners, and dress and language of their masters tended to merge with them completely in the course of a few generations.[19] The Valley People of today should not be thought of as the descendants of an immigrant alien race, they are simply descendants of Hill People who have settled in the valleys and adopted civilised customs along with the practice of Valley-type wet rice agriculture. But in making this cultural transfer they have cut themselves off completely from their former associates in the hills. In this part of the world a Buddhist cannot be a kinsman of a non-Buddhist.

Certain other aspects of the argument from ecology deserve attention. The Valley People because of their wet rice farming live in locally dense aggregates of population and this is an important factor in their cultural cohesion; in contrast, most of the Hill People, being shifting cultivators, live in small widely scattered settlements. I have no means of computing the precise figures but, very roughly, in Burma proper, the Hill country takes up ten times as much space as the Valley country but there are ten times as many Valley People as there are Hill People.

The Hill People are not in every case shifting cultivators; some of them resort to fixed cultivation on irrigated terraces. But the groups which do this are not a distinct category in any linguistic or cultural sense and their existence does not affect the general argument. Hill farming of *any* kind requires a very high labour effort in relation to yield and consequently it can very seldom provide any economic surplus over and above the immediate subsistence needs of the local population. It is the existence of such a surplus in the Valley economy which permits the Valley People to maintain their more elegant style of life.

The converse is likewise true; throughout the whole Hill region wherever a particular group has become exceptionally prosperous its members show a tendency to adopt a Shan (Thai) or Burmese style of living and to become converted to Buddhism. It follows that the contrasts of culture and language which have led to the conventional classification of 'tribes and peoples of Burma' have no intrinsic permanence. Any individual can start as a member of one category and end up in another.

Although the greater part of the 'Burma' hill country has been for centuries under the (nominal) political suzerainty of Valley Princes, the Valley influence has not been evenly distributed. Valley culture has spread only to areas where there is suitable alluvial farming land so that in some of the more remote areas an indigenous Hill population has been allowed to develop on its own without political interference from would-be Valley rulers.

If then we want to consider the nature of Hill Society as an ideal type so as to contrast it with Valley Society as an ideal type then it is here in the more remote hill areas that we can observe it.

Political structure of Hill Society

On this basis Hill Society can be said to possess the following general characteristics:

(1) The Valley pattern of a semi-divine Prince, surrounded by a harem, and ruling by divine right in his personal capacity, is wholly absent.

(2) Two contrasted patterns of authority structure stand out and are nearly always juxtaposed in immediate association . . .

These are:

(a) an ideology of rule by aristocratic chiefs. The chief is not endowed with personal charisma but holds his office by hereditary right as senior member of a royal lineage;

(b) an ideology of 'democratic' rule by a council of elders. Each elder acts as representative of a particular lineage but no one lineage is intrinsically superior to any other. The elder may achieve his office either by seniority or as a consequence of passing some test of merit.[20]

In either case offices of authority are representative offices and are derived from status at birth. The granting of office is never linked with political patronage as in the Valley Society.

It is very remarkable that both types of ideology, the aristocratic and the democratic, are regularly found to coexist side-by-side throughout the whole of the northern and western parts of the 'Burma' hill country. I will list only a few examples:

Hill Group	*Aristocratic*	*Democratic*
Kachin[21]	*gumsa*	*gumlao*
Konyak Naga[22]	*thendu*	*thenkoh*
Southern Naga[23]	Sema	Chakrima (Angami)
Central Chin[24]	Zahau	Zanniat
Western Manipur Hills[25]	New Kuki (Thado)	Old Kuki

For the more easterly hill tracts of the southern Shan States, Karenni, northern Thailand, and Laos, the ethnographic descriptions are too defective to permit confident generalisation, but here too the same two contrasted types of political ideology appear to coexist.[26] Elsewhere I have argued at length that these two types of political organisation represent different aspects of a single 'cyclic' type of system viewed at different phases of its growth.[27]

(3) In the aristocratic type of regime a single chief usually claims dominion over a number of scattered villages. Each of these villages has a headman who holds office by hereditary right. The headman's lineage and the chief's lineage are usually linked by ties of affinity.

In contrast, in the democratic regime, each village is on its own. Democratic villages are not necessarily weaker politically than aristocratic chiefdoms, for some democratic villages are relatively very large.

(4) The great majority of the Hill People are organised in exogamous unilineal descent groups of lineage type. The Karens may be an exception to this rule but the available information is inadequate and inconsistent. In contrast, among the Valley People unilineal descent groups are not a normal feature of the social structure. Where such descent groups occur, as sometimes among the aristocracy, they are not exogamous.

(5) Hill Society attains its highest elaboration in areas which are remote from the contaminating influence of Buddhist civilisation. This proposition is not self-contradictory. From the viewpoint of the external observer it is legitimate to regard the Buddhist Valley People as the *civilised* element in the total population in contrast to the animist Hill People, who are, by comparison, *barbarians*. But Hill Society has its own scale of values and these show up best when they are unadulterated. The following remarks by Scott concerning the Wa head-hunters of the Eastern Shan States might be applied to almost any of the Hill Peoples:

> Material prosperity seems to exist in inverse ratio to the degree of civilisation. The Head-hunting Wa have the most substantial villages and houses, the broadest fields, the greatest number of buffaloes, pigs, dogs and fowls. They also have the greatest conceit of themselves, the most ornaments and the least clothes. The Intermediate Wa fall some way behind in material possessions. The Tame Wa with their civilisation, find their houses dwindle to hovels, their fields shrink to plots . . . and beyond this there are Wa who put up no heads at all; some of them claim to be Buddhists, others make no claim to anything, not even the pity of their neighbours.[28]

There is a genuine paradox here. The Valley People as a whole are vastly more prosperous and sophisticated than the Hill People as a whole, yet in the context of a hill ecology the trimmings of civilisation are disadvantageous. Certain features of this pattern deserve attention.

In the first place, it is very clear that the process of interaction between the Hill People and the Valley People has not been one of simple cultural diffusion. Hills and Valleys stand in radical opposition and there is evidently a certain level at which Hill culture and Valley culture are totally inconsistent with one another just as one might say of early mediaeval Europe that Christianity and paganism were inconsistent. There are cultural elements which are common to both groups but these similarities are remarkably few. Culturally there is far more in common between the Lakher in Assam and the Lamet in Laos[29] than there is between either group and their nearest Valley neighbours. The same is true of any of the Hill Peoples throughout the area.

Yet the pattern of political relations which I have previously described might have led us to expect something different. After all, the Hill People and the Valley People are racially the same and languages are very easily changed, so what is it that keeps the two groups apart?

I do not think that the anthropologist or anyone else can say *why* the distinction exists but I think it may be illuminating to point out some of the associated correlations.

China and the Hill People

Earlier in this essay I remarked that although the Hill People of 'Burma' have for centuries come under the spasmodic political influence of Indian-style states, their most direct economic contacts have been with the Chinese. In some cases this is true even at the present time. I myself have first-hand acquaintance of a number of North Burma localities which were 'unadministered territory' throughout the period of British colonial rule; all of them were regularly visited by Chinese traders, but never by Burmese.

It is relevant here to remember that Chinese society, like that of the Hill People, is structured into a system of unilineal descent groups and also that the 'animism' of the Hill People is fundamentally a cult of dead ancestors which has many Confucianist parallels. These similarities make it possible for the Chinese and the 'Burma' Hill People to communicate with one another and to establish permanent social relationships in a way which is impossible for the Hill People and the Valley People.

Chinese villagers actually settle in the hill country and then live much like ordinary hill folk. They will even inter-marry with their 'barbarian' neighbours; but the Valley People will never do either of these things. The contrast in the pattern of marriage seems to me particularly significant.

In the Valley culture the population of each local rice plain tends to be endogamous. The Prince, who has many wives, may take daughters from neighbouring Princes but he also takes women from his own immediate followers. He receives the latter women as tribute. Thus, in terms of kinship, Valley Society as a whole forms a closed system; the Valley People do not give their women away to strangers. Furthermore, each marriage is an individual affair between a particular man and a particular woman; it does not establish an alliance between kin groups. All this is consistent with the fact that elements of Hindu caste ideology have all along been present in the Valley culture. Valley People repudiate marriage with the barbarians even when they are willing to accept their economic services.[30]

In contrast, in the Hill culture, marriage is closely mixed up with trade. Girls are married against a bride-price and the objects involved in bride-price transactions are the same sort of objects as are met with in dealings with a Chinese trader.[31] Thus the ties of affinal kinship ramify widely, following trade routes and jumping across language frontiers and political boundaries. In 1942 a Gauri acquaintance of mine from east of Bhamo found himself in a Singfo village in Assam 250 miles from home, but it took him only a day or so to persuade his hosts that he was one of their relatives.

I am not arguing that a single kinship network ramifies over the whole of the 'Burma' Hill country but everywhere in the hills a very high valuation is placed on extended kinship relations and also upon the permanence and stability of such relations. Individuals are regarded as representatives of particular lineages and particular places and they are classed on that account as friend or foe. Women who are given in marriage serve to establish a relationship between lineages – a relationship which is likely to be repeated later in further marriages or further trade. This is the antithesis of the Valley culture theory which treats women either as separate individuals or as chattel slaves. A Valley Prince receives women as tribute; a Hill chieftain gives them out as pledges of economic cooperation.

Hill culture is not a direct imitation from the Chinese but it parallels the Chinese system in a way that the Valley culture does not. Just as we can say that the Valley culture has an Indian style without implying that the Shans are Hindus or that the Burmese have a fully developed caste system, I think we can say that the Hill culture has a Chinese style without implying that Naga tribesmen are devout adherents of the Confucian ethic.

The really crucial distinction here is that between charismatic (individual) authority on the one hand and traditional office on the other. In the Valley system all authority is individual and temporary and for that reason tyrannical. The Valley tyrant does not display his merit by justice but by acts of self-glorification.

In the Hill system, as in the Chinese, all offices are vested either in particular lineages (which are conceptually immortal) or else are reserved for individuals who have achieved a particular social status (e.g. by passing examinations or by working through a graded series of sacrificial feasts). The acts of the ruler are themselves governed by rules, everything he does carries the sanction of legitimate custom.

My suggestion is that this contrast of ideologies about the nature of authority illuminates, even if it does not explain why 2000 years of Indian rule has not eliminated the radical separation between Hill and Valley society.

Summary

'Burma' is a region lying between two great centres of civilisation. Throughout history it has been influenced simultaneously from India and from China, not only at the trivial level of Court politics but fundamentally in terms of the cultural system as a whole.

But this influence has not been an indiscriminate diffusion of ideas. Politics, ecology, kinship, and economics provide in some degree separate and separable frames of reference, and I have therefore invited the historian of Burma to look upon the present as part of a continuing process of interaction between two kinds of political structure, two kinds of ecology, two distinct patterns of kinship organisation, two sets of economic interests.

There are other frontier regions where a very similar style of analysis might apply and it is on that account that I feel justified in offering this as a contribution with potential comparative value.

Notes

This paper was published in the interdisciplinary journal, *Comparative Studies in Society and History*, in 1961.

1. Lattimore, *Inner Asian Frontiers of China.* Note on References: No attempt has been made here to support my more general statements with detailed references. For Burma proper and the regions to the east the most useful select bibliography for English-language readers is that appended to Hall, *A History of South-East Asia.* Ethnographic sources for the whole region are well covered by Embree and Dotson, *Bibliography of the Peoples and Cultures of Mainland South-East Asia* (1950). For the Naga Hills area Hutton ('A Bibliography of the Naga Hills') covers nineteenth-century sources very thoroughly. I know of no general bibliography of sources for Assamese history but Mackenzie (*History of Relations with the Hill Tribes of North-Eastern Bengal*), Michell (*Report on the North-East Frontier of India*), and *Selection of Papers* (on 'Hill Tracts') give summaries of many of the key documents for the nineteenth-century period. These source books have been supplemented by Reid, *History of the Frontier Areas Bordering Assam from 1883–1941.* Leach (*Political Systems*) mentions a number of items relating to the North Burma/Assam region which do not appear in other bibliographic lists.
2. E.g. Pelliot, *Mémoires de Tcheou Ta-Kouan*, pp. 20–5. This is a translation of the only first-hand account of Angkor at the height of its splendour. The original author was a Chinese who travelled with an embassy from the Mongol Emperor in the year 1296. [Eds: The 'Mongol Emperor' mentioned here is the Yüan Dynasty Emperor of China, Ch'eng-tsung.] He distinguishes three elements in the population, the Cambodians proper in the city area, the savages who sell themselves as bond slaves to Cambodian masters and work for them in the city, and the brigands of the mountains who form a race apart. The first two categories are dependent on intensive rice agriculture.
3. This ignores the highly complex language pattern among the Valley People of eastern Assam and Manipur.
4. Pelliot, *Mémoires de Tcheou Ta-Kouan*, p. 19; Leach, *Political Systems*, p. 293.
5. Milne, *Shans at Home.*
6. Pelliot, 'Deux itinéraires de Chine en Inde'.

7. See Luce and Pe Maung Tin, 'Burma Down to the Fall of Pagan,' p. 267. Chinese sources date back to the fourth century AD. Certain of the Kachin groups of North Burma are still referred to as *p'ok* by their Shan neighbours. See Leach, *Political Systems* pp. 248f.
8. Pelliot, *Mémoires de Tcheou Ta-Kouan*, p. 10.
9. I use Weber's terminology: cf. Weber, *Theory of Social and Economic Organisation*, and *Religion of China*.
10. Hall, *History of South-East Asia*, p. 13. When Hinayana Buddhism replaced Saivite Hinduism, Pali replaced Sanskrit.
11. Hall, *History of South-East Asia*, pp. 144–6.
12. Benedict, 'Thai, Kadai, and Indonesian'; Taylor, 'General Structure of Languages Spoken in Burma'.
13. Scott and Hardiman, *Gazetteer of Upper Burma*, part 2, ii, p. 333.
14. Quaritch Wales, *Siamese State Ceremonies*, ch. 4; cf. Cady, *History of Modern Burma*, ch. 1; cf. Hall, *History of South-East Asia*, pp. 93–4. Pelliot (*Mémoires de Tcheou Ta-Kouan*, p. 16) credits the thirteenth-century Cambodian monarch with 5000 concubines.
15. Ibid., p. 14.
16. For summarised evidence see in particular Quaritch Wales (*Siamese State Ceremonies*); Graham (*Siam*); Scott and Hardiman (*Gazetteer of Upper Burma*).
17. Scott, *The Burman*, pp. 484–5.
18. In Assam there is a special term *posa* for this type of payment. Even the British authorities with their overwhelming military superiority found it convenient to make *posa* payments to the Hill tribes throughout most of the nineteenth century. Another method of appeasement was for the prince formally to grant his Hill chieftains the right to levy toll on trade caravans passing through the mountains. This practice likewise was kept up by the British colonial authorities for many years.
19. Cf. *supra*, n. 4.
20. Stevenson, *Economics of the Central Chin Tribes*.
21. Leach, *Political Systems*.
22. Von Fürer-Haimendorf, 'Gemeinschaftsleben der Konyak-Naga'.
23. Hutton, *Angami Nagas*, and *Sema Nagas*.
24. Stevenson, *Economics of the Central Chin Tribes*.
25. Shakespear, *Lushei Kuki Clans*.
26. Scott and Hardiman, *Gazetteer of Upper Burma*, part 1, i.
27. Leach, *Political Systems*.
28. Scott and Hardiman, *Gazetteer of Upper Burma*, part 1, i, p. 511.
29. Parry, *The Lakhers*; Izikowitz, *Lamet*. These two 'tribes' are about 500 miles apart.
30. Cf. Pelliot, *Mémoires de Tcheou Ta-Kouan*, p. 19; Milne, *Shans at Home*, p. 50.
31. Cf. Leach, *Political Systems*, refs. to *hpaga*.

3.4

Concerning Trobriand Clans and the Kinship Category *Tabu* (1958)

For social anthropologists Malinowski's ethnographic accounts of Trobriand Island culture are a kind of Domesday Book. Palpably incomplete, palpably imperfect, they yet transcend in some indefinable way everything of like kind. This paper is an attempt to demonstrate from Malinowski's own material that certain of his inferential conclusions were incorrect. It is with no feelings of disrespect that I offer this revision. On the contrary I consider it a tribute to Malinowski's remarkable skill as an ethnographer that he can be shown to have recorded important features of the Trobriand social system of which he himself was unaware. The conclusion which I reach at the end of my paper is a functional one which would have appealed strongly to Malinowski's imagination.

The paper has originated in this way. I have argued elsewhere that Malinowski's emphasis on the pragmatic consequences of behaviour led him to underestimate the degree to which behaviour can serve as a system of symbolic communication.[1] I have cited his view that classificatory kinship terminologies are to be explained as systems of homonyms as an example of the sociological distortion that results from this kind of pragmatism. The present paper elaborates this argument in detail.

My paper bears a certain genetic relationship to Fortes' essay 'Time and Social Structure'.[2] The common theme is that the nature of a social system can only be fully understood when we recognise adequately that any particular individual occupies successively a series of different positions in the total structure.

In brief, the problems which I seek to answer are these. First, why do the Trobrianders have four clans?

The common-sense explanation is that it is an historical accident. That no doubt is the explanation which Malinowski himself would have offered. That seems to me too simple.

As a matter of fact Malinowski fails to explain why the Trobrianders should have a clan system at all. The clans appear to play no social role as such. The effective social groupings in Trobriand society are the units which Malinowski calls sub-clans. It is these sub-clans which are the landowning units, and which operate efficiently as exogamous corporations. Yet, according to Malinowski, each of these numerous sub-clans is allocated to one or other of four totemic clans, and the number four is, it seems, important:

> Humanity is divided into four clans. Totemic nature is conceived to be as deeply ingrained in the substance of the individual as sex, colour, and stature. It can never be changed, and it transcends individual life, for it can be carried over into the next world, and brought back into this one when the spirit returns by reincarnation. This four-fold totemic division is thought to be universal, embracing every section of mankind.[3]

To use Malinowski's terminology, this is quite clearly a 'mythical charter' for something or other. But for what? Malinowski does not explain; I shall seek to do so.

My second problem concerns the tantalising Trobriand word *tabu* which Malinowski discusses at some length on several occasions.[4]

Malinowski distinguishes several meanings of this word which he regards as homonyms – i.e. as different words of similar sound. Apparently he considered that there were at least three such distinct words:

(1) *tabu* = taboo, sacred, forbidden. This, according to Malinowski, is an alien word introduced into the Trobriands by Christian missionaries.

(2) *tabu* = grandparents, ancestors, totems.

(3) *tabu* = father's sister and, by a process of extension, 'lawful woman' – i.e. a woman with whom sexual intercourse is permitted.

On Malinowski's own showing *tabu* in the Trobriands also has various further meanings, e.g. grandchild, and 'husband of any lawful woman'. It is not clear to me whether Malinowski regarded these as yet further homonyms or as extended meanings of the first three.

Now homonyms occur in most languages and, since Malinowski was a most notable linguist, we should perhaps accept his views on the matter. But this I prefer not to do. I submit the hypothesis that Malinowski was here mistaken and that there is only one Trobriand word *tabu*, all the meanings of which are closely and logically connected.

Finally I shall show how my 'solutions' to these two 'problems' tie in very nicely with a third curiosity of Trobriand ethnography, the celebrated origin myth, whereby various original ancestors are made to emerge from holes in the ground conveniently situated at known sites on ancestral property. In pursuing these enquiries we shall be led to re-examine and partly reinterpret Malinowski's views concerning the nature of Trobriand rules of incest and exogamy.

Let us start by considering the various meanings of *tabu*, regarded as a kinship category. In Malinowski's published writings there is no complete list of Trobriand kinship terminology. The nearest approximation to such a list is to be found in *The Sexual Life of Savages*, ch. XIII, section 6. However, in preparing this paper I have had the advantage of being able to consult Mr H. A. Powell, who carried out anthropological fieldwork in the Trobriand Islands in 1950/1. Mr Powell has not only filled in the gaps in Malinowski's kinship term diagram, he has also explained how in certain particulars Malinowski's diagram is in error. The points at which I rely on Mr Powell's information in lieu of Malinowski's own are noted in the text below.[5]

I must stress that I have used Mr Powell simply as an informant on matters of fact. My use of his material does not in any way imply that he agrees with my theoretical interpretations; indeed I know very well that he does not. For all that, his comments on a preliminary draft of this paper have been extremely helpful.

Considered simply as a system in itself, without regard to cultural context, Trobriand kinship terminology falls into the well-known Crow type which has long been recognised as correlated in a general way with matrilineal descent.[6] There are, however, a number of atypical features – e.g. Ego's mother's brother's wife falls into the same term category as Ego's mother. As a consequence, the system as a whole cannot be made comprehensible by a simple lineage analysis of the kind favoured by Radcliffe-Brown and his pupils.[7] Instead of arguing a priori let us then start with Malinowski's own analysis.

As I have already indicated, Malinowski's treatment of the term *tabu*, regarded as a kinship term, starts by distinguishing *tabu* meaning grandmother and *tabu* meaning father's sister as two different words. Of the latter he says:

> The primary meaning of this word [*tabu*] is 'father's sister'. It also embraces 'father's sister's daughter' or 'paternal cross-cousin' or by extension 'all the women of the father's clan'; and, in its widest sense 'all the women not of the same clan [as Ego]'. In this, its most extensive application, the word stands for 'lawful woman'. . . . For such a woman the term *lubaygu*, 'my sweetheart', may be correctly used; but this term is absolutely incompatible with the kinship designation, *lu(gu)ta*, 'my sister'. This linguistic use embodies, therefore, the rule of exogamy, and to a large extent expresses the ideas underlying this.[8]

On Malinowski's own showing, this statement is neither comprehensive nor altogether accurate. It ignores the fact that the category *tabu*, regarded as a kinship term, is used by members of both sexes and that, in either case, it includes numerous males as well as females. It is true that most 'lawful' (i.e. 'marriageable') women are classed as *tabu* by a male Ego, but this does not equate, as Malinowski seems to suggest, with 'all women not of the same clan as Ego'. On the contrary, both the wives and the daughters of the men of both Ego's own sub-clan and that of his father are ordinarily categorised by terms other than *tabu*, and this is true also of a large number of other women who, in later life, are connected affinally to Ego through his wife.

Throughout his analysis Malinowski assumes that 'prohibitions on sexual intercourse' and 'rules of exogamy' are interchangeable, coincident, descriptions of the same set of regulations; moreover, in the context cited, he states explicitly that by 'exogamy' he means 'clan incest'. In Malinowski's presentation the exogamous group is defined by the principle of matrilineal descent alone and is influenced by no other factor. His argument is that, in its widest extension, the category *tabu* serves to mark off this exogamous grouping – the women who are *tabu* are the 'lawful women' who are outside the barrier of clan incest. Using exogamy in this sense Malinowski's explanation simply fails to fit the facts which he describes.

But what better explanation can be offered?

It is a cardinal and fundamental assumption in Malinowski's analysis that words employed in kinship terminology have attached to them certain *primary* meanings and sentiments, which derive from a sociological relationship existing between the speaker and a particular individual near-kinsman. The use of kinship terms in a classificatory sense comes about through the gradual extension of these primary sentiments to a wider and wider range of individuals. Thus, to take a particular instance, the term *tama*, which a Trobriander ultimately applies to nearly all the males of his father's clan, has, in Malinowski's view, the *primary* meaning 'father' or 'mother's husband' and all extended uses of the term are derived from the initial relationship existing between a Trobriand father and his son.[9]

In my own analysis I shall make no such assumption. I do not repudiate the possibility of the 'extension' of meanings from narrow primary to wider secondary contexts, but I do not admit that words used as kinship terms must, *ipso facto*, derive their primary meaning exclusively from a kinship context, nor that the primary application is always to a particular individual rather than to a class of individuals.

For example, I agree with Malinowski that the term *tama* has a primary meaning which later undergoes extension, but, where Malinowski supposes that the primary meaning stems from the context of the nuclear family, so that *tama* = 'mother's husband', I myself would suggest that the primary meaning here stems from the identification of a particular group of males with a particular locality. My own 'primary' translation would be *tama* = 'domiciled male of my father's sub-clan hamlet'. Let me elaborate this distinction.

I fully accept Malinowski's contention that, of all the males whom the child addresses as *tama*, the speaker's own father is the one with whom Ego has the most personal contacts, but that does not make 'father' the primary meaning of *tama*, nor does it imply that every *tama* is looked upon as being, in some sense, 'a kind of father'. The fact that I have a pet dog called Peter does not make Peter the primary meaning of the word *dog*, nor does it imply that I cannot distinguish between my dog and another.

My view is that most words employed in kinship terminologies are category terms rather than individualising proper names. Malinowski insisted that *tama* refers primarily to a particular individual, the father, and to other individuals only by extension; he supposed that any other view would imply that Trobrianders cannot distinguish between one *tama* and another.[10] My own assumption, on the contrary, is that *tama* refers primarily to a category; this does not imply any suggestion that Trobrianders have any difficulty about distinguishing the roles of different individual *tama*.

Malinowski does not describe for us in detail the actual kinship composition of any particular Trobriand local community, but he explains fairly clearly what the ideal 'theoretical' composition of such a community ought to be according to the Trobrianders' own ideas. Land in the Trobriands is owned by the matrilineal sub-clans.[11] The married males of the sub-clan, numbering it would seem about a dozen individuals, live, each in his own domestic household, in a village, or section of a village, situated on or near the sub-clan land. I shall call this collectivity a sub-clan hamlet.

Here let me emphasise two things. First, the assertion that all the adult males of a sub-clan live in their own sub-clan hamlet is almost certainly an idealisation of reality. I imagine that in almost all actual cases there are some married men who are *not* living in the hamlet of their own sub-clan. But this discrepancy between fact and ideal does not, I think, affect my argument. Second, my phrase 'sub-clan hamlet' is not meant to be identical with the term 'village' as used by Malinowski.

In Malinowski's writings 'village' ordinarily means the cluster of buildings around a particular central place (*baku*). Although such a 'village' may sometimes be occupied by householders of a single sub-clan, this is not ordinarily the case.

The more usual pattern is that a village comprises several sections each of which is associated with a different sub-clan. The households forming one section of the village belong to married males of one particular sub-clan, and these men collectively exercise certain rights of ownership over parts of the garden land adjacent to the village. The houses in a village section plus the garden lands associated with this village section form a unity which I call a sub-clan hamlet. This analysis is valid even though the houses and gardens of different sections of the same village are immediately adjacent to one another.

In these terms, the 'component village of Yalumuguwa'[12] embraces two sub-clan hamlets; Omarakana[13] comprises three sub-clan hamlets, though in this case the male householders of one of the three sub-clans reside in another village. My phrase 'sub-clan hamlet' equates therefore with Malinowski's 'village section' and appears to correspond to a native Trobriand category.[14] The variety of land ownership rights that pertain to a sub-clan hamlet, considered as a corporation, is described in *Coral Gardens.*[15]

In the course of a lifetime both men and women are ordinarily resident members of two distinct sub-clan hamlets. A girl remains under the control of her parents until she marries, and then joins her husband in a new household established in the husband's sub-clan hamlet; at no stage is she a resident member of her own sub-clan hamlet. The pattern of residence for a boy is more complicated. He ceases to sleep in his parents' house at adolescence and joins a bachelor house (*bukumatulu*).[16] Bachelor houses are not necessarily identified as belonging to any particular sub-clan; boys of different sub-clans may sleep in one house. If a boy's father and his mother's brother live in different villages, he might, it seems, find bachelor accommodation in either community.[17] But a boy only sleeps in the bachelor house, he does not eat there.

From an early age a boy plays his part in garden work, but while he starts by working for his father he gradually transfers his productive effort to his mother's brother's lands.[18] So long as he contributes directly to his parents' household, he receives food from his mother; when he contributes to his mother's brother's household, he receives food from his mother's brother's wife. The economic consequences of this shift are small, for when the boy works on his mother's brother's land, the produce serves to increase the annual harvest gift (*urigubu*) which the mother's brother's household contributes to the father's household. Thus, in either case, the boy may be said to be working for his parents.

Finally, on marriage, a young man establishes a new independent household in his own sub-clan hamlet. From his garden plots he continues to make *urigubu* payments to his parents and his married sisters.

I must emphasise that although a boy ceases to sleep in his parents' house at adolescence he does not fully renounce his residence rights there until after he is married. Marriage itself is publicly established by the act of cohabitation in the household of the boy's father – *not* that of his mother's brother.[19]

We may describe all this by saying that, in the precise terminology of English law, a Trobriand male is, from the start, *domiciled* in his own sub-clan hamlet but his *residence* varies. During childhood he is resident in his father's sub-clan hamlet; after marriage he is resident in his own sub-clan hamlet; during the interval between adolescence and marriage he has a dual status with residence rights in both communities.

These facts provide the core of my analysis. My thesis is that, as a child, the male Ego identifies himself primarily with his father's household while, as an adult, he identifies himself primarily with the members of his own sub-clan hamlet considered as a corporation. I argue that this time-shift in the composition and membership of the group whom Ego (male) regards as 'people like us' is fundamental for our understanding of the nature of Trobriand kinship categories.

The position of a girl is different; though technically domiciled in her own sub-clan hamlet, she is never actually resident there. The analysis which follows is pursued solely from the viewpoint of a male Ego. A separate though comparable analysis would be necessary to explain the system of kinship categories used by a girl.

It follows from what I have said, and from Malinowski's own description of the sex and age categories in Trobriand society,[20] that any particular sub-clan hamlet, at any particular time, comprises the following categories of individuals:

A Old men – *tomwaya* or *toboma*[21]
B Old women – *numwaya* – wives of *A*, widows, etc.
C Active married men – *tovavaygile*
D Active married women – *navavaygile* – wives of *C*
E Bachelors – *to' ulatile* – 'sister's sons' to *A* and *C* and resident here only part of the time
F Young girls – *inagwadi* – and adolescent girls – *nakapugula* – still under the charge of their parents, daughters of *A, B, C, D*
G Young boys – *gwadi* – still living with their parents – sons of *A, B, C, D*

In this classification *A, C,* and *E* together comprise the locally resident owners of the sub-clan hamlet. In addition, some other male members of the sub-clan, young boys, live scattered about among other hamlets with their parents. *B, D, F,* and *G* in the above classification are all members of 'alien' sub-clans; that is to say, although their *residence* is in this hamlet, their *domicile* is elsewhere.

Let us now ignore altogether Malinowski's tendentious arguments about the way in which kinship sentiments are first established within the context of the elementary family and then extended outwards. Instead let us simply consider from first principles how a Trobriander might reasonably be expected to classify his kinsmen and acquaintance.

It seems evident from Malinowski's account that the two really fundamental economic facts in Trobriand social organisation are (1) an individual's rights to the use or produce of the land of his or her own sub-clan, and (2) the institution of *urigubu* which results from this principle of land tenure. Rights in the land are possessed by men and women alike, but only the men of the sub-clan have direct access to their land. The men therefore cultivate the land; one major share (*taytumwala*) of the produce is kept by the cultivator for the use of his own household and for seed purposes; another, usually larger, share (*urigubu*) is transferred in harvest gifts to the cultivator's mother and married sisters.[22] Let us assume that these economic facts are the ones which provide the primary criteria for distinguishing categories of kin.

It is plain that the individual Trobriand male experiences the effects of the *urigubu* institution in two distinct phases; first, as a child in his father's household, and secondly, as a married adult in his own household.

In the first phase the implications of *urigubu*-giving are lopsided. The child is a member of a household which regularly receives gifts from members of a sub-clan hamlet which he is taught from the start to regard as his own. These people, his 'mother's brothers' (*kada*), are clearly, in a formal sense, 'friends'. The friendship may indeed be subject to strain, but it is palpably advantageous to 'our household'.

In contrast, a substantial share of the produce of his own father's garden is given away to strangers – the father's mother and the father's sister – from whom Ego receives no benefits. On the contrary, in the long run, the sons of these strangers will appear on the scene and usurp the property which at present seems to be the main source of Ego's livelihood. These people too no doubt are, officially speaking, to be regarded as 'friends', but from Ego's point of view they are very disadvantageous ones. Indeed in many respects these strangers, the recipients of the father's *urigubu* gifts, might seem to be the prototype 'enemy'.

I shall here digress to remind the reader briefly of certain features of Radcliffe-Brown's theoretical discussions of taboo and joking relationships.[23]

For Radcliffe-Brown *taboo* is a technical term with a narrower range of meaning than the common Polynesian word *tabu*. He discusses taboo in terms of what he calls 'ritual avoidances' which serve to define the 'ritual status' differences existing between two persons in a single social system. The following are some of the characteristics of taboo which emerge from Radcliffe-Brown's analysis: tabooed persons are respected as sacred, they are the object of ritual avoidance and the recipients of tribute. The tabooed thing or person is 'abnormal', it is separated from that which is normal, but its quality is ambivalent; it is a source of power, but the power may have good or evil consequences, it is sacred and polluting at the same time.

The ritual behaviours which Radcliffe-Brown discusses under the general title of 'joking relationships' are an exemplification of this theme. These behaviours express 'friendship' either by manifesting taboo – e.g. ritual avoidance coupled with gift-giving – or else by the systematic breach of taboo, which amounts to much the same thing – for, in Radcliffe-Brown's argument, anyone who breaks a taboo automatically becomes taboo himself. That taboo should be used in this way to express 'friendship' is the subject of one of Radcliffe-Brown's most penetrating pieces of analysis.

He points out that marriage often serves to unite two potentially hostile groups, and that it then becomes necessary for members of these 'opposed' parties to assert, by formal behaviour, that they are 'friends'. The 'friendship' involved is of a peculiar and precariously balanced kind: it is 'a relation neither of solidarity nor of hostility but of "friendship" in which the separateness of the groups is emphasised, but open conflict between the two groups or members on the two sides is avoided'. By way of example he refers to his own description of the Andamanese *aka-yat* relationship[24] in which two individuals who scrupulously avoid one another constantly send each other presents. There seems an obvious parallel here with the Trobriand householder who avoids his married sister yet regularly sends her gifts.

Radcliffe-Brown further points out that the kind of ritual friendship which may characterise the behaviour of persons linked by ties of affinity is also frequently characteristic of the behaviour that is expected between members of alternating generations – e.g. between a grandparent and a grandchild – the fact that in some societies a man is expected to marry his 'classificatory granddaughter' exemplifies this similarity.[25]

Radcliffe-Brown's discussion is here not altogether convincing. Since he treats the relationship between grandparents and grandchildren as an example of joking relationship, one might infer that the friendship involved is one in which 'there is an appearance of antagonism, controlled by conventional rules',[26] yet elsewhere he has maintained that 'in many classificatory systems the terms for grandfather and grandmother are used . . . as implying a general attitude of friendliness, relatively free from restraint towards all persons to whom they are applied'.[27]

This contradiction disappears if we say that 'friendliness' and 'hostility' are not, properly speaking, exclusive categories; as with the case of 'sacredness' and 'pollution', each is an aspect of 'the same thing'. Radcliffe-Brown's argument would have been more convincing if he had simply opposed 'relations of solidarity', which stem from economic co-operation and common economic interest, and 'relations of separateness', which link persons who are outside this co-operative corporation. His essential theme is that all relations of this latter kind have an ambivalent friendship/hostility content; they are always formally expressed by behaviours indicating 'friendship' but, in especially critical situations, an added element of taboo is present, superimposed on the friendliness. From this digression let us now return to the Trobriand Islands.

That the relationship which links groups of Trobriand affines in bonds of 'friendship' is of a precarious kind is plain enough. Malinowski himself describes the relationship between a man and his father's sister's son as one of 'predestined emnity'.[28] This latent hostility becomes explicitly formalised in the mortuary rituals which follow the death of either the father's sister or her husband or that of either of the father's parents. On these occasions not only are the affinally linked sub-clans ritually opposed to one another in the clearest possible manner, but the affines of the deceased are very liable to be accused of murder by sorcery. 'It is characteristic of their idea of the bonds of marriage and fatherhood – which they regard as artificial and untrustworthy under any strain – that the principal suspicion of sorcery attaches always to the wife and childern.'[29]

The male Ego's own role in this situation is by no means clear-cut. As a member of his mother's sub-clan, he is an affine of his father, and thus a kind of logical ally of his father's other affines, who come near to being his father's enemies. My thesis is, however, that the young child, resident in his father's house, is taught to accept a set of kinship categories which are appropriate to the structural situation of that household. In that situation the recipients of Ego's father's *urigubu* form a highly ambivalent category of kinsmen.

Enemies who must be treated as 'friends'; dangerous people who must be appeased by gift-giving; this precisely is the context which, in Radcliffe-Brown's terminology, reflects a situation of taboo.

In Radcliffe-Brown's terms, the relationship which Malinowski describes as existing between the givers and receivers of *urigubu* is one of taboo. Consistent with this we find that a man's child is taught to class as *tabu* all the recipients of his father's *urigubu*. The category *tabu* includes:

(*a*) Ego's father's mother
(*b*) Her husband and the other males of his sub-clan
(*c*) Ego's father's sister
(*d*) Her husband and the other males of her sub-clan
(*e*) The daughters of (*a*) and (*d*).

Accordingly, instead of postulating, as Malinowski does, that the Trobrianders have several different words pronounced *tabu* I assume that they have only one such word and that its meaning approximates to Radcliffe-Brown's concept of taboo.

Malinowski tells us little of the prescribed behaviour that accompanies this verbal category, though it appears that, as Ego begins to grow up, he finds himself in an emphatic joking relationship with his father's sister.[30] On my thesis, it is not to be expected that a male Ego will be required to behave in exactly the same way towards all his *tabu*. In Radcliffe-Brown's terminology 'joking relationship' or 'ritual friendship' includes not only violent and obscene horseplay between cross-cousins but also playful friendliness between grandparents and grandchildren. If then the Trobriand relationship *tabu* is likewise one of 'ritual friendship', there is room for variation.

What seems to happen is that while Ego (male) is still a child in his father's household his 'friendship' with the immediate recipients of his father's *urigubu* is critical enough to involve a relationship of the 'obscene joking' type. But as he grows older and begins to separate off from his father's household, the social distance between himself and these paternal *tabu* steadily increases. Such *tabu*

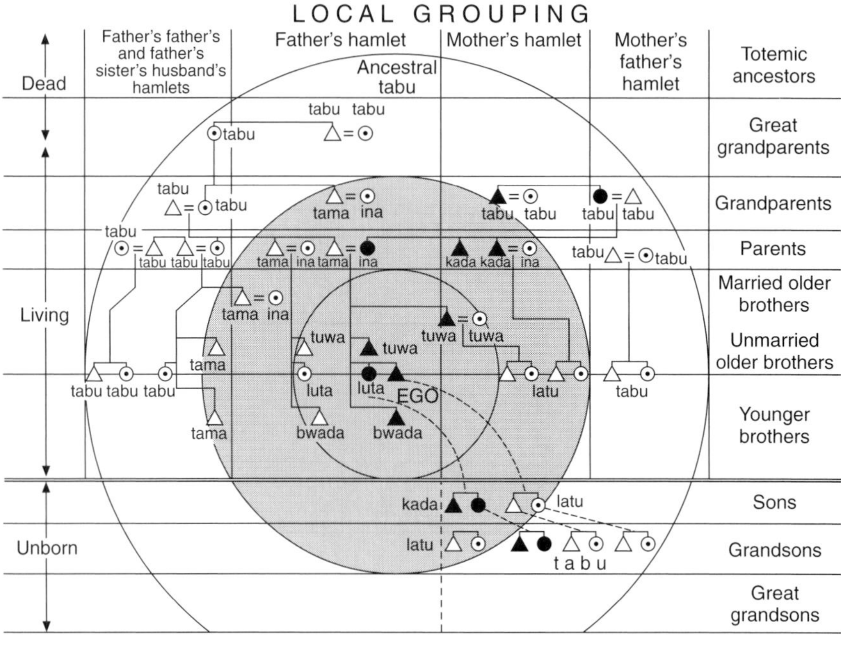

Members of Ego's sub-clan

Fig. 1. Trobriand kinship categories (unmarried male Ego).

Innermost circle – classificatory siblings – *tuwa, bwada, luta.*
Middle ring – *tama, ina, kada, latu.*
Outermost ring – *tabu.*
All within the shaded circle are 'socially close' to Ego either on account of common domicile or common residence.
All *tabu* are 'socially distant' from Ego either on account of difference in age or difference in residence.

are still 'formal friends' but the stereotype of behaviour now becomes one of playful friendliness rather than obscene horseplay. On this basis the father's sister's daughter is said to be an appropriate object for sexual liaison and ultimate marriage.[31] I shall have more to say concerning this alleged 'preferred marriage' presently.

The young male Ego's *tabu* category is not confined to the recipients of his father's *urigubu*. It extends also to a number of relatives distinguished by their age seniority and their social remoteness from Ego. Thus *tabu* includes Ego's mother's parents. In contexts which are not rigidly formal it also includes classificatory father's mother's mother's brothers and their wives, and classificatory mother's mother's brothers and their wives.[32] Note that it is social distance rather than genealogical distance that matters here. While Ego is resident with his father, it is only the males of the father's sub-clan who are *three* generations senior to Ego who may rate as *tabu*; that is to say individuals who are already, socially speaking, 'almost dead'. In contrast, the males of Ego's own sub-clan who are only *two* generations senior to himself may rate as *tabu*; but of course by the time Ego himself becomes a householder in his own sub-clan hamlet these too

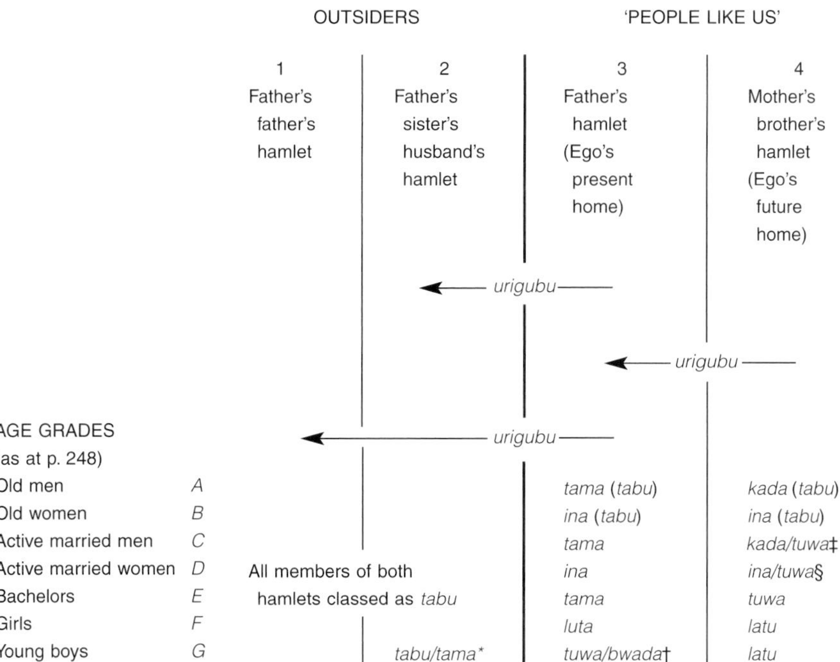

Fig. 2. Tabular version of Fig. 1.
*tama** – boys of Ego's father's sub-clan. *tuwa‡* – young married men of Ego's generation.
bwada† – boys younger than Ego. *tuwa§* – wives of men classed as *tuwa* (source Powell).

will be very old men withdrawn from social life. In relation to Ego all these elderly *tabu* are merging into the other-world of the sacred and ancestral dead.

We can represent the whole system, as so far described, by a diagram (Fig. 1). Ego at the centre is surrounded by a body of 'near kinsmen', his father's group (*tama*) and his own sub-clan group (*kada*). Beyond this 'circle of active kin relations' in all directions lie the *tabu*, the marginal kin who merge into the outer unknown of dangerous strangers and dangerous ancestral spirits.

The same argument is presented in Fig. 2, which demonstrates even more clearly that the kinship categories express differences of locality and of age status rather than genealogical relationship.

In this figure the terms listed against the leading letters *A–G* correspond to the age categories listed above.[33] Ego (male), resident in his father's hamlet, is thought of as occupying a position at the bottom of column 3. He classes all the members of his father's father's and father's sister's husband's hamlets as *tabu* except for a few young boys who are members of his own father's sub-clan.[34] He categorises the members of his father's hamlet as in column 3 and of his mother's hamlet as in column 4 regardless of their sub-clan affiliation.

Although all the information contained in these diagrams is derived directly from the genealogically arranged table of kinship terms given by Malinowski himself,[35] they suggest that the words involved have quite different 'primary meanings' from those given by Malinowski.

Tabu now appears as a general term, undifferentiated as to age or sex, comprising the whole broad category of potentially hostile 'outsiders'. The only individuals in the *urigubu*-receiving hamlets who are not categorised as *tabu* are the male *tama* who are domiciled in (and later residents of) Ego's father's hamlet.

Tama, as I have already suggested, is seen to refer to 'a domiciled male of my father's sub-clan hamlet'.[36]

Kada, tuwa, bwada are not here primarily 'mother's brother', 'elder brother', 'younger brother' but rather 'the domiciled males of my own sub-clan hamlet' categorised by age and generation. The use of *tuwa* and *bwada* for the wives of men previously classified by these terms is clearly an extension of the initial meaning.

Ina, which in Malinowski's analysis has the fundamental meaning 'mother', here becomes 'the wife of any senior male of either of my two home hamlets'.

Luta is not simply 'sister' but 'alien girls resident in my father's hamlet'. The phonemically very similar word *latu* represents a corresponding category, namely 'alien children resident in my own sub-clan hamlet'.

These last two terms need further discussion for they affect our understanding of incest and exogamy rules. For Malinowski the primary meaning of *luta* is 'own sister'; it is the fundamental incest category, 'the core of the *suvasova* taboo'.[37] By 'extension' *luta* also comes to cover, first, a number of 'sub-clan sisters' who are regarded as real kinsmen (*veyola*) and to whom the *suvasova* taboo rigidly applies, and secondly, a much wider range of 'clan sisters' who are regarded as pseudo-kinsmen (*kakaveyola*) and to whom the *suvasova* taboo applies only in modified degree.

According to Malinowski, *marriage* with *luta* of all types is strictly prohibited but *sexual intercourse* with *luta* in the *kakaveyola* category, though 'prohibited by legal doctrine', 'is frequently practised, and is, so to speak, at a premium'.[38] Unfortunately Malinowski entirely ignores the fact that most of the *luta* who are Ego's immediate next-door neighbours are not members of Ego's own sub-clan at all. This is true for example of the daughters of Ego's father born of wives other than Ego's own mother; and it is true also of most of the daughters of other males of Ego's father's sub-clan, all of whom are ordinarily resident close to Ego's own father. This is a very serious omission.

Malinowski makes a point of opposing the two categories *tabu* = 'lawful woman' and *luta* = 'prohibited woman',[39] but he couples this with a suggestion that *luta* are all 'clan sisters' and that it is the clan to which rules of exogamy and incest alike apply. But here he was surely either mistaken or misleading? The 'distant' *luta* with whom Ego is likely to be in most immediate contact, the girls with whom sex relations, though forbidden, are 'so to speak at a premium', are not his clan sisters scattered all over the island but the girls next door!

From Malinowski's elaborately detailed accounts of the amorous adventures of Trobriand childhood it appears that the sexual experiments of infancy and early adolescence are with local playmates. They are affairs which lack all seriousness. Now the most obvious playmates for a boy are the girls of his two home hamlets, the daughters of his *tama* and the daughters of his *kada*. It is surely striking that

Ego rates the first as *luta* – 'classificatory sisters' and the second as *latu* – 'classificatory daughters'.

All members of the first of these categories fall, theoretically, under the incest prohibition (*suvasova*). Relations with the second category are not incestuous (*suvasova*) but they are nevertheless improper. According to Malinowski, marriage with such a girl 'is viewed with disfavour and happens only rarely'. The verbal similarity between the two terms perhaps reflects this similarity of valuations. Malinowski's statements, taken as a whole, imply that while a boy can safely have love affairs with any of his *latu* and most of his neighbouring *luta*, he can decently marry neither.

In contrast, serious love affairs of the kind likely to lead to marriage tend to be with girls of other hamlets, most of whom fall into the *tabu* category.[40] Affairs of this latter type are described in section 6 of ch. IX of *The Sexual Life of Savages*. In some cases they evidently entail a substantial element of risk for the lovers and were formerly the occasion of paramilitary raiding parties, especially if the girls concerned lived outside the local village cluster.

In all, we are left with two equations:

(1) The girls of Ego's two home hamlets – classed like 'sisters' and 'daughters' – mostly fair game for a love affair, but not suitable for marriage – *luta* and *latu*.

(2) The girls outside Ego's two home hamlets – classed like 'potential enemies' – suitable for marriage – *tabu*.

This is a conclusion which would have satisfied Tylor.[41] It suggests quite a different picture from that given by Malinowski. In his interpretation, all pre-marital sex relations are to be regarded as trial preliminaries leading to marriage. For Malinowski the typical youthful love affair is with a *tabu*, the 'lawful woman'. Yet I feel he must be wrong. The structure that I have now presented has so many striking parallels in other societies,[42] and it makes sense in so many different ways.

Malinowski's analysis rests on the assumption that the fundamental element in the total system is 'clan exogamy'; but Trobriand clans are shadowy amorphous things with no very obvious function. Why and how should such shadowy entities maintain their exogamy? In contrast, the membership of sub-clan hamlets is clear and corporate and economically highly significant. I find it very illuminating to realise that if a Trobriander keeps to the rules which Malinowski describes it is not merely Ego's clan that becomes exogamous; it is the total population of Ego's two home hamlets that is set apart as 'people like us'.[43]

Let me emphasise again that these 'hamlets' are not spacially separate entities immediately discernible on the ground. A single village may contain households of a number of different sub-clans and the members of these sub-clans intermarry. But the hamlets are defined as entities by the rules of exogamy and the category distinctions of kinship terminology. I have already quoted Malinowski as saying 'this linguistic usage (with respect to *luta*) embodies therefore the rule of exogamy and to a large extent expresses the ideas underlying this'.[44] I would now agree with this but it is the exogamy of local grouping that I am talking about whereas Malinowski thought only of the exogamy of clans.

As to how far the *luta* category – as I have now distinguished it – forms, in fact, an exogamous category, I have no information. That it is ideally considered to be such seems clearly apparent in Malinowski.

The distinction I have now made between casual premarital love affairs with *luta* and *latu*, and serious liaisons with *tabu*, is fully consistent with the kind of meaning I have already attributed to the word *tabu*. It eliminates a striking inconsistency in Malinowski's presentation which makes it appear that marriage, a contractual arrangement of the most serious economic consequences, is the legal outcome of love affairs of the utmost casualness.

In terms of my diagram *latu* are 'the children of the married males of Ego's own sub-clan'. A category of this type is to be expected in any 'Crow-type' system of kinship terminology. Malinowski translates it simply as 'child'.[45]

As the Trobriand male child grows up he begins to separate himself off from his parents and for a while has a kind of dual residential status in both his home hamlets – that of his father and that of his mother's brother. During this phase there is little change in the way that Ego's kinsmen are categorised, but the significance of the different categories becomes modified. For example, in terms of Radcliffe-Brown's analysis which I outlined above, the relationship between Ego and his father which was formerly one of 'solidarity' now begins to assume the qualities of 'separateness' and ritual 'friendship', while, on the other hand, the relationship of Ego with the senior males of his own sub-clan, which had previously been one of 'friendship' and 'separateness' now changes to one of 'solidarity'.

It is symptomatic of this change of attitude that Ego who has previously referred to the householders of his own sub-clan hamlet collectively as *kada* (uncles) now begins to refer to the same collectivity as *tuwa* (brothers) (Mr Powell's information).

At the same time Ego's father's affines (Ego's paternal *tabu*) move outside the field of Ego's *urigubu* system altogether, they now become remote relatives barely distinguishable from total strangers (*tomakava*). Meanwhile many of the elders of his own sub-clan hamlet will have died. These men, whom Ego referred to as *tabu* while he was living with his father, remain *tabu* even though they now exist only in the world of ancestral spirits.

When finally the Trobriand male Ego marries and settles down the *urigubu* institution assumes for him a new significance. Ego is now resident in his own sub-clan hamlet along with his mother's brother. He is receiving gifts from his wife's brother's hamlet and he is also linked in ties of friendly alliance with his wife's father's hamlet – which was his wife's original home. In turn he is giving gifts to his sister's husband and to his father in the latter's capacity as mother's husband.

At this phase in the boy's development the *urigubu* can no longer be considered as an isolated institution; it is closely enmeshed with the political relationships which bind a man to his chief; it is linked through the institutionalised payments called *youlo* and *takola* with the prestige-gaining activities of the *kula* exchange; it is part of 'a veritable tangle of obligations and duties' which are finally worked out only after the death of the *urigubu* recipients.[46] It is Malinowski's thesis that the *urigubu* gifts which a man makes to the husbands of his mother and his sisters are adequately reciprocated by the various benefits, political and otherwise, which he receives in return. Malinowski does not make it very clear just why a Trobriander should have this evaluation, but we must accept the fact that it is so.

It is a symptom of this equality between givers and receivers of *urigubu* that at every phase Ego is, terminologically, in a reciprocal relationship with all the members of his *urigubu* system, other than his own father. As a child Ego classes the recipients of his father's *urigubu* as *tabu* and the givers of his father's *urigubu* as *kada*, both terms are used reciprocally. Now as an adult he uses the term *lubou* both for his sister's husband to whom he himself gives *urigubu* and for his wife's brother from whom he receives *urigubu*. The other males of the sister's husband's sub-clan who are also indirect beneficiaries of Ego's *urigubu* payments fall into the *yawa* category, which is again a reciprocal term.

Marriage establishes a *lubou* relationship between two men, namely the wife's brother and her husband. This relationship is expressed by the payment of *urigubu*. The same marriage puts the hamlets with which the two *lubou* are associated in a vaguer affinal relationship signified by the reciprocal use of the kinship category *yawa*.

The marriage of a male Ego and the marriage of his sister thus puts Ego in affinal relationship with the members of four hamlets – those of his wife's mother's brother, his wife's father, his sister's husband, and more vaguely his sister's husband's father. Nearly all these relatives are *yawa*.[47] The only exceptions are *lubou*'s brothers who are also *lubou*; *lubou*'s children who are *tabu*, unless they are members of Ego's own clan when they are *kada*; and Ego's wife's unmarried sisters, who are classed as if they were male siblings (*tuwa/bwada*). Marriage with these last is not incestuous (*suvasova*) but is strongly disapproved,[48] presumably because such polygyny would place a double load of *urigubu* liability on the one set of wives' brothers. Marriage with *kada* females is, of course, incestuous. Marriage with either *tabu* or *yawa* females is legitimate, though marriage with *tabu* is considered preferable.

Roughly speaking therefore the effect of marriage and its associated *urigubu* system is to create for Ego a new 'ring' of relatives which, in social distance, lies somewhere between the near kinsmen of the home groups and the distant marginal kinsmen classed as *tabu*. My Fig. 3 shows this argument schematically.

As in Fig. 1 Ego's total kinship system may still be thought of as a series of concentric circles centred about himself. But Ego is now located in the *kada/tuwa/bwada* group, while the *tama* are of declining significance. Indeed, by the time that both Ego's parents are dead the *tama* sub-clan will cease to be regarded as relatives at all.

Beyond the circle of these 'near kin', among whom Ego has residential status, are the affines (*lubou*, *yawa*), established as such by Ego's own marriage and the marriage of his sisters, and beyond them again are the marginal, socially remote, *tabu* relatives who lie outside Ego's personal system of *urigubu* transactions.

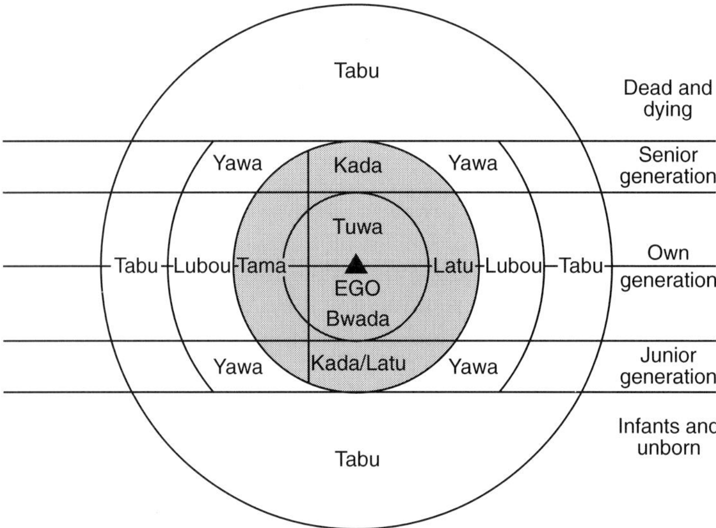

Fig. 3. Trobriand kinship categories (married male Ego).

All the affines (*yawa* and *lubou*) are potentially hostile 'aliens' whose relationship is modified into a kind of treaty friendship by the fact of marriage and *urigubu* gift-giving. It needs to be remembered that there is an avoidance relationship between a man and his sister, and though Malinowski is not very specific on the matter, it seems evident that the *lubou* relationship must be one of marked strain. So far as Ego is concerned, the relationship is based solely on the marriage bond and, if the marriage is terminated by death or divorce, the relationship is terminated also. Thereafter if the members of these affinal groups are categorised at all, they are rated simply as *tabu* or as 'total strangers' (*tomakava*).[49]

At this stage in the male Ego's development the members of his father's hamlet are also drifting away into a relationship of weak affinity, though here the relationship link is less fragile than in the case of *lubou.* Even after their mother's death, sons will continue to make *urigubu* payments to their father. On the latter's death the sons have important duties to perform in the mortuary ritual.[50] So long as either parent survives, a son cannot completely break off 'treaty relations' with his father's hamlet.

I must now make a somewhat lengthy digression to discuss Trobriand rules of preferred marriage. This is necessary not only because it has a bearing on the meaning of the term *tabu* but because it has been the subject of a good deal of unjustified theoretical speculation.[51]

According to Malinowski, Trobrianders maintain a theoretical preference for marriage with the true father's sister's daughter. It is largely on the basis of this alleged preference that Malinowski bases his argument that *tabu* has the extended meaning 'lawful woman', for, in his view, this term refers primarily to the father's sister and her daughter who are, he says, 'the prototype' of the lawful woman.[52]

The argument is unsatisfactory. Actual occurrences of patrilateral cross-cousin marriage seem to be rare and to be largely confined to the families of chiefs. Malinowski's only explanation of the rule is that it is a device whereby, in a matrilineal structure, a man, particularly a chief, may ultimately transmit his hereditary rights to his own son's son. He has not, however, demonstrated that Trobrianders themselves think of father's sister's daughter marriage as a tortuous legal subterfuge of this kind.

Nevertheless Malinowski cites his Trobriand informants as saying: 'the true *tabu* is the proper wife for us' and he is most emphatic that this means marriage with the *actual* father's sister's daughter.[53] What are we to make of this?

It is of course possible that Malinowski misunderstood his informants, and that they were merely maintaining that most actual marriages are between individuals who are in a *tabu* relationship of one kind or another. This of course is true enough. The rules of exogamy exclude women who are classed as *ina*, *luta*, *latu*, *tuwa*, *bwada*, *kada* and this only leaves *yawa* and *tabu* available. But let us consider what would be implied if Malinowski were correct in thinking that marriage with the first cousin *tabu* is preferred.

On the face of it, a marriage convention of this kind appears to be in direct conflict with the principles of *urigubu* gift giving. If normal residence behaviour is adhered to, a patrilateral cross-cousin marriage will serve to cancel out the economic bond between Ego and his father's community. While Ego will be contributing *urigubu* to his father (*tama*), his father's sister's son (*tama*) will be contributing *urigubu* to Ego. Such direct reciprocity would make nonsense of the theme that *urigubu* payments represent, among other things, tribute from a political inferior to a political superior.

Moreover it is plain that direct reciprocity of this kind makes no sense to a Trobriander. When marriage with the true father's sister's daughter *does* occur, the residence pattern is abnormal. The husband, instead of taking his wife to live with him in his own sub-clan hamlet, acquires the right to settle in his wife's sub-clan hamlet and to farm his wife's land. In other words, he goes on living in his own father's village, and farms his father's land in company with his father's sister's sons.[54] According to Malinowski this comes about through the personal affection of a father for his son.

It is quite evident that such behaviour is altogether exceptional. The only example that Malinowski cites is that of a chief's son. Further, he states that if an ordinary commoner were to encroach in this way upon his *tama*'s territorial privileges he would 'both degrade himself and suffer disabilities',[55] which perhaps means that he would receive no *urigubu* from his wife's brothers.

Malinowski[56] does give a genealogy which is said to display three patrilateral cross-cousin marriages within one short pedigree, but in point of fact only one of these is between first cousins. Moreover, although Malinowski omits to mention the fact, the same genealogy also displays two (classificatory) *matrilateral* cross-cousin marriages; the chart therefore gives little support to the view that marriage with the true father's sister's daughter is preferred.

The genealogy in question is indeed revealing, but for reasons other than those suggested by Malinowski. Since the Tabalu chiefs receive their 'tribute' in the form of *urigubu* payments from their wives' brothers, it is a matter of some political significance as to who receives the *urigubu* payments of the chief himself. About this Malinowski tells us very little, but the cross-cousin marriages in his chart all have the effect of making members of the Kwoynama sub-clan recipients of the chief's *urigubu.* Elsewhere we are told that 'this sub-clan is the very one from which a Tabalu chief ought to choose his principal wife'.[57] In doing so, he evidently marries a classificatory mother's brother's daughter (*latu*) – a relationship which is nearly incestuous.[58] The implication seems to be that, as an exception to the normal system, a practice of *bilateral* cross-cousin marriage operates between the Kwoynama and Tabalu aristocratic sub-clans which permits these two groups to exchange *urigubu* gifts without prejudice to the political status of either.[59]

The principle involved can be stated thus. Whoever marries the sister of the chief's heir is potentially in a structurally superior position, for the chief's heir must give him tribute. By marrying this girl to his own son and then insisting that the son stays where he is, the chief is not 'favouring his son', he is protecting the rights of his heir! The son pays *urigubu* to his father the chief.

The reverse case is mentioned in a rather vague way by Malinowski.[60] If a woman of high rank marries a man of lower rank, she may arrange for her son to marry the sister of her husband's heir. Again the son in question 'stays put' in his father's hamlet, instead of moving to his own. But in this case, unlike the first, he is able to transmit his irregularly acquired land rights to his own heirs – his sister's sons. This, according to Malinowski, is the mechanism whereby aristocratic sub-clans have been able to assert territorial claims in villages where they have no mythological roots.

On this analysis the preferred marriage with a father's sister's daughter, in so far as it exists, has nothing to do with the affection of fathers for their sons. It is simply a straightforward mechanism in the working of the political structure.

It is thus evident that, despite Malinowski, marriage with the 'true' *tabu* is exceptional. For anyone except the highest chiefs it is 'proper' (i.e. desirable) only in the sense that, if achieved, it permits the husband's sub-clan to encroach on the land rights of the wife. It is a status-climbing device. On the other hand the fact that Trobriand chiefs contract marriage alliances which would be more or less taboo for everyone else is strictly in accord with theoretical expectations.[61]

The system of terminology discussed above covers all the usage of a male Ego, for, as Ego grows older and acquires married children and grandchildren, the new relationships that are thereby set up are merely the reciprocals of those which Ego himself experienced as a youth. By the time that Ego and his sisters have married the various categories of relationship have received their final form.

Presented in this way the logic of the system is seen to be entirely simple and consistent. In contrast, when the terms are projected on to a genealogical diagram, as is done by Malinowski, the underlying logic is utterly incomprehensible. Anyone who doubts this opinion should compare the analysis given here with that given by Malinowski in *The Sexual Life of Savages.*

But while the term system is complete the diagrams cover the population of only eight particular sub-clan hamlets, namely:

(*a*) father's hamlet – male owners: *tama*
(*b*) own hamlet – male owners: *kada, tuwa, bwada*
(*c*) father's sister's husband's hamlet – male owners: *tabu*
(*d*) father's father's hamlet – male owners: *tabu*
(*e*) wife's brother's hamlet – male owners: *yawa, lubou*
(*f*) wife's father's hamlet – male owners: *yawa*
(*g*) sister's husband's hamlet – male owners: *yawa, lubou*
(*h*) sister's husband's father's hamlet – male owners: *yawa.*

I suggest that this is in fact the initial range of effective kinship; it is the range of active *urigubu* transactions as they affect the individual Ego.

Just how far the various categories are 'extended' beyond this immediate operational context is not clear in Malinowski's writings. Evidently, in principle, all the terms applied to Ego's own sub-clan hamlet are applicable also to all other sub-clan hamlets of Ego's clan. Similarly the terms applied to the father's hamlet should apply also to all other hamlets of the father's clan and also to the hamlet of the mother's sister's husband and so on. But I suspect that much of this wider range of kinship is notional only. Where the category is in doubt the relationship is *tabu.*

Thus construed, the term *tabu,* as used by a male adult, becomes a category of purely marginal relationship. In Radcliffe-Brown's phrase[62] – 'it is used to mark off a marginal region between non-relatives and those close relatives towards whom specific duties and over whom specific rights are recognised'. It is a negative category.[63] *Tabu* comprises all those numerous members of Ego's total society who are *not* in one way or another directly involved in the *urigubu* transactions of which Ego is either giver or receiver.

In terms of genealogy some *tabu* appear to be quite 'closely related' – e.g. the father's sister, the father's parents, the mother's parents. But in terms of structure these people are scarcely relatives at all. The households of which they are members are, socially speaking, remote from Ego; he has virtually no economic contact with them. Only the father's sister, with whom there is a formal joking relationship, is close enough to be regarded as in some respects a member of 'our group'.

Remote kinship is not only vague but ambiguous. According to Mr Powell: 'Kinship terms are used only in contexts where emphasis is on the formal aspects of kinship relations; in ordinary conversation personal names are used more frequently between, and of, persons of all ages and both sexes.' The occasions on which one would require to specify the precise kinship category of a distant clan relative must be rare. The uncertainty as to whether a distant clansman should be regarded as a clan relative (*kada, tuwa, bwada*), some sort of affine (*tama, yawa, lubou*), or scarcely a relative at all (*tabu*), is thus of no great consequence.

But this raises another issue which I mentioned at the beginning of this paper. Why do Trobrianders have a clan system at all? If, as seems to be the case, the operationally functional social groups are the sub-clans, what purpose do the clans serve, and why are there four of them?

In quite a different ethnographic context, that of the North Burma Kachins, I have pointed out that the assertion commonly made by Kachins that 'we have five clans' does not correspond to the empirical facts.[64] Nevertheless this assertion is a highly important schematic device. The Kachins need five distinct patrilineal categories if they are to explain to themselves the workings of their own society, and the fiction that there are only five clans altogether serves just this purpose. I suggest that in a comparable manner the Trobrianders need four categories to display the workings of their society, and that the four matriclans fulfil this purpose.

What happens in the Kachin case is that a Kachin will say *either* that the social world consists of five clans – Marip, Lahtaw, Lahpai, N'hkum, Maran *or* he will say that it consists of five major categories of kin: (1) *kahpu-kanau* (clan brothers), (2) *mayu* (matrilateral affines), (3) *dama* (patrilateral affines), (4) *lawu* (classificatory grandchildren, 'those below'), and (5) *lahta* (classificatory grandparents, 'those above'). Allowing for the fact that the Trobriands are matrilineal while the Kachins are patrilineal the corresponding categories in the Trobriand case would be (1) *kada, tuwa, bwada*, (2) *tama*, (3) *yawa/lubou*, (4 and 5) *tabu*. Let me elaborate this.

On the analysis I have given in this paper it would appear that the individual Trobriand male is presented with a society which appears to consist of four distinct types of sub-clan hamlet. These are

A.	People like us	(*a*) *tama* hamlets
		(*b*) *kada, tuwa, bwada* hamlets
B.	The others	(*c*) affines: *yawa, lubou* hamlets
		(*d*) marginal relatives and non-relatives: *tabu* hamlets

From the individual Ego's point of view, this has the appearance of a moiety system. Ego should not seek a wife in (*a*) or (*b*); he should seek a wife in (*c*) or (*d*), especially perhaps in (*d*), since a marriage here will increase 'our' total range of kinship alliances. *Tabu* becomes the stereotype of a suitable wife simply because it is desirable in principle to reduce the number of *tabu* groups and convert them into *yawa*. Also, as I have indicated, a man who marries a *close tabu* may achieve a step up in the rank hierarchy.

Now these four categories of the total society are *not* unilineal descent groups. They are categories of hamlets distinguished according to the kind of people who are resident therein. Nevertheless I suggest that there is a functional connection between this fourfold categorisation of Ego's kinship world and the fact that Trobrianders claim to have four clans.

The Trobriand myths of origin which form the basis of Trobriand rules of land tenure specify that the original sub-clan ancestors emerged from various holes in the ground appropriately situated in the midst of sub-clan territory.[65] It is these myths which establish that the members of the sub-clan are the owners (*toli*) of the sub-clan hamlet and its associated lands. The Trobriand sub-clan is a dispersed unit which seldom actually assembles all in one place; the sub-clan hamlet and its lands is, on the other hand, a permanent visible entity known to all. It is really an inversion of the facts to say that the continuing units in Trobriand social structure are the sub-clans and that the hamlets belong to the sub-clans. It is much closer to reality to say that the continuing units are the hamlets and that the sub-clan members belong to the hamlets by virtue of the emergence myths. How many kinds of sub-clan hamlet ought there to be in terms of Trobriand mythology?

The sub-clan emergence myths are mostly bald and perfunctory assertions of dogmatic fact, but they are supplemented by a much more elaborate story of the same type. 'Only one myth of first emergence is expanded into a long and dramatised story, and that is the myth of the first emergence of the four ancestors of the four main clans.'[66] In this myth the four totemic animals of the four clans emerge one after another from a single hole.[67] Malinowski maintains that the function of this myth is to assert the superior rank status of the Tabalu sub-clan of the Malasi clan, but his argument is weak. To me it seems plain that this 'clan' emergence myth can only be understood if considered along with the 'sub-clan' emergence myths. In that context what the myth 'says' is that while people in general are indissolubly associated with particular domains – sub-clan members with their sub-clan hamlets – there are four distinct kinds of such people.

My thesis is then that the four Trobriand clans are not really to be thought of as four unique and separate lines of descent – Trobrianders indeed seem to have little interest in pedigree. The four clans are an 'expression', a kind of model, of the fact that the Trobriand individual finds himself in a world which contains, so far as he is concerned, four kinds of localised hamlets with their associated sub-clans. From the young male Ego's point of view there are four categories of landowners – *tama, kada, yawa, tabu* – and they have four categories of daughters – *luta, latu, yawa, tabu*. This explains why the importance of the four clans seems to be constantly emphasised by the Trobrianders themselves, even though the clans scarcely exist as corporate groups and may at times be difficult to identify at all.

Conclusion

In this paper I have sought to demonstrate the advantage of approaching the analysis of a kinship terminology without any preconceived assumption that the 'primary meaning' of this or that particular word must necessarily be defined by genealogy. My general standpoint is that kinship terms are category words by means of which the individual is taught to recognise the significant groupings in the social structure into which he is born. Until we as anthropologists fully understand the nature of that social structure we can hardly hope to understand what the various category words 'mean'. Indeed the meaning of particular terms varies according to the age status of the individual within the total system.

From Malinowski's writings we can safely infer that, in Trobriand social structure, descent group affiliation and residential grouping have an almost equal importance. We can further infer that the *urigubu* payment is the primary and fundamental expression of the various relationships which result from this structure. Assuming this to be the case, I have examined the kinship term categories against the structural background. The result is what seems to me a perfect 'fit'. Where the genealogical analysis of Malinowski leads to a maze of 'anomalies' and to Malinowski's desperate expedient of the doctrine of homonyms, the present analysis displays no exceptions and can in fact be memorised in a few minutes. This consistency convinces me that the pattern I have given comes very near to the Trobrianders' own conception. Further confirmation is provided by the fit between the fourfold categories in the kinship system and the four clans. The supposed preference for patrilateral cross-cousin marriage has been demonstrated as an expression of the rules of exogamy which emerge from other elements in the structure. This much indeed Malinowski himself proclaimed, but where Malinowski argued that exogamy centred in the sub-clan and clan, I have suggested that it is based in the male Ego's dual residential status in the hamlets of his father and his mother's brother.

My further initial purpose was to demonstrate that there is an inherent consistency between all the various meanings of *tabu* which were listed at the beginning of this paper. This I claim to have done. In the context of kinship, *tabu* in all its senses is seen to refer to 'remote and potentially hostile relatives with whom Ego has no direct economic bonds but towards whom an attitude of "friendship" is expected'. It is a category of marginal relationship; it is filled with the 'dangers of the unknown' upon which Malinowski was prone to lay such stress. The category includes remote deceased ancestors and totemic spirits, and this links up the notion of 'sacred–forbidden' with that of 'distant–dangerous'.

Open hostility is not involved, *tabu* are related to one another only by intermediate links, there is no common economic interest which they are likely to fight about. But, for all that, *tabu* are dangerous people, people of power with whom you must be on good terms. It is significant that the only situations in which Malinowski mentions the *tabu* relationship as being ritually important are occasions when the *tabu* influence one another by magic.[68] The magic in these cases happens to be beneficial, but a Trobriander would never forget that any magician may very easily become a sorcerer.

I hope then that I have disposed of the idea that the various meanings of *tabu* are accidental homonyms as unrelated as *pair* and *pear*.

Yet the puzzle remains. Why should Malinowski have been so keen to insist that the various meanings of the word are wholly unrelated? Why, when he himself laid such stress on the taboo between a man and his sister, should he repudiate the logic by which a boy regards his father's sister as *tabu*?

The answer seems to be that it was because he took over uncritically from his predecessors the bland assumption that the key to the understanding of any system of kinship terminology must always be sought in rules of preferred marriage.

This belief had been dogma for Rivers, and Malinowski regarded Rivers's anthropology as the very quintessence of everything that is wrong-headed and misdirected. Yet Malinowski's pronouncements regarding the term *tabu* seem to derive from the fact that Trobrianders told him that they ought to marry their *tabu*. How could it possibly be that the term which thus described the 'lawful woman' should also mean 'forbidden, dangerous, sacred'? The only possible explanation for Malinowski was that we are here dealing with two or more entirely different words. What he failed to notice was that when a man does marry a *tabu* relative either close or remote, she and her immediate kinsmen forthwith cease to be *tabu*, and come into the much more closely bonded categories of *lubou* and *yawa*. In other words, marriage is a device whereby the dangers of *tabu* are for the time being exorcised.

Notes

'Concerning Trobriand Clans and the Kinship Category *Tabu*' was published in *The Developmental Cycle in Domestic Groups* edited by Jack Goody (1958). It was the first volume in the series Cambridge Papers in Social Anthropology, which was established under the joint editorship of Fortes, Goody, and Leach (later joined by Tambiah), as a forum for the publication of works by people associated with the Cambridge University Department of Social Anthropology. Other volumes in the series included *Aspects of Caste* (edited by Leach), *Marriage in Tribal Societies* (Fortes), *Succession to High Office* (Goody), *Dialectic in Practical Religion* (Leach), and *Councils in Action* (edited by Audrey Richards and Adam Kuper).

1. [Eds.: See 'Malinowski's Empiricism', I.1.2. above.]
2. [Eds.: The volume in which this essay by Leach originally appeared was intended by its editor, Jack Goody, to be devoted to the exploration and elaboration of the methods and claims set out in the paper by Fortes referred to here. Characteristically, Leach's contribution is, in many respects, an argument against Fortes.]
3. Malinowski, *Sexual Life of Savages* (3rd edn), p. 416. [Eds: Throughout this essay, references to Malinowski's *The Sexual Life of Savages* are to the 3rd edn (1932).]
4. Ibid., pp. 423, 450–1; *Coral Gardens*, ii. pp. 28, 113.
5. [Eds.: Powell's doctoral dissertation, 'An Analysis of Present-Day Social Structure in the Trobriands', was completed in 1956. In subsequent essays on Trobriand ethnography, such as 'Rethinking Anthropology' (see I.3.7), Leach again makes use of Powell's ethnography, and refers extensively to the dissertation.]
6. Tax, 'Some Problems of Social Organisation,' pp. 12ff.
7. Gilbert, 'Eastern Cherokee Social Organisation', p. 292.
8. Malinowski, *Sexual Life of Savages*, p. 423.

9. Ibid., p. 5.
10. Ibid., p. 447.
11. Ibid., pp. 26, 417; Malinowski, *Coral Gardens*, i, ch. 12.
12. Ibid., p. 385.
13. Ibid., p. 430.
14. Ibid.
15. Ibid., pp. 343–4.
16. Malinowski, *Sexual Life of Savages*, pp. 53–64.
17. Malinowski, *Coral Gardens*, i, pp. 36, 205, 357.
18. Ibid., pp. 60, 191.
19. Malinowski, *Sexual Life of Savages*, pp. 75, 93.
20. Ibid., p. 51.
21. Malinowski (ibid., p. 52) translates *toboma* as 'tabooed man' from the general root *boma* ('sacred', 'taboo'). This fits well with the explanation of *tabu* given below.
22. Malinowski, *Coral Gardens*, i, p. 194.
23. Radcliffe-Brown, *Structure and Function in Primitive Society*, chs 4, 5, 7.
24. Radcliffe-Brown, *Andaman Islanders*, p. 81.
25. Radcliffe-Brown, *Structure and Function*, pp. 79–80, 100.
26. Ibid., p. 112.
27. Ibid., p. 79.
28. Malinowski, *Sexual Life of Savages*, p. 13.
29. Ibid., p. 137.
30. Ibid., p. 450.
31. Ibid., p. 295.
32. Source Powell. In strict formality father's mother's mother's brothers are *tama*, mother's mother's brothers are *kada*. The informal use of *tabu* here seems to fit with the use of *toboma* for certain respected old men; cf. above, p. 248.
33. See p. 248.
34. It is possible that some members of either of these two hamlets might be members of Ego's own sub-clan. In that case he would use *kada, ina, tuwa, bwada, luta*, as appropriate in place of *tabu*.
35. Malinowski, *Sexual Life of Savages*, p. 435.
36. See above and cf. Fortes, 'Structure of Unilineal Descent Groups', p. 20.
37. Malinowski, *Sexual Life of Savages*, p. 448.
38. Ibid., p. 449.
39. Ibid., p. 423.
40. Ibid., p. 295.
41. White, 'Definition and Problem of Incest', p. 416; Tylor, 'Method of Investigating the Development of Institutions', p. 267.
42. E.g. Fortes, *Web of Kinship*, p. 249; Evans-Pritchard, *Kinship and Marriage among the Nuer*, pp. 44–8.
43. See Fig. 2, above.
44. See above, p. 245.
45. Malinowski, *Sexual Life of Savages*, pp. 434–6.
46. Malinowski, *Coral Gardens*, i, pp. 56, 406, 190, 372; *Sexual Life of Savages*, p. 136; *Argonauts*, p. 64.
47. Mr Powell has here corrected Malinowski. The term *ivata* which appears in Malinowski's lists is not used by males and I shall not discuss it. In Malinowski, *yawa* has the restricted meaning of parent-in-law.
48. Malinowski, *Sexual Life of Savages*, p. 449.
49. Ibid., pp. 4, 451; *Coral Gardens*, i., p. 192.
50. *Coral Gardens*, i, pp. 192, 206.
51. As, for example, in Homans and Schneider, *Marriage, Authority, and Final Causes.*
52. Malinowski, *Sexual Life of Savages*, p. 450.
53. Ibid., pp. 81, 86, 451.
54. Ibid., pp. 83, 86; *Coral Gardens*, i, pp. 206, 354, 385.

55. Malinowski, *Sexual Life of Savages*, p. 83n.
56. Ibid., p. 85.
57. Ibid., p. 113–14.
58. Ibid., p. 87.
59. The Kwoynama sub-clan itself possibly has a similar arrangement with their political inferiors of the Malasi clan in the village of Yalomugwa. Malinowski (*Coral Gardens*, i, p. 389) shows the Kwoynama village headman Yosivi marrying off his sister Aykare'i to his own wife's brother who is a member of the inferior Malasi sub-clan in the same village as Yosivi himself.
    Cf. also Seligman, *Melanesians of British New Guinea* (p. 718) where it is noted that *for chiefs only* the father, the children, and the sister's husbands fall into one ritual category; this would be a logical consequence of bilateral cross-cousin marriage.
60. Malinowski, *Coral Gardens*, i., pp. 362f.
61. Radcliffe-Brown, *Structure and Function*, p. 138.
62. Ibid., p. 69.
63. Malinowski, *Coral Gardens*, ii, p. 113.
64. Leach, *Political Systems.*
65. Malinowski, *Coral Gardens*, i, pp. 342ff.
66. Ibid., i, p. 343.
67. Malinowski, *Sexual Life of Savages*, pp. 419ff.
68. Ibid., pp. 185ff, 295ff.

3.5

Kinship in its Place (1961)

Regarded as a contribution to technical social anthropology, my topic might be summarised as follows: this is a study of a small peasant community subsisting by the cultivation of rice in irrigated fields of fixed size and position. The emphasis is on the relevance of kinship and marriage for the practices relating to land holding and land use. Unilineal descent is not a factor in the situation. Although the ethnography has an extremely narrow range the community has an ecology which has parallels in many parts of the world; for that reason some aspects of the analysis are of general significance.

The factual evidence is in certain respects very detailed and some parts of it have a time-depth of sixty-five years. This 'excessive' detail brings into prominence the question of how far the anthropologist's concept of social structure refers to a set of ideas or to a set of empirical facts. This is a general theoretical issue which concerns all social anthropologists.

All British social anthropologists would agree that during the period 1935–54 the most important developments in anthropological theory were concerned with the enlargement of our understanding of the nature and significance of unilineal descent groups. This work stemmed directly from a series of theoretical papers by Radcliffe-Brown[1] and from the influence of Evans-Pritchard's brilliantly simplified study of the Nuer.[2] Fortes has provided an admirably argued summary of this whole development.[3] Like all successful theses the theory of unilineal descent groups serves to generate its own antithesis.

Throughout his writings Radcliffe-Brown consistently exaggerated the importance of unilineal as opposed to bilateral (cognatic) systems of succession and inheritance. Likewise, he constantly stressed the legal aspects of kinship relations as manifested in rights of inheritance in contrast to the economic aspects manifested in work co-operation. The lineage and not the family was the focus of attention.

The bias in favour of unilineal exogamous descent structures was remarkable. In an 85-page general survey of kinship theory published in 1950 the whole Arab world was dismissed in three lines.[4] In the same essay, cognatic systems proper which, though uncommon in Africa, are widely distributed throughout the rest of the world, were treated simply as an eccentric historical peculiarity of the Teutonic tribes.[5]

Such bias should make us cautious. A number of far-reaching generalisations have been derived from Radcliffe-Brown's theoretical argument and the fieldwork which resulted from it. The generalisations stand up well in most lineage type societies. But how far do they apply in societies which do not conform to the unilineal pattern to which Radcliffe-Brown attached so much importance?

For example, it has been argued, very cogently, that in societies with a lineage structure the continuity of the society as a whole rests in the continuity of the system of lineages, each of which is a 'corporation', the life-span of which is independent of the individual lives of its individual members. But in societies which do not have unilineal descent groups, what kind of 'corporation' takes the place of the lineage in providing the nexus of continuity between one generation and the next?

By implication Fortes himself, in the paper I have cited, posed precisely this problem and a quotation may usefully serve as a text for my whole investigation.

> We see that descent is fundamentally a jural concept as Radcliffe-Brown argued in one of his most important papers;[6] we see its significance, as the connecting link between the external, that is the political and legal aspect of what we have called unilineal descent groups, and the internal or domestic aspect. It is in the latter context that kinship carries maximum weight, first, as the source of title to membership of the groups or to specific jural status, with all that this means in rights over and toward persons and property, and second as the basis of the social relations among the persons who are identified with one another in the corporate group. In theory membership of a corporate legal or political group need not stem from kinship, as Weber has made clear. In primitive society, however, if it is not based on kinship it seems generally to presume some formal procedure of incorporation with ritual initiation. . . . Why descent rather than locality or some other principle forms the basis of these corporate groups is a question which needs more study. It will be remembered that Radcliffe-Brown related succession rules to the need for unequivocal discrimination of rights *in rem* and *in personam*.[7] Perhaps it is most closely connected with the fact that rights over the reproductive powers of women are

> easily regulated by a descent group system. But I believe that something deeper than this is involved, for in a homogeneous society there is nothing which could so precisely and incontrovertibly fix one's place in society as one's parentage.[8]

It will be found that in the Sinhalese village of Pul Eliya it is locality rather than descent which forms the basis of corporate grouping, even though the final sentences of the quotation remain valid. The circumstances in which this comes about suggest some interesting reflections on Fortes's thesis.

First, it should be observed that Fortes is here writing in general terms and not exclusively of unilineal systems. Negative evidence will thus throw doubt upon the whole theory.

The issues at stake are far-reaching. If anthropologists come to look upon kinship as a parameter which can be studied in isolation they will always be led, by a series of strictly logical steps, to think of human society as composed of equilibrium systems structured according to ideal legal rules. Economic activities come to appear of minor significance and the study of social adaptation to changing circumstance is made impossible.

But an alternative possibility is to regard economic relations as 'prior' to kinship relations. In this case the continuity of the kinship system need not be regarded as intrinsic; it is, at every point in time, adaptive to the changing economic situation.

In Evans-Prichard's studies of the Nuer[9] and also in Fortes's studies of the Tallensi[10] unilineal descent turns out to be largely an ideal concept to which the empirical facts are only adapted by means of fictions. Both societies are treated as extreme examples of patrilineal organisation. The evident importance attached to matrilateral and affinal kinship connections is not so much explained as explained away.

The basic thesis which underlies these writings has been thus summarised by Fortes: 'The tendency towards equilibrium is marked in every sector of Tale society and in the society as a whole; and it is clearly *the result of the dominance of the lineage principle* in the social structure. . . . The almost complete absence of economic differentiation . . . mean(s) that *economic interests do not play the part of dynamic factors in the social structure.*'[11] But the factual evidence presented in support of this thesis is highly selected and the time-depth very shallow. To the more sceptical it might appear that, if the evidence were more specific and more historical, the discrepancies between the ideal of patrilineal descent and the facts of empirical behaviour might well become still more prominent. In that case both the 'equilibrium' and the 'dominance of the lineage principle' would be little more than academic fancies.

In later writing Fortes has treated the concept of social structure in a different way.[12] Whereas in the Tallensi books structure is a matter of jural rules, the ideal form of which can be represented as a paradigm, Ashanti social structure is shown to emerge as a statistical norm. Fortes himself does not contrast these two arguments and he perhaps intended to imply that the statistical pattern must always converge towards the normative paradigm. But this could only be a presumption. If in reality the ideal order of jural relations and the statistical order of economic relations do not converge, then the significance which we attach to the 'structure of unilineal descent groups' will need careful reconsideration.

It is may thesis that jural rules and statistical norms should be treated as separate frames of reference, but that the former should always be considered secondary to the latter.

In this book I examine the quantitative ('statistical') facts of a particular case and show that these possess a structural pattern which is independent of any ideal paradigm. This does not imply that ideal relations are irrelevant, but it does emphasise that the ideal order and the statistical order are not just one and the same thing.

In an earlier publication,[13] I have stressed this dichotomy in a different way. I there argued that the ideal order tends to be a constant which is reinterpreted to fit the changing circumstances of economic and political fact, but I also suggested that the latter – the facts of empirical reality – are, in every variation, constrained by the ideas which people hold about what is supposed to be the case.

In my Sinhalese story I want to make a different point. Here again the ideal model of society and the empirical facts are distinct. Indeed, despite tremendous empirical changes, the ideal order is still close to that described by Ievers nearly sixty years ago. The remarkable manner in which this ideal system has constrained actual behaviour is clearly demonstrated, especially in chapter VI.

But the Pul Eliya community does not only operate within an established framework of legal rules, it also exists within a particular man-made ecological environment. It is the inflexibility of topography – of water and land and climate – which most of all determines what people shall do. The interpretation of ideal legal rules is at all times limited by such crude nursery facts as that water evaporates and flows downhill. It is in this sense that I want to insist that the student of social structure must never forget that the constraints of economics are prior to the constraints of morality and law.

Although I am pleading that my specialist study of Pul Eliya has general implications, I am not proposing a classification. Since I have used a quotation from Fortes as my text, this must be stressed.

The theory of unilineal descent groups is, on the face of it, well established; it would, therefore, be tempting to offer Pul Eliya as a contrary type – a 'bilateral' as opposed to a 'unilineal' structure. I am not proposing any such typology, for I am sceptical of all typologies.

Radcliffe-Brown's generalisation that 'there are few if any societies in which there is not some recognition of unilineal descent'[14] is itself invalid, but the corollary, that no clear distinction is possible between societies which recognise unilineal descent and those which do not, is correct. There are a large number of societies which possess some of the superficial attributes of unilineal systems yet lack clearly defined unilineal descent groups. The English with their patrilineally inherited surnames provide one example; Sinhalese society is another. The precise nature of the 'unilinearity' present in these marginal cases calls for close investigation, but it would be prejudging the whole issue to assume that the presence or absence of lineages was a diacritically significant factor.

Other writers have suggested that patrilineal lineages occur in Sinhalese society.[15] In my view that is fallacious, yet it is perfectly true that the Sinhalese do possess, in certain respects, a patrilineal ideology. Is this patrilinearity of the Sinhalese an enduring characteristic of Sinhalese culture or is it a reflection of the way in which Sinhalese order their economic lives? Has it the lasting quality of a principle of law or is it simply descriptive of a temporary state of affairs?

I might put it this way. We can learn a great deal about the nature of unilineal descent groups by pursuing to its limit the terminological issue as to whether it is or is not correct to say that Sinhalese society is patrilineal. Conversely we can learn a great deal about the nature of cognatic (bilateral) systems if we pursue the question: why is it functionally useful in a society such as that of Pul Eliya, which lacks unilineal descent groups, to have a concept of descent at all? But the outcome of this enquiry will be to blur rather than to intensify the distinction between unilineal and non-unilineal systems; Pul Eliya itself does not belong to either 'type'.

Kinship as we meet it in this book is not 'a thing in itself'. The concepts of descent and of affinity are expressions of property relations which endure through time. Marriage unifies; inheritance separates; property endures. A particular descent system simply reflects the total process of property succession as effected by the total pattern of inheritance and marriage. The classification of whole societies in terms of such a parameter can only be meaningful in an extremely crude sense.

What we need to understand about a society is not whether it is patrilineal or matrilineal or both or neither, but what the notion of patrilinearity stands for and why it is there.

Again and again I found my Pul Eliya villagers asserting of a particular piece of ground that the owner's rights were *purāna* ('from the beginning') or *paravēni* ('ancestral'), even when I knew as an unquestionable fact that the land in question had recently been acquired by purchase. Why this scheme of values? What does continuity with the ancestral past 'mean' in such a society?

Such answer as I can give is a special answer which applies in its particularity only to the special case of Pul Eliya. But it is a special answer with general implications; it has relevance for the much wider issue of the distinction between unilineal and bilateral kinship systems on the one hand, and between jural and economic relationships on the other.

Finally I would add a more technical point. The case-history method of presenting anthropological arguments has now been in vogue for many years. It was practised by Malinowski and it has been practised in much the same way by some of his most vociferous critics. But case-history material in anthropological writings seldom reflects objective description. What commonly happens is that the anthropologist propounds some rather preposterous hypothesis of a very general kind and then puts forward his cases to illustrate the argument. The technique of argument is still that of Frazer. Insight comes from the anthropologist's private intuition; the evidence is only put in by way of illustration.

Now the special conditions under which the anthropologist makes his observations and his analyses make it very difficult to avoid this kind of subjectivism, and I do not pretend that I have escaped from it in this book. But I have tried to do so. The case-history material in this book is very extensive, but the cases are not simply there to illustrate a particular theoretical principle. On a larger scale the isolated examples all fit together into a single case-history, and the material is there in sufficient quantity for the reader to exercise his scepticism where and how he will. The interpretation of the evidence is of course still *my* interpretation, but I have tried to avoid offering a 'take it or leave it' solution. I claim that the evidence 'speaks for itself'. Even if this is not entirely the case I feel that I have been more honest with my readers than some of my colleagues have managed to be with theirs. The extra detail goes in at the cost of readability, but I cannot avoid that. The result is not bedside reading, but there is plenty to exercise the acrostic-making talent of the industrious undergraduate.

What then has been demonstrated by this meticulous examination of a very limited range of facts? In this final chapter I shall attempt my own assessment of where this volume stands in relation to other current work in the field of social anthropology.

The crucial distinction which separates the social anthropologist from the ethnographer is his interest in the constraint of the individual. The ethnographer is content to record 'custom', that is to say the facts which are generally true of a society in a broad sense; the individual appears only as a stereotype, a creature who conforms to custom unthinkingly and without motive. In contrast, the social anthropologist stresses that custom is synthetic and quite distinct from the behaviour of individuals; a large part of modern anthropological 'theory' is concerned with the implications of this dichotomy.

There have been several distinct approaches to this issue which differ according to the empiricist and idealist bias of the writer's underlying philosophy. Is the 'social thing' which constrains the individual a tissue of ideas or of objective facts? The several arguments can all be traced to Durkheim.

In the immediate post-war period the strongest influence in British social anthropology emanated from Oxford, where the views of Radcliffe-Brown and Evans-Pritchard were dominant, with Durkheim's *Division of Labour* and Maine's *Ancient Law* as primary sources. Individuals were presumed to be born free into a society composed of corporate institutions, the relations within which and between which provide a paradigm of social existence. The structural shape of such a corporation is intrinsically self-perpetuating and is independent of the individual life-span of its particular members. Social structure is thought of as a network of relationships between 'persons', or 'roles'. The stability of the system requires that the content of such relationships shall be permanent. In such a society every individual who fills a role finds himself under jural constraint to fulfil the obligations inherent in that role. More crudely, the customs of a society are seen as providing a body of moral norms worked out in behaviouristic form; the discrepancies between individual behaviour and customary behaviour are due simply to the inability of the average man to live up to the moral demands of his society. He is represented as knowing very well what ought to be the case, but as devising immensely complicated fictions which will absolve him from the inconveniences of virtue.

Evans-Pritchard's accounts of Nuer practices with regard to descent, residence, and sacrifice provide numerous examples of what I have in mind. It may be remarked that this whole analysis rests on the premiss that behaviour, as observed by the anthropologist, must of necessity make sense in terms of an equilibrium system. The reader should remember that both the sense and the equilibrium are purely pragmatic assumptions – they are convenient for certain practical purposes. There may well be situations in which these functionalist premisses are best abandoned.

There is another line of thought, which also comes from Durkheim, which stems from the thesis that the social is that which is *quantitatively* normal. In the *Division of Labour* norms are jural norms, rules of behaviour supported by sanctions; in *Suicide* the norm is a statistical average. Throughout the later writings both of Durkheim himself and of his followers this same ambiguity between normative and normal constantly recurs. In British anthropology it corresponds in some ways to the opposition between the Radcliffe-Brown and the Malinowski versions of functionalist doctrine.

In Radcliffe-Brown's schema society is something other than a sum of individuals, for society has the power to impose its will upon the individual through the operation of the sanctioned rules which constitute the structure of enduring corporate groups. The social anthropologist is expected to concentrate his attention upon the nature of these rules and the manner by which they are enforced.

In contrast, in Malinowski's system, despite the underlying assumption that every custom serves a utilitarian purpose and the emphatic assertion that the individual is not a 'slave to custom', no clear distinction ever emerges between customary behaviour on the one hand and individual behaviour on the other. Custom is what men do, normal men, average men.

It follows that custom, in Malinowski's conception, is like Durkheim's 'suicide rate', a symptom; it is not something imposed by rule, nor is it itself coercive, it simply corresponds to the state of affairs. Custom 'makes sense' not in terms of some external, logically ordered, moral system, but in terms of the private self-interest of the average man in that particular cultural situation.

Malinowski here evaded many issues, and the crucial one of just *how* the social fact of normal behaviour can emerge from a sum of seemingly arbitrary individual choices is one which the social anthropologist cannot legitimately avoid; but at least he did not invoke a mysticism to explain away what we do not understand.

The currently fashionable structuralist[16] concept of 'social solidarity' seems to me to be precisely such a mysticism, for it has lately begun to be treated as an ultimate explanatory device, an absolute virtue towards which all social activity is of necessity directed. The magical potency of this concept has now been expanded to the point at which Gluckman finds it sensible to explain war-like deviation from customary behaviour as itself a form of custom which has the purposive function of enhancing social cohesion.[17] This kind of double-talk can be made very persuasive, but it is a purely scholastic argument; it has no more scientific value than the comparable double-headed dogmas of the psychoanalysts.

A third way of thinking about the distinction between custom and individual behaviour derives from the difficult Durkheimian notion of 'collective representations'. Here the thesis is that the 'sacred' and the 'profane' are distinct categories of verbal and non-verbal behaviour and that the former is, as it were, a 'model' for the latter. In some developments of this argument, ritual is looked upon as providing an 'outline plan' in terms of which individuals orientate their day-to-day behaviour. The divergencies of individual behaviour from any standard norm are not then the result of moral error or of unenlightened self-interest, but arise simply because different individuals, quite legitimately, fill in the details of the ideal schema in different ways.

As I made clear in an earlier volume,[18] this last type of approach, despite its manifest idealist pitfalls, offers a number of attractions. It disposes of the twin functionalist fictions that social systems are intrinsically in stable equilibrium and that all parts of such a system are mutually consistent. Furthermore, it allows the anthropologist to take cognisance of social adaptation to changing circumstances.

But, in my view, the strict Durkheimian proposition that 'things sacred' and 'things profane' are quite separate categories, applicable to sets of events which are distinct both in time and place, is not tenable. The category distinction, to be useful, must apply to aspects of all behaviour rather than to separate items of total behaviour. 'Rituals', through which the members of a society manifest to themselves the model schema of the social structure within which they live, occur all the time, in ordinary everyday affairs just as much as in situations which are explicitly ceremonial.

No doubt it is true that, on the occasion of a wedding or a funeral or a coronation or a degree-taking ceremony or of any similar formal function, the structural relationships between the participants are quite explicitly and consciously dramatised, and therefore easy to observe, but, unless such representations are to be regarded as mere play-acting and pretence, the same kind of structural patterning should be observable in ordinary everyday affairs

In this book I have attempted to demonstrate this principle. The facts which have been discussed cover only a part of a single institutional aspect of the life of Pul Eliya villagers. The subject matter of the book is the relation between land use and kinship within that very narrow territorial framework. But my objectives are those of a social anthropologist, not of a geographer; I have sought to demonstrate that the notion of 'structural relationship' is not merely an abstraction which the anthropologist uses as a paradigm to simplify his problems of description. The social structure which I talk about in this book is, in principle, a statistical notion; it is a social fact in the same sense as a suicide rate is a social fact. It is a by-product of the sum of many individual human actions, of which the participants are neither wholly conscious nor wholly unaware. It is normal rather than normative; yet, since it clearly possesses some degree of stability, we are still faced with Durkheim's problem – what relates a suicide rate with the motivations of an individual suicide? What is it about the Pul Eliya social system which persists?

When I started writing this book, this seemed to me to be my principal problem – I wanted to understand the principles of structural continuity in this small-scale community which lacked any obvious type of exclusive ongoing corporation. There were no unilineal descent groups, no secret societies, no sects; what then were the continuing sets of relations which kept the society in being? It was only gradually that I came to realise that this whole formulation was altogether too much in the tradition of Radcliffe-Brown and the Oxford structuralists. Why should I be looking for some social entity other than the individuals of the community itself?

Because the structuralists assume that the individual is constrained by *moral* forces, it necessarily follows that the constraint is social, and we are led directly into the Durkheimian mystique which attributes the characteristics of deity to society regarded as a corporation. But if we repudiate the emphasis on moral rules and jural obligation then the problem becomes much simpler. The constraint imposed on the individual is merely one of patterning and limitation; the individual can do what he likes as long as he stays inside the group. The group itself need have no rules; it may be simply a collection of individuals who derive their livelihood from a piece of territory laid out in a particular way. The continuing entity is *not* Pul Eliya *society* but Pul Eliya itself – the village tank, the *gamgoda* area, the Old Field with its complex arrangement of *bāga* and *pangu* and *elapata*. For purely technical reasons, connected with the procedures and efficiency of irrigated rice agriculture, the arrangements of the Pul Eliya ground are difficult to alter. They are not immutable, but it is much simpler for the human beings to adapt themselves to the layout of the territory than to adapt the territory to the private whims of individual human beings.

Thus, as I stated at the beginning, Pul Eliya is a society in which locality and not descent forms the basis of corporate grouping; it is a very simple and perhaps almost obvious finding, yet it seems to me to have very important implications for anthropological theory and method.

My denigration of 'kinship structure' in favour of 'locality structure' does not rest simply on an assertion. I claim that, by the detailed presentation of the facts, I have demonstrated, for the careful reader, that what I assert to be the case is so. But having made the demonstration, at least to my own satisfaction, I am filled with scepticism. How many of the elegant structural analyses, which British social anthropologists have presented over the past twenty years, would really stand up to such microscopic treatment?

Let me be clear in my insinuations. Contemporary British social anthropologists very rightly pride themselves on the meticulous detail of their field researches, and, as functionalists, all of them operate with contextualist premisses; but for the structuralist follower of Radcliffe-Brown the context is transcendental. Behaviour takes place within a social structure which, it is maintained, is no less real because it cannot be objectively perceived. Durkheim understood, as some of his successors have not, that such a 'social structure' must necessarily be credited with the attributes of deity. The anthropologist with his wealth of detailed knowledge of the behavioural facts claims an intuitive understanding of the jural system which holds these behaviours in control. When he writes his structural analysis, it is this private intuition which he describes rather than the empirical facts of the case. The logical procedures involved are precisely those of a theologian who purports to be able to delineate the attributes of God by resorting to the argument from design.

Of course it is all very elegant, but it is not a demonstration; the structuralist anthropologist, like the theologian, will only persuade those who already wish to believe.

I am not wishing to suggest that the notion of *social*, as distinct from *material*, context is wholly without value , but it is a concept which must be used with great discretion. It is essentially a metaphysical idea, and like other such ideas it can very easily be stretched to explain, or explain away, anything you choose.

Primarily this book is offered as an example of the analysis of a particular peasant society which lacks a unilineal descent system. As such, I think it has some merits whatever may be the theoretical prejudices of the anthropological reader. But as regards theory, my purpose is to introduce a wider scepticism. It is not merely that, in societies lacking unilineal descent, some such analytical process as this becomes appropriate, but that potentially this same method, applied to societies *with* unilineal descent, might produce disconcerting results. It might even be the case that 'the structure of unilineal descent groups' is a *total* fiction; illuminating no doubt, like other theological ideas, but still a fiction.

Whether this be so or not, it is high time that social anthropologists considered the possibility; they need to take another look at the basic assumptions of the structuralist thesis. Is it, for example, due to empirical fact or to theoretical bias that, in the spate of Africanist writing on systems of kinship and marriage, the emphasis has been all on kinship to the neglect of marriage? Common descent results in social solidarity, marriage differentiates and is the ultimate source of all social fission; the argument in its various manifestations is now well known.[19]

'Social solidarity', as Radcliffe-Brown and most of his followers have used it, is a deceptive, unanalysed concept. It does not follow that those who have common interests are the most likely persons to act in co-operation; nor does the fact that two individuals are placed in the same category by third parties necessarily impose upon them any solidarity of interest or of action. In Pul

Eliya, full siblings belong by birth to the same household, and hence to the same compound group, and they necessarily have closely similar territorial rights of all kinds. This means that full siblings must learn to 'fit themselves to the ground' in much the same way, yet, from the start, full siblings are rivals for the same material assets; every man will be the gainer by the death of his brother. In contrast, relations to affinity, which lack common territorial interest, are likely to maximise economic and social co-operation. There is a *kind* of social solidarity both between siblings and between affines, but we need to make a distinction.

There is nothing in the least novel about this point of view; I am simply asking my anthropological colleagues to get back to first principles. Structuralist anthropologists are far too much inclined to dichotomise their material. Just as Durkheim tried to distribute actual behaviours between his polar categories 'sacred' and 'profane', so too the structuralists try to polarise 'things social' and 'things material.' Running right through the literature of structuralist anthropology there is an underlying assumption that the social structure of a society and the material environment are two 'things' of comparable kind. Although intrinsically interconnected, the two 'things' have independent existence and are both 'real' in a comparable sense.

But this antithesis is false. Society is not a 'thing'; it is a way of ordering experience.[20] My criticism is directed against such points as these:

(1) Evans-Pritchard in writing *The Nuer* clearly tried to integrate the analysis of 'ecology' (chs 1–3) with the analysis of 'social structure' (chs 4–6). In practice each half of the book is autonomous and makes sense without reference to the rest.

(2) Fortes remarks: 'lineage and locality are interwoven and interdependent factors of Tale social structure. But they are functionally discrete factors'[21] and, again, 'every defined social group' has 'an intrinsic connection' with 'a specific locality'.[22] Yet Fortes finds it useful to define the groups without reference to locality.

(3) Mitchell[23] in a chapter entitled 'The Lineage Framework of Villages' manages to polarise 'social groups' (based in matrilineal descent) and 'villages' (based in locality). Evidently, lineages are thought of as 'existing' independently of villages, and considered to be a 'social' phenomenon in a sense that villages are not.

(4) The whole body of assumptions implicit in the design and construction of *African Systems of Kinship and Marriage* which are summed up in Radcliffe-Brown's assertion that 'The reality of a kinship system as a part of a social structure consists of the actual social relations of person to person as exhibited in their interactions and their behaviour in respect of one another.'[24]

In contrast, I want to insist that kinship systems have no 'reality' at all except in relation to land and property. What the social anthropologist calls kinship structure is just a way of talking about property relations which can also be talked about in other ways.

I doubt whether any of my colleagues would deny this, but somehow they have worked themselves into a position in which kinship structure is treated as 'a thing in itself'; indeed a very superior sort of thing which provides a self-sufficient and self-maintaining framework for all that we observe.

My protest is not directed against the study of kinship, for this is by far the most sophisticated tool of analysis which the social anthropologist possesses, but against attempts to isolate kinship behaviours as a distinct category explainable by jural rules without reference to context or economic self-interest.

Of course every social anthropologist recognises that societies exist within a material context which is partly natural – terrain, climate, natural resources – and partly man-made – houses, roads, fields, water supply, capital assets – but too many authors treat such things as nothing more than context, useful only for an introductory chapter before getting down to the main job of analysing the social structure. But such context is not simply a passive backcloth to social life; the context itself is a social product and is itself 'structured'; the people who live in it must conform to a wide range of rules and limitations simply to live there at all.

Every anthropologist needs to start out by considering just how much of the culture with which he is faced can most readily be understood as a direct adaptation to the environmental context, including that part of the context which is man-made. Only when he has exhausted the possibility of explanation by way of normality should it be necessary to resort to metaphysical solutions whereby the peculiarities of custom are explained in terms of normative morality.

Notes

This is an extract from *Pul Eliya: A Village in Ceylon* (1961), pp. 5–12 and 296–306.

1. Reprinted in Radcliffe-Brown, *Structure and Function in Primitive Society.*
2. Evans-Pritchard, *The Nuer.*
3. Fortes, 'The Structure of Unilineal Descent Groups'.
4. 'Introduction' to Radcliffe-Brown and Forde (eds), *African Systems of Kinship and Marriage,* p. 69.
5. Ibid., pp. 15–18; cf. *Structure and Function,* p. 48.
6. Radcliffe-Brown, 'On the Concept of Function'.
7. Ibid.
8. Fortes, 'Structure of Unilineal Descent Groups', p. 30.
9. Evans-Pritchard, *The Nuer,* and *Kinship and Marriage among the Nuer.*
10. Fortes, *Dynamics of Clanship,* and *Web of Kinship.*
11. Fortes, *Dynamics of Clanship,* p. x (my italics).
12. Fortes, 'Time and Social Structure'.
13. Leach, *Political Systems.*
14. 'Introduction' to *African Systems of Kinship and Marriage,* p. 14.
15. Ryan, *Caste in Modern Ceylon,* p. 26; Pieris, *Sinhalese Social Organisation,* pp. 219–22.
16. [Eds.: The word 'structuralist' here does not refer to Lévi-Strauss. Until the mid-1960s this word was used in social anthropology to refer to what has since come to be called 'structural-functionalism'. So in the standard usage of the time Leach is referring to the writings of Radcliffe-Brown and those of his students and followers, and the pertinent contrast is with those of Malinowski.]

17. Gluckman, *Custom and Conflict*, esp. ch. 2.
18. Leach, *Political Systems*.
19. Fortes, 'Structure of Unilineal Descent Groups'.
20. Beattie, 'Understanding and Explanation in Social Anthropology', p. 55.
21. *Dynamics of Clanship*, p. 143.
22. Ibid., p. 171.
23. *The Yao Village*.
24. 'Introduction', p. 10.

3.6

Models (1964)

I have been asked to write about models, but the word model can easily mislead. Right from the start it is polymorphic. Tom's model aeroplane fits in a matchbox, Dick's is made of Plasticine, Harry's will actually fly; my wife's model hat is unique, my model car is made by the thousand; a model child is too good to be true, some model girls are too bad to be possible. The models of the social scientists are equally ambiguous but unavoidable.

It was Palmerston who said that 'half the wrong conclusions at which mankind arrive are reached by the abuse of metaphors and mistaking general resemblance or imaginary similarity for real identity' and he was probably right but society is a concept rather than a concrete thing and the social philosopher must shelter behind analogy of some sort before we can even begin to understand what he is talking about.

It seems to me that we can usefully distinguish four main types of sociological model:

(1) Analogy models. 'Society is an organism.' Of these more anon.

(2) Stabilised variable models. The ordinary analytical procedures of the theoretical economist. A social system is assumed to be the complex product of an unknown number of variables; any specific problem may then be solved (approximately) by holding the great majority of these variables constant and treating the remainder as a mathematically interdependent set. Electronic computers make it feasible to take account of far more variables than was formerly the case, so that models of this class now have great practical utility.

(3) Structural models. 'Binary oppositions' and 'distinctive features' in linguistics, 'segmentary oppositions' in social anthropology. The underlying assumption here is that the data under observation are ordered and not random. The model then purports to display the principle of order.

(4) Cognitive models. Each of us has some kind of cognitive awareness of any social system to which we belong. This is true of all societies. An individual's social behaviour is adapted to the concepts (models) through which

this awareness is expressed. Such models are embedded in facts of language and culture and their detection and interpretation is one of the prime tasks of the social anthropologist.

Of these four classes, types (1) and (2) are inventions of the social scientist himself. Type (3) has an ambiguous status, the investigator usually claims that his model corresponds to a 'real' attribute of the data, his critics will say he has made it up. Models of type (4) are the converse of (1), they are the inventions of the observed not the observer. In this essay I shall leave this last class out of consideration except to note that models of type (1) are type (4) models in the social scientist's own culture. The history of their growth is the history of social thought itself.

Until very recently all European social theories have been built on versions and combinations of models that are to be found in Aristotle's *Politics* written in the fourth century BC. Aristotle's real world was that of the Greek city state, the *polis*, the 160 or so civic republics which formed tiny islands of civilisation in the wider sea of the *ethne*, the 'nations' of rural barbarians outside. Consequently in his model world, Aristotle's *polis* is self-contained, and a great gulf separates the civilised, who are naturally free born, from the uncivilised, who are naturally slaves. This ideal *polis* is a naturally existing species entity of which the individual citizen is only a constituent part. It is so small and intimate that all the citizens can be addressed simultaneously by a single orator speaking in the public assembly.

In saying that the *polis* is a thing of nature (*physis*) Aristotle endowed it with an organic quality, with a natural propensity for growth. This view was in contrast to that which supposed that society is the outcome of convention (*nomos*). Throughout European history these have been the two dominant models of how things are. On the one hand, society is represented as a kind of living animal, the behaviour of which is best understood by supposing that, like any living thing, it always seeks to preserve itself in good health; on the other, society is a kind of machine, a man-made contrivance intended to further the interests of the individuals who have voluntarily come together to form an association. In the organic model, society is a superior being which exists in its own right. The collective will is so dominant over the individual that the latter is scarcely credited with any separate existence at all. In the mechanical model, society is artificial, a device of government, the individual is a complete person in his own right, without reference to the social whole. The dominance of the state arises from the exercise of force rather than from the nature of social life.

Which type of model you prefer is partly a matter of political sentiment and partly a matter of professional interest. Economists seem particularly addicted to the mechanisms of hydraulic engineering: they talk of 'pump priming', 'pressure heads', 'pipelines'. Military strategists start by playing with tin soldiers, proceed to chess, and finally beguile themselves with zero-sum two-person mathematical games. The flashy new profession of operational research goes the whole hog and turns social control into a problem of cybernetics and communication theory. All such models reduce the individual to a 'mere cog in the machine' and, largely for this reason, politicians usually prefer some kind of organic analogy. It allows for a much less precise statement of opinion and somehow suggests a more humane approach to human problems. Neddy,[1] it will be observed, is not only given a personal name (otherwise appropriate to donkeys) but he is concerned with 'rates of growth' rather than 'increases in production'.

In Hobbes, the state is a machine, but it is a man-made machine, which is constructed on the analogy of a human organism:

> Sovereignty is an artificial soul, as giving life and motion to the whole body of magistrates and other officers of the judicature and execution, artificial joints; reward and punishment, by which fastened the seat of the sovereignty every joint and member is moved to perform his duty, are the nerves . . . equity and laws are artificial reason and will; concord, health; see sickness; and civil war, death . . .

Rousseau inverts the argument; his state is an organism pure and simple:

> The body politic, taken individually, may be considered as an organised living body resembling that of a man. . . . The body politic therefore is also a moral being possessed of a will: and this general will, yet tends always to the preservation of the whole and of every part . . . constitutes all the members of the State . . . the rule of what is just or unjust. . . . The voice of the people is, in fact, the voice of God.

yet this monstrous divine organic Being turns out to be a mere product of convention, a creation of individual men:

> In place of the individual personality of each contracting party, this act of assertion creates a moral and collective body receiving from this act its unity, its common identity, its life and its will.

Either way the willing submission of the individual to the state is presupposed. If in protest, I point to the very obvious fact that individuals often feel themselves to be at loggerheads with the state which ordains their lives, the model is pushed still further. The organic state is made super-organic, it is said to resemble a biological family. Just as it is ignorance which leads the child to oppose its parents, so it is our childish lack of understanding which sometimes provokes us, as individuals, to doubt the god-like wisdom of the state. In state, as in family, each of the elements should consciously identify himself with the whole and with its interests – thus Hegel, and so on right through the nineteenth century down to the present day.

The context of this long dialectic between the organic and mechanical models of society was that of European political philosophy. The authors were principally concerned with the nature of authority within sovereign states of a sophisticated kind. If primitive man was considered at all, it was simply as a stereotype of contrast – a model of the hypothetical individual who stands 'outside society'.

For Hobbes, this man stood in 'continual fears, and danger of violent death': his life was 'solitary, poore, nasty, brutish and short'. For Rousseau, he was 'the Noble Savage', paradoxically the moral superior of his civilised and dominant opponent.

Yet it was Rousseau who first broke with this fashion for assuming a sharp antithesis between the civilised and the savage. He realised, a century earlier than Marx, that there can be no such thing as 'man outside society'. The humanity of man is located in his culture not in his biological nature, and culture can only be perpetuated through language and education which are products of society.

Once it is properly understood that social order is not a peculiarity of those whom we call civilised it becomes sensible to enquire as to what kind of society embraces those whom we call savages. Rousseau's insight thus gave the organic analogy a new twist. The idea that every society has an inherent vitality of its own was easily converted into the thesis that the observable varieties of human society represent stages in the natural growth of human society taken as a whole. From Condorcet onwards through Comte, Klemm, Gobineau, Spencer, Lubbock, Marx, Morgan, Engels, and a dozen others we get a whole series of 'layer cake' models of human history which purports to show the successive 'stages' of social evolution. Marx had four such stages and Morgan seven, but Aristotle's simpler concept of a straight dichotomy between the law-abiding organic state and the anarchic 'other' keeps reappearing in new disguises, though sometimes upside down.

Maine contrasted primitive man's status in an enlarged family with modern man's contractual relationships within a system of voluntary association, a shift, that is, away from the organic towards the mechanical. Very similar was Tönnies belief in a trend away from the organic *Gemeinschaft* (community) towards the contractual *Gesellschaft* (association) and also L. H. Morgan's distinction between *social organisation* (*societas*) founded on kinship and *political organisation* (*civitas*) founded 'upon territory and upon property'. Morgan wrote of the former as developing naturally through an 'organic series' while the latter is represented as a contrivance devised by ingenious statesmen. But Durkheim reversed the dichotomy and is thus more Aristotelian. He claimed 'mechanical solidarity' as an attribute of primitive society (which is presumed to consist of homologous segments) while 'organic solidarity' is characteristic of modern industrial society. Precisely the same dichotomy, under different labels, turned up again as late as 1940, as the basis for a typology of African political systems. Model-making is a very conservative occupation![2]

Actually, despite the labels mechanical/organic, Durkheim's scheme has an element of novelty. His organic model is the classical one; the individuals in society fill specialised roles in specialised institutions and thus, in the society as a whole, everyone is dependent on everyone else – hence the well-being of society is synonymous with concord within the body politic. But Durkheim's mechanical model has no connection with Hobbes' man-like automaton.

Since, by definition, primitive societies lack all the institutional apparatus which makes the state viable we have to ask how such societies can survive at all. Aristotle had supposed that, outside the *polis*, man at once indulges his passion for war. Total anarchy prevails, and the anarchy is totally destructive. But this is not true. Anthropologists have shown repeatedly that systems of order prevail even in tribes without rulers. Whence comes this order? Durkheim's thesis is that the homologous segments of such a society are self-sufficient and mutually opposed, but they are pressed together like the grains of sand in a jar. They retain their respective positions not because of their mutual dependence but because of external (mechanical) pressures. In such a system, the bond between the individual and society is a direct one, the link is between the individual and the collective whole not between the individual and other individuals. Mechanical solidarity is at its maximum when personality is near the zero point and when individuals are only reflections of the collective type. Models of this kind are congenial to anthropologists who have always been prone to eliminate the individual by saying that 'the Eskimo do this; the Hopi do that' but their relation to empirical facts seems rather remote.

There is no obvious reason why the modern sociologist should slavishly imitate the models employed by political philosophers over the last 2400 years, but tradition is hard to break. One of the most persistent of recent sociological model-makers, the anthropologist A. R. Radcliffe-Brown, found Aristotle too modern and declared himself a follower of Heraclitus! At one stage he laid it down in the most uncompromising manner that social systems are 'natural kinds'; that the first objective of a social science is the classification of these natural kinds; that the long-term objective of a social science is the discovery of 'laws', comparable to the law of gravitation; that social relationships 'exist in phenomenal reality'; that we can observe the persistence of a social structure in precisely the same sense that an astronomer can observe the persistence of the structure of the solar system. On this basis social science and natural science are one and the same, and *a* society is a natural thing in exactly the same sense as *a* lion.

Which analogy?

This perhaps is no more than an elaboration of Durkheim's principle that 'we must treat social facts as things', yet it seems to me most extraordinary that anyone should be able to persuade himself that this is quite literally the case, and still more extraordinary that he should have been able to persuade others, but so it is.

Radcliffe-Brown's doctrine that the organic nature of society is not an analogy but a fact, has had a most baneful influence, especially through its implication that integration and solidarity must be 'natural' attributes of all social systems. If you feel certain, on a priori grounds, that all forms of social stress must produce a reaction which will tend to restore or even reinforce the solidarity (i.e. organic health) of society then you will quickly persuade yourself that war is peace and conflict harmony.[3]

Although Radcliffe-Brown wrote that:

> I would like to suggest that the closest analogies which we shall get in the social sciences are not with the physical sciences but with biology and physiology. To make an analogy between a society and a physiological system is less open to fallacy than to make one between a society and a mechanical system

he did not leave the argument exactly as he found it. He saw that an organic model accounts more readily for persistence than for change and he was alive to the fact that in the course of history things do not stay put: '*A pig does not become sick and recover as a hippopotamus; but this is what a society does.*' To escape from this difficulty he laid stress on the *structure* of society as opposed to its cultural appearance. Structure, he argued, can persist even when appearance changes.

This notion of 'social structure' is an old one but it gained greatly increased currency as a result of Radcliffe-Brown's advocacy. It is itself, quite plainly, a 'model construct' though most users seem remarkably hazy as to what particular model they have in mind. In the outcome this key expression has come to mean quite different things to different people. That is always the trouble with analogy!

For Radcliffe-Brown the first and basic meaning of 'structure' was biological:

> Social structures are just as real as are individual organisms. A complex organism is a collection of living cells and interstitial fluids arranged in a certain structure . . .

But for others the word structure may first suggest a building, and still others are led to think of a set of mathematical relations which 'exists' independently of any particular manifest form. A page of music, the grooves on a gramophone record, and a pattern of sound waves may all have the same structure. If I myself use the expression social structure it is this last model which I have in mind. I would certainly hold that such a structure is real, but to say that it is 'as real as an individual organism' is a confusion of metaphors and Radcliffe-Brown seems to have confused himself.

If it is right that a social scientist should study social structure in the same way as a crystallographer studies the structure of crystals (as Radcliffe-Brown once said) then no one can complain if books on sociology come to be written in vector geometry and matrix algebra which is the latest American fad.

This form of super-jargon arises from a basic misunderstanding. Aristotle's error was to suppose that the *polis was* an organism rather than that it was *like* an organism and the same confusion befogs these latter-day Aristotles who want to use fancy mathematics to analyse social structures. For social structures, in this context, are models, not facts which exist of themselves, out there. It may be useful on occasion to say that, from certain points of view, a social structure is *like* a crystal structure (model type 1) and that therefore, for certain limited and special purposes, we can usefully think of social relationships as amenable to simple mathematical transformations (model type 2). But the key word here is *simple*. It is no good thinking that you can find out something fundamentally important about flying machines by a meticulous analysis of that model in a matchbox, and any *elaborate* mathematical analysis of social structure is a nonsense of just that kind.

It is not that I think all models worthless. The concepts of social theory are so lacking in concreteness that every social scientist *must* construct his argument around a model of some kind, and we shall then only understand what he means if he makes his model explicit. But we must be told what the model is for.

If the aim is only communication then analogy is justified, but in that case simple models achieve their purpose much better than complicated ones. For example, in all the massive volumes that have been written to explain the nature of social stratification in European class systems there is nothing so effective as Barnes's comparison between social class in a Norwegian fishing village and a fishing net folded into layers.[4] The hierarchy is stratified but the network is continuous. The visual image here makes a direct impact where the verbal formula is just jargon.

In contrast if models are to be used for solving problems, as in applied economics or operational research, then the opposite principle applies; the 'best' models are here likely to be the most complicated. If we use simple models at all we must be careful to specify our assumptions. But what we must never do is to confuse our objectives; we must not imagine that we can solve problems by means of oversimplified analogies or expound a simple metaphor with the aid of complex algebra. The model in a matchbox won't fly.

Notes

This article was written for the magazine *New Society* and published on 14 May 1964, in a series entitled 'Concepts'.

1. [Eds: Neddy – National Economic Development Council.]
2. [Eds: Leach here anticipates Kuper, *Invention of Primitive Society*.]
3. [Eds: This is a sideswipe at Gluckman's argument in *Custom and Conflict in Africa*. See also the Conclusion to *Pul Eliya* (I. 3.5: 274).]
4. [Eds: The reference here is to a paper given by John Barnes to a conference of the Association of Social Anthropologists in Oxford in 1953. The paper is reprinted as 'Class and Committees in a Norwegian Island Parish' in a volume of Barnes's essays entitled, *Models and Interpretations* (Cambridge, 1990). However, although it is implicit in it, the analogy which so much caught Leach's attention (this is not the only place in his writings where he makes reference to it) does not appear explicitly in the printed version of the paper.]

3.7

Rethinking Anthropology (1959/1961)

Let me begin by explaining my arrogant title. Since 1930 British social anthropology has embodied a well-defined set of ideas and objectives which derive directly from the teaching of Malinowski and Radcliffe-Brown – this unity of aim is summed up in the statement that British social anthropology is *functionalist* and concerned with *the comparative analysis of social structures.* But during the last year or so it has begun to look as if this particular aim had worked itself out. Most of my colleagues are giving up the attempt to make comparative generalisations; instead they have begun to write impeccably detailed historical ethnographies of particular peoples.

I regret this new tendency for I still believe that the findings of anthropologists have general as well as particular implications, but why has the functionalist doctrine ceased to carry conviction? To understand what is happening in social anthropology I believe we need to go right back to the beginning and *rethink* basic issues – really elementary matters such as what we mean by marriage or descent or the unity of siblings, and that is difficult – for basic concepts are basic; the ideas one has about them are deeply entrenched and firmly held.

One of the things we need to recognise is the strength of the empirical bias which Malinowski introduced into social anthropology and which has stayed with us ever since. The essential core of social anthropology is fieldwork – the understanding of the way of life of a single particular people. This fieldwork is an extremely personal traumatic kind of experience and the personal involvement of the anthropologist in his work is reflected in what he produces.

When we read Malinowski we get the impression that he is stating something which is of *general* importance. Yet how can this be? He is simply writing about Trobriand Islanders. Somehow he has so assimilated himself into the Trobriand situation that he is able to make the Trobriands a microcosm of the whole primitive world. And the same is true of his successors; for Firth, primitive man is a Tikopian, for Fortes, he is a citizen of Ghana. The existence of this prejudice has long been recognised but we have paid inadequate attention to its consequences. The difficulty of achieving comparative generalisations is directly linked with the problem of escaping from ethnocentric bias.

As is appropriate to an occasion when we honour the memory of Bronislaw Malinowski, I am going to be thoroughly egotistical. I shall imply my own merit by condemning the work of my closest friends. But there is method in my malice. My purpose is to distinguish between two rather similar varieties of comparative generalisation, both of which turn up from time to time in contemporary British social anthropology. One of these, which I dislike, derives from the work of Radcliffe-Brown; the other, which I admire, derives from the work of Lévi-Strauss. It is important that the differences between these two approaches be properly understood, so I shall draw my illustrations in sharp contrast, all black and all white. In this harsh and exaggerated form Professor Lévi-Strauss might well repudiate the authorship of the ideas which I am trying to convey. Hence my egotism; let the blame be wholly mine.

My problem is simple. How can a modern social anthropologist, with all the work of Malinowski and Radcliffe-Brown and their successors at his elbow, embark upon generalisation with any hope of arriving at a satisfying conclusion? My answer is quite simple too; it is this: *by thinking of the organisational ideas that are present in any society as constituting a mathematical pattern.*

The rest of what I have to say is simply an elaboration of this cryptic statement.

First let me emphasise that my concern is with *generalisation*, not with *comparison*. Radcliffe-Brown maintained that the objective of social anthropology was the 'comparison of social structures'. In explaining this he asserted that when we distinguish and compare different types of social structure we are doing the same kind of thing as when we distinguish different kinds of sea-shell according to their structural type.[1] *Generalisation* is quite a different kind of mental operation.

Let me illustrate this point.

Any *two* points can be joined by a straight line and you can represent this straight line mathematically by a simple *first*-order algebraic equation.

Any *three* points can be joined by a circle and you can represent this circle by a quadratic or *second*-order algebraic equation.

It would be a *generalisation* to go straight on from there and say: any n points in a plane can be joined by a curve which can be represented by an equation of order $n - 1$. This would be just a guess, but it would be true, and it is a kind of truth which no amount of comparison can ever reveal.

Comparison and generalisation are both forms of scientific activity, but different.

Comparison is a matter of butterfly collecting – of classification, of the arrangement of things according to their types and sub-types. The followers of Radcliffe-Brown are anthropological butterfly collectors and their approach to their data has certain consequences. For example, according to Radcliffe-Brown's principles we ought to think of Trobriand society as a society of a particular structural type. The classification might proceed thus:

Main type:	societies composed of unilineal descent groups
Sub-type:	societies composed of matrilineal descent groups
Sub-sub-type:	societies composed of matrilineal descent groups in which the married males of the matrilineage live together in one place and apart from the females of the matrilineage

and so on.

In this procedure each class is a sub-type of the class immediately preceding it in the tabulation.

Now I agree that analysis of this kind has its uses, but it has very serious limitations. One major defect is that it has no logical limits. Ultimately every known society can be discriminated in this way as a sub-type distinct from any other, and since anthropologists are notably vague about just what they mean by 'a society', this will lead them to distinguish more and more societies, almost *ad infinitum*.

This is not just hypothesis. My colleague Dr Goody has gone to great pains to distinguish *as types* two adjacent societies in the northern Gold Coast which he calls LoWiili and LoDagaba. A careful reader of Dr Goody's works will discover, however, that these two 'societies' are simply the way that Dr Goody has chosen to describe the fact that his field notes from two neighbouring communities show some curious discrepancies. If Dr Goody's methods of analysis were pushed to the limit we should be able to show that every village community throughout the world constitutes a distinct society which is distinguishable as a type from any other.[2]

Another serious objection is that the typology-makers never explain why they choose one frame of reference rather than another. Radcliffe-Brown's instructions were simply that 'it is necessary to compare societies with reference to one particular aspect . . . the economic system, the political system, or the kinship system' . . . this is equivalent to saying that you can arrange your butterflies according to their colour, or their size, or the shape of their wings according to the whim of the moment, but no matter what you do this will be science. Well perhaps, in a sense, it is; but you must realise that your prior arrangement creates an initial bias from which it is later extremely difficult to escape.[3]

Social anthropology is packed with frustrations of this kind. An obvious example is the category opposition patrilineal/matrilineal. Ever since Morgan began writing of the Iroquois, it has been customary for anthropologists to distinguish unilineal from non-unilineal descent systems, and among the former to distinguish patrilineal societies from matrilineal societies. These categories now seem to us so rudimentary and obvious that it is extremely difficult to break out of the straitjacket of thought which the categories themselves impose.

Yet if our approach is to be genuinely unbiased we must be prepared to consider the possibility that these type categories have no sociological significance whatsoever. It *may* be that to create a class labelled *matrilineal societies* is as irrelevant for our understanding of social structure as the creation of a class *blue butterflies* is irrelevant for the understanding of the anatomical structure of lepidoptera. I don't say it is so, but it may be; it is time that we considered the possibility.

But I warn you, the rethinking of basic category assumptions can be very disconcerting.

Let me cite a case. Dr Audrey Richards's well-known contribution to *African Systems of Kinship and Marriage* is an essay in Radcliffe-Brownian typology making what is rightly regarded as one of the 'musts' of undergraduate reading.[4]

In this essay Dr Richards asserts that '*the* problem' of matrilineal societies is the difficulty of combining recognition of descent through the woman with the rule of exogamous marriage, and she classifies a variety of matrilineal societies according to the way this 'problem' is solved. In effect her classification turns on the fact that a woman's brother and a woman's husband jointly possess rights in the woman's children but that matrilineal systems differ in the way these rights are allocated between the two men.

What I object to in this is the prior category assumptions. Men have brothers-in-law in all kinds of society, so why should it be assumed from the start that brothers-in-law in matrilineal societies have special 'problems' which are absent in patrilineal or bilateral structures? What has really happened here is that, because Dr Richards's own special knowledge lay with the Bemba, a matrilineal society, she has decided to restrict her comparative observations to matrilineal systems. Then, having selected a group of societies which have nothing in common except that they are matrilineal, she is naturally led to conclude that matrilineal descent is *the* major factor to which all the other items of cultural behaviour which she describes are functionally adjusted.

Her argument I am afraid is a tautology; her system of classification already implies the truth of what she claims to be demonstrating.

This illustrates how Radcliffe-Brown's taxonomic assumptions fit in with the ethnocentric bias which I mentioned earlier. Because the type-finding social anthropologist conducts his whole argument in terms of particular instances rather than of generalised patterns, he is constantly tempted to attach exaggerated significance to those features of social organisation which happen to be prominent in the societies of which he himself has first hand experience.

The case of Professor Fortes illustrates this same point in rather a different way. His quest is not so much for types as for prototypes. It so happens that the two societies of which he has made a close study have certain similarities of structural pattern for, while the Tallensi are patrilineal and the Ashanti matrilineal, both Tallensi and Ashanti come unusually close to having a system of double unilineal descent.

Professor Fortes has devised a special concept, 'complementary filiation', which helps him to describe this double unilineal element in the Tallensi/Ashanti pattern while rejecting the notion that these societies actually possess double unilineal systems.[5]

It is interesting to note the circumstances which led to the development of this concept. From one point of view 'complementary filiation' is simply an inverse form of Malinowski's notion of 'sociological paternity' as applied in the matrilineal context of Trobriand society. But Fortes has done more than invent a new name for an old idea; he has made it the corner-stone of a substantial body of theory and this theory arises logically from the special circumstances of his own field experience.

In his earlier writings the Tallensi are often represented as having a somewhat extreme form of patrilineal ideology. Later, in contrast to Rattray, Fortes placed an unambiguously matrilineal label upon the Ashanti. The merit of 'complementary filiation', from Fortes's point of view, is that it is a concept which applies equally well to both of these contrasted societies but does not conflict with his thesis that both the Tallensi and the Ashanti have systems of unilineal descent. The concept became necessary to him precisely because he had decided at the start that the more familiar and more obvious notion of double unilineal descent was inappropriate. In retrospect Fortes seems to have decided that double unilineal descent is a special development of 'complementary filiation', the latter being a feature of all unilineal descent structures. That such category distinctions are contrived rather than natural is evident from Goody's additional discrimination. Goody asserts that the LoWiili have 'complementary descent rather than a dual descent system'. Since the concept of 'complementary filiation' was first introduced so as to help in the distinction between 'filiation' and 'descent' and since the adjective 'complementary' cannot here be given meaning except by reference to the word 'descent', the total argument is clearly tautologous.[6]

Now I do not claim that Professor Fortes is mistaken, but I think he is misled by his prior suppositions. If we are to escape both from typology making and from enthnocentric bias we must turn to a different kind of science. Instead of comparison let us have generalisation; instead of butterfly collecting let us have inspired guesswork.

Let me repeat. Generalisation is inductive; it consists in perceiving possible general laws in the circumstances of special cases; it is guesswork, a gamble, you may be wrong or you may be right, but if you happen to be right you have learnt something altogether new.

In contrast, arranging butterflies according to their types and sub-types is tautology. It merely reasserts something you know already in a slightly different form.

But if you are going to start guessing, you need to know *how* to guess. And this is what I am getting at when I say that the form of thinking should be mathematical.

Functionalism *in a mathematical* sense is *not* concerned with the interconnections between parts of a whole but with the principles of operation of partial systems.

There is a direct conflict here with the dogmas of Malinowski and Radcliffe-Brown. Malinowski's functionalism required us to think of each society (or culture, as Malinowski would have put it) as a totality made up of a number of discrete empirical 'things', of rather diverse kinds – e.g. groups of people, 'institutions', customs. These 'things' are functionally interconnected to form a delicately balanced mechanism rather like the various parts of a wrist-watch. The functionalism of Radcliffe-Brown was equally mechanical though the focus of interest was different.

Radcliffe-Brown was concerned, as it were, to distinguish wrist-watches from grandfather clocks, whereas Malinowski was interested in the general attributes of clockwork. But *both* masters took as their starting-point the notion that a culture or a society is an empirical whole made up of a limited number of readily identifiable parts and that when we compare two societies we are concerned to see whether or not the same kinds of parts are present in both cases.

This approach is appropriate for a zoologist or for a botanist or for a mechanic but it is *not* the approach of a mathematician nor of an engineer and, in my view, the anthropologist has much in common with the engineer. But that is *my* private bias. I was originally trained as an engineer.

The entities which we call societies are not naturally existing species, neither are they man-made mechanisms. But the analogy of a mechanism has quite as much relevance as the analogy of an organism.

This is not the place to discuss the history of the organic analogy as a model for society, but its arbitrariness is often forgotten. Hobbes, who developed his notion of a social organism in a very systematic way, discusses in his preface whether a mechanical or an organic analogy might be the more appropriate for his purpose. He opts for an organism only because he wants to include in his model a metaphysical prime mover (i.e. God – life force).[7] In contrast Radcliffe-Brown employed the organic analogy as a matter of dogma rather than of choice[8] and his butterfly-collecting followers have accepted the appropriateness of the phrase 'social organism' without serious discussion. Against this complacency I must protest. It is certainly the case that social scientists must often resort to analogy but we are not committed to one type of model making for all eternity.

Our task is to understand and explain what goes on in society, how societies work. If an engineer tries to explain to you how a digital computer works he doesn't spend his time classifying different kinds of nuts and bolts. He concerns himself with principles, not with things. He writes out his argument as a mathematical equation of the utmost simplicity, somewhat on the lines of: $0 + 1 = 1$; $1 + 1 = 10$.

No doubt this example is frivolous; such computers embody their information in a code which is transmitted in positive and negative impulses denoted by the digital symbols 0 and 1. The essential point is that although the information which can be embodied in such codes may be enormously complex, the basic principles on which the computing machines work are very simple. Likewise I would maintain that quite simple mechanical models can have relevance for social anthropology despite the acknowledged fact that the detailed empirical facts of social life display the utmost complexity.

I don't want to turn anthropology into a branch of mathematics but I believe we can learn a lot by starting to think about society in a mathematical way.

Considered mathematically society is not an assemblage of things but an assemblage of variables. A good analogy would be with that branch of mathematics known as topology, which may crudely be described as the geometry of elastic rubber sheeting.

If I have a piece of rubber sheet and draw a series of lines on it to symbolise the functional interconnections of some set of social phenomena and I then start stretching the rubber about, I can change the manifest shape of my original geometrical figure out of all recognition and yet clearly there is a sense in which it is the *same* figure all the time. The constancy of pattern is not manifest as an objective empirical fact but it is there as a mathematical generalisation. By analogy, generalised structural patterns in anthropology are not restricted to societies of any one manifest structural type.

Now I know that a lot of you will tell me that topology is one of those alarming scientific mysteries which mere sociologists had best avoid, but I am not in fact proposing anything original. A very good simple account of the nature of topology appears in an article under that title in the current edition of the *Encyclopaedia Britannica.* The author himself makes the point that because topology is a non-metrical form of mathematics it deserves especial attention from social scientists.

The fundamental variable in topology is the degree of connectedness. Any closed curve is 'the same as' any other regardless of its shape; the arc of a circle is 'the same as' a straight line because each is open-ended. Contrariwise, a closed curve has a greater degree of connectedness than an arc. If we apply these ideas to sociology we cease to be interested in particular relationships and concern ourselves instead with the regularities of pattern among neighbouring relationships. In the simplest possible case if there be a relationship p which is intimately associated with another relationship q then in a topological study we shall not concern ourselves with the particular characteristics of p and q but with their mutual characteristics, i.e. with the algebraic ratio p/q. But it must be understood that the relationships and sets of relationships which are symbolised in this way cannot properly be given specific numerical values. The reader should bear this point in mind when he encounters the specimens of pseudo-mathematics which occur later in this paper.

All propositions in topology can also be expressed as propositions in symbolic logic,[9] and it was probably a consideration of this fact which led Nadel to introduce symbolic logic into his last book.[10] My own view is that while the consideration of mathematical and logical models may help the anthropologist to order his theoretical arguments in an intelligent way, his actual procedure should be non-mathematical.

The relevance of all this to my main theme is that the *same* structural pattern may turn up in *any* kind of society – a mathematical approach makes no prior assumption that unilineal systems are basically different from non-unilineal systems or patrilineal structures from matrilineal structures. On the contrary, the principle of parity leads us to discount all rigid category distinctions of this kind.

Let me try to illustrate my point with an example. To be appropriate for the occasion I shall take my example from Malinowski.

Most of you will know that Malinowski reported, as a fact of empirical ethnography, that the Trobrianders profess ignorance of the connection between copulation and pregnancy and that this ignorance serves as a rational justification for their system of matrilineal descent. From the Trobriand point of view 'my father' (*tama*) is not a blood relative at all but a kind of affine, 'my mother's husband'.[11]

However, alongside their dogmatic ignorance of the facts of life, Trobrianders also maintain that every child should resemble its mother's husband (i.e. its father) but that no child could ever resemble a member of its own matrilineal kin.

Malinowski seems to have thought it paradoxical that Trobrianders should hold both these doctrines at the same time. He was apparently bemused by the same kind of ethnocentric assumptions as later led a Tallensi informant to tell Professor Fortes that 'both parents transmit their blood to their offspring, *as can be seen from the fact* that Tallensi children may resemble either parent in looks'.[12] This is mixing up sociology and genetics. We *know*, and apparently the Tallensi assume, that physical appearance is genetically based, but there is no reason why primitive people in general should associate ideas of genetic inheritance with ideas about physical resemblance between persons. The explanation which the Trobrianders gave to Malinowski was that a father impresses his appearance on his son by cohabiting repeatedly with the mother and thereby 'moulding' (*kuli*) the child in her womb,[13] which is reminiscent of the Ashanti view that the father shapes the body of his child as might a potter.[14] This Trobriand theory is quite consistent with the view that the father is related to the son only as mother's husband – that is, an affine and not as a kinsman.

There are other Trobriand doctrines which fall into line with this. The father's sister is 'the prototype of the lawful woman',[15] which seems to be more or less the equivalent of saying that the father (*tama*) is much the same sort of relation as a brother-in-law. Again, although, as Powell has shown,[16] marriage with the father's sister's daughter is rare, the Trobrianders constantly assured Malinowski that this was a very right and proper marriage. Evidently in their view the category *tama* (which includes both father and father's sister's son) is very close to that of *lubou* (brother-in-law).[17] The similarity is asserted not only in verbal expression but also in the pattern of economic obligation, for the harvest gift (*urigubu*) paid by a married man is due *both* to his mother's husband (*tama*) *and* to his sister's husband (*lubou*).[18]

From my point of view this cluster of Trobriand beliefs and attitudes is a 'pattern of organisational ideas' – it specifies a series of categories, and places them in a particular relationship with one another as in an algebraic equation. But Malinowski was biased by his down-to-earth empiricism, by European prejudices, and by his interest in psychoanalysis, and he refused to accept the Trobriand doctrine at its face value. Instead he refurbished his concept of 'sociological paternity' which he had originally devised to fit a quite different context, that of patrilineal organisation among the Australian Aborigines.[19]

On this earlier occasion Malinowski had used 'sociological paternity' to show how relations between parents and children and between spouses derive from customary rules and not from any universal facts of biology or psychology, but in the later application of these ideas to Trobriand circumstances he shifts his ground and the argument becomes confused by the introduction of naïve psychological considerations.

On the face of it 'sociological paternity', as used in *The Sexual Life of Savages*, seems to mean that even in a society which, like the Trobriands, denies the facts of 'biological paternity', sociological attitudes which pertain to paternity, as *we* understand it, may still be found. So far, so good. But Malinowski goes further than this. Instead of arguing, as in the Australian case, that kinship attitudes have a purely social origin, he now insists that social attitudes to kinship are rooted in universal psychological facts. The paternal relationship contains elements which are necessarily present in the father/child relationship of *all* societies, no matter what the circumstances of custom and social structure may be. This is all very confusing. On the one hand the reader is told quite plainly that the Trobriand child is taught to think of his father as a non-relative, as an individual with the special non-kinship status of mother's husband. But on the other hand the reader is forced to conclude that this Trobriand mother's husband is related to the mother's child 'as a sociological father', that is to say by ties of kinship as well as by ties of affinity. The argument, as a whole, is self-contradictory.

You may well think that this is a very hairsplitting point to make a fuss about. How can it possibly make any difference whether I think of a particular male as my father or as my mother's husband?

Well, all I can say is that anthropologists do worry about such things. Professor Fortes, Dr Goody, and Dr Kathleen Gough are so disturbed by my heretical views on this subject that each of them has recently taken time off to try to bruise my head with their private recensions of Malinowski's argument.[20]

The heart of the controversy may be stated thus. To Englishmen it seems obvious that the relation between brothers-in-law is radically different from the relation between father and son. By that we mean that the rights and duties involved in the two cases are quite different *in kind*. The first relation is one of affinity; the second is one of filiation.

It also seems obvious to us that the relation between mother and son, though different from the relation between father and son, is nevertheless of the same general kind – it is again a relation of filiation. Now Fortes and his followers maintain that this is universally the case – that the relations between a child and *either* of its parents are of the same basic kind, relations of filiation. Fortes asserts that it is necessary to maintain this because any other view 'would make the incest taboo nonsensical'. Thus, like Malinowski, he is prepared on dogmatic psychological grounds to repudiate the Trobrianders' views of their own social system.[21]

The contrary approach, which is my heresy, is that we must take each case as it comes. If the Trobrianders say – as they do say both in word and deed – that the relation between a father and his son is much the same as the relation between male cross-cousins and as the relation between brothers-in-law, but absolutely different from the relation between a mother and her child, then we must accept the fact that this is so. And in that case we only delude ourselves and everyone else if we call such a relationship *filiation*.

My disagreement with Professor Fortes on this matter turns on this point. It seems to me that in his use of the term 'complementary filiation' he is trying to establish as a universal a special ethnographic phenomenon which he happens to have observed among the Tallensi and the Ashanti.

For my part I have no anxiety to demonstrate anything. I am interested only in discerning *possible* general patterns in the peculiar facts of particular ethnographies.

Let us see if we can examine this issue, not as a problem of comparative social structure, nor of verbal polemic, but as a case of generalised (mathematical) structural pattern.

The cardinal principle of Malinowski's anthropological method was that we should view the system as a whole and examine the interconnections between the parts. Thus, in his view, all the following Trobriand facts are closely interconnected:

(1) A father is deemed to have no biological connection with his child.

(2) A child shares the blood of its mother and her siblings; a father is related to his child as 'mother's husband'.

(3) Marriage is virilocal; a boy at marriage sets up house in the hamlet of his mother's brother and his wife joins him there. After marriage brothers and sisters live in different hamlets. They must avoid one another.

(4) An individual's own 'blood relatives' – his matrilineal kin – are never suspected of sorcery or witchcraft; affinal relatives, including wives and children, are often so suspected.

(5) Children are thought to resemble their fathers but not their mothers.

(6) During a man's lifetime his wife's brother gives him an annual gift of food.

(7) At his death his lineage kinsmen make large payments to his wife's lineage. All activities connected with the disposal of the corpse are carried out by members of the wife's lineage.

The list of relevant interconnected facts could be extended indefinitely, but these are the items to which Malinowski himself seems to have attached most weight (see Fig. 1).

All of us now accept this principle of the functional interconnection of items of cultural behaviour, but *generalisation* calls for an exactly opposite treatment of the data. If we are to generalise, a small cluster of interconnected facts must be treated as an isolate expressing a particular principle of social mechanism.

Now consider Fig. 2 and regard it as a generalised version of the centre of Fig. 1. I want to consider the relations of filiation *not* in relation to the system as a whole but in relation to one another.

In talking about 'function' in a *generalised* way it is not sufficient to specify relationship between particular empirical facts; we must give a genuine mathematical sense to our concept of function and start thinking in terms of ratios and the variations of ratios.

So now please forget about my list of cultural characteristics and turn your attention to the diagram (Fig. 2). Try to think of this as a mathematical

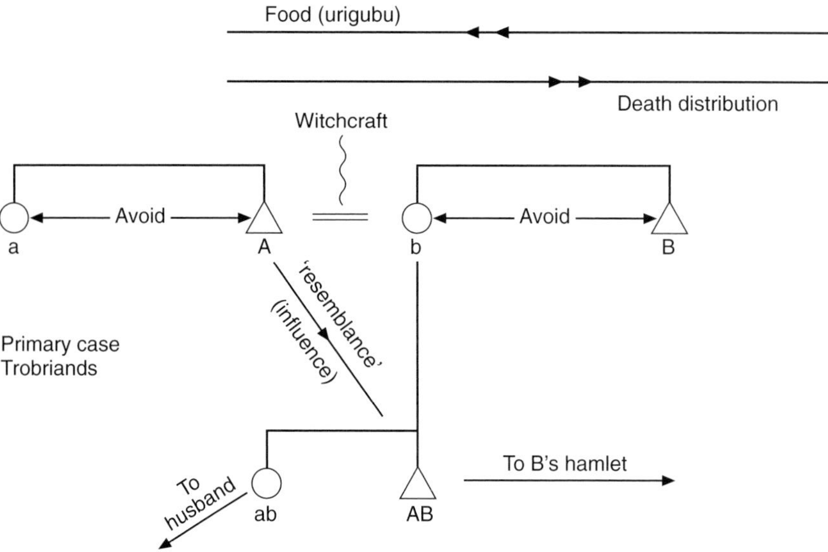

Fig. 1. Relevant Trobriand facts.

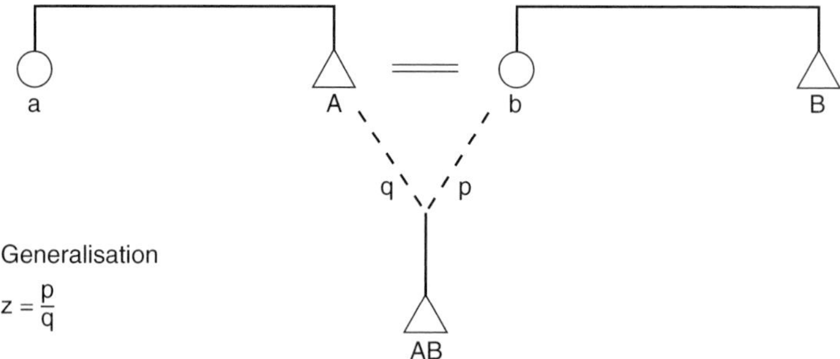

Fig. 2. Generalised diagram of filiation.

expression and forget for the moment that it was originally derived from Trobriand ethnography. I want to 'generalise' this pattern. Instead of using a value-loaded term like *filiation* we will use algebra. Filiation with the father = q, filiation with the mother = p.

The ratio p/q is a mathematical function which varies along with variations of p and q. As indicated above I want to think of these items as topological variables rather than as measurable quantities.

If we call this function z it is clear that z has an infinite number of values between 0 and infinity. The Trobriand case evidently represents one extreme:

$$q = 0;\ p = 1;\ z = \text{infinity}$$

The opposite extreme would be:

$$p = 0;\ q = 1;\ z = 0$$

And there is also an interesting special case somewhere in the middle:

$$q = p;\ z = 1$$

In the great majority of cases we must expect both p and q to have values but the exceptional cases where either p or q is zero are clearly of great interest.

I am *not* trying to argue that we can use mathematics to solve anthropological problems. What I do claim is that the abstraction of mathematical statement has great virtues in itself. By translating anthropological facts into mathematical language, however crude, we can get away from excessive entanglement in empirical facts and value-loaded concepts.

When mathematicians write down equations it doesn't worry them overmuch whether any particular instance is going to turn out 'real' or 'imaginary', but I am prepared to admit that the only kinds of structural pattern which interest anthropologists are those which actually occur.

Well, do my equations represent real or imaginary situations?

For example, what about $z = 0$; $q = 1$; $p = 0$? Obviously an impossible case, for this would imply a society in which a child is not related to its mother, which is absurd. But wait a minute. Why is it absurd? Why is it more absurd than Malinowski's case where a child in unrelated to its father? Mathematically speaking the two cases are precisely on a par; the virtue of mathematical statement is that it allows us to see at once the similarities of pattern in this sense.

Now the Malinowski of *The Family among the Australian Aborigines* would have accepted this equivalence for he argued quite explicitly that maternity as well as paternity is sociologically determined.[22] But to the later Malinowski, who ridiculed Briffault for his notion of group motherhood,[23] it would certainly have seemed absurd to talk about 'children who are not related to their mothers'. In all his Trobriand writings Malinowski was confused by a bias derived from Freudian psychology which made it impossible for him fully to distinguish relationships of a biological and psychological kind from purely sociological relationships; Malinowski's successors – notably Professor Fortes – have, I believe, been hampered by precisely this same excessive involvement in the empirical facts of the case.

Of what sort of society could we say that a child is unrelated to its mother – in the sense that there is no bond of social filiation between mother and child? Clearly the converse of the Trobriand argument applies. If there is a society in which the relation between a child and its mother is utterly unlike that between a child and its father but has much in common with the relations between cross-cousins and between brothers-in-law, then this mother/child relationship is not sensibly described as one of filiation. It is rather a relationship of affinity traced through the father.

There are many forms of ideology which might form the basis for such a pattern of ideas. The essential requirement is that the *p* and *q* relationships should be symbolised as different not only in quality but in kind. The Tikopia are a case in point. They say that the substance of the child originates in the father's semen and derives nothing from the body of the mother. Nevertheless the limbs of the child are fashioned by the Female Deity – a being who seems to be a mystical aspect not only of the mother herself but of her whole patrilineage.[24]

An analogous contrast is provided by the common Asiatic belief that the bony structure of the child's body derives from the father's semen while the soft fleshy parts are made of the blood and the milk of the mother.[25] The North Burma Kachins supplement this with a metaphysical argument. They say that the child acquires its soul (*minla*) only at the moment of birth when it begins to breathe so that this soul is not in any sense derivative from the mother. For that matter the *minla* is not properly speaking hereditary at all; the child acquires this soul from its immediate environment and it is therefore important that a child be born in its father's house.[26] Consequently, a localised patrilineage is known as a *dap* (hearth), i.e. the persons born and raised in one section of one house.

In the same Assam/Burma societies which emphasise in this way the substantial unity of the child with its father's body and with its father's house, we find that the language of kinship contains a special general category which might be translated as 'affinal relatives on the wife's side'. This category includes not only all the men rated as 'wife's brother' and 'father-in-law' but also all those classed as 'mother's brother' as well as all the women classed as 'mother'. (Examples of such broad affinal categories are the Jinghpaw term *mayu* and the Lakher term *patong*.[27])

All these are different ways of asserting both that the *p* and the *q* relationships are radically different, and that the maternal relationship approximates to affinity, but this is not enough. Something more than metaphor and metaphysics is necessary if I am to convince you that in these societies the mother/child relationship is in sociological terms one of affinity rather than of filiation.

Fortunately, from my point of view, we possess an extremely detailed ethnography of one of these groups, the Lakher.[28] Unlike some of their neighbours the Lakher recognise divorce and divorce is frequent. They consider however that the child of a properly married man is exclusively his and that his divorced wife has no rights in the child whatsoever. It follows that if a woman has a son and a daughter by two different husbands the children are deemed to be unrelated to one another. Therefore they may marry without restraint. In contrast, the son and the daughter of one man by two different mothers stand in an incestuous relationship to one another.[29]

This surely is the case we are looking for. Just as the Trobriands are an extreme case in the sense that the father has no consanguineous ties with his wife's children but is bound only to their mother as an affine, so also the Lakher are an extreme case in the sense that the mother has no kinship ties with her husband's children but is bound only to their father as an affine.

It would of course finally clinch the argument if I could show that the rules allow a Lakher male to marry his own divorced mother, but I am afraid that neither the Lakher nor their ethnographer seem to have considered this bizarre possibility!

However there are a variety of other Lakher customs which support my thesis. For example, the death due (*ru*)[30] is paid on behalf of a deceased *male* by his eldest son (or other male heir) to his *pupa*, that is, to a male of the deceased's mother's patrilineage. But in the case of a deceased *female* it is paid by her husband to a male of the deceased's own patrilineage. Should her husband be dead it is payable by her youngest son. If we assume that a common logic pervades these substitutions it is evident that the payment is made from males of the husband's lineage (*ngazua*) to males of the wife's lineage (*patong*) and that the payment reasserts the survival of an affinal tie temporally severed by death. But it will be noted that in these transactions a deceased woman's son can act as deputy for her husband, that is to say, the son is deemed to be related to the mother as an affine (*ngazua*).

No *ru* is payable for unmarried persons but a different death due called *chhongchhireu* is, in this case, paid by the father of the deceased to the mother's brother of the deceased; again an indication that the mother's brother is thought of as an affinal relative.[31] Among some Lakher groups still another death due called *chachhai* is payable by the heir of a deceased male to the deceased's wife's brother. The Lakher explained this last institution by saying that 'a man by dying has abandoned his wife so his heir must pay a fine to the dead man's relations as compensation for the inconsiderate conduct in leaving his wife without a protector'. Here again then the obligation is viewed as an aspect of affinity, and not of uterine kinship; the fact that the 'heir' in question would ordinarily be the wife's son is not considered.

Although I cannot demonstrate that the Lakher would tolerate sex relations between a man and his own mother, it is the case that among the very similar Kachin (where divorce is impossible) such relations would be treated as adultery (*shut hpyit*) rather than as incest (*jaiwawng*).[32] Also in the contrary case, a Trobriand man may cohabit regularly with his own daughter or step-daughter without committing the sin of incest (*suvasova*) even though such relations are considered morally objectionable on other grounds.[33] Malinowski says that such relations could never be legitimised as marriage but it is not clear what he means by this. A Trobriand marriage is legitimate when the wife's matrilineal kinsmen pay *urigubu* harvest gifts to the husband.[34] In the case of a man cohabiting with his own daughter this requirement is fulfilled in any case. The Trobriand moral objection is in fact precisely on these grounds. Since the husband is already receiving *urigubu* payments on account of his wife he cannot expect to have sexual access to the daughter as well.[35]

We should note that in both the 'extreme' cases the affinal alliance between the lineage of the father and the lineage of the mother is expressed in enduring and elaborately defined economic obligations. The requirement that a married Trobriand son should contribute *urigubu* harvest gifts to his father has its counterpart in the payment due from a Lakher male to his mother's brother and his mother's brother's sons. Both sets of payments have their basis in a contract of marriage and are in no way connected with any recognition of common bodily substance.[36]

That at any rate is my reading of the evidence, though those who disagree with me can doubtless turn the matter back to front. Parry himself, under the influence of Hutton, assumed that the peculiarities of the mother's brother/sister's son relationship, which he recorded for the Lakher, demonstrated 'traces of a very recent matrilineal system'.[37] Although this evolutionist doctrine seems to me totally mistaken, it is only marginally different from the views currently advocated by Fortes and Goody.[38] The latter argues that, in a patrilineal system in which property is transmitted between male agnates, the 'children of the residual siblings' (i.e. the children of the sisters) are, as it were, second-class members of the patrilineage – hence the sister's son has 'a shadowy claim' upon the property of the mother's brother by virtue of his mother's position in his mother's brother's patrilineage.[39] There may well be societies where this is so but it seems to me to be going right against the evidence to suggest that the Lakher is one of them.

I maintain, on the contrary, that the evidence shows unambiguously that the obligations which link a Lakher man to his *pupa* (mother's brother or mother's brother's son) and also to the *pupa* of his mother are part of a complex of economic obligations established by marriage. They are obligations between males of patrilineages linked by marriage alliance and they do *not* have their roots in notions of filiation between mother and son.

The patrilineal Lakher case is not unique of its kind. Long ago Philo reported of the Spartans that a man might marry his mother's daughter by a different father. McLennan, in noting this fact, deemed it incredible and brushed it aside as an obvious ethnographic error.[40] Nevertheless McLennan's comments deserve quotation for they show that he fully appreciated the significance of such a case. His text has: '. . . the report of Philo, that the Spartans allowed a man to marry his sister-uterine, but not his sister-german, or by the same father . . . we hold it to be incredible – as discordant with old law as with the habits of the Lacedaemonians'. But to this he adds a footnote: 'The reader may suspect that this is a relic of strict agnatic law. But for the reasons stated in the text, we hold that view to be excluded. *The system of relationship through males only has never, in any well authenticated case, been developed into such a rule as this*' (my italics).

There is also the case of the Tikopia who seem to treat cohabitation between half-siblings of the same father as incestuous, whereas the marriage of half-siblings of the same mother is merely odd.[41] The facts here are that in Tikopia divorce and widow remarriage are both uncommon and there is a general dislike of marriage between very close kin so that the possibility of half-sibling domestic unions does not often arise. Firth reports on two cases only. Cohabitation between half-siblings of the same father was tolerated but the union was sterile and strongly disapproved. In contrast, a domestic union of half-siblings of the same mother had produced a large and flourishing family which suffered no stigma.

No doubt the majority of human societies fall somewhere between my two extremes. Usually a child is related to both its parents because of direct ties of filiation and not simply because its parents happen to be married. I agree too that, for a substantial proportion of these intermediate cases, Fortes's concept of 'complementary filiation' may have analytical utility, but the general pattern must include the limiting extremes, so I prefer my algebraic formulation.

In a way this is all very elementary. Those of you who teach social anthropology may protest that, leaving out the algebra, this is the sort of thing we talk about to first-year students in their first term. And I agree; but *because* you leave out the algebra, you have to talk about descent and filiation and extra-clan kinship and sociological paternity and so on and your pupils get more and more bewildered at every step. In contrast what I am saying is so easy that even professors ought to be able to understand! It is not algebra that is confusing but the lack of it. After all, you professionals have long been familiar with both the Trobriand and the Kachin ethnographic facts, but I suspect that you have *not* until this moment perceived that they represent two examples of the same pattern – you have been unable to perceive this because you were trapped by the conventional categories of structural classification. Now that I have pointed out the mathematical pattern the similarity is obvious (Fig. 3, (a), (b)). But let me repeat. I am not telling you to become mathematicians. All I am asking is: don't start off your argument with a lot of value-loaded concepts which prejudge the whole issue.

The merit of putting a statement into an algebraic form is that one letter of the alphabet is as good or as bad as any other. Put the same statement into concept language, with words like paternity and filiation stuck in the middle of it, and God help you!

My time is running short and I don't suppose that I have convinced you as yet that my technique of 'generalisation' really tells us anything new, but let me try again.

So far we have dealt with only half the story. My first variable, *z*, which is the ratio between matrifiliation and patrifiliation, corresponds, at an ethnographic level, to variations in the ideology of genetic inheritance.

At the two extremes the Trobriand child derives its substance exclusively from its mother's blood, while the Kachin child is the bony product of its father's semen. In more normal cases where children are filiated to both parents (as with the patrilineal Tallensi) the child gets its physical substance from both parents.

But this does not take into account Malinowski's curious statement that the Trobriand child should resemble its mother's husband and not its mother or any clan relative of the mother. Nor have I explained what Kachins are getting at when they say that the flesh and blood of a child come from its mother, though not its bone.

I won't bother you with the algebra this time but I hope you can see that if we take the Trobriand evidence to be extreme in one direction then the opposite

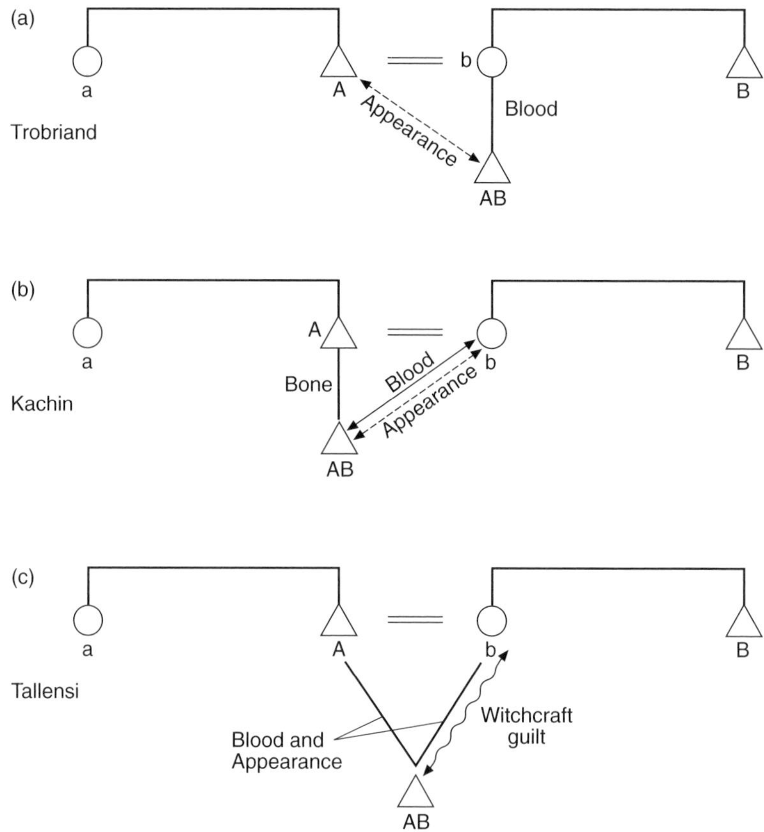

Fig. 3. Mystical influence.

extreme would be a society in which children resembled their mothers but not their fathers. And this is precisely what we do find. The North Burma Kachins have a patrilineal organisation very similar to that of the Lakher whom I mentioned just now but, despite their patriliny, they consider that a child should resemble its mother and not its father – the exact antithesis, you see, of Malinowski's case.

In the field this baffled me completely. This was because I had too many empirical facts. The main fact was a prize pig. The Government, at enormous expense, had imported a prize Berkshire boar all the way from England. The villagers were instructed to castrate their own male pigs and have all their sows served by the boar. The boar was a sensation; no one would talk about anything else – a regular nine days' wonder; but active co-operation in the scheme was virtually nil. It was then that I learnt that Kachin pigs derive all their physical characteristics from the sow; that being so, what on earth is the use of a prize boar?

Matrilineal pigs seemed to me a curious phenomenon so naturally I pursued the matter. I then learnt that the same thing applies to humans too – the mother feeds the child in her womb and at her breast and on that account a man's face (*myi-man*) comes from his maternal affines (this word for face, as in the Chinese equivalent, means 'reputation' as well as 'physiognomy'). The idea that appearances and reputations both come from the mother's side fits in with the idea that wives who are witches can infect by contagion both their husbands and children. The supreme manifestation of this is when a woman dies in childbirth; such a woman is deemed to be a witch of the most noxious kind and in former days all the possessions of her husband's household, including the house itself, had to be burnt so as to disinfect the community.

The crucial point to note here is that witch influence was thought to be transmitted in the food which the woman prepared – the husband was quite as liable to infection as the children. The original sources make it plain that Kachin witchcraft is contagious rather than hereditary. In structural terms Kachin witchcraft is associated with affinity, *not* filiation.[42]

If we compare this Kachin case with the Trobriand one it becomes clear that we are concerned with a single pattern of ideas which, in its general form, embodies something *other than* the notion of filiation. In both societies there is a concept of filiation which is thought of as genetic influence and is symbolised by the dogma of common substance; but there is also something different, the idea of mystical influence which can be independent of *any* tie of blood or bone.

There is more to all this than a mere quibble over the use of words and the interpretations of symbols. Fortes[43] has said that 'complementary filiation can be thought of as the kinship reciprocal of affinal relationship in the marriage tie', but this terminology is bound to lead to confusion. In the first place, since the phrase 'complementary filiation' only has meaning in association with unilineal descent, Fortes's argument would imply that affinal relations only occur in the presence of unilineal descent, which is plainly absurd. But secondly, in view of the distinction which Fortes draws between filiation and descent his formula amounts to an assertion that 'affinal relationship in the marriage tie' is a category applicable only to relations between individuals. But empirically this is not the case. The Jinghpaw expression *mayu/dama* and analagous categories elsewhere denote relationships of enduring affinal alliance between whole groups of persons. It is quite misleading to think of such group relationship as 'reciprocal' of any particular relationship between an individual parent and an individual child.

Elsewhere I have shown how such relations of enduring affinal alliance are expressed in the transfer of goods and in notions of differential political status.[44] But here I am referring to something both more general and more metaphysical. My proposition is that the relationship which we denote by the word 'affinity' is very commonly given cultural expression as 'mystical influence', but that this in turn is only a special instance of something more general, the logical opposition between unity through incorporation and unity through alliance.

In each of my examples (Fig. 3) we see that certain ideas cluster together to form a pattern (a topological 'set'), and the elements in the pattern divide up to form a category opposition. Thus with Trobrianders – mystical influence is linked with physical appearance but opposed to blood relationship. With Kachins – mystical influence is linked with physical appearance, flesh, and food but opposed to bone relationship. With Tallensi – genetic influence is associated with blood *and* bone *and* physical appearance and can be derived from both parents, but this is opposed to a form of mystical influence called *tyuk* and a tendency to witchcraft, both of which are derived from the mother's relatives only. In this last case the opposed categories overlap but even so, as Fortes shows clearly, the two kinds of influence, the genetic and the mystical, are, in the Tallensi view, quite distinct.[45]

The category distinctions involved in these different cases are all of much the same kind but they are *not* identical and it would be misleading to try to fit them into a typology by tagging them with precisely defined labels such as filiation, descent, and affinity. Instead I suggest that the facts can be generalised into a formula which would run something like this:

> A marriage creates an alliance between two groups, A and B. The children of the marriage may be related to either or both of these groups by incorporation, either permanent or partial, but they can also be related to either or both the groups by virtue of the marriage alliance itself. The symbols I have been discussing – of bone and blood and flesh and food and mystical influence – discriminate on the one hand between permanent and partial incorporation, and on the other between incorporation and alliance. These are variables which are significant in all societies and not merely in unilineal systems of a particular type.

The value of such generalisation is that it invites us to re-examine familiar material from a fresh point of view. For example, my cases indicate that the distinction between incorporation and alliance is always expressed in the difference between common substance and mystical influence – and surely, this is just what the Tikopia are talking about when a man refers to his own son as *tama* (child) but to the son of his sister's husband as *tama tapu* (sacred child)? But you won't find that recorded in the pages of *We, the Tikopia.*

Perhaps I may elaborate that point. The exceptional detail of Firth's ethnographic material is a standing invitation for every reader to try to 'rethink' the particular explanations which Firth himself offers us. Firth's discussion of the *tuatina/tama tapu* (mother's brother/sister's son) relationship is very extensive but nowhere does it serve to explain why the latter should carry the epithet 'sacred child'. Firth's general position seems to be similar to that adopted by Goody in the article which I have criticised above; the reader of *We, the Tikopia* gets the impression that the sister's son has a sort of second-class membership in Ego's patrilineage (ramage) and that the relationship is one which Fortes and Goody would describe as 'extra-clan kinship'. As I understand it, Firth considers that the gifts which the *tama tapu* receives from his *tuatina* originate in rights of inheritance based in some kind of principle of descent.[46] Yet this hardly seems consistent with the fact that although a man has certain rights of usufruct in land belonging to his mother's patrilineage, he loses these rights as soon as his mother is dead.[47]

In contrast I would suggest that the description 'sacred child' has a logical fit with the notion that the child is formed in the mother's womb by the Female Deity associated with the mother's patrilineage[48] and that the same Female Deity has temporary charge over a man's soul during the intricate processes of transition from life to death.[49] This implies surely that the sister's child has a mystical rather than a substantial link with members of Ego's patrilineage? Firth's meticulously detailed record of Tikopian attitudes towards the *tuatina/tama tapu* relationship seems fully in accord with this. The Tikopia themselves appear to regard this relationship as an affinal link between whole lineages rather than as a simple tie between individuals.[50]

But let me repeat. Polemic apart, the principal generalised hypothesis which has so far emerged from this essay is that, in *any* system of kinship and marriage, there is a fundamental ideological opposition between the relations which endow the individual with membership of a 'we group' of some kind (relations of incorporation), and those other relations which link 'our group' to other groups of like kind (relations of alliance), and that, in this dichotomy, relations of incorporation are distinguished symbolically as relations of common substance, while relations of alliance are viewed as metaphysical influence.

The first part of this hypothesis has obvious links with the distinction between the 'internal' system and the 'external' system which has been stressed by Homans and by Fortes.[51] The latter part, though related to Fortes,[52] is novel.

At first sight it might be supposed that the proposition is readily disproved, for although it is true that in many societies the threat of supernatural attack ('metaphysical influence') is expected to come from 'outsiders' – notably affinal kin and political associates – there are well-known instances where the contrary is the case. Thus, in matrilineal Ashanti, the witch is habitually a lineage kinsman[53] and the same is true of the patrilineal Tiv.[54] Furthermore throughout patrilineal Polynesia it is the father's sister who must be particularly respected lest she invoke supernatural sanctions.[55]

But my proposition is not quite so easily disposed of. The 'mystical influence' which has been discussed in this paper is of the same kind as that which we English denote by the word Fate, which the Tallensi denote by the term *yin*, and which Fortes has distinguished under the phrase 'prenatal destiny'.[56] It is a power beyond human control. My thesis – and here for once Professor Fortes and I seem to be in agreement – is that in any particular case the ideas concerning such *uncontrolled* mystical influence must serve to specify something about the social structure. An individual is thought to be subject to certain kinds of mystical influence because of the structural position in which he finds himself and not because of the intentional malice or favour of any other individual.

Doctrines of this sort are quite distinct from those which credit particular individuals with the capacity to punish wrongdoers or attack their enemies by secret supernatural means.

Some examples will serve to illustrate this distinction.

In the ideology of Kachin witchcraft the witch is presumed to be an unconscious and involuntary agent; she brings disaster upon her husband and her children, not because she wishes to do so, but because she has the misfortune to be the host of a witch spirit (*hpyi*). She is a person tainted with contagion through no fault of her own and hence (in my terminology) she affects her victims through 'uncontrolled mystical influence'. Contrast with this the Ashanti doctrine which presumes that witches are adult persons, fully conscious of their misdeeds, who receive special training and initiation into their nefarious arts.[57]

This Ashanti witchcraft is not 'uncontrolled mystical influence' in my sense of the term but a form of 'controlled supernatural attack'. In this respect it is analagous to such conceptions as the threat of the father's sister's curse in Samoa, or the threat of the chief's sorcery in the Trobriands and Tikopia; the individuals who wield such *controlled* supernatural authority are persons who command respect.[58]

Monica Wilson's Nyakyusa material brings out this distinction very clearly. In Nyakyusa belief 'good' and 'bad' witchcraft are both regarded as forms of 'controlled supernatural attack', but whereas a bad witch *acquires* his witchcraft unconsciously by influence from his father's wife, a good witch ('defender') *acquires* his witchcraft intentionally by taking medicines.[59]

Kachin evidence illustrates the same point in a different way. Kachins carry out 'controlled supernatural attack' by invoking the Spirit of Cursing, called *Mătsa Kănu.*[60] This name is a combination of two kinship categories *tsa* (father-in-law, mother's brother) and *nu* (mother); it embodies a formulation of the Kachin theory that the power of cursing and the power of witchcraft are of the same kind and emanate from the same source – namely the affinal relatives on the mother's side (*mayu*). The witch emits this power *unconsciously* having been infected by an uncontrolled mystical influence: the man who curses an opponent invokes precisely the same power but does so *consciously.*

As a demonstration that my procedure of topological generalisation has some practical utility I propose now to develop this distinction so as to provide a gloss on one of the classical topics of anthropological theory.

Anthropologists have a wide and varied range of functionalist explanations as to why custom should so often require a man to display some special, rather bizarre, form of behaviour towards a father's sister or a mother's brother. Mostly these explanations focus in arguments about ambiguities in principles of descent and rights of inheritance.[61] Each type of explanation throws illumination on appropriately selected case material but none of them is at all convincing as a contribution to general theory. The material which I have now presented suggests that the whole topic might fruitfully be considered from quite a new point of view, namely the degree of coincidence between notions of 'uncontrolled mystical influence' on the one hand and notions of 'controlled supernatural attack' on the other. These opposed variables may be thought of as forming a topological set.

For brevity let us denote 'uncontrolled mystical influence' by the symbol *x* and 'controlled supernatural attack' by the symbol *y* and then consider the incidence of the *x* and *y* notions as reported from the societies which we have been discussing throughout this paper.

TIKOPIA:	*x* and *y* are separated. *x* comes from the mother; *y* from the father's sister.
LAKHER (KACHIN):	*x* and *y* coincide, both come from the *patong* (*mayu*), that is the mother's brother's patrilineage.
TROBRIANDS:	*x* and *y* do not necessarily coincide but may do so. *x* comes from the father; *y* comes from affinal relatives (as an expression of malice) or from the chief (as an expression of legitimate authority).
ASHANTI:	*x* and *y* are separated. *x* comes from the father; *y* from adult women of Ego's matrilineage.
TALLENSI:	*x* and *y* are separated. *x* derives from uterine kin; *y* from Ego's patrilineal ancestors.

This pattern variation is far from random, for the degree of coincidence between *x* and *y* corresponds to the degree to which affinal alliance plays a part in the ongoing political structure of the society. As I have shown elsewhere the Kachin and the Lakher are societies in which the affinal ties of chiefs and lineage headmen have a structural permanence comparable to that provided by the idea of lineage perpetuity in unilineal descent systems.[62] In contrast among the Tikopia, the Tallensi, and the Ashanti there are no 'relations of perpetual affinity' which can serve to express enduring political relations of superordination and subordination. But in this respect the Trobrianders provide an intermediate case, for, while they have no ideal of permanent affinal relationship, they use the *urigubu* harvest payment, which is normally an obligation due to affines, as a device for expressing the tributary obligations of a village headman to his chief.

The general inference therefore is that, where *x* and *y* coincide, relations of affinity are being used to express political dominance.

The reader who wishes to verify my algebraic generalisations for himself will find the following references useful:

TIKOPIA

Evidence concerning the father's sister's curse and the mystical influence of the Female Deity has been cited above. In Tikopia the form of marriage serves to emphasise its lack of *political* importance. Once a marriage has been established a rather complex set of obligations is set up between the lineage of the husband and the lineage of the wife, but the marriage itself purports to be a 'marriage by capture' in which the parents of the bride remain ignorant of what is afoot until all is *fait accompli*. This marriage by capture is 'characteristic mainly of chiefly families',[63] and seems to amount to an explicit denial that the chiefs are using marriage for political ends.

LAKHER

Parry: 'It is *ana* (taboo) for a maternal uncle to curse or insult his nephew. . . . The highest term of respect in use among the Lakhers is *papu* (my maternal uncle) not *ipa* (my father); a villager addressing the chief always calls him *papu*.'[64] Kachin behaviour is similar; a chief is addressed as *tsa* (mother's brother). *Tsa* possess particular potency at cursing (*mătsa*).[65]

TROBRIANDS

Malinowski: 'It is characteristic of their ideas of the bonds of marriage and fatherhood which they regard as artificial and untrustworthy under any strain that the principal suspicion of sorcery attaches always to the wife and children.'[66]

Here the mystical influence of father over children is separated from the controlled supernatural attack of children against father. On the other hand Malinowski also shows the father to be in control of female sorcerers who are liable (unless the father is properly placated) to attack his pregnant daughter,[67] and in numerous contexts we are told how the chief exercises his authority with the aid of professional sorcerers who obey his command.[68] Here the mystical influence of the father may coincide with the supernatural attack of the father–chief.

It should be remarked that the chief's relationship to his village headmen is typically that of father (*tama*) or brother-in-law (*lubou*). The tribute which a chief receives from his political subordinates is, from another point of view, the *urigubu* (harvest payment) paid to a father or to a brother-in-law.[69]

ASHANTI

For ideas about supernatural attack see Rattray.[70] Ashanti often marry near kin and approve of reciprocal cross-cousin marriage. In traditional Ashanti this was carried to the extreme that the royal family and also certain professional guilds had an almost caste-like aspect.[71] However this type of small group endogamy did not result in a structure in which ties of marriage alliance could serve political ends.

TALLENSI

For ideas about supernatural influence see especially Fortes.[72] Since a Tallensi may not marry any near kinswoman, however she be related, it is self-evident that marriage cannot here serve as a relationship of perpetual political alliance in the sense which I have been discussing.

This finding has a bearing upon the argument of Fortes,[73] for, with certain qualifications, Fortes's Oedipus theology corresponds to my *x* ('uncontrolled mystical influence'), while his Job theology corresponds to my *y* ('controlled supernatural attack'). In the West African examples which Fortes has discussed, *x* and *y* are complementary notions which tend to cancel out – the inescapable consequences of personal Fate modify the arbitrary dictates of an all powerful God and vice versa, but my additional evidence shows that this seeming balance is fortuitous. There are some societies where Fate and Implacable Deity are to be found personified in one and the same affinal personality, and in such cases the relation between religious ideas and political authority takes on a very different and very special aspect – the *mana* of the King and the *mana* of the witch coalesce in the person of the all powerful Father-in-Law.

Without the algebra, my x/y proposition reads thus: '*uncontrolled mystical influence* denotes a relation of alliance; *controlled supernatural attack* denotes a relation of potential authority of attacker over attacked or vice versa. Where the presumed source of *controlled supernatural attack* is the same as the presumed source of *uncontrolled mystical influence* that source is in a position of political authority *vis-à-vis* Ego.' In this form we have an hypothesis which might, in principle, be subjected to test. In practice I suspect that the establishment of convincing negative instances may prove rather elusive. For example the material which Firth has recently provided about the relation between spirit mediums and their familiars in Tikopia and elsewhere looks at first sight as if it ought to provide an excellent test case, but I rather think that, so far as my hypothesis is concerned, this particular evidence could be interpreted in several different ways.[74] But here at any rate is a matter which invites investigation.

This whole digression into the structural implications of metaphysical belief has been introduced only by way of illustration. The insights which emerge relate to facts which cut right across the conventional categories of anthropological discussion and my objective has been to demonstrate by example how an excessive interest in the classification of ethnographic facts serves to obscure rather than to illuminate our perception of social reality. And here I revert to the point from which I started.

I am constantly amazed by the feats of mental gymnastics which anthropologists perform in their efforts of produce universal definitions and discriminations; notable examples are Gough's definition of marriage and Fortes's discrimination between filiation, affinity, and descent.[75] My harsh view is that the value of such butterfly-collecting activity is quite ephemeral and that the categories which result from it should always be highly suspect. This applies equally to the vague topological entities of my own analysis and to the polished concepts of Professor Fortes. We need to understand that the establishment of classifying categories is never more than a temporary *ad hoc* expedient. Most such categories have ceased to serve any useful purpose long before they achieve the distinction of appearing in print.

So far as our immediate discussion is concerned I readily admit that, in any given social system, we shall always find some kind of notion of corporate kinship which stands opposed to some kind of notion of marriage alliance as p is to q, but what we can usefully compare as between different societies are not these particular *p*s and *q*s (regarded as separate institutions) but the ratio of p to q considered as a mathematical function. Or, in non-metrical language, we need to think of the relationships which link children to their parents and the parents to one another as constituting a 'neighbourhood system' – a topological space.

No doubt many of you will want to dismiss my whole argument as a futile exercise in bogus mathematics. I don't accept that. I believe that we social anthropologists are like the mediaeval Ptolemaic astronomers; we spend our time trying to fit the facts of the objective world into the framework of a set of concepts which have been developed a priori instead of from observation.

It is some years since Professor Firth drew attention to the alarming proliferation of structuralist terminology.[76] He noted with dismay that maximal, major, and minimal lineages had been supplemented by medial, inner, and nuclear lineages; effective lineages were distinguished from morphological lineages; social relations had acquired focal fields, vertebral principles, and constellations of ties and cleavages.[77]

That was in 1951, but the process has continued. We now have not merely filiation but complementary filiation, not merely siblings but residual siblings. Of such cycles and epicycles there is no end.

The trouble with Ptolemaic astronomy was not that it was wrong but that it was sterile – there could be no real development until Galileo was prepared to abandon the basic premiss that celestial bodies must of necessity move in perfect circles with the earth at the centre of the universe.

We anthropologists likewise must re-examine basic premisses and realise that English language patterns of thought are not a necessary model for the whole of human society.

Malinowski's basic premiss was that the elementary family is a universal institution. Fortes would qualify this but retains a dogmatic view of the functional utility of incest which is very similar to Malinowski's. This leads logically to an acceptance of English categories and to the assumption that our words consanguinity and affinity have some universal value. It is this which leads anthropologists to treat the words sibling, filiation, descent, and affinity as absolute technical terms which can be distinguished from one another by a priori reasoning without reference to ethnographic evidence.

My contrary thesis is that ethnographic facts will be much easier to understand if we approach them free of *all* such a priori assumptions. Our concern is with what the significant social categories are; not with what they ought to be.

If you feel you must start with assumptions then let them be logical (that is mathematical) assumptions – such as that the social relation between brothers must of necessity be in some sense the opposite of the social relation between brothers-in-law. But do not drag in private psychological theories behind a smokescreen of technical terms.

All I have tried to do here is to show that an unprejudiced re-examination of established ethnographic facts which does *not* start off with a battery of concepts thought up in a professorial study may lead to some unexpected conclusions.

And that must be my conclusion – stick to the facts of the case, and exercise your imagination; but don't get so personally involved in the situation that you cannot distinguish between the empirical facts and your private analytic concepts.

In this first Malinowski Memorial Lecture I have set out to demonstrate, from a single small example, that Malinowski still has no rival in the penetration of his ethnographic observation. Where Malinowski's work was limited was that it was too exclusively Trobriand; his theoretical concepts were designed to fit Trobriand data just as, latterly, Fortes's concepts have been designed to fit Tallensi and Ashanti data. But it is still possible to base speculative generalisations on Malinowski's facts, and I believe that speculative generalisation, even if it often proves wrong, is very well worth while. Even from tonight's popshy we may have learnt a little.

Notes

Each year since 1959 the Malinowski Memorial Lecture has been delivered at the London School of Economics. Speakers are invited by the school, and the text of each lecture is now, by custom, published in the *Journal of the Royal Anthropological Institute.* 'Rethinking Anthropology' was the title of the first Malinowski Memorial Lecture, delivered by Leach in December 1959. It was published in 1961 as the title essay in a collection of Leach's papers. Then, as now, many British anthropologists from outside London attend the Malinowski lecture, and it is relevant to an understanding of the impact Leach hoped to achieve to know that he could be confident that most of the anthropologists he criticises by name – Fortes, Goody, Richards – would have been present.

1. Radcliffe-Brown, 'Letter to Lévi-Strauss', p. 109.
2. Goody, *Social Organisation of the LoWiili.*
3. Radcliffe-Brown, 'On Social Structure', p. xii.
4. Richards, 'Some Types of Family Structure among the Central Bantu'.
5. Fortes, 'The Structure of Unilineal Descent Groups', p. 33, and 'Descent, Filiation, and Affinity: A Rejoinder to Dr Leach'.
6. Fortes, *Dynamics of Clanship*, pp. 134, 200ff, 'Kinship and Marriage among the Ashanti', p. 287, 'Structure of Unilineal Descent Groups', p. 34, and 'Descent, Filiation, and Affinity'; Goody, *Social Organisation of the LoWiili*, p. 77.
7. Hobbes, *Leviathan*, p. 5.
8. Radcliffe-Brown, *A Natural Science of Society*, pp. 82–6, and 'On Social Structure', pp. 3, 10.
9. See Carnap, *Introduction to Symbolic Logic*, ch. G.
10. Nadel, *Theory of Social Structure.*
11. Malinowski, *Sexual Life of Savages*, p. 5.
12. Fortes, *Web of Kinship*, p. 35; my italics.
13. Malinowski, *Sexual Life of Savages*, p. 176.
14. Rattray, *Ashanti Law and Constitution*, p. 9.
15. Malinowski, *Sexual Life of Savages*, p. 450
16. Powell, 'Social Structure in the Trobriands', p. 314.
17. Malinowski, *Sexual Life of Savages*, pp. 86, 451.
18. Malinowski, *Coral Gardens*, i, pp. 386, 413–18.
19. Malinowski, *The Family among Australian Aborigines*, pp. 170–83.
20. Fortes, 'Descent, Filiation, and Affinity'; Goody, 'Mother's Brother and Sister's Son in West Africa', pp. 83, 86; Gough, 'Nayars and the Definition of Marriage'.
21. Fortes, 'Descent, Filiation, and Affinity', p. 194.
22. Malinowski, *The Family among Australian Aborigines*, p. 179.
23. Malinowski, 'Parenthood', pp. 144–7.
24. Firth, *We, the Tikopia*, p. 481.
25. Lévi-Strauss, *Les Structures élémentaires de la parenté*, ch. 24.
26. Gilhodes, *The Kachins*, pp. 134, 175.
27. See Leach, 'Jinghpaw Kinship Terminology', 'Structural Implications of Matrilateral Cross-Cousin Marriage', and 'Aspects of Bridewealth and Marriage Stability'.
28. Parry, *The Lakhers.*
29. Ibid., p. 293.

30. Ibid., pp. 418–19.
31. Ibid., p. 428.
32. Leach, *Political Systems*, p. 137; cf. Goody, 'Comparative Approach to Incest'.
33. Malinowski, *Sexual Life of Savages*, pp. 445–9.
34. Powell, 'Social Structure in the Trobriands', p. 349.
35. Malinowski, *Sexual Life of Savages*, p. 446.
36. Parry, *The Lakhers*, p. 244.
37. Ibid., p. xiii.
38. Fortes, 'Descent, Filiation, and Affinity'; Goody, 'Mother's Brother and Sister's Son'.
39. Goody, 'Mother's Brother and Sister's Son', pp. 82–3.
40. McLennan, *Studies in Ancient History*, p. 177.
41. Firth, *We, the Tikopia*, p. 330.
42. Gilhodes, *The Kachins*, pp. 182–5, 296; Hanson, *The Kachins*, pp. 143ff, 173–4; Leach, *Political Systems*, pp. 179ff.
43. Fortes, 'Descent, Filiation, and Affinity'.
44. Leach, 'Structural Implications of Matrilateral Cross-Cousin Marriage'.
45. Fortes, *Web of Kinship*, p. 35; also index refs. to *yin*.
46. Firth, *We, the Tikopia*, pp. 224–5, 279ff.
47. Ibid., p. 391.
48. Ibid., p. 481.
49. Firth, *The Fate of the Soul*, p. 17.
50. Firth, *We, the Tikopia*, p. 213.
51. Homans, *The Human Group*; Fortes, 'Descent, Filiation, and Affinity', p. 194.
52. Fortes, *Oedipus and Job*.
53. Rattray, *Religion and Art in Ashanti*, p. 30.
54. Bohannan and Bohannan, *The Tiv of Central Nigeria*, p. 85.
55. Firth, *We, the Tikopia*, p. 222; Mabuchi, 'Kinship Rituals among Malayo-Polynesian Peoples'.
56. Fortes, *Oedipus and Job*.
57. Rattray, *Religion and Art in Ashanti*, pp. 28–31.
58. Mead, *Social Organisation of Manu'a*, p. 146, and *Kinship in the Admiralty Islands*, pp. 309, 310, 315, 356; Firth, *We, the Tikopia*, p. 222; Malinowski, *Crime and Custom*, pp. 85f; Firth, 'Problem and Assumption in the Anthropological Study of Religion', p. 145.
59. Wilson, *Good Company*, pp. 24, 98–102.
60. Gilhodes, *The Kachins*, pp. 292–3.
61. E.g. Goody, 'Mother's Brother and Sister's Son'.
62. Leach, 'Structural Implications', and 'Aspects of Bridewealth and Marriage Stability'.
63. Firth, *We, the Tikopia*, p. 539.
64. Parry, *The Lakhers*, pp. 244–5.
65. For references regarding the political significance of Lakher marriage see Leach, 'Aspects of Bridewealth and Marriage Stability'.
66. Malinowski, *Sexual Life of Savages*, p. 137.
67. Ibid., p. 190.
68. Malinowski, *Crime and Custom*, pp. 85–6.
69. Malinowski, *Coral Gardens and their Magic*, i, pp. 392–7, 414; Powell, 'Social Structure in the Trobriands', p. 481.
70. Rattray, *Ashanti*, ch. 2, and *Religion and Art in Ashanti*, pp. 28–31.
71. Rattray, *Ashanti*, p. 301; *Religion and Art in Ashanti*, chs 29, 30.
72. Fortes, *Oedipus and Job*; and the references to *yin* in Fortes, 'Time and Social Structure'.
73. Fortes, *Oedipus and Job*.
74. Firth, 'Problem and Assumption', pp. 141–6.
75. Gough, 'Nayars and Definition of Marriage', p. 32; Fortes, 'Descent, Filiation, and Affinity'.
76. [Eds.: As in *Pul Eliya* (see I.3.5, n. 16) the word 'structuralist' here refers not to Lévi-Straussian structuralism, but to anthropological writings of the 1940s, 1950s, and early 1960s of the kind now generally referred to as 'structural-functionalism'.]
77. Firth, Review of Fortes, *Web of Kinship*.

Section 4

The Place of Ambiguity: Classification and Taboo

Though rooted in van Gennep's *Rites of Passage* (see introduction to Section 2 above), much of Leach's work on totemism and taboo, most notably his 'Animal Categories and Verbal Abuse' (I.4.2), takes off from his enthusiastic but guarded reaction to Lévi-Strauss's *The Savage Mind* (see I.1.10 above). Leach praises Lévi-Strauss's work for opening up new lines of enquiry, but still feels that the author has not pushed his ideas far enough; he finds himself preoccupied as much with some hypothetical missing chapters that Lévi-Strauss might have written as with those that are actually in the book.

Leach reads *The Savage Mind* as an extended gloss on *Totemism* and on its argument that what lies behind totemism are not utilitarian concerns – 'animals are good to eat' – but rather those of an intellectual system – 'animals are good to think with'. But why do people adopt ritual attitudes to animals? Why are some animals esteemed, others not considered edible at all, whilst yet others, however edible, must positively not be eaten? Leach feels that, in his pursuit of a rational system underlying the irrationality of religious belief, Lévi-Strauss has thrown out the baby with the bath water: 'our author proposes to show the logic of religious categories, but on the way he is led to ignore precisely the aspects of the phenomenon which are the most specifically religious' (I.1.10). What is missing is some consideration of the sacred. Note, however, that this is not Durkheim's sacred, which marks a specific category of events or activity as ritual. For Leach 'ritual' is an aspect, not a type, of behaviour (see Section 2 above) and the sacred is a source or index of *values*, a position consistent with his earlier linking of aesthetics (ritual) and ethics in *Political Systems* (See I.2.1: 153).

Leach raises further questions. Lévi-Strauss took his examples from exotic Australian clans and compared them to Indian castes.[1] But if 'la pensée sauvage' is common to all peoples, what would a totemic system look like in a society which, instead of being segmented into discrete groups, was based on gradations of social distance from a given individual – as in a cognatic system such as our own? And if Lévi-Strauss was right that culture is structured like a language and Leach right that the verbal and behavioural aspects of ritual are inseparable (see Section 2 above), might there not be a consistency between linguistic taboos and behavioural taboos? These are some of the questions that Leach set out to answer in 'Animal Categories', one of a series of essays which together make up what Leach considered to be Lévi-Strauss's missing chapters, his own theory of Taboo.[2]

In 'Animal Categories', Leach uses an analysis of some very British 'totemism' as a test case to conclude that, in addition to Lévi-Strauss's binarism, we need graduated scales: 'more sacred and less sacred', close/far, more-like-me/less-like-me (I.4.2: 342). But Leach had already begun to experiment with these ideas in 'Babar's Civilisation Analysed' (I.4.1). Like 'Once a Knight' (I.2.7), this piece is at once both playful and serious; and each deals with material close to home: the former with savage practices, the latter with savage thought. It is probably no coincidence that it was with reference to a childish French version of animal categories that Leach first sketched the germ of the argument that he later developed more formally and in greater detail with reference to their more risqué adult British counterparts.

In 'Babar's Civilisation' (I.4.1) and 'Animal Categories' (I.4.2), Leach works out his theory of taboo on fairly familiar material. Later, in 'Kimil' (1971), he applied it to Radcliffe-Brown's *Andaman Islanders*, another touchstone ethnography (along with the Trobrianders and the Tikopia) of a truly 'primitive society'. The Andamanese category 'kimil' is the equivalent of Leach's 'taboo' and, in his analysis, Leach brings his concern with food taboos in line with his earlier interest in the ritualisation of time (see also I.2.4; I.2.5). Though Leach was generally hostile to Radcliffe-Brown's functionalism and his idea of anthropology as a 'natural science' (see I.1.7), both he and Lévi-Strauss recognised a proto-structuralist streak in some of Radcliffe-Brown's work – Lévi-Strauss with respect to his work on totemism,[3] Leach with respect to his analysis of Andamanese myth.[4] Leach also sees merit in Radcliffe-Brown's notion of 'social value' concluding, in effect, that if the good side of Radcliffe-Brown's functionalism is structuralist, good structuralism must also be tempered by functional considerations: 'We *do* need a quantitative notion of social value of some sort.'[5]

'Profanity in Context' (I.4.4), which uses the schema of social distance worked out in 'Animal Categories', provides a good example of how Leach reworked his more academic pieces for a popular audience. Here he extends his analysis from everyday forms of verbal abuse to the more specifically religious context of blasphemy, to comment on a *cause célèbre* of the moment. But it also underscores another dimension of Leach's concern with religion which differentiates him from Lévi-Strauss – his interest in sexuality and repression in line with Freud's *Totem and Taboo*. 'Animal Categories' was written for a symposium held under the auspices of a Congress of Psychology and, in it, Leach emphasises the inseparability of taboo's anthropological, psychological, and linguistic dimensions (I.4.2: 324). In 'Profanity' (see also II.2.1 and II.3.3), Leach explores the links between human sexuality and divine potency. The narrow line between the two is a matter of context. In the right, privileged hands, veiled metaphoric expression of such links is a matter of science or theology; openly expressed by ordinary mortals, these same links become vulgar blasphemy; when acted upon they can lead to war.

The potential danger of unacknowledged sexuality comes to the fore in 'The Nature of War' (I.4.3), one of Leach's best-known papers and the clearest synthesis of his ideas on taboo. In essence, Leach argues, war is a form of ritual activity, something which combines both practical and metaphysical concerns. The rational causes of war – political or economic gain – are clear enough, but unless we understand and recognise its fundamentally irrational nature we are in for trouble. Because 'we, too, are savages under the skin' (I.4.3: 343), we can gain insight by understanding the underlying metaphysical rationale of sacrifice, the hunting of animals, and head-hunting as practised amongst tribal peoples.

On the one hand, these activities are ritual devices concerned with the manipulation of ambivalent power that is perceived to lie in the relation between categories: humans/animals, ourselves/our enemies, kin/affines, men/gods. The terms on the far side of these binary relations – 'affines', 'enemies', and 'God' – become assimilated to one another. By killing 'others', people bridge relations, capture souls, and appropriate power to themselves. Because 'society is a network of persons held together by links of power' (I.4.3: 345), war, like marriage, is inherent in the structure of society. 'To ask men to give up the institution of war is the same kind of request as asking them to give up marriage and the worship of God' (I.4.3: 355).

On the other hand, power is also a dimension of individual experience. In childhood, power lies outside the self, notably in relation to parents. In adulthood, it is grafted onto a theology of life and death and experienced most intensely in sexual relations. War is not a matter of rational common sense; its essence lies in a 'category mistake' which links divine potency, killing, and male sexuality (I.4.3: 356). Irrational though all this might be, the solution lies not in repression or denial but in understanding and sublimation through the provision of less harmful ritual games as legitimate and acceptable outlets for aggressive drives.

Later, Leach wrote as follows:

> The elimination of metaphysics is not such a simple matter as some humanist philosophers have supposed. The fact that we are simultaneously both animals and human beings really does pose a problem as to how the two categories can be distinguished. It is no doubt all to the good that we should rid ourselves of the delusion that our mortal bodies are inhabited by immortal souls, but in claiming to be human beings we are asserting our capacity for exercising moral choice and that implies moral responsibility. And that responsibility is far-reaching. Whether we like it or not all living species on this earth are at our mercy and in our charge. That is a situation which the tidy competitive regularities of Darwinian evolutionary theory did not take into account.[6]

Leach's analyses of taboo speak also of himself. In 'Profanity', he distinguishes between the metaphoric–synthetic mode of religious discourse and the metonymic–analytic mode of science (I.4.4: 358): a distinction which must also apply to the subject matter of anthropology on the one hand; and to anthropological analysis on the other; and, in the last analysis, also to the distinction between life and thought. As anthropologist, Leach places himself on the metonymic side: he uses this mode to dissect the workings of different manifestations of religious symbolism, showing each to be a variant expression of common underlying patterns not only rooted in a universal mode of thinking, as Lévi-Strauss would claim, but also stemming, in part, from the universal experiences of early childhood. Comparative analysis reveals such manifestations as both culturally arbitrary and also subject to various kinds of politico-ritual manipulation (see also the Introduction to Section 2 above). As such, they are suspect: Leach was as wary of involvement in organised religion as he was of involvement in ritual.

But as a person, Leach appears sometimes to have placed himself on the metaphoric side. His insistence that 'religious behaviour cannot be based upon an illusion' (I.2.3: 172) relates, in part, to his conviction that the anthropological analysis of religion cannot side-step the values, implied by Durkheim's 'sacred', which mediate between thought and life. But binarism, whether the all-pervasive Lévi-Straussian version or Durkheim's more restricted sacred/profane, is not enough. A diffuse religiosity pervades much of Leach's thought: there is always an ambiguity in the sacred, a tension between the emergence and control of potency, always something 'in the middle', lying between two opposed terms. That something, a manifestation of power, is what he called 'taboo'.

Leach agrees with Lévi-Strauss's insistence 'that the basic preoccupation of myth is with the ambiguous borderline between what is animal and what is human, what is natural and what is cultural',[7] a preoccupation which both authors themselves also share. In part it is manifest in the ethnographic record with which they are concerned, but it is also a psychological issue: the borderline is also that between the culturally arbitrary and the psychologically necessary and universal (and thus also 'natural'). But here their psychologies diverge, Lévi-Strauss's towards the cognitive, Leach's towards the analytical. For Leach it is also an epistemological issue: where does anthropology begin and psychology or biology end? Leach's intense engagement with these disciplines is manifest in his enthusiastic participation in interdisciplinary gatherings – in 'Animal Categories' it is with the psychologists; in 'Ritualisation' (I.2.2 above) with the biologists – and in his sparring with ethology and sociobiology (II.4.8). It is also a moral issue: where does the anthropologist's role as academic end and his role as public figure begin? In 'Anthropos' (II.5) he provides a summation of his epistemological stance; in his Reith Lectures (II.4.4), a summation of his moral position. They are two sides of the same coin.

Notes

1. See Lévi-Strauss, *The Savage Mind*, ch. 4, 'Totem and Caste'; also 'The Bear and the Barber.'
2. In 'Kimil' (1971), Leach lists these essays as those which are I.1.10, I.2.5, I.3.4, I.4.2, I.4.3, and II.2.1 in this collection (p. 24).

3. Lévi-Strauss, *Totemism*, pp. 89–91.
4. Leach, 'Kimil', p. 25.
5. Ibid., p. 46.
6. Leach, *Humanity and Animality* (1972), p. 20.
7. Leach, 'Kimil', p. 27.

4.1

Babar's Civilisation Analysed (1962)

It is adult rather than childish preference which from time to time awards a classic accolade to particular characters in nursery literature. Two generations back it was Alice and Peter Rabbit, then, save our souls, Winnie-the-Pooh, and today Babar. What is it that the adults find so remarkable? Why does Babar reign among the immortals?

Perhaps it is simply the author's prophetic insight into French politics: Babar, born *c.* 1933, is a long-nosed gentleman who returns to his devastated country in the midst of a disastrous war against the rhinoceroses; under his paternal rule as *Général-Président* the elephants achieve unheard-of prosperity; Babar, like his human counterpart[1] now travels in a Citröen DS19 and leads a genteel bourgeois existence in a country château remote from the turmoil of Celesteville politics.

Or should we look for Freudian symbolism? Any overdressed European male must surely derive considerable exhibitionist delight from seeing himself displayed as an elephant, whichever end you approach the matter. And no doubt there are all sorts of other possibilities as far-fetched or as obvious as you will.

But let us consider some matters of fact. The Old Lady (La Vieille Dame) recurs in all the stories. She is a direct link with mundane reality and she is the only human character of any consequence. The others such as Fernando, a circus owner, a nameless sea captain, sundry Arabs and Africans, etc. make only brief appearances, usually in crowd scenes. The Old Lady has no personal name. In the earlier (Jean de Brunhoff) books the geography is a nice blend of North Africa and southern or even central France. Real places are never mentioned by name, but the pictures imply that it is just a short scamper from darkest Africa to the banks of the Seine. A later (Laurent de Brunhoff) volume jumbles up Arabs and kangaroos. This seems to me a mistake; it is the wrong kind of inconsistency.

Babar himself is a thoroughly civilised elephant who sleeps in a bed, reads the newspaper, drives a car, and so on. To wear no clothes is a mark of savagery. This is a characteristic both of pre-Babar elephants and of post-Babar black men ('savages'). The increasing opulence of the elephant ruling class – the consequences no doubt of an oil strike in the South Sahara – has regularly been marked by the ever-increasing complexity of their human attire.

Elephant society is strictly on a par with that of men, and intermingles with it directly without evoking astonishment on the part of either the elephants or the humans. This land of the elephants is merely a different country, as England is to France. Other animals occupy further countries in a similar way, but it is not the case that *all* animal species are elevated to an identical para-human status. There is a definite hierarchy. Rhinos, though unpleasant fellows, are as civilised as elephants; they fight on equal terms; and an elephant airline employs a rhino as pilot. Likewise Zephir, the monkey playmate of the younger elephants, has a monkey land of his own complete with a monkey fiancée, Princess Isabel. But the other animals, which are humanised in the sense that they attend parties and generally participate in Celesteville high jinks, all seem to be on a slightly lower plane – Asiatics as against Europeans perhaps? A Michelin guide to Babar's zoology would run something like this:

**** CIVILISED RULERS
White Men, Elephants, Rhinoceroses, Monkeys

*** SERVILE COLONIAL POPULATIONS:
Black Men, Dromedaries, Hippopotamuses, Kangaroos

** HUMANISED ANIMALS (appearing only occasionally and then as individuals):
Lion, Tiger, Giraffe, Deer, Tortoise, Mouse, Porcupine, Lizard. Various exotic birds (e.g. Flamingo, Ibis, Pelican, Marabout)

* WILD BEASTS (hostile to elephants as they would be to man):
Crocodile, Snake

DOMESTIC ANIMALS

Domestic animals, e.g. horses, cows, sheep, goats, pigs, frequently appear in the pictures but never as 'characters' in the story; they remain domestic animals quite devoid of human qualities. Animals which rate as pets for humans (i.e. cats and dogs) are eliminated altogether with one exception: when Babar goes in search of Father Christmas – a sort of fantasy within a fantasy – he is accompanied by a talking dog (which is rather surprisingly called Duck).

The allocation of names in Babar's world has a definite pattern. The Old Lady, the only 'real' human, has no name. Babar's closest associates, that is those who are closest to being human, have names appropriate to real humans or to pets: Babar, Celeste, Pom, Flora, Alexander, Arthur, Zephir, Isabel, Eleanor (a mermaid), Cornelius.

Beyond this there is a list of Celesteville elephants who have 'real' occupations but fanciful names. Tapitor, the shoemaker, Pilophage, the officer, Capoulosse, the doctor, Barbacol, the tailor, Podula, the sculptor, Hatchibombotar, the road sweeper, Doulamor, the musician, Olur, the mechanic, Poutifour, the farmer, Fandago, the scholar, Justinien, the painter, Coco, the clown, and Ottilie, a girl friend of Arthur. The names of the rhinos are rather similar: Rataxes, Pamir, Baribarbottom. Likewise the minor characters associated with Zephir: Huc and Aristobel are monkeys; Aunt Crustadel and Polomoche are 'monsters' which look like nursery toys, and it is never stated whose aunt they are. None of the three-,

Fig. 1. From *Babar the King* by Jean de Brunhoff.

two-, or one-star animals has a personal name except the tortoise, who on one occasion is called Martha.

It will be seen that Babar's world is very urban. The humanised animals and birds are those one might meet in a zoo, behind bars. The list of professions suggests the atmosphere of a small-town street.

The naming pattern has the effect of setting up class discriminations even within the category of four-star animals. The reader is coerced into making a self-identification with one or the other of the members of Babar's own household; the rest of the universe of humanised animals is then ranged round about in categories of inferior status.

The ethnographers provide us with other evidence concerning Babar's ideas of social class. Though Babar is elected as 'King', he is not an hereditary aristocrat. There is no suggestion that he is a relative of the previous monarch who died from eating a poisonous mushroom. Nor do any of Babar's associates carry hereditary titles such as Count; they are all Mr and Mrs plain and simple. True, Babar has covered the walls of his new château with portraits of sixteenth-century 'ancestors', but this is obviously a completely fake piece of snobbery. Further evidence of class sensitivity may be seen in the fact that Babar marries his cousin Celeste, and that the only other elephant outsider with whom the family have intimate relations is another cousin, Arthur. When Babar and Celeste amuse themselves in the Celesteville Garden of Pleasure they play tennis with Mr and Mrs Pilophage, Pilophage being a military officer. In the same context, General Cornelius plays bowls with a sort of intellectual elite: Fandango the scholar, Podula the sculptor, Capoulosse the doctor. But Babar does not associate with tradesmen.

All this is as it should be. It is important that the comfortable bourgeois adult readers should not have their basic assumptions about social relationships in any way disturbed. Babar has the prejudices of a middle-class *colon* of the 1930s.

I have a theory about all this. I think that Babar appeals to adults because the fantasy is so carefully contrived, so fully under control. In the ordinary way we tend to categorise living creatures in terms of social distance, depending upon the degree of remoteness from 'myself', thus:

	1	2	3	4
ME	VERY NEAR	NEAR	FAR	VERY FAR
	very tame	tame	wild	very wild
	pets	domestic animals	familiar wild animals	unfamiliar wild animals
	inedible	edible	some edible	inedible
	family members	neighbours	strangers	total strangers, savages
	incest	marriageable	some marriageable	not marriageable

The categories of animals and humans falling into columns 1 and 4 are both abnormal and sacred, and the sacredness is in both cases marked by the taboo on edibility and sex relations.

This I admit is a complicated matter. The English have tended to accept biblical injunctions so that all meat-eating creatures and creeping things are inedible, also horses. But the French eat snails and frogs and horses. In Canton the restaurants serve up dog and snake as delicacies, also unborn mice and a soup made of bird saliva. Cannibal connoisseurs consider human rumpsteak delicious. But the point is that eating and sex are both matters of social convention and in all cases there is a 'very near' and a 'very far' category, *both* of which are alike inedible and sexually illegitimate.

I find it significant that almost all the humanised beasts in the Babar books belong to column 4, whereas surely the child's natural interests must lie in columns 1 and 2? Children's books in which the leading characters are humanised pets and humanised domestic animals are published with great regularity but seem to have no staying power – this can only be because the adults disapprove. But why? Might not the explanation be something like this:

For the child, fantasy is obvious. The category distinction real/unreal (true/false) is vague and unimportant; for the adult it is crucial. And in the adult's painfully constructed image of the real world the categories which are very close – those relating to the parts and excretions of the body – to family relations, to pets and familiar creatures – are the basic discriminations which serve as a rather shaky foundation for a vast superstructure of precisely defined linguistic concepts. As we get older the uncertainty of these early discriminations becomes a source of great anxiety, sex and excretion become 'obscene', they are loaded with a taboo which infects even Chanticleer and the harmless pussycat. Small wonder then that the adult finds this kind of country uncomfortable. We may blandly assure ourselves that we thoroughly approve of childish fantasy, but at the same time we want to be quite sure that the real and the unreal never get muddled up in our own imagination. Alice can do what she likes on the other side of the looking-glass or down the rabbit hole, but not too close please, not too close. If you want to see a real elephant go to the zoo: I don't want any of Mr Ionesco's rhinoceroses around here if you please.

Notes

This essay first appeared in *New Society* in December 1962. The text which appears here was reprinted in Egoff, Stubbs, and Ashley (eds), *Only Connect* (1969).

1. [Eds: The reference is to Charles de Gaulle.]

4.2

Animal Categories and Verbal Abuse (1964)

The central theme of my essay is the classical anthropological topic of 'taboo.' This theme, in this guise, does not form part of the conventional field of discourse of experimental psychologists; yet the argument that I shall present has its psychological equivalents. When psychologists debate about the mechanism of 'forgetting' they often introduce the concept of 'interference', the idea that there is a tendency to repress concepts that have some kind of semantic overlap.[1] The thesis which I present depends upon a converse hypothesis, namely, that we can only arrive at semantically distinct verbal concepts if we repress the boundary precepts that lie between them.

To discuss the anthropological aspects of language within the confines of space allotted to me here is like writing a history of England in thirty lines. I propose to tackle a specific theme, not a general one. For the anthropologist, language is a part of culture, not a thing in itself. Most of the anthropologist's problems are concerned with human communication. Language is one means of communication, but customary acts of behaviour are also a means of communication, and the anthropologist feels that he can, and should, keep both modes of communication in view at the same time.

Language and taboo

This is a symposium about language but my theme is one of non-language. Instead of discussing things that are said and done, I want to talk about things that are not said and done. My theme is that of taboo, expression which is inhibited.

Anthropological and psychological literature alike are crammed with descriptions and learned explanations of apparently irrational prohibitions and inhibitions. Such 'taboo' may be either behavioural or linguistic, and it deserves note that the protective sanctions are very much the same in either case. If at this moment I were really anxious to get arrested by the police, I might strip naked or launch into a string of violent obscenities: either procedure would be equally effective.

Linguistic taboos and behavioural taboos are not only sanctioned in the same way, they are very much muddled up: sex behaviour and sex words, for example. But this association of deed and word is not so simple as might appear. The relationship is not necessarily causal. It is not the case that certain kinds of behaviour are taboo and that, therefore, the language relating to such behaviour becomes taboo. Sometimes words may be taboo in themselves for linguistic (phonemic) reasons, and the causal link, if any, is then reversed; a behavioural taboo comes to reflect a prior taboo. In this paper I shall only touch upon the fringe of this complex subject.

A familiar type of purely linguistic taboo is the pun. A pun occurs when we make a joke by confusing two apparently different meanings of the same phonemic pattern. The pun seems funny or shocking because it challenges a taboo which ordinarily forbids us to recognise that the sound pattern is ambiguous. In many cases such verbal taboos have social as well as linguistic aspects. In English, though not I think in American, the word *queen* has a homonym *quean*. The words are phonetically indistinguishable (KWĪN). Queen is the consort of King or even a female sovereign in her own right; quean which formerly meant a prostitute now usually denotes a homosexual male. In the non-human world we have queen bees and brood queen cats, both indicating a splendid fertility, but a quean is a barren cow. Although these two words pretend to be different, indeed opposites, they really denote the same idea. A queen is a female of abnormal status in a positive virtuous sense; a quean is a person of depraved character or uncertain sex, a female of abnormal status in a negative sinful sense. Yet their common abnormality turns both into 'supernatural' beings; so also, in metaphysics, the contraries God and the Devil are both supernatural beings. In this case, then, the taboo which allows us to separate the two ambiguous concepts, so that we can talk of queens without thinking of queans, and vice versa, is simultaneously both linguistic *and* social.

We should note that the taboo operates so as to distinguish two identical phonemic patterns; it does not operate so as to suppress the pattern altogether. We are not inhibited from saying KWĪN. Yet the very similar phonemic pattern produced by shifting the dental N to bilabial M and shortening the medial vowel (KWĬM) is one of the most unprintable obscenities in the English language. Some American informants have assured me that this word has been so thoroughly suppressed that it has not crossed the Atlantic at all, but this does not seem entirely correct as there is dictionary evidence to the contrary.[2] It is hard to talk about the unsayable but I hope I have made my initial point. Taboo is simultaneously both behavioural and linguistic, both social and psychological. As an anthropologist, I am particularly concerned with the social aspects of taboo. Analytical psychologists of various schools are particularly concerned with the individual taboos which centre in the oral, anal, and genital functions. Experimental psychologists may concern themselves with essentially the same kind of phenomenon when they examine the process of forgetting, or various kinds of muscular inhibition. But all these varieties of repression are so meshed into the web of language that discussion of any one of the three frames, anthropological, psychological, or linguistic, must inevitably lead on to some consideration of the other two.

Animal categories and verbal obscenities

In the rest of this paper I shall have relatively little to say about language in a direct sense, but this is because of the nature of my problem. I shall be discussing the connection between animal categories and verbal obscenities. Plainly it is much easier to talk about the animals than about the obscenities! The latter will mostly be just off stage. But the hearer (and the reader) should keep his wits about him. Just as queen is dangerously close to the unsayable, so also there are certain very familiar animals which are, as it were, only saved by a phoneme from sacrilege or worse. In seventeenth-century English witchcraft trials it was very commonly asserted that the Devil appeared in the form of a Dog – this is, God backwards. In England we still employ this same metathesis when we refer to a clergyman's collar as a 'dog collar' instead of a 'God collar.' So also it needs only a slight vowel shift in *fox* to produce the obscene *fux*. No doubt there is a sense in which such facts as these can be deemed linguistic accidents, but they are accidents which have a functional utility in the way we use our language. As I shall show presently, there are good sociological reasons why the English categories *dog* and *fox*, like the English category *queen (quean)*, should evoke taboo associations in their phonemic vicinity.

As an anthropologist I do not profess to understand the psychological aspects of the taboo phenomenon. I do not understand what happens when a word or a phrase or a detail of behaviour is subject to repression. But I can observe what happens. In particular I can observe that when verbal taboos are broken the result is a specific social phenomenon which affects both the actor and his hearers in a specific describable way. I need not elaborate. This phenomenon is what we mean by obscenity. Broadly speaking, the language of obscenity falls into three categories: (1) dirty words – usually referring to sex and excretion, (2) blasphemy and profanity, and (3) animal abuse – in which a human being is equated with an animal of another species.

These categories are not in practice sharply distinguished. Thus the word 'bloody,' which is now a kind of all-purpose mildly obscene adjective, is felt by some to be associated with menstrual blood and is thus a 'dirty' word, but it seems to be historically derived from profanity – 'By our Lady'. On the other hand, the simple expletive 'damn!' – now presumed to be short for 'damnation!' – and thus a profanity – was formerly 'god-dam' (God's animal mother) an expression combining blasphemy with animal abuse. These broad categories of obscenity seem to occur in most languages.

The dirty words present no problem. Psychologists have adequate and persuasive explanations of why the central focus or the crudest obscenity should ordinarily lie in sex and excretion. The language of profanity and blasphemy also presents no problem. Any theory about the sacredness of supernatural beings is likely to imply a concept of sacrilege which in turn explains the emotions aroused by profanity and blasphemy. But animal abuse seems much less easily accounted for. Why should expressions like 'you son of a bitch' or 'you swine' carry the connotations that they do, when 'you son of a kangaroo' or 'you polar bear' have no meaning whatever?

I write as an anthropologist, and for an anthropologist this theme of animal abuse has a very basic interest. When an animal name is used in this way as an imprecation, it indicates that the name itself is credited with potency. It clearly signifies that the animal category is in some way taboo and sacred. Thus, for an anthropologist, animal abuse is part of a wide field of study which includes animal sacrifice and totemism.

Relation of edibility and social valuation of animals

In his ethnographic studies the anthropologist observes that, in any particular cultural situation, some animals are the focus of ritual attitudes whereas others are not; moreover, the intensity of the ritual involvement of individual species varies greatly. It is never at all obvious why this should be so, but one fact that is commonly relevant and always needs to be taken into consideration is the edibility of the species in question.

One hypothesis which underlies the rest of this paper is that animal abuse is in some way linked with what Radcliffe-Brown called the ritual value of the animal category concerned. I further assume that this ritual value is linked in some as yet undetermined way with taboos and rules concerning the killing and eating of these and other animals. For the purposes of illustration, I shall confine my attention to categories of the English language. I postulate, however, that the principles which I adduce are very general, though not necessarily universal. In illustration of this, I discuss as an appendix to my main argument the application of my thesis to categories of the Kachin language spoken by certain highland groups in north-east Burma.

Taboo is not a genuine English word, but a category imported from Polynesia. Its meaning is not precisely defined in conventional English usage. Anthropologists commonly use it to refer to prohibitions which are explicit and which are supported by feelings of sin and supernatural sanction at a conscious level; incest regulations provide a typical example; the rules recorded in Leviticus xi. 4–47, which prohibited the Israelites from eating a wide variety of 'unclean beasts,' are another. In this paper, however, I shall use the concept of food taboo in a more general sense, so that it covers all classes of food prohibition, explicit and implicit, conscious and unconscious.

Cultural and linguistic determination of food values

The physical environment of any human society contains a vast range of materials which are both edible and nourishing, but, in most cases, only a small part of this edible environment will actually be classified as potential food. Such classification is a matter of language and culture, not of nature. It is a classification that is of great practical importance, and it is felt to be so. *Our* classification is not only correct, it is morally right and a mark of our superiority. The fact that frogs' legs are a gourmet's delicacy in France but not food at all in England provokes the English to refer to Frenchmen as Frogs with implications of withering contempt.

As a consequence of such cultural discriminations, the edible part of the environment usually falls into three main categories:

(1) Edible substances that are recognised as food and consumed as part of the normal diet.

(2) Edible substances that are recognised as possible food, but that are prohibited or else allowed to be eaten only under special (ritual) conditions. These are substances which are *consciously tabooed.*

(3) Edible substances that by culture and language are not recognised as food at all. These substances are *unconsciously tabooed.*

Now in the ordinary way when anthropologists discuss food taboos they are thinking only of my second category; they have in mind such examples as the Jewish prohibitions against pork, the Brahmin prohibition against beef, the Christian attitude to sacramental bread and wine. But my third category of edible substances that are not classed as food deserves equal attention. The nature of the taboo in the two cases is quite distinct. The Jewish prohibition against pork is a ritual matter and explicit. It says, in effect, 'pork is a food, but Jews must not eat it.' The Englishman's objection to eating dog is quite as strong but rests on a different premise. It depends on a categorical assumption: 'dog is not food.'

In actual fact, of course, dogs are perfectly edible, and in some parts of the world they are bred for eating. For that matter human beings are edible, though to an Englishman the very thought is disgusting. I think most Englishmen would find the idea of eating dog equally disgusting and in a similar way. I believe that this latter disgust is largely a matter of verbal categories. There are contexts in colloquial English in which man and dog may be thought of as beings of the same kind. Man and dog are 'companions'; the dog is 'the friend of man'. On the other hand man and food are antithetical categories. Man is not food, so dog cannot be food either.

Of course our linguistic categories are not always tidy and logical, but the marginal cases, which at first appear as exceptions to some general rule, are often especially interesting. For example, the French eat horse. In England, although horsemeat may be fed to dogs, it is officially classed as unfit for human consumption. Horsemeat may not be sold in the same shop that handles ordinary butchers' meat, and in London where, despite English prejudice, there are low foreigners who actually eat the stuff, they must buy it in a shop labelled *charcuterie* and not *butcher*! This I suggest is quite consistent with the very special attitude which Englishmen adopt towards both dogs and horses. Both are sacred supernatural creatures surrounded by feelings that are ambiguously those of awe and horror. This kind of attitude is comparable to a less familiar but much more improbable statutory rule which lays down that swan and sturgeon may only be eaten by members of the Royal Family, except once a year when swan may be eaten by the members of St John's College, Cambridge! As the Editor of the *New Yorker* is fond of telling us, 'There will always be an England!'

Plainly all such rules, prejudices, and conventions are of social origin; yet the social taboos have their linguistic counterparts and, as I shall presently show, these accidents of etymological history fit together in a quite surprising way. Certainly in its linguistic aspects horse looks innocent enough, but so do dog and fox. However, in most colloquial English, horse is *'orse* or *'oss* and in this form it shares with its companion *ass* an uncomfortable approximation to the human posterior.[3]

The problem then is this. The English treat certain animals as taboo – sacred. This sacredness is manifested in various ways, partly behavioural, as when we are forbidden to eat flesh of the animal concerned, partly linguistic, as when a phonemic pattern penumbral to that of the animal category itself is found to be a focus of obscenity, profanity, etc. Can we get any insight into why certain creatures should be treated this way?

Taboo and the distinctiveness of nameable categories

Before I proceed further, let me give you an outline of a general theory of taboo which I find particularly satisfactory in my work as an anthropologist. It is a theory which seems to me to fit in well with the psychological and linguistic facts.

In the form in which I present it here, it is a 'Leach theory' but it has several obvious derivations, especially Radcliffe-Brown's discussions of ritual value, Mary Douglas's thinking (still largely unpublished) on anomalous animals,[4] and Lévi-Strauss's version of the Hegelian–Marxist dialectic in which the sacred elements of myth are shown to be factors that mediate contradictories.

I postulate that the physical and social environment of a young child is perceived as a continuum. It does not contain any intrinsically separate 'things'. The child, in due course, is taught to impose upon this environment a kind of discriminating grid which serves to distinguish the world as being composed of a large number of separate things, each labelled with a name. This world is a representation of our language categories, not vice versa. Because my mother tongue is English, it seems self-evident that *bushes* and *trees* are different kinds of things. I would not think this unless I had been taught that it was the case.

Now if each individual has to learn to construct his own environment in this way, it is crucially important that the basic discriminations should be clear-cut and unambiguous. There must be absolutely no doubt about the difference between *me* and *it*, or between *we* and *they*. But how can such certainty of discrimination be achieved if our normal perception displays only a continuum? A diagram may help. Our uninhibited (untrained) perception recognises a continuum (Fig. 1).

Fig. 1. The line is a schematic representation of continuity in nature. There are no gaps in the physical world.

We are taught that the world consists of 'things' distinguished by names; therefore we have to train our perception to recognise a discontinuous environment (Fig. 2).

Fig. 2. Schematic representation of what in nature is named. Many aspects of the physical world remain unnamed in natural languages.

We achieve this second kind of trained perception by means of a simultaneous use of language and taboo. Language gives us the names to distinguish the things; taboo inhibits the recognition of those parts of the continuum which separate the things (Fig. 3).

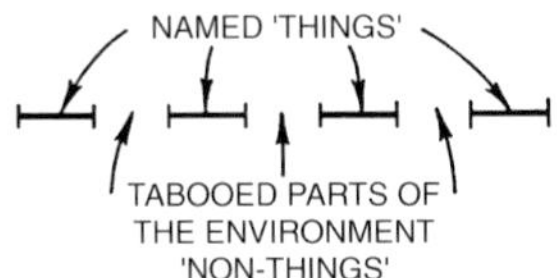

Fig. 3. The relationship of tabooed objects to the world of names.

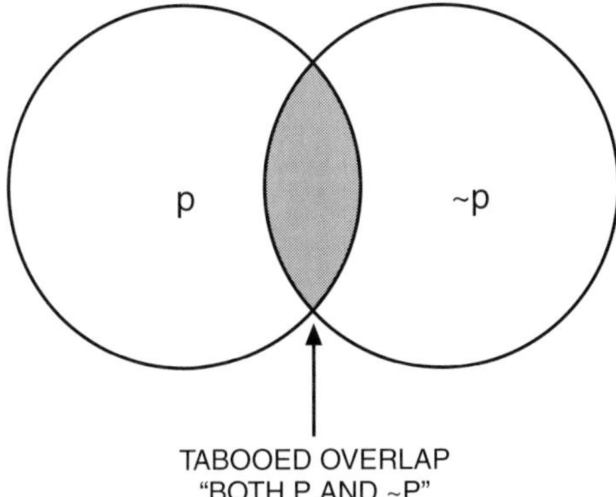

Fig. 4. The relationship between ambiguity and taboo.

The same kind of argument may also be represented by a simplified Venn diagram employing two circles only. Let there be a circle p representing a particular verbal category. Let this be intersected by another circle $\sim p$ representing the 'environment' of p, from which it is desired to distinguish p. If by a fiction we impose a taboo upon any consideration of the overlap area that is common to both circles, then we shall be able to persuade ourselves that p and $\sim p$ are wholly distinct, and the logic of binary discrimination will be satisfied (Fig. 4).

Language then does more than provide us with a classification of things; it actually moulds our environment; it places each individual at the centre of a social space which is ordered in a logical and reassuring way.

In this paper I shall be specially concerned with verbal category sets which discriminate areas of social space in terms of 'distance from Ego (self)'. For example, consider the three sets (a), (b), (c).

(a) Self . . . Sister . . . Cousin . . . Neighbour . . . Stranger
(b) Self . . . House . . . Farm . . . Field . . . Far (Remote)
(c) Self . . . Pet . . . Livestock . . . 'Game' . . . Wild Animal

For each of these three sets, the words, thus arranged, indicate categories that are progressively more remote from Self, but I believe that there is more to it than that. I hope to be able to show that, if we denote these word sets as

(a)	A1	B1	C1	D1	E1
(b)	A2	B2	C2	D2	E2
(c)	A3	B3	C3	D3	E3

then the relational statement A1 : B1 : C1 : D1 : E1 is the same as the relational statement A2 : B2 : C2 : D2 : E2 or the relational statement A3 : B3 : C3 : D3 : E3. In other words, the way we employ the words in set (c), a set of animals, allows us to make statements about the human relationships which belong to set (a).

But I am going too fast. Let us go back to my theory of taboo. If we operate in the way I have suggested, so that we are only able to perceive the environment as composed of separate things by suppressing our recognition of the non-things which fill the interstices, then of course what is suppressed becomes especially interesting. Quite apart from the fact that all scientific enquiry is devoted to 'discovering' those parts of the environment that lie on the borders of what is 'already known,' we have the phenomenon, which is variously described by anthropologists and psychologists, in which whatever is taboo is a focus not only of special interest but also of anxiety. Whatever is taboo is sacred, valuable, important, powerful, dangerous, untouchable, filthy, unmentionable.

I can illustrate my point by mentioning diametrically contrasted areas where this approach to taboo fits in well with the observable facts. First, the exudations of the human body are universally the objects of intense taboo – in particular, faeces, urine, semen, menstrual blood, hair clippings, nail parings, body dirt, spittle, mother's milk.[5] This fits the theory. Such substances are ambiguous in the most fundamental way. The child's first and continuing problem is to determine the initial boundary. 'What am I, as against the world?' 'Where is the edge of me?' In this fundamental sense, faeces, urine, semen, and so forth, are both me and not me. So strong is the resulting taboo that, even as an adult addressing an adult audience, I cannot refer to these substances by the monosyllabic words which I used as a child but must mention them only in Latin. But let us be clear, it is not simply that these substances are felt to be dirty – they are powerful; throughout the world it is precisely such substances that are the prime ingredients of magical 'medicines'.

At the opposite extreme, consider the case of the sanctity of supernatural beings. Religious belief is everywhere tied in with the discrimination between living and dead. Logically, *life* is simply the binary antithesis of *death*; the two concepts are the opposite sides of the same penny; we cannot have either without the other. But religion always tries to separate the two. To do this it creates a hypothetical 'other world' which is the antithesis of 'this world'. In this world life and death are inseparable; in the other world they are separate. This world is inhabited by imperfect mortal men; the other world is inhabited by immortal non-men (gods). The category god is thus constructed as the binary antithesis of man. But this is inconvenient. A remote god in another world may be logically sensible, but it is emotionally unsatisfying. To be useful, gods must be near at hand, so religion sets about reconstructing a continuum between this world and the other world. But note how it is done. The gap between the two logically distinct categories, this world/other world, is filled in with tabooed ambiguity. The gap is bridged by supernatural beings of a highly ambiguous kind – incarnate deities, virgin mothers, supernatural monsters which are half man/half beast. These marginal, ambiguous creatures are specifically credited with the power of mediating between gods and men. They are the object of the most intense taboos, more sacred than the gods themselves. In an objective sense, as distinct from theoretical theology, it is the Virgin Mary, human mother of God, who is the principal object of devotion in the Catholic Church.

So here again it is the ambiguous categories that attract the maximum interest and the most intense feelings of taboo. The general theory is that taboo applies to categories which are anomalous with respect to clear-cut category oppositions. If A and B are two verbal categories, such that B is defined as 'what A is not' and vice versa, and there is a third category C which mediates this distinction, in that C shares attributes of both A and B, then C will be taboo.

But now let us return to a consideration of English animal categories and food taboos.

Animal and food names in English

How do we speakers of English classify animals, and how is this classification related to the matters of killing and eating and verbal abuse?

The basic discrimination seems to rest in three words:

Fish creatures that live in water. A very elastic category, it includes even crustacea – 'shell fish'.

Birds two-legged creatures with wings which lay eggs. (They do not necessarily fly, e.g. penguins, ostriches.)

Beasts four-legged mammals living on land.

Consider Table 1. All creatures that are edible are fish or birds or beasts. There is a large residue of creatures, rated as either *reptiles* or *insects*, but the whole of this ambiguous residue is rated as not-food. All reptiles and insects seem to be thought of as evil enemies of mankind and liable to the most ruthless extermination. Only the bee is an exception here, and significantly the bee is often credited with quite superhuman powers of intelligence and organisation. The hostile taboo is applied most strongly to creatures that are most anomalous in respect of the major categories, e.g. snakes – land animals with no legs which lay eggs.

The fact that birds and beasts are warm-blooded and that they engage in sexual intercourse in a 'normal' way makes them to some extent akin to man. This is shown by the fact that the concept of *cruelty* is applicable to birds and beasts but not to fish. The slaughter of farm animals for food must be carried out by 'humane' methods;[6] in England we even have humane rat traps! But it is quite proper to kill a lobster by dropping it alive into boiling water. Where religious food taboos apply, they affect only the warm-blooded, near-human, meat of birds and beasts; hence Catholics may eat fish on Fridays. In England the only common fish subject to killing and eating restrictions is the salmon. This is an anomalous fish in at least two respects; it is red-blooded and it is simultaneously both a sea fish and a freshwater fish. But the mammalian *beasts* are much closer to man than the egg-laying *birds*. The Royal Society for the Prevention of Cruelty to Animals, the Anti-Vivisection League, Our Dumb Friends League and such

Table 1. English-language discriminations of living creatures

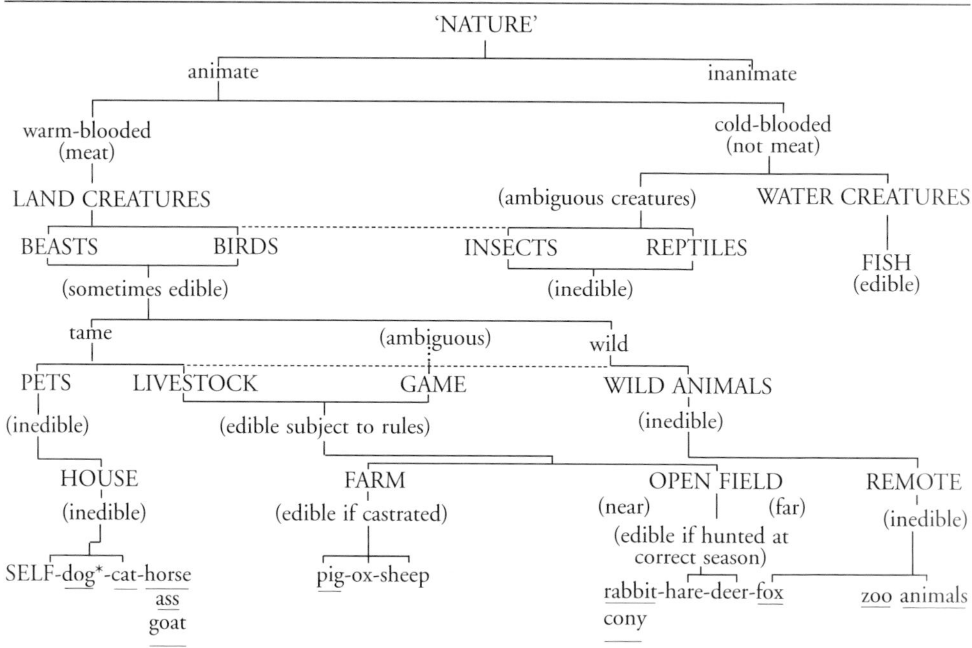

* The species underlined on the bottom line are those which appear to be specially loaded with taboo values, as indicated by their use in obscenity and abuse or by metaphysical associations or by the intrusion of euphemism.

organisations devote most of their attention to four-footed creatures, and as time is short I shall do the same.

Structure of food and kinship terminologies

Anthropologists have noted again and again that there is a universal tendency to make ritual and verbal associations between eating and sexual intercourse. It is thus a plausible hypothesis that the way in which animals are categorised with regard to edibility will have some correspondence to the way in which human beings are categorised with regard to sex relations.

Upon this matter the anthropologists have assembled a vast amount of comparative data. The following generalisation is certainly not a universal, but it has a very wide general validity. From the point of view of any male Self, the young women of his social world will fall into four major classes:

(1) Those who are very close – 'true sisters', always a strongly incestuous category.

(2) Those who are kin but not very close – 'first cousins' in English society, 'clan sisters' in many types of systems having unilineal descent and a segmentary

lineage organisation. As a rule, marriage with this category is either prohibited or strongly disapproved, but premarital sex relations may be tolerated or even expected.

(3) Neighbours (friends) who are not kin, potential affines. This is the category from which Self will ordinarily expect to obtain a wife. This category contains also potential enemies, friendship and enmity being alternating aspects of the same structural relationship.

(4) Distant strangers – who are known to exist but with whom no social relations of any kind are possible.

Now the English put most of their animals into four very comparable categories:

(1) Those who are very close – 'pets', always strongly inedible.

(2) Those who are tame but not very close – 'farm animals', mostly edible but only if immature or castrated. We seldom eat a sexually intact, mature farm beast.[7]

(3) Field animals, 'game' – a category toward which we alternate friendship and hostility. Game animals live under human protection but they are not tame. They are edible in sexually intact form, but are killed only at set seasons of the year in accordance with set hunting rituals.

(4) Remote wild animals – not subject to human control, inedible.

Thus presented, there appears to be a set of equivalents:

incest prohibition	inedible
marriage prohibition coupled with premarital sex relations	castration coupled with edibility
marriage alliance, friend/enemy ambiguity	edible in sexually intact form; alternating friendship/hostility
no sex relations with remote strangers	remote wild animals are inedible

That this correspondence between the categories of sexual accessibility and the categories of edibility is rather more than just an accident is shown by a further accident of a linguistic kind. The archaic legal expression for game was beasts of venery. The term venery had the alternative meanings, hunting and sexual indulgence.

A similar accident yields the phonemic resemblance between *venery* and *venerate* which is reminiscent of that between *quean* and *queen*. Sex and authority are both sources of taboo (respect) but in contrary senses.

A fifth major category of English animals which cuts across the others, and is significantly taboo-loaded, is vermin. The dictionary definition of this word is comprehensively ambiguous:

> mammals and birds injurious to game, crops, etc.; foxes, weasels, rats, mice, moles, owls, noxious insects, fleas, bugs, lice, parasitic worms, vile persons.

Vermin may also be described as *pests* (i.e. plagues). Although vermin and pests are intrinsically inedible, rabbits and pigeon, which are pests when they attack crops, may also be classed as game and then become edible. The same two species also become edible when kept under restraint as farm animals. I shall have more to say about rabbits presently.

Before we go further, let me review the latest part of my argument in rather different form. The thesis is that we make binary distinctions and then mediate the distinction by creating an ambiguous (and taboo-loaded) intermediate category. Thus:

p	both p and $\sim p$	$\sim p$
man	'man–animal'	not man
(not animal)	('pets')	(animal)
TAME	GAME	WILD
(friendly)	(friendly/hostile)	(hostile)

We have already given some indication that ritual value (taboo) attaches in a marked way to the intermediate categories *pets* and *game*, and I shall have more to say about this, but we shall find that even more intense taboo attitudes are revealed when we come to consider creatures which would only fit into the interstices of the above tabulation, e.g. goats, pigs, and horses which are not quite pets, rabbits which are not quite game, and foxes which are wild but treated like game in some respects (see bottom of Table 1).

In Table 2 are listed the more familiar names of the more familiar English animals. These name sets possess certain linguistic characteristics.

Nearly all the house pets, farm, and field (game) animals have monosyllabic names: dog, cat, bull, cow, ox, and so on, whereas among the more remote wild beasts monosyllables are rare. The vocabulary is most elaborated in the farm category and most attenuated in the inedible house-pet and wild-beast categories.

Thus farm animals have separate terms for (1) an intact male, (2) an intact female, (3) a suckling, (4) an immature female, (5) a castrated male (e.g. bull, cow, calf, heifer, bullock, with local variants). This is not surprising in view of the technical requirements of farming, but it seems odd that the pet vocabulary should be so restricted. Thus dog has only: dog, bitch, pup, and of these bitch is largely taboo and seldom used; cat has only: cat, kitten.

If sex discrimination must be made among pets, one can say 'bitch' and 'tom cat.' This implies that a dog is otherwise presumed male and a cat female. Indeed cat and dog are paired terms, and seem to serve as a paradigm for quarrelling husband and wife.

Among the field animals all males are *bucks* and all females *does*. Among the wild animals, in a small number of species we distinguish the young as *cubs*. In a smaller number we distinguish the female as a variant of the male: tiger – tigress; lion – lioness; but most are sexless. Fox is a very special case, exceptional in all respects. It is a monosyllable, the male is a *dog*, the female a *vixen*, the young a

Table 2. English sub-categories of familiar animals

	Female	Male	Infant	Young male[a]	Young female[a]	Castrated male	Baby language	Carcass meat
Dog	Bitch		Puppy				Bow wow	
Hound			Whelp				Doggy	
Cat		(Tom)	Kitten				Pussy	
Goat	(Nanny)	(Billy)	Kid				?	(Mutton)
Pig	Sow	Boar	Piglet	Hogget[b]	Gilt	Hog[c]	Piggy	Pork, bacon, ham
						Porker		
Ass							Ee-yaw	
Horse[d]	Mare	Stallion	Foal	Colt	Filly	Gelding	Gee-gee	
Cow (ox)[e]	Cow	Bull	Calf		Heifer	Steer	Moo-cow	Veal; beef[f]
						Bullock		
Sheep	Ewe	Ram	Lamb	Teg			Baa-lamb	Mutton
Fowl	Hen	Cock	Chick	Cockerel	Pullet	Capon	?	Chicken
Duck	Duck	Drake	Duckling				Quack-quack	
Goose	Goose	Gander	Gosling					
Pigeon			Squab					
Rabbit	Doe	Buck					Bunny	
Hare	Doe	Buck	Leveret					
Deer	Doe	Buck						Venison
	Hind	Stag[g]						
Swan			Cygnet					
Fox	Vixen	Dog	Cub[h]					

[a] *Other sex distinctions:*
Most birds other than duck and goose may be distinguished as cocks and hens.
Then whale, walrus, elephant, moose, and certain other large animals are distinguished as bulls and cows.
Lion and tiger are presumed male since they have feminine forms lioness, tigress.
The female of certain other species is marked by prefixing the pronoun 'she'; thus, she-bear.

[b] *Hogget* – a boar in its second year. The term may also apply to a young horse (colt) or to a young sheep (teg).

[c] *Hog* – may also refer to pigs in general as also *swine*.

[d] Note also *pony*, a small horse suitable for children.

[e] *Ox (Oxen)* – properly the term for the species in general, but now archaic and where used at all refers to a castrated male. The common species term is now *cow (cows)* or *cattle*. Cattle is in origin the same as capital = 'live stock'. The archaic plural of *cow* is *kine* (cf. *kin*).

[f] *Beef* – in singular = dead meat, but *beeves* plural refers to live animals = bullocks.

[g] *Hart* – an old stag with sur-royal antlers.

[h] *Cub (whelp)* – includes young of many wild animals: tiger, bear, otter, etc.

cub. Elephants and some other 'zoo animals' are distinguished as bulls, cows, and calves, a direct borrowing from the farm-animal set.

A curious usage suggests that we are ashamed of killing any animal of substantial size. When dead, bullock becomes *beef*, pig becomes *pork*, sheep becomes *mutton*, calf becomes *veal*, and deer becomes *venison*. But smaller animals stay as they are: lamb, hare, and rabbit, and all birds are the same alive or dead. Goats are 'nearly pets' and correspondingly (for the English) goat meat is nearly inedible. An English housewife would be outraged if she thought that her mutton was goat!

Animal abuse and eating habits

Most of the monosyllables denoting familiar animals may be stretched to describe the qualities of human beings. Such usage is often abusive but not always so. Bitch, cat, pig, swine, ass, goat, cur (dog) are insults; but lamb, duck, and cock are friendly, even affectionate. Close animals may also serve as near-obscene euphemisms for unmentionable parts of the human anatomy. Thus cock = penis, pussy = female pubic hair, and, in America, ass = arse.

The principle that the close, familiar animals are denoted by monosyllables is so general that the few exceptions invite special attention. The use of phonetically complex terms for 'close' animals seems always to be the result of a euphemistic replacement of a tabooed word. Thus *donkey* has replaced *ass*, and *rabbit* has replaced *coney*. This last term now survives only in the fur trade where it is pronounced to rhyme with Tony, but its etymological derivation is from Latin *cuniculus*, and the eighteenth-century rabbit was a cunny, awkwardly close to *cunt*, which only became printable in English with the licensed publication of *Lady Chatterley's Lover*. It is interesting that while the adult cunny has switched to the innocuous rabbit, baby language has retained bunny. I gather that in contemporary New York a Bunny Club has at least a superficial resemblance to a London eighteenth-century Cunny House.[8]

Some animals seem to carry an unfair load of abuse. Admittedly the pig is a general scavenger but so, by nature, is the dog and it is hardly rational that we should label the first 'filthy' while making a household pet of the second. I suspect that we feel a rather special guilt about our pigs. After all, sheep provide wool, cows provide milk, chickens provide eggs, but we rear pigs for the sole purpose of killing and eating them, and this is rather a shameful thing, a shame which quickly attaches to the pig itself. Besides which, under English rural conditions, the pig in his backyard pigsty was, until very recently, much more nearly a member of the household than any of the other edible animals. Pigs, like dogs, were fed from the leftovers of their human masters' kitchens. To kill and eat such a commensal associate is sacrilege indeed!

In striking contrast to the monosyllabic names of the close animals, we find that at the other end of the scale there is a large class of truly wild animals, most of which the ordinary individual sees only in a zoo. Such creatures are not classed as potential food at all. To distinguish these strangers as lying outside our English social system, we have given them very long semi-Latin names – elephant, hippopotamus, rhinoceros, and so forth. This is not due to any scholastic perversity; these words have been a part of the vernacular for a thousand years or so.

The intermediate category of fully sexed, tame–wild, field animals which we may hunt for food, but only in accordance with set rules at special seasons of the year, is in England now much reduced in scope. It now comprises certain birds (e.g. grouse, pheasant, partridge), hares, and, in some places, deer. As indicated already, rabbits and pigeons are both marginal to this category. Since all these creatures are protected for part of the year in order that they may be killed in the other, the collective name *game* is most appropriate. Social anthropologists have coined the expression *joking relationship* for a somewhat analogous state of affairs which is frequently institutionalised between affinally related groups among human beings.

Just as the obscene rabbit, which is ambiguously game or vermin, occupies an intermediate status between the farm and field categories (Table 1), the fox occupies the borderline between edible field and inedible wild animals. In England the hunting and killing of foxes is a barbarous ritual surrounded by extraordinary and fantastic taboos. The intensity of feeling aroused by these performances almost baffles the imagination. All attempts to interfere with such customs on the grounds of 'cruelty' have failed miserably. Some aspects of fox-hunting are linguistic and thus directly relevant to my theme. We find, for example, as commonly occurs in other societies in analogous contexts, that the sacredness of the situation is marked by language inversions, the use of special terms for familiar objects, and so on.

Thus foxes are hunted by packs of dogs and, at the conclusion of the ritual killing, the fox has its head and tail cut off, which are then preserved as trophies, but none of this may be said in plain language. It is the fox itself that can be spoken of as a *dog*, the dogs are described as *hounds*, the head of the fox is a *mask*, its tail a *brush*, and so on. It is considered highly improper to use any other words for these things.

Otters, stags, and hares are also sometimes hunted in a comparable ritual manner, and here again the hunting dogs change their identity, becoming either hounds or beagles. All of which reinforces my original hypothesis that the category *dog*, in English, is something very special indeed.

The implication of all this is that if we arrange the familiar animals in a series according to their social distance from the human Self (Table 1, bottom) then we can see that the occurrence of taboo (ritual value), as indicated by different types and intensities of killing and eating restrictions, verbal abuse, metaphysical associations, ritual performance, the intrusion of euphemism, etc. is not just randomly distributed. The varieties of taboo are located at intervals across the chart in such a way as to break up the continuum into sections. Taboo serves to separate the Self from the world, and then the world itself is divided into zones of social distance corresponding here to the words farm, field, and remote.

I believe that this kind of analysis is more than just an intellectual game; it can help us to understand a wide variety of our non-rational behaviour. For example, anyone familiar with the literature will readily perceive that English witchcraft beliefs depended upon a confusion of precisely the categories to which I have here drawn attention. Witches were credited with a power to assume animal form and with possessing spirit familiars. The familiar might take the form of any animal but was most likely to appear as a dog, a cat, or a toad. Some familiars had no counterpart in natural history; one was described as having 'paws like a bear but in bulk not fully as big as a coney'. The ambiguity of such creatures was taken as evidence of their supernatural qualities. As Hopkins, the celebrated seventeenth-century witchfinder, remarked, 'No mortal alone could have invented them.'

But my purpose has been to pose questions rather than to offer explanations. The particular diagrams which I have presented may not be the most useful ones, but at least I have established that the English language classification of familiar animals is by no means a simple matter; it is not just a list of names, but a complex pattern of identifications subtly discriminated not only in kind but in psychological tone. Our linguistic treatment of these categories reflects taboo or ritual value, but these are simply portmanteau terms which cover a complex of feeling and attitude, a sense perhaps that aggression, as manifested either in sex or in killing, is somehow a disturbance of the natural order of things, a kind of necessary impiety.

A non-European example

If this kind of analysis were applicable only to the categories of the English language it would amount to no more than a parlour game. Scientifically speaking, the analysis is interesting only in so far as it opens up the possibility that other languages analysed according to similar procedures might yield comparable patterns. A demonstration on these lines is not easy: one needs to know a language very well indeed before one can play a game of this kind. Nevertheless it is worth trying.

Kachin is a Tibeto-Burman language spoken by hill tribesmen in north-east Burma. Since it is grammatically and syntactically wholly unlike any Indo-European language it should provide a good test case. At one time I spoke the language fluently though I cannot do so now. I have a first-hand anthropological understanding of Kachin customary behaviours.

Kachin is essentially a monosyllabic language in which discrimination is achieved by varying the 'prefixes' of words rather than by tonal variation, though, as in other Tibeto-Burman languages, tones play their part. It follows that homonyms are very common in this language, and the art of punning and *double entendre* is a highly developed cultural feature. A special form of lovers' poetry (*nchyun ga*) depends on this fact. A single brief example will suffice as illustration:

Jan du	gawng lawng	sharat a lo
At sunset	the clapper of the cattle bell	swings back and forth.
Mai bawt	gawng nu	sharat a lo
The (buffalo's) short tail	and the base of the bell	are wagged.[9]

Nothing could be more superficially 'innocent' than this romantic image of dusk and cattle bells. But the poem takes on a very different appearance once it is realized that *jan du* (the sun sets) also means 'the girl comes (has an orgasm)' while *mai bawt* (the short tail) is a common euphemism for the human penis. The rest of the Freudian images can easily be worked out by the reader!

On the other hand, it cannot be said that the Kachin is at all 'foul-mouthed.' Precisely because of his cultivated expertness at *double entendre*, he can almost always appear to be scrupulously polite. But verbal obscenities do exist, including what I have called animal abuse; the latter are mainly concentrated around the dog (*gwi*).

Kachins are a primitive people living in steep mountainous forest country. Their diet consists mainly of rice and vegetables, but they keep cattle, pigs, and fowls. There are very few edible creatures which they will not eat, though they draw the line at dogs and rats and human beings. The domesticated animals are killed only in the context of a sacrificial ritual. The meat of such sacrifices is eaten by members of the attendant congregation, and sacrifices are frequent. Despite this frequency, the occasion of a sacrifice is a sacred occasion (*na*) and there is a sense in which all domestic animals are sacred.

Until very recently the Kachins had an institution of slavery. It is an indication of their attitude to animals rather than of their attitude to slaves that a slave was classed as a *yam*, a category which includes all domesticated animals. It is also relevant that the word *ni* meaning near also means tame.

The linguistic correlates of all this are not simple. In general, everything that has a place in ritual occasions falls into the wide category *wu* (*u*) meaning pollution. This has sundry sub-categories:

(a) birds
(b) various species of bamboo
(c) creatures classed as *nga* – mainly fish and cattle
(d) creatures classed as *wa* – mainly human beings and pigs.

Ignoring the human beings and the bamboo, this is a category of polluted foods, i.e. foods which may properly be eaten only in the context of sacrifice. It contrasts with ordinary clean food and meat (*shat, shan*). Other creatures such as dog (*gwi*) and rat (*yu*) may sometimes be offered in sacrifice, but these would not be eaten except as part of some special magical performance. I have arranged these and other terms (Table 3) on a scale of social distance comparable to that shown for English-language categories in Table 1. The parallels are very striking.

Table 3. Kachin categories of familiar animals (for comparison with bottom three lines of Table 1)

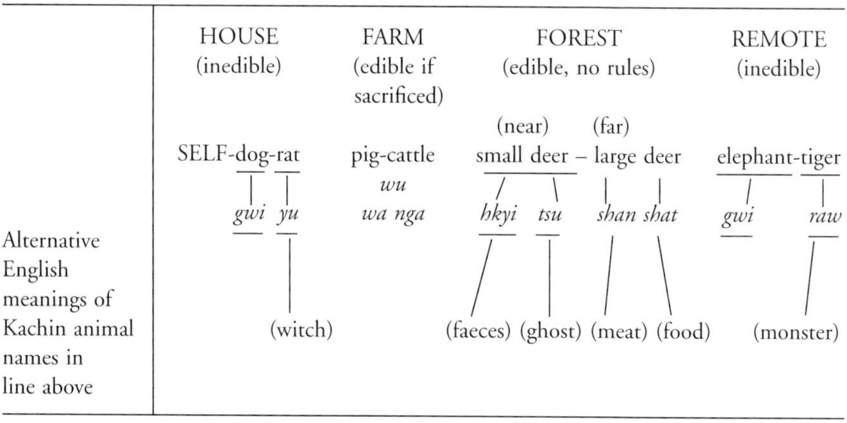

	HOUSE (inedible)	FARM (edible if sacrificed)	FOREST (edible, no rules)	REMOTE (inedible)
	SELF-dog-rat	pig-cattle	(near) small deer – (far) large deer	elephant-tiger
	gwi *yu*	*wu* *wa nga*	*hkyi* *tsu* *shan* *shat*	*gwi* *raw*
Alternative English meanings of Kachin animal names in line above	(witch)		(faeces) (ghost) (meat) (food)	(monster)

Let us consider the items in this table reading from left to right, that is to say, from very close to very far.

The closest creatures are the dog and the rat. Both are inedible and heavily loaded with taboo. To call a man a dog is an obscenity; *yu* (rat) also means witchcraft. In some contexts it may also mean affinal relative on the wife's or mother's side. For a variety of structural reasons which I have described in other publications, a Kachin's feelings towards these *mayu ni* are ordinarily highly ambivalent. My wife's mother, a strongly incestuous category, is *ni*, which we have already seen also means very near, and tame.

The domesticated creatures that are edible if sacrificed have been considered already. These 'farm' creatures are much more closely identified with the self than the corresponding English categories. They are as human as slaves; they all live in the same house as their owners. The term *wa* (pig) also means man, father, tooth. It is veritably a part of 'me'!

In the English schema I suggested that field (game) animals have the same structural position, in terms of social distance, as the category of potential wives. In the Kachin case the category of animals comparable to English game are the forest animals hunted for meat. They live in the forest (*nam*). Now the Kachin have a prescriptive rule of marriage which requires a man to marry a girl of a certain category; this category is also *nam*. But in other respects the Kachin case is the inverse of the English situation. An Englishman has free choice in obtaining a wife, but he must go further afield than a first cousin; on the other hand he hunts his game according to precise rules. In contrast the Kachin has his category of possible wives defined in advance and, as first preference, should choose a particular first cousin (the mother's brother's daughter). But he is subject to no rules when he hunts in the forest.

The creatures of the forest which are thus obtained for meat by hunting are mainly deer of various sizes. The smaller ones are found close to the village. Like the English rabbit these are regarded as vermin as well as game, since they raid the rice fields. The larger deer are found in the deep forest. There are in all four categories of deer: *hkyi* and *tsu* are both small species living close in, *shan* and *shat* are large creatures living far out. All these words have homonym meanings: *hkyi*: faeces, filth; *tsu*: a disembodied human spirit, ghost; *shan*: ordinary (clean) meat food; *shat*: ordinary (clean) food of any kind.

Thus the pattern is quite consistent. The more remote animals are the more edible, and the homonym meanings of the associated words become less taboo-loaded as the social distance is increased.

However, the overall situation is not quite so simple. Monkeys of many kinds abound. They are sometimes eaten, occasionally tamed as pets, and their blood is credited with magical aphrodisiac qualities. They seem to be thought of as wild animals rather abnormally close to man, like the little deer *tsu*. A monkey is *woi*, a term which also means grandmother. The status of squirrels is very similar. The squirrel figures prominently in Kachin mythology, since it was the death of a squirrel that led man to become mortal. Squirrels are hunted and eaten, but again the attitude is ambiguous. Squirrels are *mai* (tails), but *mai* as we have already seen means a human penis.

Moreover, as remoteness is increased, we finally reach, as in English, a category of unknown and therefore inedible creatures, and the pattern is then reversed. There are two great beasts of the forest which the ordinary Kachin knows about but seldom sees. The first is the elephant, called *magwi* but also *gwi*. Since *gwi* is a dog this may seem odd, but the usage is very similar to that by which the English call the male fox a dog. The other is the tiger (*sharaw*, *raw*) which stands as the prototype for all fabulous monsters. *Numraw*, literally woman tiger, is a creature which figures prominently in Kachin mythology; she (?) has many attributes of the Sphinx in the Oedipus story, an all-devouring horror of uncertain sex, half man, half beast.[10]

This overall pattern, as displayed in Table 3, is certainly not identical to that found in English, but it is clearly very much the same kind of pattern, and the resemblances seem too close to be the product of either mere accident, as that phrase would ordinarily be understood, or the obsessional prejudices of myself as investigator. I suggest that the correspondences are at least sufficient to justify further comparative studies. On the other hand, I readily agree that it is easy to be overpersuaded by such evidence, especially when dealing with a language such as Kachin where the incidence of homonyms is very high.

In writing of English I suggested that there was a correspondence between the sequence of sex relationships: sister (incest); cousin (premarital relations possible, no marriage); neighbour (marriage possible); stranger (marriage impossible); and the sequence of 'edibility relationships' displayed in Table 1. How far does this apply for Kachin? How does one make the comparison? The difficulty is that Kachin has a kinship system quite different from that of English. True sisters are a strongly incestuous category, but remote classificatory clan sisters are persons with whom liaisons are possible but marriage is not. Elder sister is *na* and younger sister is *nau*. The homonyms are *na*, a sacred holiday, an occasion on which a ritual sacrifice is made; *nau*, a sacred dance occurring on *na* occasions to the accompaniment of sacrifice. This of course fits very nicely with my thesis, for Table 3 can now be translated into human as opposed to animal relationships (in Table 4) thus:

Table 4. Kachin categories of human relationships

	incest	no marriage, illicit relations	marriage	remote nonrelative
Self	*ni*	*nalnau*	*nam*	*raw**
	mother-in-law	'sister'	marriageable cross-cousin	
	near	sacred occasion	forest	forest fire
	(inedible)	(edible if sacrificed)	(edible)	(inedible)

* There are two relevant homonyms of *raw* = tiger. *Raw* as a verb means cease to be related; it applies in particular when two affinally related groups cease to recognise their relationship. *Raw* also means forest fire. It is thus the dangerous aspect of the forest, where *nam* is friendly.

Perhaps all this is too good to be true, but I think that it deserves further investigation.

Those who wish to take my argument seriously might well consider its relevance to C. Lévi-Strauss's most remarkable book *La Pensée sauvage* (1962). Though fascinated by that work I have also felt that some dimension to the argument is missing. We need to consider not merely that things in the world can be classified as sacred and not sacred, but also as more sacred and less sacred. So also in social classification it is not sufficient to have a discrimination me/it, we/they; we also need a graduated scale close/far, more-like-me/less-like-me. If this essay is found to have a permanent value it will be because it represents an expansion of Lévi-Strauss's thesis in the direction I have indicated.

Notes

This paper was originally published as a chapter in E. H. Lennenberg (ed.), *New Directions in the Study of Language*, (1964)the proceedings of the symposium on 'Language and the Science of Man' held under the auspices of the 16th International Congress of Psychology.

1. Postman, 'The Present Status of Interference Theory'.
2. The *Oxford English Dictionary* says nothing of the obscenity but records *Quim* as a 'late Scottish variant' of the now wholly obsolete *Queme* = 'pleasant'. Partridge, *Dictionary of Slang*, prints the word in full (whereas he balks at f*ck and c*nt). His gloss is 'the female pudenda' and he gives *queme* as a variant. Funk and Wagnalls (*New 'Standard' Dictionary of English Language*) and Webster (*New International Dictionary of the English Language*), latest editions, both ignore the term, but Wentworth and Flexner, *Dictionary of American Slang*, give: '*quim* n. 1 = queen; 2 (taboo) = the vagina.' That this phonemic pattern is, in fact, penumbral to the more permissible *queen* is thus established.

   The American dictionaries indicate that the range of meanings of *queen* (*quean*) is the same as in English, but the distinction of spelling is not firmly maintained.
3. English and American taboos are different. The English spell the animal *ass* and the buttocks *arse* but, according to Partridge, *Dictionary of Slang*, *arse* was considered almost unprintable between 1700 and 1930 (though it appeared in the *Oxford English Dictionary*). Webster's 3rd Edition spells both words as *ass*, noting that *arse* is a more polite variant of the latter word,

which also has obscene meaning, sexual intercourse. Funk and Wagnalls (*New 'Standard' Dictionary of English Language*) distinguish *ass* (animal) and *arse* (buttocks) but do not cross-reference. Wentworth and Flexner (*Dictionary of American Slang*) give only *ass* but give three taboo meanings, the rectum, the buttocks, and the vagina.

4. [Eds: See Douglas, *Purity and Danger*, and 'Self Evidence'; also Bulmer, 'Why the Cassowary is not a Bird', and Tambiah, 'Animals are Good to Eat and Also Good to Prohibit'.]
5. An interesting and seemingly unique partial exception to this catalogue is 'tears'. Tears can acquire sacredness, in that the tears of saints have been turned into relics and tears are proper at sacred situations, e.g. funerals, but tears are not, I think, felt to be dirty or contaminating after the manner of other exudations.
6. The word *humane* has become distinguished from *human* only since the seventeenth century.
7. Two reasons are usually offered for castrating farm animals. The first, which is valid, is that the castrated animal is more amenable to handling. The second, which I am assured is scientifically invalid, is that a castrated animal produces more succulent meat in a shorter time.
8. In general, birds fall outside the scope of this paper, but while considering the ambiguities introduced by the accidents of linguistic homonyms we may note that all edible birds are *fowl* (i.e. foul = filthy); that pigeon has replaced *dove*, perhaps because of the association of the latter with the Holy Ghost; and that the word *squabble* (a noisy quarrel, particularly between married couples) is derived from *squab*, a young pigeon.
9. All Kachin linguistic usages cited here except the obscene connotations of *jan du* can be verified from Hanson, *Dictionary of the Kachin Language.*
10. This greatly simplifies a very complex mythological category. The *numraw* (also *maraw*) are 'luck' deities, vaguely comparable to the Furies (*erinyes*) of Greek mythology. The *numraw* are not always female nor always of one kind. *Baren numraw* lives in the water and seems to be thought of as some kind of alligator, *wa numraw* is presumably a wild boar, and so on.

4.3

The Nature of War[1] (1965)

> This ideal of *glory* and *grandeur* – which consists not merely in considering nothing wrong that one does, but in priding oneself on every crime one commits, ascribing to it an incomprehensible supernatural significance . . .
>
> Leo Tolstoy, *War and Peace.*

If going to war were governed wholly by reason, twentieth-century man would be enjoying perpetual peace. This essay discusses some non-rational causes of war which are encountered among primitive peoples. But do not be deceived by the circumstances that I write about head-hunters. We, too, are savages under the skin. Whatever instincts we possess are shared also by cannibals and pygmies, bushmen and Australian Aborigines.

When modern nations go to war it is as a means to an end; some apparent objective can always be specified in rational terms – conquest, the defence of territory, the assertion of economic rights. But with primitive peoples this is seldom the case. Primitive warfare is a kind of ritual game; any benefits that it may bring are metaphysical rather than material, virtue rather than loot. There is a ritual element in modern warfare also but it is overlaid by more rational concerns. It is all the more dangerous because it is so easily ignored.

Every society must bring the aggressive instincts of its individual members under control. This can never be achieved simply by outright repression or by moral precept, but only by sublimation, that is by providing legitimate outlets for dangerous feelings. Until very recently warfare has always been looked upon as an orthodox, ritualised, emotionally satisfying outlet of this kind. Most human societies have been organised around the presumption that the primary occupation of all young adult males is fighting, and that peace is an interlude between wars rather than the other way about. The manly virtues (heroism, courage, bravery, honour, and the like) all find their primary definition in a context of war.

The moral values which underlie such verbal categories fit in with our psychological dispositions, which remain the same with or without H-bombs and poison gas. Any nation which now, in the light of reason, seeks genuinely to abandon the use of war as an instrument of policy will need to discover alternative forms of valour. Yesterday's hero, whatever his failings, had the moral virtues of a soldier; the new James Bond equivalent is a sadistic, sexually indiscriminate, man of violence. That should be warning enough. Some may feel that moon rocketry is so obviously futile that it can only be a cloak for far more lethal forms of experiment, yet as a sublimated form of aggression space travel has advantages over head-hunting.

Head-hunting is an unusual and no doubt deplorable form of human activity but it is warfare on a minimal scale and if we are searching for the essence of the matter this may be where we should look. Head-hunting institutions have been reported from various parts of the world, notably South America, New Guinea, Borneo, and Assam. They have much in common, though details vary from place to place. The generalisations which follow are based mainly on the literature relating to the Nagas of Assam and the Dyaks of Central Borneo.

Head-hunting raids are not carried out indiscriminately but in response to special circumstance. The most typical circumstance is misfortune in the form of crop failure or death. Whenever a distinguished individual dies, the whole local community must go into mourning and submit to various kinds of ritual restraint. The young men must go out on a head-hunt before these mourning restraints can be removed. The head-hunt itself is simply an organised raid on some neighbouring group, the objective of which is not to conquer but to kill. Evidence of the killing is provided by bringing back the skulls of the dead enemy. Valour, in our sense, is not an issue. The head of an infant or of an old woman serves as well as that of a warrior. These skulls then become the focus of an elaborate ritual celebration.

The sense of triumph which is expressed in the display of the trophy heads has magical consequences:

(1) It removes the evil consequences of the previous death and permits the lifting of the mourning ban.

(2) It is felt to be generally beneficial to the community in that it improves the fertility of the crops, and brings individual prosperity and prestige to members of the war party.

Formerly this personal prestige was so marked that no young man could hope to win a wife unless he had first participated in a head-hunt. The close link between physical aggression and sexual aggression is plainly manifested in various details of the associated rituals. The head-hunt is felt to be an expression of male virility, a fertilising, health-restoring act of a magical kind.

The ideology which surrounds the severed heads is very complicated. In these societies, as in most others, great importance is attached to the requirement that a corpse shall be disposed of with proper ritual. The souls of those who receive the proper rites will rest in peace; the souls of those who die violent or unnatural deaths cannot receive proper mortuary rites and on that account turn into dangerous ghosts. We are familiar with the same kind of belief in our own society where the souls of suicides and murdered men are thought to haunt the scenes of their suffering precisely because of the irregularity of their death and burial. Now a man killed by a head-hunting war-party dies a violent death and the removal of his head makes it impossible for his own kin to give the corpse proper rites. On both counts his soul is bound to become a ghost. Feelings about this go very deep. Consider for example the horror and shock with which the British reacted to a recent South Arabian incident in which two British soldiers were not merely killed but also decapitated. The British authorities quickly recovered the corpses but then went to great lengths to recover the heads.

It would take much too long to discuss in detail just why the 'head' rather than any other part of the anatomy has this peculiarly emotive force. According to orthodox psychoanalytic theory the human head is a common symbolic displacement for the human phallus. Ethnographic evidence shows that this kind of symbolic association is very common in religious ritual.[2] Certainly in head-hunting a strong sexual element is involved. To decapitate a head from a corpse is a symbolic equivalent for emasculation. It is probably relevant that the most common forms of mutilation imposed on enemy corpses, other than decapitation and scalping, are cutting off the hands and cutting off the genitals.

By taking the enemy head the killers ensure that the soul of their victim shall become a ghost, but by appropriate ritual procedures the captors of the head can enslave the ghost and make it work on their behalf, rather like the slave genie of Aladdin's lamp. Thus the captive heads in a head-hunting society are more than just trophies; they are objects of power which are believed to bring metaphysical benefit to the community of their captors.

Of what relevance is all this for an enquiry into the Nature of War? I am not suggesting that modern European warfare is simply an enlarged Borneo head-hunt, but rather that many of the same social and psychological drives are involved in both. We may gain some insights into the general phenomenon if we analyse the symptoms of this special case.

Society, however we conceive it, is a network of persons held together by links of power. The individual who apprehends society in this way has to proceed by logical steps. He must first be able to see how one person differs from another person and he must then be able to appreciate that two persons, though different, may yet be linked together. Viewed in this way power does not lie in persons or in things but in the interstices between persons and between things, that is to say *in relation*. Every individual must go through this concept-forming process, first distinguishing the self from the non-self and then apprehending the relationship between the self and the other. On a grander scale the same is true of society; we recognise what we are as a community by seeing how we differ from and how we are related to 'the others'.

Power, the influence of relationship, is ambivalent. On one side it is dominance; on the other submission. In human affairs one man's advantage is always balanced by some other man's disadvantage. Power in itself is amoral, bringing benefits to one, disaster to another. But from the point of view of the individual power always lies on the outside; power is the influence I have on others, the influence others have on me. It is what joins me to the others, it is betwixt and between, and it is dangerous stuff. The other side of this image of how things are is the feeling that every unintended thing that happens, fortunate or unfortunate as the case may be, is due to influence from outside. It follows that any action we may take which seeks to modify the present state of affairs must be concerned with modifying relationships between 'us' and 'the others'.

I am not suggesting that head-hunters argue among themselves in this abstract fashion, but this is the logic behind what they do and perhaps behind what we do also.

The self and the soul

We do not need to go all the way with Freud to agree firstly that the adult's view of the world must be tied in with his childhood experiences and secondly that the child's view of the world is a response to the socialising discipline he receives at the hand of the adults around him, notably his own parents. Inevitably this external world appears as a dangerous place, arbitrarily and unpredictably friendly or hostile, dispensing benefits at one moment and punishments the next. But, for the child, power, whether good or bad, is always 'out-there'; the self is impotent.

In adult life this childhood experience has to be grafted to a theology of life and death. There is an almost universal theory that the difference between a live creature and a dead one is that the 'life' or 'soul' has abandoned the latter. The 'soul' is conceived of as a kind of substance which exists on a metaphysical plane even when it is detached from the body. It is the persisting immortal part of me; the central indestructible essence of self. It follows that the living parents, who administered arbitrary and unpredictable justice when I was a child, still survive on a metaphysical plane after they are dead and continue to administer arbitrary and unpredictable justice to their surviving descendants. This influence of the souls of the dead upon the fortunes of the living derives from the state of relationship which is felt to exist between the living 'here' and the dead 'out-there'.

A great deal of religious ritual has the professed purpose of altering this relationship.

But where is 'out-there'? Theology is confused and self-contradictory on this point. The categories of verbal and ritual expression seem always to imply at least three kinds of 'out-there' which are distinguished by their distance from the self, the degree to which they are felt to be understood and under control, and their influence upon the self. Crudely stated the three categories are:

(1) The near out-there, that which corresponds to the English concept of *home.*

(2) The far out-there, the great unknown.

(3) A crucially important intermediate zone which is neither altogether unknown nor fully predictable.

The boundaries of these categories keep changing as we pass through life. For the young child 'the near out-there' is restricted to the limits of the immediate domestic family of parents and children, while 'the great unknown' may start a few yards beyond his front doorstep, but for an adult 'home' extends at least to the frontiers of the local community and often very much further.

In most primitive societies the content of my three categories would be:

(1) The near out-there (home): the local village community, kinsfolk, friends, tame animals, witches.

(2) The far out-there (the great unknown): total strangers, large wild animals, ancestors, gods, major demons.

(3) The intermediate out-there: village fields and familiar hunting grounds, wild animals of the more familiar sorts, affinal relatives with whom 'we' exchange wives, enemies against whom 'we' make war, ghosts.

There is no straightforward distinction between friendly home and hostile beyond. The out-there is morally ambiguous. Home is mostly friendly and reliable but it contains hostile elements; beyond the limits of home, the world is always dangerous and often hostile but relations with it are essential. We depend upon the outside world for our sustenance. Food and wives both come from beyond the immediate home, and our souls too.

Theology is understandably reticent about just *how* the immortal soul comes into being, but many, perhaps most, peoples profess to believe that the souls of the living derive in the first place from some kind of pool of souls or of soul stuff which exists all the time in the far 'out-there', in the land of the dead, and that it is to this same far 'out-there' that our own dead souls must ultimately return. Thus 'we' are engaged in a constant interchange of souls with 'the others'; the dead are replaced by the newly born. This idea, of a permanently enduring exchange relationship between ourselves and the powers of the remote unknown, is linked up with two deeply rooted physiological experiences, firstly the infantile metabolic sequence of eating and excretion, and secondly the adult experience of sex, whereby the male gift of semen is reciprocated by the gift of a child. These physiological exchanges between the self and the other are loaded with intense emotional feelings which are readily transformed into metaphysical notions concerning the exchange of souls between known and unknown. Eating and excretion are both commonly subject to the most elaborate ritual taboos and either may feature as sacraments in the fullest sense. Both in religious mysticism and on the psychoanalyst's couch the ecstacy of the sexual act may be felt as a foretaste of death.

On a more material plane the sexual interchange between individual man and individual woman may serve as the prototype for a social relationship in which a marriage alliance serves to link together not merely two individuals but two whole sets of kinsfolk. Since rules of exogamy usually require that a wife shall not be a close kinswoman of her husband, the perpetuation of community through the birth of children then comes to depend upon the establishment and maintenance of marital interchange between 'us' and 'the other'. In such circumstances relationships of affinal alliance may be felt to have something in common with the relationship between the living and the dead and the whole institution becomes heavily loaded with metaphysical potency. As like as not wives and brothers-in-law are felt to be potential witches. Modern Europeans like to think that they are free from such childish superstitions, but consider for a moment our English attitude to cleanliness.

Cleanliness

When we clean anything we endeavour to reach the 'thing itself', the pure essence. We try to distinguish the thing from its environment. In the process the marginal stuff, which tends to confuse the boundary between what we treat as 'the thing itself' and 'the rest', comes to seem out of place and we describe it as *dirt.* Dirt is thus defined by context, *it is matter out of place*; soil is dirty in the kitchen but not in the garden. From another point of view dirt is what lies between one clean category and another. That dirt is the ambiguous stuff which tends to confuse the edges of our nice clean categories is most clearly seen if we examine the dirtiest kinds of dirt, which are always the exudations of the human body: faeces, menstrual blood, semen, urine, sweat, etc. The dirtiness of such things arises in the first place because, in the process of the child's category formation, the substances are ambiguous, they are neither 'me' nor 'not-me'; they present the child with a basic uncertainty as to the boundary of the clean self, the 'true' self. Because 'dirt' thus defined contaminates the 'essential me' it is powerful dangerous stuff. Thus we arrive at an extraordinary but very fundamental (and almost universal) paradox in human thought: the true me, the essential me, is the 'clean' me, that is the me with the dirt removed, the me with the potency removed. *So the essential 'I' is not only clean but also sexless and impotent.*

From this false logic derive all kinds of ascetic rituals which consist, in their simplest form, of removing portions of the human body in order to attain ritual

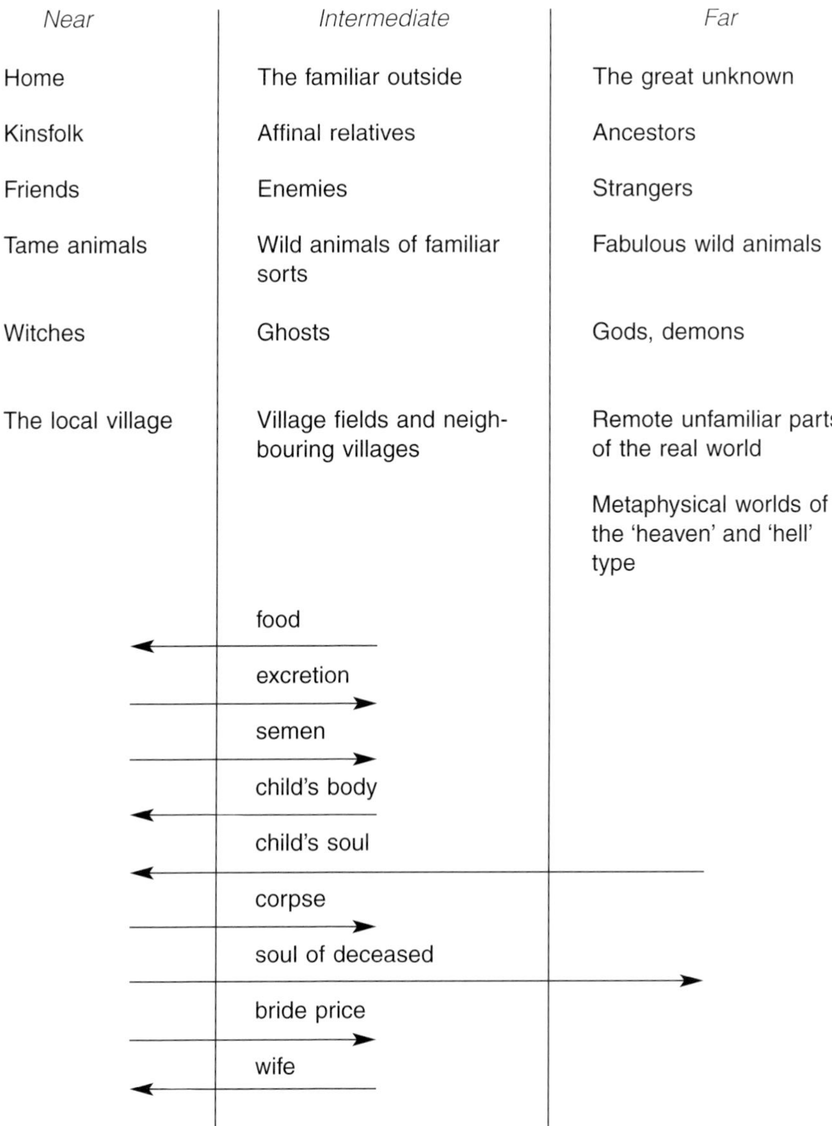

Fig. 1. 'Out-there'.

cleanliness: circumcision and shaving are the most obvious examples, but of a similar kind are the ritual removal of teeth, the cutting off of finger joints, and in extreme cases actual castration. As we shall see presently such ritual acts of body mutilation belong to the same set of ideas as animal sacrifice. They are cleansing rituals. The celebrant moves closer to the divine by discarding a part of his mundane 'dirt', which is the relationship which ties him to the world. The logical outcome of the pursuit of ritual cleanliness by this ascetic path is monastic quietism such as is found, in its most extreme form, in Buddhism. The ideal Buddhist monk pursues cleanliness to a point at which he avoids all physical contact with other human beings. His aim is total passivity, total sexlessness, total avoidance of aggression. In other words he achieves his ritual cleanliness at the cost of life itself. He continues to breathe, but he is socially dead.

There is a kind of pseudo-consistency between this line of thought and the further argument that the dirt which is so carefully removed in order to reach the pure essence of the clean individual must itself be the stuff of life, the stuff of influence, the power of God. Thus we find that throughout the world the extrusions of the body, excreta, urine, menstrual blood, semen, hair clippings, finger nails, foreskins, and, most of all, the detached human phallus, are treated as magical objects, things which have power in themselves or which are vehicles of the power of God. It is in this sense that the trophy heads of the head-hunter are treated as objects which are potent in themselves.

If power lies not in things but in the interstices between things, in relationships, then it may easily be located in 'dirt', the stuff which lies in the interstices between 'clean' categories. The two arguments are the same. The stuff of dirt is a materialisation not only of power but of relationship. Anthropologists who are familiar with such forms of matter as 'witchcraft substance' and 'soul stuff' will take this in their stride; if others find it too difficult let it suffice that, carried to extremes, the dichotomy between cleanliness and material dirtiness sometimes becomes polarised:

(1) The essence of Man is the clean passive monk.

(2) The essence of God (that is of Non-Man) is the potency of aggressive sexuality considered as a thing in itself, most appropriately and most commonly symbolised by the human phallus.

But this schema carries with it the strange idea that the power of God is contaminating in the same way as dirt is contaminating, and this implies that God manifests Himself in epidemics, disasters, earthquakes. We become aware of the supernatural when the predictable orderliness of nature and/or of human society suddenly breaks down.

This line of thought leads to an inversion of the monk's ascetic role. In many societies it is assumed that the path to holiness is not through ascetisism but through ecstacy. A human being who achieves an ecstatic frenzy and no longer behaves like a human being at all is treated as 'inspired by God'. Holy men of this kind usually adopt bizarre, transvestite, ambiguous forms of dress and are physically very dirty. They manifest their power by repudiating membership of all 'normal' clean categories. In his trance state the ecstatic medium claims to straddle the gap between this world and the other. The behaviour of the ascetic monk and the ecstatic medium are respectively intended to evade and to make use of the supremely dangerous potency which lies in the relationship between this world and the other world, that is in the category distinction between life and death. The ritual killing of men and animals is likewise concerned with the control of this particular brand of metaphysical influence.

But first let us consider the nature of killing in general.

Killing

Killing is a classifying operation. We kill our enemies; we do not kill our friends. The resulting category set differs widely as between one society and another. In our own case creatures which are felt to be remote from man, such as insects and fish, can usually be killed quite indiscriminately. But most warm-blooded mammals and birds which have close relations with man, either as predators or as domestic food animals or as pets, are treated with greater respect. We kill them, but only according to set rules of time and place and manner. On the other hand there is here also a special category, vermin which may be exterminated at will.

The killing of men is subject to similar conventions. Human beings who are not 'true men' because they are of a different colour and therefore a different 'race' (i.e. species) have very commonly been classified as vermin, to be hunted down for slavery as in West Africa, exterminated like rats as in Tasmania, or used for target practice as on the north-west frontier of India. Killing of this sort must be excluded from the category of war proper, despite the fact that many so-called wars of colonial conquest have had this form. War proper is an enterprise which entails approximately equivalent risk for both sides. He who kills may get killed himself. In war, as distinct from a rat hunt, the enemy are deserving of respect. Warfare is between men and other men, not men and beasts.

And for those whom we recognise as true men the rules are quite clear: 'Thou shalt not kill except in specific ritual circumstances as shall later be specified', namely (1) in carrying out an execution, a 'legitimate' punishment of one of 'our group', and (2) in war, a 'legitimate killing' of one of 'the others'. In the latter case the proceedings are far from indiscriminate. All sorts of 'rules of war' are supposed to apply. It is proper only to use 'conventional' weapons; enemy wounded must be given proper care; prisoners must be treated with respect; war graves must be recorded; it is unsporting to launch a major attack on Christmas Day, and so on. Such formalities are reminiscent of the English rules for killing grouse and foxes. The killing is a ritual matter, and it is only the ritual which turns yesterday's murder into tomorrow's noblest duty.

We are prone to say of those who die in battle that they have 'sacrificed their lives on behalf of their country'. What do we mean by this? Let us examine the concept of *sacrifice.*

Sacrifice

The ideas about power and soul stuff and cleanliness and interstitial relationships which have been discussed earlier are all relevant. Sacrifice usually entails the ritual killing of an animal. In this respect it resembles the formalised hunting of game or of wild animals rather than the extermination of vermin. Hunting and sacrifice are also similar in that a special relationship (a special potency) already links the slayer with his victim, even before the act. With a few very specialised exceptions a sacrificial animal is always a domestic animal which is the property of the 'giver' of the sacrifice, that is, of the individual who expects to benefit most from the performance of the rite. In the case of formal hunting, although the victim is wild, the hunt itself (e.g. fox-hunting in England) constitutes an institution which permanently links the hunter with the hunted. The sentiments which the relationship entails are markedly ambivalent. In our own society big-game hunters and fox-hunters alike commonly profess to 'love' the animals which they destroy; they react with outraged indignation if anyone suggests that their activities are cruel.

The relationship which associates the victim with his slayer before the event is intensified by the ritual preliminaries to the killing and by the killing itself. The creature that is finally slain is in a mystical sense a part of the killer's own self. The traumatic similarity between the two kinds of killing is shown by the way in which the slayer, sacrificer and hunter alike, often retains a portion of the victim (e.g. the skull, the horns, the brush, the jawbone) as a memorial of his murderous triumph. Such mementoes of death preserve a kind of vicarious relationship with the deceased as do gravestones and war memorials. They evoke in the mind of the beholder some echo of the potency which the original killing generated.

But hunting and sacrifice are not identical. In some respects they are converse. In hunting the act of killing invigorates, in sacrifice it horrifies. The general pattern is perfectly illustrated by the biblical story of Abraham and Isaac. It is Abraham's only son, his most precious possession, a very part of himself, which has to be killed; the eventual killing of the animal, 'the ram caught in a thicket', is only a substitute for this act of self-mutilation. It is the self-mutilation which is magically effective. It is precisely in such a temper that a nation at war sends its sons to the slaughter. The more dreadful the carnage the more beneficial the mystical consequences.

Sacrifice always has elements of a cleansing operation, of cutting away the dross, of setting the sacrificer free from the contamination of his present circumstance.

Since the Christian religion has no place for animal sacrifice we may be inclined to dismiss such institutions as relics of the barbarous. Yet it is easy to show that even in quite mundane affairs our psychological attitudes are similar. On two separate occasions in my life I have been in foreign lands when one or more members of the small local British population has been required to depart in a hurry. On both occasions there was strong moral pressure from the other local Englishmen which required the wanderer to destroy his pets, rather than allow these beloved creatures to live on in relationships with someone else. In this way, the wanderer (and his pets) would be set free. By killing his pets he shakes the dust from his feet. Somewhat oddly, this killing of pets was on both occasions justified as an act of 'kindness' to the pets themselves. The logic of sacrifice is very close to this. The victim which is killed is a sanctified creature. It is itself liberated and made god-like by the act of killing.

In societies which have sacrificial institutions of the more ordinary kind the occasions for making a sacrifice are well defined. The most typical precipitating causes fall into two classes:

(1) the occurrence of misfortune: death, illness, drought, pestilence, etc.
(2) social initiations: at puberty, marriage, accession to office, etc.

In the first case the sacrifice aims to remove the evil influence, in the second it permits readjustments in an established mesh of human relationship. In both cases the sacrificial performance is supposed to bring about a modification of the overall structure of power relationships between gods and men and between men and other men.

If we ask the performers of a sacrifice to explain what they are doing, we are likely to get obscure and self-contradictory answers. A very common statement is that the sacrifice is 'a gift to the gods', and that the gods, on accepting the gift, will be compelled to reciprocate by granting benefits to the sacrificers. Such a theory rests upon a very naive kind of theology. Gods and men are presumed to be beings of comparable species. The Gods live *there*, in the other world, much as men live *here*, in this world, and the relations between the two are such as exist between nations engaged in trade or in war or in the contraction of political alliance.

Naïve theologies of this sort are certainly quite common among primitive peoples but they are quite inadequate as 'explanations' of sacrifice. Even if it makes sense to offer gifts to an unseen deity, the logic by which the killing of a domestic animal can be thought to constitute such a gift is left obscure. And indeed there can be no rational explanation for such an irrational idea. Even so the general structure of the thought processes involved is comprehensible. We must accept the fact that there is a nearly universal feeling that the most potent of all relationships is that which distinguishes the living from the dead and links them together. The power involved, the very power of God Himself, is so terrible that ordinarily we shun it and put it out of mind. But the death of anything, whether natural or accidental or artificially contrived, activates the relationship because it forces us to think about it. A ritual killing does in a very real sense 'generate the power of God' simply because it obliges the beholder to contemplate the mystery of the difference between life and death. The logic by which mystical benefit is felt to accrue from a sacrificial killing then runs something like this: a sacrificer kills a mundane part of himself. In doing this he cuts himself free from the potency of relationships which tie him down to his present situation. But, in addition, the act of killing separates a soul from a body and by identification with the victim the sacrificer is able to feel that it is in fact his own soul that has been thus released (and 'given' to the gods). The true self of the sacrificer has been cleansed; momentarily he has moved himself away from the contaminating imperfections of life here in this world towards the ineffable perfections of life there in the other world. Such magical ideas are not really so far removed from our own. It is much less than a century since 'bleeding' was considered the beneficent medical panacea for all ills.

But if the sacrificial killing of a kinsman or of a tame domestic animal is in some sense a cleansing operation which strengthens the killer's identification with the immortal by rejecting his identification with the mortal, the ritual killing of enemies ought to have an exactly opposite implication. Sacrificial killing projects soul stuff away from the home towards the potencies outside; the killing of enemies projects potencies towards the home. In the case of head-hunting this is quite explicit; the souls of the dead are brought back captive in the heads of the slain and then function as a fertilising, life-renewing force in the homes of the slayers. Similar ideas occur in much less fanciful forms of warfare. Even for us, slaughter of the enemy is not simply a means of averting immediate practical danger. It has a mystical force. The killing gives psychological satisfaction in itself.

Marriage

We may be able to comprehend this curious reciprocity more clearly if we consider certain aspects of marriage. It is murder to kill a member of 'our own group'; it is a deed of valour to kill an enemy. Likewise it is incest to have sex relations with a woman of our own group; but legitimate and proper to have sex relations with a wife, that is with a woman who was originally one of the enemy. One of the few universals of human society is that marriage is always in some degree exogamous. 'Our' young men must find their brides in the ambivalently friendly/hostile outside world.

For a great many primitive peoples the alliance of affines which is established by a marriage is seen as the direct antithesis to a relationship of war. Ethnographers repeatedly give reports of informants who tell them 'We marry our enemies.' Marriage in such society is a means of perpetuation, but it is also a political and economic contract; the husband acquires a wife, but the brother-in-law acquires a bride-price. Bride-price may take many forms; in societies where it is associated with an institution of sacrifice, the same kinds of animals that are sacrificed feature also in the bride-price payments.

It was argued earlier (Fig. 1) that the structure of exchange relationships established by a marriage between 'us' and the 'out-there' is directly comparable to that experienced in the sexual act, or in eating, or in living and dying. To this set of transactions we can now add warfare.

There is often an explicit association between cycles of marriage alliance and cycles of ritualised warfare. Group A marries with Group B and forms an alliance; they quarrel, probably over a woman; they go to war; they make peace, by forming an alliance, that is by inter-marriage, and the cycle starts again. The allies of today are the enemies of yesterday and the enemies of tomorrow. In such a context, when a political alliance is established by a marriage, it is not sufficient just to transfer a wife to her husband. There must be elaborate ceremonial, gifts and counter-gifts and often a holocaust of sacrifices to dead ancestors to remove the taint of previous enmity. But, besides the killings, there must also be gifts of live animals which pass from the bridegroom's party to the bride's party.

In such marriages live animals are given away to 'the enemy' in exchange for a woman who will bring future benefit in the form of children; this closely parallels the ideology of sacrifice where the souls of sacrificed animals are said to be 'given' to the god in exchange for future benefits in the form of health and prosperity. Thus, in sum, there is an equation between 'affinal relatives', 'the enemy', and 'God'. In the context of head-hunting the captured enemy head is treated as a part of the other world, an object potent in itself. So also in the context of marriage the wife who is brought in from outside is a creature of inherent danger; not only a source of children but also a potential witch.

Women are necessarily given out as wives as well as taken in. Sometimes the exchange is direct, sometimes indirect, but always the element of reciprocity is there. Whereas sacrifice (the giving of souls to the outside) balances the ritual slaying of enemies (the taking of souls from the outside), so also the giving of sisters balances the taking of wives. Both systems, one metaphysical, the other physical, constitute structures of relationship of the same kind, and many primitive peoples would certainly hold that warfare is 'necessary for survival' *in just the same sense* as marriage is 'necessary for survival'. In our enlarged modern world the people we marry are not the same as the people we fight, and this kind of equation no longer applies, but it may still be worth reflection that to ask men to give up the institution of war is the same kind of request as asking them to give up marriage and the worship of God.

But how does this analysis of the elements of head-hunting bear on the nature of war? Modern warfare is conducted with massive support from the most sophisticated scientific apparatus; it seems the very antithesis of a natural phenomenon. Yet, regardless of cost, the leaders of all nations, including even the smallest and least formidable, feel impelled to invest in tanks and aircraft and guided missiles. Such men are acting out parts in an established drama and the drama has them in thrall; they cannot control what they do. But even a dance of death must have a cause. Causes lie at different levels, not only the elemental drives of the individual human psyche and the 'rational' motives of political and economic gain, but also functions which lie within the structure of society as such.

Socialisation is a process of restraint rather than repression. Man has created institutions which channel the dangerous aggressive urges of the individual into modes of expression which are relatively harmless to the home society, whatever the consequences may be for those in the world outside. Warfare, religious ritual, and exogamous marriage are all institutions of this kind. My essay has been designed to show up some of the interconnections between these three frames of reference as well as their links with basic underlying motives of the individual.

Running through everything that I have said is a principle of duality. This has its ultimate paradigm both in our human recognition of the difference between life and death, and in our animal recognition of the difference between the sexes. In every case, both in reality and in ritual, fertility and life are the outcome of an activation of the relationship between the 'I' and the 'other' which results from male aggression (which may be either sexual or combative). In a sexual context the 'other' is a woman;' in a head-hunting context, it is 'the enemy'; in a sacrificial context, it is 'God'. The fact that in the case of sacrifice the aggression is directed against the self (as an act of self-mutilation) rather than against the 'other' is not of great relevance, for in the immediate context of a sacrificial killing there is a mystical merging of the donor, the victim, and the god and there is a sense in which the aggression is directed against all three.

The unpleasant implication of my argument is that this is true also of modern war. In a mystical sense warfare, precisely at its most horrible moments, establishes a momentary bridge between this world and the other. Illogically, yet very fundamentally, the slaughter of the enemy and the slaughter of one's own side are *both* felt to be 'the supreme sacrifice', a mystical sexual union of man and God.

Mystical notions of this sort are not amenable to common sense. It would be quite wrong to suppose that just because it is self-evident that warfare is disastrous it is equally self-evident that warfare should be avoided. Disasters are manifestations of divine intervention and some may feel that to court disaster is the surest way of summoning God to our aid. Likewise we should not imagine that an exaggerated pacifist disposition is a secure safeguard against indulgence in warlike violence. Puritan ascetics can all too easily persuade themselves that, as saints of God, their duty calls them to bring fire and slaughter upon the heathen. Holy wars in defence of peace are of great antiquity.

What is to be done about it? Is the moral of my story simply that human society suffers from a kind of collective death wish, so that the sublimated satisfaction of our animal drives urges us like Gadarene swine to rush headlong to destruction? I think this *is* the implication of my story, but the fact that we suffer from a collective death wish does not mean that we must respond to it. For the trouble lies in a 'category mistake'. There is a very widespread human tendency to make an association between the notion of 'divine power' on the one hand and two different manifestations of aggression on the other: 'killing' and 'male sexuality'. This is a curious triangle of ideas and it seems to arise because, even at the sub-human animal level of existence, killing and male sexuality are very closely interlocked. But there is no necessity for us to make this kind of identification, and the more thoroughly we can understand what we are doing the more likely it is that we shall free ourselves from our predicament.

It is much too simple a formula to say that we kill things, including the enemy and ourselves, because we are afraid of our own sexuality, but that is roughly the drift of my argument. If we all had a clearer more rational understanding of the way that sexual drives operate, we might be much less inclined to fly off the handle and start imitating the ritual dances of Borneo head-hunters.

Notes

This paper is an expansion of one read to a conference on 'Factors in the Aetiology of War' (Oxford, 10–12 July 1964). The original paper was printed in the *Bulletin of the Medical Society for the Prevention of War*. The expanded text, reproduced here, was published in *Disarmament and Arms Control* in 1965.

1. In preparing this paper I have borrowed ideas indiscriminately from the writings of sundry anthropological colleagues but in particular from J. H. Hutton, M. Fortes, C. Lévi-Strauss, Mary Douglas, and J. R. Goody.
2. See Berg, *The Unconscious Significance of Hair*; Leach, 'Magical Hair' (II.3.2).

4.4

Profanity in Context (1977/1980)

Until fairly recently, when it became permissible to print 'four-letter words' without restriction, the serious literature on this topic (which everyone finds absorbingly interesting) either took the form of pornography, dressed up as scholarship, or else became buried in specialised dictionaries of argot or journals of linguistics. And even then editors had their problems. As late as 1957 a scholarly journal published by the University of Toronto which printed an item about the difference between vocal and printed versions of bawdy songs carried the footnote: 'The Canadian Criminal Code has made it necessary to delete thirty-six lines of verse from the examples given in this article: These lines, of course, deal with the very things about which the author writes.'

Things are now rather better, but Edward Sagarin's *The Anatomy of Dirty Words* (1962) has yet to be improved upon. In the present essay I am not so much concerned with 'dirty words' as such as with the relationship between 'dirty words' and other words and with the contexts in which the use of such words comes to be considered a profanity.

Profanity here has the weak general sense of 'the vulgar language of abuse', but there is also a strong sense where it equates with blasphemy. The two meanings are closely related so the surprising prosecution of *Gay News* for publishing a blasphemous libel provides a convenient starting-point.[1]

The verdict evoked a long correspondence in *The Times* which served to confirm my own assessment of the matter. Opinion was very divided. The theologians were mostly put out, they regretted that the prosecution had been started at all. Deities, after all, can presumably look after themselves, so if a human judge and jury feel that they must inflict punishment upon their fellows for insulting the Almighty it must be because they fear that in His indignation He will inflict quite indiscriminate punishment upon the general public if they do not. This view of divine retribution is common enough in primitive society but it is an odd interpretation of the ethics of Christianity!

But leaving the Deity aside, why did the judge and jury feel so shocked? I suggest that it may be relevant that

(1) The offending matter was illustrated poetry and not prose. The mode of expression was thus purportedly metaphoric–synthetic, which is the normal convention for all religious discourse.

(2) The poem had an adorational theme which used the metaphor of homosexual relationship to express the love of the poet for his God. But the references to homosexual intercourse were very explicit. They were cast in the metonymic–analytic mode, which is the form of speech in which we ordinarily talk about practical mundane affairs.

(3) Neither the poet nor the channel of publication could claim special privileged status. *Gay News* was not a 'learned', 'scientific', 'medical', or 'theological' journal; James Kirkup's renown as an established poet was too restricted to allow him to get away with it.

My thesis is that the prosecution's success depended upon the combination of these factors rather than on the content of the poem in isolation. When the present Bishop of Kingston, speaking in plain prose with the authority of a recognised theologian, suggested some years ago that Jesus may have been homosexual there was some fluttering of journalistic dovecots but no major scandal ensued.

The issue then is one of context. Broadly speaking, behaviour which is tabooed in a secular context is behaviour which is characteristic of a sacred context. In secular contexts we endeavour, so far as possible, to keep metaphor and metonymy apart; in sacred contexts we systematically mix them. For the purposes of such analysis sexual intercourse and the associated discourse of lovers is a sacred context. I hope to justify that last, perhaps surprising, proposition during the course of my paper.

This is not the place to elaborate a full-scale framework of structuralist theory but some further explanation of the contrast between metaphor and metonymy may be called for. Metaphor is synthetic; it is the 'unmotivated' assertion of similarity, the associations are arbitrary: 'My love is a rose.' In metaphor quite contradictory assertions are acceptable as equally and simultaneously true. 'God is a Father', 'God is a Son', 'God is a Holy Spirit.' Metonymy is analytic; it is the recognition of association by contiguity; it is a matter of taking things to pieces and showing what is the case by distinguishing one thing at a time, in sequence, as in anatomical dissection or logical demonstration.

In all ordinary vernacular languages normal conversation tends to mix up the metaphoric and metonymic poles of expression, but it is a peculiar feature of our contemporary industrial society that a special type of discourse – logical, mathematical, scientific – from which metaphor is largely excluded has acquired exceptional prestige – and this is discriminated from a complementary field of discourse, that of 'art', from which metonymy is largely excluded.

In this modern context the paradox of the Christian religion, particularly in its Protestant forms, is that it tries to have it both ways. Christians explicitly affirm that the 'truth' of the Gospel story is metonymic and actual (as in science and history), as well as metaphoric and symbolic (as in painting and poetry).

In a formal sense the central mystery of Christianity has always been that Jesus was both an ordinary mortal man capable of ordinary human suffering and also an immortal God born into this world by supernatural means; but, in the context of contemporary society, which separates the metonymic from the metaphoric to an unprecedented degree, it has become increasingly difficult to accept this challenge to common sense.

If Jesus was an ordinary mortal he should have had ordinary human sexual appetites. A variety of Christian mystics, including St Teresa and St John of the Cross, have expanded on this point, though they have usually done so by resort to metaphor. Likewise many mediaeval Christmas carols contain picturesque references to the sexual attributes of the Deity which Mrs Whitehouse would almost certainly rate as obscene if she understood what they meant. But latterly, with our metonymic insistence on calling spades spades, the theology of educated laymen has been slipping back from dyophysite orthodoxy (Christ-Jesus is fully Man as well as fully God) into monophysite heresy (God and Man are beings of wholly different kinds) so that the anatomical attributes of Jesus Christ cannot be thought about. A few professional theologians have used their privileged position as 'authorities' to discuss such matters, but for lay Christians, who have usually been taught at school, not only that logical, metonymic thinking is 'correct', but also that 'sin' equates with 'sex', it seems rather obvious that a sinless Christ must also be sexless.

This leads back to my earlier point that profanity is always delimited by social context. Although the verbal content is far from arbitrary it is only in certain contexts that the relevant words are thought to be shocking, and it is always the situation of profanity, rather than the words as such, which generates excitement. In the vocabularly of verbal expletives all the words are metaphoric of the same thing . . . whatever that thing may be. Any one word is the equivalent of any other: fuck, shit, Christ, bugger, damn, and a score of others may all be evoked by precisely the same situation according to the personal predilection of the speaker.

However there are some interesting and rather puzzling complications and variations. In any one context and for any one speaker there is a hierarchy of intensity for such 'swear words', though the principle on which the hierarchy is based is not obvious. The facts are difficult to research because of the lack of reliable literary evidence and the operation of euphemism. Most English males of my own social class and generation would have felt that the sequence in which the five taboo words listed above have been arranged places them in declining order of 'badness'. I am told that females of the same species rarely used sexual terms at all; they usually found adequate cathartic release in very attentuated, euphemised, 'religious' terms such as 'hell-(p)', 'Hades'. On the other hand at just this same period (*c.* 1930) there were workshop situations where all the male operatives used the word 'fucking' as a kind of all-purpose adjective to slow down the rate of discourse, for example, 'give me that fucking hammer to drive this fucking nail into this fucking board'. In this context this word, which was still shocking for the middle class and still legally unprintable on grounds of obscenity, carried no 'expletive' quality whatsoever. At the present time differences in such usages as between the sexes, members of particular social classes, and particular local districts have probably been much reduced, but there is still an immense amount of variation. And in any case it is always the situation rather than the lexicon which decides whether or not any particular expression is or is not a profanity and the gravity of that profanity.

And so also in the *Gay News* case, it was the event rather than the content which really mattered. It was quite obvious, for example, that a high proportion of those who felt driven to let off steam by writing to *The Times* had not actually ready the offending poem. Moreover nearly all of those who challenged the fairness of the judicial verdict relied upon an argument about context rather than content. And this seems very reasonable. It certainly seems likely that at least some of the very restricted readership for whom the poem was originally intended would have seen the author's sexual fantasy as adorational and serious. But in the Establishment Christianity represented by the judiciary, the Deity is male, sexless, and authoritarian; consequently, in an English Court of Law, any explicit mixture of human sexuality with divine asexuality constitutes gross disrespect to the Establishment itself.

At this point let me cut a few corners and offer a preliminary definitional hypothesis: 'It is a general principle of human thinking that incongruity of context, "matter out of place", ("dirt" in the language of Lord Chesterfield and Mary Douglas), evokes sentiments of alarm, awe, and respect. Blasphemy–profanity, both in the strong and in the weak sense, is the offence of treating a congeries of incongruities with disrespect and thus blurring the distinction between the religiously awful and the comic.'

Where does comedy come into it? Not perhaps on the surface but underneath. 'Swearing' and laughter are both psychologically cathartic.

Laughter is a very complicated psycho-physical reaction and it should not be taken for granted that all situations which are considered to be comic have something in common; but it is very obvious that, in any total inventory of joke stories and practical jokes, two broad categories would be extremely prominent: (1) 'dirty jokes', focused around sexual and excretory activity, and (2) 'role reversal jokes', in which the social persons to whom we are ordinarily expected to defer – policeman, magistrate, business manager, schoolmaster, vicar, mother-in-law, leaders of any kind – are shown up as ridiculous. But if pushed too far this kind of frivolity becomes sacrilege.

Here again fashions change. The extent to which the caricaturists of the Rowlandson era made a mock of the ruling monarch (who in those days exercised genuine political power) would today be considered quite intolerable; on the other hand, over the years, mocking the Deity has become decreasingly dangerous. Even if *Gay News* can still be fined for blasphemy, Mr Kirkup runs no risk of being burnt at the stake for heresy. (I should however make clear that, whatever *The Times* correspondents may have imagined, no intentional mockery of the Deity was in fact involved.)

There are many ways by which the dignity of office may be mocked. Many of them involve the inappropriate use of the uniforms and insignia by which the legitimacy of the office and its authority are ordinarily affirmed. But sexual undertones are usually discernible; fancy dress and music-hall or pantomime comedy is very frequently transvestite.

One of the relevant 'incongruities' in such cases is that which comes through in the ambivalent meaning of our English word 'potency' (and its opposite 'impotence'). In common usage potency (= power) is an attribute of God, of persons in authority, of the prime movers of machines, and of males in sexual intercourse. In polite discourse these several meanings are kept apart; so much so that the actual word 'potency' (as distinct from 'power') is now seldom used except in a sexual context. But the fact that very similar metaphors crop up in many different languages shows that the cross-references must be based in some fundamental kind of natural common sense.

The outrage in the *Gay News* case was that the poet pointedly equated sexual potency with divine potency, an equation which Protestant Christianity has declared to be taboo, though in the great majority of human societies this equation is taken for granted. In Saivite Hinduism, for example, the metonymic sign of Deity is a *lingam* which is almost explicitly a human phallus. Half a century ago Katherine Mayo, a Mary Whitehouse of her day, made a proper killing out of this topic and was closely imitated by many others. *Mother India* went through twelve impressions between 1927 and 1930 while Arthur Miles's *The Land of the Lingam* went through four impressions in the course of two months in 1933! It is thus interesting that the plain rectilinear Crusaders' Cross, which is now standard in Protestant Churches, and which was adopted as a Christian symbol relatively late, has historical links with the Egyptian *ankh* (the sign for 'life') which was also, in origin, a stylised phallus.

Let me come clean about what I am saying here. *Power* lies at the interface between separable categories. If A and B are recognised as separate entities in dynamic relationship, then power flows either from A to B or from B to A and the channel through which it flows is the interface boundary which is common to both. The metaphorical equivalence of the potency of sexual intercourse and the potency of Deity thus turns on the fact that in sexual embrace the sensory distinction between 'I' and 'Other' disappears, while in a context of religious worship the distinction between the devotee and his deity disappears, and death becomes life.

Perhaps it will help if I put the same argument in rather a different way. Mystical ideas (such as 'the power of God') are synthetic and metaphorical. They are generated in the first place by the superimposition of a variety of non-congruent ideas which are somehow felt to belong together. At the bottom of all such piled-up metaphors there is always a 'primitive' notion, derived from the thinker's own childhood, which expresses the ultimate category distinction of human consciousness, the difference between 'I' and 'Other'. As the Freudians have very well understood, these primary verbal symbolisations of the 'I'/'Other' opposition are inextricably entangled with the oral, anal, and genital experiences of early childhood. If I am to develop the consciousness of myself as distinct from 'Other' I must learn that my mother's breast is not part of me, that my faecal excretions are not part of me, but also, ultimately and in a very complicated sense, that my genitals are both part of me and part of 'Other'.

In our kind of social system we contrast mystical ideas with rational thought. Where mystical ideas are synthetic and metaphoric, one thing piled on top of another in ambiguity and confusion, rational thought depends upon analysis and metonymic association, upon taking complexities to pieces and looking at each of them in turn, one at a time, one after another. The links between the pieces are logical and mechanical like the relationships which bring together the various named components of the human anatomy; by contrast, the links between the component elements of mystical ideas are quite arbitrary and depend simply upon the *assertion* of similarity or identity.

I have already made the point that our literate, high-technology, 'scientific' system attempts, to an unusual degree, to keep the metonymic and metaphoric poles of thinking apart; but, besides that, our modern education leads us to deny that poetic (metaphoric) imagery can lead to any sort of truth. Scientific method is a procedure for eliminating metaphoric error.

Even in less materialistic societies the need to avoid total confusion has always made it necessary to establish conventional rules which will discriminate metonymic relations from metaphoric relations and thus allow the actor to perceive his surroundings as full of separate 'things' rather than just a mess of superimposed sensory stimuli. For we only manage to recognise things as things and events as events by refusing to recognise the spatial and temporal boundaries where one chunk of space-time merges into the next. This is what cultural conventions are all about.

We become aware of the existence of the world around us because of sensory inputs which reach the brain through our eyes, ears, nose, skin, tongue, etc. but we interpret those inputs according to preconceived expectations which are to a large extent determined by the way we have been reared and the way the categories of our language usage cuts things up. We inhabit a *man-made* world, not simply because generations of men have operated upon it by clearing forests, building houses and roads and machines and so on but because we can only recognise the world through the conceptual model which we make with verbal categories in our minds. That world, the model of reality which we hold in our heads and the expression of the model which we have imposed on the world out-there, has to be orderly so that we can understand it and, as it were, find our way about in it. The model world is made orderly by rules; rules which say that certain kinds of verbal and behavioural categories must be kept apart and not mixed up. The rules vary very greatly from one society to another; the infringement of such rules is what constitutes a profanity, a breach of taboo, in the context of that society.

Well that is all very grand and theoretical but what has it really got to do with sexual obscenity, knocking off policemen's helmets, or jokes about the mother-in-law?

Perhaps you will begin to see the connection if I draw your attention to another set of verbal associations which crop up repeatedly in all sorts of different linguistic contexts. Cock = male bird = human penis has been around in various European contexts at least since the Athens of the fourth century BC. In the United States the bird has now become a 'rooster'. Latin *cunnus* is the source of English *cunt* and late mediaeval French *con*. But French *connil*, *connin* = English *coney* was the animal we now call a rabbit. In sixteenth-century French love poetry and English Puritan tracts this play on words is explicit, as also in the eighteenth-century term *cunny-house* = brothel. But where coney turned into rabbit for adults, it turned into *bunny* for children, whence it has re-emerged as a title suitable for the ambiguous ladies in *Playboy* magazine's various entertainments for men! Pussy = domestic cat = female pubic hair. In England ass = donkey but in various dialects arse = buttocks is pronounced ass; but in the United States ass = buttocks ≠ donkey!

A common principle seems to be at work. On the one hand there is a tendency to use the names of very close and familiar animals as metaphors for the private parts of the human anatomy; on the other we encounter a puritanical sensitivity which vetoes the animal metaphor as well as the sexual organ for which it stands.

A variety of other domestic animals are made to serve a rather similar purpose which is likewise double-faced. It is a rather *mild* form of *derogatory abuse* to identify Other with any of the following: pig, dog, bitch, ass, goat, goose, cat. But another set of 'close' animals are used as epithets of *affection*: chick, lamb, kitten, dove, mouse, duck. A few wild animals which have no legitimate status in the domestic home serve in this way as a rather *severe* form of *abuse*. It is far more offensive to call someone an ape or a reptile or a rat than an ass, a goat, or a goose. There are two intriguing exceptions to this general pattern. Although it is a domestic animal, 'swine' is rather strongly abusive, perhaps because it is felt to be a foreign word (German *Schwein*) rather than normal English. To call someone an owl is the equivalent of goose. But the owl is wild, not tame; furthermore, according to literary tradition, it is linked with Minerva in her capacity as the Goddess of Wisdom! And there are other cases too where the literary ancestry can be traced all the way back to Aesop's Fables. But antiquity is not the point; such usages would not have survived if they did not somehow seem appropriate. I would emphasise again that most of the epithets are *mild*; the abusive variants are scurrilous rather than obscene. Nevertheless they lie right on the boundary of polite speech as is shown by the fact that, at least in American English, *a silly ass* is barely distinguishable from a *silly prick*.

But why do we find this kind of animal imagery 'appropriate'? Appropriate for what? What is at issue, I suggest, is the representation of *power*. As I argued earlier, power lies in the interface of separable categories; but power itself is then an ambiguity, both A and not-A, and when we try to express such ambiguities through the symbolism of language or behaviour we generate a logical contradiction which is emotionally upsetting and which then evokes censorship and taboo. Here is an example. In the course of the evolution of the English language the Old English morpheme *cwene* (woman), which survives in Dutch as *kween* (a barren cow) and is closely linked with the English four-letter obscenity *quim* (cunt), came to mean (a) a female monarch and (b) a prostitute. This not only constitutes a perfect example of the A/not-A formula but also corresponds to the religious ideology of Catholicism where Mary the Sinless Virgin is a sort of double of Mary Magdalene, the Repentant Sinner. But the overlap of these sensitive religious–sexual–political ideas was intolerable. First *queen* (the monarch) was discriminated from *quean* (the prostitute) by using a different spelling, and then *quean* (the prostitute) was virtually dropped from the lexicon altogether.

The point about domestic animal metaphors is that they allow such paradoxes to be talked about without provoking a drastic sequence of taboo reactions. Sometimes of course the process breaks down – the American rejection of the 'cock' and 'ass' metaphors are cases in point – but on the whole it works. Because we cannot take our domestic animals very seriously – they are, after all, like children, fully under our control – our pets allow us to evoke in permissible form, vicariously and at one remove, the deepest and most private sexual experiences. Pussy on my lap, who is also a vicious cat, is quite safe from prosecution for blasphemy or obscenity. Even the tough-minded Dr Kinsey found it polite to write 'petting to climax' instead of 'mutual masturbation'. But why pets and domestic animals?

The point here is that the basic discrimination which separates 'I' from 'Other' becomes a transformation not only of the opposition Man/God but also of Tame/Wild, Humanity/Animality, and in the anthropologist's language, Culture/Nature. Man everywhere has to define himself as a disciplined human being against the uncontrollable Other, 'Nature in the Wild' out there. But living creatures do not form in this respect a single unitary class; some are close, some are far; some are friends, some are enemies; some we can control, some are beyond our control. Looked at in this way the spectrum represented by the categories: pets, farm animals, game animals, wild animals, places them in a hierarchy 'near' to 'far', 'tame' to 'wild', 'controllable' to 'uncontrollable' and can serve as an 'appropriate' metaphor or transformation for other such spectra. For example, see the schema in Fig. 1.

To read this schema assume that each horizontal line is a transformation (metaphoric substitution) for any other. The three columns A, B, C between them cover the whole of the interface between the opposed major categories I/Other, Common Man/God. Power (potency) is manifested in the subcategories associated with each of the three columns but the potency gets greater as we move from left to right; likewise attitudes of respect and taboo become

	A	B	C	
I				Other
Common Man				God
	pets	farm animals	game animals	wild animals
	members of my domestic family	neighbours	affines	strangers
	incest: unmentionable sex behaviour	illegitimate but recognised sex behaviour	legitimate sex behaviour (marriage)	no sexual relations
	policeman	magistrate	earthly ruler	
	priest	saint	incarnate deity	
	joking coupled with affection	joking coupled with hostility	formalised 'joking relationships'; 'privileged familiarity'	
	weak obscenity	strong obscenity	blasphemy	
	common use of animal joking metaphors	relatively uncommon use of animal joking metaphors	animal metaphors unusual but, when used, regarded as highly offensive	

Fig. 1. Schema of potency and obscenity.

intensified as we move from left to right. You can make fun about the *dog* collar worn by the vicar but you come close to blasphemy if you point out that *dog* written backwards reads *god*! When joking behaviour appears in column C it is highly formalised as in a game. Hence we play ritualised games with our *game* animals carefully preserving them at one time of the year and hunting them with elaborate ritual at another. The 'joking relationships' between affines which have repeatedly been described by social anthropologists take on this same formalised unspontaneous form, as do mother-in-law jokes in our own society. A widely syndicated strip cartoon which appears daily in the *Cambridge Evening News* has produced roughly one such joke a week for the past ten years or more!

We can now get back to the original issue of profanity and incongruity. Profanity of the kind which arouses passionate scandal (for example that exhibited in the *Gay News* case) occurs when the conventions implied in my schema are ignored. For example, the ultra-hostile strong obscenity *mother-fucker* implies that I is accusing a neighbourly Column B Other of incest. As Sagarin has noted, this term is 'unique in its ability to incite aggressive anger even among people who have developed an armour of defence against the insults derived from obscenity'. According to the theory I am advancing in this paper the enormous emotive force of this expression, in this particular context, arises because of its interface (potency) position between Columns A and C (given a cultural background impregnated with Christian theological ideas).

In Column A, according to Freud, accusations of incest with the mother are constantly thought about but never mentioned, while in Column C the incest of the Deity with His own mother constitutes the inexpressible essence of the mystery of the Incarnation.

And this takes us back to the *Gay News* case. James Kirkup's poem nowhere employs the language of obscenity but the images evoked by the poem may well have evoked echoes of such obscene language in the minds of the judge and jury. In particular, verse four, which has come in for special denunciation, may have evoked the crudely sexual, though not particularly emotive, Column B obscenity *cocksucker*. In that case the jury may have felt completely outraged that such language, even by implication, should be shifted to Column C.

But if this is a valid interpretation of what happened then it would seem that the members of the jury were not very well informed about the finer contextual nuances of obscene language! Earlier on I recorded the use of *fucking* as an all-purpose adjective which is entirely devoid of emotive content, and similarly Sagarin notes of *cocksucker* that 'a man addicted to the use of this word may find it handy thirty or forty times during an evening of conversation'; it is applicable to members of either sex, to 'any reprobate, any contemptible person, anyone who is to be insulted or defamed, anyone crossing one's path'. I admit that many English people do find this term peculiarly offensive though just why this should be so is far from clear; it is not self-evident that it is any 'worse' than its inverse, the adjective *henpecked*! Although Kirkup did not in fact use the word (or any other obscenity) comparison of his text with what has been written about it by the legal pundits (for example M. S. Samuels in *The Times* correspondence of 25 July 1977) suggests that it was only because he *might* have so used it that the jury could conclude that the poem was 'so obscene or scurrilous as to vilify the Christian religion and be calculated or tend to arouse strong feelings of resentment which could lead to a breach of the peace'.

Robert Graves once told the story of how a patient in a military hospital when asked by the lady visitor where he had been wounded could only reply: 'I'm sorry, Ma'am; I don't know: I never learnt Latin.' Perhaps if blasphemy by verbal association becomes a general fashion we shall need, in common prudence, to amend the well-known formula to 'The Law is a Derrière'.

Notes

This essay first appeared in the journal *New Scientist*, 20 October 1977. The text which appears here is a slightly expanded version, which was published in Cherfas and Lewin (eds), *Not Work Alone* (1980).

1. In June 1976 the magazine *Gay News* published a poem called 'The Love that Dares to Speak its Name', by James Kirkup. The poem was a fantasy of a Roman centurion describing his homosexual love for Jesus. Mrs Mary Whitehouse, self-appointed guardian of decency in Britain, brought a private prosecution against the editor, publisher, and distributor of *Gay News*, charging them with blasphemous libel. The case was heard in July 1977 and the jury returned a verdict of guilty by a majority of ten to two (the smallest majority allowed in English law). The editor was fined £500 and given a nine-month prison sentence, suspended for eighteen months. The publisher was fined £1000. The Criminal Division of the Appeal Court heard their appeal in February 1978 and delivered judgment a month later. It upheld the verdict of the lower court, but quashed the prison sentence. Finally, in February 1979, the House of Lords also upheld the original verdict of guilty, but again by the smallest possible majority of three to two. To reprint the poem here would be to invite a further prosecution for blasphemous libel.

References

Ahern, Emily, 'The Problem of Efficacy: Strong and Weak Illocutionary Acts'. *Man* (n.s.), 14/1 (1979).

Anderson, J., *Mandalay to Momien* (London, 1871).

Anon., 'Rule in Class'. *New Society* (15 August 1974).

Ardrey, Robert, *The Territorial Imperative* (New York, 1966).

Arens, W., *The Man-Eating Myth* (Oxford, 1978).

Ashley Montagu, M. F., *Coming into Being among the Australian Aborigines* (London, 1937).

—, *Man and Aggression* (New York, 1968).

Aslib (Association of Special Libraries and Information Bureaux, London), 'Symposium on Classification'. *Aslib Proceedings*, 14/8 (1962).

Austin, J. L., *How to Do Things with Words* (Oxford, 1962).

Austin, L., 'Procreation among the Trobriand Islanders'. *Oceania*, 5 (1934).

Baines, J., 'Temple Symbolism'. *Royal Anthropological Institute News*, 15 (1976).

Banerjea, J. N., 'The Hindu Concept of God', in K. W. Morgan (ed.), *The Religion of the Hindus* (New York, 1953).

Barnes, John, *Models and Interpretations* (Cambridge, 1990).

Bataille, Georges, *Eroticism* (London, 1962).

Bateson, Gregory, *Naven* (Cambridge, 1936).

—, *Steps to an Ecology of Mind* (London, 1972).

—, *Mind and Nature: A Necessary Unity* (London, 1979).

Beals, Alan R., *Gopalpur: A South Indian Village* (New York, 1962).

Beard, Mary, 'Frazer, Leach, and Virgil: The Popularity (and Unpopularity) of *The Golden Bough*'. *Comparative Studies in Society and History*, 34 (1992).

Beattie, John, 'Understanding and Explanation in Social Anthropology'. *British Journal of Sociology*, 10 (1959).

—, *Other Cultures* (London, 1964).

Benedict, P. K., 'Thai, Kadai, and Indonesian: A New Alignment in Southeastern Asia'. *American Anthropologist*, 44 (1942).

Benedict, Ruth, *Patterns of Culture* (London, 1935).

—, *The Chrysanthemum and the Sword* (Boston, 1946).

Bentzen, Aage, *Introduction to the Old Testament*, 4th edn (Copenhagen, 1958).

Berg, Charles, *The Unconscious Significance of Hair* (London, 1951).

Berndt, R. M., and C. H. Berndt, *Sexual Behaviour in Western Arnhem Land* (New York, 1951).

Bernstein, Basil, *Class, Codes, and Control* (London, 1971).

Bertalanffy, L. von, *General Systems Theory: Foundations, Development, Applications* (New York, 1968).

Besterman, T., *A Bibliography of Sir James Frazer, O. M.* (London, 1934).

Bettelheim, Bruno, *Symbolic Wounds* (London, 1955).

Bloch, Maurice, 'Symbols, Song and Dance and Features of Articulation'. *Archives européennes de sociologie*, 15 (1974).

—, *From Blessing to Violence* (Cambridge, 1986).

Boas, Franz, *Primitive Art* (Oslo, 1927).

Bohannan, Paul, *Social Anthropology* (New York, 1963).

Bohannan, Laura, and Paul Bohannan, *The Tiv of Central Nigeria* (London, 1953).

Bourdieu, Pierre, *Outline of a Theory of Practice* (Cambridge, 1977).

Bowra, Maurice, 'Dance, Drama, and the Spoken Word'. *Philosophical Transactions of the Royal Society of London*, Series B, 251 (1966).

Brandon, S. G. F., 'The Myth and Ritual Position Critically Considered', in S. H. Hooke (ed.), *Myth, Ritual, and Kingship* (Oxford, 1958).

Brend, W. A., *Sacrifice to Attis* (London, 1936).

British Museum, *Handbook to the Ethnographical Collections*, 2nd edn (London, 1925).

Brown, George, *Melanesians and Polynesians* (London, 1910).

Buffon, George-Louis Leclerc, *Histoire naturelle, générale et particulière*, 18 vols (Paris, 1785–91).

Bulmer, R., 'Why the Cassowary is Not a Bird'. *Man*, 2 (1967).

Butler, E. M., *The Myth of the Magus* (Cambridge, 1948).

Cady, John F., *A History of Modern Burma* (Ithaca, 1958).

Carnap, Rudolf, *Introduction to Symbolic Logic and its Applications* (New York, 1958).

Carrapiett, W. J. S., *The Kachin Tribes of Burma* (Rangoon, 1929).

Carstairs, G. Morris, *The Twice-Born* (London, 1957).

Cartland, B., *Romantic Royal Weddings* (London, 1984).

Cartman, J., *Hinduism in Ceylon* (Colombo, 1957).

Cassianus, J., *Works* (trans. E. S. S. Gibson), in H. Wace and P. Schaff (eds), *Nicene and Post Nicene Fathers*, Series 2, vol. 11 (Oxford, 1894).

Chadwick, W. O. (ed.), *John Cassian: A Study in Primitive Monasticism*, 2nd edn (Cambridge, 1968).

—, *Western Asceticism: Selected Translations from the* Vitae Patrum, *the Conferences of Cassian and the Rule of Benedict* (London, 1958).

Charbonnier, Georges (ed.), *Conversations with Claude Lévi-Strauss* (London, 1969).

Chauvet, S., *Art de Nouvelle Guinée* (Paris, 1930).

Chavannes, A.-C., *Anthropologie, ou science générale de l'homme* (Lausanne, 1788).

Cherfas, J. and R. Lewin (eds), *Not Work Alone: A Cross-Cultural View of Activities Superfluous to Survival* (London, 1980).

Cherry, C., *On Human Communication* (Cambridge MA, 1957).
Cheyne, T. K., and J. S. Black, *Encyclopaedia Biblica*, 4 vols (London, 1899–1903).
Chomsky, Noam, *Syntactic Structures* (The Hague, 1957).
Clifford, James, and George E. Marcus (eds), *Writing Culture: The Poetics and Politics of Ethnography* (Berkeley, 1986).
Coedès, G., *Angkor: An Introduction* (Hong Kong, 1963).
Cook, S. A., 'Jews', in *Encyclopaedia Britannica*, 14th edn (1929).
Cooke, S. M., 'Nazarite', in James Hastings (ed.), *Encyclopaedia of Religion and Ethics*, vol. 9 (Edinburgh, 1917).
Cornford, F. M., 'Mystery Religions and Pre-Socratic Philosophy'. *Cambridge Historical Magazine*, 14 (1926).
Crapanzano, Vincent, *Tuhami: Portrait of a Moroccan* (Chicago, 1980).
Crawley, E., *The Mystic Rose* (London, 1927).
Darwin, Charles R., and A. R. Wallace, *Evolution by Natural Selection* (London, 1858).
Deng, F. M., *The Dinka of the Sudan* (New York, 1972).
Desai, D., *Erotic Sculpture of India* (New Delhi, 1975).
Diamond, Stanley, *In Search of the Primitive* (New Brunswick, 1974).
Diodorus Siculus, *Diodorus of Sicily*, 10 vols, ed. and trans. C. H. Oldfather (London, 1934).
Dodds, E. R., *The Greeks and the Irrational* (Berkeley, 1951).
Douglas, Mary, 'Taboo'. *New Society* (12 March 1964).
—, *Purity and Danger: An Analysis of the Concepts of Pollution and Taboo* (London, 1966).
—, 'The Contempt of Ritual'. *New Society* (31 March 1966).
—, 'The Meaning of Myth: With Special Reference to "La Geste d'Asdiwal"', in E. R. Leach (ed.), *The Structural Study of Myth and Totemism* (London, 1967).
—, 'Correspondence: Virgin Birth'. *Man* (n.s.), 4/1 (1969).
—, *Natural Symbols: Explorations in Cosmology* (London, 1970).
—, 'Smothering the Differences – Mary Douglas in a Savage Mind about Lévi-Strauss'. *The Listener* (13 September 1970).
—, 'The Healing Rite'. Review of V. W. Turner, *The Forest of Symbols* and *The Drums of Affliction. Man* (n.s.) 5 (1970).
—, 'Deciphering a Meal'. *Daedalus* (Winter 1972).
—, 'Self Evidence'. The Henry Myers Lecture, Royal Anthropological Institute, 1972. Published in *Implicit Meanings: Essays in Anthropology* (London, 1975).
—, Review of Luc de Heusch, *Le Roi ivre ou l'origine de l'état. Man* (n.s.), 8 (1973).
—, *Evans-Pritchard* (Glasgow, 1980).
—, 'Betwixt, Bothered, and Bewildered': Review of Leach and Aycock, *Structuralist Interpretations of Biblical Myth. New York Review of Books* (20 December 1984).
Douglas, Mary, and Aaron Wildavsky, *Risk and Culture: An Essay on the Selection of Technical and Environmental Dangers* (Berkeley, 1982).
Dowson, J., *A Classical Dictionary of Hinduism* (London, 1903).
Driver, S. R., *et al.*, *The International Critical Commentary* (London, 1895–1951).

Dumont, Louis, 'Definition structurale d'un dieu populaire tamoul: Aiyanar, le Maitre'. *Journal asiatique* (1953).
—, *Une Sous-caste de l'Inde du sud* (Paris, 1957).
—, *Homo hierarchicus: essai sur le système des castes* (Paris, 1966).
Durkheim, Emile, *Quid secundatus politicae scientiae instituendae contulerit* (Bordeaux, 1892).
—, *De la Division du travail sociale* (Paris, 1893). English version, *The Division of Labour in Society* (Glencoe IL, 1947).
—, *Les Règles de la méthode sociologique* (Paris, 1895). English version, *The Rules of Sociological Method*, trans. Sarah A. Solovay and John H. Mueller, 8th edn, G. E. G. Catlin (ed.) (Glencoe IL, 1938).
—, *Les Formes élémentaires de la vie religieuse: le system totémique en Australie*, 2nd edn (Paris, 1925 [1912]); English version, *The Elementary Forms of the Religious Life* (London, 1954).
—, *Sociologie et philosophie* (Paris, 1924). English version, *Sociology and Philosophy*, trans. D. F. Pocock (London, 1953).
Dwyer, Kevin, *Moroccan Dialogues* (Baltimore, 1982).
Eggan, Fred, *Social Organisation of the Western Pueblos* (Chicago, 1950).
Eggan, Fred (ed.), *Social Anthropology of North American Tribes* (Chicago, 1937).
Egoff, S., G. Stubbs, and L. Ashley (eds), *Only Connect: Readings in Children's Literature* (Toronto, 1969).
von Einem, Herbert, *Michelangelo* (London, 1973).
Eliot, Charles, *Hinduism and Buddhism: An Historical Sketch*, 3 vols (London, 1921).
Embree, J. F., and L. O. Dotson, *Bibliography of the Peoples and Cultures of Mainland South-East Asia* (New Haven, 1950).
Engels, Friedrich, *Der Ursprung der Familie* (Stuttgart 1884). English version, *The Origin of the Family, Private Property, and the State* (London, 1972).
Enriquez, C. M., *A Burmese Arcady* (London, 1923).
Epstein, I., *The Babylonian Talmud: Seder Nashi VIII Kiddushin*, trans. H. Freedman (London, 1936).
Erikson, Erik, 'Ontogeny of Ritualisation in Man'. *Philosophical Transactions of the Royal Society of London*, Series B, 251 (1966).
Eusebius Pamphili, Bishop of Caesarea, *Historia Ecclesiastica* (Basel, 1523).
Evans-Pritchard, E. E., *The Nuer: A Description of the Modes of Livelihood and Political Organisation of a Nilotic People* (Oxford, 1940).
—, *The Divine Kingship of the Shilluk of the Nilotic Sudan* (Cambridge, 1948).
—, *Kinship and Marriage among the Nuer* (Oxford, 1951).
—, *Nuer Religion* (Oxford, 1956).
Ewing, W., 'Hair', in James Hastings (ed.), *A Dictionary of the Bible*, vol. 2 (Edinburgh, 1899).
Faral, E., 'Sur le Rite de la "capilature" dans quelques textes médiévaux', in M. Williams and J. A. de Rothschild (eds), *A Miscellany of Studies in Romance Languages and Literature Presented to L. E. Kastner* (Cambridge, 1932).
Fardon, Richard, *Mary Douglas: An Intellectual Biography* (London, 1999).

Filby, P. W., 'Life with the Frazers', typescript in Cambridge University Library (1958).
Finley, I. M., 'Myth, Memory, and History'. *History and Theory*, 4 (1965).
Finsch, O., *Samoafahrten: Ethnologisches Atlas* (Leipzig, 1888).
—, *Ethnologische Erfahrungen und Belegstucke aus der Südsee*, pt 2 (Vienna, 1891).
Firth, Raymond, *The Kauri-Gum Industry: Some Economic Aspects* (Wellington, 1924).
—, *The Primitive Economics of the New Zealand Maori* (London, 1929).
—, 'Marriage and the Classificatory System of Relationship'. *Journal of the Royal Anthropological Institute*, 60 (1930).
—, 'Report on Research in Tikopia'. *Oceania*, 1 (1930).
—, 'Totemism in Polynesia'. *Oceania*, 1 (1930).
—, *Art and Life in New Guinea* (New York, 1936).
—, *We, the Tikopia: A Sociological Study of Kinship in Primitive Polynesia* (London, 1936).
—, *Primitive Polynesian Economy* (London, 1939).
—, *The Work of the Gods in Tikopia*, 2 vols (London, 1940).
—, *Malay Fishermen: Their Peasant Economy* (London, 1946).
—, Review of Fortes, *The Web of Kinship among the Tallensi. Africa*, 21 (1951).
—, *Elements of Social Organisation* (London, 1951).
—, *The Fate of the Soul.* The Frazer Lecture 1951 (Cambridge, 1955).
—, 'Alfred Reginald Radcliffe-Brown' Obituary Notice. *Proceedings of the British Academy*, 42 (1956).
—, 'Ceremonies for Children and their Social Frequency in Tikopia'. *Oceania*, 27 (1956).
—, *Economics of the New Zealand Maori*, rev. edn of Firth, *Primitive Economics* (Wellington, 1959).
—, *Social Change in Tikopia: Re-Study of a Polynesian Community after a Generation* (London, 1959).
—, 'Problem and Assumption in the Anthropological Study of Religion'. *Journal of the Royal Anthropological Institute*, 89 (1959).
—, *History and Traditions of Tikopia* (Wellington, 1961).
—, *Essays on Social Organisation and Values* (London, 1964).
—, *Malay Fishermen: Their Peasant Economy*, rev. and enl. edn (London, 1966).
—, *Tikopia Ritual and Belief* (London, 1967).
—, *Rank and Religion in Tikopia: A Study of Polynesian Paganism and Conversion to Christianity* (London, 1970).
—, 'The Sceptical Anthropologist? Social Anthropology and Marxist Views of Society'. *Proceedings of the British Academy*, 58 (1972).
—, *Symbols: Public and Private* (London, 1973).
—, 'Speech Making and Authority in Tikopia', in Maurice Bloch (ed.), *Political Language and Oratory in Traditional Society* (London, 1975).
—, *Tikopia–English Dictionary* (Auckland, 1985).
Firth, Raymond (ed.), *Two Studies of Kinship in London* (London, 1956).

—(ed.), *Man and Culture: An Evaluation of the Work of Bronislaw Malinowski* (London, 1957).

—(ed.), *Themes in Economic Anthropology* (London, 1967).

Firth, Raymond, Jane Hubert, and Anthony Forge, *Families and their Relatives: Kinship in a Middle-Class Sector of London: An Anthropological Study* (London, 1969).

Firth, Raymond, and B. S. Yamey (eds), *Capital, Savings, and Credit in Peasant Societies: Studies from Asia, Oceania, the Caribbean, and Middle America* (London, 1964).

Firth, Rosemary, *Housekeeping among Malay Peasants* (London, 1943).

Flourens, P., *Histoire des travaux et des idées de Buffon* (Paris, 1845).

Forde, Daryll, *Marriage and the Family among the Yakö* (London, 1941).

Forster, E. M., *Howard's End* (London, 1910).

Fortes, Meyer, *The Dynamics of Clanship among the Tallensi: Being the First Part of an Analysis of the Social Structure of a Trans-Volta Tribe* (London, 1945).

—, *The Web of Kinship among the Tallensi: The Second Part of an Analysis of the Social Structure of a Trans-Volta Tribe* (London, 1949).

—, 'Time and Social Structure: An Ashanti Case Study', in Meyer Fortes (ed.), *Social Structure: Studies Presented to A. R. Radcliffe-Brown* (Oxford, 1949).

—, 'Kinship and Marriage among the Ashanti', in A. R. Radcliffe-Brown and Daryll Forde (eds), *African Political Systems* (London, 1950).

—, 'The Structure of Unilineal Descent Groups', *American Anthropologist*, 55 (1953).

—, 'Descent, Filiation, and Affinity: A Rejoinder to Dr Leach'. *Man*, 59 (1959).

—, *Oedipus and Job in West African Religion* (Cambridge, 1959).

—, 'Religious Premises and Logical Technique in Divinatory Ritual'. *Philosophical Transactions of the Royal Society of London*, Series B, 251 (1966).

Fortes, Meyer (ed.), *Social Structure: Studies Presented to A. R. Radcliffe-Brown* (Oxford, 1949).

Fortes, Meyer, and E. E. Evans-Pritchard (eds), *African Political Systems* (Oxford, 1940).

Fortune, R. F., *Sorcerers of Dobu* (London, 1932).

Foucault, Michel, *Les Mots et les choses: une archéologie des sciences humaines* (Paris, 1966). English version, *The Order of Things: An Archaeology of the Human Sciences* (New York, 1970).

Fox, R. B., 'The Pintubo Negritos: Their Useful Plants and Material Culture'. *Philippines Journal of Science*, 81 (1952).

Fränkel, H., *Wege und Formen früh-griechischen Denkens* (Munich, 1955).

Frazer, J. G., 'On Certain Burial Customs as Illustrative of the Primitive Theory of the Soul'. *Journal of the Anthropological Institute*, 15 (1885).

—, 'Totemism', in *Encyclopaedia Britannica* (London, 1888).

—, *The Golden Bough*, 2 vols (London, 1890); 12 vols (London, 1914); 3 vols (London, 1937); 1-vol. abridgement (London, 1922).

—, *Passages from the Bible: Chosen for their Literary Beauty and Interest by J. G. Frazer, M. A., Fellow of Trinity College, Cambridge* (London, 1895).

—, 'The Origins of Circumcision'. *Independent Review* (November 1904).

—, 'The Beginnings of Religion and Totemism among Australian Aborigines'. *Fortnightly Review* (n.s.), 78 (1905).

—, *Adonis, Attis, Osiris* (London, 1906; later vols 5 and 6 of *The Golden Bough*, 3rd edn).

—, 'Beliefs and Customs of the Australian Aborigines'. *Man*, 9 (1909).

—, *Totemism and Exogamy*, 4 vols (London, 1910).

—, *Pausanias' Description of Greece* (London, 1898).

—, *Ovid's Fasti* (with an English translation by J. G. Frazer) (New York, 1931).

—, *The Belief in Immortality and the Worship of the Dead*, 3 vols (London, 1913–24).

—, *Folklore in the Old Testament*, 3 vols (London, 1918–22).

—, *The Fear of the Dead in Primitive Religion* (London, 1933).

—, *Totemica: A Supplement to Totemism and Exogamy* (London, 1937).

—, *Anthologia Anthropologica: The Native Races of Africa and Madagascar*, R. A. Downey (ed.) (London, 1938).

Freedman, Maurice (ed.), *Social Organisation: Essays Presented to Raymond Firth* (London, 1967).

Freud, Sigmund, *Totem and Taboo* (London, 1919).

—, 'The Occurrence in Dreams of Material from Fairy Tales' (1913), in James Strachey (ed.), *The Standard Edition of the Works of Sigmund Freud*, vol. 12 (London, 1953).

—, 'A Mythological Parallel of a Visual Obsession' (1916), in James Strachey (ed.) *The Standard Edition of the Works of Sigmund Freud*, vol. 14 (London, 1953).

—, *An Autobiographical Study* (New York, 1952).

Friedman, Jonathan, 'Tribes, States, and Transformations', in Maurice Bloch (ed.), *Marxist Analyses and Social Anthropology* (London, 1975).

Fuller, C. J., and Jonathan Parry, 'Petulant Inconsistency? The Intellectual Achievement of Edmund Leach'. *Anthropology Today*, 5/3 (1989).

Fuller, Peter, 'A Chat of Analysts'. *New Society* (31 July 1975).

Funk and Wagnalls, *New Standard Dictionary of the English Language* (New York, 1961).

von Fürer-Haimendorf, C., 'Das Gemeinschaftsleben der Konyak-Naga von Assam'. *Mitteilung der anthropologische Gesellschaft in Wien*, 71 (1941).

—, *The Konyak Nagas* (New York, 1969).

Gallie, W. B., *Peirce and Pragmatism* (London, 1952).

Gardner, D. S., 'Performativity in Ritual: The Mianmin Case'. *Man* (n.s.), 18 (1983).

Geertz, Clifford, *Peddlars and Princes* (Chicago, 1963).

—, 'Religion as a Cultural System', in Michael Banton (ed.), *Anthropological Approaches to the Study of Religion* (London, 1966).

—, *Islam Observed* (Chicago, 1968).

—, *The Interpretation of Cultures* (New York, 1973).

—, *Negara: The Theatre State in Nineteenth-Century Bali* (Princeton, 1980).

—, *Works and Lives* (Stanford, 1988).

Geertz, Clifford, and Hildred Geertz, *Kinship in Bali* (Chicago, 1975).

van Gennep, Arnold, *Les Rites de passage* (Paris, 1908/9). English version, *The Rites of Passage* (London, 1960).

George, E. C. T., 'Memorandum of the Enumeration of the Tribes Inhabiting the Kachin Hills', and 'Memorandum on the Kachins of our Frontier', in *Census of India* (Calcutta, 1891).

Gerth, H., and S. Mills, *Character and Social Structure: The Psychology of Social Institutions* (London, 1954).

Getty, A., *Ganesha: A Monograph on the Elephant-Faced God* (Oxford, 1936).

Gilbert, W. H., 'Eastern Cherokee Social Organisation', in Fred Eggan (ed.), *Social Anthropology of North American Tribes* (Chicago, 1937).

Gilhodes, C., *The Kachins: Religion and Customs* (Calcutta, 1922).

Ginsberg, Morris, *On the Diversity of Morals* (London, 1956).

Glass, Patrick, 'The Trobriand Code: An Interpretation of Trobriand War Shield Designs'. *Anthropos*, 81 (1986).

—, 'Oedipal or Tudavan? The Trobriand Nuclear Complex Revisited'. *Canberra Anthropology*, 19 (1986).

Gluckman, Max, *Custom and Conflict in Africa* (Oxford, 1955).

—, *The Judicial Process among the Barotse of Northern Rhodesia* (Manchester, 1955).

—, 'Les Rites de passage', in Max Gluckman (ed.), *Essays on the Ritual of Social Relations* (Manchester, 1962).

—, *The Ideas in Barotse Jurisprudence* (New Haven, 1965).

Goody, Jack, *The Social Organisation of the LoWiili* (London, 1956).

—, 'A Comparative Approach to Incest and Adultery'. *British Journal of Sociology*, 7 (1956).

—, 'Fields of Social Control among the Lo Dagaba'. *Journal of the Royal Anthropological Institute*, 87 (1957).

—, 'The Mother's Brother and the Sister's Son in West Africa'. *Journal of the Royal Anthropological Institute*, 89 (1959).

—, 'Religion and Ritual: The Definitional Problem'. *British Journal of Sociology*, 12 (1961).

—, 'Inheritance, Social Change, and the Boundary Problem', in Jack Goody (ed.), *Comparative Studies in Kinship* (London, 1969).

Gougaud, L., *Ermites et reclus: études sur d'anciennes formes de la vie religieuses* (Ligugé, 1928).

—, 'Chevelure', in *Dictionnaire de Spiritualité*, vol. 2 (Paris, 1953).

Gough, E. Kathleen, 'The Nayars and the Definition of Marriage'. *Journal of the Royal Anthropological Institute*, 89 (1959).

Graham, W. A., *Siam*, 2 vols (London, 1924).

Gramsci, Antonio, *Quaderni del carcere* (Turin, 1975).

—, *The Modern Prince and Other Writings*, trans. L. Marks (New York, 1957).

Graves, R., and R. Patai, *Hebrew Myths: The Book of Genesis* (London, 1964).

Great Britain Naval Intelligence Division, *Pacific Islands*, 4 vols. Geographical Handbook Series B. R. 519A–C (London, 1943–5).

Groddeck, Georg, *The World of Man: As Reflected in Art, in Words, and in Disease* (London, 1934).
Haddon, A. C., *The Decorative Art of British New Guinea* (Dublin, 1894).
Hall, D. G. E., *A History of South-East Asia* (London, 1955).
Hallpike, C. R., 'Social Hair'. *Man* (n.s.), 4 (1969).
Hanson, O., *A Dictionary of the Kachin Language* (Rangoon, 1906).
—, *The Kachins: Their Customs and Traditions* (Rangoon, 1913).
Harper, E. B., 'A Hindu Village Pantheon'. *Southwestern Journal of Anthropology*, 15 (1959).
Harris, Marvin, *The Rise of Anthropological Theory: A History of Theories of Culture* (New York, 1968).
Harrison, Jane, *Prolegomena to the Study of Greek Religion*, 3rd edn (Cambridge, 1922 [1903]).
—, *Themis: A Study of the Social Origins of Greek Religion*, 2nd edn (Cambridge, 1937 [1912]).
—, *Ancient Art and Ritual*, 2nd edn (Oxford, 1951 [1913]).
Harrisson, Tom, *Savage Civilisation* (London, 1937).
Hartland, E. S., *The Legends of Perseus*, 3 vols (London, 1894–1906).
—, *Primitive Paternity*, 2 vols (London, 1909–10).
Hastings, James (ed.), *A Dictionary of the Bible*, 5 vols (New York, 1898–1904).
—(ed.), *Encyclopaedia of Religion and Ethics*, 12 vols (Edinburgh, 1908).
Hefele, C. J., *Histoire des conciles*, vol. 1, pt 2 (Paris, 1907).
Herskovits, M. J., *Man and his Works* (New York, 1948).
Hertz, H. F., *A Practical Handbook of the Kachin or Chingpaw Language* (Calcutta, 1943).
Hobbes, Thomas, *Leviathan, or Matter, Form, and Power of a Commonwealth, Ecclesiasticall and Civill*, ed. Michael Oakshott (Oxford, 1957 [1651]).
Hocart, A. M., *Caste: A Comparative Study* (London, 1950).
—, *Kings and Councillors* (Chicago, 1970).
Hodgen, M. T., *Early Anthropology in the Sixteenth and Seventeenth Centuries* (Philadelphia, 1964).
Hogbin, H. I., *Law and Order in Polynesia* (London, 1934).
—, *Experiments in Civilisation: The Effects of European Culture on a Native Community in the Solomon Islands* (London, 1939).
Homans, G. C., *The Human Group* (London, 1951).
Homans, G. C., and David M. Schneider, *Marriage, Authority, and Final Causes* (Glencoe IL, 1955).
Hooke, Samuel H. (ed.), *Myth, Ritual, and Kingship* (Oxford, 1958).
Hose, C., and W. McDougall, *The Pagan Tribes of Borneo*, 2 vols (London, 1912).
Hoyle, F., *The Nature of the Universe* (Cambridge, 1950).
Hubert, Henri, Review of Fowler, *The Roman Festivities at the Period of the Republic. L'Année sociologique*, 4 (1899–1900).
—, 'Le Rituel'. *L'Année sociologique*, 5 (1900–1).
Hubert, Henri, and Marcel Mauss, 'Essai sur la nature et la fonction du sacri-

fice'. *L'Année sociologique*, 2 (1897–8). English version, *Sacrifice: its Nature and Function*, trans. W. D. Halls with foreword by E. E. Evans-Pritchard (London, 1964).
—, 'Esquisse d'une théorie générale de la magie'. *L'Année sociologique*, 7 (1902–3).
—, 'L'Origine des pouvoirs magiques dans les sociétés australiennes', in *Mélanges d'histoire des religions* (Paris, 1909).
—, 'Etude sommaire de la représentation du temps dans la religion et la magie', in *Mélanges d'histoire des religions* (Paris, 1909).
Hudson, Liam, 'Degree Class and Attainment in Scientific Research'. *British Journal of Psychology*, 5 (1974).
Hugh-Jones, Stephen, *Edmund Leach 1910–1989* (Cambridge, 1989).
Hutton, J. H., *The Angami Nagas* (London, 1921).
—, *The Sema Nagas* (London, 1921).
—, 'A Bibliography of the Naga Hills with some Adjacent Districts', Appendix 6 to J. P. Mills, *The Ao Nagas* (London, 1926).
—, 'The Significance of Headhunting in Assam'. *Journal of the Royal Anthropological Institute*, 58 (1928).
—, 'Introduction', in N. E. Parry (ed.), *The Lakhers* (London, 1932).
—, *Caste in India* (Cambridge, 1946).
—, 'The Mixed Culture of the Naga Tribes'. *Journal of the Royal Anthropological Institute*, 95 (1965).
Ievers, R. W., *Manual of the North-Central Province, Ceylon* (Colombo, 1899).
Ingold, Tim (ed.), *The Concept of Society is Theoretically Obsolete* (Manchester, 1990).
Irwin, J., '"Asokan" pillars: a reassessment of the evidence'. *Burlington Magazine* (in four parts: November 1973; December 1974; October 1975; November 1976).
Ishida, E., 'Mother–Son Deities', *History of Religions*, 4 (1964).
Iyer, L. K. A., *The Mysore Tribes and Castes*, 4 vols (Mysore, 1928–35).
Izikowitz, K. G., *Lamet: Hill Peasants in French Indochina* (Göteborg, 1951).
Jakobson, R., and M. Halle, *Fundamentals of Language* (The Hague, 1956).
Jakobson, R., and Claude Lévi-Strauss, 'Les Chats de Charles Baudelaire'. *L'Homme*, 2 (1962).
Jarvie, I. C., *The Revolution in Anthropology* (London, 1964).
Jastrow, M., 'An Assyrian Law Code'. *Journal of the American Oriental Society*, 41 (1921).
Jesse, W., *The Life of George Brummell Esq. commonly called Beau Brummell*, 2 vols (London, 1927).
Jones, Ernest, 'Mother-Right and the Sexual Ignorance of Savages'. *International Journal of Psycho-Analysis*, 6 (1925).
Kaberry, P. M., 'Spirit Children and Spirit Centres of the North Kimberley Division, West Australia'. *Oceania*, 6 (1936).
—, *Aboriginal Women* (London, 1939).
Kawlu Ma Nawng, *History of the Kachins of the Hukawng Valley*, trans. and annotated by J. L. Leyden (privately printed, Bombay, 1942).

Keesing, Roger M., *Cultural Anthropology: A Contemporary Perspective*, 2nd edn (New York, 1981).

Kenyatta, Jomo, *Facing Mount Kenya* (London, 1938).

Kerényi, K., *The Gods of the Greeks* (London, 1951).

—, 'The Trickster in Relation to Greek Mythology', in Paul Radin (ed.), *The Trickster: A Study in American Indian Mythology* (London, 1956).

Kirk, G. S., *Myth: Its Meaning and Functions in Ancient and Other Cultures* (Cambridge, 1970).

Kroeber, A. L., 'California Kin Terms'. *University of California, Publications in American Archaeology and Ethnology*, 12 (1917).

—, *The Nature of Culture* (Chicago, 1952).

Kroeber, A. L., and Clyde Kluckhohn, *Culture* (Cambridge MA, 1952).

Kuhn, Thomas S., *The Structure of Scientific Revolutions* (Chicago, 1962).

Kuper, Adam, *Anthropology and Anthropologists: The Modern British School*, rev. edn (London, 1983).

—, 'An Interview with Edmund Leach'. *Current Athropology*, 27 (1986).

—, *The Invention of Primitive Society* (London, 1988).

La Metrie, J., *L'Homme machine* (Leiden, 1747).

Lafitau, J.-F., *Moeurs des sauvages amériquains, comparées aux moeurs des premiers temps* (Paris, 1724).

Lam, H. J., 'Classification and the New Morphology', *Acta Biotheoretica* (1948).

Lamarck, J.-B.-P.-A. de Monet de, *Philosophie zoologique, ou Exposition des considérations relatives à l'histoire naturelle des animaux* (Paris, 1809).

Lang, A., and J. J. Atkinson, *Social Origins and Primal Law* (London, 1903).

Lattimore, Owen, *Inner Asian Frontiers of China* (New York, 1940).

Leach, E. R., 'Boat Construction in Botel Tobago'. *Man*, 37 (1937).

—, 'The Yami of Koto-sho: A Japanese Colonial Experiment'. *Geographical Magazine*, 5/6 (1937).

—, 'Economic Life and Technology of the Yami of Botel Tobago'. *Man*, 38 (1938).

—, *Social and Economic Organisation of Rowanduz Kurds*. London School of Economics Monographs on Social Anthropology (London, 1940).

—, 'Jinghpaw Kinship Terminology: An Experiment in Ethnographic Algebra'. *Journal of the Royal Anthropological Institute*, 75 (1945). Reprinted in E. R. Leach, *Rethinking Anthropology* (London, 1961).

—, 'Pilot Survey of Sarawak. Report on the Possibilities of a Social Science Survey of Sarawak', Report for the Colonial Social Science Research Council (London, 1948).

—, 'Some Features of Social Structure among Sarawak Pagans'. *Man*, 48 (1948).

—, 'A Melanau (Sarawak) Twine-Making Device, with Notes on Related Apparatus from North East Malaya'. *Journal of the Royal Anthropological Institute*, 79 (1949).

—, 'Some Aspects of Dry Rice Cultivation in North Burma and British Borneo'. *The Advancement of Science*, 6/21 (1949).

—, *Social Research in Sarawak: A Report on the Possibilities of a Social Economic Survey of Sarawak* (London, 1950).

—, Review of Fortes, *The Web of Kinship among the Tallensi. Man*, 50 (1950).
—, 'A Kagaram Tomb Post from the Belaga Area of Sarawak'. *Man*, 50 (1950).
—, Review of Mauss (ed. Lévi-Strauss), *Sociologie et anthropologie. British Journal of Sociology*, 2/1 (1951).
—, 'The Structural Implications of Matrilateral Cross-Cousin Marriage'. *Journal of the Royal Anthropological Institute*, 81 (1951). Reprinted in E. R. Leach, *Rethinking Anthropology* (London, 1961).
—, 'Cronus and Chronos'. *Explorations: Studies in Culture and Communication*, 1 (1953). Reprinted in E. R. Leach, *Rethinking Anthropology* (London, 1961).
—, *Political Systems of Highland Burma: A Study of Kachin Social Structure* (London, 1954).
—, 'Primitive Time Reckoning', in Charles Singer *et al.* (eds), *A History of Technology*, vol. 1 (Oxford, 1954).
—, 'Aesthetics', in E. E. Evans-Pritchard *et al*, *The Institutions of Primitive Society* (London, 1954).
—, 'A Trobriand Medusa?'. *Man*, 54 (1954).
—, 'Time and False Noses'. *Explorations: Studies in Culture and Communication*, 5 (1955). Reprinted in E. R. Leach, *Rethinking Anthropology* (London, 1961).
—, 'The Epistemological Background to Malinowski's Empiricism', in R. Firth (ed.), *Man and Culture: An Evaluation of the Work of Bronislaw Malinowski* (London, 1957).
—, 'Aspects of Bridewealth and Marriage Stability among the Kachin and Lakher'. *Man*, 57 (1957). Reprinted in E. R. Leach, *Rethinking Anthropology* (London, 1961).
—, 'Concerning Trobriand Clans and the Kinship Category *Tabu*', in Jack Goody (ed.), *The Developmental Cycle in Domestic Groups* (Cambridge, 1958).
—, Review of Radcliffe-Brown, *A Natural Science of Society*, and Nadel, *The Theory of Social Structure. Man*, 58 (1958).
—, 'Magical Hair', Curl Bequest Prize Essay 1957. *Journal of the Royal Anthropological Institute*, 88 (1958).
—, 'Hydraulic Society in Ceylon'. *Past and Present*, 5 (1959).
—, Review of Lynch, *The Image of the City. American Anthropologist*, 63 (1960).
—, 'Some Prejudiced Thoughts on Race Prejudice'. *Cambridge Opinion*, 18 (1960).
—, *Pul Eliya – A Village in Ceylon: A Study of Land Tenure and Kinship* (Cambridge, 1961).
—, *Rethinking Anthropology* (London, 1961).
—, 'Golden Bough or Gilded Twig?'. *Daedalus*, 90/2 (Spring 1961).
—, 'Lévi-Strauss in the Garden of Eden: An Examination of Some Recent Developments in the Analysis of Myth'. *Transactions of the New York Academy of Sciences*, Series 2, 23/4 (1961).
—, 'The Frontiers of "Burma"'. *Comparative Studies in Society and History*, 3/1 (1961).
—, 'Asymmetric Marriage Rules, Status Difference, and Direct Reciprocity: Comments on an Alleged Fallacy'. *Southwestern Journal of Anthropology*, 17/4 (1961).

—, 'Genesis as Myth'. *Discovery*, 23/5 (1962). Reprinted in Edmund Leach, *Genesis as Myth and Other Essays* (London, 1969).

—, 'Classification in Social Anthropology'. *Aslib Proceedings*, 14 (1962).

—, 'Pulleyar and the Lord Budda: An Aspect of Religious Syncretism in Ceylon'. *Psychoanalytic Review*, 49/2 (1962).

—, 'Beasts and Triangles'. *New Society*, 1/1 (4 October 1962).

—, 'Nostalgia', Review of Evans-Pritchard, *Essays in Social Anthropology. New Statesman*, 64/1657 (14 December 1962).

—, 'Babar's Civilisation Analysed'. *New Society*, 1/12 (20 December 1962).

—, Review of Lévi-Strauss, *Le Totémisme aujoud'hui* and *La Pensée sauvage. Man*, 63 (1963).

—, 'Sins or Rules'. *New Society*, 1/27 (4 April 1963).

—, 'Sociology or Nothing'. Review of Jayawardena, *Conflict and Solidarity in a Guianese Plantation*; Gulliver, *Social Control in an African Society*; Douglas, *The Lele of the Kasai*; Middleton and Winter (eds), *Witchcraft and Sorcery in East Africa. New Statesman*, 66/1687 (9 August 1963).

—, 'Anthropological Aspects of Language: Animal Categories and Verbal Abuse', in E. H. Lenneberg (ed.), *New Directions in the Study of Language* (Cambridge MA, 1964).

—, 'Models'. *New Society*, 3/185 (14 May 1964).

—, 'Telstar et les aborigènes ou "La Pensée sauvage"'. *Annales: Economies, Sociétés, Civilisations*, 19/6 (1964). English version published in Emmet and MacIntyre (eds), *Sociological Theory and Philosophical Analysis* (New York, 1970).

—, 'New Hat'. Review of Lévi-Strauss, *Totemism*, and other anthropology books. *New Statesman*, 69/1771 (19 February 1965).

—, 'Paths and Deserts'. Review of Evans-Pritchard, *The Position of Women in Primitive Society and Other Essays*, and Lienhardt, *Social Anthropology. Times Literary Supplement* (13 May 1965).

—, 'The Cult of Informality'. *New Society*, 6/145 (8 July 1965).

—, Review of Lévi-Strauss, *Mythologiques, Le Cru et le cuit. American Anthropologist*, 67/3 (1965).

—, 'Warfare, Headhunting, and Sacrifice'. *Proceedings of the Medical Association for the Prevention of War*, 1 (1965).

—, 'The Nature of War'. *Disarmament and Arms Control*, 3/2 (1965).

—, 'Testament of an English Eccentric'. Review of Lord Raglan, *The Temple and the House. New York Review of Books*, 5/3 (1965).

—, 'Men and Ideas. Frazer and Malinowski: On the "Founding Fathers"'. *Encounter*, 25/5 (1965). Reprinted in *Current Anthropology*, 7/5 (1966).

—, 'Claude Lévi-Strauss: Anthropologist and Philosopher'. *New Left Review*, 34 (1965).

—, 'The Legitimacy of Solomon: Some Structural Aspects of Old Testament History'. *European Journal of Sociology*, 7/1 (1966). Reprinted in Edmund Leach, *Genesis as Myth and Other Essays* (London, 1969).

—, 'Ritualisation in Man in Relation to Conceptual and Social Development', in Julian Huxley (ed.), 'A Discussion on Ritualisation of Behaviour in Animals and Man'. *Philosophical Transactions of the Royal Society of London*, Series B, 251/772 (1966).

—, 'The Face Disguised'. *Sunday Times Magazine* (4 December 1966).
—, 'Don't say "Boo" to a Goose'. Review of Lorenz, *On Aggression*, and Ardrey, *The Territorial Imperative. New York Review of Books*, 7/10 (15 December 1966). Reprinted in *Man and Aggression* ed. M. F. Ashley Montagu (New York, 1968).
—, 'Virgin Birth', Henry Myers Lecture 1966. *Proceedings of the Royal Anthropological Institute* (1966). Reprinted in Edmund Leach, *Genesis as Myth and Other Essays* (London, 1969).
—, 'Introduction' in E. R. Leach (ed.), *The Structural Study of Myth and Totemism* (London, 1967).
—, 'An Anthropologist's Trivia'. Review of Malinowski, *A Diary in the Strict Sense of the Term. Guardian* (11 August 1967).
—, 'Brain-Twister'. Review of Lévi-Strauss, *The Savage Mind* and *Mythologiques: du miel aux cendres. New York Review of Books* 9/6 (12 October 1967).
—, 'Introduction', in E. R. Leach (ed.), *Dialectic in Practical Religion* (Cambridge, 1968).
—, *A Runaway World? The Reith Lectures 1967* (London, 1968).
—, 'Ritual', in David L. Sills (ed.), *International Encyclopaedia of the Social Sciences*, vol. 13 (New York, 1968).
—, *Genesis as Myth and Other Essays* (London, 1969).
—, 'Planning and Evolution', *Journal of the Town Planning Institute*, 55 (1969).
—, 'What Kind of Community?' *New Society*, 13/345 (8 May 1969).
—, 'The Prejudices of Claude Lévi-Strauss'. Review of Charbonnier, *Conversations with Claude Lévi-Strauss. The Listener*, 82 (31 July 1969).
—, *Culture and Nature or La Femme sauvage.* The Stevenson Lecture, Bedford College, University of London, 1968 (London, 1969).
—, *Lévi-Strauss* (London, 1970). (Subsequent editions: London, 1974, 1985, 1996. Page references are to the 1996 edition.)
—, 'Frazer Reconsidered'. Review of Downie, *Frazer and The Golden Bough. Guardian* (30 July 1970).
—, 'Kimil: A Category of Andamanese Thought', in Pierre Maranda and Elli Kongas Maranda (eds), *Structural Analysis of Oral Tradition* (Philadelphia, 1971).
—, 'Mythical Inequalities'. Review of Douglas, *Natural Symbols. New York Review of Books*, 16/1 (28 January 1971).
—, 'The Structure of Symbolism', in Jean La Fontaine (ed.), *The Interpretation of Ritual: Essays in Honour of A. I. Richards* (London, 1972).
—, 'The Influence of Cultural Context on Non-Verbal Communication in Man', in Robert A. Hinde (ed.), *Non-Verbal Communication* (Cambridge, 1972).
—, *Humanity and Animality.* 54th Conway Memorial Lecture (London, 1972).
—, 'Baboon Tract'. Review of Tiger and Fox, *The Imperial Animal. New Society*, 20/508 (22 June 1972).
—, 'Melchisedech and the Emperor: Icons of Subversion and Orthodoxy'. Presidential Address. *Proceedings of the Royal Anthropological Institute* (1972).
—, 'The Study of Man in Relation to Science and Technology'. Two Cantor Lectures, delivered at the Royal Society of Arts. *The Royal Society of Arts Journal*, 121/5203 (1973).

—, 'Levels of Communication and Problems of Taboo in the Appreciation of Art', in Anthony Forge (ed.), *Primitive Art and Society* (Oxford, 1973).
—, 'Impressionistic Ethnographer'. Review of Lévi-Strauss, *Tristes Tropiques. New Scientist,* 61/880 (10 January 1974).
—, 'Anthropology Upside Down'. Review of Hymes, *Reinventing Anthropology. New York Review of Books,* 21/5 (4 April 1974).
—, 'Integration, Race, and Ethnicity'. *Royal Anthropological Institute Newsletter,* 2/8 (1974).
—, 'Variation in Man: Culture and Breeding'. *Patterns of Prejudice,* 8/5 (1974).
—, 'Freedom and Social Conditioning'. Raymond Priestley Lecture, University of Birmingham, 1974. *Educational Review,* 27/2 (1975).
—, 'Cultural Components in the concept of Race', in F. J. Ebling (ed.), *Racial Variation in Man* (London, 1975).
—, 'Jesus, John, and Mary Magdalene'. *New Society,* 34/690 (25 December 1975).
—, *Culture and Communication: The Logic by which Symbols are Connected* (Cambridge, 1976).
—, 'Social Anthropology: A Natural Science of Society?'. The British Academy Radcliffe-Brown Lecture 1976. *Proceedings of the British Academy,* 62 (1976).
—, 'Oh Come, All Ye Faithful'. Review of Lévi-Strauss, *Structural Anthropology II. Spectator,* 238/7752 (29 January 1977).
—, 'All that Glitters is not Gold'. *Times Higher Education Supplement* (25 February 1977).
—, 'Anthropos', in *Enciclopedia Einaudi,* vol. 1 (Turin, 1977).
—, *Custom, Law, and Terrorist Violence.* Munro Lectures 1977 (Edinburgh, 1977).
—, 'Reconsiderations: *The Golden Bough*'. *Human Nature* (February 1978).
—, 'Cultura/Culture', in *Enciclopedia Einaudi,* vol. 4 (Turin, 1978).
—, 'Etnocentrismi', in *Enciclopedia Einaudi,* vol. 5 (Turin, 1978).
—, 'Does Space Syntax Really Constitute the Social?', in D. Green, C. Hazelgrove, and M. Spriggs (eds), *Social Organisation and Settlement, British Archaeological Report, International Supplementary Series,* 47/2 (1978).
—, 'Of Ecstasy and Rationality', in Mick Csáky (ed.), *How Does it Feel?: Exploring the World of Your Senses* (London, 1979).
—, 'Taste and Smell', in Mick Csáky (ed.), *How Does it Feel?: Exploring the World of Your Senses* (London, 1979).
—, 'Long Pig, Tall Story'. Review of Arens, *The Man-Eating Myth. New Society,* 49/882 (30 August 1979).
—, 'Raymond Firth', in *International Encyclopaedia of the Social Sciences,* vol. 18 (New York, 1979).
—, *L'Unité de l'homme et autres essais* (Paris, 1980).
—, 'Profanity in Context'. Slightly amended version of 'Profanity and Context' [*New Scientist,* 76/1074 (1977)], in Jeremy Cherfas and Roger Lewis (eds), *Not Work Alone: A Cross-Cultural View of Activities Superfluous to Survival* (London, 1980).
—, 'Malinowskiana: On Reading A Diary in the Strict Sense of the Term, Or the Self-Mutilation of Professor Hsu'. *Royal Anthropological Institute Newsletter,* 36 (1980).

—, 'Natura/Cultura', in *Enciclopedia Einaudi*, vol. 9 (Turin, 1980).
—, 'The Ecology of Mental Process: A Life of Gregory Bateson'. Review of Lipset, *Gregory Bateson: The Legacy of a Scientist. Nature*, 288 (1980).
—, 'Cairo Essays'. Review of Douglas, *Evans-Pritchard. London Review of Books*, 2/23 (4 December 1980).
—, 'A Poetics of Power'. Review of Geertz, *Negara. New Republic*, 184 (4 April 1981).
—, 'Happily Ever After?'. Review of various books about the Royal Wedding. *New Statesman*, 102/2627 (24 July 1981).
—, 'Symbolic Locks'. Review of Obeyesekere, *Medusa's Hair. Times Literary Supplement* (18 December 1981).
—, *Social Anthropology* (Oxford/London, 1982).
—, 'Frazer, Sir James George, 1854–1941', in Justin Wintle (ed.), *Makers of Nineteenth-Century Culture 1800–1914* (London, 1982).
—, (with D. Alan Aycock) *Structuralist Interpretations of Biblical Myth* (Cambridge, 1983).
—, 'The Kula: An Alternative View', in Jerry W. Leach and Edmund Leach (eds), *The Kula: New Perspectives on Massim Exchange* (Cambridge, 1983).
—, 'The Shangri-La That Never Was'. Review of Freeman, *Margaret Mead and Samoa. New Society*, 63/1062 (24 March 1983).
—, 'The Gatekeepers of Heaven: Anthropological Aspects of Grandiose Architecture'. *Journal of Anthropological Research*, 39/3 (1983).
—, 'The Integration of Minorities', in Ben Whitaker (ed.), *Minorities: A Question of Human Rights?* (Oxford, 1984).
—, 'Glimpses of the Unmentionable in the History of British Social Anthropology'. *Annual Review of Anthropology*, 13 (1984).
—, 'Sri Minaksi and her Tamil Cousins'. Review of Shulman, *Tamil Temple Myths. Semiotica*, 49/1/2 (1984).
—, 'Notes on the Mythology of Cambridge Anthropology'. *Cambridge Anthropology*, 9/1 (1984).
—, 'Michelangelo's Genesis: A Structuralist Interpretation of the Central Panels of the Sistine Chapel Ceiling'. *Semiotica*, 56/1 and 2 (1985). Revised version of that published in the *Times Literary Supplement* in 1977.
—, 'Middle America'. Review of Howard, *Margaret Mead*, and Bateson, *With a Daughter's Eye. London Review of Books*, 7/4 (7 March 1985).
—, 'Reflections on a Visit to Nemi: Did Frazer Get it Wrong?'. *Anthropology Today*, 1/2 (1985).
—, Review of Singer, *Man's Glassy Essence. American Ethnologist*, 12/2 (1985).
—, 'The Big Fish in the Biblical Wilderness'. 19th Ernest Jones Lecture 1985. *International Journal of Psychoanalysis*, 13 (1986).
—, 'Lévi-Straussiana'. Review of Lévi-Strauss, *The View from Afar. Partisan Review* (1986).
—, 'Naming of Dogs'. Review of Lévi-Strauss, *The View from Afar. London Review of Books*, 8/5 (20 March 1986).
—, 'Fishing for Men on the Edge of the Wilderness', in Robert Alter and Frank Kermode (eds), *The Literary Guide to the Bible* (London, 1987).

—, 'C. S. Peirce in Tamil Nadu'. Review of Daniel, *Fluid Signs. Semiotica*, 64/3/4 (1987).

—, 'Late Mediaeval Representations of Saint Mary Magdalene'. *Psychoanalytic Review*, 75/1 (1988).

—, *Noah's Second Son* (Cambridge, 1988). Reprinted in *Anthropology Today*, 4/4 (1988); with a few textual changes.

—, 'Corpo', in *Enciclopedia delle Scienze Sociale* (Rome, 1988).

—, 'Writing Anthropology'. Review of Geertz, *Works and Lives. American Ethnologist*, 16/1 (1989).

—, 'Tribal Ethnography: Past, Present, Future', in E. Tonkin, M. McDonald, and M. Chapman (eds), *History and Ethnicity* (London, 1989).

—, 'Masquerade: The Presentation of Self in Holi-Day Life'. *Cambridge Anthropology*, 13 (1990).

Leach, Edmund, and John Drury, *The Great Windows of King's College Chapel Cambridge* (Cambridge, 1988).

Leach, Jerry W., and Edmund Leach (eds), *The Kula: New Perspectives on Massim Exchange* (Cambridge, 1983).

Leenhardt, Maurice, *Arts de l'Océanie* (Paris, 1947).

Lennenberg, E. H. (ed.), *New Directions in the Study of Language* (Cambridge MA, 1964).

Lévi-Strauss, Claude, 'L'analyse structurale en linguistique et en anthropologie', *Word* (Journal of the Linguistic Circle of New York) 1/2 (1945). *La Vie familiale et sociale des Indiens Nambikwara* (Paris, 1948).

—, *Les Structures élémentaires de la parenté* (Paris, 1949).

—, *Introduction à Marcel Mauss*, Sociologie et anthropologie (Paris, 1950). English version, *Introduction to the Work of Marcel Mauss* (London, 1987).

—, 'The Structural Study of Myth'. *Journal of American Folklore*, 68 (1955). Modified version in *Structural Anthropology* (New York, 1963).

—, *Tristes Tropiques* (Paris, 1955). English version, *A World on the Wane* (omitting several chapters) (London, 1961).

—, 'La Geste d'Asdiwal'. *Annuaire de l'Ecole Practique des Hautes Etudes (Sciences Religieuses) 1958–9* (Paris, 1960). English version, in Claude Lévi-Strauss, *Structural Anthropology II* (New York, 1976).

—, *Anthropologie structurale* (Paris, 1958). English version, *Structural Anthropology*, trans. Claire Jacobson and Brooke Grundfest Schoepf (New York, 1963; London, 1968).

—, *Entretien avec Claude Lévi-Strauss*, ed. George Charbonnier (Paris, 1961). English version, *Conversations with Claude Lévi-Strauss* (London, 1969).

—, *Le Totémisme aujourd'hui* (Paris, 1962). English version, *Totemism*, trans. Rodney Needham (London, 1964).

—, *La Pensée sauvage* (Paris, 1962). English version, *The Savage Mind* (London, 1966).

—, 'The Bear and the Barber'. *Journal of the Royal Anthropological Institute*, 93 (1963).

—, *Le Cru et le cuit* (Paris, 1964). English version, *The Raw and the Cooked*, trans. J. and D. Weightman (London, 1970).

—, *Du Miel aux cendres* (Paris, 1966). English version, *From Honey to Ashes*, trans. J. and D. Weightman (London, 1973).

—, *L'Homme nu* (Paris, 1968). English version, *The Naked Man*, trans. J. and D. Weightman (London, 1978).

—, *La Voie des masques* (Paris, 1979). English version, *The Way of the Masks* (London, 1983).

Lienhardt, Godfrey, 'Modes of Thought', in E. E. Evans-Pritchard *et al.* (eds), *The Institutions of Primitive Society* (London, 1954).

—, *Divinity and Experience: The Religion of the Dinka* (Oxford, 1961).

Linnaeus, Carolus (Carl von Linné), *Systema naturae sive regna tria naturae systematice proposita per classes, ordines, genera, et species* (Leiden, 1735).

Linton, R., and P. S. Wingert, *Arts of the South Seas* (New York, 1946).

Lipset, David, *Gregory Bateson: The Legacy of a Scientist* (Englewood Cliffs, 1980).

Locke, John, *An Essay concerning Human Understanding* (London, 1694).

Lorenz, Konrad, *On Aggression* (New York, 1966).

—, 'Ritualisation in the Psycho-Social Evolution of Human Culture'. *Philosophical Transactions of the Royal Society of London*, Series B, 251 (1966).

Luang Boribol Buribhand and A. Griswold, *Images of the Buddha in Thailand* (Bangkok, 1957).

Luce, G. H., 'Economic Life of the Early Burman'. *Journal of the Burma Research Society*, 30 (1940).

Luce, G. H., and Pe Maung Tin, 'Burma Down to the Fall of Pagan, Part I'. *Journal of the Burma Research Society*, 29 (1939). [Part II was never published.]

Lucian of Samosata, *De Dea Syria*, trans. Tookes (London, 1820).

Mabuchi, T., 'Two Types of Kinship Ritual Among Malayo-Polynesian Peoples'. *Proceedings of the 9th International Congress of the Institute of Religion, Tokyo* (1958).

Mackenzie, A., *History of the Relations of the Government with the Hill Tribes of the North-Eastern Frontier of Bengal* (Calcutta, 1884).

Maine, Henry S., *Ancient Law*, 9th edn (London, 1883).

de Malesherbes, C. G. L., *Observations sur l'histoire naturelle de Buffon et Daubenton* (Paris, 1798).

Malinowski, Bronislaw, *The Family among the Australian Aborigines: A Sociological Study* (London, 1913).

—, 'The Natives of Mailu: Preliminary Results of the Robert Mond Research Work in British New Guinea'. *Transactions and Proceedings of the Royal Society of South Australia*, 39 (1915).

—, 'Baloma: The Spirits of the Dead in the Trobriand Islands'. *Journal of the Royal Anthropological Institute*, 46 (1916).

—, 'War and Weapons among the Trobriand Islanders'. *Man*, 20 (1920).

—, *Argonauts of the Western Pacific: An Account of Native Enterprise and Adventure in the Archipelagos of Melanesian New Guinea* (London, 1922).

—, 'The Problem of Meaning in Primitive Languages', in C. K. Ogden and I. A. Richards (eds), *The Meaning of Meaning* (London, 1923).

—, 'Science and Superstition of Primitive Mankind'. Review of J. G. Frazer, *The Golden Bough*. *Nature*, 111 (1923).

—, 'Psychoanalysis and Anthropology'. Letter to editor. *Nature*, 112 (1923).

—, 'Magic, Science, and Religion', in J. A. Needham (ed.), *Science, Religion, and Reality* (London, 1925).

—, *Crime and Custom in Savage Society* (London, 1926).

—, *Myth in Primitive Psychology* (London, 1926). Reprinted in *Magic, Science, Religion and Other Essays* (Boston, 1948).

—, *Sex and Repression in Savage Society* (London, 1927).

—, *The Sexual Life of Savages in North West Melanesia*. Preface by Havelock Ellis (London, 1929).

—, 'Parenthood: The Basis of Social Structure', in V. F. Calverton and S. D. Schmalhausen (eds), *The New Generation* (London, 1930).

—, 'Culture', in *Encyclopaedia of the Social Sciences*, vol. 6 (New York, 1931).

—, *The Sexual Life of Savages in North West Melanesia*, 3rd edn with new foreword (London, 1932).

—, 'Introduction', in H. I. Hogbin, *Law and Order in Polynesia* (London, 1934).

—, *Coral Gardens and their Magic: A Study of Methods of Tilling the Soil and of Agricultural Rites in the Trobriand Islands*, 2 vols (London, 1935).

—, *The Foundations of Faith and Morals: An Anthropological Analysis of Primitive Beliefs and Conduct with Special Reference to the Fundamental Problems of Religion and Ethics* (Durham, 1936). Reprinted in Malinowski, *Sex, Culture, and Myth* (New York, 1962).

—, 'Foreword', in M. F. Ashley Montagu, *Coming into Being among the Australian Aborigines* (London, 1937).

—, 'Introductory Essay: The Anthropology of Changing African Cultures', in *Methods of Study of Culture Contact in Africa* (London, 1938). Reprinted from *Africa*, vols 7, 8, and 9.

—, *A Scientific Theory of Culture and Other Essays* (Chapel Hill, 1944).

—, *The Dynamics of Culture Change* (London, 1945).

—, *Freedom and Civilization* (London, 1947).

—, *Magic, Science, Religion and Other Essays* (Boston, 1948).

—, *Sex, Culture, and Myth* (New York, 1962).

Malson, L., *Les Enfants sauvages* (Paris, 1964).

Man, E. H., 'On the Aboriginal Inhabitants of the Andaman Islands'. *Journal of the Anthropological Institute*, 12 (1882–3). Reprinted as *On the Aboriginal Inhabitants of the Andaman Islands* (London, 1885).

Maranda, P., and E. K. Maranda (eds), *Structural Analysis of Oral Tradition* (Philadelphia, 1971).

Marriott, McKim, 'Little Communities in an Indigenous Civilization', in McKim Marriott (ed.), *Village India* (Chicago, 1955).

Martin, E., *The Gods of India* (New York, 1914).

Marx, Karl, *Theses on Feuerbach* (1845). English version, *Concerning Feuerbach* (London, 1973).

—, *Capital: A Critique of Political Economy* (Chicago 1925–6 [1867–79]).
Mauss, Marcel, *Manuel d'ethnographie* (Paris, 1947).
—, 'Essai sur le don: forme et raison de l'échange dans les sociétés archaiques'. *L'Année sociologique* (n.s.), 1 (1923–4). English version, *The Gift* (London, 1954).
Mayo, K., *Mother India* (London, 1935).
McLennan, J. F., *Primitive Marriage* (London, 1865).
—, *Studies in Ancient History*, 1st series, including reprint of *Primitive Marriage* [1865] etc. (London, 1876).
Mead, Margaret, *Coming of Age in Samoa* (London, 1928).
—, *Social Organisation of Manu'a*. Bishop Museum Bulletin no. 36 (Honolulu, 1930).
—, *Kinship in the Admiralty Islands.* American Museum of Natural History Anthropology Papers no. 34 (New York, 1934).
Meggitt, M. J., *Desert People* (Sydney, 1962).
Merton, Robert K., *Social Theory and Social Structure* (Glencoe IL, 1951).
Michell, St J. F., *Report (Topographical, Political and Military) on the North-East Frontier of India* Confidential (Calcutta, 1883).
Mills, J. P., *The Rengma Nagas* (London, 1937).
Milne, L., *Shans at Home* (London, 1910).
Mitchell, J. Clyde, *The Yao Village* (Manchester, 1956).
Montaigne, M., 'Des Cannibales' (1579), in *Essais* (Paris, 1598).
Montesquieu, Ch.-L., *De l'Esprit des lois*, 2 vols (Geneva, 1748). English version, *The Spirit of the Laws of Baron de Montesquieu*, trans. Thomas Nugent (New York, 1949).
Morgan, Lewis Henry, *Systems of Consanguinity and Affinity of the Human Family* (Washington DC, 1871).
—, *Ancient Society; or Research in the Lines of Human Progress from Savagery through Barbarism to Civilization* (Chicago, 1877).
Morgenstern, J., *Rites of Birth, Marriage, Death, and Kindred Occasions among the Semites* (Cincinnati, 1966).
Morris, Desmond, *The Naked Ape* (London, 1967).
Munn, Nancy D., 'The Effectiveness of Symbols in Murngin Rite and Myth', in R. F. Spencer (ed.), *Forms of Symbolic Action* (Seattle, 1969).
—, 'The Spatial Presentation of Cosmic Order in Walbiri Iconography', in Anthony Forge (ed), *Primitive Art and Society* (Oxford, 1973).
Murdock, G. P., *Social Structure* (New York, 1949).
Nadel, S. F., *The Nuba: An Anthropological Study of the Hill Tribes in Kordofan* (Oxford, 1947).
—, *The Foundations of Social Anthropology* (London, 1951).
—, *The Theory of Social Structure* (London, 1957).
Nagel, E., and J. R. Newman, *Gödel's Proof* (New York, 1958).
Needham, Rodney, 'The System of Teknonyms and Death-Names of the Penan'. *Southwestern Journal of Anthropology*, 4 (1954).
—, 'Surmise, Discovery, and Rhetoric', in *Remarks and Inventions: Skeptical Essays about Kinship* (London, 1974).

Neumann, F., 'Introduction', in *The Spirit of the Laws of Baron de Montesquieu*, trans. Thomas Nugent (New York, 1949).
Nilsson, M. P., *Geschichte der griechischen Religion*, 2nd edn (Munich, 1955).
Norbeck, Edward, *Religion in Primitive Society* (New York, 1961).
Obeyesekere, Gananath, *Medusa's Hair: An Essay on Personal Symbols and Religious Experience* (Chicago, 1981).
Onians, Richard Broxton, *The Origins of European Thought about the Body, the Mind, the Soul, the World, Time, and Fate* (Cambridge, 1951).
Onslow, P., 'Hair, Weaving of', in W. Smith and S. Cheetham (eds), *A Dictionary of Christian Antiquities*, 2 vols (London, 1875).
Palmer, P. M., and R. P. More, *The Sources of the Faust Tradition from Simon Magus to Lessing* (New York, 1936).
Pareto, V., *Trattato di sociologia generale* (Turin, 1916).
Parker, H., *Ancient Ceylon* (London, 1909).
Parry, N. E., *The Lakhers* (London, 1932).
Parsons, Talcott, *Essays in Sociological Theory: Pure and Applied* (Cambridge MA, 1949).
Parsons, Talcott, and R. F. Bales *et al.*, *Family Socialisation and Interaction* (Glencoe IL, 1955).
Parsons, Talcott, and E. A. Shils (eds), *Towards a General Theory of Action* (Cambridge MA, 1951).
Partington, J. Edge, and C. Heape, *An Album of Weapons, Tools, Ornaments, Articles of Dress, etc., of the Natives of the Pacific Islands* (privately printed, 1890–8).
Partridge, Eric, *A Dictionary of Slang and Unconventional English* (London, 1949).
Pelliot, Paul, 'Deux itinéraires de Chine en Inde à la fin du VIIIème siècle'. *B.E.F.E.O.* (Hanoi, 1904).
—, *Mémoires sur les coutumes du Cambodge de Tcheou Ta-Kouan*. In *Oeuvres posthumes de Paul Pelliot*, vol. 3 (Paris, 1951).
Peters, E., 'The Proliferaton of Segments in the Lineage of the Bedouin of Cyrenaicia'. *Journal of the Royal Anthropological Institute*, 90 (1960).
Petty, W., *The Petty Papers* (London, 1927).
Pfeiffer, Robert H., *Introduction to the Old Testament* (London, 1952).
Pieris, Ralph, *Sinhalese Social Organisation: The Kandyan Period* (Colombo, 1956).
Pinkerton, J., *A General Collection of the Best and Most Interesting Voyages and Travels in all Parts of the World*, 17 vols (London, 1808–14).
Plato, *Phaedo*, in H. Cary (trans.), *Five Dialogues of Plato bearing on Poetic Inspiration* (London, 1910).
Popper, K. R., *The Poverty of Historicism* (London, 1957).
Postman, L., 'The Present Status of Interference Theory', in Charles N. Cofer (ed.), *Verbal Language and Verbal Behavior* (New York, 1961).
Powell, H. A., 'An Analysis of Present-Day Social Structure in the Trobriands'. PhD thesis (London, 1956).
Prichard, J. C., *Researches into the Physical History of Mankind* (London, 1813).
Propp, Vladimir, *The Morphology of the Folktale* (Bloomington, 1958).

Purcell, B. H., 'Rites and Customs of Australian Aborigines'. *Zeitschrift für Ethnologie*, 25 (1893).

Quaritch Wales, H. G., *Siamese State Ceremonies* (London, 1931).

Rabinow, Paul, *Reflections on Fieldwork in Morocco* (Berkeley, 1977).

—, 'Representations are Social Facts: Modernity and Post-Modernity in Anthropology', in James Clifford, and George E. Marcus (eds), *Writing Culture: The Poetics and Politics of Ethnography* (Berkeley, 1986).

von Rad, Gerhard, *Theologie des Altes Testaments*, vol. 1, *Die Theologie der geschichtlichen Überlieferungen Israels* (Munich, 1957). English version, *Old Testament Theology*, vol. 1, *The Theology of Israel's Historical Tradition* (London, 1962).

—, *Genesis* (London, 1961).

Radcliffe-Brown, A. R., 'The Sociological Theory of Totemism'. *Proceedings of the 4th Pacific Science Congress* (Java, 1929). Reprinted in A. Radcliffe-Brown, *Structure and Function in Primitive Society* (London, 1952).

—, 'The Social Organisation of Australian Tribes'. *Oceania Monographs*, 1 (1930–1).

—, *The Andaman Islanders*, 2nd edn (London, 1933 [1922]).

—, On the Concept of Function in Social Science'. *American Anthropologist*, 37 (1935). Reprinted in A. R. Radcliffe-Brown, *Structure and Function in Primitive Society* (London, 1952).

—, 'Taboo'. The Frazer Lecture 1939. Printed in A. R. Radcliffe-Brown, *Structure and Function in Primitive Society* (London, 1952).

—, 'On Social Structure'. *Journal of the Royal Anthropological Institute*, 70 (1940). Reprinted in A. R. Radcliffe-Brown, *Structure and Function in Primitive Society* (London, 1952).

—, 'Religion and Society'. *Journal of the Royal Anthropological Institute*, 75 (1945). Reprinted in A. R. Radcliffe-Brown, *Structure and Function in Primitive Society* (London, 1952).

—, *The Nature of a Theoretical Natural Science of Society: Notes on a Discussion in a Seminar at the University of Chicago, 1937* (Mimeograph: University of Chicago Bookstore, Chicago, 1948).

—, 'Introduction', in A. R. Radcliffe-Brown and Daryll Forde (eds), *African Systems of Kinship and Marriage* (London, 1950).

—, 'The Comparative Method in Social Anthropology'. *Journal of the Royal Anthropological Institute*, 81 (1951).

—, *Structure and Function in Primitive Society* (London, 1952).

—, Letter Addressed to Claude Lévi-Strauss (dated 1952), quoted in part in Sol Tax *et al.* (eds), *An Appraisal of Anthropology Today* (Chicago, 1953).

—, *A Natural Science of Society*. Foreword by Fred Eggan (Glencoe IL, 1957).

Radcliffe-Brown, A. R., and Daryll Forde (eds), *African Systems of Kinship and Marriage* (London, 1950).

Radin, Paul, *The Trickster: A Study in American Indian Mythology*. With commentaries by C. G. Jung and Karl Kerényi (London, 1956).

Lord Raglan, *The Hero* (London, 1936).
—, *The Temple and the House* (New York, 1964; London, 1978).
Rattray, R. S., *Ashanti* (London, 1923).
—, *Religion and Art in Ashanti* (London, 1927).
—, *Ashanti Law and Constitution* (London, 1929).
Ratzel, F., *The History of Mankind*, 3 vols (London, 1896–8).
Read, Herbert, *Education through Art* (London, 1943).
Read, Kenneth, *The High Valley* (New York, 1965).
Reid, R., *History of the Frontier Areas Bordering Assam from 1883 to 1941* (Shillong, 1942).
Richards, Audrey I., 'Some Types of Family Structure among the Central Bantu', in A. R. Radcliffe-Brown and Daryll Forde (eds), *African Systems of Kinship and Marriage* (London, 1950).
Ricoeur, Paul, 'Structure et herméneutique'. *Esprit* (November 1963).
Rivière, P., 'Myth and Material Culture: Some Symbolic Interrelations', in R. F. Spencer (ed.), *Forms of Symbolic Action* (Seattle, 1969).
Roheim, Geza, *Animism, Magic, and the Divine King* (London, 1930).
—, 'Psycho-Analysis of Primitive Cultural Types'. *International Journal of Psycho-Analysis*, 13 (1932).
Roscher, W. H., *Lexikon der griechischen und romischen Mythologie* (Leipzig, 1884).
Rose, H. J., *A Handbook of Greek Mythology* (London, 1928).
Roth, W. E., 'Superstition, Magic, and Medicine'. *North Queensland Ethnographic Bulletin*, 5 (1903).
Rousseau, Jean-Jacques, *Discours sur l'origine et les fondements de l'inégalité parmi les hommes* (Amsterdam, 1755).
—, *Du Contrat social* (Amsterdam, 1762).
—, *Emile* (Amsterdam, 1762).
Royal Anthropological Institute, *Traditional Art of the British Colonies* (London, 1947).
—, *Edmund Leach: a Bibliography*. Royal Anthropological Institute Occasional Paper no. 42 (London, 1990).
Russell, Bertrand, *Marriage and Morals* (London, 1929).
—, *Human Knowledge* (London, 1948).
Ryan, Bryce, *Caste in Modern Ceylon* (New Brunswick, 1953).
Ryle, Gilbert, *The Concept of Mind* (London, 1949).
Sagarin, E., *The Anatomy of Dirty Words* (New York, 1962).
Sahlins, Marshall, *Islands of History* (Chicago, 1985).
Saliba, J. A., 'The Virgin Birth Debate in Anthropological Literature: A Critical Assessment'. *Theological Studies*, 36 (1975).
Sartre, Jean-Paul, *Critique de la raison dialectique* (Paris, 1960).
Schapera, Isaac, *Native Land Tenure in the Bechuanaland Protectorate* (London, 1943).
—, *Migrant Labour and Tribal Life* (London, 1947).

—, 'The Sin of Cain'. *Journal of the Royal Anthropological Institute*, 85 (1955).

Schmidt, W., 'Der Konzeptionsglaube australischer Stämme'. *International Archive of Ethnography*, 46 (1952).

Schniewind, J., 'A Reply to Bultmann', in H. W. Bartsch (ed.), *Kerygma and Myth: A Theological Debate* (London, 1953).

Scott, J. G. (Shway Yoe), *The Burman, His Life and Notions* (London, 1896).

Scott, J. G., and J. P. Hardiman, *Gazetteer of Upper Burma and the Shan States*. Part I, 2 vols; Part II, 3 vols (Rangoon, 1900/1901).

Searle, John R., *Speech Acts* (Cambridge, 1969).

Selection of Papers, Selection of Papers regarding the Hill Tracts between Assam and Burma and on the Upper Brahmaputra (Calcutta, 1873).

Seligman, C. G., *The Melanesians of British New Guinea* (Cambridge, 1910).

Shakespear, J., *The Lushei Kuki Clans* (London, 1912).

Shannon, C., and W. Weaver, *The Mathematical Theory of Communication* (Urbana, 1949).

Sharp, Lauriston, 'Social Organisation of the Yir-Yiront Tribe'. *Oceania*, 4 (1934).

—, 'Ritual Life and Economics of the Yir-Yiront of Cape York Peninsula'. *Oceania*, 5 (1934).

Sills, David L. (ed.), *International Encyclopaedia of Social Sciences* (New York, 1968).

Sinding-Larsen, S., 'A Re-Reading of the Sistine Chapel', in *Acta ad Archaeologiam et Artum Historiam Pertinentia*, 4 (Rome, 1969).

Slotkin, J. S. (ed.), *Readings in Early Anthropology* (London, 1965).

Smith, William Robertson, *Kinship and Marriage in Early Arabia* (London, 1885).

—, *Lectures on the Religion of the Semites* (London, 1889).

Smith, W. R., and T. K. Cheyne, 'Nazarite', in T. K. Cheyne and J. S. Black (eds), *Encyclopaedia Biblica* (London, 1901).

Snouk Hurgronje, C., *Mecca in the Latter Part of the Nineteenth Century* (Leyden, 1931).

Sollas, W. J., *Ancient Hunters and their Modern Representatives* (London, 1911).

Soustelle, J., *La Vie quotidienne des Azteques à la veille de la conquète espagnole* (Paris, 1955).

Spencer, B., and F. J. Gillen, *The Native Tribes of Central Australia* (London, 1899).

Spencer, Herbert, *Social Statics* (London, 1851).

Sperber, Dan, *Le Symbolisme en générale* (Paris, 1974). English version, *Rethinking Symbolism* (Cambridge, 1975).

Spiro, Melford E., 'Religion: Problems of Definition and Explanation', in Michael Banton (ed.), *Anthropological Approaches to the Study of Religion* (London, 1966).

—, 'Virgin Birth, Parthenogenesis, and Physiological Paternity: An Essay in Cultural Interpretation'. *Man* (n.s.), 3 (1968).

Srinivas, M. N., *Religion and Society among the Coorgs of South India* (Oxford, 1952).

Stanner, W. E. H., 'The Daly River Tribes: The Theory of Sex'. *Oceania*, 4 (1933).

Stebbing, Susan, *A Modern Introduction to Logic* (London, 1945).

Steinberg, Leo, 'The Line of Fate in Michaelangelo's Painting'. *Critical Inquiry*, 6 (1980).

von den Steinen, Karl, *Die Bakairi Sprache* (Leipzig, 1892).

—, *Unter den Naturvölkern Zentral-Brasiliens* (Berlin, 1894).

Steiner, Franz B., *Taboo* (London, 1956).

Stevenson, H. N. C., *The Economics of the Central Chin Tribes* (Bombay, n.d. [1943]).

Strauss, Leo, 'Interpretation of Genesis'. Typescript of a lecture delivered at University College, London (25 January 1957).

Strehlow, C., *Die Aranda und Loritja Stämme in Zentral-Australian* (Frankfurt, 1907–21).

Strong, James, *The Exhaustive Concordance of the Bible* (London, 1894).

Suter, K., and K. Stearman, *Aboriginal Australians.* Minority Rights Group Report no. 35 (1994).

Tambiah, S. J., 'Animals are Good to Eat and Also Good to Prohibit'. *Ethnology*, 7 (1969).

—, 'The Galactic Polity: The Structure of Traditional Kingdoms in Southeast Asia', in Stanley Freed (ed.), *Anthropology and the Climate of Opinion* (New York, 1977).

—, 'A Performative Approach to Ritual'. *Proceedings of the British Academy*, 65 (1979).

Tax, Sol, 'Some Problems of Social Organisation', in Fred Eggan (ed.), *Social Anthropology of North American Tribes* (Chicago, 1937).

Taylor, L. F., 'General Structure of Languages Spoken in Burma'. *Journal of the Burma Research Society*, 39 (1956).

Thompson, D. F., 'The Hero Cult, Initiation, and Totemism on Cape York: The Knowledge of Physical Paternity'. *Journal of the Royal Anthropological Institute*, 63 (1933).

Thompson, Sir D'Arcy Wentworth, *On Growth and Form*, 2 vols (Cambridge, 1917; new edn, 1942).

Tiger, Lionel, and Robin Fox, *The Imperial Animal* (London, 1972).

de Tolnay, C., *The Sistine Chapel* (New Brunswick, 1945).

Topley, Marjorie, 'Chinese Women's Vegetarian Houses in Singapore'. *Journal of the Malayan Branch of the Royal Asiatic Society*, 27 (1954).

Turner, Victor W., 'The Syntax of Symbolism in an African Religion'. *Philosophical Transactions of the Royal Society of London*, Series B, 251 (1966).

—, *The Forest of Symbols* (Ithaca, 1967).

—, 'Liminality and Communitas', in *The Ritual Process* (New York, 1969).

Tylor, E. B., *Primitive Culture: Researches into the Development of Mythology, Philosophy, Religion, Art, and Custom*, 2 vols (London, 1871).

—, 'On a Method of Investigating the Development of Institutions: Applied to

Laws of Marriage and Descent'. *Journal of the Royal Anthropological Institute*, 58 (1888).
Tyson, E., *Orang-Outang, Sive Homo Silvestris, or the Anatomy of a Pigmie* (London, 1699).
Vaihinger, H., *The Philosophy of 'As If'* (London, 1924).
Valeri, V., *Kingship and Sacrifice: Ritual and Society in Ancient Hawaii* (Chicago, 1985).
Vico, Giambattista, *The New Science of Giambattista Vico*, trans. from 3rd edn (1744) T. B. Bergin and M. H. Fisch (New York, 1961).
Vidich, A. J. Review of Gerth and Mills, *Character and Social Structure*. *Man*, 185 (1954).
Vierkandt, A., 'Wundt', in *Encyclopaedia of the Social Sciences*, vol. 15 (New York, 1935).
Wardlaw, C. W., *Phylogeny and Morphology* (London, 1952).
Warner, W. L., *A Black Civilisation* (New York, 1937).
Warren, F. E., 'Tonsure', in W. Smith and S. Cheetham (eds), *A Dictionary of Christian Antiquities*, 2 vols (London, 1875).
Weber, Max, *The Theory of Social and Economic Organisation*, trans. A. R. Henderson and T. Parsons, ed. T. Parsons (London, 1947).
—, *The Religion of China* (Glencoe IL, 1951).
Webster, N., *New International Dictionary of the English Language* (London, 1934).
Webster, W. D., *Illustrated Catalogues of Ethnographic Specimens*, vol. 2, no. 20 (Bicester, 1900).
Wentworth, H., and S. B. Flexner, *A Dictionary of American Slang* (New York, 1961).
Whitaker, B. (ed.), *Minorities: A Question of Human Rights* (London, 1984).
White, L. A., 'The Definition and Prohibition of Incest'. *American Anthropologist*, 50 (1948).
Whitehead, Alfred North, *Science and the Modern World* (Cambridge, 1927).
Widengren, G., 'Early Hebrew Myths and their Interpretation', in S. H. Hooke (ed.), *Myth, Ritual, and Kingship* (Oxford, 1958).
Wiener, N., *Cybernetics* (New York, 1948).
Wilken, G. A., 'Über das Haaropfer', in *Revue coloniale internationale* (Amsterdam, 1886).
Wilkins, W. J., *Hindu Mythology: Vedic and Puranic* (Calcutta, 1913).
Wilson, Edward O., *Sociobiology: The New Synthesis* (Cambridge MA, 1975).
Wilson, G., and M. Wilson, *The Analysis of Social Change* (Cambridge, 1945).
Wilson, Monica, *Good Company* (London, 1949).
—, 'Nyakyusa Ritual and Symbolism'. *American Anthropologist*, 56 (1954).
Winograd, T., 'The Process of Language Understanding', in Jonathan Benthall (ed.), *The Limits of Human Nature* (London, 1973).
Wittgenstein, Ludwig, *Tractatus Logico-Philosophicus* (London, 1922).
Wootton, A. J., 'Talk in the Homes of Young Children'. *Sociology*, 8 (1974).

Worringer, W. R., *Form in Gothic*, trans. and ed. and with an intro. by Herbert Read (London, 1927).
Yalman, Nur, '"The Raw: the Cooked :: Nature: Culture" – Observations on *Le Cru et le cuit*', in E. R. Leach (ed.), *The Structural Study of Myth and Totemism* (London, 1967).
Zimmer, H. R., *Myths and Symbols in Indian Art and Literature* (New York, 1946).
—, *Philosophies of India*, ed. Joseph Campbell (New York, 1951).
—, *The Art of Indian Asia*, 2 vols (New York, 1955).

Index